"Once again Doug Campbell sets the cat among the pigeons! Through careful argumentation, laced with a mass of radically new suggestions, he builds an original case for a ten-letter corpus of authentic Pauline letters in a historical sequence never before proposed. All Pauline scholars, whether convinced or not, will need to give this book the careful attention it deserves."

— JOHN BARCLAY
Durham University

"A sharp, imaginative, painstaking study. . . . Like a puzzle master, Campbell fits together clues large and small to form a compelling whole. . . . To take Campbell's disciplined analysis seriously may mean, for some, to reframe Paul rather dramatically. But to ignore his argument is to miss an opportunity to check accumulated habits and prejudices that may, for a host of intellectual and theological reasons, 'frame' unjustly Paul's actual, complicated, exigency-driven correspondence."

— ALEXANDRA BROWN
Washington and Lee University

Let no one consider this wasted labor,
nor the investigation itself a sign of idle curiosity.
For knowing the chronological sequence of the epistles
is of great help in our studying them.

Chrysostom, *Homilies on Romans,* Preface

FRAMING PAUL

An Epistolary Biography

Douglas A. Campbell

WILLIAM B. EERDMANS PUBLISHING COMPANY
GRAND RAPIDS, MICHIGAN / CAMBRIDGE, U.K.

Published 2014 by

Wm. B. Eerdmans Publishing Co.

2140 Oak Industrial Drive N.E., Grand Rapids, Michigan 49505 /

P.O. Box 163, Cambridge CB3 9PU U.K.

Printed in the United States of America

19 18 17 16 15 14   7 6 5 4 3 2 1

Library of Congress Cataloging-in-Publication Data

Campbell, Douglas A. (Douglas Atchison), 1961-

Framing Paul: an epistolary biography / Douglas A. Campbell.

pages   cm

Bibliographical references and index.

ISBN 978-0-8028-7151-0 (pbk.: alk. paper)

1. Paul, the Apostle, Saint. 2. Bible. Epistles of Paul —

Criticism, interpretation, etc.   I. Title.

BS2506.3.C365   2014

225.9′2 — dc23

2014015190

www.eerdmans.com

To Rachel,

my smokin' hot foxy lady

for thirty years and counting

HUT	Hermeneutische Untersuchungen zur Theologie
ICC	International Critical Commentary
JSNTSup	Journal for the Study of the New Testament: Supplement Series
KEK	Kritisch-exegetischer Kommentar über das Neue Testament (Meyer-Kommentar)
LBS	Linguistic Biblical Studies
LCL	Loeb Classical Library
LNTS	Library of New Testament Studies
LPS	Library of Pauline Studies
MdB	Le Monde de la Bible
MTB	Münchner Theologische Beiträge
NBBC	New Beacon Bible Commentary
NICNT	New International Commentary on the New Testament
NIGTC	New International Greek Testament Commentary
NovTSup	Novum Testamentum Supplements
NPNF[1]	*Nicene and Post-Nicene Fathers,* Series 1
NPNF[2]	*Nicene and Post-Nicene Fathers,* Series 2
NTC	The New Testament in Context
NTD	Das Neue Testament Deutsch
NTL	New Testament Library
NTOA	Novum Testamentum et Orbis Antiquus
PFES	Publications of the Finnish Exegetical Society
PG	Patrologia graeca [= Patrologiae cursus completus: Series graeca]. Edited by J.-P. Migne. 162 vols. Paris, 1857-86.
PL	Patrologia latina [= Patrologiae cursus completus: Series latina]. Edited by J.-P. Migne. 217 vols. Paris, 1844-64.
PS	Pauline Studies
RB	*Revue biblique*
RBén	*Revue bénédictine*
SBLDS	Society of Biblical Literature Dissertation Series
SBLSBS	Society of Biblical Literature Sources for Biblical Study
SBLSymS	Society of Biblical Literature Symposium Series
SNTSMS	Society for New Testament Studies Monograph Series
SP	Sacra Pagina
STAC	Studien und Texte zu Antike und Christentum
SUNT	Studien zur Umwelt des Neuen Testaments
ThKNT	Theologischer Kommentar zum Neuen Testament
TSK	*Theologische Studien und Kritiken*
TU	Texte und Untersuchungen

TV	Theopolitical Visions
TZ	*Theologische Zeitschrift*
TZT	*Tübinger Zeitschrift für Theologie*
VCSup	Supplements to Vigiliae christianae
WBC	Word Biblical Commentary
WMANT	Wissenschaftliche Monographien zum Alten und Neuen Testament
WUNT	Wissenschaftliche Untersuchungen zum Neuen Testament
ZAC	*Zeitschrift für Antikes Christentum / Journal of Ancient Christianity*
ZNW	*Zeitschrift für die neutestamentliche Wissenschaft und die Kunde der älteren Kirche*
ZPE	*Zeitschrift für Papyrologie und Epigraphik*
ZTK	*Zeitschrift für Theologie und Kirche*
ZWKB	Zürcher Werkkommentare zur Bibel
ZWT	*Zeitschrift für wissenschaftliche Theologie*

An Extended Preface

The origins of this project lie — as is often the case — with some of my teachers in graduate school. Richard Longenecker was writing his excellent commentary on Galatians (1990) when I was in the program at the University of Toronto in the late '80s, and his students were intimately familiar with his extensive defense of the "South Galatian" hypothesis. (The book-length introduction was circulating in manuscript.) But, rather unusually, this defense was crafted in conversation with the views of his colleague in the Toronto School of Theology, and one of our other teachers, John Hurd, from whom Longenecker always encouraged his students to learn. Thus, we were all familiar with John Knox's arguments, along with Hurd's (1983 [1965]) superb development of his views in specific relation to 1 Corinthians. Peter Richardson also was interested in biographical issues and brought a fertile mind to any such discussions. So biographical issues were vigorously in play at Toronto in relation to the study of Paul. Then I had a stroke of luck.

The external examiner for my doctoral thesis on Romans 3:21-26, Robert Jewett, recruited because of his expertise in Romans (as seen eventually in his magisterial 2007 commentary), was also, fortuitously, a biographical and chronological expert (1979). And of all these senior figures, it was Jewett who subsequently mentored me through my first post, in the Department of Religion at the University of Otago, facilitating numerous conversations at SBL to the benefit and great appreciation of an unimportant lecturer from Dunedin, New Zealand. By this time, a number of things had become apparent to me.

It was clear that most Pauline scholars were continuing to work with either an Acts-based chronology that had serious problems or with a muddled approach that switched between Acts-based and epistolary systems essentially opportunistically and hence unjustifiably. Moreover, the field still lacked a convincing and stringently epistolary account of Paul's life; somewhat incredibly, despite its main contours having been elucidated by Knox in 1950, this puzzle had yet to be solved. So I bent my mind to an answer and ended up working on it rather obsessively. (On one summer holiday, I spent far too much time ignoring my family and scribbling different chronological solutions in the sand on the beach.) But I did feel after this period in the early '90s that I had crafted a workable solution. Indeed, its basic outline appears here. Still, quite a bit had to happen before it could be fully articulated, twenty or so years later.

In 1996 I accepted a post at King's College London and was forced to take a big step up in terms of academic rigor. The doctoral seminars chaired by Graham Stanton and vigorously driven by Francis Watson are still one of my fondest academic memories. Faced with the pressures of navigating a university in the United Kingdom during one of its worst funding crises, I found it difficult to press ahead with large research projects like a Pauline chronology. But I was still passionately committed to the issue and taught it frequently in class. Then in 2000 I was able to spend a year in Germany, courtesy of a von Humboldt scholarship and the kind invitations of Peter Lampe and Robert Jewett, where I was able to press my understanding of two key elements within my broader chronological hypothesis to the appropriate depth.

One was an Acts datum and so will not feature centrally here: the interpretation of an inscription from Chytri on Cyprus that possibly attests to the presence of Sergius Paul[l]us there during the reign of Tiberius. If my reading of the damaged inscription in these terms is correct, then it is an enormous problem for any literal, Acts-based chronology — what I would call a sequential use of the Acts evidence — but a vindication of Knox's views. (It is also, nevertheless, a fundamental vindication of what I would call the episodic veracity of Acts.) I had to check the inscription personally, however, before the study could be published, necessitating a visit to the Metropolitan Museum in New York, and also to get my findings past the eagle-eyed Joyce Reynolds, so it appeared in print only in 2005.

The other key element was what I often speak of as "the Aretas datum," that is, the one possibly datable event in Paul's life supplied by Paul himself and hence an incident of almost immeasurable importance for the Pauline scholar: his escape from an ethnarch appointed by King Aretas IV to govern the city of Damascus (2 Cor 11:32-33). I simply had to know whether this event was precisely datable, and reliably so. And, rather to my surprise, I found that one quite specific solution — an escape somewhere between late 36 and early 37 CE — was easily the most plausible reading and was reassuringly solid. Like most dense articles on chronological questions in learned journals, this proposal (2002) has not attracted much attention. Fortunately, however, it has yet to be refuted, and it figures centrally in what follows.

In 2003 I moved to a post at Duke University in the United States, where I was surrounded by congenial and deeply learned colleagues in the Divinity School and the Department of Religion, and at UNC-Chapel Hill.[1] In this supportive environment, I could move forward and complete the major projects that had been gestating for so long. I first turned my attention to the construal of many of Paul's most famous texts in terms of something usually called "justification" — an interpretative discourse about which I had long nursed suspicions. I finished this project in 2007 (with the book appearing in 2009), after which I began a broader theological reading of Romans. But it seemed best to break this off temporarily in 2012 and turn back to chronological matters in an effort to bring those to an appropriate conclusion. During this period, the Duke environment brought four further things to my developing biographical project that have greatly enriched it and for which I am profoundly thankful.

First, my massive project on justification, possible only because of Duke's extensive support (not to mention my wife's), was also an education into the problematic interweaving of theological and biographical concerns within current Pauline scholarship. I learned that a particular account of Paul's life — including, most importantly, a particular account of the production of his letters — was being used to buttress a particular account of his soteriology. This was not in itself objectionable, but it was being done dishonestly, or at least sloppily. Evidence from Acts was being used to deploy the letters, while the evidence of the letters themselves was being introduced under the control of that framework, and even, when necessary, narcotized (see esp. my 2009, 143-64, 515-18). Moreover, I found that the same prejudices and consequent vicious methodological circularity were influencing decisions of authorship.

I also became aware of the intertwining of authorship issues with prior ecclesial commitments. Duke is rooted in the Methodist tradition, but its branches spread to many other traditions, including Catholicism. And in this setting, I became increasingly offended by the marginalization I was seeing of Pauline letters deemed too Catholic — sometimes simply because they emphasize the church! At Duke, it is clear that this is an especially insidious argument. Thus, it became even more apparent that my own chronological

---

1. At Duke Divinity School, in NT, Joel Marcus, Richard Hays, and Susan Eastman, then C. Kavin Rowe (and now Ross Wagner and Brittany Wilson); in the Department of Religion, E. P. Sanders at first, then Mark Goodacre; and at UNC-Chapel Hill, Bart Ehrman and Zlatko Plese.

work would need to be more than just a chronology; it would need to answer a range of fundamental questions about the letters, including questions about their very authenticity.

Second, Duke fosters a famous doctoral program, and I was able to benefit from the learning of the outstanding students entering it. Of course, they would often begin by being "Campbellized" chronologically, but as their studies developed, they generally ended up, as the proverb goes, knowing more than their teacher. And I am not ashamed to acknowledge their importance to this project.

Stephen Carlson achieved a profound expertise in Galatians, in text-critical work, and already knew a great deal about pseudepigraphy. (Through him I also met and learned much from Mike Holmes. Although I have resisted Holmes's account of Ignatius and Polycarp here in chapter 6, I am utterly convinced by his text-critical eclecticism in ultimate dependence on Zunz, which is in play tacitly through everything that follows.) Robert Moses (2014) crafted a powerful account of Paul's much-neglected discourse concerning "the powers," one that generated further critical insight into the authenticity (or not) of the letters. Colin Miller (forthcoming 2014) brought patristic interpretation to bear on Romans in conversation with Alasdair MacIntyre, opening new avenues on Paul's actual reading in an ancient, as against a modern, Western, setting, and generating new perspectives on his ecclesial material. Moving closer to my time of writing, Tom McGlothlin brings a deep awareness of the patristic interpretation of ethics and resurrection to bear on Paul. And various brilliant students from the UNC doctoral program have also contributed to my thinking — Ben White composed a sparkling engagement with the second-century battle for Paul's identity, a debate most Pauline scholars have yet to come to grips with in its latest developments (see his 2011 essay, which is used in ch. 6); Jason Staples generated a radical new perspective on the rationale underlying Paul's conversion of pagans (and simply brings a sharp eye to the interpretation of any Pauline material; see his 2011); and Ken Olsen knows a great deal about Eusebius. But two Duke students have been especially important for what follows.

T. J. Lang has grown into something of a constant academic companion. His eclectic and creative interests are threaded through a great deal of the argument that follows (indeed, in ways too numerous to list), but his use of patristic sources to analyze Paul's neglected "mystery" or "divine secret" discourse has been particularly helpful. This research opens up important new perspectives on Ephesians and Colossians in conversation both with Paul's uncontested texts and with Christian thinkers in the second and third centuries. The specific challenges of his latest work in this vein involve rethinking where Paul's corpus should be centered, and doing so in a way that resists the subliminal imposition of modern categories and assumptions.

And Hans Arneson has developed an extraordinary learning in the complex debates surrounding 2 Corinthians; he has drawn together, in effect, a genealogy of error in this arena. We have learned from one another in chronological matters for many years now, but his brilliant insights into this letter have been nothing less than vital additions to this project's opening stages. I eagerly anticipate the publication of his field-changing work in due course.

All of which is to say that the doctoral students at and associated with Duke have greatly enriched this project in quite specific ways, requiring more than the acknowledgment of a generic debt of gratitude. But Duke has also helped me in a third significant way.

"Interdisciplinarity" is currently something of a buzzword at the university, but irrespective of its use for the purposes of self-definition, this project is deeply invested in research that crosses traditional disciplinary boundaries. Indeed, although I have tried to keep engagements with secondary literature to a minimum — the main argument and its engagement with the primary sources being sufficiently complex — I have wherever possible gestured toward interdisciplinary avenues that I think illuminate puzzles in Paul's interpretation significantly and are worthy of further exploration. Computer-assisted research has been especially important in this effort.

I have constantly utilized ORBIS, a computer-assisted tool for plotting ancient travel generated recently under the leadership of Walter Scheidel at Stanford (see ORBIS 2013; Scheidel, Meeks, and Weiland 2012; Scheidel 2013). And I have had a series of delightful conversations with experts around the world working in a field that is itself fundamentally interdisciplinary: the computer-assisted — or "nontraditional" — ascription of authorship. (John Burrows, Joe Rudman, Andris Abakuks, and David Mealand — all busy people — have been especially gracious in response to my urgent queries.) The need for a reasonable grasp of statistics has prevented most NT scholars from engaging with this field, and the most sophisticated studies that have done so in relation to Paul are isolated and now somewhat out of date. My introduction of this material here is by no means definitive, but it is highly instructive, and the field is simply begging for deeper utilization with respect to Paul.

Duke has also enriched this project with contributions from its leading (sociological) organizational theorists — figures like Mark Chaves and Martin Ruef (and I am grateful, as always, to Christian Smith for some of the initial sociological help) — and from its ongoing dialogue in neurobiology.

The presence of the latter in my analysis is somewhat indirect, mainly with reference to a standard work of behavioral economics by Daniel Kahneman (2011), and this needs to be used cautiously. But exploration of the interface between the humanities and the exciting work on the human brain currently being undertaken by scientists and medical researchers is simply in the air at Duke, and so it has been inhaled here, so to speak, at least for a breath or two, and applied to some of the questionable methodologies observable within the Pauline field, yielding a tentative explanation in terms of newly recognizable cognitive biases. (I expect a seminal contribution here shortly in relation to Paul from my colleague Susan Eastman.)

And of course Duke provides a number of brilliant classicists who can assist the struggling *Neutestamentler* from time to time — in my case, Mary Boatwright and William Johnson. The latter in particular has greatly influenced my developing understanding of the fundamentally cross-cultural nature of Pauline interpretation and the resulting fragility of many of the judgments Pauline scholars tend to make about ancient reading and editorial practices. Johnson (esp. 2000; 2010) should be required reading for NT scholars.

But my move to Duke in 2003 did not just enrich this project in the foregoing three, somewhat standard academic ways. It brought me to live in a fairly conservative state — North Carolina — in the United States of America, where I was confronted with a modern discourse that has profoundly influenced the life of my entire family.

For one reason and another, in 2005 my wife and I were brought face to face with the dynamics of judgment and incarceration in the United States. We learned firsthand what it was all about and were deeply shocked as we followed a young person through a process of arrest, evaluation, judgment, and imprisonment. This personal engagement — which was possible only because of the courage of my wife, Rachel — eventually linked hands with a move by the Divinity School (spearheaded by Bishop Ken Carder) to address issues of incarceration. I was and still am privileged to be part of this growing effort, which now extends to classes on justice and imprisonment — most importantly, including field trips — and classes taught *in* prisons with mixed groups combining students with people doing time. (These are facilitated by some of our former students under the auspices of "Project TURN"; see http://www .newmonasticism.org/turn.php.) I have learned a lot from all of this. I have been prompted to engage not only with questions directly related to justice and imprisonment but also with the growing alternative to punitive responses known as "restorative justice." (This is usefully introduced by Zehr 2002, but see also Pranis 2005; it is discussed in a little more detail in ch. 3.) Moreover, my engagement has affected both the way I read Paul and my perceptions of his interpretation by some of the secondary literature.

I have realized that modern scholars are not deeply attuned to their own cultural and political presuppositions about justice, judgment, and conflict resolution, and so tend to project these unwittingly onto Paul, unaware of the danger of anachronism and the existence of many alternatives. Further, modern scholars are not deeply attuned to the context of incarceration — a context informing *five* of the *thirteen* canonical letters bearing Paul's name. By this I mean that most modern scholars are — in a certain sense, understandably — unfamiliar with the concrete practicalities and difficulties that attend imprisonment, and with the impact that such dynamics have on any writing undertaken while incarcerated. Again, I do not do much more than introduce these issues here, but they are in play, and helpfully so (see ch. 5). These avenues too beg for further exploration.

But the contribution of the harsher side of the U.S. context to Paul's interpretation does not stop here. As I just noted, the practices of restorative justice provide new lenses for viewing conflict and its resolution (recalling the title of Zehr's seminal work in 1990), and these prove helpful for the Pauline scholar at certain other critical points as well. Things that were not apparent to me previously suddenly come into view (see ch. 2).

In short, in a fourth contribution, my location at Duke in North Carolina, in the United States, has profoundly shaped my reading of Paul, and at the most fundamental level: his framing. We might say that *where* we read Paul — whether in a study, at a café, on a bus — directly affects what we see (see Charles [Chuck] Campbell and Saunders 2000), and reading him in a prison helps us see a lot. So although I struggle daily with my concerns about the horrific side of the U.S. prison-industrial complex (see Schlosser 1998; Gawande 2009), I am thankful for the ways it has opened my eyes to important dimensions in Paul's life and letter writing that I had not seen before.

In sum, Duke has tremendously enriched the frame I originally developed for Paul's life and letters so long ago at Otago, in the early '90s, and I am therefore grateful for the long delay in its articulation and publication. I have been able to "road-test" this framework in numerous settings, finding that it has generally held up well under pressure. No test, however, has been more searching than the Duke doctoral seminar, and the final touches to the frame that have resulted from this latest set of contexts have considerably enhanced it.

I have titled this project "Framing Paul," drawing on a useful methodological insight from Derrida (explained most lucidly by B. Johnson 1980 [1978]; see further in ch. 1). He is suggesting here that the way we frame the object of our investigation inevitably controls what we see, but the biases and interpretative acts involved with this framing tend to be hidden unless we name them explicitly. They often hide in Pauline investigation, as elsewhere, under the ostensibly neutral notion of "context." But every constitution of a historical context is itself an interpretative act — an act of framing. Just how we frame Paul is clearly critical, unavoidable, and yet often corrupt in methodological terms.

So I suggest here undertaking this exercise afresh, with reference initially only to the data in the letters. Our key initial sources are epistolary; hence, this project is subtitled "An Epistolary Biography." But the subtitle is meant to suggest further that we must use this data to reach the key initial judgments not only *from* but also *about* the letters. We must ask what basic circumstances surrounded and elicited them, *as well as,* essentially simultaneously — and in dependence only on their own data — which letters are authentic, and which (if any) need to be partitioned because they were subject to later acts of editorial collation. So the biography we are constructing is very much an epistolary one: the biography of the genesis of Paul's letters, and a biography sourced principally and primarily from the letters.

It is probably clear by now that this epistolary biography may be a very difficult thing to achieve. However, without such a biography, I am not sure how much coherent historical-critical work on Paul is ultimately even possible. An initial limited biographical frame in solely epistolary terms needs to lie at the beginning, and then at the heart, of everything else in historical-critical terms that Pauline scholars do. It is my hope that the following analysis, or something of its kind, will ultimately prove persuasive.

DC
Durham, N.C.

CHAPTER ONE

An Extended Methodological Introduction

1. A Starting Point

Victor Furnish gave voice in an excellent summary article in 1989 to a central challenge within Pauline interpretation: the extraordinary diversity of Paul's writings, especially at first glance. Even allowing for the assignment of some or even most of the canonical letters written in Paul's name to other authors — a move that will be scrutinized carefully in due course — the remaining letters are still characterized by a remarkable variation in argumentation, structure, and expression. Just Romans and 1 Corinthians, whose authenticity is usually uncontested, when placed side by side, seem to come not infrequently from overtly different places in conceptual terms. Meanwhile, adding only 2 Corinthians and Galatians to the comparison diversifies the overall situation further, creating a fundamental methodological challenge. How are interpreters to supply a unified account of various aspects of Paul himself as his texts strain in multiple directions?

An important response to this phenomenon was articulated by J. C. Beker (1984 [1980]) in a classic study that is now less read than it ought to be. It is Beker's initial methodological proposal that concerns us here. He observed that any reconstruction of Paul's thinking must navigate an interplay within his texts between "contingency" and "coherence." This proposal seemed to capture much that Pauline scholars had been trying to do, justly passing into standard scholarly parlance, at least for his generation.

"Contingency" denotes the occasionality of Paul's texts. The interpretative posture being identified here is, more expansively, the conviction that Paul's letters were crafted and dispatched to deal with quite specific circumstances in the communities to which they were addressed, and hence were shaped significantly by Paul's perceptions of those particular circumstances. All interpretation of Paul, at any level, must therefore take this dimension into account programmatically. Every statement is not merely a word of and from Paul but also, as Beker famously said, "a word on target" (1984 [1980], 12). (This axiom will be nuanced in due course.)

Beker's hypothesis speaks immediately to the phenomenon of diversity with which we began. It could be that Paul crafted his letters to speak to specific communities so successfully that the very different communities to which he wrote thereby elicited very diverse communications. If Paul, something like a chameleon, changed his structures, arguments, and terms to reflect the very different situations of his auditors, then any collection of his letters would contain an initially bewildering array of colors and patterns. This is not ultimately surprising if we are explaining a rhetorical chameleon responding to diverse environments — or, in perhaps more positive terms, a good missionary contextualizing his message.

Having said this, however, Beker also insisted that Paul's letters were nevertheless informed significantly by what he called Paul's "coherence" — a term that can confuse as much as it clarifies, so it needs to be defined carefully. Coherence denotes for Beker certain important convictions on Paul's part about God's activity in Christ and its implications. Beker claimed that a constant coherence in basically this sense is discernible within all of Paul's different letters — a "deep structure" underlying all the occasional argumentation.[1] (He argued more specifically that it was "apocalyptic," suitably defined, but we do not need to explore this particular proposal just yet.)

---

1. His use of the language of structuralism, presumably in distant dependence on the work of Noam Chomsky, is somewhat unfortunate, since it mobilizes false analogies. Some structuralists (notably, Propp and Greimas) claimed that various folk stories contained underlying formulae that could be discerned across individual instances, allowing the derivation of actantial maps of texts that identified standard actors such as heroes and helpers. Beker might have been appealing to this basic notion with his claim concerning coherence. But this claim is problematic. There is arguably no "underlying" structure or "deeper" entity in stories and texts. Stories do not move through spaces that have shallow and deep locations, as a submarine might move across the ocean closer to or farther away from the water's surface. Observable similarities between texts are possibly better explained in terms of a shared tradition and set of practices, equally recognizable to authors and readers or auditors. This proposal does, however, open up important explanatory opportunities for Paul's texts, provided that they are pursued correctly. Overlapping narratives might become apparent as readers sensitive to these possibilities analyze and compare texts. But these are not "deep structures." (The method is pursued famously and rather more responsibly by Hays 2002 [1983]; B. Longenecker 2002 is a further useful overview and assessment of the method with respect to Pauline analysis.)

But Beker did not just name two important dynamics within Pauline explanation. He named them in relation to one another. By identifying the importance of both contingency and coherence, Beker insisted that Paul's conceptuality could not simply be read out of Paul's texts automatically or in any straightforward way; his texts are not simply coherent. Their basic texture is irreducibly contingent. Paul's coherence can be recovered only through the patient interpretation of their occasional expression. Yet any occasional accounts of these texts must nevertheless be informed, he insisted in equal measure, by some account of Paul's coherence at work within them. Paul's contingent texts are infused in some way with an overarching coherence. A single chameleon, we might say, underlies the shifting colors and patterns.

Few if any scholars today accept the exact terms in which Beker set up his dialectical interpretative hypothesis; however, all do accept its basic claims and tend to proceed accordingly: with accounts within any explanation of a Pauline text of its contingency, its coherence, and the interplay between these two dynamics. Indeed, historical work on Paul, whether in toto or in part, is effectively impossible in any other terms. Given the brute fact of textual diversity, an utterly coherent account — the view that Paul is simply providing propositions exclusively drawn from his own theological system — is untenable. Clearly, Paul is overtly circumstantial in much that he writes. But the equally obvious facts of textual overlap coupled with, at the least, occasional moments of sustained argument within letters, not to mention terms and claims held in common across different texts, entail that some degree of coherence must be in play as well. Paul must hold certain propositions constant within and between sentences for much of the time, or his words would be simply random — meaningless — which they patently are not. All scholars in effect concede, then, that contingency and coherence are in play in some sense within all Pauline interpretation, and hence the question of their relationship is posed automatically. Beker's formulation captures the complex ways in which Paul's letters both overlap with and diverge from one another in terms that are essentially undeniable. And given its importance, we ought now to probe it a little more deeply.

2. A Conundrum

When we press on Beker's account, we quickly discover that to name the problems of contingency, coherence, and their relationship within Pauline explanation more broadly is by no means to have resolved them. Beker himself tends to jump straightaway from this prescient articulation to a particular solution rather as a magician pulls a rabbit out of a hat (see, e.g., 1984 [1980], 16-19). He does try to justify his thesis in due course. But his frequent restatements and difficulties (see esp. xiv-xxi)[2] indicate that further work on the account of the problem needs to be done before any proposed solution can be successful.

The difficulty begins to emerge when we realize that there are significant variations in the ways key interpreters have understood and correlated the basic dynamics of contingency and coherence. We can consider five important and rather different accounts of their relationship here first.

(i) A more traditional account of Paul tends to read him as a thinker who takes pains to articulate at any given moment only what accords with a carefully constructed prior theological orchestration. The circumstances surrounding each letter therefore catalyze the deployment of some of these resources but do not shape or elicit them in any stronger sense. It is possible simply to extract from the letters the data and arrange it topically without further ado, yielding a description of Paul's conceptuality that holds together overtly and intelligibly as a theological account. As a result, Paul's letters are viewed as largely coherent in propositional and even logical terms, merely mediated by their contingency or circumstances.

This is of course a maximal account of Paul's coherence, although its nature is also being envisaged in certain terms. And most modern interpretation of Paul has been deeply unconvinced by it. But it represents one basic approach to the correlation of contingency and coherence in Paul, arguably lingering in the topical approach of many of the major current accounts of Paul's theology.[3] We can turn now to consider its polar opposite.

2. Beker suggests at one point that "the coherent center of Paul's thought is constituted by a symbolic apocalyptic field, originating out of a profound experience, which comes to expression in an apocalyptic grammar" (xx).

3. See, e.g., the topical organization of Dunn (1998) and Schreiner (2001). The famous earlier treatments of Whiteley (1964) and Ridderbos (1975 [1966]) are also indicative. Schnelle (2005 [2003]), with its initial biographical discussion, is a partial exception discussed in more detail shortly, although ultimately it still treats Paul's thought topically (387-597). More fully exceptional is J. Becker (1993 [1989]), which is biographical throughout. As we turn to note Bultmann's vastly influential work, we step from specialized treatments of Paul per se to treatments of Paul's thought within the broader ambit of NT theology as a whole. But the same judgment tends to be appropriate there. Bultmann himself treats Paul's thought entirely under two topical headings — "Man Prior to the Revelation of Faith" (1951-55, 1:190-269) and "Man under Faith" (1:270-352). Recent major contributions to NT theology are reviewed helpfully by

(ii) Some interpreters suggest a maximal account of Paul's contingency that minimizes the role of any coherence — so, for example, the reading offered by Heikki Räisänen.[4] Räisänen argues that Paul is a demonstrably ad hoc thinker, manufacturing statements and positions for temporary rhetorical and local advantage. We might say, then, that in each letter he basically tells his auditors whatever their itching ears want to hear, as long as this maintains his own objectives within their situation (and these can be viewed rather diversely, whether in terms of power, money, loyalty, and so on). It is therefore fruitless to search for any overarching coherence, because Paul is a conceptual opportunist. A slightly less cynical variation on this basic approach that also appears at times in Räisänen's analyses suggests, rather, that he is deeply confused. Paul would deploy coherence if he could, but he cannot hold together the issues that he is debating in a coherent fashion, arguably because his different positions cannot be held together. He tends to paint himself into corners. Different letters — and even some letters within themselves, such as Romans — articulate incommensurate conceptualities, although the overall result is the same: an essentially contingent corpus informed by no basic coherence at all.

Most scholars feel, however, that Paul's coherence cannot be dissolved completely into momentary rhetorical advantage or confusion, even if at times it can be. So they posit accounts of contingency and coherence that lie somewhere between these two options.

(iii) Beker clearly gestures toward an alternative account of contingency that takes Paul's coherence more seriously than does Räisänen, without losing sight of the influence of circumstances on the texture of Paul's texts, as a more traditional account tends to. We have already noted its main suggestions and so will only summarize them here. According to Beker, Paul contextualizes his material within the forms and situations of his auditors so that his letters take on a very different texture for each spe-

---

Rowe (2006); see also Matera (2005). (Rowe's monumental review treats Stuhlmacher 1991-99; Gnilka 1994; Strecker 2000 [1996]; Vouga 2001; Hahn 2001-5 [2002]; and Wilckens 2002-5; as well as Caird 1994; Esler 2005; I. Marshall 2004, 209-488; and Thielman 2005; noting in closing the more expansive Childs 1992.) To these figures we should now add, at the least, Swartley (2006, 189-253); and Matera (2007, 99-258). Topical treatments are evident throughout.

4. Most famously 1987 [1983]; but see also 1988. His corresponding account of NT theology can be found in 2000 [1990].

cific situation. This sensitive hermeneutical behavior on his part does not entail, however, that his coherence has been lost. Rather, it has merely been *translated* into local idioms, in response to specific local issues — a dynamic account of the presentation of the gospel that Beker rather admires. So a reversal of this process by the Pauline interpreter should be able to recover the coherence that is at work within the letters. We do not reduce Paul's letters directly to coherence, as in option one, but neither do we abandon coherence altogether, as in option two.

But is this all we need to say? Other scholars have suggested that other key dynamics within this process need to be recognized.

(iv)　E. P. Sanders can represent a fourth principal option (at least, in his famous early publications 1977 and 1983).[5] Sanders articulates an account of the relationship between contingency and coherence in Paul that lies in effect between Räisänen's and Beker's. Like Beker, he is persuaded that coherence can be recovered from Paul's texts in relation to certain pressing issues that his communities forced him to address. However, like Räisänen, he is not convinced that this coherence is always commensurate. According to Sanders, different issues raised by different situations in different communities can lead Paul to draw on different clusters of coherence as he responds. Within each cluster and in response to certain questions these communications are coherent, but the clusters are not especially coherent when placed side by side. (Although Sanders claims that his account of Paul is coherent in another sense from Beker, namely, that it explains coherently why Paul is often conceptually incoherent: Paul responds consistently to different questions with different systems. But this is of course a very different notion of coherence from Beker's.)[6] In short, Sanders sees Paul's coherence as possessing areas

---

5. And more so in 1983 than his more famous 1977 (which treats Paul directly in 431-523). To reiterate, I am referring here to what we might dub the "early" or "classic" Sanders; for the views of the "later" Sanders, which are introduced momentarily, see his 2008.

6. Sanders has recently clarified that he distinguishes conceptual coherence in Paul from systematizing. The former is, in his definition, a certain sort of "clumping" or "clustering" of notions together; the latter is, in his definition, a more hierarchical and rigid taxonomical ordering of ideas or notions (2008, 325-30). He is happy to use coherence (in his definition) to describe Paul's thought, but not systematizing. Here, however, I am using Beker's definition of coherence, which is probably more like the "systematizing" that Sanders rejects, although Beker too would doubtless reject the suggestion that Paul systematized in quite the way that

of what we might call unresolved material. Not everything has been strictly correlated in systematic terms. But there are bunches or clusters of coherent material activated discernibly by different issues.[7]

Up to this point, our main options have basically assumed that the phenomenon (or not) of conceptual coherence in Paul can be explained in essentially synchronic terms that nevertheless hold firm diachronically: he makes perfect sense consistently at all times; he makes no consistent sense at any time; he translates consistently in every situation; or he draws intelligibly on particular clusters of coherence in relation to particular questions as they arise. But we need now to consider a rather different explanatory angle on our central problem that abandons this assumption.

(v) Some scholars have argued that Paul changes his mind about certain things, which introduces a further explanatory dynamic.[8] As certain

---

Sanders describes this in 2008, i.e., essentially taxonomically. However, Beker thinks that Paul's underlying conceptuality is a "core" of convictions about the Christ event that is translated in different contexts, and this is in fact a reasonable account of what many contemporary theologians would recognize as "systematic theology," where the eschewal of overly rigid systematizing and of taxonomies is widespread. So, e.g., Karl Barth in his *Church Dogmatics* clearly attempts to provide a rigorous account of appropriate Christian thinking, i.e., of systematic theology; indeed, his conceptualizing could hardly be more systematic. But he firmly repudiates any suggestion that his rich account *is* a "system," along with the very possibility that God's activity in Christ *can* be systematized — the sort of conceptual orchestration that both Sanders and Beker also reject. And this realization concerning the actual nature of most systematic Christian thinking limits the force of its repudiation in relation to Paul. It seems that if the descriptor "systematic" can be understood in more flexible and appropriate terms, then it can be applied to Paul's thinking, at least as a possibility. (Whether it *is* the best account of his underlying thought must wait for the framing of his letters.)

7. Lakoff (2002) provides an interesting point of comparison when he analyzes the "bi-conceptual" nature of most current American voters; two fundamental and quite different conceptual models inform their political activity. The situation has a straightforward explanation in underlying bodily terms, namely, the simultaneous coexistence of different worldviews within the brain. Once both have been introduced, political decision making is then in part a matter merely of activation, a view of mental and bodily activity that reinforces Sanders's intuitive sense of the same operating in Paul in soteriological and ethical terms.

8. A classic account of this is also regrettably superficial: Buck and Taylor (1969). Buck's approach lay at the center of a cluster of developmental analysts that included Riddle (1940) and Hurd (1983 [1965]). R. Longenecker, my Doktorvater, also emphasized development in Paul's thinking strongly, although he did not publish any sustained treatment of it. However, the approach is noted briefly in his 1998. More rigorous is Tatum (2006); he has influenced his Doktorvater, Sanders (see now 2008).

contingencies arose, such interpreters suggest, Paul was forced to think through new questions that had not yet occurred to him. And the result was, they suggest — perhaps not surprisingly — that he modified his coherence. That is, he did not merely apply a coherent position that was already in place just waiting to be deployed. Nor did he make up something altogether new. His existing coherence was altered by this engagement. There are minimal and maximal suggestions in this regard. Minimalists suggest that Paul introduced minor alterations, and perhaps only to positions that later tradition would view as secondary matters. Perhaps he adjusted his views on local church government. Perhaps he changed his mind on whether church leaders should be paid. More worryingly, however, he might have changed his mind about the future fate of deceased Christians, at which point we are edging toward a more maximal account of his development. Indeed, some go so far as to suggest that each new circumstance bequeathed to Paul a significant new set of terms and arguments that then resonates traceably through subsequent letters, fading, but still detectable, as it becomes less pertinent.

This view clearly introduces a further significant variable into the possible correlation between contingency and coherence in Paul's texts. Minimal developmental advocates see Paul's coherence modifying in a nuanced fashion in relation to each contingency; maximalists detect a rather small initial reservoir of coherence that is augmented significantly by each new situation. Hence, not only does Paul's coherence shift, but it grows, although in each case just how much and in what sense is fiercely debated. It is enough for now, however, simply to note this basic suggestion.

Although it is tempting to place these options on a continuum, and not altogether improper at times to do so, their accounts are not mutually exclusive. They propose (in Beker's terms) different, at times overlapping, hermeneutics concerning the relationship between contingency and conceptuality. But more worryingly, it is apparent on reflection that these could easily interchange from text to text and situation to situation. At one moment, Paul could draw on innate tradition and prior conceptuality directly and simply and then apply it (option one). At another moment, he could feel a strong rhetorical need to create a certain dynamic. But lacking the traditional resources, he might make something up or deploy a rather random appeal (option two). Alternatively, on a given issue, he might draw on his most important convictions but translate them carefully into local idiom (option three). Then again, he might switch between different and somewhat unresolved traditions and conceptualities as still another issue arises (option four). However, as certain situations arise, it might be that he is prompted to engage instead in some hard thinking, modifying his principal coherence and proceeding to think and to argue accordingly (option five). In short, all these options could plausibly be in play at some point within Paul's letters and hence need to be drawn upon for accurate explanation by the Pauline interpreter. So articulating clearly the relationship between contingency and coherence in Paul is a deeply challenging task. And it is about to get even more so.

Although Pauline scholars work fairly frequently with the foregoing approaches, they tend to direct far less attention to the *nature* of Paul's coherence, which can be conceived in oddly stereotypical and anachronistic terms. We need to appreciate that different options exist here as well, a situation that can be illuminated further if we initiate a brief conversation with George Lindbeck (1984).

Lindbeck famously suggested that theological conceptuality can take different forms. (He is of course concerned with modern theological movements, but his insights are still instructive, suitably modified, for the interpreter of Paul.) He identifies three basic modes. The first is strictly propositional — "cognitivist" — this being the bête noire that many interpreters resist attributing to Paul. The second is more experiential — "experiential-expressive," as he puts it. The third, overlooked in Lindbeck's view for far too long, is traditioned — his designation is "cultural-linguistic."

Lindbeck's views are subtle, and have been paralleled and developed in many ways, but for our purposes here it suffices to appreciate his argument that conceptuality per se does not exist apart from language, and that language does not exist apart from practices, habits, and communities, which themselves possess a history. These claims suggest that Paul's coherence should not necessarily be conceived of fundamentally as a distinguishable schema arranged propositionally within his own mental universe, which is inserted in some way into his texts as he engages with local circumstances. Indeed, this looks suspiciously like a prejudicial construct animated by the post-Cartesian predilections of much modern Western philosophy. Nor should it necessarily be understood as a translation of an underlying primordial religious experience of God, which risks reifying anachronistically some of the central claims of modern liberal Protestantism and even of European romanticism. Paul's conceptuality might have a fundamentally different *nature* from these explanatory suppositions. It might be embedded in a broader community and within various traditions as a set of habits and practices (understanding these in a certain way) that are adjusting to changing contexts. And language would consequently articulate this conceptuality in a different mode from what we might expect — principally as reformulated narrative and tradition (and here we link hands with Lakoff).

We do not need to pronounce here on the validity of Lindbeck's well-known assertions. They suffice to introduce further possibilities into our unfolding consideration of Beker's approach to Paul. Lindbeck challenges the Pauline interpreter to be open to the problem of divergence — not to mention anachronism — in the way that Paul's coherence is conceptualized. He suggests that the analysis of Paul's thinking might often contain an unexamined endorsement of individualism and interiorization — a demonstrably culture-bound and fallacious account. Further, he opens up the particular possibility that Paul's conceptuality is very unlike our own, perhaps being more broadly Aristotelian in mode, or at least distinctively ancient rather than modern and so frequently communal, narrative, and traditioned.[9] And the task of the Pauline interpreter in relation to Beker's program has now become even more complex than it was before. Not only must she coordinate contingency and coherence, but she must remain open to the different possibilities concerning the shape of Paul's coherence within that coordination, not to mention Paul's location vis-à-vis his broader community.

We might be tempted to throw up our hands at this point and say, "Who cares?" — that is, to abandon the quest for the historical Paul's thinking. But many people care deeply about this situation. For those who attend to Paul's writings in historical mode, if only to some degree, the situation is deeply disturbing.[10] His coherence is — to borrow a Matthean image — a pearl of great price (13:45-46), and we need to find some way of buying it if we can. But in order to do so, we need to appreciate that the challenge is no longer merely complex. This situation and its central methodological conundrum as Beker has formulated it *is almost entirely unresolvable.* The differences between these fundamentally different options cannot be adjudicated except in a certain, carefully defined way. Conversely, the way that these options are adjudicated at present seems almost invariably to be circular and incoherent, trapping much modern Pauline interpretation in a morass of corrupt conclusions.

---

9. The modern recovery of his discourse is associated especially with the work of Alasdair MacIntyre (see his 1988; 1990; 2007 [1981]).

10. It is the more so if his writings, read in these basic terms, are viewed as authoritative, if not infallible.

3. The Solution in Outline: A Framing Account

In order to assess the plausibility of the different options concerning Paul's coherence, both in nature and in influence, the interpreter *must* be able to articulate, at least in rough terms, the circumstances through which any coherence is being expressed. Moreover, the circumstances *must* be known across at least some, and ideally all, of the letters. Only this allows the interpreter to reach valid judgments about the probity of the different views of Paul's coherence being offered, although even then it clearly remains a difficult task.

Unless we know the basic circumstances surrounding the composition of a letter, we simply cannot tell whether Paul primarily is deploying his own conceptuality, is making things up in an ad hoc manner to influence those circumstances directly, is contextualizing within those circumstances, or is drawing on different conceptualities for the different questions those circumstances generate. All these widely differing accounts of the text would be entirely possible, because we have no way of filtering out the contribution from the circumstances, not knowing them. And without knowing the circumstances of his other letters as well, we cannot make any progress on these vital issues. *Only a comparative analysis within which the contribution of circumstances to the composition of more than one letter can be controlled* (at least to some degree) *offers any hope of valid judgments on questions of contingency and coherence.* (And it is this realization above all that rules out atomistic, piecemeal approaches to Pauline interpretation, working from each letter individually, as a sufficient interpretative act.)[11]

If a basic account of some or even all the relevant letters' contingencies is in place, then the interpreter can control for the contribution of contingency across the different situations and reach a judgment about the nature and role of Paul's coherence. As Paul operates coherently in relation to different circumstances — assuming that he does — the Pauline interpreter should be able to identify that coherence. And this identification can then perhaps be cross-checked with the opposite situation, namely, his responses to similar

---

11. The careful address of individual letters in their own terms is an important interpretative move in certain situations, and will be undertaken here esp. in chs. 4, 5, and 6; it is usually referred to later as the text's "immediate implied exigence" — the account that a letter supplies of its own immediate exigence. But my claim here is that broader judgments about the nature of Paul's thinking will be impossible if analysis stays at this level. Indeed, deeper analysis even of an individual letter will ultimately be frustrated as well, since judgments about the contributions of Paul's theology will be impossible, as will accurate assessments of any implications flowing from adjacent letters and situations in Paul's life.

contingencies, where his coherence should hold reasonably steady, if he possesses it. The presence of both comparative scenarios will allow the Pauline
interpreter to adjudicate between the different options posited in explanation
of the dialectic between contingency and coherence in Paul's texts. And this
all suggests that *any valid Pauline interpretation in any historical respect must
begin with a workable account of the letters' circumstances in relation to one
another.* We must tell the story of their interrelated composition. This is the
sine qua non of all valid historical interpretation of Paul. Furthermore, this
implication needs to be appreciated in all its programmatic force.

Any interpretation of *any* Pauline text in historical-critical terms that
extends beyond textual superficialities and claims in terms of immediate
exigence presupposes that the interpreter knows the story within which that
text is embedded. If this story is wrong by way of methodological overreach
or contamination, then the analysis is probably significantly flawed as well.
How much current Pauline exegesis is mistaken because the historical story
of the letters it presupposes is corrupt? The figure might be disturbingly
high.

We should go on to note immediately that this story will have a certain
distinctive shape. It will be the story of the circumstances in which Paul wrote
his letters, so it will have a biographical quality. It will not be a complete biography in the sense of an intellectual biography; we are pursuing this preliminary biography so that we can write that thicker, richer account on its basis.
Moreover, it will need to extend past Paul, to a degree, into his relationships
with his communities, and into some of their significant relationships with
one another in turn, although only the relevant contingent information at
these points is required; not every biographical detail that can be gleaned from
the texts informs the circumstances that surround the letters' composition. In
short, Pauline interpreters working in historical mode desperately need — to
draw at this moment on Derrida — the Pauline story that *frames* the letters.[12]
(And there are other good reasons for this project to be minimal,[13] although it

---

12. Framing is explained helpfully by B. Johnson (1980 [1978]), as noted earlier.

13. If what I have argued up to this point is broadly correct, then interpreters will need
to agree on this framing account if they are to move forward into richer explanations of Paul's
life and thought. This frame will need to be the basis for some consensus. The simpler, then,
not to mention the clearer, the better. Interpreters tend to find such framing discussions complex and forbidding. The analysis of the details of Paul's life, and of things like the dates when
he arrived in certain cities, can lead interpreters down various rabbit holes (and into entire
warrens). We need at all costs, then, to enhance this account's clarity and accessibility, and this
can presumably be assisted by minimizing what we need to agree on.

is emphatically not an "atomistic" account.[14]) Once this is appreciated, we can turn to consider the nature of the evidence that must underlie its derivation — another vital discussion.

4. The Frame's Arguments

4.1 Avoiding Vicious Circularity

Put at its simplest, we need to appreciate that certain arguments must be avoided when constructing this frame or it will be compromised irretrievably. And the key constraint here is actually quite simple. We must at all costs, during the construction, avoid introducing judgments concerning interpretative dimensions in Paul that we are going to reach later on, after the frame has been completed — and so are based on it. This seems to be a fairly obvious caution, but it is violated so frequently by Pauline interpreters that it needs to be grasped with complete clarity.

If, for example, we introduce convictions about Paul's coherence into our initial frame, we will generate a corrupt explanation in several respects. First, we have no basis for this privileging of our conceptual convictions; it is merely arbitrary. Second, this arbitrary privileging contaminates our framing account, distorting it and rendering it effectively useless as a control. Third, if we go on to claim eventually that this frame underwrites our conceptual convictions, then we fail to recognize the vicious circularity both undergirding and invalidating our conclusions.

14. This framing account is still an integrated explanation of a significant swath of Paul's life and hence in part an explicit rejection of methodological atomism. We cannot assume that the broader explanation of Paul will emerge if we work independently on its smaller constituent units — that localized interpretation, done well, will simply lead to the crafting of small explanatory blocks that can fit together in only one way, so that, by doing this repeatedly, we can gradually build up a convincing overarching edifice. To be sure, there is a partial truth in this approach. But the Pauline data is linguistic and thus unstable. In effect, the building blocks change shape depending on the broader explanations of the field that are in play. Linguistic data will shift depending on the rules, practices, and connotations thought to be operative. Localized interpretation that is insensitive to this will consequently risk endorsing a questionable overarching explanation in the name of a naïve presuppositionless objectivity, invalidly of course. It is better, then, to appreciate that Pauline explanation is seeking to grasp an integrated field of evidence of great complexity that shifts, to a degree, depending on the explanations being brought to bear at any given moment. Hence, explanations must be attempted at a suitably controlled and broad level — in this case, in an account that frames all the letters together. This seems to be the correct explanatory unit for our discussion.

This concern is no straw man. For example, Udo Schnelle has relatively recently provided a benchmark account of Paul's thought that both distinctively and impressively recognizes its integration with his biography. Yet Schnelle excludes from the outset six of the thirteen canonical letters bearing Paul's name from his complex and subtle theological reconstruction, assigning them to a Pauline "school" (2005 [2003], 146-51). This exclusion takes place on the grounds that "in all the deutero-Paulines, Paul's emphasis on the doctrine of justification, as found in Galatians and Romans, remarkably subsides. Apocalyptic motifs in Christology likewise decline in importance, and an emphasis on present eschatology prevails. The focus is on matters of church order and problems of ethics that have emerged because of the altered situation in the life of the church (the appearance of false teachers; coming to terms with the failure of the parousia)" (150).

Schnelle gives a faithful account of the thinking of most Pauline analysts here. But what is remarkable is the overt circularity present in the a priori assertion of each of these claims if they are introduced at the most basic level of his analysis, which they are. For this case to hold, Pauline interpreters must know that Galatians and Romans contain a "doctrine of justification" and, moreover, that this is a constant for Paul, necessarily appearing in all his authentic works irrespective of contingency. And they must know the same things in turn concerning "apocalyptic motifs in Christology," and the same things in reverse in relation to "present eschatology," "church order," and "ethics" (i.e., that the authentic Paul did not emphasize these and no circumstances ever unfolded that might have led him to address them). But they can know these things only after the historical Paul has first been reconstructed in toto and the circumstances surrounding the composition of his letters controlled so that this picture of his contingency has emerged. Hence, to build these assumptions into that reconstruction at the outset is to vitiate the entire process. Schnelle's construction must now be suspect in fundamental terms. The very shape of his account of the Pauline data must be viewed as problematic.

We cannot appeal to Paul's principal theological convictions when framing, because we do not yet know what they are.[15] Similarly, we cannot appeal

---

15. But there should be a palpable sense of relief when discussions of things like "Paul and the law" are liberated from their inextricable tangle with various biographical claims. Multiple biographies of Paul and the law are possible, and adjudicating between them is largely impossible when all the data and all the explanatory levels are on the table at the same time. *Paul's view of the law should be assisted if not controlled by a biographical frame that is already in place, and on grounds that are independent of the adjudication of the issue.*

to his lexical choices, at least strongly, because we do not yet know whether he is a hermeneutical chameleon, adapting his lexicon to local circumstances, as against someone with a very rigid and limited lexicon. (Claims concerning the lexical encyclopedia available culturally to him in general terms will still be relevant.) Moreover, we do not yet know what the circumstances are to which he might be adapting. And so on.[16] We can, in short, use only evidence and argumentation that do not beg important later questions.[17] Where question-begging arguments are offered, we must rebuff them.[18]

One might respond to these strictures with the concern, "What arguments are left?" So some clarifications concerning the nature of the evidence underlying the frame should now be helpful. Indeed, the rest of this book will unfold rather like a classic treasure hunt.

4.2 The Appropriate Roles of Criticism and Doubt

Just as fictional treasure hunters face an overt problem — usually, piecing together subtle clues into a map that leads the heroes to a buried store of ancient riches — so we face the overt problem of the Pauline letters' frame. And just as the fictional investigators must sift a mass of evidence for the relevant pieces of information, that is, the clues, and decode their cryptic messages, we too must sift a data pool for the appropriate pieces of evidence and fit them together. But we need to give some thought to just what our clues might consist of.

We have already established that certain clues must *not* be introduced. We cannot introduce claims based on concealed judgments that have not yet been generated by our overarching investigation, injecting vicious circularity into the process. The treasure hunter should not simply decide in advance of her investigation that the treasure is hidden in a particular room or house, or even on a specific island. Moreover, we need to be attentive to the different

---

16. This approach will also allow a useful control over the influence of presuppositions derived from tradition. Such presuppositions are not in themselves necessarily bad, but they can function unhelpfully.

17. Resisting such arguments psychologically is a different matter. Kahneman (2011) documents numerous ways in which such methodological vigilance can falter, and we will call upon his exposés frequently in what follows.

18. These constraints sharply limit the value for this effort of the vast majority of the secondary literature addressing matters of Pauline biography and the circumstances surrounding the composition of the letters, as will become apparent in much that follows.

levels of confidence that we can place in alternative construals of our ancient and fragmentary data. Frequently, this data admits of multiple explanations; we need to proceed with construals that are certain or at least highly probable — as against probabilistic and only corroborative, or merely possible and thus little more than broadly supportive. We will need to be alert to the infiltration of evidence from this last category up through the hierarchy to the first, that is, possible readings masquerading as probable or even certain evidence. And we need to be sensitive to the correct methodological functions of criticism and doubt, since it will be easy to cast doubt in general terms on the small clues that underpin much of the reconstruction of the Pauline frame, a consideration worth exploring in more detail.

Descartes suggested, in a classic argument widely influential in the modern period, that everything is in effect guilty until proved innocent. The result was, rather famously, the reduction of all certain knowledge to the conviction that his mental processes at least guaranteed his existence. In other words, he used radical doubt as a fundamental method. Everything must be doubted until it can be demonstrated indubitably to be true.

Now, it can certainly be granted that it is helpful at times to reorient paradigms and to strip away faulty thinking, and radical doubt seems to achieve these advances. But the Cartesian method has struggled to get anywhere significant and has, moreover, been subjected to ferocious critique, not least from Wittgenstein, who pointed out (characteristically indirectly) that the use of language implies participation in a broader linguistic community, which is in turn difficult to detach from a complex broader reality that cannot be doubted in the first instance without lapsing into utter incoherence. So Descartes's key initial claims are in fact delusional. Unfortunately, however, the critical method, which played such a significant role in the rise of the modern university, has had a long dalliance with Cartesianism, so the latter tends to live on, haunting the corridors of the academy like a restless shade. It allowed figures like Kant to reject tradition out of hand and to argue from simpler and more certain first principles, although Kant too struggled to develop his principles with the certainty and extension that he really sought. It is not a completely crass oversimplification to suggest, then, that many modern Pauline scholars, shaped in part by the traditions at work in the modern university, seem to assume, at least at times, that the "critical" assessment of evidence simply involves the application of doubt in a generic way, ultimately in the manner of Descartes. It is a posture of comprehensive skepticism. One must be unconvinced until one is convinced of something's probity on certain grounds. But I would suggest that when practiced in this generic and universal manner, this is an invalid and self-defeating methodology and a false understanding of criticism.[19]

We have already gestured toward the method's invalidity by way of a failure to account for language, but it is worth adding here that this method will lead us in Pauline studies to precisely nothing. Everything the Pauline scholar claims can be doubted on Cartesian grounds. One of the method's great difficulties in general is reaching in any significant way into what we might call immediate external reality (and certain scholars have gone on to struggle mightily with this), which falls far short of any reconstruction of the past. There have not been many rigorously Cartesian historians. And it follows that any partial application of the method is inconsistent as well. That is, any scholar laying claim at any point in historicist terms to something originally true in relation to Pauline reconstruction cannot turn at another point and make a Cartesian claim, because that would be fundamentally incoherent. But if the programmatic practice of doubt is self-defeating, then we ought to pry the notion of criticism loose from its dead hand.

Criticism, correctly conceived, is the application of the appropriate feedback from any data under consideration to any hypothesis currently being suggested to account for it. Hypotheses are not ultimately endorsed without the appropriate data (although we should add that the sort of feedback that critics expect will depend, most importantly, on the nature of the object under investigation, i.e., on the actual nature of the data). Criticism assesses this central explanatory relationship. And doubt can be an important part of the process. Appropriate doubt is directed at a hypothesis when it fails to account for the relevant data, at which point it should be modified or abandoned, and this irrespective of its relationship to tradition. Interpreters will have difficulty deriving and initially processing hypotheses without tradition, so tradition remains essential, but it is not unquestioned. The critical process is thus broader than the mere presence of doubt and is by no means reducible to it. Indeed, it begins in exactly the opposite way, somewhat fideistically, with the positing

19. A lively introduction to the roles of Cartesian and post-Cartesian "critical" thinking within the modern university can be found in Readings (1996, esp. 44-69). Deeper critiques specifically of the Cartesian subject are C. Taylor (1989); MacIntyre (1990); and, in an important earlier treatment that dialogues especially informatively with Bultmann, Thielicke (1974 [1968]). More accessible overviews of the entire development of this discourse are supplied by Gellner (1988) and Poole (1991). I cover some of this territory in ch. 9 of my 2009 (295-309). Also significant is Hauerwas (2002), the issues becoming apparent as he contrasts the thinking of William James and Reinhold Niebuhr, two doyens of modernity, with Karl Barth, the scourge of modernist thinking within theology.

of an appropriate hypothesis in explanation of a given problem in a data set, sensitive to the nature of that data and the methods appropriate to evaluation, with doubt potentially entering the process at a later stage. Appropriate, essentially scientific criticism, we might say then, never takes place in a vacuum, and neither does appropriate doubt; both are always considering the relationship between evidence and its interpretation.[20] The following reconstruction therefore welcomes both criticism and doubt at the appropriate points but is uninterested in criticism and doubt per se.[21]

We will rely on slender snippets of evidence in what follows, because that is all that we have — occasional and fragmentary remains of conversations that took place millennia ago. But we do have evidence, and it will not do to dismiss parts of the following reconstruction with a generic claim that "this is insufficient" or "there is still not enough evidence." If this is the evidence that we have and it explains the data in the best existing fashion, then the correct scientific conclusion must be to endorse it and not to complain that we need more data that unfortunately does not exist.

With these brief methodological clarifications in place, we can turn to the important practical question that remains: Can this reconstruction actually be achieved? Does the Pauline treasure hunter, in effect, have sufficient clues to find the cache of lost riches? The short answer is yes, and the reason for my confidence lies in the fact that the way forward has already been indicated in all essentials by John Knox, although much yet remains to be done. It is as if a basic map has already been drawn indicating where the treasure lies buried, but the difficult journey there has yet to take place, and one or two unforeseen challenges need to be navigated on the way.

---

20. Polanyi (1964 [1958]) has been particularly seminal for my understanding here (see also his more accessible 1966). Many of the critical theological consequences are grasped and articulated peerlessly by T. F. Torrance (see esp. his 1969a; 1969b; 1971; 1976).

21. How might we recognize inappropriate doubt masquerading as valid criticism? Such doubt generally does not attend to the actual data and its explanation, falsifying it directly. It begs the question. Or, more commonly, it suggests a comparative situation but fails to supply the comparison; a given argument might be pronounced insufficient to convince, but what exactly establishes argumentative sufficiency is not stated (and usually cannot be). Of course, such judgments are meaningless without an overt standard or measure of sufficiency. And that measure is the data itself in relation to the broader object under investigation and the current explanation in play! Do these actually match up, or is a problem discernible in their relationship(s)? If the latter, the appropriate critical process should elicit doubt, along with the modification or abandonment of the hypothesis. Modification or the clear provision of an explanatory alternative is a signal that the appropriate critical method and doubt are operative. Without these elements, a doubting critic runs the danger of merely posturing.

5. Completing Knox

I suggest that John Knox articulated some time ago all the main moves that need to be made in relation to the data to generate a reliable account of the Pauline frame.[22] Just why it has taken the world of Pauline scholarship so long to recognize this is an interesting question, but it should not detain us here. Certainly, he has not lacked support altogether.[23] It must suffice to say that I will try in what follows to update, occasionally correct, and thereby complete Knox's project, and this should result in a persuasive account of the Pauline frame.

Knox made two distinguishable and especially significant proposals in this regard. First, he drew a vital distinction between different sources in the data. This has been much misrepresented, however, so we will have to re-present that suggestion here, and to articulate it further, since it lacks precision with respect to our current concerns. Second, he sketched out an argument that can, through a series of specific steps, derive a frame plausibly from that data without begging any key questions. After much further research and reflection, I would suggest that this argument cannot be improved upon in basic terms. Once again, however, it requires considerable further articulation, along with, at times, slight correction.

We should now pause to consider the two key dimensions in Knox's work in more detail, since they underpin so much of what follows. We will take up his initial clarifications with respect to the sources in the remainder of this chapter and then move on in the rest of the book to work out his second contribution in detail. That is, we will spend most of our time reconstructing the Pauline frame by way of a series of carefully argued steps through the data as Knox basically suggested them. But before proceeding to that task, we must appreciate clearly his claims about the sources.

---

22. His key work is 1987 [1950], esp. pp. 31-52, with the epistolary evidence treated on pp. 31-41. It was anticipated by 1936 and 1939, and intriguing subsequent reflections followed in 1983 and 1990.

23. Some have already been mentioned, notably, Hurd (1983 [1965]); Buck and Taylor (1969); Tatum (2006). Sanders (1977, 432) provides passing support. But see also Hare (1987 [1950], ix-xxii), in the introduction to Knox (1987 [1950]); Donfried's entry concerning Pauline chronology in the *ABD* (1992); and, perhaps most significantly, Luedemann (esp. 1984 [1980]; but see also 1989a; 1989b [1983]). Jewett (1979) is also an important figure, who is close to Knox in certain respects but charts his own course in others.

5.1 Handling the Sources Appropriately

Knox introduced a strong distinction concerning the sources within the broader pool of available data (see 1987 [1950], esp. 17-28, rhetorically antic-ipated by 3-16) — a distinction that has been much misunderstood. Further reflection suggests, however, that it is both simple and incontestable.

Knox observed that Paul's authentic letters are "primary," meaning that they come from his own hand and hence directly from the circumstances that enfolded them. Their data is close to the events in question; it emerged directly out of the events, at times functioning causally within them. Over against this, the data concerning Paul in the book of Acts, the second princi-pal historical reservoir for his life, is something of an unknown quantity. We do not know who wrote Acts, when, where, or — perhaps most importantly — why. We do not know — and certainly not at first glance — what the re-lationship was between the author and Paul. So this data is of "secondary" status over against the primary epistolary data. It is an unknown quantity that might come from much later on and at some remove from Paul himself. It follows that we ought to begin our reconstruction of the Pauline frame with the epistolary data *and with this alone.* Acts' secondary data cannot be allowed to intrude into the processing of the epistolary material or it will in effect contaminate it.

Once the epistolary data has been processed successfully and some sort of explanatory frame derived, then the data from Acts can be introduced into an exquisitely controlled situation. We will be able finally to derive just the judgment that many have been seeking for so long — a sense of the ac-curacy of the book's account of Paul, which can be derived by comparing its data with the Pauline material. Any bias in the Acts account will be overtly detectable and so could be corrected by the modern Pauline interpreter. In-deed, having noted the overt advantage of this situation, it is frustrating to observe how frequently Pauline interpreters flout this principle and muddle epistolary and Acts data together from the outset. In my experience, a great deal of the confusion generally present in Pauline biography derives from the failure to prescind from this practice. Once Knox's key distinction has been abandoned, there is no way back — no coherent way to correct a situation that has descended into methodological chaos. When the advantages of preserving this distinction and following this rule are so great, and the disadvantages of violating it so debilitating, it is puzzling why more scholars do not seem to hold to it. But the reason may lie in some pervasive misunderstandings that we should now consider.

(i) Neither Knox nor I would claim that Paul's data is perfect or completely unbiased. Paul is clearly imparting his own rhetorical bias to many of his biographical claims. But there is Pauline data pertinent to framing concerns that might have been somewhat inadvertent to Paul himself (where his biography is not an overt issue but biographical details arise in passing), and this can be mined for information with less risk of deceptive bias. Admittedly, Paul is at times deeply invested in narrating his activities appropriately — that is, where competing and frequently unflattering accounts of his behavior are being offered by others. However, we must appreciate that Knox's claim concerning a chasm in initial quality between the data in the letters and that found in Acts is an essentially comparative judgment. The Acts data is initially opaque, irrespective of what we make of Paul. It could be spun out of thin air, for all we know. So the distinction between the two data sets remains valid in spite of Paul's obvious imperfections.

(ii) Unfortunately, many advocates of the importance of Knox's work in Pauline studies have launched vigorous and essentially independent attacks on the veracity of Acts.[24] This tactic might have derived, at least in part, from the conviction that Pauline interpreters need to have their faith in Acts' story of Paul shaken in order to appreciate Knox's approach (and we touch on this to some extent in our fourth point here). But I suspect that this has done more harm than good. In the first instance, it is unnecessary. No prior judgment needs to be reached about Acts in order to appreciate Knox's distinction concerning the respective initial value of the two sets of sources in historical terms. It stands on its own merits. Second, this strategy actually obscures the control that Knox's approach provides for the reception of Acts. Acts should be evaluated later in the light of the epistolary data, because this is the clearest and most objective point from which to judge that book's veracity. Initial attacks consequently obscure and even short-circuit this important practice. And third, this attack creates a rhetorically plausible if ultimately invalid way of undermining Knox's entire approach.

If Knox's position is held to be linked tightly to the independent discrediting of Acts, then any demonstration of Acts' veracity can be held conversely to overthrow Knox's approach in its entirety. This is of course a bad argument, because it overlooks what he actually suggests

---

24. See, to a degree, Knox himself (1987 [1950], 3-16); but also (i.a.) Hurd (1983 [1965], 13-42); and Luedemann (1984 [1980], 1-19; 1989a).

and does not refute his central claim; it largely misses the point. But it is rhetorically effective if Knox's advocates do in fact undertake sweeping indictments of Acts that can be countered.

However, we have just seen that such indictments are unnecessary and even distorting. From this point on, then, I suggest that the application of Knox's proposals to Pauline framing be detached from independent critiques of Acts. We must let Knox's own method show us how to evaluate Acts later on, for better or worse. An interesting possibility now presents itself.

(iii) Knox affirmed the importance of original source material over later and less-determined data. So in effect, he privileged Paul's eyewitness information as the correct starting point for the Pauline interpreter. It follows that if Acts contains eyewitness information, then that information must be elevated to evidence of the first rank. And at first glance, Acts does lay claim to eyewitness data (see Lk 1:2-3; Acts 16:10-17; 20:5–28:31). We will have to evaluate this carefully in due course, open to the possibility that data from Acts will join the epistolary evidence in the most basic layer of material undergirding the construction of the Pauline frame. We cannot begin with this evidence (because it is not overtly firsthand), but we can certainly affirm it if that judgment ultimately proves appropriate, and our investigation in accord with Knox's strictures will provide the most controlled way of reaching such a judgment. Moreover, simply in general terms, it may be possible to affirm the veracity of a great deal of the data in Acts in the light of Knox's methodology. The result of a strict application of Knox's approach could be a stunning validation of Acts.[25] But we will have to wait and see whether this proves to be the case.

(iv) Even as we must prescind from preliminary critiques of Acts and remain open to its function at times as a primary source, so too must we be alert to its inappropriate use and reject this. The field of Pauline studies is not aided by the frequent presence of what is effectively an Acts fundamentalism. This generally holds as accurate the individual episodes within Acts *and* the sequence in which they are placed by the narrative, *along with* the temporal intervals that the narrative periodically supplies. In short, everything that Acts says is true, and even in the order in which Acts says it.[26] A dogged defense of the Acts frame for Paul, both episod-

---

25. It is often overlooked that Knox himself believed that his reconstruction provided "a strong affirmation of the historical value of Acts" (1987 [1950], 10).

26. We cannot really make this claim without appealing to doctrines of inspiration

ically and sequentially, is by no means limited to scholars who explicitly endorse a historicist account of inspiration in terms of inerrancy, as we might at first expect. It is widespread outside these traditions, so we need to ask what else might be going on. I suggest that something as simple and as powerful as unexamined psychological and explanatory dependence may be in play. We must learn to recognize this, and to resist it.

Most Pauline interpreters have not been raised to think about Paul as John Knox recommends. The Paul of the church and of popular discourse is either the Paul of Acts or one inextricably and uncritically infused with Acts data. This is simply in place, like an ancient but familiar operating system installed years ago in the minds of interpreters so that they can run other programs and undertake other tasks. This story therefore almost certainly frames most interpreters' more detailed and expansive work on Paul, and there is a painful explanatory price to be paid if it is to be rigorously reexamined — an onerous wiping clean of the relevant hardware and installation of new and unfamiliar software. Hence, it is entirely understandable that alterations in fundamental explanatory structures would be resisted, and they certainly are in the matter of Pauline biography.[27]

Precisely because of this necessary struggle against the psychological availability of framing explanations rooted in Acts data, we need to make a completely fresh start.[28] We must attempt a comprehensive analysis of Paul's life informed only by epistolary data.

---

and inerrancy, and I will appeal to neither here. But even for those that do, I suggest that the situation does not need to be this rigid. A cursory comparison of the Gospels suggests that variation in the sequence of stories has widespread canonical legitimation. The stakes are consequently lower in relation to the sequence of the data in Acts as against the veracity of the individual episodes — what we can call sequential as against episodic reliability. So the possibility raised by Knox's approach that the arrangement of Acts is informed by literary and theological considerations as against strict chronological order ought to occasion no alarm. And we can safely leave judgments about the veracity of individual episodes in Acts until later on, when we can begin to compare stories about Paul from Acts with the gleanings about the same events gathered from the letters.

27. Kahneman (2011, esp. 7-9, 129-45 [chs. 12-13], 425-27 [app. A, originally published in 1974]) documents the advantages that explanations of data characterized by "ease" and "availability" have over explanations not so characterized.

28. When a negotiation has been initially primed with a false and deeply distorting anchor, further negotiations must stop entirely and the terms of the debate be psychologically reset. Kahneman's somewhat flamboyant advice in this regard: "If you think the other side has made an outrageous proposal, you should not come back with an equally outrageous counter-offer, creating a gap that will be difficult to bridge in further negotiations. Instead you should

With these caveats in place concerning Knox's first crucial contribution to this debate — the distinction between primary, initially epistolary data and secondary data drawn largely from Acts — we should consider more closely some of the specific implications of addressing initially just the epistolary data, a consideration that Knox himself largely overlooked. That is, we must ask exactly how the epistles ought to be approached once we have realized that we need to begin with their data exclusively.

As we saw earlier, we are not yet interested in a comprehensive biography of the apostle. This would attempt too much. We need only to frame his letters with a minimal reconstruction, on the basis of which we can attempt richer descriptive accounts of his life and thought later on. In order to move forward, then, and to generate an initial frame for Paul's letters from the data present in letters, we will need to answer *five* specific questions and little more: questions about the letters' authenticity, integrity, sequence, intervals, and reference. That is, in order to derive a frame for Paul's letters *from* Paul's letters, we must reach judgments about which letters he actually wrote (authenticity) and whether different original letters have been editorially pieced together into their current canonical form (integrity). And at the same time, we need to order them relative to one another (sequence) and, if possible, ascertain the length of the gaps between them in absolute temporal terms (intervals). Moreover, we need as far as possible to anchor any developing sequence to other events taking place at the time (reference), thereby ultimately generating dates and an absolute chronology overall. If we drop one of these questions from our explanatory quest, then we lose the ability to construct a frame (although some might argue that we do not, strictly speaking, need to solve the question of reference; we might be able to frame the letters independently of external events — an issue we will discuss further shortly). If we answer them all, however, then we do generate a useful framing account. Consequently, these five questions will be our particular focus through the analysis of Paul's epistolary data that follows. Their mutual necessity is the principal reason why the following is not just a "Pauline chronology," an exercise that generally does not attend simultaneously to questions of authenticity. A Pauline frame is both less and more than a Pauline chronology. It does not address all the questions of chronology raised by Paul's life but only those necessary to frame the letters. At the same

---

make a scene, storm out or threaten to do so, and make it clear — to yourself as well as to the other side — that you will not continue the negotiation with that number on the table" (2011, 126). The present study is in a certain respect, by concentrating almost entirely on epistolary material, storming out of the room if Acts data is introduced prematurely into framing.

time, in framing the letters it has to address more than merely chronological questions, and in a particular methodological fashion not always discernible in chronological treatments of Paul. And at this point we must introduce a significant corrective to Knox (thereby drawing a further distinction between reconstructions of the Pauline frame and most chronologies).

In his most famous work on Paul, Knox basically sketched out the key contours of Paul's life and thought; he was concerned with the big picture. So he did not reflect in depth on some of the methodological issues that we have just considered. As a result of this oversight, he went on to make a mistake when dealing with what I have identified here as the issue of authenticity, which he addressed only vestigially in any case, although his thinking here ultimately developed in an interesting way.[29]

If we exclude question-begging argumentation from our initial analysis of the epistolary data and maintain a similar vigilance against illegitimate Cartesian doubt, then when considering the question of authenticity we cannot at the outset simply exclude as an obvious matter any letters bearing Paul's name. We must make a case for exclusion with respect to each putative Pauline letter; epistolary data is in effect innocent until proved guilty. Consequently, all thirteen letters in the canon bearing Paul's name must be carefully evaluated for their authenticity during framing.[30]

With this important if surprising correction in place concerning the issue of epistolary authenticity, our consideration of Knox's famous source distinction is complete. We can now turn to the second set of key insights in

---

29. See esp. his 1990.

30. A consideration of just these letters in what follows will be "sufficient trouble for the day." Moreover, if we cross the threshold from authentic to pseudonymous letters within the canonical material, it is improbable that further authentic epistolary material will be found outside the canon. If a canonical letter is demonstrably shown to be pseudonymous, then the other ancient letters bearing Paul's name outside the canon will likely prove to be pseudonymous as well in due course, namely, *3 Corinthians, Laodiceans,* the *Letter to the Alexandrians,* and Paul's contributions in the *Letters of Paul and Seneca,* since these generally seem like less persuasive and skillful forgeries than any canonical counterparts would be (although none have yet been identified). A brief introduction to these texts and the issues can be found in Pervo (2010, 96-116), although this is not a methodologically reliable book. Similar considerations apply to Ehrman (2013, 425-32 [*3 Corinthians*], 439-45 [*Laodiceans*], 521-22 [*Letters of Paul and Seneca*]). The question of Hebrews arises here as well in an interesting way. Because it does not bear Paul's name explicitly, we will not consider its Pauline authorship. This question must be faced in due course, but precisely because it does not bear that explicit mark, it must, strictly speaking, make its way (or not) into the Pauline corpus from the outside in rather than vice versa. This investigation too is best undertaken elsewhere.

Knox's work that assists us when framing Paul: his actual case for a frame. In my view, Knox is again basically right, although he made some important mistakes as he developed his case, which will necessitate some revisions as we move forward.

5.2 The Reconstruction's Key Steps in Knox

Knox did not just identify the key methodological distinction within the sources at the outset of rigorous Pauline reconstruction. He also gestured toward the way in which, in a series of steps, the all-important epistolary data could be seen to yield a coherent and largely complete frame of Paul's apostolic career, and hence of the period during which he composed his letters. Knox argued his case in five steps (1987 [1950], 32-42).

First, he established a sequence for Paul's three longest letters — Romans and 1 and 2 Corinthians — by noting the way in which they all speak of an important collection of money destined for Jerusalem. This activity orders them as follows, covering a period of roughly one calendar year: 1 Corinthians — 2 Corinthians — Romans.

Second, he argued for the insertion of Galatians into the middle of this sequence, largely by suggesting (partly in dependence on others) that Galatians 2:10 is speaking of the collection as well. This critical move linked Galatians' uniquely extensive and detailed prehistory, especially concerning Jerusalem, to the sequence already in place. And Knox now knew that Paul undertook a visit to Jerusalem just before the main letter sequence, his second visit; and another some fourteen years before that, his first. Given that Romans anticipates a further visit to Jerusalem to deliver the collection, Knox now hypothesized that three visits to Jerusalem occurred during Paul's apostolic career. Moreover, Paul's call must have occurred some three years before the first visit. Hence, after these simple moves, a fairly extensive sequence and frame for Paul's apostolic work is in place.

Third, although Knox did not explore the point in any detail, he did note in passing that a reference might be detectable within this data in relation to Paul's escape from an ethnarch appointed by King Aretas to govern the city of Damascus (1987 [1950], 67), which the apostle speaks of somewhat oddly in 2 Corinthians 11:32-33. Almost certainly, this immediately predated his first visit to Jerusalem as an apostle (Gal 1:18-20). If this event could be referenced, then the sequence already developed in relative terms could be anchored to broader events. And Knox basically got the dating of this event right, that is, around 37

CE, although for rather ironic reasons.[31] Paul's call had to occur, then, around 34 CE, his first visit to Jerusalem around 37, his second around 51, the letters 1 Corinthians, 2 Corinthians, and Galatians had to have been composed in 51-53, and Romans, anticipating a third visit to Jerusalem, in 54. The entire frame was now anchored in relation to external events through a key reference, although for Knox this was drawn from Acts (see his 1987 [1950], 67-68).

Fourth, Knox introduced the letters still unaccounted for into this framework. As we have already intimated, he fell victim at this point to vicious circularity, not to mention uncritical doubt, so he did not consider correctly all the extant epistolary evidence bearing Paul's name. Nevertheless, those letters he deemed authentic were inserted where he thought most appropriate into the existing framework, which is the right procedure.

Fifth, and finally, Knox introduced the evidence of Acts into his reconstruction, although under the control of the material he had already derived from epistolary data. Where he detected a clash, he modified or dropped the information from Acts. Consequently, although the content of the various visits by Paul to Jerusalem recounted by Acts matched up rather nicely with the visits apparent in the letters, Knox reduced the five visits found in Acts to the three attested by the letters, and again, I think he fundamentally got the correlations right (1987 [1950], 35, 44). Indeed, I think that Knox got most things right in this series of steps and the resulting frame, so we will essentially trace it out again in what follows. However, it will need to be adjusted at several key points, which can be usefully anticipated here.

5.3 Beyond Knox

The elaboration and correction of Knox's case will take place in six analytic steps spread through five chapters. (Steps two and three are best treated in a single discussion.)[32]

---

31. In fact, he was not convinced that any precise time spans for this event can be determined, other than that it must have occurred before Aretas's death in 40 CE. He generated his chronological schema by calculating the intervals and the basic frame and then tying it to an event described in Acts: Paul's trial before Festus. He dated this to 55 CE (again, basically correctly in my view), citing Tacitus, *Annals* 13.14-15; Josephus, *Jewish Antiquities* 20.8-9; and Eusebius's *Chronicon*. In my view, his framework is basically out from this point by one year, and then more imprecise later on.

32. Knox's final move, which presupposes the detailed analysis of a great deal of data from Acts, is best undertaken in a separate study.

(i) The backbone of Knox's reconstruction is the stringing together of
1 Corinthians, 2 Corinthians, and Romans in relation to the collection
of money for the community in Jerusalem. But this step has become
rather more complex recently than it was in Knox's day — although it
was complex enough then. This collection has been narrated in many
different ways by modern scholars. And if 2 Corinthians is partitioned in
certain ways, as many scholars advocate, then Knox's broader argument
is problematized if not invalidated. There are more letters in play than
just canonical 2 Corinthians; these begin to spread out temporally, and
some fail to reference the collection. The partitioning of 2 Corinthians
will in any case raise the whole question of the "interim events" that unfolded between the composition of 1 Corinthians and certain pieces (at
least) of what is now 2 Corinthians. Complex reconstructions of these
events will tend to undermine Knox's claims concerning a straightforward sequence.[33] And we encounter the issue of partition in relation to
Romans as well, since scholars have long nursed various suspicions about
chapter 16. So we must revisit Knox's articulation of a backbone for the
broader framing project and see whether it is still viable in the light of
this complex research on Romans and 2 Corinthians.

I will, however — to tip my hand — end up arguing for a great simplification with respect to much modern explanation of this material, suggesting that the simplest account of the collection is the most plausible,
and that complex reconstructions of the interim events rest too much
on possible — and not enough (if ever) on certain or even probable —
readings of the data, while similar considerations apply to the partition
of both Romans and 2 Corinthians. So we will end up affirming Knox's
basic claim at this point, if not simplifying it still further.

But we will introduce a relatively new interpretative dimension that
is often overlooked when considering the location of letters — what

33. Strictly speaking, partitioning 2 Cor does not *necessarily* raise a complex set of interim events, i.e., a complex reconstruction between 1 Cor and what is left of 2 Cor in its traditional position, and vice versa. We will assess the precise methodological relationship between
partition theories of 2 Cor and reconstructions of the interim events in due course. Furthermore, the complication of this sequence in various ways, due to partition and/or complex
interim events, does not necessarily entail the abandonment of a framing project altogether. But
that project would have to be significantly reconceived, as it is, e.g., in Tatum's (2006) important
study. Tatum is not persuaded that, among other things, the issue of reference can be addressed
plausibly. He (among others) is also unconvinced by Knox's first step here, namely, the strict and
relatively simple sequencing through one calendar year of 1 Cor, 2 Cor, and Rom, in that order.

Charlotte Hartwig and Gerd Theissen (2004) have dubbed *Nebenadressat,* or "addressees alongside." Paul's letters were written for and spoken to a primary audience, which is named explicitly, but we learn from the letters in this initial sequence that their composition and performance were not limited to that principal audience. Other, secondary audiences in effect overheard these letters, thereby constituting audiences alongside the original addressees, as Paul was well aware. A new attentiveness to this dimension in Paul's letters provides important corroborative evidence concerning their composition. So here too we will go beyond Knox in a supplementary fashion.

(ii) The introduction of Galatians into the epistolary backbone oriented by the collection of money for Jerusalem is perhaps the most important step in the entire argument. It locks Galatians, which supplies so much information about critical events in Paul's earlier ministry, to the large letters already positioned next to one another. I do not disagree with Knox that this is what ought to happen or that his judgment here is right. However, I am unsatisfied with the arguments he adduces in its support — essentially, the solitary and rather fragile claim that Galatians 2:10 refers indubitably to the collection. So I will try to strengthen this critical move, in two principal ways.

First, I will increase the data in play, and hence the leverage on the move, by introducing as much data as I can into the backbone prior to considering Galatians. Some years ago, I thought that this meant inserting both 1 Thessalonians and Philippians into the sequence. I have recently been persuaded that 1 Thessalonians belongs elsewhere and only Philippians belongs here; nevertheless, this positioning alone is important. When the astonishing appropriateness of the location of Philippians just prior to Romans — during a trial in Corinth — is grasped, the introduction of Galatians into the sequence becomes more compelling. In addition, I will argue for a slightly new interpretative angle on material many scholars excise from Philippians as an interpolation — 3:2–4:3 — material that, understood correctly, contributes significantly to framing considerations.

Following this new insertion, we will reconsider Knox's suggestion that Galatians, and 2:10 in particular, references the collection. I will argue that the presence of the collection in Galatians is rather more subtle than Knox supposed, yet still detectable, and hence Knox's original claim can be deployed as an important secondary, corroborative argument in support of this location for Galatians.

(iii) Knox noted that a datable event could possibly be detected in Paul's epis-
       tolary data, something of which many scholars seem to be unaware.[34]
       He gestured specifically toward what we will call "the Aretas datum"
       (1987 [1950], 67). However, he did not press forward to a precise analysis,
       a point where the present project will go further than his proposals. I
       will argue that the event can be dated specifically, between the fall of 36
       and the spring of 37 CE, and that this priceless chronological insight can
       anchor the rest of the biographical material.[35] The other potential date
       Knox noted derives from Acts and so will not be addressed here, and his
       mistake in relation to authenticity led him to overlook the only other
       possible datable external reference found in a Pauline letter, which will
       be noted here momentarily. In these discussions, then, we will be rather
       more consistent and precise than Knox was in the important matter
       of absolute dating, although pressing forward along lines that he has
       already identified.

(iv)   Following these three opening and very important explanatory steps,
       Knox turned to consider where Paul's other letters might fit into his
       developing frame. We have had cause, however, to question his incon-
       sistent limitation of the evidence under consideration. So where Knox
       considered only a few letters, we must broaden the discussion to a con-
       sideration of all the canonical letters bearing Paul's name that have yet
       to feature within his schema (although one has already been located,
       namely, Philippians). This single step in Knox will expand into three
       as we consider the relevant groups of remaining epistolary material —
       the Thessalonian correspondence; the interrelated cluster of Philemon,
       Colossians, and Ephesians; and 1 and 2 Timothy and Titus. Certain dis-
       tinctive considerations will have to be brought to bear in relation to each
       cluster of letters, since questions of authenticity arise with special force
       during these steps in the overall argument.

       We turn initially to consider the Thessalonian correspondence, and
       some surprises again await us. We encounter here for the first time the
       way in which a rigorous application of Knox's methodology, coupled
       with a rejection of invalid, circular argumentation, opens up important
       new angles on epistolary questions long considered closed.

       First Thessalonians is the first letter that does not seem to fit into the

---

34. The denial of this claim is documented in more detail in the final section of ch. 3,
where I attempt to refute it.

35. The case is argued in detail in my 2002 and summarized here in ch. 3.

epistolary sequence already enumerated. It seems earlier. But the frame of reference now in play opens up the fascinating possibility that it could be *much* earlier, that is, anytime within the 40s CE, although at this point we cannot say exactly when. But its similarity to 1 Corinthians invites further explanation. So we will consider as well whether Paul kept and circulated copies of his letters that had been sent to other destinations, ultimately opening an important avenue of explanation concerning the creation of the original Pauline letter collection, along with new insights into the letters' original receptions. (By now we will have added two new methodological considerations to Knox's case in terms of Paul's ancient epistolary reception: the phenomena of *Nebenadressat* and of copies of letters circulating in places other than their named destinations.)

After the consideration of 1 Thessalonians, it seems most obvious to turn to 2 Thessalonians. And here we learn that many of the reasons usually adduced for this letter's pseudonymity are rooted in false methodology and, often, an oddly fragile biography (that is, in something approaching an Acts fundamentalism). We will find that a judgment of authenticity seems surprisingly solid, and this opens up further fascinating possibilities for the frame.

Second Thessalonians seems to contain strong references to "the Gaian crisis," which unfolded from 39 through early 41 CE. Suitably interpreted, this offers a second critical reference or date, one that fits nicely with our first — the Aretas datum — which stemmed from late 36 to early 37 and was associated with Damascus and Jerusalem. The links between 2 Thessalonians and 1 Thessalonians now draw both letters into this early and dramatic phase in the mission of the church, although the present allusion is not as delimited as the Aretas datum. First and Second Thessalonians — probably, for certain fragile reasons, in this order — turn out to be our earliest extant sources for Paul and may, moreover, be dramatically earlier than most scholars have previously suspected, being written during the early 40s CE. They have always been fascinating and important texts, but if these judgments hold good, then their value for the Pauline interpreter increases still more. To possess sources from this phase within the expansion of the early church, perhaps just over a decade after the death and reported resurrection of its founder, would be nothing short of extraordinary.

(v) We must now try to position Philemon, Colossians, and Ephesians in relation to this developing frame, as well as to make the appropriate judgments about their authenticity.

Few scholars in fact question the authenticity of Philemon, perhaps because it seems rather innocuous. But it cannot be positioned with any confidence in relation to the broader Pauline frame without a consideration of at least Colossians. And of course we have a new perspective for adjudicating the authenticity of Colossians by now within our overall discussion. Its authenticity can be addressed in the terms that were introduced to adjudicate 2 Thessalonians, including appeals to the modern, statistically assisted analysis of style, that is, to "nontraditional authorship ascription." Much previous analysis seems worryingly out of date in this regard. And both Colossians and Ephesians obviously raise the further issue of dependence, since these two texts are so closely intertwined. But our analysis of 1 Thessalonians in relation to 1 Corinthians will already have opened up a new angle on this phenomenon. We noted there the possibility of letter copies being kept in the Pauline circle and appearing in nondesignated churches, to which we should now add considerations of orality and performance. (The seminal methodological figure concerning orality is Walter Ong.)[36] And in view of these considerations, it seems that nothing decisive stands against a preliminary affirmation of the authenticity of Colossians. Certainly, there is insufficient data at this point to reject its authenticity, so it will remain for the time being within the Pauline group.

The numerous connections between Philemon and Colossians now connect both letters with the nearby Lycus valley. (The recent Stanford project on ancient travel supervised by Walter Scheidel — ORBIS — becomes exceptionally helpful at this juncture.)[37] Moreover, they seem to hover just before the principal epistolary sequence that has already been identified, so sometime around Paul's second visit to Jerusalem, when so many vital issues concerning the shape of the early Christian mission were negotiated — something they may now shed light on.

Ephesians fares similarly, although it seems most likely to have been composed first, insofar as this distinction remains relevant. Derivation from Colossians would cause difficulties for authenticity, but determining the causality of this relationship is in my view impossible on stylistic grounds alone, especially when considerations of Paul's incarceration, orality, and resulting compositional dynamics are taken into account. The composition of texts in prison is a common phenomenon within the

36. See esp. his 2000 [1967]; 2002; 2012 [1982].
37. See ORBIS (2013); also Scheidel, Meeks, and Weiland (2012); Scheidel (2013).

Christian tradition, but it is not well understood by modern scholars, largely owing to its peculiar context. A brief consideration of some of the dynamics surrounding the production of prison literature is therefore instructive.

If Ephesians is authentic, however, it seems necessary to affirm its identity as the letter to the Laodiceans mentioned in Colossians 4:16, now often thought to be lost. (So we find that it has been hiding in plain sight.) This takes the collection of Pauline letters judged authentic and sequenced thus far to ten.

(vi) It remains only to consider 1 and 2 Timothy and Titus. The most appropriate letter to evaluate first is Titus, since it seems to fit most obviously into our developing frame.

The correct method for evaluating authenticity is quite well established by this point in our project. We consider a letter's account of its immediate circumstances or exigence. We then ask whether and where it fits into our developing critical biography. After this, we address issues of style and dependence, the former suitably informed by modern statistical analyses and the latter by suitably nuanced explanations concerning the circulation and composition of Paul's letters. Then finally, we probe for possible mistakes by a putative pseudepigrapher, for example, blatant anachronisms.

Titus struggles more with respect to these considerations than the other disputed letters have, leading ultimately to a judgment of pseudepigraphy, and similar dynamics then play out with 1 Timothy. This letter arguably contains explicit anachronisms, along with other difficulties for authenticity. However, the situation with respect to 2 Timothy is more finely balanced.

Arguably nothing decisive is apparent that might lead to an immediate judgment of pseudepigraphy. But there is a steady accumulation of doubts leading ineluctably in that direction. So these three letters do ultimately end up being grouped together as "the Pastorals," and are excluded from further involvement within the construction of the preliminary frame — although it needs to be emphasized that all preliminary framing judgments are provisional. This leaves the number of canonical Pauline letters judged authentic at this preliminary stage, on internal grounds, at ten, with the sequence established by the end of chapter 5, at which point we turn to consider quickly a useful corroborative contention.

The shape of the original Pauline letter collection is arguably apparent in the data surrounding Marcion, who seems to have inherited an edition of Paul's letters composed of just these ten — an important correlation — that was apparently addressed, rather elegantly, to seven churches (see also Rev. 2:1–3:22). That is, Marcion seems to have worked with a collection of Paul's letters that contained Galatians, 1 and 2 Corinthians, Romans, 1 and 2 Thessalonians, Laodiceans (Ephesians), Colossians and Philemon, and Philippians. But he seems not to have known of 1 and 2 Timothy or Titus, suggesting that those letters might have been composed, at least in part, against his program. This attestation can be challenged; hence, our discussion also has to address briefly certain considerations in the evidence of Clement, Ignatius, Polycarp, Irenaeus, and Eusebius. Nevertheless, it will be suggested that the simplest explanation of this complex situation — which has just been noted — is also the most persuasive. And this evidence concerning transmission does seem to be a useful confirmation of our judgments reached on internal grounds. That the two lines of investigation match up exactly can increase our confidence in the entire disposition.

In sum, after these six steps, it seems that we will be able to offer an epistolary frame for Paul in two senses — that all the letters initially deemed authentic will now be nicely framed in terms of their circumstances, perhaps to a surprising level of detail, and that the evidence underlying this frame will be entirely epistolary and hence primary. Our task will be complete. But one final issue needs to be briefly considered before this initial methodological discussion draws to a close — namely, the ongoing status of this reconstruction once it has been successfully derived.

By the end of the argument, we will have generated an account that frames Paul's authentic letters. This will have been derived in the correct way, using the appropriate arguments and evidence. We will have used initially only epistolary material, and will have processed it using arguments sensitive to problems of vicious circularity, different levels of construal, and the appropriate deployments of criticism and doubt. We will have resisted inappropriate atomization and tacit psychological dependence on Acts. The result should be an account that frames Paul's letters by rigorously answering the key questions of authenticity, integrity, sequence, intervals, and reference. This can then serve as the basis for richer explanations of other aspects of Paul, which can now proceed in a way that avoids begging the question and similar problems. But there is one final issue hanging, concerning the relationship between those later, richer explanations and this frame that has been derived in first position, as a preliminary explanation, and hence in a deliberately restricted and controlled fashion. Does this frame need to be held constant during those later investigations, come hell or high water, so to speak, or can it be judiciously modified? In short — is it, to a degree, also *provisional*?

I think the answer to this question is yes. The frame is provisional, provided its possible later modification is undertaken appropriately.

It seems to me that the careful examination of texts later on might lead to comprehensive accounts that encourage us to reverse some of our initial judgments. So, for example, a student of Colossians might be able to show in due course how all the complex theological concerns of that letter just do not fit plausibly with those apparent now in the other nine letters presently judged authentic and that it ought to be excluded from the Pauline canon. Or a student of 2 Timothy might succeed in running this analysis in the opposite direction, arguing that that letter ought to be included — and the grounds for the initial exclusion of 2 Timothy are not that strong. Both analyses would accept the way that our preliminary frame has established the burden of proof. And it only seems fair to concede that these arguments, and others like them, are possible. Our framing account is provisional. However, it is vital for us to appreciate that any later arguments of this nature, seeking to reverse the frame's judgments at particular points, will carry certain specific explanatory burdens.

Any such suggested modifications will have to show how the original framing decision that turns out to be incorrect can be corrected in a way that does not undermine the rest of the frame that is currently being used to make that case. If it fails to do this, it will risk falling back into vicious circularity. Put a little more colloquially, it will be sawing off the branch that it is sitting on. Hence, alternatively — if the branch is indeed being sawed off — an entirely different frame will have to be demonstrably derived that still supports its judgments, and this looks like a difficult task. The risk lying in wait here is the collapse of all the data into an unframed situation, at which point we are back to the central conundrum with which this chapter began — the inability to adjudicate between any of the main interpretative options for Paul at the most basic levels of contingency and coherence, this being the very distinction that makes a complaint about the authenticity of Colossians possible.

Consequently, we should affirm that the framing account being offered here is provisional. But any future modifications will have to be undertaken very carefully indeed if we are not to return unwittingly to a fundamentally distorted and confused situation. A preliminary frame might turn out to be rather better than a modified frame that is really no frame at all.

With this caution concerning the frame's provisional nature duly noted, we can now turn to the fascinating but difficult task of reconstructing it in detail. And we will begin where Knox did: with the reconstruction of a critical one-year sequence that can serve as the frame's backbone. This is argued in relation to 1 Corinthians, 2 Corinthians, and Romans, and their apparent concern, at least at times, with a collection for the saints in Jerusalem.

CHAPTER TWO

The Epistolary Backbone:
Romans and the Corinthian Correspondence

1. The Initial Disposition

As the introduction noted, Knox began his reconstruction of the Pauline frame by sequencing Paul's three longest letters together on the basis of their references to a collection of money intended for Jerusalem. We need now to scrutinize the relevant evidence, along with Knox's account of it, a little more closely.[1]

First Corinthians, written from Ephesus in Asia (16:8), provides what

---

1. The collection is much discussed. B. Longenecker is an excellent guide (2010, 157-89). (He himself is particularly concerned to distance Gal 2:10 from the collection. This argument is assessed in more detail when Gal is introduced into our developing frame in chap. 3.) Unfortunately, however, if contamination from Acts evidence is to be resisted, the vast majority of this material must nevertheless be set to one side as methodologically corrupt — see, e.g., Georgi (1991 [1965]); Wedderburn (2002); and Downs (2006, 2008), to name just a few.

Luedemann is one of the few remaining helpful treatments in terms of the correct approach and its consistent prosecution (1984, 22, 77-100, esp. 77-94). His critique of Georgi's classic analysis is a nice example of the way epistle-based analysis must sift and reject analyses making premature appeals to Acts data (1984, 72-88 and associated notes *passim*). However, he loses his way from p. 94, when he introduces a visit and a lost letter by Paul to Corinth between 1 and 2 Cor. This throws his detailed chronology off, stretching a two-year to a four-year sequence (1984, 99; note, these claims are also based on some simple *non sequiturs,* which are puzzling in such an otherwise precise argument). As we will see in detail shortly, these hypotheses, although widely advocated, greatly complicate matters, and rest on overly fragile epistolary evidence. The same problems dog Tatum's otherwise brilliant analysis (2006, 94-122). Consequently, Knox's original reconstruction, despite being dated, remains simpler and better, although he relies too heavily on Gal 2:10 (1987 [1950], 32-42). I will try to set things on a firmer footing in what follows.

seems to be the first snapshot in a broader story.[2] Paul apparently responds in 16:1-4 to a query from the Corinthians concerning exactly how to undertake a collection of money destined for the Christians in Jerusalem (see v. 3). He recommends collecting money personally and regularly, once a week, as he has just instructed the Galatians (vv. 1-2).

This snapshot reveals that the rationale and origin of the collection are already in place for both Paul and the Corinthians. Meanwhile, Paul does not commit to accompanying the money to Jerusalem personally, even if this is clearly possible (v. 4), although it is helpful to observe that Paul's character-izations of money tend to be carefully nuanced, and especially in relation to the Corinthians. He does anticipate Corinthian delegates being sent in some association with letters of recommendation (see v. 3, although the Greek ac-count of just who is writing the letters is initially ambiguous).[3]

Second Corinthians contains a long and fascinating exhortation about this project in what are now our chapters 8 and 9. At first glance, this seems to be a second snapshot of a further stage in the collection's progress, which is now apparently in some difficulties. Paul writes this time from Macedonia (see esp. 2:13 and 7:5),[4] and the involvement of the Macedonians with the project is discussed at length, apparently in part to stir the competitive Corin-thians to more extensive action. There is no mention of the Galatians or of the collection's ultimate destination in Jerusalem, although the absence of the former is probably more significant ultimately than of the latter. The discus-sion's addressees are in fact characterized throughout in regional terms, Paul mentioning "Achaia" in 9:2 (see also 1:1). And Paul is not alone in this under-

---

2. [16:1] Περὶ δὲ τῆς λογείας τῆς εἰς τοὺς ἁγίους ὥσπερ διέταξα ταῖς ἐκκλησίαις τῆς Γαλατίας, οὕτως καὶ ὑμεῖς ποιήσατε. [2] κατὰ μίαν σαββάτου ἕκαστος ὑμῶν παρ᾽ ἑαυτῷ τιθέτω θησαυρίζων ὅ τι ἐὰν εὐοδῶται, ἵνα μὴ ὅταν ἔλθω τότε λογεῖαι γίνωνται. [3] ὅταν δὲ παραγένωμαι, οὓς ἐὰν δοκιμάσητε δι᾽ ἐπιστολῶν τούτους πέμψω ἀπενεγκεῖν τὴν χάριν ὑμῶν εἰς Ἰερουσαλήμ· [4] ἐὰν δὲ ἄξιον ᾖ τοῦ κἀμὲ πορεύεσθαι, σὺν ἐμοὶ πορεύσονται.

3. Verse 4 might suggest that the letters come from Paul, if in the softly adversative fashion possible for the conjunction δέ it considers a different travel arrangement from the one just described in v. 3: see ἐὰν δὲ ἄξιον ᾖ τοῦ κἀμὲ πορεύεσθαι, σὺν ἐμοὶ πορεύσονται. If Paul considers it appropriate to accompany the collection, that is, in an arrangement different in certain respects from the one envisaged in v. 3, then the Corinthian delegates will go with him, and implicitly not therefore with his letters of recommendation. If the conjunction is directly continuative, however, then the origin of the letters must be from the Corinthians.

4. 2:13: οὐκ ἔσχηκα ἄνεσιν τῷ πνεύματί μου τῷ μὴ εὑρεῖν με Τίτον τὸν ἀδελφόν μου, ἀλλὰ ἀποταξάμενος αὐτοῖς ἐξῆλθον εἰς Μακεδονίαν· 7:5: Καὶ γὰρ ἐλθόντων ἡμῶν εἰς Μακεδονίαν οὐδεμίαν ἔσχηκεν ἄνεσιν ἡ σὰρξ ἡμῶν ἀλλ᾽ ἐν παντὶ θλιβόμενοι· ἔξωθεν μάχαι, ἔσωθεν φόβοι.

taking. His companion Titus has been involved in some way (see esp. 8:6, 16-17, 23; 12:18) and will apparently revisit Corinth shortly (see 2:12-13; 7:6-7, 13-16), accompanied by two unnamed delegates from the Macedonian congregations. Paul declares his intention to come to Corinth himself on what he identifies as his third visit to the city (12:14; 13:1). But the small delegation introduced in chapter 8 will precede him, presumably along with 2 Corinthians itself, and Paul seems to be hoping that this will redress certain matters before his arrival, matters seemingly including an apparent lack of enthusiasm for the project.

Romans provides a third snapshot of the collection's progress from what seems to be a still later stage (see 15:25-32).[5] Paul's concern at this point in writing is his reception in Judea and not the progress of the collection itself among the Aegean churches. Paul writes Romans in the house of Gaius and hence apparently in Corinth (see 1 Cor 1:14; Rom 16:23). The collection is now as complete as presumably it ever will be, although, as in 2 Corinthians, only Macedonia and Achaia are mentioned as participants. And Paul seems poised to deliver it to Jerusalem himself (see 1 Cor 16:4), accompanied by various other Christians who will act in part as porters and guards of the money.

We do not need to undertake a detailed reconstruction of the rationale, symbolism, and politics of the collection here.[6] (These will be probed in a little more depth when we turn to consider Gal 2:10 in the next chapter.) Our interest is simply in its contribution to framing. And we are fortunate indeed that this data sequences Paul's three longest letters unequivocally in the order 1 Corinthians — 2 Corinthians — Romans. We will consider possible disruptions to this contention shortly, principally by way of challenges to some of the letters' integrity. But this is the simplest and clearest point at which to begin framing.[7] Fortunately, we have enough information here to gauge some intervals as well.

---

5. [15:25] Νυνὶ δὲ πορεύομαι εἰς Ἰερουσαλὴμ διακονῶν τοῖς ἁγίοις. [26] εὐδόκησαν γὰρ Μακεδονία καὶ Ἀχαΐα κοινωνίαν τινὰ ποιήσασθαι εἰς τοὺς πτωχοὺς τῶν ἁγίων τῶν ἐν Ἰερουσαλήμ. [27] εὐδόκησαν γὰρ καὶ ὀφειλέται εἰσὶν αὐτῶν· εἰ γὰρ τοῖς πνευματικοῖς αὐτῶν ἐκοινώνησαν τὰ ἔθνη, ὀφείλουσιν καὶ ἐν τοῖς σαρκικοῖς λειτουργῆσαι αὐτοῖς. [28] τοῦτο οὖν ἐπιτελέσας καὶ σφραγισάμενος αὐτοῖς τὸν καρπὸν τοῦτον, ἀπελεύσομαι δι' ὑμῶν εἰς Σπανίαν· [29] οἶδα δὲ ὅτι ἐρχόμενος πρὸς ὑμᾶς ἐν πληρώματι εὐλογίας Χριστοῦ ἐλεύσομαι. [30] Παρακαλῶ δὲ ὑμᾶς, ἀδελφοί, διὰ τοῦ κυρίου ἡμῶν Ἰησοῦ Χριστοῦ καὶ διὰ τῆς ἀγάπης τοῦ πνεύματος συναγωνίσασθαί μοι ἐν ταῖς προσευχαῖς ὑπὲρ ἐμοῦ πρὸς τὸν θεόν, [31] ἵνα ῥυσθῶ ἀπὸ τῶν ἀπειθούντων ἐν τῇ Ἰουδαίᾳ καὶ ἡ διακονία μου ἡ εἰς Ἰερουσαλὴμ εὐπρόσδεκτος τοῖς ἁγίοις γένηται, [32] ἵνα ἐν χαρᾷ ἐλθὼν πρὸς ὑμᾶς διὰ θελήματος θεοῦ συναναπαύσωμαι ὑμῖν.

6. See most famously perhaps Georgi (1991 [1965]). The modern debate is summarized well by B. Longenecker (2010).

7. If these judgments need to be revisited and revised — or even abandoned — in the light of later decisions and debates, then this should of course take place.

First Corinthians states that it was written before the feast of Pentecost
and also contains distinctive allusions to the feast of Passover (see 5:6-8; 16:8).
This points to composition in the spring of the relevant year. As we will see
in more detail shortly, the letter was preceded by a Corinthian communication to Paul, which was probably preceded in turn by a letter from Paul to
the Corinthians that must have contained his first instructions concerning
the collection. And we learn from 2 Corinthians that Paul's instructions were
issued to the Corinthians in the year previous to that letter (see the reference
"last year," ἀπὸ πέρυσι, which occurs twice in this discussion, in 8:10 and 9:2).
This data combines to suggest — at least initially — that 2 Corinthians was
written in the same year as 1 Corinthians. It follows, moreover, that both letters
were composed in the year following the inauguration of the collection with
the Corinthians. But 1 Corinthians also contains a brief projected itinerary on
Paul's part that we will examine more closely in due course (16:5-9).[8]

It anticipates a journey to Corinth by way of Macedonia, followed most
probably by a winter sojourn at Corinth. At this point, no good reasons are
apparent in the sources to suggest that this itinerary changed, so we can assume
until proved otherwise that 2 Corinthians was written during Paul's journey
through Macedonia, as planned, and Romans was written at this itinerary's
conclusion, in Corinth, after that winter, also as planned. Hence, Paul's subsequent movements as charted by our data about the collection match his
announced itinerary in 1 Corinthians 16 exactly — a journey from Asia to
Macedonia and then south to Corinth in Achaia. Moreover, Paul's imminent
departure for Jerusalem with the collection suggests the composition of Romans after the winter, as planned, and so in the spring of the following year,
when travel, especially over long distances by sea, became more manageable
(although these considerations should not be pressed too hard).[9] We thus
arrive at the following reconstruction — whose integrity in Knox's original
reconstruction can now be affirmed, with the important proviso that more
detailed examinations of contested data later on do not overthrow it:

. . . [collection begins] . . .
// year change //

8. [16:5] Ἐλεύσομαι δὲ πρὸς ὑμᾶς ὅταν Μακεδονίαν διέλθω· Μακεδονίαν γὰρ διέρχομαι,
[6] πρὸς ὑμᾶς δὲ τυχὸν παραμενῶ ἢ καὶ παραχειμάσω, ἵνα ὑμεῖς με προπέμψητε οὗ ἐὰν
πορεύωμαι. [7] οὐ θέλω γὰρ ὑμᾶς ἄρτι ἐν παρόδῳ ἰδεῖν, ἐλπίζω γὰρ χρόνον τινὰ ἐπιμεῖναι
πρὸς ὑμᾶς ἐὰν ὁ κύριος ἐπιτρέψῃ. [8] ἐπιμενῶ δὲ ἐν Ἐφέσῳ ἕως τῆς πεντηκοστῆς· [9] θύρα
γάρ μοι ἀνέῳγεν μεγάλη καὶ ἐνεργής, καὶ ἀντικείμενοι πολλοί.
9. See Scheidel, Meeks, and Weiland (2012); Scheidel (2013); ORBIS (2013).

$$\dots 1 \text{ Cor} - 2 \text{ Cor} - \text{Paul VC3}^{10} -$$
$$// \text{ year change } //$$
$$- \text{ Rom} - \text{Paul VJ}^{11} \dots$$

With this initial sequence and set of intervals in place, we need now to consider its various links in more detail. And we will begin at the right-hand end, so to speak, with Romans, the latest letter in the sequence.

2. The Integrity of Romans

It was fashionable for a time to assert that Romans 16, suitably edited, was a separate letter from the rest of the material now appearing in our canonical Romans (a view discussed in more detail shortly). If the assertion is true, we will have to add another authentic letter to our developing frame by splitting Romans into a long and a short epistle.

$$\dots [\text{collection begins}] \dots$$
$$// \text{ year change } //$$
$$\dots 1 \text{ Cor} - 2 \text{ Cor} - \text{Paul VC3} -$$
$$// \text{ year change } //$$
$$- \text{ Rom 1-15 / Rom 16} - \text{Paul VJ} \dots$$

This decision will have important implications for any detailed account later on of the provenance of Romans — whether it was originally sent to Rome or to somewhere else, most probably Ephesus, or whether it was a circular letter sent to many destinations, perhaps including Rome and Ephesus. Hence, this claim merits more detailed examination. The historian of Paul attempting to frame his original letters is interested in any case in whether the canonical letters possess integrity in the sense that they are intact single letters largely as Paul composed and dispatched them, as against, at least in some cases, orchestrated collations of several original letters by an anonymous editor. Paul's frame can change dramatically depending on the judgments reached concerning epistolary integrity. And the case for partitioning Romans because of the conviction that some or all of Romans 16 was originally a separate letter is probably as strong a case for partition

---

10. VC: visit to Corinth. See the full list of biographical abbreviations in the front matter.
11. VJ: visit to Jerusalem.

as we ever encounter in Paul. So it can serve as a useful threshold for this particular methodological suggestion.

We need to consider first the significance of disorder in the manuscript tradition. It was the discovery of p⁴⁶, usually dated around 200 CE, that led to the most well-known advocacy of partition concerning Romans 16, by T. W. Manson (1991 [1962]), now most accessibly found in Donfried (1991, 3-15). This early manuscript indicates that Romans circulated at some early stage with the doxology usually found at 16:25-27 positioned at the end of chapter 15. Manson argued that this evidence was an important corroboration of the earlier suggestion, made largely on internal grounds, that Romans 16 was originally addressed to Ephesus and circulated independently of the rest of Romans, being joined to Romans 1-15 to create canonical Romans only at some later stage. The case for an independent Romans 16 is not reducible to the evidence from p⁴⁶, but we will focus for the moment on the function of disorder in the manuscript tradition as evidence for early editorial collation.

We can certainly grant that this evidence could attest to a claim of collation, presumably in various ways. An editor might have deliberately collated two (or more) original Pauline letters when forming the original edition of the Pauline letter collection. Or, alternatively, an earlier editor of "Romans" alone might have appended a much shorter letter after the longer text of Romans proper — perhaps mistakenly, perhaps in confusion, and perhaps entirely deliberately, thinking that this was a responsible decision. The synthesized document would then have been inherited by the editor of the later collection proper (and so on). Serious disorder in the manuscript tradition in terms of length, such as we find in Romans, would then derive from the existence of copies of the letters in their original form coexisting and persisting after the publication of the edited collection, thereby causing confusion for scribes as they later encountered more than one version of the given letter. Manuscript confusion *could* thereby attest to this earlier editorial decision to collate letters that the modern historian ought now to partition.

However, if the evidence is to attest *decisively* to this sort of original editorial situation, then collation also needs to be the *only* possible explanation for such manuscript confusion, and the number of different versions of Romans evident in the tradition suggests immediately that it is not. Romans circulated widely in at least fourteen- and sixteen-chapter versions as a result of later modifications — Marcion often being blamed for generating the short version[12]

---

12. Although H. Y. Gamble (1977) suggests this is unfair; I am not so sure (see, to a degree, my arguments here in ch. 6).

— and chapter 16 itself is a tangle of variations attesting to many different later versions. (There are in fact as many as fourteen major attested textual forms if the case is argued in traditional genealogical terms; see Lampe 1985b, summarized in 2003 [1989], 154-55.) Given these dynamics, it is very difficult to determine whether later manuscript confusion denotes an early collation of original letters, which would support a hypothesis of partition, or a later mutilation of parts of the published letter collection by figures functioning in the manner attributed to Marcion. Either explanation is compatible with the simple data of manuscript confusion. Hence, it seems that the presence of manuscript confusion is not necessarily good evidence for early editorial collation. Indeed, it seems largely irrelevant.

But is confusion in the manuscript tradition still of partial value in the opposite sense? Could this be necessary — as against sufficient — evidence of collation, so that, at the least, we would be entitled to reject all claims of partition that could *not* point to manuscript confusion? Unfortunately, this contention too looks unlikely.

This would suppose that editorial collation within the first corpus left original evidence intact, and the mere fact of manuscript confusion does not establish this. There may have been no significant influence on the manuscript tradition from independent copies after the first Pauline letter collection was published with its carefully collated letters. The original letters and their copies may have been very scarce and so been effectively silenced by the popularity of the later, edited version. In this case, all the confusion in the manuscript tradition evident today would derive from later scribal alterations and mistakes. But original compilation could still have taken place, none of which would necessarily be attested to by manuscript confusion.

So we must discard the correlative contention from manuscript confusion for assertions of partition as well, and this evidence must therefore be discarded on both sides of the question. Its presence cannot count decisively for this claim, but neither can its absence count decisively against it (although its presence could still function as corroborative evidence of earlier collation). But another important methodological question has been raised in passing by this consideration of manuscript variation that we should now consider in more detail: the behavior of the editor of the original Pauline letter collection.

Almost every claim of partition in a Pauline letter invokes conscious editorial activity at some level in the relevant act or acts of collation, with a number of original letters being combined, whether elegantly or clumsily, into "canonical letters." Such claims need to offer a plausible account of this behavior. But we do not know the identity of the original editor or the exact date and circumstances of the collection. (We will investigate this last question carefully in due course but will be forced to pull up short of the judgments we need here.) So we are forced to reconstruct practices of ancient editorial behavior more generally, conscious that our sources are scarce and that ancient practices of collation probably differed as greatly from modern conceptions as ancient practices of reading differ from modern ones. The differences here are potentially vast. (W. Johnson's 2010 benchmark study of ancient elite reading practices is instructive; see also his 2000.)

The vital question of ancient editorial activity is treated surprisingly lightly in the relevant literature. It is probably fair to claim that H.-J. Klauck's (2003) work is currently dominant. But even his learned treatment is distressingly limited in purview, focusing largely on the preserved correspondence surrounding Cicero. Klauck's data — contrary to the way it is sometimes presented[13] — establishes important explanatory constraints on any suggestions of partition in relation to the putative behavior of ancient editors.

Klauck's research affirms that letters could be composed over time and hence shift in direction quite significantly in the light of new information. (His principal example of this is a letter by M. Caelius Rufus preserved in Book 8 of *Ad familiares;* see 8.6.5; Klauck 2003, 141-43; 2006 [1998], 164.) This seems a decisively proven insight. Klauck also notes the presence, although comparative rareness, of interpolations, observing that these are often explicable by way of quotation. Other preserved letters are sometimes quoted within correspondence, and even letters within letters. But strictly speaking, these are then not interpolations at all but, precisely, quotations. Moreover, both techniques are authorial, and this will need to be borne in mind in what follows. In the vital matter of ancient editorial activity, Klauck's researches are considerably less decisive.

In the enormous correspondence preserved in general relation to Cicero — which is a fraction of the correspondence originally published — he finds only approximately fifty compilations, and this is relatively few. His survey spans more than eight hundred extant letters. Klauck emphasizes here the need for relatively simple explanations of any collation — principally, two different letters fused together, one lacking an ending and the other a beginning. And it is at just this point that we must raise an important query.

This very mode of perceived collation raises the entire question of editorial intention. Are such collations evidence of original editorial intent, or

---

13. Even, to a degree, contrary to the way *he* presents it. Some of his final conclusions seem rather problematically derived from his actual evidence and argumentation.

perhaps of original editorial carelessness — which would be entirely understandable given the task facing Cicero's original editor and executor, Tiro (who was also his secretary) — or perhaps of later scribal carelessness in transmission coupled with the vagaries of transmission itself? Few manuscripts of Cicero's correspondence are now extant, the time lapses between their reproduction are long, and knowledge of the history of their transmission is severely limited. These vagaries make it impossible to rule out the possibility that all the compilations detected by Klauck stem from scribal error, whether by Tiro or later scribes, and not from deliberate editorial policy. We have no *decisive* evidence of this last practice from the material. Indeed, the nature of the compilations that Klauck detects indicates the comprehensive plausibility of an explanation strictly in terms of transmission (i.e., carelessness, haste, and the later jumbling together of material). Hence, his research does not establish that ancient editors collated and compiled epistolary manuscripts into new artificial epistolary syntheses deliberately. But Klauck's research is instructive in another key relation.

Klauck establishes compilation, irrespective of its origin, by what we might call hard evidence of contradiction within a single published letter, that is, when two different and irreconcilable dates are apparent within one text or, in essentially the same terms, when datable episodes that are contradictory can be detected. Cicero affords many of these, because of his close involvement with the Roman civil war. These terse factual contradictions allow a firm judgment of compilation. And this seems entirely fair. The presence of this type of evidence can undergird a plausible claim of partition — what we can call "telltale contradictions."

Armed with this knowledge, we can turn to Paul and the case of Romans 16 and posit its appending to the rest of Romans in the presence of hard evidence of contradiction, something that would probably establish deliberate ancient editorial collation.[14] But it seems that we have nothing of this nature

---

14. It seems unlikely that compilations in the original Pauline letter collection would have been accidental. The letter openings and endings, carefully preserved in every canonical letter except Hebrews, would have to have been removed. And suitable connections would have to have been supplied between strips of material from different letters that have apparently been joined, namely, δέ in Rom 16:1 and 2 Cor 10:1 (at the least). Many of the suggestions of collation, including the most plausible in relation to Rom 16, posit interpolation or insertion. This *must* have involved deliberate editorial activity. These considerations all suggest that if editorial collation of different Pauline letters has taken place, it was not inadvertent but quite self-conscious. This realization does not resolve the broader question whether compilation did in fact take place. But in effect it "raises the stakes" for the following discussions. If partition

in the text of Romans 16 over against the rest of canonical Romans. The internal or substantive arguments in this regard are all only probabilistic, which is to say that reasonable alternative construals of the relevant data remove any putative contradictions, and this judgment is affirmed in subsequent scholars' rejection of the hypothesis.

Manson's classic case reprises an earlier case made originally by David Schulz (1829; see Manson 1991 [1962], 12-13). The suggestion is that Romans 16 seems to have been addressed not to Rome but to Ephesus, with the rest of canonical Romans (most probably) being addressed to Rome (see 1:7). If it holds good, this is in effect an internal contradiction, suggesting in turn the partition of the canonical letter. A single letter could hardly have been sent both west to Rome and east to Ephesus.

The suggestion is argued on a number of more specific grounds:

(i) Paul has an implausible number of personal friends in Romans 16 and knows too much about the people he greets to be addressing Rome, since he has never been there;

(ii) the overt connections of some of the people are with Asia — principally, Prisca and Aquila, from whom we last hear in a Pauline letter written from Asia (see 1 Cor 16:19), and Epaenetus, "the first fruits of Asia" (Rom 16:5) — a reasonable argument at this stage in the construction of the frame; and

(iii) the exhortations of 16:17-20 are too aggressive for a church unknown to Paul.

(iv) I would add that vv. 1-2 are a pristine example of a letter of recommendation. It is plausible to suggest that Paul wrote short letters of this nature, which are well attested in his day, to facilitate the reception of his delegates and helpers, and this would be a largely self-sufficient explanation of an independent letter — in this case, Romans 16:1-20 (see Klauck 2006 [1998], 72-77). That is, the cause of this short letter would have been Paul's desire to recommend his client Phoebe to the Ephesian community.[15]

---

of a Pauline letter is proved demonstrably to be necessary, then we may step beyond Klauck's evidence and posit deliberate ancient editorial collation. Absent this proof, however, it is not demonstrated that such behavior ever took place. All collation evident in ancient letter collections would be entirely attributable to carelessness and mistakes.

15. The presence of δέ in 16:1, linking the following material overtly to something preceding, would have to be explained as a later editor's decision to smooth over the seam at this point in the canonical letter (see also 2 Cor 10:1). However, this is not especially implausible.

But none of these arguments necessarily generates an explicit contradiction. The relevant pieces of data are all equally explicable in a letter written to Rome, and there are strong counterarguments to the hypothesis of an Ephesian destination. In direct rebuttal, we should note:

(i) Paul arguably uses extended personal greetings to establish personal rapport as against simply to maintain it, as Colossians 4:10-14 might attest. Moreover, his information about Rome is presumably quite good, especially if his coworkers Prisca and Aquila are there, along with converts from Asia.

(ii) Mobility in the ancient Mediterranean was comparatively good, so it would not have been implausible for businesspeople associated with Ephesus to be associated at some other time with Rome (see the famous instance of the craftsman Flavius Zeuxis, who sailed from the east to Rome seventy-two times according to *CIG* 3920; noted by Lampe 2003 [1989], 158; see also ORBIS 2013). Moreover, only three people named in Romans 16 need to have migrated to Rome — Prisca, Aquila, and Epaenetus. This is not implausible (and especially if Acts data is taken into account, notably 18:2, but this will not be emphasized here).

(iii) The contention about the aggressive material in 16:17-20 depends on the reconstruction of ancient rhetorical practices and their appropriateness — a delicate matter that we will consider carefully in relation to 2 Corinthians in this chapter's final major section. Suffice it for now to say that while 16:17-20 might seem offensively aggressive to modern commentators, the fiery warnings may well have been unexceptionable within the harsher world of ancient polemic. And they may, moreover, have accorded exactly with one of the letter's key strategies (see Lampe 2003 [1989], 159-60; D. Campbell 1994, 315-36; 2009, 469-518, esp. 496-98 and 513-15). It is important to observe as well that they concern outsiders and not the addressees themselves.

(iv) Paul's letters are unusually long and complex in relation to the papyri, so they are generally treated as "mixed types" that contain numerous instances within them of various epistolary genres. It is therefore not necessarily surprising to find a recommendation for someone embedded at the end of a much longer letter primarily concerned with other things. Furthermore, this material seems to characterize the principal letter bearer (see Head 2009a; 2009b) and so makes excellent sense just where it is positioned canonically.[16]

---

16. And no special pleading is necessary for the presence of δέ in 16:1. We should also

(v) Some of the people greeted in Romans 16 seem in any case to have belonged in Rome; see especially the allusions to members of the elite Roman and Jewish households there — "those members of the household of Aristobulus" (v. 10), "those of Narcissus" (v. 11b), and the slave named for the Herodiani ("Herodiana" in v. 11a) (see Lampe 1991, 216-30; and, in much more depth, Lampe 2003 [1989], 153-83, esp. 157).[17]

It seems, then, that the hypothesis is currently faltering. The putative contradiction in terms of incompatible destinations seems more apparent than real. However, the claim might receive stronger attestation from a consideration of letter theory. In my view, the best argument for the partition of Romans 16 is the possible presence within the canonical text of two sets of Pauline letter endings. If true, this would be unprecedented and might well suggest the presence of two originally separate letters now melded into one, although it would not necessarily denote an original destination for Romans 16 of Ephesus.[18] I will lean here primarily on the work of Jeffrey Weima (see esp. his 1994a and 1994b).

Weima notes how Paul's letter endings sculpt formulaic elements into contingently appropriate conclusions in a manner as careful and considered as his letter openings. Consequently, they almost always contain four stereotypical elements, although these can be internally complex and occur in different orders:

---

note that it seems odd to break an original letter at 15:33, where a peace wish occurs, one of Paul's typical closing formulae (Ὁ δὲ θεὸς τῆς εἰρήνης μετὰ πάντων ὑμῶν, ἀμήν). One must then posit the deliberate editorial introduction of further material at this point (including the introduction of a δὲ), together with the excision of the beginning of the shorter letter, the excision of its ending, and a final appending of the original ending of the longer letter. And this all seems oddly complicated.

17. Lampe also argues that simply in statistical terms, and taken altogether, the names in Romans 16 correlate better with Rome than with Ephesus (see Lampe 2003 [1989], 157, 164-83), but it is hard to know just how much weight to give this claim.

18. This independent letter would probably be best understood as a letter sent to Rome with the letter bearers who were carrying the rest of Romans, and not as a largely independent note sent to Ephesus; the arguments for that provenance have already collapsed. So we should imagine Phoebe arriving at a tenement church and presenting herself with Rom 16:1-20 first — essentially her letter of introduction — and following this with a presentation and discussion of Rom 1:1-15:33 + 16:21-24, perhaps also with 16:25-27 included somewhere. Of course, the latter presentation would unfold only if the short introductory letter got her through the door, so to speak.

A: Peace benediction
B: Hortatory section
C: Greetings
   These could be in the first, second, or third person;
   could include a kiss greeting;
   and could include an autograph.
D: Grace benediction

Paul's letter endings could also contain other elements mingled with these — doxologies, expressions of joy, postscripts, and so on. However, the four key elements noted above are almost invariably present, and absent only for obvious reasons; so, for example, it seems understandable that Galatians does not contain greetings. And consequently, it seems significant that all four principal elements are at first glance present at the end of Romans *twice*. Like the opening and the transition to the letter body, the ending of Romans seems to be especially complex.

Peace benedictions (A) arguably occur in both 15:33 and 16:20:

15:33: Ὁ δὲ θεὸς τῆς εἰρήνης μετὰ πάντων ὑμῶν, ἀμήν.

16:20a: ὁ δὲ θεὸς τῆς εἰρήνης συντρίψει τὸν σατανᾶν ὑπὸ τοὺς πόδας ὑμῶν ἐν τάχει.

The characteristic beginnings of hortatory sections (B) are discernible in 15:30 and 16:17:

15:30: Παρακαλῶ δὲ ὑμᾶς, ἀδελφοί, διὰ τοῦ κυρίου ἡμῶν Ἰησοῦ Χριστοῦ καὶ διὰ τῆς ἀγάπης τοῦ πνεύματος συναγωνίσασθαί μοι ἐν ταῖς προσευχαῖς ὑπὲρ ἐμοῦ πρὸς τὸν θεόν, κ. τ. λ.

16:17: Παρακαλῶ δὲ ὑμᾶς, ἀδελφοί, σκοπεῖν τοὺς τὰς διχοστασίας καὶ τὰ σκάνδαλα παρὰ τὴν διδαχὴν ἣν ὑμεῖς ἐμάθετε ποιοῦντας, καὶ ἐκκλίνετε ἀπ' αὐτῶν· κ. τ. λ.

Greetings (C) occur in a long block in 16:3-16 but then recur in vv. 21-23. The first block of greetings is primarily imperative ("greet one another"), but it finishes with a more typical kiss greeting and a general greeting in the third person. The later material is personal and so in the first, second, and third person.

16:16: ἀσπάσασθε ἀλλήλους ἐν φιλήματι ἁγίῳ. ἀσπάζονται ὑμᾶς αἱ ἐκκλησίαι πᾶσαι τοῦ Χριστοῦ.

16:21: Ἀσπάζεται ὑμᾶς Τιμόθεος ὁ συνεργός μου καὶ Λούκιος καὶ Ἰάσων καὶ Σωσίπατρος οἱ συγγενεῖς μου.

Finally, grace wishes (D), which were Paul's personal autograph, occur twice within the manuscript tradition, at 16:20b (the majority of the MSS; omitted in D*vid, F, G) and 16:24 (see esp. D [adding also 16:25-27], F, G; although other MSS place this material after 16:25-27, and a few, like Ψ, have both):

16:20b: Ἡ χάρις τοῦ κυρίου ἡμῶν Ἰησοῦ μεθ᾽ ὑμῶν.

16:24: Ἡ χάρις τοῦ κυρίου ἡμῶν Ἰησοῦ Χριστοῦ μετὰ παντων ὑμῶν. ἀμήν.

This evidence is quite impressive at first glance — enough to make one think long and hard about compilation. However, these doublets may be more apparent than real.

Romans 16:20a is not necessarily a peace wish but may emerge from the short, sharp exhortation Paul fashions at this point, and in particular from the scriptural intertexts that he seems to be invoking (see Pss 8:6 and 110:1;[19] along with Gen 3). The exhortation beginning in 15:30 arguably flows directly out from the letter body and so does not necessarily function as a concluding exhortation within a letter ending. This would leave 16:17-20 as the sole parenetic subsection within the letter ending proper, which would be typical. This important exhortation may then arguably interrupt Paul's greetings, which resume after the climactic proclamation in v. 20 of victory over Satan, reducing the apparent double sets of greetings to one. And the shift from general and collective greetings to personal greetings in a Pauline letter ending is attested elsewhere (see 1 Cor 16:19 and, to some degree, Phil 4:21-22). Finally, the doublet of autographing grace wishes may well be due to manuscript confusion caused, among other things, by the later addition of vv. 25-27 at the end of chapter 16. Certainly, few manuscripts attest to the presence of two grace wishes. Most merely differ over the exact form and position of one.

In sum, then, it seems that the evidence in terms of letter form is insuf-

---

19. 1 Cor 15:25-27 is an important parallel text; this material is discussed briefly in my 2009 (697 and nn. 63 and 64).

ficiently decisive to warrant the separation of Romans 16:1-20 from the rest of the canonical letter on the grounds that it was originally a distinguishable letter. The evidence of epistolary doublets seemed potentially decisive but was not borne out unambiguously by the actual data, although it was "a near run thing."[20] And with this judgment, the suggestion concerning the partition of Romans 16 seems to have failed overall. However, this failure has still been instructive.

It has established in a preliminary way an explanatory threshold for judgments of partition in relation to a canonical letter. We can posit the occasional haphazard collation of letters by ancient editors with a degree of confidence in the presence of telltale contradictions. In the case of a decisive instance in Paul, this would allow us to augment Klauck's implicit conclusion with the claim that such compilations were probably at times deliberate decisions by an original editor, as against original editorial mistakes or mistakes in transmission. But in the absence of such contradictions in Paul — here specifically, in Romans 16 in relation to the rest of Romans — or of any similarly probative contentions, such as incontestable doublets of letter formulae, we have no reason yet to believe that ancient editors did act in this way in general or that Paul's editor did so in particular.[21] As Klauck and many others have indicated, the way ancient editors influenced the reception of ancient authors in published collections seems to have been primarily with the technique of pseudepigraphy — that is, more colloquially, forgery — and not of compilation. So we must remain especially attentive in what follows to suggestions of pseudepigraphy. Unfortunately, the principal ancient way of authentication, namely, an autograph in the hand of the letter's author, is now lost to us. With the first scribal copy of a Pauline original that did not include an authenticating mark by Paul himself, later readers lost the ability to adjudicate authenticity in these terms (except perhaps when the text denotes the presence of such an autograph, an issue we will discuss in further detail when it arises). We will address the question of pseudepigraphy carefully in due course, although principally this will take place in chapters 4, 5, and 6, when we discuss 2 Thessalonians in relation to 1 Thessalonians, then Colossians and Ephesians, and finally Titus along with 1 and 2 Timothy.

---

20. The Duke of Wellington's comment to Marshall Blücher on meeting his Prussian ally after the battle of Waterloo.

21. The best cases for deliberate editorial modification from Paul's general period are probably Polycarp's letter to the Philippians and the epistle to Diognetus. The former is not directly applicable, however (it is discussed in ch. 6). An authentic letter seems to have been pseudonymously augmented. And the latter is only artificially epistolary and has an extremely fragile history of transmission.

The question of partition in relation to the Pauline letters is by no means over. We will turn shortly to consider the letter most widely supposed to contain partition in Paul, namely, 2 Corinthians. But before doing so we will address a frequently unnoticed methodological dimension brought into play by Romans — *Nebenadressat* — and the links in the developing frame that seem to be present prior to 1 Corinthians. The insights we gain in these two areas will help us when we turn to consider the difficult questions surrounding 2 Corinthians.

3. *Nebenadressat* ("Addressees Alongside")

Charlotte Hartwig and Gerd Theissen published a fascinating thesis in 2004 that arguably deserves more attention from the scholarly world than it has so far enjoyed.[22]

Hartwig begins by observing that the Corinthians — along with any Macedonian delegates present, whom she does not mention — undoubtedly heard their direct acknowledgment in Romans 15:26: εὐδόκησαν γὰρ Μακεδονία καὶ Ἀχαΐα κοινωνίαν τινὰ ποιήσασθαι εἰς τοὺς πτωχοὺς τῶν ἁγίων τῶν ἐν Ἰερουσαλήμ. It seems likely that Paul crafted this statement to affirm the listening Achaians and Macedonians as well as to inform the Roman Christians (230). Certainly, they would have felt affirmed by this statement. But I would observe further that Paul goes on to add an admonitory statement in v. 27 that seems less relevant to the Romans than to the assembled participants in the collection at the letter's point of origin: εὐδόκησαν γὰρ καὶ ὀφειλέται εἰσὶν αὐτῶν· εἰ γὰρ τοῖς πνευματικοῖς αὐτῶν ἐκοινώνησαν τὰ ἔθνη, ὀφείλουσιν καὶ ἐν τοῖς σαρκικοῖς λειτουργῆσαι αὐτοῖς. Presumably, the Roman Christian auditors who were former pagans could *infer* from this that they ought to be generous materially with any poor Jewish Christians in their midst. But the direct force of the statement is to reframe — for those Corinthians and Macedonians who were listening — the Aegean collectors' generosity within the standard ancient obligation of reciprocity. This money is *owed* whether the collectors are delighted by the opportunity to give or not. And this suggests in turn that Hartwig is right to hypothesize that other material in the rest of

---

22. I have seen it occasionally cited but never used substantively, except minimally in Theissen's later work. See only a passing annotation in Schnabel (2004, 39 n. 95). The argument is based primarily on Hartwig's Heidelberg dissertation of 2001, so I will attribute the position to her in what follows. Stirewalt provides useful background for the phenomenon without going on to recognize it (2003, 10-11).

Romans not directly addressing the Corinthians would nevertheless function within Paul's communicative relationship with them. She goes on to make a number of useful observations about the original composition of Romans. This was of course a largely oral event. Paul would have been processing the material that eventually went into this extraordinary letter with himself, his companions, and his hosts over a period of time. And this would not have been just, or even primarily, "an inner dialogue" (231). (Perhaps one should envisage an advanced seminar led by a professor with the ultimate goal of writing a paper.) Romans is a complex and crafted letter that must have been written in sections and stages. Indeed, we can detect the voice of some of the participants in this "seminar" when the text includes the doxological response of "amen" (see 1:25; 9:5; 11:36; and perhaps 16:27), along with any similar comments (see 16:22: ἀσπάζομαι ὑμᾶς ἐγὼ Τέρτιος ὁ γράψας τὴν ἐπιστολὴν ἐν κυρίῳ). We could add that considerable processing of Scripture was probably going on as well, which, if undertaken in broadly midrashic terms, would ordinarily have involved much oral recitation and discussion.[23]

But Hartwig notes that the Corinthian correspondence itself must also have been involved in these oral deliberations in some way. The Corinthians would doubtless have been continuing to process Paul's "weighty" letters, which they had received over the previous calendar year. And it is both exciting and vexing to think that they therefore had an extended opportunity to query Paul about everything he had written to them. This rolling discussion would have interwoven with the composition of Romans.

Moreover, we should recall that the final form of the letter was read out first to the Corinthians and the Macedonian delegates, not to the Romans, and we are even able to name some (or perhaps all) of this audience (see Rom 16:21-23). As Hartwig observes, those named as greeting the Romans specifically must have heard the letter. ("Wer Grüsse ausrichten lasst, ist in der Regel über den Brief informiert, der seine Grüsse enthält"; 232.) So the first listeners to "Romans" were Timothy, Lucius, Jason, Sosipater, Tertius, Gaius, Erastus, and Quartus, all of whom were in Corinth.

On the basis of this evidence, Hartwig posits three possible modes of intertextuality in relation to Romans (233-34): (1) a reshaping of polemical Corinthian material in Romans in a less polemical form; (2) a development

---

23. A useful entry point into some of the debates surrounding this phenomenon is Stanley and Porter (2008). An intriguing suggestion emphasizing this general point is Jaffee (2001), namely, that "oral" Torah and its disputes refer not to additional material but strictly to matters of pronunciation or prosody.

of material from the Corinthian correspondence in the light of the crises Paul had experienced since formulating it (i.e., in Asia and vis-à-vis the Corinthians themselves); and (3) a continuation of his relationship with the Corinthians as Romans corrected and completed material from the letters they already knew.

It is the third possibility here that is especially important for our developing frame. (The first two modes would apply to later theological reconstructions that can take place only after the frame is in place, as the introduction pointed out.) But Hartwig's case needs to be supplemented before we pursue it further.

There is a gap between Hartwig's initial observations and her conclusion. It does not follow from the mere orality of the original situation surrounding the composition of Romans that Paul was deliberately addressing the Corinthians in addition to the stated recipients at Rome. The Corinthians could have been largely inadvertent listeners who were being edified in passing; they could have been merely listening in on another conversation. But the very volume of material from the Corinthian correspondence that recurs in Romans speaks against this simpler account of the rhetorical situation. Romans reiterates a considerable amount of material recognizable from 1 Corinthians and 2 Corinthians. (This is especially evident in the parenetic section of Romans.)[24] And only three possibilities suggest themselves in initial explanation of this, two of which can be discarded quickly as unlikely, leaving us with Hartwig's account.

This overlapping material could be drawn from Paul's own theological reservoir — from his coherence. He simply repeats this material in his communications because it is standard.[25] But then we would expect to see it in all, or at least most, of his other letters, and we do not. It occurs almost entirely in 1 Corinthians and Romans (and to a lesser extent in 2 Cor). Alternatively, this material could be tailored to quite specific circumstances — as indeed it seems to be in relation to Corinth. But then the specific circumstances at Corinth and Rome would have to be identical, and this seems unlikely. That they could be similar in one or two respects seems possible, but to be identical in all the relevant respects strains credulity — especially given that Paul

24. The mere fact of overlap between the Corinthian correspondence and Romans has been noted quite frequently in the past. Manson (1991 [1962]) reprises it briefly but accurately in the classic article already noted.

25. This is basically Karris's (1991 [1973], 65-84) explanation of the recurrence of material from 1 Cor 8 and 10 in Rom 14, which discusses the weak and the strong. However, this rationale has been decisively refuted by (i.a.) Donfried (1991 [1974], 102-24); see also my remarks in 2009, 488.

did not found the Roman church. So we are left with a widespread reprise of Corinthian material in Romans that is inexplicable except in the terms that Hartwig suggests. In Romans, *Paul is deliberately echoing his earlier material addressed originally to Corinth in part to continue to address Corinth.* This does not preclude the material's usefulness at Rome, suitably restated. But *both* audiences are in view. Paul's epistolary rhetoric has multiple targets, and this is entirely understandable once we recall the complex process of composition that unfolded at the letter's place of origin. The text developed over time and apparently quite deliberately in relation to multiple addressees.

It remains only to appreciate that while the heavily reiterated material establishes Hartwig's conclusion, her inference about the rhetorical texture of Romans must now extend beyond this reiterated material. The Corinthians will be informed by *everything* that is written in Romans. Insofar as this material does address specific contingencies in Romans, we would expect it to be less directly relevant to Corinth (that is, unless the two contingencies overlapped, which seems possible in single and general instances but implausible to any great extent). But much as modern congregations can still be informed by careful historical reconstructions of Paul's address to an ancient community, the Corinthians would benefit from listening in on this overtly Roman material. This raises a methodological question concerning how to distinguish between what we might call more direct and more indirect material in Romans in relation to both the Corinthians and the Romans. However, an inability on our part to reach decisive judgments here in all respects does not invalidate the basic dynamics in play. We simply reach the limits of modern historicizing at this point.

This basic realization generates two significant conclusions for the modern Pauline interpreter. First, interpreters must learn to interpret Paul's rhetoric in terms of multiple audiences that include a letter's origin as well as its destination, plus presumably its receptions en route, if these can be determined.

Second, we will receive assistance when trying to locate a letter in the frame from a consideration of its apparent *Nebenadressat*. Clearly, this methodological angle on framing must be used demonstrably and cautiously. However, suitably applied, it will have the potential to generate important corroborative evidence for the places of composition of some of Paul's letters that are more puzzling in this respect than Romans. The composition of Romans at Corinth, surrounded by the Corinthian correspondence, strongly establishes the validity of this type of investigation. We will therefore try from this point onward to be attentive to echoes of a letter's place of origin as well as its destination.

4. Extending the Front End:
A Previous Letter to Corinth and a Corinthian Reply

In 1 Corinthians 5:9-13 Paul writes a pungent paragraph referring to a letter. Most translations and modern scholars take this to be a reference to a letter written by Paul previously to Corinth and now lost (at least in large measure). But the situation is not completely clear-cut.

[5:9] Ἔγραψα ὑμῖν ἐν τῇ ἐπιστολῇ μὴ συναναμίγνυσθαι πόρνοις, [10] οὐ πάντως τοῖς πόρνοις τοῦ κόσμου τούτου ἢ τοῖς πλεονέκταις καὶ ἅρπαξιν ἢ εἰδωλολάτραις, ἐπεὶ ὠφείλετε ἄρα ἐκ τοῦ κόσμου ἐξελθεῖν. [11] νῦν δὲ ἔγραψα ὑμῖν μὴ συναναμίγνυσθαι ἐάν τις ἀδελφὸς ὀνομαζόμενος ἢ πόρνος ἢ πλεονέκτης ἢ εἰδωλολάτρης ἢ λοίδορος ἢ μέθυσος ἢ ἅρπαξ, τῷ τοιούτῳ μηδὲ συνεσθίειν. [12] τί γάρ μοι τοὺς ἔξω κρίνειν; οὐχὶ τοὺς ἔσω ὑμεῖς κρίνετε; [13] τοὺς δὲ ἔξω ὁ θεὸς κρινεῖ; ἐξάρατε τὸν πονηρὸν ἐξ ὑμῶν αὐτῶν.

The aorist Paul uses here in v. 9 might be an epistolary aorist and hence a reference to the material he has written previously in 1 Corinthians itself: "I have written to you already in *this* letter [instructions] not to associate with immoral people." He could then be repeating this reference in v. 11: "But now I write to you [the instructions] not to mix together if someone named a brother should be an immoral person." Clearly, some sort of interpretative clarification is taking place, namely, that Paul's instructions concerning the avoidance of association with certain sorts of lurid sinners do not entail avoiding contact with non-Christian sinners. He is referring, he says here, only to lurid sinners within the Christian community. Christians are not to judge outsiders in this way but *are* to judge insiders, expelling evildoers if they are present.

If Paul's clarification applies to 1 Corinthians only, then it must apply to 5:1-8, since Paul has not yet addressed sexual immorality up to this point in the letter (although he now proceeds to do so at length; see 5:1–7:40 and 10:6-30). And this seems possible. In 5:1-8 he dictates how the Corinthians are to expel from their midst a person who has committed incest.[26] Hence, the question is more finely balanced than many seem to suppose. But:

26. [5:1] Ὅλως ἀκούεται ἐν ὑμῖν πορνεία, καὶ τοιαύτη πορνεία ἥτις οὐδὲ ἐν τοῖς ἔθνεσιν, ὥστε γυναῖκά τινα τοῦ πατρὸς ἔχειν. [2] καὶ ὑμεῖς πεφυσιωμένοι ἐστὲ καὶ οὐχὶ μᾶλλον ἐπενθήσατε, ἵνα ἀρθῇ ἐκ μέσου ὑμῶν ὁ τὸ ἔργον τοῦτο πράξας; [3] ἐγὼ μὲν γάρ, ἀπὼν τῷ σώματι παρὼν δὲ τῷ πνεύματι, ἤδη κέκρικα ὡς παρὼν τὸν οὕτως τοῦτο κατεργασάμενον· [4] ἐν τῷ ὀνόματι τοῦ κυρίου ἡμῶν Ἰησοῦ συναχθέντων ὑμῶν καὶ τοῦ ἐμοῦ πνεύματος σὺν

(i) Paul's language is odd if he is merely engaging in a clarification of vv. 1-8 by way of a rhetorical flourish. If it was never his intention that vv. 1-8 be construed restrictively, then the opening to v. 11 in particular cannot be read adversatively and thus seems redundant (see νῦν δὲ ἔγραψα ὑμῖν). This material makes perfect sense, however, as a specifically present (νῦν) adversative *correction* — and in fairly forcible terms (see οὐ πάντως in v. 10) — to an existing interpretation *that must then have been caused by a previous communication,* which in context would be a letter.

(ii) The first epistolary aorist used here references a letter in arthrous terms. Hans Arneson (2014) has failed to find a decisive instance from contemporary sources in which an arthrous reference in this manner does not refer to *another* letter. (His observation applies to statements in the indicative; see also Rom 16:22: ἀσπάζομαι ὑμᾶς ἐγὼ Τέρτιος ὁ γράψας τὴν ἐπιστολὴν ἐν κυρίῳ.)

(iii) Paul's characterization of what he has written is not, strictly speaking, correct if it is a reference to vv. 1-8. He has not spoken of social ostracism in general, although this could be inferred from the context, but of expulsion from the assembly. More importantly, he has not said that all the sexually immoral are to be expelled but only a particular egregious practitioner (ἀρθῇ ἐκ μέσου ὑμῶν ὁ τὸ ἔργον τοῦτο πράξας . . . τὸν οὕτως τοῦτο κατεργασάμενον . . . παραδοῦναι τὸν τοιοῦτον), although again a more general application could perhaps be inferred from the context (see the citation of Deut 17:7 in v. 13). Quotation was often quite precise in the ancient world, letters often being immediately available to check references (see esp. Klauck 2003, 151-52). Paul's correction would make better sense, then, if he had written explicitly at some point, μὴ συναναμίγνυσθαι πόρνοις (or its close equivalent). This could be the case if he had written it in a previous letter, but it is not literally the case here.

(iv) Some sort of prior communication between Paul and the Corinthians concerning sexual ethics seems to have taken place. Sexual immorality seems to have been an ongoing problem at Corinth, as it was presumably for many of Paul's pagan converts (see 2 Cor 12:21; 13:2), so it is entirely plausible that Paul addressed it. More distinctively, the Corinthians seem

---

τῇ δυνάμει τοῦ κυρίου ἡμῶν Ἰησοῦ, [5] παραδοῦναι τὸν τοιοῦτον τῷ σατανᾷ εἰς ὄλεθρον τῆς σαρκός, ἵνα τὸ πνεῦμα σωθῇ ἐν τῇ ἡμέρᾳ τοῦ κυρίου. [6] Οὐ καλὸν τὸ καύχημα ὑμῶν. οὐκ οἴδατε ὅτι μικρὰ ζύμη ὅλον τὸ φύραμα ζυμοῖ; [7] ἐκκαθάρατε τὴν παλαιὰν ζύμην, ἵνα ἦτε νέον φύραμα, καθώς ἐστε ἄζυμοι· καὶ γὰρ τὸ πάσχα ἡμῶν ἐτύθη Χριστός. [8] ὥστε ἑορτάζωμεν μὴ ἐν ζύμῃ παλαιᾷ μηδὲ ἐν ζύμῃ κακίας καὶ πονηρίας ἀλλ᾽ ἐν ἀζύμοις εἰλικρινείας καὶ ἀληθείας.

to have asked Paul a series of questions about sexual ethics to which he responds in much of 1 Corinthians. These seem to include challenges to some prior injunctions from Paul on theological grounds, and apparently from rather different directions (see 6:12-20; 7:1, 25; 11:2-16; a classic account of these is provided by Hurd 1983 [1965]). So we can affirm with confidence the existence, before the Corinthians' response to Paul, of a communicative "space" from Paul himself that included sexual ethics. And this would be occupied appropriately by a letter from Paul.

For these reasons, we may tentatively conclude that a letter from Paul preceded a return communication from the Corinthians to Paul (and this will be corroborated later in the light of 2 Cor 10:10, if our identification of the Letter of Tears proves sustainable). This opens up the possibility in turn that Paul sometimes "corrects" existing interpretations of his material at Corinth (so M. Mitchell 2003). But Paul's response is also informed by a great deal of information about the situation in Corinth.

We know of an oral report from "those of Chloe's household" (1 Cor 1:11), and of a letter from Corinth (see esp. 7:1). Sosthenes coauthors 1 Corinthians with Paul (1:1), although only Acts associates him with Corinth (18:17). But Paul is also apparently being informed by Stephanas (see 1 Cor 1:16; 16:15-16), likely a convert from Athens who had since emigrated to Corinth. It is hard to tell whether the two slaves Fortunatus ("Lucky") and Achaicus ("Greek") are to be identified with those from Chloe's household already mentioned, were companions and/or retainers of either Stephanas or Sosthenes, or were simply further delegates of the Corinthian congregation. They probably came from a Latin-speaking house, however, so it seems most likely on balance that they were sent by Gaius (see Rom 16:22-23). Certainly, they came from Achaia. So the information about Corinth flowing to Paul in Ephesus was clearly rich.

Unfortunately, it is impossible to give a precise account of the movements of all these parties in relation to one another. We can surmise only that the delegation from Chloe seems to have been a more unauthorized report and so could have traveled separately from any official party to Paul, the latter presumably carrying the letter from the Corinthians to Paul. So we will simply posit a cluster of Corinthian visits to Paul in Ephesus at this time.

We also do not know exactly when all these parties from Corinth arrived in Ephesus. It is impossible to say whether they arrived during the previous year, before the onset of winter, allowing Paul the winter season to compose a response; whether they arrived during the winter, perhaps traveling largely overland, or risking a direct winter crossing at considerable expense and personal danger; or whether they arrived in the spring, entailing that Paul then composed 1 Corinthians rather more quickly. And the different parties may have done different things. So we will simply posit a set of Corinthian arrivals at Ephesus during this time span. Fortunately, not much turns on further precision here.

Just when these figures traveled back to Corinth is also hard to say, although it is by no means impossible that they all traveled back together, accompanied by Timothy (1 Cor 4:17; 16:10-11), whom Paul then expected to return to him in Ephesus. So we will simply posit a generic Corinthian set of returns as well, and 1 Corinthians most likely went with this party.

We can say with more confidence that Paul's first communication at this time with Corinth, which we have tentatively inferred was epistolary, took place in the previous year, and it seems to have included, at the least, controversial instructions about sexual ethics, along with a statement concerning the inauguration of the collection for the saints in Jerusalem. Reconstructing the rest of the previous letter's content is a more delicate business. Further topics in the Corinthian reply open up the possibility of their presence in Paul's prior letter, although sometimes little more than this. But we can safely leave definitive judgments here until a later moment within our broader reconstruction.

The Corinthian reply does not need to be reconstructed in detail here either. It seems to have contained a query about diet, specifically concerning meat sacrificed to idols (8:1), and also seems — not entirely unfairly — to have cited a slogan from that context in relation to sex (see 10:23). The reply also apparently made a query concerning spiritual gifts (12:1), and added a request for a visit from Apollos (16:12), this last remark in particular requiring further consideration with respect to the developing frame.

First Corinthians is, especially in its first main section, much concerned to define Paul's position in relation to the Corinthians over against Apollos (see 1:18–4:21), with almost four chapters of sustained engagement. There is, moreover, apparently a group at Corinth who are partisans of Apollos (1:12), even as there are partisans of Paul and of Cephas. We must therefore posit the presence of direct contact between some of the Corinthians and Apollos prior to this moment in the frame. Had various Corinthians been exposed to Apollos elsewhere, perhaps in Ephesus, presumably including being baptized by him (1:14-15), and then emigrated back to Corinth, taking their partisanship with them? Or had Apollos traveled to Corinth and succeeded in converting and baptizing some Corinthians there? It seems unlikely that Cephas ever traveled to Corinth, yet he seems to have had Corinthian supporters (1:12), so both options seem initially possible.

But Paul speaks about Apollos in a way that suggests his actual presence at Corinth at some point. In particular, in 3:6 he says, "I planted, Apollos watered." This analogy makes little sense unless Apollos was present at Corinth sometime after Paul's founding visit. And it then seems likely in the light of this that when Paul says in 3:10, "In accordance with the gift of God which was given to me, I laid the foundation like a wise master builder, and another built on it," he is referring to Apollos again (and the Greek should even arguably be translated deictically: Κατὰ τὴν χάριν τοῦ θεοῦ τὴν δοθεῖσάν μοι ὡς σοφὸς ἀρχιτέκτων θεμέλιον ἔθηκα, ἄλλος δὲ ἐποικοδομεῖ, that is, ". . . *that* other person . . ."). So we will posit a visit by Apollos to Corinth before much of this sequence, although at exactly which point is difficult to say. The Corinthian reply seems to have asked for his return, so he must have left Corinth and is apparently residing now in Ephesus, although this is somewhat indistinct too. Apollos may have been in Corinth at roughly the same time as the arrival of Paul's first letter, or he may have been there before it.

. . . Apollos VC[27] / [PLC][28] — Corinthian VEs / [Corinthian reply][29] . . .
// year change //
. . . 1 Cor — 2 Cor — Paul VC3 —
// year change //
— Rom — Paul VJ . . .

An important realization that has emerged from this analysis of the front end of the epistolary backbone is that Paul can interpret his earlier letters within his later communications (see esp. M. Mitchell 2003). But he is operating in an ongoing and frequently somewhat difficult relationship with a congregation, the management of which is almost certainly his main concern. So such interpretation is never an entirely neutral activity. That is, Paul is not merely correcting a misunderstanding of what he wrote earlier, although he might be doing this. He is managing the reception of an earlier communication in a way that he considers more constructive and helpful than the way it seems to be understood currently by the Corinthians. Hence, his interpretation of the

27. VC: visit to Corinth (VE: visit to Ephesus; VJ: visit to Jerusalem). See the full list of biographical abbreviations in the front matter.
28. [PLC]: Previous Letter to Corinth from Paul, brackets suggesting that it is now lost, at least in large measure. (We will later consider briefly the possibility of identifying 2 Cor 6:14–7:1 with part of PLC.) Note that this is the most likely point for the collection's inauguration with the Corinthians.
29. A formal written reply from the Corinthians to PLC, delivered to Paul in Ephesus.

correct understanding of an earlier letter may seem to us somewhat egregious. The reception he is correcting may even be a more accurate reading in the original terms than the one he later supplies. But the later position is the one he nevertheless wants the Corinthians to carry forward, for any number of reasons. (He might have overstated something or even made a mistake; his earlier advice might have contained ambiguities or unintended consequences that he does not want to endorse; a new situation might call for different advice, here generated by way of reinterpretation of something already read; and so on.)

We cannot demonstrate the presence of this fundamentally rhetorical hermeneutic in relation to Paul's own texts within his remarks in 1 Corinthians 5:9-13, because almost certainly we lack the text that he is commenting on — his previous letter to Corinth. (There is one other possibility here that will be considered in due course.) But this is an interpretative practice to which we must now be alert, and it will be especially important to bear in mind when we address Paul's statements scattered through 2 Corinthians about a letter written previously, which we must shortly try to identify.

5. The Interim Events and the Identification of the Letter of Tears

5.1 Basic Positions

By this point in our reconstruction, we have considered a partition hypothesis in relation to Romans 16, establishing a basic methodological threshold for that hypothesis, although 2 Corinthians will also provide a strong case for partition in a Pauline letter on slightly different grounds. The phenomenon of *Nebenadressat* has been introduced. And a tentative reconstruction of events prior to the composition of 1 Corinthians has been undertaken, noting especially the way that Paul might reinterpret his earlier communications within a sequence. Hence, the front and back ends of our existing short sequence have been briefly explored. Armed with these insights, we now need to consider 2 Corinthians and the sequence surrounding it in detail, addressing the links between 1 and 2 Corinthians, and between 2 Corinthians and Romans, in full.

We will first investigate the earlier span, stretching between 1 and 2 Corinthians, which covers what are often dubbed "the interim events." Interpreters populate this part of Paul's life with various journeys and communications to and from Corinth, although the number and complexity of these events vary significantly between reconstructions. The interval between 1 Corinthians and 2 Corinthians can seem frighteningly complex, and the academic debates surrounding it most certainly are. But only after preliminary judgments have been made about the events that led up to the composition of 2 Corinthians will we be able to reconstruct what follows this letter with any confidence.

We should note immediately that there are two major contentions that must be pondered. Second Corinthians refers not infrequently to a previous letter that Paul has sent to Corinth. At one point, Paul states that he "wrote this with many tears" (see ἔγραψα ὑμῖν διὰ πολλῶν δακρύων in 2:4), so we will designate this letter for the moment the "Letter of Tears" (LT). We need to identify this letter if we can. Is it 1 Corinthians (1 Cor = LT?), as the church fathers often thought? Or is it a lost letter that we must interpose into our existing sequence between 1 Corinthians and 2 Corinthians, as many modern scholars have supposed (1 Cor — [LT] — 2 Cor)?

The resolution of this question is complicated by another contention frequently heard today: that 2 Corinthians is a collation of two or more letters originally by Paul. (Some important advocates of this approach suggest that it was composed of as many as five originals plus a letter fragment.) If this is the case, then it raises the further question whether a piece of 2 Corinthians should be identified with the Letter of Tears — although if the collation that is our canonical 2 Corinthians is complex, we will have to ask where the various letters or letter fragments belong in any case. So explanation potentially spills out here beyond the interval between 1 and 2 Corinthians, and probably beyond one calendar year as well, and greatly complicates our entire account of this part of the frame.

These, then, are the two major issues our framing project has to face when reconstructing the section of the frame between 1 Corinthians and 2 Corinthians: a letter identification (LT) and a question of partition (2 Cor). But their resolution is complicated by a third cluster of issues, namely, the reconstruction of all the other events that seem to have taken place during this interval. In particular, various people seem to have made visits from Paul's location in Ephesus to Corinth, although just how they linked up again with Paul is debated. So we will need to make sense of at least one visit by Titus, although possibly more than one (see 2 Cor 2:12-13; 7:5-7, 13-15; 8:16-24; 12:17-18). We will need to consider a possible visit by Apollos (see 1 Cor 16:12), and the possible advent of certain "super-apostles" (see 2 Cor 10:12–11:23, etc.). And we will need to consider whether Paul himself made a second visit to Corinth during this interval.

We know that he visited Corinth for a second time at some point, because it is apparent in 2 Corinthians that his forthcoming visit is his third (see 2:2-3; 12:14; 12:20–13:2). But it will obviously change the dynamics of this interval considerably if his second visit actually fell within it rather than took place before it. And this question is bound up with the question of his broader travel plans at the time, at least some of which are announced in 1 Corinthians and 2 Corinthians (see 1 Cor 16:3-9; 2 Cor 1:15-17). These questions overlap in turn with the question concerning the actual problem(s) Paul seems to be facing at Corinth, an issue then connected with the identification of an "offender" who seems to be mentioned in 2 Corinthians (see 7:12; and perhaps also 2:5).

So there are many further balls at this point that the Pauline interpreter must juggle, along with the usual ones. And we must think about which one should be tossed up first. I suggest that it is most appropriate to begin with the question of identification, addressing the reconstruction of some of the other interim events in the light of our initial answer. We can proceed after this to a consideration of partition in 2 Corinthians. The broader debate seems to have proceeded this way in historical terms. Perhaps more importantly, however, there seem to be good methodological grounds for arguing in this order.

Judgments concerning partition tend to draw, if not to rest, upon particular views of the relationship between Paul and the Corinthians. But early on in the investigation, those views would not yet have been formally determined. Moreover, later on, when they are being determined, they would be interlaced with complex hypotheses of partition and resulting fragmentation of the canonical sources, making the precise evaluation of the historical claims in play difficult, to say the least. It seems wiser, then, to bring what insights we can derive minimally and rigorously about the interval between 1 Corinthians and 2 Corinthians to bear on the complicated question of partition, and not to proceed in the other direction. And this means trying first to identify the Letter of Tears, at least in terms of the preliminary possibilities.[30]

---

30. Thrall's (1994, 1:1-77) excellent discussion is also an excellent example of the explanatory distortions that result from beginning the argument with partition. She provides an impressively precise and fulsome account of all the relevant questions but begins with the question of "separation" (i.e., of chs. 10-13 from 1-9). Unfortunately, she also overlooks the correct location of the burden of proof during this early discussion. This leads to her early affirmation of a basic partition hypothesis largely on the grounds that its critics do not provide arguments for unity sufficient to convince her. In similar terms, she then repudiates the "identification" hypothesis (i.e., of chs. 10-13 with the Letter of Tears), ending up with a sequence of a lost Letter of Tears, 2 Cor 1-8, a separate ch. 9, and then a later letter, some of which remains in chs. 10-13. And this particular partition theory then controls her consideration of the other key historical questions and data — the identification of the offender (see 2 Cor 2:5; 7:12) and the explanation of Paul's travel plans (see 1 Cor 16:3-9; 2 Cor 1:15-16). These events are effectively inserted into her existing sequence, and any independent and at times countervailing information is thereby effectively silenced. (Where an alternative voice speaks at these points, she tends again to assign

5.2 The Shape of the Letter of Tears

We need first to try to detect the "shape" of the letter written previous to 2 Corinthians from Paul's characterization of it in 2 Corinthians. We know already from 1 Corinthians that Paul can recharacterize his earlier letters, so this evidence will have to be used advisedly. However, this is the obvious place to start our inquiry. Once we know what basic shape the Letter of Tears had, we can ask what extant letters or pieces of letters are candidates for matching it.

We can glean vestigial data concerning the Letter of Tears from many parts of canonical 2 Corinthians, although it is discussed in the most detail in 2:1-11 and 7:5-14. Smaller pieces of evidence can be found in places such as 3:1; 5:12; 10:9-11; and 13:10 (see also 6:4; 10:12, 18; 12:19). Despite this steady trickle of data, however, certain results are extremely hard to come by. Paul's references are vague, and perhaps deliberately so. We can infer only the following four short characterizations on the basis of his more scattered comments just noted:

  (i) This letter seems to have been perceived, at least by some, as threatening, frightening, and "heavy" (see 10:9-11; 13:10; see also 1:23–2:3).

  (ii) It seems to have included some sort of "recommendation" by Paul that was arguably inappropriate, at least in part because he seems to have lacked suitable letters of recommendation himself from the Corinthians' point of view (so 3:1; 5:12; see also 6:4; 10:12, 18; 12:19).

  (iii) It would not be surprising, to say the least, if this letter addressed factionalism at Corinth, which seems to have been an ongoing problem (see esp. 12:20; 13:2).

  (iv) In a similar vein, it would not be at all surprising if this letter addressed sexual immorality, which also seems to have been an ongoing problem (see 12:21; 13:2; see also esp. 1 Cor 5:1-13).

In sum, the Letter of Tears could be characterized as heavy or frightening; it involved recommendation; and it upbraided the Corinthians for, among other

---

the burden of proof incorrectly and thereby to defuse the challenges rhetorically.) By beginning with the question of identification, addressing the overt historical questions (if we can) after this, and only then turning to consider partition, the following analysis should avoid these sorts of problems. Having said this, if a case for contradictions sufficient to establish the partition of 2 Cor could be made outright, we could begin with this. However, I do not know of one. Claims concerning such "contradictions" tend to appeal to reconstructions of the Corinthians and their relationship with Paul — at which point we are entitled to address the identification of the Letter of Tears first, and probably should.

things, factionalism and sexual immorality. What can we add to this initial picture from a consideration of its more detailed characterizations — first, from 2:1-11?

Verses one through four especially suggest that Paul's letter caused what he now calls "grief" (λύπη) among the Corinthians — an emotional or affective state *and* a complex cultural construct somewhat different for ancient Roman and Hellenistic auditors than it is for modern Western scholars (see respectively Tomkins 2008, esp. 289-350; and Welborn 2011). This is strong language characterizing the letter's impact. Paul goes on to say that he wrote this letter "out of much suffering and constriction of heart . . . and with many tears" (2:4), and these comments connect with other references in 2 Corinthians to a discourse concerning the heart, both Paul's and the Corinthians' (see esp. 6:11-13). But in 2:4 he is characterizing his motivation in composing the letter, which should color its (current!) reception.

We learn from this — cutting a long story short — that the Letter of Tears has had a devastating impact on the Corinthians, so that their very relationship with Paul is probably in jeopardy. In the language of the day, their hearts are now constricted and narrowed against him (see 6:12-13). The *topos* of grief therefore allows Paul to try to narrate the impact of the Letter of Tears in a way that overcomes certain negative results from this impact and opens up the Corinthians' affections to him once more, thereby restoring their relationship. He tries to achieve this broad goal in several ways.

In vv. 1-4 we see him suggesting many things:

(i)   The impact of the Letter of Tears was only ever supposed to be temporary, allowing Paul to reestablish a more fundamental relationship of mutual joy (see 1:24; 2:2, 3). Indeed, the letter having had its effect, the planned visit can now be joyful (see 2:3: καὶ ἔγραψα τοῦτο αὐτό, ἵνα μὴ ἐλθὼν λύπην σχῶ ἀφ' ὧν ἔδει με χαίρειν, πεποιθὼς ἐπὶ πάντας ὑμᾶς ὅτι ἡ ἐμὴ χαρὰ πάντων ὑμῶν ἐστιν).

(ii) The intent was also to avoid a stern visit (see 1:23b: ὅτι φειδόμενος ὑμῶν οὐκέτι ἦλθον εἰς Κόρινθον).

(iii) Paul wrote the letter with a suffering heart. In fact, the constriction he felt at the time was a constriction caused by suffering (see 2:4a: ἐκ γὰρ πολλῆς θλίψεως καὶ συνοχῆς καρδίας ἔγραψα ὑμῖν; see 6:12-13). Moreover, he wrote with many tears, indicating his deep concern for the letter's recipients (see 2:4b: διὰ πολλῶν δακρύων). Thus, any infliction of grief by the letter was accompanied by Paul's own deep suffering and concern.

(iv) Indeed, his main intention in the Letter of Tears was not primarily to grieve the Corinthians but that they might know how much he loved them (see 2:4c: οὐχ ἵνα λυπηθῆτε ἀλλὰ τὴν ἀγάπην ἵνα γνῶτε ἣν ἔχω περισσοτέρως εἰς ὑμᾶς) — things to which his suffering heart and tears bore witness.

(v) Most importantly, Paul suggests that the impact of the letter should have been precisely one of "grief" in the sense of hurt (see λύπη or λυπῶ in 2:1, 2 [2x], 3, 4). Such hurt could be inflicted by close friends or by family members for various reasons; this was the socio-emotional register that Paul suggests should have informed the reception of the Letter of Tears. The impact of the letter was the hurt experienced analogous to a stinging rebuke from a father who disciplines because he loves so much (and so on). The pain it caused was the pain of grief.

In vv. 5-8 we see some further developments:

(i) For the first and only time, in v. 5a, Paul may suggest that he himself has been grieved by something and someone directly: Εἰ δέ τις λελύπηκεν, οὐκ ἐμὲ λελύπηκεν. This is a negation, so we cannot tell immediately whether Paul is qualifying his own grief or denying it altogether. But some feeling of grief on his part is likely. In the same breath, he suggests more clearly that someone has caused grief at Corinth: Εἰ δέ τις λελύπηκεν, οὐκ ἐμὲ λελύπηκεν, ἀλλὰ ἀπὸ μέρους, ἵνα μὴ ἐπιβαρῶ, πάντας ὑμᾶς. And he goes on to establish an ingenious narrative of grieving causality.

Someone has done something that has caused grief to Paul but apparently not to the Corinthians directly and immediately. Presumably, this is some awful sin. Paul has consequently written to the Corinthians and inflicted grief on them — the grief that they should have felt originally from this sinner. And they seem now to have responded, at least in this instance, with the appropriate communal disapprobation. So the origin of the grief is actually the sin in the Corinthians' midst, to which they ought to have responded immediately. And Paul is only reflecting back on them in the Letter of Tears their own initially inadequate response to the incident.

(ii) Equally importantly, Paul now urges the Corinthians to refrain from punishing the one causing the grief unduly (vv. 5b-11). The majority have apparently inflicted dishonor on this figure (v. 6: ἱκανὸν τῷ τοιούτῳ ἡ ἐπιτιμία αὕτη ἡ ὑπὸ τῶν πλειόνων). They are to forgive even as Paul has forgiven, in order that they may not fall prey to a satanic scheme (see ἵνα μὴ πλεονεκτηθῶμεν ὑπὸ τοῦ σατανᾶ), presumably by overwhelming the dishonored person and prompting a drastic response such as permanent exclusion or even suicide. This exhortatory narrative achieves several further goals for Paul. In the first instance, it urges forgiveness and *reintegration* for someone who has caused grief. The impact of the grief is not to spill over into more permanent communal damage.

(iii) But presumably, this action applies also to Paul himself, the one who has signally inflicted grief on the Corinthians, although in his view legitimately. Implicitly, this cause of grief as well should not be allowed to last but should be met with forgiveness, so that Satan's schemes might not be permitted to prosper.

(iv) Further, this allows Paul to praise the Corinthians for responding to the letter constructively and correctly, at least at this point. In so doing, they have attested to their obedient character (see v. 9: . . . εἰ εἰς πάντα ὑπήκοοί ἐστε), a response that Paul hopes will extend to all his injunctions. Indeed, Paul's language indicates a rather lofty goal — obedience in *everything*. The text also states that the Letter of Tears sought an "attestation of character" in the form of "submission" (v. 9: εἰς τοῦτο γὰρ καὶ ἔγραψα, ἵνα γνῶ τὴν δοκιμὴν ὑμῶν), although this and the preceding call for obedience are fairly generic goals.[31]

Much the same dynamics are then evident in 7:5-14, although with a narrative twist. There Paul praises the Corinthians, possibly after a long apostolic interlude, for responding to the grief inflicted by the previous letter, as they have become repentant in a constructive way (see the reintroduction of grief in vv. 8 [2x], 9 [3x], 10 [2x], and 11 [1x]). He goes on to suggest that they have demonstrated "purity in relation to a matter" (11b: ἐν παντὶ συνεστήσατε ἑαυτοὺς ἁγνοὺς εἶναι τῷ πράγματι), and this is presumably an instance of

---

31. We should appreciate that this narration does not even require a specific incident in order to apply. It could apply to a particular category of wrongs identified by the Letter of Tears, or to several — to whatever sin has offended the majority of the community after initially offending Paul but that allows reintegration (although presumably all sins could be forgiven, with the appropriate response to their rebuke). But we have little specific information about the activity or activities in question beyond this. (I am grateful to Hans Arneson for pointing to these interpretative possibilities; he himself suggests that another, rather different reading is also possible — that the Corinthians are being urged to submit "to everyone," reading the accusative phrase with reference to generic people as against instructions. There is much to ponder in this suggestion, although I will not build on it here.)

constructive repentance. But somewhat frustratingly for the modern historian, he provides few further details concerning the actual wrong in question — the *pragma* in relation to which the Corinthians have zealously demonstrated themselves to be "pure." Our only further clues are that they seem to have demonstrated other characteristics here as well: "exertion, defense [lit. apology], indignation, alarm, longing, zeal, and punishment" (see v. 11a: ἰδοὺ γὰρ αὐτὸ τοῦτο τὸ κατὰ θεὸν λυπηθῆναι πόσην κατειργάσατο ὑμῖν σπουδήν, ἀλλὰ ἀπολογίαν, ἀλλὰ ἀγανάκτησιν, ἀλλὰ φόβον, ἀλλὰ ἐπιπόθησιν, ἀλλὰ ζῆλον, ἀλλὰ ἐκδίκησιν). So clearly, some issue has been addressed quite strongly.

Paul then goes on in v. 12 to reject a negative account of the origins of the Letter of Tears and to (re)characterize its motivation once again, in terms consistent with his characterization in chapter 2: ἄρα εἰ καὶ ἔγραψα ὑμῖν, οὐχ ἕνεκεν τοῦ ἀδικήσαντος οὐδὲ ἕνεκεν τοῦ ἀδικηθέντος ἀλλ᾽ ἕνεκεν τοῦ φανερωθῆναι τὴν σπουδὴν ὑμῶν τὴν ὑπὲρ ἡμῶν πρὸς ὑμᾶς ἐνώπιον τοῦ θεοῦ. A positive response to something in the Letter of Tears by the Corinthians is again taken as evidence of their obedience, here described in v. 12b as their zeal for Paul in the sight of God (see 2:9). And this shifts the current reception of the earlier letter away from the wronging and wronged parties, who clearly *were* in view in some way in the Letter of Tears. Paul is now able to praise the Corinthians, to affirm their loyal relationship to him, and to deflect attention — which he seems to want to do — from a particular earlier situation, or perhaps simply from a generic situation of communal wrongdoing. The focus of the letter's reception is now on the Corinthians' positive response and not on their prior toleration of wrongdoing or on the wrongdoer and the injured party.

In short, there seems to be a close similarity between Paul's rhetorical tactics as they appear in his two most detailed characterizations of the Letter of Tears, in chapter 2 and chapter 7. He praises the Corinthians' reception of that letter by way of some specific response(s). In the former instance, he praises their application of disapprobation and communal shame, although he asks for its cessation. In the latter, he praises their zealous purity in a particular matter involving someone wronging and someone wronged against. (We will probe this material for more details shortly, when we consider the possible identities of the offender and the offended, and the incident[s] in question.)

What have we learned, then, about the Letter of Tears from this more detailed look at its characterizations by Paul in 2:1-11 and 7:5-14?

We have found considerable reinforcement for the notion that it was perceived by the Corinthians as "heavy" or "frightening." But we have also learned that the Corinthians had responded positively in Paul's view, at least at one point, by addressing an issue that the Letter of Tears had identified.

Chapter 7 details a response to wronging and wronged parties, although Paul now clearly wants to shift the focus away from the incident itself and the figures involved. It suggests a degree of transparency about this, a forceful address, and a degree of closure; the Corinthians are now pure and innocent in this matter and even seem to have exercised punishment in relation to it. The incident alluded to in chapter 2 is more ambiguous — if indeed it was a particular incident — but the text also implies a communal action of disapprobation against a sinner or group of sinners that Paul urges should now be supplemented by forgiveness and reintegration.

In sum, we can now strengthen our earlier characterization of the Letter of Tears considerably and add a fifth dimension to our description:

(i) This letter seems to have been perceived as threatening, frightening, and "heavy" — and emphatically so. It hurt!

(ii) It included "recommendation" by Paul that some seem to have argued, in response, was inappropriate.

(iii) It would not be surprising if this letter addressed factionalism at Corinth, and this would almost certainly have involved discussing Paul's leadership.

(iv) In a similar vein, it would not be at all surprising if this letter addressed sexual immorality.

(v) It addressed one or more issues that the Corinthians seem to have dealt with before the composition of 2 Corinthians. Chapter 7 denotes an incident involving wrongdoing that was resolved. Chapter 2 denotes an incident or incidents that could result in forgiveness and reintegration after the infliction of communal disapprobation.

This, then, is the substantive "space" that the Letter of Tears occupies within the rhetoric of 2 Corinthians. We need now to consider the candidates that can fill it appropriately. And we will begin with a traditional and surprisingly effective option.

5.3 First Corinthians as the Letter of Tears

Given these descriptive parameters, is it plausible to identify 1 Corinthians with the Letter of Tears? Modern scholarship tends to answer this question emphatically in the negative. But until the modern period, church commentators were entirely comfortable with this suggestion. We will consider here first

whether 1 Corinthians could be the Letter of Tears. After this, we will consider
whether any evidence suggests that it should be.

At first glance, it seems clear that nothing prohibits an identification of
1 Corinthians with the Letter of Tears, and this is an important realization. The
outline of the Letter of Tears discernible within 2 Corinthians is not especially
specific. And 1 Corinthians potentially matches the five characteristics already
identified quite nicely.

(i) First Corinthians is a periodically aggressive, judgmental, and even sting-
     ing letter and so seems appropriately described as "weighty," judging,
     and even harsh or overbearing. In the course of an extended comparison
     between Apollos and himself — to which we will return — Paul develops
     his relationship with the Corinthians in terms of a father and his foolish
     children over against tutelage by a pedagogue. Paul reflects here the
     considerable authority of the father in ancient culture, especially within
     the Roman household, which was a potentially threatening persona. He
     concludes this section in 4:21 with the ominous interrogation, τί θέλετε;
     ἐν ῥάβδῳ ἔλθω πρὸς ὑμᾶς ἢ ἐν ἀγάπῃ πνεύματί τε πραΰτητος. (He fur-
     ther depicts the Corinthians in a decidedly infantile position. So, for
     example, in 3:1-2 he states, Κἀγώ, ἀδελφοί, οὐκ ἠδυνήθην λαλῆσαι ὑμῖν
     ὡς πνευματικοῖς ἀλλ᾽ ὡς σαρκίνοις, ὡς νηπίοις ἐν Χριστῷ. γάλα ὑμᾶς
     ἐπότισα, οὐ βρῶμα· οὔπω γὰρ ἐδύνασθε. ἀλλ᾽ οὐδὲ ἔτι νῦν δύνασθε.)
     When he addresses the role of Apollos at Corinth, he again threatens
     those who build inappropriately on the foundation that he, a master
     builder, has already laid. Their work will be tested with fire and if re-
     vealed to be shoddy, incinerated; and those who build destructively will
     themselves be destroyed.

         In chapter 5 Paul goes on, despite his personal absence, to consign
     someone to Satan, and to prohibit association with any immoral per-
     son within the congregation — something defined more broadly than
     in terms of sexual immorality. In 6:9-10 he suggests that ignoring this
     advice will result in definitive eschatological exclusion. He rebukes some
     of the Corinthians strongly in chapter 11 for their behavior during wor-
     ship and at the Lord's Supper. He berates disorder in chapters 12 and 14.
     And he makes short shrift of those denying Christ's bodily resurrection
     in chapter 15, where he notes caustically in passing, in v. 34: ἐκνήψατε
     δικαίως καὶ μὴ ἁμαρτάνετε, ἀγνωσίαν γὰρ θεοῦ τινες ἔχουσιν, πρὸς
     ἐντροπὴν ὑμῖν λαλῶ.

         Thus, 1 Corinthians is at times clearly a weighty letter that could understandably be construed by its auditors as overbearing and bullying or, in like measure, deeply painful in its criticisms and serial disapproval. It points at times to shameful lapses in the community's ethic — in particular, to the celebrated instance of incest.

(ii) Paul undertakes an extended and pointed comparison between Apollos and himself from 1:18 through to the end of chapter 4. Here he advocates the superiority of his epistemology, of his preaching and account of wisdom, and of his ministry among the Corinthians, which he likens to his building well with rich materials as against badly with rubbish. The argument concludes with a straightforward claim of ultimate authority over the Corinthians on Paul's part; he is their father, who has begotten them. The Corinthians might have many pedagogues — that is, supervisory servants, perhaps of dubious background and sincerity — but they have only the one, loving parent, who is thereby entitled to discipline them stringently. It seems, then, that Paul could be construed as recommending himself and his ministry here over against Apollos (and possibly also over against Cephas).

(iii) The issue of factionalism is implicit in much that has been said and is an overt theme for much of 1 Corinthians. The principal rivalry at Corinth seems to have been between Paul and Apollos, but there is also apparently loyalty on the part of some to Cephas (see 1:12). (The existence and possible reference of "a Christ party" is difficult to determine; see 1:12b; 3:23; 4:10; see also perhaps 2 Cor 13:3.) First Corinthians is concerned with this issue for much of the time (and it might lie behind many of Paul's later discussions in the letter as well, e.g., ch. 15).

(iv) Sexual immorality is clearly an issue in 1 Corinthians. Paul addresses it stridently in chapter 5 and in 6:9-20, alluding to it further in 7:2; 10:8; and 15:33. One Corinthian seems to "have had his father's wife" (5:1). Other sexual immorality seems to be present as well. The use of prostitutes seems to be taking place (6:15-20), something that would be largely unexceptionable for pagans but would have deeply offended Jewish sensibilities.

(v) First Corinthians provides several possible candidates for characteristic (v) in the Letter of Tears, the incident(s) and aftermath of wrongdoing alluded to in 2 Corinthians 2 and 7. The wrongdoing in chapter 7 has apparently been addressed firmly by the Corinthians; the wrongdoing in chapter 2, having been addressed, now needs to be met with forgiveness and reintegration. We will consider some candidates for the incident in chapter 7 first, aware that a more detailed discussion of this data will follow.

Some of the church fathers suggested that the incestuous man identified in 1 Corinthians 5 was the figure spoken of in 2 Corinthians 7.[32] The situation was presumably resolved by his expulsion, which "punishment" would have "purified" the Corinthians. However, this is not the only possibility. Second Corinthians 7 could allude to 1 Corinthians 6:1-8 and the apparent defrauding or robbery within the community by someone whom Paul asked the Corinthians to judge for themselves rather than take to an external court.[33] Alternatively, the Corinthians could have begun to celebrate the Lord's Supper in a more orderly and sensitive way, or to have abandoned offensive feasting on meat, purchased in the city's market, that had been previously sacrificed to idols. Or Paul might even be alluding here to a restoration of the appropriately traditional gender codes at Corinth — the resumption of correct dress and decorum by certain women during their assembly for worship. Any or all of these things could have been addressed constructively by the Corinthians from Paul's point of view and so have elicited his positive response in chapter 7.

Some of these alternatives could then also underlie the incident or incidents alluded to in 2 Corinthians 2. Paul might be recommending the reintegration of the incestuous man into the community — provided, of course, that he had repented. Similarly, he could be recommending the reintegration of repentant fornicators more generally, and perhaps specifically of those who had previously visited prostitutes. He could be recommending the reintegration of the wrongdoer tried and convicted by the Corinthians of some form of fraud or robbery. Or his instructions could be judged general enough to cover all these types of reintegration. Moreover, such reintegration could plausibly include the forgiveness of women who had been dressing and worshipping inappropriately. (The grammar is masculine but could include this activity.)

Clearly, and rather significantly, 1 Corinthians provides numerous possibilities for this particular feature of the Letter of Tears — what we could call things the Corinthians had gotten right.

We should now consider briefly whether any decisive arguments stand against a possible identification.

---

32. Thrall notes in particular its discussion by Tertullian ("[this] traditional view was well-established by the time of Tertullian"; 1994, 1:61-62) and Chrysostom (PG 61:422; 1994, 1:61-65).

33. Thrall (1994, 1:68, esp. n. 454) notes support for this view from Krenkel and Windisch; and her own view, discussed in more detail shortly, is not far from it.

Thrall traces modern critical objections to the identification to F. Bleek (1830; 1869 [1866], 431-36) in the early nineteenth century; however, his arguments are not overwhelming.[34] Thrall's survey adds further objections (see 1994, 1:57-61), some of which can be engaged here usefully, albeit briefly. Thrall argues (i) that Paul is the one who has been offended against and grieved directly (see 2 Cor 2:5 and 7:12) and that this is not apparent in 1 Corinthians; and (ii) that the "Painful Letter" is concerned with only one incident (see again 2 Cor 2:5 and 7:12), while 1 Corinthians deals with a wide-ranging variety of incidents (59-60).

But, against (i), we need merely note that Paul is only a possible identification for the offended figure in 2 Corinthians, and perhaps not even a likely one, as we will see in more detail shortly. So this is not a decisive refutation. (Any argument based on a particular claimed identification of the offended party in 2 Corinthians will necessarily prove fragile.) The rebuttal also presupposes that Paul's second visit intervened between 1 and 2 Corinthians, a position that will be tested shortly. If the visit is best located elsewhere, the contention collapses. Against (ii), we should note that 2 Corinthians 2 and 7 do not necessarily denote the same incident. But even if they are connected, it is unlikely that the Letter of Tears as a whole addressed only this one issue as Thrall suggests (thereby disqualifying an identification with the complex 1 Corinthians). We have already determined five probable features of the letter, to which we should add an unexpected Pauline itinerary and probably some discussion of the collection as well. Thus, the Letter of Tears was almost certainly complex. And in support of this suspicion, we should recall that all of Paul's extant letters addressing churches contain multiple concerns. There is no extant example of a Pauline letter to a church that focuses on just one

---

34. Bleek did not interpose a visit from Paul between 1 Cor and 2 Cor, but he did hold that the Letter of Tears was lost (see esp. 1830). He was convinced that 2 Cor 7 could not denote the incestuous figure in 1 Cor 5; nor could 1 Cor 16:3-9 explain the defensiveness of 2 Cor 1:13-15; nor were the travels of Titus explicable without an intervening letter. (Titus is the information source evidently lying behind much of 2 Cor, but 1 Cor is sent to Corinth with Timothy. It seems reasonable to suppose, then, that Titus visited in the interim with a letter.) But these are hardly decisive objections to a possible identification between 1 Cor and the Letter of Tears. The first is misdirected; the figure in 2 Cor 7 might align with some other figure criticized in 1 Cor (see more on this shortly). The second is merely assertive (and see the discussion of the travel plans that follows here in §5.4). And the third objection is clearly invalid, given the number of visits by delegates without letters apparent elsewhere in Paul's epistles (see esp. Timothy in 1 Thess 3:1-6 and Phil 2:19-24, texts that will be discussed in more detail in chs. 4 and 3 respectively; on Paul's delegates in general, see esp. M. Mitchell's important corrective remarks in 1992).

issue.[35] So Thrall's claim that the Letter of Tears addressed only the issue in view in 2 Corinthians 2 and 7, even granting that the same issue is in view, seems questionable.[36]

In sum, it seems that the identification of 1 Corinthians with the outline of the Letter of Tears that we can detect in 2 Corinthians is initially plausible, and that nothing decisive stands in the first instance against it. But can we press on from mere possibility to probability? Three standard questions concerning the interim events will need to be discussed as we do so: Paul's travel plans (see §5.4 immediately), the timing of his second visit to Corinth (§5.5), and the possible identity of the offender (§5.6). After these discussions, we will be able to make a more confident judgment about the hypothesis.

5.4 The Travel Plans

I am going to lean in this subsection on an argument first made by Theodor Zahn (1909 [1897]) that was brought to my attention by Hans Arneson.[37]

We already noted in the first major section in this chapter that the two travel plans found in 1 and 2 Corinthians match one another and subsequent events nicely. We need now to grasp the implications of this synchrony for our current question, which necessitates exploring some of these events in greater detail.

In 1 Corinthians 16:3-9 we learn that at the time of writing Paul intends to leave Ephesus at Pentecost and then pass through Macedonia en route to

---

35. Philemon is only a partial exception, as ch. 5 will suggest.

36. Fredrickson (2001) offers an impressive and subtle reconstruction of the Letter of Tears using ancient evidence from Paul's period concerning the composition of letters associated with tears. He concludes that the Letter of Tears is lost but its content can be inferred, at least in part, from this evidence. However, the evidence amassed is not incompatible with Paul's (re)characterization in 2 Cor of the composition of 1 Cor. So Fredrickson's data can function as a thickening of the descriptive situation without excluding this hypothesis.

37. See also Hyldahl (1973; 1986). When I first encountered this argument, it offended almost every preconception I had ever nursed, taught, or defended about the situation. But on reflection, I found it extremely hard to counter, eventually becoming convinced of both its plausibility and its importance. In an explanatory area fraught with complexity and fragility, it seems to me that Arneson and those like him are right to insist that it is the simplest, clearest, and most dependable contention that we have. Hence, although it has involved some painful reformulation on my part, I am grateful for this correction and its insights, and will try to build on them here. The travel plans are — rather significantly — the last issue addressed by Thrall in her comprehensive critical introduction (see 1994, 1:60-61, 69-74[-77]; references to earlier works, xxii-xxiii).

Corinth. The collection is in progress, so he will presumably collect money from Macedonia before arriving in Corinth. And he will then spend some time in Corinth — probably a winter — before deciding whether to accompany the entire collection to Jerusalem himself in the spring. These are Paul's stated intentions in 1 Corinthians 16. And both 2 Corinthians and Romans map onto them very neatly.

Second Corinthians was indeed written from Macedonia, to which Paul had just traveled from Asia by way of Troas, apparently as planned. At the time of writing, the collection is in progress, although Paul is clearly concerned about the Corinthians' participation. And Romans was then written from Corinth with Paul poised to return to Jerusalem with the collected money and hence most likely in the spring. So everything fits together exactly. But what has all this to do with the identification of the Letter of Tears, and with its possible correlation with 1 Corinthians?

At the beginning of the letter body in 2 Corinthians, Paul apologizes extensively for a *change* in travel plans (see esp. 1:12-24; see also 2:1-3). He is currently passing through Macedonia en route to Corinth, engaged (among other things) with the collection, but this is revealed to be a problematic *shift* in plans, and one that has made Paul rather vulnerable at Corinth. Before his current plan, which is now unfolding, he had apparently promised the Corinthians that he would undertake this trip and activity by way of Corinth on both ends, so to speak, so that they would end up seeing him twice, or, as Paul puts it, "would benefit twice" (see ἵνα δευτέραν χάριν σχῆτε in 1:15b). He would travel from Asia to Corinth, from Corinth to Macedonia, and then back to Corinth, so we can refer to this as the "Travel Plan Corinth First," or TPCF. This was his original, or at least earlier, plan. But Paul is now apparently being forced, in 2 Corinthians, to defend its alteration in the Letter of Tears to a "Travel Plan Macedonia First," or TPMF. Paul's vulnerability is especially evident in the apology he makes for this new plan in 1:17-19:

[17] τοῦτο οὖν βουλόμενος μήτι ἄρα τῇ ἐλαφρίᾳ ἐχρησάμην; ἢ ἃ βουλεύομαι κατὰ σάρκα βουλεύομαι ἵνα ᾖ παρ' ἐμοὶ τὸ ναὶ ναὶ καὶ τὸ οὒ οὔ; [18] πιστὸς δὲ ὁ θεὸς ὅτι ὁ λόγος ἡμῶν ὁ πρὸς ὑμᾶς οὐκ ἔστιν ναὶ καὶ οὔ. [19] ὁ τοῦ θεοῦ γὰρ υἱὸς Ἰησοῦς Χριστὸς ὁ ἐν ὑμῖν δι' ἡμῶν κηρυχθείς, δι' ἐμοῦ καὶ Σιλουανοῦ καὶ Τιμοθέου, οὐκ ἐγένετο ναὶ καὶ οὒ ἀλλὰ ναὶ ἐν αὐτῷ γέγονεν.

The repeated denial of the phrase "yes *and* no" here is striking — see vv. 17b (with double emphasis, i.e., lit. "yes yes and no no"), 18b, and 19b (and implicitly in this last verse twice). This suggests that the shift in travel plans in the Letter of Tears from TPCF to TPMF has made Paul vulnerable to a criticism at Corinth of *inconsistency;* he often says A but then does B, his critics are apparently accusing, or even says A and B, and hence lacks integrity. In parlance well known from modern American political discourse, this shift in plans has proved that Paul is "a flip-flopper," and then as now, this is a serious liability. Drawing on powerful moral analogies of straightness, demonstrations of inconsistency generate pejorative connotations of bentness, waywardness, and fundamental immorality (see definitively Lakoff 2002). To "shift" in something is to be "shifty." Indeed, it is interesting to note that Paul spends some time in the initial sections of Galatians attributing these undesirable notions to the Jerusalem leadership and claiming notions of firmness for himself (see esp. 2:11-14, but also 1:10; 2:2, 6, 9; 4:12). But Paul's flexible mission practice, articulated especially in 1 Corinthians (see 1 Cor 9:19-23), along with some of the criticisms he counters elsewhere in 2 Corinthians (see 10:10-11), combine to suggest that this is an entirely plausible understanding of at least part of his broader difficulties at Corinth. His shift in itinerary is being used by his critics at Corinth as further evidence of a changeability that denotes an underlying lack of character.

Paul's rhetorical recharacterization of the damaging and painful letter sent previously to 2 Corinthians, the Letter of Tears, which contained this shift in plans, overlaps with his attempt to deflect this charge of inconsistency. Paul sent the Letter of Tears, he says, *instead of making his planned visit to Corinth* so that his next visit to Corinth would not be a grievous affair but one that brought joy (and so on) — the grievous issues having been addressed by the Letter of Tears and its immediate aftermath, and Paul's relationship with the Corinthians, he hopes, having survived this astringent interlude. The Letter of Tears in effect took Paul's place in Corinth within the earlier itinerary, as did Titus (whose movements we will consider in more detail shortly), to spare the Corinthians grief and pain. Of course, this disclaimer is not strictly to the point, because Paul could still have traveled to Corinth after the Letter of Tears as originally planned in TPCF, but for reasons that we will note shortly, he decided not to do so. And we come now to the first crucial inference for our current discussion.

When we think about all of this carefully, it becomes difficult to avoid the conclusion that 1 Corinthians must be the Letter of Tears. If we identify 1 Corinthians with the Letter of Tears, all the data fits together with complete integrity, whereas any other narration, which is inevitably more complex, tends to lapse into implausibility at various points. The problem-free narration supplied by the simple construal of the data — in which 1 Corinthians is the Letter of Tears — will be described here first, and then we will identify the accumulating difficulties of more complex alternative narrations.

As we have already seen, the plan to visit Macedonia before visiting Corinth (i.e., TPMF) is evident explicitly in 1 Corinthians (16:3-9); hence, it is certainly plausible to suggest that 1 Corinthians was the letter that announced this change in itinerary. The initial travel plan of TPCF would then have been present in the letter sent prior to 1 Corinthians, in the previous year, which is now lost — the Previous Letter to Corinth [PLC]. We already have good reason to suspect the existence of this letter, and it seems reasonable to suppose that it contained a travelogue. If this is in fact the case, it would explain the subtle redundancies that seem to be present in Paul's announcement of TPMF, which would be displacing TPCF, in 1 Corinthians 16:3-7.

Paul emphasizes there that he will be passing through Macedonia en route to the Corinthians, stating the point twice in immediate succession in v. 5: Ἐλεύσομαι δὲ πρὸς ὑμᾶς ὅταν Μακεδονίαν διέλθω· Μακεδονίαν γὰρ διέρχομαι. Paul goes on to emphasize in v. 6 that he wants to spend some time with the Corinthians, perhaps even a winter. And then in v. 7 he repeats his wish to spend time with them, adding, in another redundancy, that this will entail no mere passing visit or short stay, "if the Lord permits."

These flourishes are insufficient by themselves to establish that a different travel plan existed in the Previous Letter to Corinth prior to the announcement of TPMF in 1 Corinthians. They could perhaps be explained if false expectations had been raised in 1 Corinthians 4:18-21 of a direct visit. (See perhaps esp. v. 19b: ἐλεύσομαι δὲ ταχέως πρὸς ὑμᾶς ἐὰν ὁ κύριος θελήσῃ; this is Thrall's rebuttal in 1994, 1:71.) Or Paul could merely be communicating pedantically. However, given the existence of our developing frame, these flourishes now receive a better explanation, namely, that they *are* announcing a different itinerary and duly apologizing for it. He is now going through Macedonia first, hence the double emphasis; but the result will be not merely a passing visit to Corinth, as on the front end of TPCF, and perhaps on the second, return leg of the journey as well, but a long stay. Moreover, all these plans remain as ever under the sovereignty of God, who is entitled to change them and apparently already has.

This plausible reading clearly falls short of being a probative contention, but it is strong enough to function corroboratively. And this tight fit with the data continues in relation to the other letters involved.

Second Corinthians apologizes at length for the change in plans in 1 Corinthians / the Letter of Tears, arguing in various ways for Paul's consistency in important matters. It also suggests, as we just noted, that 1 Corinthians / the Letter of Tears was sent instead of Paul himself to avoid a personal visit and the infliction of grief on the congregation by an apostle angry about various unaddressed sins — practices such as theft and incest. So the shift is defended in numerous ways. Moreover, 2 Corinthians is clearly located in the middle of the changed plan, which was announced in 1 Corinthians, with Romans occurring at the end.

This evidence all combines to suggest that Paul seems to have decided prior to writing 1 Corinthians to "triangulate" the Corinthian situation. Rather than traveling directly to the city and confronting the set of difficult problems there that he had been learning about from various sources over the winter (from visits by various Corinthians, along with the written Corinthian reply), he seems to have decided to try to gain some time and traction prior to his arrival, partly by way of the clever use of third parties. He would send a powerful letter to Corinth (1 Cor) instead of visiting directly. He would travel to Macedonia first and then send some Macedonians on ahead of him to Corinth (or, alternatively, he might want to arrive with their support in company). In this way, he would take a group of loyal supporters with him to Corinth. Moreover, he could send delegates to check on the Corinthians during the interval — most notably Titus — who could circle the Aegean in the opposite direction and rendezvous with him to the north. (One supposes that Titus was a more imposing figure than Timothy.) And, as things turned out, Paul even had time to send another letter (2 Cor) and group of delegates prior to his visit, when he learned that his first letter had had a positive impact — at least, suitably interpreted.

It was almost certainly a risk to change his original plan of a direct, and ultimately double, visit to Corinth. But clearly, Paul viewed it as a calculated one. He was going to have to offend the Corinthians deeply in any case as he addressed a slate of congregational problems, and he was already vulnerable to charges of inconsistency by virtue of his missionary practice. However, by changing his route he would buy time for a letter or two to do their work, along with the appropriate delegates. And this might eventually enable a more successful entry to Corinth, especially as he arrived with the additional leverage provided by Macedonian support, which could help him in multiple ways. It was thus the very gravity of the Corinthian situation, transmitted through numerous sources and apparent by the spring, that prompted this new tactical approach, with its switch from TPCF to TPMF — one that was risky, but ultimately seems to have succeeded (at least in part).

These decisions generate the following, relatively simple sequence of events:

Fall:	[Previous Letter to Corinth], with TPCF
	Corinthian visitors and written Corinthian reply at some point in the interim
// year change //	
Spring:	1 Corinthians / Letter of Tears, with TPMF, sent from Ephesus (probably with Timothy)
	Paul leaves Ephesus for Macedonia, probably at Pentecost, although possibly earlier; Titus leaves Ephesus for Corinth
	Paul links up with Titus in Macedonia
Summer:	2 Corinthians, with apology for TPMF, sent from Macedonia with Titus
Fall:	Paul arrives in Corinth on his third visit to the city
// year change //	
Spring:	Romans composed with the collection in hand from Corinth

The most important things to appreciate about this narrative explanation at this point in our discussion are that it is exact, economic, and explicit. Everything fits together precisely. All the events match up, as they should. And everything is explained. Certainly, nothing vital is left unexplained. Moreover, all the data needed to sustain the account is extant or explicit. We have neither less nor more data than we need. Hence, we will now need decisive reasons for a departure from this reconstruction. And in fact only a few potentially decisive points of leverage against it are apparent, all of which tend to collapse on closer examination.

The foregoing reconstruction must be abandoned if the Letter of Tears cannot be identified with 1 Corinthians and must be presumed lost, thereby interposing other communications and travel plans into the sequence. However, our brief survey of the outline of the Letter of Tears in 2 Corinthians suggested that this line of argument is not promising, and especially when Paul's propensity to recharacterize the reception of his earlier letters is taken into account (see also the recharacterization of the Previous Letter by 1 Cor). Indeed, I know of no decisive arguments against the identification of 1 Corinthians with the Letter of Tears.[38]

It could of course be claimed that the Letter of Tears is better explained

---

38. It is significant that Thrall primarily construes the argument in the other direction, assessing whether there are decisive reasons to identify the Letter of Tears with 1 Cor.

by a piece of 2 Corinthians once it has been partitioned — for example, by chapters 10-13, as suggested most famously by Hausrath — but this hypothesis needs to be assessed in the next major section in our discussion, when we consider the possible partition of 2 Corinthians. If we decide there in favor of partition, then a piece of 2 Corinthians might conceivably displace 1 Corinthians as the best identification of the Letter of Tears. But this eventuality will depend on a decisive case for partition there, which will not be presupposed here.

Another reason for abandoning the simple narrative currently in place might be the need to insert Paul's second visit to Corinth into this sequence, after 1 Corinthians. Like the presence of a lost letter, this would introduce new travel information that would disrupt our present narrative. We will find, however, that this proposal is a good illustration of how further clusters of difficulty arise when any more complex narrative of Paul's travel data is introduced to explain this period in his life, and I will argue for staying with the unproblematic and simpler explanation already in place. That is, we will end up not inserting Paul's second visit to Corinth here, for what seem to me to be quite good reasons. In order to appreciate these, however, we need to grasp first the explanatory corollaries that any more complicated narrative generates, so our more detailed discussion of this option will begin here.

5.5 Paul's Second Visit to Corinth

Second Corinthians attests, as we already know, to the arrival of the Letter of Tears in Corinth in lieu of Paul himself. It also attests that the Letter of Tears contained the offensive travel plan in which Paul would now visit Corinth only after passing through Macedonia first — TPMF. Formerly, he had promised the Corinthians a direct and ultimately a double visit — TPCF — so that the Corinthians "would have a second blessing" (see ἵνα δευτέραν χάριν σχῆτε in 1:15). Hence, the data in 2 Corinthians necessitates that the letter prior to it, the Letter of Tears, changed Paul's travel plans from TPCF to TPMF. Prior to the arrival of the Letter of Tears, the Corinthians were in eager expectation of TPCF. Upon its arrival, they learned of the disappointing TPMF, which they duly criticized for its inconsistency. Second Corinthians responded apologetically but did not abandon TPMF (and indeed could not, because it was halfway through that plan, being written from Macedonia).

We noted in the previous subsection that this data fits together smoothly and economically when the Letter of Tears is identified with 1 Corinthians. First Corinthians announced TPMF. The original plan, TPCF, can then reasonably be attributed to the Previous Letter, written the previous year. And nothing additional now needs to take place between 1 Corinthians / the Letter of Tears and 2 Corinthians; the extant and implicit letters explain the data. But with the nonidentification of 1 Corinthians and the Letter of Tears, the information in 2 Corinthians concerning the Letter of Tears and its embarrassing shift in travel plans really has to be introduced into the general sequence of letters as additional steps unfolding somewhere *after* 1 Corinthians, *which was already committed to TPMF.* This entails not merely the introduction of the Letter of Tears announcing TPMF but an introduction prior to the Letter of Tears of TPCF — although *after* 1 Corinthians and its endorsement of TPMF.[39] This has to be done in order to account for the embarrassing shift by the Letter of Tears, prior to 2 Corinthians, from TPCF to TPMF. And these extra steps in the relationship between Paul and the Corinthians will prove problematic however we try to parse them.

An initial step toward simplification could arguably be taken by denying the presence of TPCF in the Previous Letter, and we have already seen that there is no decisive proof of this. The flourishes present in Paul's announced itinerary in 1 Corinthians 16:3-9 are arguably explicable on different grounds from the announcement of a new itinerary replacing the one presented in the Previous Letter. So this reduces the number of embarrassing changes in play. First Corinthians presumably, then, just reiterates TPMF from the Previous Letter, albeit a little clumsily with this concession. We end up with the following sequence (which has been slightly simplified from the sequence supplied previously, to aid clarity):

Fall: [Previous Letter to Corinth], with TPMF
// year change //
Spring: 1 Corinthians, reiterating TPMF
Implicit change in travel plans from TPMF to TPCF
Midsummer: [Letter of Tears], reinstating TPMF
Late summer: 2 Corinthians, with apology for change back to TPMF, sent from Macedonia
Fall: Paul arrives in Corinth
// year change //
Spring: Romans composed with the collection in hand from Corinth

39. This seems rather more likely than an ongoing struggle by Paul to defend TPMF in *three* successive letters, with escalating difficulty — in 1 Cor, [LT], and then 2 Cor.

The presence of an otherwise unknown communication between Paul and Corinth between 1 Corinthians and the Letter of Tears that shifts his travel plans from TPMF to TPCF looks rather embarrassing at first glance, not to mention the further change taking place from the Letter of Tears onward (i.e., back to TPMF). However, a relatively simple and persuasive answer seems to resolve these problems, namely, Paul's second visit to Corinth. We know that Paul made three visits to Corinth ultimately, and inserting his second into this sequence seems to resolve the explanatory lacuna surrounding the shift from TPMF to TPCF rather nicely: he announced this plan himself when he was at Corinth. However, the introduction of a second visit into the sequence generates a still more complex narrative:

Fall: [Previous Letter to Corinth], with TPMF
// year change //
Spring: 1 Corinthians, reiterating TPMF
Early summer: *Paul makes second visit to Corinth; TPCF announced*
                 Paul returns to Ephesus; TPCF now expected in Corinth
Midsummer: [Letter of Tears], reinstating TPMF, delivered to Corinth
                 Paul leaves for Macedonia (TPMF); Titus leaves for
                 Corinth
Late summer: 2 Corinthians, with apology for TPMF, sent from
                 Macedonia
Fall: Paul arrives in Corinth on his third visit to the city
// year change //
Spring: Romans composed with the collection in hand from
                 Corinth

To reiterate: this more complex sequence looks helpful initially, because at least it seems to be able to explain how the Corinthians' expectations were firmly reset to TPCF after the receipt of 1 Corinthians with its announcement of TPMF. But when we press on its details, various aspects of the explanation begin to unravel into unexplained, and even inexplicable, problems. In order to appreciate these, we need to consider the nature of Paul's visit, which can be construed in different ways. There are two main alternatives: the view endorsed by Thrall that Paul at this point actually began the first leg of TPCF (see also Barrett 1973); and the view endorsed by Furnish that Paul made "a flying visit" to Corinth to deal with some crisis, returning immediately to Ephesus after its apparent failure. Each of these views has certain strengths, often over against the other, but careful consideration suggests that both suffer ultimately from debilitating weaknesses.

(1) The Hypothesis That Paul's Second Visit to Corinth Began TPCF

Margaret Thrall (1994, 1:49-57) suggests that Paul went to Corinth at this time on the first leg of his new travel plan, TPCF. There is therefore no need to posit some more-sinister account for his visit, which he seems to have decided to undertake in relation to the collection (see 2 Cor 1:15-16). However, she posits an unexpected departure by interpreting 2 Corinthians 2:5 and 7:12 (etc.), as many do, with reference to Paul himself, and the second visit therefore as a grievous one in certain respects. Some personal insult was unexpectedly inflicted on Paul, and of such severity that he withdrew from the congregation and the city, returning to Ephesus. The Letter of Tears, which duly followed to try to repair some of the damage, inaugurated — or actually reinstated — TPMF, but the letter was focused largely on the issue of Paul's rejection and is now unfortunately lost.

Thrall's explanation of the relevant data is characteristically tidy. But there are problems. First, we should note her corollaries, which make her hypothesis extremely fragile.

It is difficult for interpreters to explain why Paul had to leave Corinth, apparently somewhat suddenly, and then issue a series of communiqués to try to retrieve a situation that seems bad. The most plausible explanation, Thrall suggests, is some terrible and largely unexpected crisis related to Paul himself. This narrative entails the construal of 2 Corinthians 2:5a, preferably along with 7:12, in strict relation to Paul, and really also necessitates a monolithic account of the Letter of Tears. The statements in 2 Corinthians refer rather cryptically and euphemistically to some dreadful public humiliation of the apostle by his enemies at Corinth (or, alternatively, perhaps by his aggrieved supporters). It also interprets the second visit as grievous.

Unfortunately, on this last point the Greek is unhelpful, as Theodoret noted some time ago.[40] Certainly, when writing 2 Corinthians Paul is anticipating a possibly grievous visit, his third to the city, and so has sent a letter that inflicts grief, ostensibly to try to avoid a visit of this nature. It is reasonable to suppose that if a visit by him had just taken place at this time but failed, then it too could have been grievous. However, we cannot tell incontrovertibly from the Greek Paul uses in 1:23; 2:1; 2:3; 12:21; and 13:2 whether a forthcoming grievous visit is to be another grievous visit or merely another visit that in this case might prove to be grievous. This crit-

---

40. See PG 82:385; comments in Thrall (1994, 1:51, esp. n. 322).

ical question, at best, lacks any clear answer from the data, but 1:16 stands explicitly against it.[41]

It may be granted that Thrall's reconstruction rests at every point on possible construals of the Greek data. But these are by no means certain and so offer no decisive support for the cogency of the scenario. Moreover, if it can be shown eventually that 2:5 and 7:12 do not refer to Paul's personal involvement in the Corinthian situation preceding the Letter of Tears, then the explanation of his departure from Corinth after his second visit collapses into incomprehensibility. Because of these ambiguities, the location of Paul's second visit to Corinth here within the frame — at least in Thrall's terms — is now positioned on a razor's edge. And while these explanatory riders look risky, three other clusters of problems raise even deeper concerns.

(i) Thrall makes a seemingly initially successful claim about Paul's visit to Corinth at this time by appealing to the report of TPCF supplied by 2 Corinthians 1:15-16. She hypothesizes that Paul went to Corinth on this visit as the first leg precisely of TPCF. However, she interposes several further shifts in travel plans into the unfolding relationship between Paul and the Corinthians after this and before the Letter of Tears and 2 Corinthians, as she must — a crisis at Corinth and a return by Paul to Ephesus, followed by the dispatch of the Letter of Tears that supposedly introduces TPMF again over against an expectation at Corinth of TPCF. But in the light of these further events, it now becomes apparent that Thrall has no reason to suppose that Paul's initial visit to Corinth at this time *was* in fulfillment of TPCF. TPCF is in place *after he leaves,* and is controverted by the Letter of Tears. It is as if she plays this card in her

---

41. See 1:23: Ἐγὼ δὲ μάρτυρα τὸν θεὸν ἐπικαλοῦμαι ἐπὶ τὴν ἐμὴν ψυχήν, ὅτι φειδόμενος ὑμῶν οὐκέτι ἦλθον εἰς Κόρινθον; 2:1: Ἔκρινα γὰρ ἐμαυτῷ τοῦτο τὸ μὴ πάλιν ἐν λύπῃ πρὸς ὑμᾶς ἐλθεῖν; 2:3: καὶ ἔγραψα τοῦτο αὐτό, ἵνα μὴ ἐλθὼν λύπην σχῶ ἀφ' ὧν ἔδει με χαίρειν; 12:21: μὴ πάλιν ἐλθόντος μου ταπεινώσῃ με ὁ θεός μου πρὸς ὑμᾶς καὶ πενθήσω πολλοὺς τῶν προημαρτηκότων καὶ μὴ μετανοησάντων; and 13:2: προείρηκα καὶ προλέγω, ὡς παρὼν τὸ δεύτερον καὶ ἀπὼν νῦν, τοῖς προημαρτηκόσιν καὶ τοῖς λοιποῖς πᾶσιν, ὅτι ἐὰν ἔλθω εἰς τὸ πάλιν οὐ φείσομαι. The ambiguity of the Greek has been noted for a long time; Thrall (1994, 1:50-51) records this observation in Theodoret. That the Greek is ambiguous if not unhelpful for the assumption that Paul's pending visit in 2 Cor would be *another* grievous visit is established decisively by 1:16a: . . . καὶ δι' ὑμῶν διελθεῖν εἰς Μακεδονίαν καὶ πάλιν ἀπὸ Μακεδονίας ἐλθεῖν πρὸς ὑμᾶς κ.τ.λ. It is clear that in 1:16 πάλιν does *not* denote a duplication of content by the second visit; this would entail the incorrect notion that Paul was visiting the Corinthians again *from Macedonia,* when patently he is not. He is merely visiting *again* — this time from Macedonia as against from Asia.

hand twice, which of course she cannot really do. And we are left, as a result, not knowing why Paul went to Corinth on this visit within her reconstruction.

(ii) Paul's return *to Ephesus* after this visit now deepens this explanatory opacity. As we have just seen, Thrall hypothesized that Paul's second visit was taking place as the first leg of TPCF. But if she is right about this, then Paul's return from Corinth to Ephesus is incomprehensible. It makes no sense for him not to go on to Macedonia, and there seem to be no reasons for him to return to Ephesus, where his business is complete. Hence, both legs of Paul's visit to Corinth at this time have collapsed into incomprehensibility. (And Thrall is now vulnerable to Furnish's alternative reconstruction that claims to be able to explain these events.)

(iii) Thrall nevertheless supposes that Paul left the Corinthians with a firm expectation of a third visit in place by way of a direct visit, TPCF. These expectations were dashed by the announcement (again) of TPMF in the Letter of Tears, eliciting the apology found in 2 Corinthians. However, the nature of this apology now seems odd in various respects.

It is silent concerning all the plans and events prior to the latest developments, that is, the Previous Letter, 1 Corinthians, and Paul's second visit. And this is no innocuous silence. Paul is defending himself in 2 Corinthians against a criticism of shiftiness; one would expect that he would use a shift *back* to something in place previously in his defense. The announcement of TPMF by the Letter of Tears is the reinstatement of the original plan as announced (according to this hypothesis) by the Previous Letter and reiterated by 1 Corinthians. Yet none of this is mentioned. Equally significantly, Paul defends none of the other embarrassing shifts, in particular, his sudden visit to Corinth and his craven return to Ephesus. Only *one* shift is mentioned and apologized for — from TPCF to TPMF, effected in the Letter of Tears.

In direct association with this, the timing of Paul's apology now seems odd. As we saw earlier, the apology concerns a criticism from Corinth of changeableness: "with Paul it is always 'yes and no.'" Changes in Paul's plans began, however, much earlier than 2 Corinthians, during the second visit (at least), when Paul arrived at Corinth directly in defiance of TPMF as announced in 1 Corinthians, instating (or worse, reinstating) TPCF (change one at least). This was exacerbated by his return to Ephesus (change two). Then the Letter of Tears announced TPMF *again* (change three). So *three* changes at least, and possibly four took place (i.e., if TPCF was in place in the Previous Letter, prior to 1 Cor). This

means that the rhetorical risks of any change in travel plans vis-à-vis
Corinth would have been plainly apparent in the conversation well before the Letter of Tears. We would reasonably expect an apology in that
letter, *and not in the one that follows it.* That Paul's apology occurs only in
the later letter suggests that Paul did not realize his changed plan would
create such a vulnerability at Corinth; it was somewhat unexpected. But
this is the case only if the Letter of Tears' shift to TPMF is his first announced change, as the simpler narrative suggests (where LT = 1 Cor).
Thrall has interposed several more steps in the conversation, beginning
with a personal visit by Paul to Corinth, his second overall, and followed
by a lost letter, the Letter of Tears. The delayed timing of Paul's apology
for the shift in plans effected by the Letter of Tears now becomes difficult
to explain, along with its oddly simplified focus.

These three clusters of difficulty range from unsupported assertions and the
introduction of areas of incomprehension to points of outright difficulty. And
taken together, they suggest that this narrative hypothesis is less coherent than
the simpler account introduced earlier (i.e., where LT = 1 Cor and Paul's second
visit is not introduced into the interim events). However, the hypothesis that
positions Paul's second visit to Corinth in the interim exists in an important
alternative variation that may succeed in avoiding these problems.

(2) The Hypothesis of a Flying Visit

Victor Furnish approaches this sequence of events in different terms from
Thrall's (although they are far less thoroughly discussed). Paul, he suggests,
"[makes an] emergency ('sorrowful') visit to Corinth, prompted by Timothy's
alarming report about a situation there. Paul himself has a traumatic confrontation of some kind with one of the members of the congregation and returns
to Ephesus after only a short stay, apparently determined to return en route to
Macedonia" (1984, 41, 54-55).[42] He goes on to suggest that the next key event

42. I will not press Furnish's exegetical corollaries here — in particular, his dependence
on the suppositions that (i) 1 Cor was sent in the fall of the previous year, and (ii) Timothy
visited Corinth independently of 1 Cor, returning after its dispatch and thereby catalyzing Paul's
immediate departure for Ephesus with further news of the Corinthian situation. Regarding
(i), we should note that the dispatch of 1 Cor in the spring seems more likely (see 5:6-8 and
16:8). Regarding (ii), we should note that the view that Timothy accompanied 1 Cor seems
more likely than the alternative, although uncertainty surrounding his movements cannot be

is the dispatch of a third letter to Corinth from Ephesus — the "letter of tears," now lost (55). Paul, who has been imprisoned at Ephesus, then travels upon his release to Troas and on to Macedonia, thus effecting what we have been calling TPMF. Hence, Paul's second visit to Corinth is viewed by Furnish as what we moderns would call a "flying visit."[43]

One of the strengths of this hypothesis is that it seems to overcome some of the problems initially apparent in Thrall's account. Thrall was not entitled to introduce TPCF in explanation of Paul's second visit to Corinth. Nor could she explain why Paul went back to Ephesus after he was humiliated at Corinth. But Furnish does not have these particular difficulties. With this second visit portrayed as a flying visit, Paul seems always to have intended to return to Ephesus. But closer consideration suggests that this advantage has been purchased at too high a price. Furnish now runs into debilitating problems that Thrall managed to avoid, and he fails to avoid the other problems apparent in Thrall's account. In short, he has jumped from the frying pan into the fire.

(i) Closer scrutiny suggests that Furnish's initial purchase of plausibility over against Thrall by refusing to use TPCF to explain Paul's second visit to Corinth, attributing it instead to a flying visit, does not actually resolve the difficulties apparent at this point in the explanatory narrative. Paul has just written a long, powerful letter (1 Cor) to deal with a slate of problems there. And he will follow this with at least one more long, powerful letter (2 Cor), and perhaps with several. What data do we have, then, concerning a matter so urgent that Paul had to make a flying visit

---

excluded. There is ambiguity in 1 Cor 16:10-11; however, 4:17 indicates that Timothy has been sent directly to Corinth and therefore presumably with the letter (4:17: Διὰ τοῦτο ἔπεμψα ὑμῖν Τιμόθεον, ὅς ἐστίν μου τέκνον ἀγαπητὸν καὶ πιστὸν ἐν κυρίῳ, ὃς ὑμᾶς ἀναμνήσει τὰς ὁδούς μου τὰς ἐν Χριστῷ Ἰησοῦ, καθὼς πανταχοῦ ἐν πάσῃ ἐκκλησίᾳ διδάσκω; 16:10-11: Ἐὰν δὲ ἔλθῃ Τιμόθεος, βλέπετε, ἵνα ἀφόβως γένηται πρὸς ὑμᾶς· τὸ γὰρ ἔργον κυρίου ἐργάζεται ὡς κἀγώ· [11] μή τις οὖν αὐτὸν ἐξουθενήσῃ. προπέμψατε δὲ αὐτὸν ἐν εἰρήνῃ, ἵνα ἔλθῃ πρός με· ἐκδέχομαι γὰρ αὐτὸν μετὰ τῶν ἀδελφῶν). So, like Thrall, Furnish rests on particular exegetical claims in relation to — at minimum — ambiguous data, which renders his reconstruction fragile. In the presence of a viable alternative that makes no such appeals, we need to ask why we should adopt his account.

43. I thought initially that the expectations of travel within this hypothesis might be anachronistic and unworkable, but ORBIS (July 25, 2013) suggests that a journey from Ephesus to Corinth during June would have taken only 3.8-4.6 days, and the return journey, utilizing more favorable winds, even less time — 2.9-3.6 days. So, although it seems counterintuitive, Paul could have been there and back in under a week.

to deal with it? Such visits respond in general to crises or emergencies. What crisis was present at Corinth at this time that was not being dealt with, at least initially, by a letter and the appropriate delegates? What problem is apparent after this so-called visit had taken place that could be dealt with only by that immediate personal visit? None. There is no obvious emergency in view to explain a visit in these terms. The hypothesis of an immediate flying visit to Corinth at this time to put out some fire in the congregation consequently begs the question and leaves the sequence unexplained at its critical point — while resting on fundamentally ambiguous Greek. We do not really know why Paul made this visit. The emergency that sparked the sudden alteration in plans is strangely opaque, and especially when we recall that Paul is visiting in any case quite soon, in about two months. This leaves Furnish's account in much the same position as Thrall's — with an explanatory lacuna at the key moment.

(ii) And this reconstruction does not resolve problem (iii) from above — the incongruity in various respects of Paul's later apology in 2 Corinthians for his changeableness evidenced by the announcement of his revised travel plan in the Letter of Tears. The flying visit to Corinth still introduces as many changes into Paul's plans and the Corinthians' expectations as a supposed inauguration of TPCF, that is, three to four. So both the delay and the omissions in the apology offered in 2 Corinthians for these changes remain puzzling.

In view of these difficulties, we must judge Furnish's variation on Paul's second visit to be as problematic as Thrall's. But can his alternative narrative be rescued from these problems in a slightly simplified form?

The initial difficulties in the reconstructions of Thrall and Furnish (i and ii in Thrall and i in Furnish) derive from the suggestion that Paul made his second visit to Corinth during the interim between 1 and 2 Corinthians. Neither Thrall nor Furnish can explain why he went to Corinth at this time, nor can Thrall explain why he then returned rapidly to Ephesus. But these problems can presumably be avoided if we follow the alternative rendering of the Greek accounts of the visits and push Paul's second visit earlier than the interim events, a hypothesis Thrall attributes primarily, in the modern period, to Bleek.[44] All we know from the epistolary data is that Paul was concerned

---

44. Thrall (1994, 1:50-53). She dialogues with Bleek (1830) but notes Bleek's references to still earlier advocates of the view.

during this second visit with sexual immorality, which was presumably a fairly generic issue with respect to his pagan converts (see 2 Cor 13:2; cf. 1 Thess 4:1-8). So all we would need to conclude is that it was a second visit by Paul to Corinth that we cannot yet date precisely but that seems to have preceded this part of the frame — and our developing frame has plenty of room for this visit to have taken place, with Paul's mission to the area occurring at some time during the 40s. Does this simplification resolve our difficulties?

It resolves some but not all of them, and once again, closer scrutiny suggests that its initial advantages are purchased at a price. (Note that these difficulties dog the remaining explanation of the interim events, not the placement of Paul's second visit to Corinth earlier in the overarching frame.)

(i) The introduction of TPCF into the sequence prior to the lost Letter of Tears' offensive reintroduction of TPMF now becomes opaque — and yet this is vital! It must happen at some point. Locating Paul's second visit during the interim did at least achieve this, Paul himself arguably resetting the Corinthian expectations from TPMF as announced in 1 Corinthians to TPCF. We must now posit a visit by someone else during this period to Corinth, although we have no data for such a visit and no reason to posit one — or to posit this change in plans. So this explanation seems to have difficulties equivalent to explanations involving Paul and his second visit at this time, and it seems that no real progress has been made. The opacities apparent in positing a visit by Paul during the interim have merely been transferred to someone other than Paul, who is even more dimly perceived.

(ii) The timing and nature of the apology in 2 Corinthians are still unresolved. That is, Paul's travel plans still contain the same number of changes within the sequence — however we get them introduced there — and this generates the same difficulties in terms of the odd lateness and strange simplicity of the apology in 2 Corinthians. Indeed, the root of our difficulties here is now plainly apparent.

The various problems that dog all the more complex explanations of this period in Paul's life lie in a simple supposition — the multiplication of the travel plans that takes place when the Letter of Tears is not identified with 1 Corinthians.

First Corinthians is overtly committed to TPMF. But 2 Corinthians apologizes for a change from TPCF to TPMF that was effected by a letter written previously to it — the Letter of Tears. If the Letter of Tears is distinguished from 1 Corinthians and identified with a lost letter, or perhaps with some fragment from 2 Corinthians itself, we must posit an additional set of shifts in Paul's travel plans that must then be explained. We must suppose that the Letter of Tears announced TPMF, altering expectations from TPCF offensively. And we must therefore introduce TPCF prior to that letter. But we know that 1 Corinthians is committed to TPMF, ostensibly before this, so we end up with the following sequence: TPMF (1 Cor) — TPCF (implicit prior to the Letter of Tears) — TPMF (announced in the Letter of Tears) — apology for the introduction of TPMF in the Letter of Tears (2 Cor). And this sequence tends to break down in ways that we have already noted. The introduction of TPCF between 1 Corinthians and the Letter of Tears is effectively impossible to explain without generating further opacities and implausibilities. Inserting a visit by Paul to Corinth at this point, while initially an appealing move, generates as many difficulties as it solves. And in any reconstruction, 2 Corinthians offers an apology for the change that took place just previous to it; however, the apology is odd if it comes only after several stages and changes, and fails in fact to mention two of them. It is both late and oversimplified. Yet all these problems disappear at a stroke if we simply identify the Letter of Tears with 1 Corinthians. This cuts out all the difficulties that have been generated by the multiplication of events.

We know immediately when TPCF was introduced — in the Previous Letter, prior to 1 Corinthians! This is entirely plausible. And 1 Corinthians is of course itself the offensive letter, written in tears, that altered expectations to TPMF. Hence, no implausible insertions now need to take place resetting Corinthian expectations after 1 Corinthians to TPCF and then back to TPMF. Moreover, the apology in 2 Corinthians now occurs in exactly the right place and exactly the right terms — after the *first* announcement of TPMF, in 1 Corinthians, which changed expectations from TPCF, this being the only change in travel plans that needed to be explained.

In short, it seems that there are good reasons for preferring the relatively simple narrative laid out earlier that was premised on the identification of the Letter of Tears with 1 Corinthians. Hence, we will continue to do so, at least for the time being. And with this hefty nudge toward the superiority of the simplest possible account of the frame in relation to Paul's stated travel plans, we can turn to consider a second indication in favor of the simpler reconstruction, although it is less decisive than the foregoing. In doing so, we pick up the last standard topic of debate concerning this part of Paul's life, namely, the identification of "the offender" (see esp. 2 Cor 2:5 and 7:12).

5.6 The Offender

Arguably, Paul's affirmation of the Corinthians in 2 Corinthians 7:8-12 most plausibly resumes the specific situation addressed by 1 Corinthians 6:1-8, a view that Thrall attributes originally to Krenkel (1890, 305-6), which was endorsed by Windisch (1970 [1924], 238-39), and that Thrall goes on to support in a particular variation (1994, 1:67-69; see also 1987, 74-76). If this connection holds good, then it will further corroborate the identification of 1 Corinthians with the Letter of Tears.[45]

We should first note, following Krenkel and Windisch, that certain linguistic signals seem to suggest this connection.

The verb ἀδικέω is rare in Paul. (It occurs only seven times: in 1 Cor 6:7, 8; 2 Cor 7:2, 12; Gal 4:12; Col 3:25; Phlm 18.) It generally denotes "inflicting injury of an illegal kind upon a person or thing," or, in modern legal parlance, "offending" (Thrall 1994, 1:67, drawing on Zahn 1909 [1897]), a meaning apparent in each Pauline instance. So its connotations were forensic in the literal sense. Second Corinthians 7 suggests that some instance of illegal offending within the congregation has been addressed by the Letter of Tears. The grammar suggests that both figures were male. It seems highly significant that this specific language is found within 1 Corinthians only in 6:1-8, which is addressing litigation within the congregation — "brother with brother." Paul is upset there that the Corinthians are settling a legal dispute within the congregation in the local court instead of dealing with it internally.

To this we should add that πρᾶγμα occurs in both passages as well, and seldom elsewhere in Paul (Rom 16:2; 1 Cor 6:1; 2 Cor 7:11; 1 Thess 4:6). This signifier could take a general sense denoting merely an "event" or "undertaking" or "matter" (BDAG, mngs. 1-4). But it could denote, more specifically, a "lawsuit" or "dispute" (BDAG, mng. 5). The more general meaning seems likely in 1 Thessalonians 4:6, and probable in Romans 16:2. (That Phoebe would be in Rome because of a lawsuit is not impossible, but the indefinite nature of Paul's exhortation suggests that the more general sense is in view; the Roman Christians are probably not being asked in 16:1-2 to support Phoebe in what-

---

45. 2 Cor seems to follow directly from a letter that preceded it. In 2 Cor 7 (and 2) this is identified as the Letter of Tears. So any sense that events presupposed and addressed by 1 Cor are being resumed by 2 Cor, here in 7:8-12, supports an identification of the Letter of Tears with 1 Cor. Having said this, the identification between 2 Cor 7 and 1 Cor 6 is too indefinite for this argument to function as definitive evidence of the identification of 1 Cor with the Letter of Tears in its own right. But it is useful evidence in corroboration of that hypothesis once it has been established on other grounds, which is the case here.

ever lawsuit she might get involved with.) But the specific sense of a lawsuit is undoubtedly in view in 1 Corinthians 6:1, its only occurrence in the letter. And it seems likely that this more specific sense is in view in 2 Corinthians 7:11 as well. Not only does the list of praiseworthy actions assembled by Paul in this verse to affirm the Corinthians contain forensic acts (note esp. ἀπολογία and ἐκδίκησις), but the immediately following verse (12) contains two instances of the indelibly forensic verb already noted, ἀδικέω.

Hence, a double connection of distinctive forensic signifiers — ἀδικέω *and* (the forensic use of) πρᾶγμα — links 1 Corinthians 6 and 2 Corinthians 7 uniquely. A connection between the two sets of events presupposed by these passages therefore seems highly likely. And such an identification makes excellent sense in rhetorical terms.

Paul's use of πρᾶγμα in 2 Corinthians 7:11 draws specific attention to the only other πρᾶγμα extant in relation to the Corinthians, namely, the incident addressed in 1 Corinthians 6:1-8, where it is plausible to suppose that the Corinthians had responded positively to Paul's instructions. They may well have proceeded to set up an internal court and to discipline technically illegal behavior within the church by members against one another — presumably fraud or theft of some sort.[46] Significantly, Paul's commands here in 1 Corinthians 6 were not countercultural in the way that his instructions about leadership and sexual behavior were, and so presumably were rather easier for the Corinthians to obey. It is, moreover, entirely unsurprising to suppose that high-status, wealthy members of the congregation had little difficulty acting rigorously against low-status, poor members who were involved with technically illegal offenses in material terms — theft and the like — which were typical acts of resistance by low-status constituents against local power brokers in hierarchical societies (see the classic analysis of such behavior by Scott 1990). The congregation's bold turn to internal discipline and rejection of redress through the local courts would constitute an appropriate instance of life-giving repentance, eliciting Paul's praise for this act of obedience to at least *this* aspect of the Letter of Tears.

---

46. Thrall (1994, 68-69) posits a more complex narrative involving the collection and Paul to accommodate her prior decisions that 2 Cor 2:5 and 10 denote a personal insult of some sort to Paul and that Paul's second visit is after 1 Cor but before 2 Cor 1–8. Her ingenious account does succeed in embracing all these dynamics but is lacking almost entirely in direct attestation. And it is of course only as good as these prior assumptions, which our analysis here suggests are unnecessary, and even arguably unlikely (i.e., the suggestion that Paul's grief over the Corinthians derives from a personal insult in some relation to his apostleship; this situation does not seem to be behind Paul at the time of writing 2 Cor, so it cannot explain the sense of closure in 2:5-10 and 7:8-15).

Moreover, it is plausible to suppose that this is one of the few sets of instructions that the Corinthians had been able to enact. Paul is still deeply concerned about their sexual immorality and factionalism as he writes 2 Corinthians (see esp. 12:20-21); clearly, considerable progress had yet to take place on those fronts. This eliminates a fundamentally positive response in 2 Corinthians to everything addressed in 1 Corinthians 1–7 except 6:1-8. And praise for a successful legal situation does not respond appositely to putative alterations in inappropriate behavior during banqueting or in decorum during worship, or repentance from incorrect assumptions about bodiliness and the resurrection, the concerns of the rest of the letter aside from the collection (see chs. 8-10, 11-14, and 15, respectively). Hence, there are few plausible candidates in 1 Corinthians / the Letter of Tears — outside of the institution of an internal court as mandated by 1 Corinthians 6:1-8 — for a positive response by the Corinthians to that letter's instructions, once their later failures and the response's specifics have been taken into account. But a positive response to 1 Corinthians 6:1-8 makes excellent sense of the data.

In short, a reference by 2 Corinthians 7:8-12 to the redress of a situation denoted by 1 Corinthians 6:1-8 seems to be signaled by the linguistic markers involved, and corroborated by its broader situational and rhetorical suitability. And this identification functions in turn to corroborate the identification of 1 Corinthians with the Letter of Tears, the letter that appears to have immediately preceded 2 Corinthians, with chapter 7 in 2 Corinthians praising a communal response by the Corinthians, prompted by that letter, to figures who had offended and been offended.[47]

The main objection to an identification of 1 Corinthians with the Letter of Tears at this stage in our broader discussion must now derive from the

---

47. Whether this identification lies behind 2 Cor 2:5-11 is harder to decide. It is certainly possible, and the incident of the offender described in 2 Cor 7:8-12 is probably meant to be included there. That the original Corinthian appeals to secular courts would "grieve" Paul, and thereby explain 2 Cor 2:5, seems reasonable. His comments in 1 Cor 6:2, 4, 5, and 7 are biting and strident. But it seems possible that in 2 Cor 2 Paul is deliberately providing a way for anyone who had been rebuked and perhaps alienated by an aggressive communal response to any of the problems identified by 1 Cor/LT to be reintegrated into the community, where this was appropriate. While this reintegration would include the defrauding or thieving wrongdoer of 1 Cor 6, who would indeed have been shamed by the majority of the community, although not necessarily for that reason expelled, it could also include the repentant fornicator, the repentant eucharistic drunkard, and perhaps even the repentant prophetess. (Further, the ending of Rom — where only male voices speak — might indicate that Paul's reestablishment of traditional gender roles had been heeded.) I am grateful to Hans Arneson for pointing out to me this possible broad function for Paul's treatment of repentance and reintegration in 2 Cor 2.

claims that 2 Corinthians should be partitioned and that one of the pieces produced looks like a better candidate for the Letter of Tears than 1 Corinthians. This hypothesis will also have to explain the interim events satisfactorily, a challenging gauntlet to run, although it is only fair to note that 2 Corinthians could be partitioned independently of the simplified sequence of events just established. (That is, 1 Corinthians could still be identified with the Letter of Tears and 2 Corinthians partitioned after it. Advocates of the partition of 2 Corinthians in these terms would have to position the relevant parts of 2 Corinthians within any developing sequence with the appropriate immediacy after 1 Corinthians / the Letter of Tears. Our simplified sequence would act in this fashion only as a caveat, and not as a decisive refutation.) But before addressing the partition of 2 Corinthians, it will be helpful to clarify the remaining interim events, leaning here as ever on the principle of explanatory parsimony.

5.7 A Summary of the Interim Events

I have already suggested that even advocates of more complex reconstructions of the interval between 1 Corinthians and 2 Corinthians — which are generated principally by the nonidentification of the Letter of Tears with 1 Corinthians — are best served by locating Paul's second visit to Corinth earlier than this sequence. And if 1 Corinthians is identified with the Letter of Tears, as seems most likely at this stage in our broader argument, it is impossible to locate this second visit between 1 Corinthians / the Letter of Tears and 2 Corinthians in any case, because Paul's apology for his travel plans in 2 Corinthians 1 excludes such a visit, thereby deciding the grammatical ambiguities in favor of a nongrievous and earlier second visit. Paul did apparently admonish the Corinthians at some point during this visit about correct sexual practices, but this is hardly surprising for the apostle to the pagans, given his Jewish and Christian expectations in this regard and his converts' pagan cultural origins. We do not yet know exactly where to place this visit, but we do know that it should be placed before the Previous Letter, when the controversial travel plans first apparently began to be announced. And at least one visit by Titus to Corinth has taken place before the dispatch of 2 Corinthians, because Paul enthuses in the letter over Titus's positive reception by the Corinthians (see 2 Cor 2:12-13; 7:5-7, 13-15; 8:16-24; 12:17-18). We will consider shortly whether this data suggests more than one visit, but the existence of one prior visit is fundamentally plausible.

Paul's plan, TPMF, seems to have involved sending Titus to Corinth, to rendezvous ultimately with him in Troas or, failing that, in Macedonia. Titus would travel directly across the Aegean to Achaia, visit Corinth, and then travel north to Macedonia, presumably heading upon arrival in an easterly direction along the Ignatian Way and, if necessary, across to Troas. Paul would travel north initially from Ephesus through Asia, cross to Macedonia, and then presumably travel west along the Ignatian Way. Their paths would therefore cross at some point — possibly as early in the process, for Paul, as Troas. Given the travel time required, Titus clearly left on his journey to the west rather earlier than Paul left on his to the north.[48] Somewhat ironically, with Titus's eventual return to Corinth with Paul, *he* would in fact carry out Paul's original itinerary of TPCF.

Many good reasons can be supplied for Paul's dispatch of Titus to Corinth at this time. Titus could report to Paul on the aftermath of the stinging 1 Corinthians / Letter of Tears. He could discern the progress (or not) of the collection, which might well have suffered as a result of 1 Corinthians / the Letter of Tears. And he could report on the movements of another significant figure whom we must now briefly consider.

In 1 Corinthians 16:12 Paul responds to an apparent request in the Corinthian letter for a visit from Apollos. (Περὶ δὲ Ἀπολλῶ τοῦ ἀδελφοῦ, πολλὰ παρεκάλεσα αὐτόν, ἵνα ἔλθῃ πρὸς ὑμᾶς μετὰ τῶν ἀδελφῶν· καὶ πάντως οὐκ ἦν θέλημα ἵνα νῦν ἔλθῃ· ἐλεύσεται δὲ ὅταν εὐκαιρήσῃ.) It is easy to overinterpret this statement, so we will simply suggest at this point that it contains positive and negative implications. Paul endorses Apollos's visit, and in immediate terms. He seems to be urging him to travel to Corinth with all the brothers who are carrying the letter. However, Apollos does not accede, either to Paul's request or to the Corinthians'. He is "not at all" willing to come immediately (πάντως οὐκ), although he seems to intend a visit at a later, "more

---

48. ORBIS (July 25, 2013) calculates that a journey from Ephesus to Troas in May would have taken between 3 and 6 days. We have already seen that a journey from Ephesus to Corinth around this time of year would have taken about the same time: 3.8-4.6 days. A journey from Corinth to Troas by way of Thessalonica and Philippi would have taken a further two to three weeks of travel time: 5-8.2 days to travel from Corinth to Thessalonica using coastal sea routes, 3.8-4.3 days to travel from Thessalonica to Philippi by sea, and roughly the same by road, and 4.9-6 days to travel from Philippi to Troas. This all suggests that in order to effect a rendezvous in Troas, Titus had to leave two to three weeks ahead of Paul. For Paul to "overshoot" that rendezvous, meeting Titus in Macedonia, however, suggests that he left Ephesus earlier than planned, and data supports this suspicion (2 Cor 1:8). Paul's departure just a week after Titus's departure, possibly under duress, would explain what actually happened.

appropriate" time. There is, then, at the least, an absence of either obedience or direct cooperation with respect to Paul. Relations between them are potentially strained, although still fundamentally positive, because it is hard to envisage Paul endorsing this visit otherwise. If we take Paul's report concerning Apollos at his word, we can surmise that Apollos did make a second visit to Corinth, and this may affect our understanding of Titus's role as well. There is now one more party we must briefly consider.

In the last major section of canonical 2 Corinthians, Paul spends much time engaging with figures he calls at one point "super-apostles" (see τῶν ὑπερλίαν ἀποστόλων in 11:5). We will need to posit the arrival of these figures in Corinth prior to 2 Corinthians as well, and almost certainly prior to Titus's visit; he brings information about them to Paul in Macedonia that then informs 2 Corinthians. Alternatively, however, we could pursue explanatory parsimony aggressively and suggest identifying these figures with Apollos and his colleagues and retainers.[49] Certainly, there is a surprising amount of data that supports this identification and not a lot to be said against it. The identification, if sustained, suggests that Paul's relationship with Apollos was precarious — as we might expect, given what was said to the Corinthians, not to mention to any listening Ephesians, through most of 1 Corinthians 1:18–4:21. In this scenario, Apollos's second visit to Corinth did greatly exacerbate factionalism, and Paul's relationship with Apollos soured completely. Titus's visit seems to have been the more necessary because of this. That is, it seems that Titus may have been sent to gauge not just the reception of 1 Corinthians / the Letter of Tears and the state of the collection but the nature and results of Apollos's second visit. And it would follow from this that Titus visited Corinth after Apollos. Fortunately, we do not need to decide on the possible identification of Apollos and his companions with the super-apostles when framing. We can simply note this in passing as a possible explanatory simplification.

The only other interim event that must be noted is an Asian crisis that

---

49. Furnish's (1984, 48-54) survey of the main options is a useful and judicious starting point. A benchmark study emphasizing methodological rigor in any identification of Paul's opponents — and undertaken originally under Furnish's supervision — is Sumney (1990). An important and imaginative account of 1 Cor that includes provocative characterizations of Apollos is Wire (1990). Our later discussion of Col, in ch. 5, is also arguably relevant here; the issue of Paul's opponents recurs there. However, preliminary framing tries to avoid strong judgments based on particular characterizations of the opponents, in view of their fragility and tendency to beg key questions, preferring the reverse procedure — clues concerning the identity of the opponents being derived from the frame.

made Paul despair of life itself (see 2 Cor 1:8-11). It is unlikely that this preceded Titus's visit to Corinth, because he would presumably have reported such a crisis to the Corinthians and Paul's disclosure of the situation in 2 Corinthians 1 would then be redundant (or, at the least, would probably have acknowledged this). Moreover, Paul uses a disclosure formula, suggesting further that this was something unknown to the Corinthians, which had happened more recently than Titus's visit (see Οὐ γὰρ θέλομεν ὑμᾶς ἀγνοεῖν, ἀδελφοί, ὑπὲρ τῆς θλίψεως ἡμῶν τῆς γενομένης ἐν τῇ Ἀσίᾳ).[50] If the crisis led to a premature departure by Paul from Ephesus, then this would also explain why he slightly overshot his apparent rendezvous point with Titus in Troas, although this contention is not especially weighty. And with this judgment, there is little need to pursue things further here.[51]

In the light of this discussion, the interim events have been simplified by being reduced to three visits to Corinth — and perhaps even to two, if Apollos's party is identified with the super-apostles — along with an event in Ephesus that took place after these. We have pushed Paul's second visit to Corinth earlier than the main sequence, where we must also posit a first visit by Apollos. These decisions yield the following account to date of the sequence that lies at the heart of the epistolary frame — a relatively simple one.

. . . Paul VC2[52] . . .

// year change(s) //

. . . Apollos VC1 / [PLC][53] — Corinthian VEs / [Corinthian reply] —

// year change //

— 1 Cor — Apollos VC2 / super-apostles VC[54] — Titus VC1 —

Asian crisis

— 2 Cor / Titus VC2 — Paul VC3 . . .

// year change //

. . . Rom — Paul VJ . . .

50. Paul's use of disclosure formulae is discussed in more detail in ch. 4.

51. We will return to consider this dramatic event in more detail when we introduce data from Acts into the epistolary frame in a subsequent study.

52. VC: visit to Corinth (VE: visit to Ephesus; VJ: visit to Jerusalem). See the full list of biographical abbreviations in the front matter.

53. It should be recalled that we do not know exactly how these two events were positioned in relation to one another, that is, Apollos's first visit to Corinth and Paul's dispatch of his first letter in this sequence, previous to our 1 Cor.

54. This arrangement prescinds from judging whether Apollos and his circle should be identified with the super-apostles.

With these provisional judgments in place, we turn finally to address the complex and fascinating question of partition in relation to 2 Corinthians.

6. The Integrity of 2 Corinthians

The frame will be affected considerably by our decisions here. We could multiply letters to Corinth through this critical phase in Paul's ministry, and might even be forced to abandon Knox's local argument in so doing. Or we might retain the current, relatively simple sequence. Somewhat unfortunately, these important decisions are surrounded by extraordinarily complex debates. So I will take an initial step toward simplification by observing that underneath all the clashing readings, contentions, and reconstructions lies one essentially straightforward question: Is there evidence that makes the partition of 2 Corinthians necessary? If we have to answer "yes" at any point, then we can engage at that moment and in that relation with the ensuing complications. But if we answer "no" throughout, then many complications do not arise. The burden of proof lies on the advocates of partition, since our initial data appears to be a single letter; that is, canonical 2 Corinthians seems initially to be a fairly typical Pauline letter with a recognizable beginning, letter body or middle, and ending. We will need decisive contentions from advocates of partition, then, to lead us to the judgment that this initial position of integrity ought to be abandoned. Advocates of partition tend to make three basic types of claims in support of their hypothesis: in terms of (1) rhetorical "shift"; (2) letter form; and (3) "telltale contradictions." The first of these is especially important, because it undergirds claims of partition and indicates where that partition ought to take place; methodologically speaking, it does double duty. Hence, its discussion will be the most extensive in what follows. The second and third types of claims are more straightforward and so will be dealt with more briefly after our consideration of the implications of shift.

6.1 Claims in Terms of "Shift"

Advocates of both unity and partition in 2 Corinthians acknowledge rhetorical shifts in the texture of the letter. Four are especially important (we will count the shifts back out of a section within the initial shift into it and so as one basic movement). In canonical sequence, interpreters detect:

I   a shift beginning at 2:14 and running essentially through 7:4, which is a long discussion concerned primarily with Paul's apostleship;

II within this long block of material, a much shorter section running from 6:14 through 7:1 that is admonitory, is concerned with some form of sin, and quotes Scripture in a catena;

III a shift in chapters 8 and 9 to distinctive financial concerns that seem almost immediately to link up with 1 Corinthians 16:1-4 and to anticipate Romans 15:25-28b and 31, and so to denote the important collection of money for the saints in Jerusalem that runs like a thread through this entire period (some scholars would split this material up further into two separate letters); and

IV a shift at the beginning of chapter 10 to what seems at first glance to be a much more aggressive apostolic defense than 2:14–7:4, running through at least 13:10 (13:11-13, a seemingly more irenic final section, is sometimes partitioned from 10:1–13:10 largely for that reason, but this perception of shift need not hold us up here).

Two features of these shifts need to be noted before we proceed. Some are simply abrupt switches of content and apparent direction — shifts I-III. But one contains marked switches of what is commonly called "tone" in relation to what precedes as well — shift IV (10:1–13:10). However, "tone" is a rather misleading account of the shift in question; strictly speaking, tone is a nontextual or paralinguistic dimension added to a written text by its presenter at the time of its performance, and we can supply very different tones to the same texts through different performances of them, as any actor will attest. It is more accurate, then, to speak of a *rhetorical* shift in a certain, quite specific sense. The shift at 10:1 seems not merely abrupt, that is, as a sudden change in textual direction; it seems also to be a change in persuasive strategy, with an aggressive and even sarcastic argumentation and implied authorship that have not been evident in the letter before.

Arguments concerning both types of shift will be addressed in what follows, building from contentions in terms of shift alone through to the implications of dramatic rhetorical shift.

Advocates of partition make a particular argument in relation to these textual shifts (making analogous arguments in due course with respect to letter form and putative contradictions). They claim that the abruptness and perhaps also the rhetorical changes apparent at these junctures cannot be explained by a single integrated account of the letter, that is, by a letter that was a (relatively) unified compositional act on Paul's part that was sent and then read out to the

Corinthians in one principal — albeit presumably repeated — performance. The shifts in the texture of 2 Corinthians can only be explained, they suggest, by the way that the relationship between Paul and the Corinthians changed dramatically over a certain period of time, something reflected in a series of different letters composed at different stages in a tempestuous relationship. These letters were only later embodied in a single canonical letter through deliberate editorial policy, but they obviously retained their originally disparate rhetorical textures, which can then be duly recovered by the sensitive historical interpreter. In short, only a causal explanation can account for the text's shifts.[55]

We now need to examine various elements in this general case more closely, progressing in seven steps from a careful look at its corollaries through to a brief consideration of countervailing explanations (and we will conclude, when all is said and done, that the advocacy of partition on the basis of shift is unpersuasive).

(1) An Editorial Caveat

We should immediately introduce what we might call an editorial caveat for the explanation of these shifts in terms of partition. More work remains to be done on this issue, but for the moment we will lean — like most — on the benchmark work of Hans-Josef Klauck. As already noted, Klauck identifies some redacted letters in the Ciceronian corpus, although he fails to demonstrate that these were deliberate as against careless redactions. For the sake of argument, however, we will set aside the important unresolved question whether deliberate ancient editorial activity is attested here at all. For our present purposes, we need only to note that *if* ancient editorial activity took place, it was, in Klauck's words, "simple" (2003, 154). He means by this that letters were glued together in blocks or strips, usually with the ending of one and the beginning of another missing. Arguably, shorter letters could appear in these compilations as well, so it may be that a simple redactional process could still incorporate more than two ancient letters in a series. The implications of this observation for our current question are helpful.

Granting the possibility of the deliberate ancient editorial synthesis of

55. It is interesting to note that this might thereby be a classic appeal on the part of the cognitive "System 1" to a causal explanation of a perceived and unexplained anomaly in a given data set that might in fact possess a simple, perhaps merely statistically random, rationale; see Kahneman (2011, esp. 74-78, 109-18, 186, 207). This is not the last time we will need to note this potential explanatory danger.

letters, we would expect blocks of material laid end to end *but not interpolations* in the sense of a block of material appearing in the middle of a letter, one having been carefully inserted into the middle of another (which presumably would have been a more complex editorial act, involving a careful splicing operation as against a mere addition). Thus, we might expect an editorial synthesis of letters A, D, F, and M in the form of A-D-F-M, or even M-D-A-F (that is, violating the original chronological order of the letters). But we would not expect, on the basis of the evidence in Cicero, a redacted letter in the form of, say, M-A-M-F-D-F. Klauck construes such "interpolations" in Cicero in terms of authorial techniques, generally of quotation. And this evidence raises an important constraint for suggestions of collation in 2 Corinthians with respect to what we might call "Klauckian simplicity."

There is ancient editorial attestation — and possible at that — only for the redaction of letters in blocks or strips, so only compilations in those terms are initially plausible. This places question marks against shifts I and II above, along with the separation of 13:11-13, all of which would involve interpolations, or their equivalent, and consequently violate this attestation. On the basis of Klauckian simplicity, only shifts III and IV seem plausible, although these might contain variations. We will primarily consider from this point on, then, the possible partition of 2 Corinthians into chapters 1-7, 8-9 (or 8 and 9), and 10-13, remaining aware that these strips or blocks, if representative of earlier original letters, are not necessarily in their original chronological order. Editorial suggestions concerning 2 Corinthians remain plausible for these shifts, while editorial explanations of the other perceived shifts have been significantly problematized.

(2) Anachronism — the Patristic Evidence

It was indicated earlier that the case for partition frequently depends on the presence of an explanatory threshold within the text constituted by what we might call unacceptable rhetorical shift (that is, unacceptable without positing an editorial and hence essentially causal explanation for it). But while this suggestion can certainly be granted initially in the sense that shocking shift does invite explanation and could conceivably be explained in causal and even deliberate editorial terms, we must take care to avoid anachronism. It is tempting for modern interpreters to pronounce themselves unconvinced by the text's dynamics and then go on to affirm an editorial explanation. However, this may in the first instance simply be a failure on the part of the modern interpreter to understand the text in terms of reading expectations that belong to a very distant culture. How are we to test the various claims made in this regard, and in particular, to provide controls on modern interpretative hubris?

One way of moving self-consciously out of modern interpretative expectations and closer to the ancient encyclopedias in play is through a consideration of the patristic discussion of 2 Corinthians. We are fortunate to possess a set of sustained homilies on 2 Corinthians by Chrysostom. And it seems significant that he apparently did not articulate the difficulties with the various rhetorical shifts in 2 Corinthians that modern interpreters do. That is, he did not find the shifts in Paul's rhetorical texture so extreme that he felt compelled to posit a causal and editorial explanation. He certainly detected shifts. But equally informatively, he sometimes detected shifts at different points in the text from those identified by modern interpreters.[56] These observations should give us pause.

(3) Alternative Local Explanation

Our consideration above of possible ancient editorial practice raised a question mark over the editorial explanation of shifts I and II (i.e., 2:14–7:4 and 6:14–7:1), with suspicions deepening as the patristic evidence was introduced. But we can approach this question from another angle, namely, whether perceived shifts can be explained in alternative, effectively more "local" terms. It will be most helpful to focus initially on shift II, or 6:14–7:1, since this is the most abrupt unit and its editorial explanation as an interpolation is widely accepted. Somewhat ironically, editorial dynamics call the suggestion of an interpolation here into question, although these are not the only grounds for doubting an editorial account of its presence in canonical 2 Corinthians.

In this relation, I have yet to come across a definitive refutation of Gordon Fee's case, made in 1977, that 6:14–7:1 is comprehensible as an integrated part of 2 Corinthians, and makes demonstrably better sense construed in this way than as an interpolation, whether from another Pauline text or even from a non-Pauline reservoir (so, e.g., Betz 1973).[57]

---

56. M. Mitchell's (2001) warnings about the appropriate and inappropriate use of patristic evidence are important (see also her 2002a, a more detailed treatment of Chrysostom in relation to Paul). Ambrosiaster, being a Latin speaker, is not as useful as Chrysostom, but he was still probably exposed to rhetoric and so is informative (translated and edited accessibly in Bray 2009, 207-65; Bray 2006 is a more disparate collection of comments from the patristics on 2 Cor, which are again frequently instructive).

57. Fee's view is supported by (i.a.) Goulder (1994).

Fee (1977, 144-47) observes that claims of non-Pauline vocabulary are overstated. Indeed, the vocabulary seems at times more likely to be drawn from Paul than from any other NT reservoir, although we are not emphasizing this sort of argument at present, because of its methodological constraints (see further in chs. 4, 5, and 6). Fee then makes two principal complementary arguments that are helpful for our present discussion. He points out how editorial considerations problematize the suggestion that the fragment is an interpolation. And he articulates the integration apparent between the fragment and various concerns discernible in 1 Corinthians, which could plausibly have elicited this set of exhortations from Paul as a digression in a later letter.

Concerning editorial activity, Fee draws on Plummer's observations to reject the possibility of careless interposition, which is unlikely given the neat sentences demarcating the fragment and its context (142-43). But the only remaining possibility — of deliberate editorial insertion — now raises more problems than it solves. If scholars cannot discern reasons why *Paul* included this material here, then the situation is not resolved or even improved by suggesting that an ancient editor deliberately did so. An editor working in such terms lacks discernible reasons for acting in this way as well; indeed, his/her behavior is perhaps even more puzzling than Paul's because he/she *inserted* the material quite deliberately, whereas Paul merely *digressed*. Absent any obvious rationale for doing so, such behavior simply looks unlikely. Hence, a consideration of ancient editorial practice undermines the suggestion that an interpolation is present at this point in 2 Corinthians. (Fee also observes that the insertion is not as neat as an interpolation arguably requires in any case [161]; 7:2 seems resumptive of 6:13a, yet running the two together creates a redundancy: [6:13] τὴν δὲ αὐτὴν ἀντιμισθίαν, ὡς τέκνοις λέγω, πλατύνθητε καὶ ὑμεῖς . . . [7:2] Χωρήσατε ἡμᾶς· οὐδένα ἠδικήσαμεν [κ.τ.λ.].)

Complementing the problem of putative editorial practice, Fee argues that concerns from 1 Corinthians can explain the concerns evident in 6:14–7:1, thereby demonstrating how original considerations, now only partially apparent, can offer a richer set of interpretative options for troubling material than editorial hypotheses. (This realization will be supplemented by the further compositional and performative considerations we will discuss in the next subsection.) Fee posits an ongoing concern on Paul's part about the Corinthians feasting in idol temples (see 1 Cor 8–10; see also the characterizations of the Corinthian congregation as a temple in 3:9a-17), a reading that can neatly explain the fragment's concerns (see esp. 2 Cor 6:16a: τίς δὲ συγκατάθεσις ναῷ θεοῦ μετὰ εἰδώλων; ἡμεῖς γὰρ ναὸς θεοῦ ἐσμεν ζῶντος). I would add only that it is unnecessary to delimit this concern as tightly as Fee does. A concern about visiting idol temples suffices to explain Paul's anxieties in 2 Corinthians 6:14–7:1, whether for food, as Fee opines, for sex, for celebration, for mere phatic participation, or for some combination of these activities. The fragment would then be an aside prompted by Paul's strong exhortations to the Corinthians in 6:11-13, grounded in much preceding argument (i.e., 2:1–6:10), to be wide open in heart and affection toward him and his coworkers even as he is to them. (See [6:11] Τὸ στόμα ἡμῶν ἀνέῳγεν πρὸς ὑμᾶς, Κορίνθιοι, ἡ καρδία ἡμῶν πεπλάτυνται· [12] οὐ στενοχωρεῖσθε ἐν ἡμῖν, στενοχωρεῖσθε δὲ ἐν τοῖς σπλάγχνοις ὑμῶν· [13] τὴν δὲ αὐτὴν ἀντιμισθίαν, ὡς τέκνοις λέγω, πλατύνθητε καὶ ὑμεῖς.) Paul pauses to clarify his deep concern that the Corinthians nevertheless be utterly constricted with respect to certain pagan cultural options, notably, to indiscriminate sex and direct participation in demonic worship. So the presence of the digression seems intelligible in terms of the local prompts, while its explanation in terms of editorial decisions is opaque.

In short, considerations of style and vocabulary, possible ancient editorial practice, and recognizable broader contextual relevance, along with a careful look at the seams in question, all combine to suggest that 2 Corinthians 6:14–7:1 is best explained as a digression on Paul's part and not as an interpolation. (An alternative now might be to posit quotation; see more on this possibility in ch. 3, and Klauck's [2003, 151-52] brief comments are highly suggestive.) So this judgment establishes an important local threshold in the evidence concerning perceptions of abrupt rhetorical shift and its explanation.

Despite our modern interpretative sensibilities, the shift apparent between 6:13/6:14 and 7:1/7:2 (i.e., shift II) is not necessarily best explained causally and editorially — editorial considerations proving more difficult here than local considerations — but rather in more traditional, integrated terms, with reference to some of the concerns and complications in Paul's ongoing relationship with the Corinthians. And with this benchmark in place, it seems that the other contentions in the data in terms of abrupt shift, the shifts beginning at 2:14 (I), 8:1 (III), and 10:1 (IV), could well subside into more traditional explanations as well. The shift at 2:14 is now problematized in particular, because it has already been called into question, alongside 6:14(–7:1), by Klauck's implicit query concerning the reality of editorial interpolations. If shift II should not be explained in ancient editorial terms, then it follows that shift I does not need to be either. Moreover, shift III, although acceptable in editorial terms, does not seem abrupt enough, viewed alongside I and II, to necessitate such explanation. The unusually complex series of conjunctions used in 9:1, περὶ μὲν γάρ, also seems directly continuative within this block of material (i.e., chs. 8 and 9), as

Stowers's (1990) research in particular suggests. At this point, then, arguments for partition at shifts I, II, and III seem to be struggling.

(4) Original Performative Signals

It should be helpful at this moment in our discussion to augment our gathering suspicions about editorial explanations of shift with some considerations in favor of comprehending such shifts as part of the original communication between Paul and Corinth. Modern interpreters trying to comprehend strong rhetorical changes in Paul's text when it was first performed possess explanatory resources unavailable to advocates of editorial explanations.

We noted earlier Klauck's research affirming that ancient letters could be composed over time. In the case of Paul, such pauses in epistolary composition would be understandable, given the unusually long and complex nature of his letters.[58] Paul's letters must have been written over a period of time and could consequently have involved significant compositional and temporal pauses, which may in turn have involved shifts in concern and resulting rhetoric. Certainly, we ought to speak of compositional resumptions. Moreover, ancient authors and auditors were familiar with shifts, as well as shifts and returns, because of the common phenomenon of digressions, which are a standard feature of all oral discourse and were theorized about quite extensively in Paul's day.[59] These pauses and digressions could be communicated relatively easily to a letter's auditors by performative signals.

When a letter was read out to its listeners, its reader was effectively involved in the text's performance, at which point two bodies of additional communication became operative. The reader supplemented the written text with additional information through its verbalization in an oral event — prosody — thereby contributing features such as speed and intonation to the words that had been written down (which were only, strictly speaking, signifiers). More-

---

58. Klauck (2003, 141-43, 153-54), here rehabilitating a much derided suggestion by Lietzmann (1969) concerning 2 Cor, echoed by de Boer (1994) in relation to 1 Cor, as well as, to a lesser extent, Bahr (1966) concerning Paul's postscripts.

59. Garland (1985, esp. 173) and D. Watson (1988, esp. 71-72) cross swords over the occurrence of a digression in Phil, but their methodology is both instructive and transferable; the key rhetorical resources are provided in a classic analysis by Wuellner (1979). The standard introduction to insights derived from orality is Ong, who is especially important for our reflections in ch. 5; see his 2000 [1967]; 2002; 2012 [1982]. His remarks on the redundancy of oral discourse are helpful here (2012 [1982], 39-41).

over, the verbalization of the text would be cocooned by a thicket of nonverbal cues, or additional paralinguistic prompts; some theorists suggest that as much as 60 to 65 percent of the information communicated in certain "live" contexts derives from nonverbal elements.[60] (One aspect of nonverbal communication in the ancient world open to some investigation is the use of gestures.)[61]

These additional interpretative resources suggest that what seem to a modern interpreter to be unacceptable rhetorical shifts could possibly have been communicated reasonably effectively in an original "live" setting, because of the richness of the initial situation's extra- and nonverbal cues. But such cues are essentially hidden once the text has become a historical artifact that is read, usually silently, at some remove from its original performed situation. These considerations consequently suggest another interpretative threshold: if a shift is possibly acceptable in terms of an original performance of the text, then that shift cannot function as decisive evidence of compilation. Having said this, it is possible that there are a few written cues in partial explanation of some of the shifts in 2 Corinthians with which interpreters have struggled. It is to these that we now turn.

(5) Explicit Signals of Integration

We already noted in passing Fee's observation that 2 Corinthians 7:2a seems resumptive as against merely continuative, when we would expect the latter if in the original letter 6:13 read straight on to 7:2. The Greek suggests, then, albeit subtly, a deliberate digression rather than an editorial interpolation. Similarly, 7:5a is arguably resumptive of 2:12-13 (conceding Weiss's 1959 [1917] division of the text here for the sake of argument; it should nevertheless be emphasized in passing that the assignment of 7:4 to what precedes it in the

---

60. This figure is advocated by J. K. Burgoon (1994). I discuss nonverbal communication briefly in 2009 (531-32). Guerrero, Devito, and Hecht (1999) is a useful introduction to the field. Nonverbal communication addresses the suggestiveness of (1) kinesics (bodily movements including eye behavior, although the latter is so significant that it is sometimes addressed separately as oculesics); (2) physical appearance; (3) olfactics (codes of smell such as perfume); (4) vocalics (which overlaps with prosody); (5) proxemics (codes of space); (6) haptics (codes of touch); (7) chronemics (codes of time); and (8) environmental features, which can be given or contrived.

61. See Boegehold (1961); Graf (1992); Aldrete (1999); Shiell (2004). On the complexities of ancient reading practices, and their frequent distance from our own, see now esp. W. Johnson (2000; 2010).

text and not to what follows is, on closer scrutiny, an almost bizarrely insensitive judgment):[62]

[2:12] Ἐλθὼν δὲ εἰς τὴν Τρῳάδα εἰς τὸ εὐαγγέλιον τοῦ Χριστοῦ καὶ θύρας μοι ἀνεῳγμένης ἐν κυρίῳ, [13] οὐκ ἔσχηκα ἄνεσιν τῷ πνεύματί μου τῷ μὴ εὑρεῖν με Τίτον τὸν ἀδελφόν μου, ἀλλὰ ἀποταξάμενος αὐτοῖς ἐξῆλθον εἰς Μακεδονίαν. . . .

[7:5] . . . καὶ γὰρ ἐλθόντων ἡμῶν εἰς Μακεδονίαν οὐδεμίαν ἔσχηκεν ἄνεσιν ἡ σὰρξ ἡμῶν ἀλλ' ἐν παντὶ θλιβόμενοι· ἔξωθεν μάχαι, ἔσωθεν φόβοι. [6] ἀλλ' ὁ παρακαλῶν τοὺς ταπεινοὺς παρεκάλεσεν ἡμᾶς ὁ θεὸς ἐν τῇ παρουσίᾳ Τίτου.

A strict continuation is certainly not impossible here, allowing the suggestion of interpolation, but it is arguably puzzling in various respects.

Paul switches grammatically from first person singular to first person plural. And the contribution of γάρ is opaque (a merely connective δέ would be more understandable), although the meaning of this highly flexible conjunction should not be pressed too hard. Perhaps most importantly, the narrative of rest (ἄνεσις) shifts subtly between these two texts. In 2:12-13 Paul's failure to find relief is caused specifically by his failure to rendezvous with Titus at Troas (τῷ μὴ εὑρεῖν με Τίτον τὸν ἀδελφόν μου). In 7:5-6, however, on arriving in Macedonia, Paul's group fails to find rest because it suffers in many respects — from violence without and anxieties within (ἐν παντὶ θλιβόμενοι· ἔξωθεν μάχαι, ἔσωθεν φόβοι). Titus then arrives in a divine appointment to encourage the struggling apostolic band.

The development of the motif of anxiety in 7:5-6 is not in itself problematic for a putative continuation. However, the narrative of anxiety specifically

62. See πολλή μοι παρρησία πρὸς ὑμᾶς, πολλή μοι καύχησις ὑπὲρ ὑμῶν· πεπλήρωμαι τῇ παρακλήσει, ὑπερπερισσεύομαι τῇ χαρᾷ ἐπὶ πάσῃ τῇ θλίψει ἡμῶν. The first and fourth clauses in this verse seem to reference the preceding analysis of apostolic ministry, as the theory of partition suggests; Paul has spoken "frankly" there and has frequently emphasized his sufferings (although "frank" speech on his part is even better connected with the bulk of chs. 10-13). However, the second and third clauses fail to reference anything plausible in what precedes but do seem to connect explicitly with material that follows in the canonical letter, that is, with material beyond the seam that Weiss proposes — Paul's boasting over the Corinthian reception of Titus, his encouragement over his meeting with Titus, and so on. (The final clause also seems best explained by material that follows immediately, namely, Paul's joy on meeting with Titus and his learning then of the positive response by many of the Corinthians to the Letter of Tears.)

in relation to Titus in 2:12-13 is not resumed or developed *at all* in 7:5-7, and this is more troubling. This shift — along with the shift from singular to plural subjects — makes perfect sense, however, if the long digression of 2:14–7:4 has intervened. The development would reflect the sustained concern of the digression with apostolic suffering, and Paul's specific reason for leaving Troas and traveling to Macedonia would be a detail long left behind. Nevertheless, the basic story present in 2:12-13 resumes in 7:5-6: Paul fails to meet Titus in Troas and so travels on to Macedonia, and there the hoped-for rendezvous does finally take place, a basic narrative Paul resumes after a long epistolary interlude. The resumption allows him to return to the direct address of personal and epistolary matters at Corinth, although he shifts the grounds of his anxiety here partly in view of the recently concluded digression.

This leaves only one shift in play (IV), at 10:1, although it is especially significant. The text simply supplies δέ, which is, strictly speaking, continuative, sometimes with slight adversative force. But much more can and should be said about this key transition, which appeals as none of the others do to particular rhetorical dynamics.

(6) Rhetorical Questions

We need at this point in the broader discussion to revisit the editorial suggestion concerning 2 Corinthians in more detail, focusing the hypothesis now on shift IV (i.e., 9:15/10:1). And this necessitates recalling some key features of modern Pauline explanation.

All modern scholars acknowledge that Paul's letters are broadly rhetorical in the sense that they are fundamentally persuasive documents. They presuppose throughout groups of people who in the apostle's view need to be persuaded to change in certain ways from their current dispositions or, concomitantly, to maintain certain postures over against other advocates of change whom he regards as unhelpful if not illegitimate and dangerous.[63] Hence, Paul's epistolary rhetoric generates an image of a situation that has elicited it — specifically, an implied audience, behind which an empirical audience originally lay and concerning which Paul has received information that is often disturbing — generally referred to in what follows as the text's immediate implied exigence.[64] (Note that we have supplemented this notion with the

---

63. The classic analysis is Perelman and Olbrechts-Tyteca (1969 [1958]).
64. The useful language of exigence stems originally from Bitzer (1968). Its important

recognition of possible *Nebenadressat* but have not displaced it.) In the case of Corinth, Paul is quite well informed, having received information about its situation from multiple sources. The difficulty with which many modern interpreters struggle in 2 Corinthians in this particular respect — the transition from chapters 1-9 to 10-13 — is, quite simply, the apparent incompatibility of the rhetorics and therefore of the implied audiences in view within the single canonical letter. In formal terms, we might ask how Paul can say A in one part of the letter, presupposing audience A', and B in another, suggesting audience B'. Thus, Margaret Thrall observes that in 2 Corinthians 1–7 Paul writes — presumably primarily — of reconciliation, and his "tone" is one of joy and confidence. But beginning in 10:1, "he suddenly bursts out into a torrent of reproaches, sarcastic self-vindication, and stern warnings" (Thrall 1994, 1:5, citing Plummer's classic analysis). Similarly, she suggests that the transition from earnest pleas for generosity in chapters 8 and 9 to a "threatening and reproachful discourse" in chapters 10-13 "would surely prove counterproductive" (6). In 7:7-16 the congregation supports Paul, but in 10:1-11 they support his critics, the super-apostles. In 8:11 and 9:2 they respond willingly to the collection, but in 12:16-18 they seem to have criticized his envoys (6). And that final text raises a further question over the relationship between this visit and the one by Titus and two other brothers anticipated in 8:16-24. (The presence of these suspicions makes the continued use of Titus for the collection odd as well, perhaps along with Paul's earlier optimism about its completion.) Margaret Mitchell summarizes the posture with characteristic precision: "[There is] a definitive break in tone, style, and content between 9:15 and 10:1 . . . [entailing an] enormous difference in historical situation in the two contexts (a confident fundraising appeal versus a bitter defense against personal insult)" (2005, 319; see also the excellent summary in Furnish 1984, esp. 30-32).

Thrall entertains criticisms of these contentions, and other positive considerations in favor of unity, but finds them "unconvincing" (6-13). Hence, she judges finally that "it is preferable to conclude that chaps. 10-13 belong to a separate letter" (13). That is, the dramatic rhetorical transition in 2 Corinthians, especially at 9:15/10:1, implies a transition to a different set of issues in relation to the target audience, to the point where many modern interpreters have simply become unconvinced that the same audience can be in view — at least at the same time. These differences can be comprehended, advocates of partition suggest, if a certain story is told of Paul's tempestuous relationship

---

methodological contributions become especially salient from ch. 4 onward, so it is best introduced in more detail there.

with the Corinthians, but not otherwise. We should now tease out some of the frequently unnoticed corollaries within this argument.

This explanation of shift in terms of partition actually rests on certain important assumptions: (i) that modern interpreters can grasp a serious rhetorical mistake within an ancient setting, that is, generate a sense of inappropriate rhetoric cross-culturally (something we have already been exploring, although not yet in quite the extreme terms posed by shift IV); and (ii) that the congregation was fundamentally unified. And sustaining these assumptions will, in my view, prove very difficult. We will briefly scrutinize the first assumption here, and turn in the next subsection to a consideration of the second.

We should note first Thrall's pithy contention that the transition from pleas for generosity in chapters 8 and 9 to a "threatening and reproachful discourse" in chapters 10-13 "would surely prove counterproductive" (6). Thrall assumes that she can recognize a discourse that would be oddly incompetent on reception in ancient Corinth. This generates a hypothetical conditional of the following form: "If Paul had said B, having just said A, then the effect would have been utterly inappropriate. But Paul was not this incompetent; he was competent. Therefore, we contend that he would not and so did not actually say B immediately after A; rather, he deployed these rhetorics in different letters." Clearly, this is a fragile inference.

We have no concrete evidence, given the nature of this hypothetical inference, of an actual case of such rhetorical incompetence from Paul. As a *negative hypothetical conditional,* it is the nature of the argument to have no actual internal evidence. ("If A is the case, then it leads to B, but B is unlikely; therefore, A is not the case." This argument provides no evidence for the key claim that A leading to B *would* be unlikely; the progression has simply been denied and not demonstrated.) Furthermore, this is a modern conjecture about an ancient reception. We should ask at the least, then, for a concrete instance of an analogous rhetorical offense as a check on modern interpretative biases, but such evidence tends to be lacking. Certainly, Thrall provides none. And we ought to conduct our inquiry without psychologizing, that is, without basing important judgments on assumptions about Paul's probable motivations, which cannot be reconstructed.

In short, for the claim to prove valid that abrupt rhetorical shift entails partition, we need evidence from Paul's cultural location demonstrating the clumsiness of the rhetorical moves being rejected by modern scholars as unacceptably clumsy. Without this evidence, any modern sense of interpretative offense risks anachronism. Indeed, the possible cross-cultural inappropriateness of this sort of judgment by a modern interpreter is simply being erased in a manner that is disturbingly colonial.[65]

This problem is enough to give the modern interpreter pause. However, an even more worrying aspect of the case for partition in relation to dramatic rhetorical shift derives from the second assumption noted above, namely, that the Corinthian congregation was fundamentally unified.

(7) The Nature of the Congregation

The claim that change in the Corinthian relationship with Paul over time is the only possible explanation of the rhetorical shift in question rests on the assumption that the congregation is of one mind. Indeed, for the temporal explanation to hold by itself, thereby vindicating an editorial analysis of 2 Corinthians, the Corinthians must be unified in all significant respects (i.e., precisely in relation to all markers of response and shift over against Paul). If this was the case, then any perceived shifts in audience — any rhetorical changes reflecting a change in the implied audience — should be explained by a change in the entire congregation. However, if the congregation was at all fractured, or even merely complex — and what congregation is not?! — then the explanatory monopoly maintained by the temporal explanation of shift no longer holds. The shifts in question could be explained equally well in terms of space, so to speak, as against time, and the former would not need to mobilize a problematic editorial scenario in support. The rhetorical shifts evident in 2 Corinthians might be explained alternately, that is, as Paul pivots this way and that to address different problems within a highly complex and fractured congregational situation.

Advocates of partition are aware of this explanatory rider. However, I am

65. Some useful checks on modern interpretative hubris have already been mentioned; see W. Johnson (2000; 2010). The behavioral and cognitive biases involved are helpfully explicated by Kahneman, esp. when discussing "expert intuition" (2011, 234-44). Kahneman's suggestion is that expert intuition is more trustworthy in a high-validity environment, in which immediate, stable, and perceptible feedback can be received regularly — an environment where "the effects of . . . actions are likely to be quickly evident" (242). It is far less trustworthy in a low-validity environment, where feedback is sporadic, and this is arguably the situation of the modern interpreter of Paul's prose. Those possessing competence in the linguistic perceptions under discussion are long dead and hence not available to correct modern interpretative biases and consequent mistakes. In this situation, "experts may not know the limits of their own expertise" (242) — thus calling for caution in judgments concerning phenomena such as ancient rhetorical shifts.

not convinced that they have established it adequately, or refuted the countervailing position concerning possible congregational complexity.

It is not unfair for them to claim in the first instance that 2 Corinthians
is littered with terms of general address. Paul speaks frequently to a plural
audience (i.e., πρὸς ὑμᾶς, etc.). And this could suggest at first glance that
he is addressing the entire congregation throughout the letter, so that any
rhetorical shifts still address everyone. However, Paul speaks in these general
terms in all his letters, so the necessary inference of this argument is that all
his congregations were perfectly unified, which seems unlikely — or that
the general markers conceal congregational complications, at least at times.
Moreover, general markers are used frequently in 1 Corinthians, where Paul
explicitly identifies deep divisions within the congregation (see esp. 1:11-12,
along with the broader resonances of these observations through the rest of
the letter). This all suggests that a plural address by Paul does not necessarily
entail anything more than a generalizing or "blanket" address that could conceal more specific concerns, rather as many sermons today address specific
issues within a congregation in general terms without identifying the people involved explicitly. Those addressed usually know who they are, and the
rest of the congregation is still instructed by the general line of admonition,
whether they know what is really going on or not. (That Paul also uses more
specific addresses at times is true, and must be carefully marked, but this
does not entail that his general addresses are not also specific at times; the
suggestion that this follows is a false entailment — a non sequitur — which
Thrall fails to notice; see 1994, 1:7.) Moreover, divisions seem to have been
especially the case *at Corinth*.

The Corinthian church was the product of different missionaries —
the Pauline team, Prisca and Aquila, and Apollos — and derived from very
different contexts, whether from pagan situations, apparently including "the
street" (see 1 Cor 5:10; 6:9-11), or from the Jewish subculture at Corinth. It
therefore was born in diversity and most likely continued to operate in those
terms.

Suffice it to say that advocates of partition still need to make their case
for consistent congregational unity at Corinth, and I am not confident that
this will be possible. It will risk begging the question (i.e., in the sense that
these shifts might be evidence of congregational division), and overt data (i.e.,
of division) seems to stand directly against it. We can add finally that Paul
does arguably mark his problematic tirade through much of chapters 10-13
with indications of a specific addressee, namely, the partisan(s) of the super-
apostle(s) within the congregation. That is, a turn to a specific group within

the Corinthian church is arguably signaled, and this would explain the shift in question, although in terms of "space" and not time.[66] Note first 10:1: Αὐτὸς δὲ ἐγὼ Παῦλος παρακαλῶ ὑμᾶς διὰ τῆς πραΰτητος καὶ ἐπιεικείας τοῦ Χριστοῦ, ὃς κατὰ πρόσωπον μὲν ταπεινὸς ἐν ὑμῖν, ἀπὼν δὲ θαρρῶ εἰς ὑμᾶς.

It seems likely that Paul is quoting a Corinthian criticism here — ὃς κατὰ πρόσωπον μὲν ταπεινὸς ἐν ὑμῖν, ἀπὼν δὲ θαρρῶ εἰς ὑμᾶς — which must come from a specific source in the Corinthian congregation and not from the entire group simultaneously. This criticism functions to qualify the force of the exhortation, παρακαλῶ ὑμᾶς. It also initiates a particular set of concerns that are developed and responded to quite consistently through much of chapters 10-13. The address in v. 2 is even more specific, targeting "those who view us as walking in a fleshly manner." It is these people toward whom Paul hopes he will not have to be as bold as he currently fears: δέομαι δὲ τὸ μὴ παρὼν θαρρῆσαι τῇ πεποιθήσει ᾗ λογίζομαι τολμῆσαι ἐπί τινας τοὺς λογιζομένους ἡμᾶς ὡς κατὰ σάρκα περιπατοῦντας. Verses 8 and 9 then arguably articulate further criticisms at Corinth.

When Paul lays claim to a certain sort of excessive boasting of his authority in v. 8 (περὶ τῆς ἐξουσίας ἡμῶν), he defines it as constructive, not destructive (ἧς ἔδωκεν ὁ κύριος εἰς οἰκοδομὴν καὶ οὐκ εἰς καθαίρεσιν ὑμῶν), echoing the same terminology from elsewhere in the section (see 12:19; 13:10). In a similar vein, v. 9 rejects the suggestion that he has been trying to frighten the Corinthians with his letters: ἵνα μὴ δόξω ὡς ἂν ἐκφοβεῖν ὑμᾶς διὰ τῶν ἐπιστολῶν. The rationale for these concerns seems to become apparent in v. 10, which explicitly quotes a Corinthian criticism: ὅτι αἱ ἐπιστολαὶ μέν, φησίν, βαρεῖαι καὶ ἰσχυραί, ἡ δὲ παρουσία τοῦ σώματος ἀσθενὴς καὶ ὁ λόγος ἐξουθενημένος. Paul's personal presence is "weak" (a criticism that will shortly receive much fuller development in the section in terms of the ancient fool).[67] But his letters are "powerful." And these criticisms align nicely with the hints of Corinthian criticism already assembled, and seem to facilitate a set of integrated attacks on the apostle.

The apostle's heavy letters are actually bullying attempts to intimidate, some of them seem to have suggested. This is unattractive in and of itself. But perhaps worse, his personal presence is unimpressive. Hence, his letters do not

---

66. Thrall (1994, 1:6-7, esp. n. 41) surveys this case; she traces it back to Rückert's (1837) critique of Semler and Weber, but sees the view reiterated in De Wette (1841); Hodge (1974 [1859]); Beyschlag (1871); Holtzmann (1879); and P. Hughes (1962).

67. Treated definitively in Welborn (2005).

need to be taken seriously, because when Paul himself shows up, he will not act as they threaten. Nor should his leadership be boasted of or advocated in the interim at Corinth by his followers (or indeed by the church as a whole); he is certainly no visiting celebrity. The two dynamics in combination suggest, furthermore, a fundamentally inconsistent figure, and thus one that lacks integrity and cannot be trusted. (Both criticisms also unite in the characterization of Paul as a fool, who in ancient terms was a ridiculous but bullying figure; see more on this just below.) And it must be conceded that this is a formidable critique not altogether lacking in evidence.

Clearly, these criticisms of Paul are rooted in specific concerns, and in particular phrases and words. Hence, the text is involved primarily with the originator of the words and any local support for them, even though the letter refrains from naming names. (This is itself a recognizable rhetorical strategy.) As if to acknowledge the limited scope of these powerful calumnies, Paul characterizes his focus in v. 11 in generic but limited terms, using the indefinite demonstrative pronoun: "Any such person should consider this . . ." (τοῦτο λογιζέσθω ὁ τοιοῦτος, ὅτι οἷοί ἐσμεν τῷ λόγῳ δι᾽ ἐπιστολῶν ἀπόντες, τοιοῦτοι καὶ παρόντες τῷ ἔργῳ.; see elsewhere in 2 Cor esp. 2:6, 7; 11:13). This anonymous but specific address returns in association with the important criticism of Paul as a fool, which begins in 11:16 (πάλιν λέγω, μή τίς με δόξῃ ἄφρονα εἶναι . . .; see 11:16 [2x], 19; 12:6, 11).

The entire congregation did not hatch the criticism that Paul seemed like a fool. It began with someone specific, presumably much as the criticism that Paul had "caught" them deceitfully did as well (see 12:16). And we can only speculate about how far this criticism spread. Presumably, some Corinthians endorsed it, some went along with it, and some did not. But Paul's careful language of limitation suggests that not everyone necessarily advocated it. Indeed, his text thereby allows his readers the space to locate themselves *either* as the direct target of his rebuttal or *alongside* the rhetorical conflict, as observers.

Much of the rest of the section is devoted to his squaring the circles just noted, that is, arguing that these perceived inconsistencies are legitimate in various respects. But Paul's response is of course intertwined with a critique of the super-apostles, who seem to have been allied in some way with the Corinthian critique of Paul's presence, letters, and inconsistencies. This aspect of the text will not be pressed here, but it is worth noting that the super-apostles are also possible evidence of further division at Corinth, thereby corroborating the evidence of division within the congregation that was apparent first in 1 Corinthians. And this is especially the case if the key super-apostle — the ringleader, so to speak — was Apollos. But while this connection can be raised when framing, now is not the time to explore it in detail. Suffice it to say that advocates of partition on grounds of shift will need to establish that the Corinthian loyalties had been *entirely* reoriented to the super-apostles; otherwise, the presence of these figures must constitute further evidence of a divided congregation. And this will be difficult to do. The burden of proof lies on the advocate of partition and the demonstration of unity, because the earlier evidence, found in 1 Corinthians, is of division, as are general expectations of groups and congregations. Moreover, this case's prospects are not promising when some of Paul's final statements seem to suggest directly that the congregation was divided.

In 12:20 Paul identifies partisanship at Corinth as one of the two major sins he hopes the Corinthians will have repented of prior to his arrival so that he will not have to act sternly to discipline them: φοβοῦμαι γὰρ μή πως ἐλθὼν οὐχ οἵους θέλω εὕρω ὑμᾶς κἀγὼ εὑρεθῶ ὑμῖν οἶον οὐ θέλετε· μή πως ἔρις, ζῆλος, θυμοί, ἐριθεῖαι, καταλαλιαί, ψιθυρισμοί, φυσιώσεις, ἀκαταστασίαι. And this concern seems to be reiterated with some of the concluding exhortations of 13:11: καταρτίζεσθε, παρακαλεῖσθε, τὸ αὐτὸ φρονεῖτε, εἰρηνεύετε. (The other sin that especially concerns Paul is of course sexual immorality; see 12:21.) I do not know of any feasible way around this evidence for advocates of congregational uniformity. (Some would excise 13:11-13 from the end of chs. 10-13 and attach it to a more suitable letter, but this violates the principle of Klauckian simplicity in terms of editorial practice, and seems egregious to boot.) In short, Paul's letter ends with explicit evidence of Corinthian division — just the scenario that can explain a dramatic shift in rhetoric from 10:1.

If Paul's text contains hints of a shift from 10:1 to specific addressees — addressees entertaining certain criticisms of him and unsettling loyalties to other leaders — then the case for partition on the basis of unacceptable rhetorical shift at this point in canonical 2 Corinthians will struggle. It is not necessary to prove this reading here. These hints suffice to indicate the difficulty of the task facing the advocate of partition in this regard, who must now show how 2 Corinthians 10-13 cannot be read in such a way. In other words, an interpretative monopoly will need to be established concerning 2 Corinthians 10-13. Such a reading is certainly possible. But with the burden of proof resting on the advocate of partition on these grounds, mere possibility is no longer enough. And a demonstration at this higher level of rigor looks difficult enough for us to continue to frame 2 Corinthians for the time being in unified terms and to await with interest any later demonstrations of the need to partition it. The possibility of any such later demonstration is not being excluded; we may yet return to the partition of 2 Corinthians (although most probably after, not before, Paul's trip to Macedonia when he was en route from Ephesus to Corinth on TPMF). But a clear and irrefutable path to that judgment will have to be charted — at least in terms of rhetorical "shift."

However, contentions in terms of shift have arguably been the weakest claims for partition within the broader debate. We turn now to consider the two briefer but stronger sets of assertions undergirding composite interpretations: claims in terms of letter form and of straightforward telltale contradictions.

6.2 Claims in Terms of Letter Form

We considered earlier in this chapter the contention that letter form can be a significant indicator of compilation and hence of the need for partition when framing. It seemed at first glance as if the ending of Romans preserved two sets of formulae typical for the Pauline letter ending, and if true, this would be an argument for the presence of compilation. However, the all-important doublets proved spurious on closer examination. Considerations of letter form also play an important role within the broader debate over possible compilation in 2 Corinthians, although in a rather different sense. Hans Dieter Betz (esp. 1985) has suggested that chapters 8 and 9 preserve small discrete letters recognizable in general terms. He argues more specifically that both chapters were official advisory letters written in the basic mode of deliberative rhetoric, and he suggests, largely in view of this, that they were both originally distinct communications. This suggestion accords with the principle of Klauckian simplicity — just — and so seems plausible on ancient editorial grounds. But Betz's ingenious analysis is unconvincing on two further grounds.

First, Paul's letters are demonstrably longer and more complex documents than the vast majority of the extant papyrus correspondence, necessitating the judgment that they are "mixed" types of letters containing many genres and types of rhetoric. The identification of particular epistolary styles and modes of persuasion in one part of a canonical letter does not therefore entail the separation of that material from its surrounding text. Indeed, we have already found invalid the suggestion that Romans 16 should be separated from the rest of the canonical text when, taken in isolation, it is a pristine example of a letter of recommendation. Clearly, Paul could include patches of material within his epistles that were analogous to short, complete letters of a certain type that were circulating in his day. Betz's learned identifications of the genres and rhetorics operative in 2 Corinthians 8 and 9 can therefore be granted but still fall short of functioning as decisive evidence for compilation.

Second, Betz separates chapters 8 and 9 largely by appealing to redundancy. Observing that chapter 9 seems unnecessarily repetitive,[68] he argues that it was originally separate, making Paul's rhetorical appeals concerning the collection rather more concise. He points to the regional sense of the discussion as well (see esp. v. 2, but also v. 4), suggesting that chapter 9 addressed the Christians in Achaia as a whole, presumably including the Corinthians, but also, at the least, the Cenchreans (see Rom 16:1).

However, this argument too is insufficient. It may be granted that redundancy is *possible* evidence of compilation, and the regional sense of the discussion may support this in turn, but repetition is by no means *necessary* evidence that decisively demonstrates the original claim. In order to be valid, the case requires that chapters 8 and 9 are too overtly redundant to come plausibly from the same communication by the apostle, a type of argument that we have already found grounds to criticize. That is, this claim begs the question. Paul may have been quite a redundant communicator at times, as 2 Corinthians 8 and 9 might suggest — and redundancy is a standard feature of pedagogy, not to mention of communication in general, especially in an oral setting (so Ong 2012 [1982], 39-41). Hence, we may simply have to view this material as clumsily constructed. Or, alternatively, it may be that an argument deemed clumsy by modern interpreters would have been heard by ancient Corinthians as nicely weighted, given the fragile state of their relationship with Paul and the delicate nature of the matter at hand. (And so on.)

So Betz's elegant suggestion regarding the original insertion of 2 Corinthians 8 and 9 into the broader composite document known to us canonically as 2 Corinthians must be regarded as unproved. (And we have already noted the important counterargument, made principally by Stowers (1990), that 9:1 begins with an overtly continuative set of connectives, namely, περὶ μὲν γάρ.) Hence, until proved otherwise, the preliminary frame will continue to include chapters 8 and 9 within 2 Corinthians. Decisive arguments for their separation in terms of letter form are not yet apparent. And with this judgment, we come to the final group of claims made in support of original compilation — in many respects, the most important and potentially decisive set.

---

68. The redundancy of 9:1 is held to be esp. overt: περὶ μὲν γὰρ τῆς διακονίας τῆς εἰς τοὺς ἁγίους περισσόν μοί ἐστιν τὸ γράφειν ὑμῖν κ.τ.λ.

6.3 Claims of Telltale Contradictions

Klauck (2003, 137-40, 145-48) argued for the compilation of some of Cicero's letters on the basis of what we have dubbed "telltale contradictions," that is to say, concrete evidence of unavoidable temporal contradictions. If one part of a letter contained a particular reference or situation and another part of the letter explicitly reflected a quite different reference or situation (i.e., a difference implausible in terms of a mere lapse of time during composition), then Klauck concluded that compilation had occurred. And this seems entirely fair. Straightforward contradictions within an ancient letter suggest rather strongly that it is in fact a composite document. So these arguments will prove the most important and potentially decisive in relation to the partition of 2 Corinthians. However, there are very few such arguments. We have just gestured toward one in the previous subsection, namely, the suggestion that chapter 9 is redundant. But redundancy is not the same thing as a direct contradiction — an important realization. In fact, there is one principal argument in play within the broader debate that lays claim to a direct contradiction within 2 Corinthians.

C. K. Barrett (1982 [1969], 118-31) famously suggested that the two references in canonical 2 Corinthians to a visit by Titus to Corinth are incommensurable.

In chapters 7 and 8 Titus is about to be dispatched to Corinth by Paul to assist the collection (see 7:13-15; 8:6, 16). He will be accompanied by two other brothers who are recommended but not named, and Paul gives thanks for the enthusiasm (ostensibly) apparent in this entire endeavor: [8:16] Χάρις δὲ τῷ θεῷ τῷ δόντι τὴν αὐτὴν σπουδὴν ὑπὲρ ὑμῶν ἐν τῇ καρδίᾳ Τίτου, [17] ὅτι τὴν μὲν παράκλησιν ἐδέξατο, σπουδαιότερος δὲ ὑπάρχων αὐθαίρετος ἐξῆλθεν πρὸς ὑμᾶς. [18] συνεπέμψαμεν δὲ μετ᾽ αὐτοῦ τὸν ἀδελφὸν οὗ ὁ ἔπαινος ἐν τῷ εὐαγγελίῳ διὰ πασῶν τῶν ἐκκλησιῶν. In 12:18, however, Paul refers to a *previous* visit to Corinth by Titus and another unnamed companion, although in very similar language: παρεκάλεσα Τίτον καὶ συναπέστειλα τὸν ἀδελφόν· μήτι ἐπλεονέκτησεν ὑμᾶς Τίτος? Παρακαλῶ, the strong verb of exhortation, is used here again, as well as συναποστέλλω, the verb of delegation. So Barrett argues, critically, "The coincidence of language is such that the identification of this visit to Corinth with that described in Chapter 8 is scarcely open to question" (127). And if he is right, this data looks like a blatant contradiction. If these references are to the same visit, then 2 Corinthians must be composite. A *future* visit in chapter 8 is viewed as a *past* visit in chapter 12.

However, Barrett's case for the all-important identification of the two descriptions of a visit by Titus to Corinth rests on the similarity in the language.

And this is problematic. Similar language does not entail similar reference. One could, for example, use very similar words to describe the election of a president but refer every four or eight years to someone completely different. Moreover, similarity of language in the matter of encouraging and sending delegates is possibly not that surprising, and similarity of language within what is arguably the same letter would be utterly unsurprising. Paul has presumably read and reread what precedes, so the resurfacing of earlier phraseology in a later discussion of a similar activity is to be expected. Important counterevidence to Barrett's contention is also apparent. Certain clues in the data suggest that the two visits, despite their phraseological similarities, are not references to the same visit.

The delegation in chapters 8 and 9 includes two important accompanying brothers, whereas the one in 12:18 mentions only one. Moreover, we know from chapters 2 and 7 that Titus has visited Corinth prior to the visit anticipated in chapters 8 and 9 (assuming a degree of unity here).[69] There seems little reason, then, at least initially, not to suppose that 12:18 refers to the earlier visit, in the appropriately past terms, when Titus seems to have been accompanied by only one brother.

For these reasons, it seems that Barrett's putative contradiction collapses, at which point we should turn to consider one other contribution of this nature. Margaret Mitchell (2005, 325; 2010, esp. 68-69) has made an argument similar to Barrett's, suggesting that Paul's temporal references to "last year" in 8:10 and 9:2 refer to different years:

[8:10] καὶ γνώμην ἐν τούτῳ δίδωμι· τοῦτο γὰρ ὑμῖν συμφέρει, οἵτινες οὐ μόνον τὸ ποιῆσαι ἀλλὰ καὶ τὸ θέλειν προενήρξασθε ἀπὸ πέρυσι· . . .

[9:2] οἶδα γὰρ τὴν προθυμίαν ὑμῶν ἣν ὑπὲρ ὑμῶν καυχῶμαι Μακεδόσιν, ὅτι Ἀχαΐα παρεσκεύασται ἀπὸ πέρυσι, καὶ τὸ ὑμῶν ζῆλος ἠρέθισεν τοὺς πλείονας.

This is a subtle but important argument: 8:10 refers to the Corinthians "beginning" the collection in the previous year (see προενήρξασθε), while 9:2 refers to the "preparedness" of the Corinthians in the previous year (see παρεσκεύασται). Mitchell suggests, not unfairly, that these references are ir-

---

69. And 8:6 arguably refers to a previous visit as well, still more pointedly: εἰς τὸ παρακαλέσαι ἡμᾶς Τίτον, ἵνα καθὼς προενήρξατο οὕτως καὶ ἐπιτελέσῃ εἰς ὑμᾶς καὶ τὴν χάριν ταύτην.

reconcilable. Chapter 8 seems to indicate that the Corinthians were just beginning their collection in the previous year, but chapter 9 suggests that it was largely complete, or "prepared," in the previous year, its completion being used by Paul to goad the Macedonians into action. So these references seem to function within letters written originally at different times — letters that can then be further demarcated using (i.a.) Betz's observations, regional terms, and redundancies.

But for this argument to hold, Mitchell's readings must be decisively superior to the alternatives, and I am not convinced that they are. In particular, the "preparedness" of the Corinthians that Paul speaks of in 2 Corinthians 9 is evidently not complete, as the following verse in the letter says directly: ἔπεμψα δὲ τοὺς ἀδελφούς, ἵνα μὴ τὸ καύχημα ἡμῶν τὸ ὑπὲρ ὑμῶν κενωθῇ ἐν τῷ μέρει τούτῳ, ἵνα καθὼς ἔλεγον παρεσκευασμένοι ἦτε. The Corinthians have *said* that they are prepared, but Paul is clearly concerned that the money is not yet collected. And this suggests that the preparedness in question was the preparedness to contribute, as against the preparedness of having contributed — just the preparedness, in other words, that is apparent in chapter 8. The Corinthians were willing to participate in the previous year and seem to have done *something*. But they have not yet done *enough*. Their "doing" must yet be "completed" (v. 11).

Given the reasonableness of these alternatives, it seems that Mitchell's ingenious claim that the two situations are contradictory is exaggerated. The situations contradict given certain readings of the data, but equally plausible readings eliminate any contradictions. Thus, the argument must be judged inadequate as a decisive demonstration of original compilation within 2 Corinthians as a whole. And with the collapse of Mitchell's contention — at least at this early stage of the discussion — all the initially plausible arguments for telltale contradictions in the data have proved invalid.

Our preliminary and provisional conclusion in this section overall on the suggestion of partition in 2 Corinthians, then, is that such hypotheses are fascinating but fragile and highly unstable. I am very fond of partition theories — as well as complex accounts of the interim events — and so am a somewhat reluctant advocate of the position unfolding here.[70] However, I am at present

70. These are well introduced by Vegge (2008, 12-34), although, as a student of Bieringer's, Vegge is not ultimately sympathetic to them. He organizes the main options into five phases that developed in relation to one another, along with one motley group of more individual theories: (1) Semler; (2) Hausrath-Kennedy(-Plummer/Watson); (3) Weiss-Bultmann(-Barrett); (4) (early) Schmithals-Bornkamm; and (5) Semler-Windisch; along with (6) various more

unpersuaded by suggestions of partition. Consequently, I have ended up minimizing and simplifying the frame at every point. In something like a Corinthian digression, we have ended up at the end of this section back where we started, with the conclusion of the previous section: 1 Corinthians is the Letter of Tears, and 2 Corinthians remains the single letter that follows it, being followed itself, at this stage in our discussion, by Romans. And it seems, further, that Knox's account of the frame in this all-important first reconstructed step has been fundamentally vindicated. The best account of the frame at present is:

... Paul VC2 ...
// year change(s) //
... Apollos VC1 / [PLC] — Corinthian VEs / [Corinthian reply] —
// year change //
— 1 Cor (LT) — Apollos VC2 / super-apostles VC — Titus VC1 —
Asian crisis
— 2 Cor / Titus VC2 — Paul VC3 ...
// year change //
... Rom — Paul VJ ...

And with this part of the frame in place, we now turn to the critical questions surrounding the insertion of Galatians into its main sequence.

---

distinctive theories, e.g., from the later Schmithals. More sympathetic to the entire enterprise, and making an original and significant contribution, is M. Mitchell (2005). Mitchell organizes the theories principally in terms of how many letters canonical 2 Cor is partitioned into — two, three, or five — subdividing these categories helpfully when necessary in terms of the resulting question of order. (2 Cor 6:14–7:1 is not usually counted as a letter in these reconstructions but is viewed as a fragmentary interpolation or some such.)

CHAPTER THREE

Augmenting the Backbone: Philippians and Galatians

1. Locating Philippians

We come now to a pivotal step in Knox's approach to framing Paul: the insertion of Galatians into the epistolary sequence that is already in place (i.e., 1 Cor — 2 Cor — Rom). If this proves possible, an extensive and workable frame for Paul's missionary career will be generated immediately, because Galatians contains so much significant framing information, especially in its first two chapters. (This will be parsed carefully in due course.) However, Knox's approach requires augmentation at this critical moment. His case for the insertion of Galatians into the epistolary spine is weak, relying almost entirely on overconfident claims about Galatians 2:10 (1987, 36-40, citing Burton 1920 in support). We will use his argument here eventually, but only suitably elaborated, and with the appropriate degree of confidence — as a corroborative contention. And this entails a search for more probative contentions to begin with.

One way of finding these is by considering something Knox failed to address. If other letters can be inserted into the epistolary spine more obviously than and prior to Galatians, then this might introduce further information that assists the insertion of Galatians itself. (Alternatively, it might speak against inserting Galatians here — something we would need to know.) We might, in other words, be able to gain more leverage on this vital issue if we could expand the spine in any way beyond the sequence 1 Cor — 2 Cor — Rom before assessing Galatians. And I suggest that we can, principally by way of Paul's letter to the Philippians. A rigorous examination of Philippians first will turn up surprisingly strong contentions in favor of locating it here, and this will open up stronger contentions in turn with respect to Galatians. Indeed, arguably the location of Philippians will turn out to be the initial key to the location of Galatians.

Philippians was composed during an imprisonment, and we should note some aspects of this data before moving on to make a case for the letter's location.

1.1 Paul's Place of Imprisonment

Philippians is often placed in an imprisonment at Rome, but this opinion needs to be challenged. That Paul is imprisoned at the time of writing, and partway through a capital trial, is clear (see 1:7, 13, 14, 17, 20). At the beginning of the letter he speaks positively of this incarceration. Because of this, he claims, the knowledge of Christ has spread "to the whole of the Praetorium/ Praetorian [Guard], as well as to everyone else" (see 1:13: ὥστε τοὺς δεσμούς μου φανεροὺς ἐν Χριστῷ γενέσθαι ἐν ὅλῳ τῷ πραιτωρίῳ καὶ τοῖς λοιποῖς πᾶσιν). At the end of the letter he sends special greetings to the Philippians "from those who belong to Caesar's household" (see 4:22: ἀσπάζονται ὑμᾶς πάντες οἱ ἅγιοι, μάλιστα δὲ οἱ ἐκ τῆς Καίσαρος οἰκίας).

These comments could be references respectively to the Praetorian Guard, which was located almost entirely at Rome, and to the imperial household — the *familia Caesaris* — which was centered in Rome as well and so could conceivably have yielded some converts (see esp. Rom 16:11b, "those of the household of Narcissus," who were almost certainly members in turn of the *familia Caesaris*). Construal of the data in these terms seems, moreover, to dovetail with the way that the book of Acts concludes, with Paul imprisoned at Rome (see 28:16-31). And perhaps the influence of generations of Hollywood biblical blockbusters should not be discounted at this point, in which gorgeously appareled Roman villains sport foolishly with Christians in the empire's capital. In short, a Roman provenance is not an unfair understanding of the relevant data, and it accords with some of our imaginative proclivities. However, it is not the only possible construal.

"The Praetorium" is a reference in the rest of the NT, as in much other literature at this time, to "the governor's residence" (see Mt 27:27; Mk 15:16; Jn 18:28 [2x], 33; 19:9; Acts 23:35), so called in part because the Roman governor in NT times was usually a *propraetor*. The term probably came originally from the Latin designation for the residence of the *praetor* in a legion's camp. But the word was doubly useful in provincial terms. The rapid expansion of the empire over the previous century had forced the senate to broaden its gubernatorial pool from proconsuls to propraetors, only two consuls being elected every year in Rome as against ten praetors. Later imperial provinces could draw on figures as far down the aristocratic social scale as equestrians, leading to provincial government by people like Pontius Pilate, but as the NT data attests, the original Latin designation for the governor's residence seems to have stuck. It was the place where the governor, who was not infrequently a propraetor, lived.

Similarly, the phrase "Caesar's household" was the name of the Roman imperial "family," members of which could be found dotted all over the empire. That is, although the majority of this group was probably at Rome, a large number of its members were involved with administration on the emperor's behalf (for example, administering estates in some capacity), and an equally large number had retired, often after manumission around the age of thirty, to some provincial location.[1] That members or former members of Caesar's household would be found in a city that also housed a governor's residence is therefore entirely unsurprising. And this suggests that Philippians could have been written from an imprisonment in any provincial capital at the time, many of which Paul visited during his travels and in some of which he undoubtedly ran into legal difficulties.

In direct support of the provincial possibility, the epistolary data tells us that Paul suffered multiple imprisonments. Second Corinthians 11:23, in particular, boasts that he has been in prison many more times than his opponents (see "in prisons many times"; ἐν φυλακαῖς περισσοτέρως), and v. 25 suggests that he has been disciplined with an official Roman beating three times by this point in his missionary work. We may plausibly assume an episode of incarceration in each of these cases as well, and most likely in areas under a Roman type of jurisdiction, since this was a Roman punishment.[2] Moreover, five of the canonical thirteen letters were written from prison —

---

1. For more details, see Weaver (1972); Millar (1977, esp. 69, 159, 173, 177-78); also Fuhrmann (2012, esp. 196). A conspicuous example of this was Gaius Julius Zoilus, the great benefactor of the city of Aphrodisias in the Roman province of Asia, but formerly a slave of Julius Caesar who was manumitted by Augustus (then Octavian); see R. Smith (1993).

2. Specifically, τρὶς ἐραβδίσθην, or beaten three times with rods *(virgis caedere)*. The punishment would have been at the hand of a Roman *lictor* (lit. "rod-carrier"), a figure who attended Roman magistrates. The lictor's *fasces,* a bundle of rods often bound with an ax *(secures),* was carried as a symbol of authority. For this punishment, however, the rod used would have been a practical rather than a ceremonial staff of wood. See further Fuhrmann (2012). The most likely scenario for these incarcerations would have been the detention of Paul after some disturbance to await local and then, if necessary, gubernatorial trial.

an extraordinary statistic (see, in possible addition to Philippians, Philemon, Colossians, Ephesians, and 2 Timothy). So we are entitled on the basis of the epistolary evidence to consider carefully whether the incarceration that Paul is experiencing in Philippians corresponds to one of these many earlier imprisonments, as well as, more specifically, whether it fits anywhere within our developing frame, which at present encompasses roughly a year and a half of intense activity around the shores of the Aegean. A church community is also visible in the letter at the place of Paul's incarceration, so we should ask specifically whether Paul was imprisoned when writing Philippians in Ephesus, the capital since Augustus of the province of Asia; in Thessalonica, the capital of Macedonia; or in Corinth, the capital of Achaia.[3] Our response to this query needs to begin somewhat obliquely, with a consideration of the letter's integrity, which has been called into question almost as much as the integrity of 2 Corinthians.[4]

1.2 The Implications of Philippians 3

Although not as widespread as they once were, extensive doubts about the integrity of canonical Philippians are still common, and with some reason. In an excellent treatment, Garland observes that "the key argument against the unity of Philippians is the different tone that distinguishes the beginning of chap. 3. It is described as 'a break so harsh as to defy imagination,' a switch from 'eirenical calm' to 'violent hysteria.' It does seem that Paul wheels inexplicably from a cordial expression of concern for the Philippians in 1:1–2:30 to a scathing philippic against 'dogs, evil workers and mutilators' in 3:2 without an appropriate transition" (1985, 144, quoting Goodspeed and Houlden respectively). Garland goes on to add that Paul's "train of thought" seems to have a "disjunction," while "4:4 seems to follow more intelligibly from 3:1a than does 3:2" (144). That is, the anomalous material seems to have an overt beginning and ending. The disjunction is intimately bound up with the new focus of the letter's attention within the distinctive section. A group of opponents is in view that seems either to be characterized in rather different terms from earlier in the letter (1:15, 17, 18; 2:15) or, more likely, to be a fundamentally different group

3. Useful background on Ephesus can be found in Trebilco (1991; 2007 [2004]).

4. An excellent survey — although not ultimately sympathetic to partition — is provided by Garland (1985, 141-59). Koperski (1993, 599-603) analyzes the origins of the modern hypothesis — again, a little unsympathetically. A briefer and more recent canvassing of the issue can be found in D. Watson (2003, 157-61).

from those figures and hence unannounced and unanticipated until its sudden dramatic entrance in 3:2.

Complementing these structural and substantive differences, Paul's imprisonment is not in view within the section. Moreover, the consternation caused by the sudden transition can be buttressed by suggestions that the epistolary formulae τὸ λοιπόν and χαίρετε in 3:1 are best read as "finally" and "farewell," and are more appropriately positioned at the end of a letter than at this midpoint in 3:1a. Hence, as Garland says: "All of these observations seem to point to the conclusion that chap. 3 was originally a separate fragment, written on a different occasion (perhaps even to a different church), that was later joined to 1:1–2:30 (3:1) by someone other than Paul" (1985, 145).

Doubts concerning 4:10-20 can then be introduced alongside those already mustered in relation to 3:2–4:3. Paul's response of gratitude to the Philippians for their gift seems oddly extended and indirect. Moreover, "not only is it delayed in the course of the letter, it seems to have been delayed in the course of time" (146). This section is arguably positioned somewhat awkwardly within the letter's closing formulae, and would have been considerably delayed in terms of time if Paul had had to wait weeks or even months for Epaphroditus's recovery (see 2:25-30) before penning a letter from somewhere as distant from Philippi as Rome. So once again these concerns are arguably best met with an act of partition, 4:10-20 having originally been "a separate thank you note dashed off by Paul immediately upon his receipt of the gift" (146), and then subsequently combined with later letters to Philippi into the canonical Philippians. And a passing remark by Polycarp, in his epistle to the Philippians, that Paul "wrote letters to you" (ὑμῖν ἔγραψεν ἐπιστολάς) might even confirm these suspicions (Pol. Phil 3:2).

However, we have reason to doubt that a hypothesis of original collation, to be resolved in our period by partition, is the best response to this data. We have already introduced the suspicion that ancient editors did not act in this sophisticated interpolative fashion; that is, the foregoing hypothesis violates the editorial principle of Klauckian simplicity. Canonical Philippians would have been composed, according to this supposition, basically in terms of A — B — A — C — A, and this seems unlikely. Nevertheless, much of the raw data deployed in favor of partition is undeniable and requires explanation. So we will try to articulate a different account of it in what follows, a task that will necessitate some detailed engagement with the data in question. We will have to study closely, in particular, the abrupt transition in 3:1 and the resulting distinctive section within Philippians of 3:2–4:3.

(1) Preliminary Interpretative Questions Concerning 3:2–4:3

Five local interpretative questions concerning 3:1a and 1b need to be addressed before we can move forward in broader terms. Fortunately, they do not all need to be decided, but they should be helpful in giving us some sense of the interpretative options involved, as well as, eventually, some interpretative purchase on the broader situation.

[3:1a] Τὸ λοιπόν, ἀδελφοί μου, χαίρετε ἐν κυρίῳ.

[3:1b] τὰ αὐτὰ γράφειν ὑμῖν ἐμοὶ μὲν οὐκ ὀκνηρόν, ὑμῖν δὲ ἀσφαλές.

Two localized questions arise initially in v. 1a: (i) the interpretation of τὸ λοιπόν; and (ii) the significance of Paul's exhortation to the Philippian brothers to rejoice, especially in relation to exhortations to do the same found elsewhere in Philippians.

(i) The phrase τὸ λοιπόν does not modify a substantive directly in 3:1a and so seems best construed, as in 4:8, as an adverbial expression constructed with the article and the neuter adjective of λοιπός. The signifier can take a variety of different senses. λοιπός refers, as a rough rule of thumb, to things remaining (so BDAG), and the phrase τὸ λοιπόν can consequently demarcate items sequentially, whether merely what remains or the last item in a series. It can also supply inferential information ("well then," "therefore," "and so"). And it can function with reference to time that remains, and so mean "in the future," "henceforth," or "from now on." In view of all these options, we just cannot say in the first instance which sense the phrase takes in 3:1a. An inferential sense looks the most awkward, but even that does not seem impossible. We should recall, moreover, that the phrase is being used here with the vocative "brothers" (ἀδελφοί), which is usually a transitional signal in Paul's letters. So we must turn to the other questions arising in the immediate context in the hope that the answer to one of those will help our broader deliberations more decisively. What we can say now is that τὸ λοιπόν is not necessarily functioning in 3:1 to signal the end of a letter — the sense of "finally" or some such. So it cannot be used as decisive evidence of partition. It could equally easily be signaling a transition.

(ii) The suggestion that the instance of χαίρω in 3:1a means "farewell" indubitably, and therefore denotes the presence of another letter in the text here, can actually be dismissed fairly quickly. It is far more likely that this verb is functioning in 3:1a as it does in the other ten instances in Philippians, as a reference to joy. Paul's exhortation in 3:1a to the Philippians to be joyful is merely one in a series of such references that thread through the canonical letter (see 1:18 [2x]; 2:17 [2x, counting an instance of συγχαίρω], 18 [ditto], 28; 3:1; 4:4 [2x], 10), a thread whose density is unparalleled in his other extant writings.[5] It is worth noting especially carefully Paul's following exhortation to joy, in 4:4, where, as in 2:17 and 18, he provides a double instance without apology: Χαίρετε ἐν κυρίῳ πάντοτε· πάλιν ἐρῶ, χαίρετε. Again, we cannot yet say much more than this. So we need now to turn to the three further questions arising in relation to v. 1b in the search for interpretative leverage on the broader situation.

(iii)   We should first consider the meaning of ὀκνηρός. Many commentators prefer a translation informed by hesitation in the face of events causing anxiety or fear, hence "troublesome," in the sense of being troubled. So the NRSV renders 3:1b: "To write the same things to you is not troublesome to me." But this is not the only possible sense of ὀκνηρός. It could denote hesitation in the face of activity per se. And if the activity was simply work or work-related, it could therefore suggest "shrinking," "idle," "timid," or even "sluggish" (see Reed 1996, 73). Moreover, the former group of construals — that is, "troublesome" in the sense of troubled — seems to prejudge the remaining interpretative questions in relation to vv. 1b and 2; it assumes a connection between the verses, which is disputed, along with an aggressive reading of Paul's imperatives in v. 2, which is also disputed.[6] But the latter

---

5. See Rom (4x); 1 Cor (6x); 2 Cor (8x); Gal (0x); Eph (0x); Phil (11x); Col (2x); 1 Thess (2x); 2 Thess (0x); 1 Tim (0x); 2 Tim (0x); Titus (0x); Phlm (0x).

6. Most notably by Kilpatrick (1968), suggesting that the strong meaning of the verb βλέπετε, "beware of," is followed "almost without exception" (citing Garland 1985, 165) by either an object clause using μή and the aorist subjunctive or future, or by the preposition ἀπό, but never by a direct object. In the last instance, the verb takes the less alarming meaning "consider" or "take due note of," allowing the material in question to function in an exemplary fashion (see, e.g., 1 Cor 1:26; 10:18; 2 Cor 10:7; Col 4:17; Mk 4:24). But Kilpatrick's observations do not account for all of the data, and his suggested interpretations seem to be placed on a continuum rather than in a disjunctive relationship. He consequently underemphasizes the semantic possibility that βλέπετε means keeping a lookout, which is not a warning per se but can still refer in a non-exemplary fashion to something negative (see, e.g., Mk 13:23). And this realization undermines much of Garland's positive response to the challenges of Phil 3, since he argues that Paul is directing the Philippians' attention there to Jews and Judaism as a generic negative example.

group of construals — in terms primarily of hesitation — is, as Reed (1996) observes, an epistolary staple, and furthermore, is often associated with the verb γράφειν. In addition, the meaning "troublesome" [i.e., troubling] is unattested in the papyri in an epistolary context. Reed concludes persuasively that the phrase ἐμοὶ μὲν οὐκ ὀκνηρόν in v. 1b is most probably a predicate nominative construction in the first of two complementary claims about the act of repetitive writing just referenced, best rendered, "To write the same things is not a matter of hesitation for me [i.e., because it is burdensome work or onerous]." But this decision does not help us with the remaining interpretative questions. Our options are all still open, even as the rhetorical shift in the passage is still unexplained.

(iv) With respect to the meaning of ἀσφαλές, used in the second complementary phrase, ὑμῖν δὲ ἀσφαλές, Reed observes correctly that different interpretations are quite possible again. ἀσφαλές could denote something "assured from danger" or "safe," or something "trustworthy," "unfailing," "not liable to fall, immovable, steadfast," and hence "certain, dependable" (77). But interpreters have in the past wrongly privileged the first option here, again apparently influenced by a polemical reading of v. 2 based on interpretative judgments that we have yet to establish. So it seems that we must at the moment remain open again to both semantic possibilities for ἀσφαλές. Paul could be balancing his claim that "to write the same things is not on my part a matter of the slightest hesitation [despite the work involved]" with a claim that "on your part this is a matter that safeguards [you]" *or* ". . . that will contribute to your steadfastness." Fortunately, there is not a great deal of semantic distance between these two readings. However, by this point in our analysis, with four lexical and syntactical issues addressed, we have yet to make decisive progress on the broader questions. And so we come now to what is possibly the key question in the entire local debate.

(v) What is the reference of the phrase τὰ αὐτά in v. 1b? We need to begin here by asking whether it is functioning anaphorically, to what has just been written (ἀδελφοί μου, χαίρετε ἐν κυρίῳ), or cataphorically, with reference to what follows (Βλέπετε τοὺς κύνας, βλέπετε τοὺς κακοὺς ἐργάτας κ.τ.λ.). Two main considerations, assisted by a third, would suggest that the function of the expression is cataphoric:

(a) It is at just this point that much of the evidence assembled in favor of partition throws its weight — somewhat ironically — behind a cataphoric reference. As we noted earlier, the letter shifts dramatically in v. 2. Its rhetoric becomes aggressive, perhaps even polemical, and focuses in detail on a group possessing numerous Jewish character-istics that has nevertheless only — at the least — been hinted at thus far in the canonical letter (see 1:27-30). And Paul's location in prison fades from sight. This abrupt shift to a sustained polemic about a dif-ferent concern in v. 2 is perplexing, prompting numerous scholars in the past to posit partition. However, a cataphoric reference for v. 1b explains this shift explicitly, in part by simply announcing it, although in terms that we will have to parse carefully in a moment. Paul seems to be telling his auditors specifically in v. 1b, immediately prior to this shift, that he is now "writing the same things," and not "hesitating" to do so on grounds of their onerous nature. Moreover, this will help their "steadiness" or even "safeguard them." The text, on this cataphoric reading, acknowledges the rhetorical disjunction, and the latter therefore seems to be good evidence *for* this reading.

(b) Just as a cataphoric reference for 1b seems to speak to one of the most obvious and problematic aspects of the letter's data, an anaphoric reference, to Paul's repeated exhortation to be joyful in v. 1a, would leave the shift from v. 2 onward unexplained. Concomitantly, it seems oddly heavy-handed for Paul to use an overt explanation merely to guide interpretation of a resumed exhortation of three words, χαίρετε ἐν κυρίῳ. That this exhortation in 3:1a does not merit such attention seems confirmed by the parallel exhortation that oc-curs later, in 4:4: Χαίρετε ἐν κυρίῳ πάντοτε· πάλιν ἐρῶ, χαίρετε. This is twice as long as 3:1a but elicits no apology — merely the statement by Paul that he is going to say "'rejoice' again."[7] And, in reinforce-ment of these suspicions, we should recall that 3:1a contains its own epistolary orientations in any case without v. 1b, namely, the phrase τὸ λοιπόν coupled with the vocative ἀδελφοί. The exhortation to joy does not need further orientation beyond these two distinct epistolary markers.

(c) As if to confirm the syntactical self-sufficiency of 3:1a, v. 1b is asyn-detic. No connecting particle connects 1b with what precedes, and this suggests the beginning of a new section and hence a cataphoric

---

7. Reed (1996, 80) correctly notes the argument of O'Brien (1991, 351) in this sense: "Would this simple and natural summons (which occurs again twice in 4:4!) have called forth an apology for repetition?" — a point made earlier by Lightfoot (1896, 125-26).

function for v. 1b. By way of comparison, this is not the case in 2:17b-18, an overtly continuing set of exhortations ([17] . . . χαίρω καὶ συγχαίρω πᾶσιν ὑμῖν· [18] τὸ δὲ αὐτὸ καὶ ὑμεῖς χαίρετε καὶ συγχαίρετέ μοι).

On these grounds, we can regard a cataphoric function in v. 1b as highly likely. We need now to consider how this judgment affects our understanding of this critical transitional text more broadly.

Paul is stating in 3:1b that "to write the same things to you is, on my part, not a matter of the slightest hesitation [i.e., despite the work involved], and is, on your part, a thing that is dependable [or perhaps even something of a safeguard]." The dramatic rhetorical shift to new material then follows in 3:2, softening the "polemical" interpretation of v. 2 to an emphatic exhortation to vigilance: "Keep a careful lookout for those dogs; be vigilant concerning those workers of evil things; keep watch for those mutilators." Hence, a new group enters the picture, while Paul's incarcerated situation fades from view. But the letter then explicitly resumes the material that tapered off in 3:1a in 4:4, with a return to an emphatic exhortation to joy. And in view of all this data, I suggest, as Klauck (2003, 152) opined in passing,[8] that the most obvious explanation — as well as, in many respects, the simplest — is the supposition that in 3:2–4:3 Paul is quoting from a previous letter to the Philippians (at which point Polycarp's observation returns to mind).[9] Paul effectively announces this quotation in 3:1b by stating that for him *to write the same things* to the

---

8. Klauck also gestured toward an accompanying study by D. Watson (2003), but this, although a trenchant defense of the letter's unity, does not develop the possibility that 3:2–4:3 is a quotation of a previous letter.

9. This possibility has been noted by a handful of scholars; O'Brien (1991, 351) tabulates M. R. Vincent (1897), J. H. Michael (1922), and I.-J. Loh and E. A. Nida (1977). Moreover, when other commentators reject it, the arguments tend to be strangely weak. O'Brien simply asserts that "too much weight should not be placed on . . . [the] evidence [of Polycarp]" (351). No reasons are given for dismissing this significant information or the other evidence supporting the reading. Bockmuehl opines that there are "several" problems with the view, going on to enumerate two: (1) that this meaning is unlikely because "there is in fact no clear reference to previous letters" and "[w]e might expect a more explicit mention of such a document"; and (2) "it is significant that Paul literally says he is writing 'the same things' . . . not that he is writing 'once again' " (1997, 178). But objection 1 ignores the actual evidence in question, 3:1b, which is an explicit reference, and objection 2 is groundless. Presumably Paul could refer to his act of rewriting and quotation as he wanted to — here as "writing the same things will be helpful/not burdensome" rather than "[I am now] writing a [piece of another] letter once more."

Philippians is not onerous, that is, despite his difficult location, the repetition involved, and perhaps even the difficulty of consulting a copy of the earlier letter. Rather, given his concern about these dangerous figures (dangerous, that is, in Paul's view), this repetition will be something that safeguards them or, at the least, that they can depend on.

This theory has the significant advantage that all the powerful considerations previously advanced in favor of a hypothesis of interpolation now pivot away from that supposition and support this new suggestion instead. Every disjunction is explicable in terms of the differing circumstances of the earlier letter, when Paul apparently was addressing certain figures, whom we will consider in more detail momentarily, and was not incarcerated. His principal concerns when writing the later letter, our canonical Philippians, have shifted a little from the previous epistle. He is currently responding, within an imprisonment, to the generosity of the Philippians, to the recovery of Epaphroditus, and so on. But that earlier situation is clearly still sufficiently close for him to reiterate some of his earlier instructions. A further advantage of the theory is that it does not run afoul of the principle of Klauckian simplicity in relation to ancient editorial behavior but accords with standard ancient epistolary practice. In short, the hypothesis that 3:2–4:3 is an excerpt from a previous letter to Philippi that is explicitly announced in 3:1b — the broader letter breaking off and resuming at 3:1a and 4:4[10] — explains everything both adequately and plausibly.[11] By way of contrast, advocates of partition now have a difficult row to hoe, although their suspicions that a fragment of other correspondence is intruding into 3:2–4:3 have been vindicated.[12] So we will build on the quotation

---

10. Paul's exhortation to the Philippians to be joyful in 4:4 functions as a precise repetition of 3:1a and hence as a direct resumption of the line of thought initiated then: Τὸ λοιπόν, ἀδελφοί μου, χαίρετε ἐν κυρίῳ. . . . Χαίρετε ἐν κυρίῳ πάντοτε· πάλιν ἐρῶ, χαίρετε.

11. It could be suggested, against this, that Paul is reproducing previous speech or oral teaching here instead. But not much turns on this explanatory variation, which seems less likely than a quotation of an earlier text in any case. Paul's use of a "burden" formula makes sense only if he is burdened by an act of written repetition; certainly, he never refers to the epistolary transmission of earlier oral teaching in terms of hesitation and burden. Quotation makes better sense of 3:1b than a reference to earlier teaching as well. That is, the brevity of the actual claim is well explained if Paul is referring here to what was in effect his "writing the same things [that I wrote previously]." The expanded version would have been bad Greek with an obvious redundancy. However, as a reference to "writing the same things [that I *said* previously]," the claim as he worded it would entail a puzzling omission.

12. The best contention in favor of partition was in terms of shift. But if the hypothesis of a quotation in Phil 3:2–4:3 is correct, then this contention simply collapses, functioning instead to reinforce the quotation hypothesis.

hypothesis in what follows, positing a previous letter by Paul that has been lost, the Previous Letter to Philippi [PLP], which must be distinguished carefully from the Previous Letter to Corinth. Unlike the Previous Letter to Corinth, part of the Previous Letter to Philippi has been fortuitously preserved by Paul's own reproduction of it in a quotation in Philippians 3:2–4:3.[13] And with this judgment, we arrive at the next critical step within our broader argument.

(2) The Nature of the Opponents

As far as we know, Paul wrote the Previous Letter to Philippi because of the opponents in view within the material he quotes in Philippians 3:2–4:3. No other reason is apparent for that letter's composition in this text; it is little more than a carefully composed comparison and critique (see otherwise only 4:2-3). It therefore seems likely that either these figures or news of them arrived where Paul was and thereby elicited the composition and dispatch of the Previous Letter to Philippi fairly immediately, with its exhortations to vigilance and instructions concerning how to respond specifically to their agenda should they arrive in Philippi. "Keep a lookout for these figures," Paul says repeatedly, the implication being that they are not yet present there, although their silhouette is perhaps dimly traceable on the horizon. We must now examine the opponents more closely, since we may be able to trace their outline and/or trajectory in relation to other letters, thereby developing our broader frame.

Here, however, we are starting to walk into another proverbial minefield in Pauline studies. The reconstruction of the apostle's opponents is an academic industry that goes back to the dawn of the modern interpretative era, with F. C. Baur.[14] So it is important to be aware that I have no intention of walking all the way through, so to speak. We will pick our way into it just as far as we need to go and no farther. It is not necessary for our present purposes in

13. This judgment might suggest revisiting 2 Cor 6:14–7:1 in these terms as well. That passage is not introduced as a quotation as clearly as Phil 3:2–4:3 is, but otherwise many of the features of the data are similarly disjunctive. And with Paul's practice of quotation established by the Philippian instance, the introductory silence in 2 Cor is no longer as problematic as it was.

14. See Baur (2003 [1845]), although, strictly speaking, this activity predates Baur considerably; he is just the seminal figure in relation to whom the "modern" scholarly period tends to be dated. Sumney (1990) remains a critical methodological contribution to this entire area of analysis in Paul, as is Barclay (1987); their strictures eliminate much that has been said on this question in the past.

terms of framing to achieve a comprehensive reconstruction of the opponents. Indeed, if the success of the frame depended on this, then the project might as well be abandoned; we would be involved with a full-fledged historical reconstruction, which is precisely what we are trying to avoid. The frame is supposed to provide an objective basis for this sort of reconstruction to take place later on without begging critical historical questions in relation to the frame itself. So how are we to proceed at this early methodological stage once the issue of the opponents has been raised?

Fortunately, we need only to achieve certain minimal conclusions that will enable framing judgments and nothing more. Specifically, we need only to identify the same opponents from letter to letter, and to distinguish one group from another if that is also necessary. We need only to know, in more formal terms, whether in Letter A we are dealing with group X or group Y (if there is a group Y in play as well), as against in Letter B, and so on. We do not need to know everything about the opponents after this — the origins, nature, and agenda of group X, along with Paul's multiple responses in all their depth. So the amount of evidence in play is rather less than we find in most discussions of Paul's opponents, and the resulting portrait less complete, although it is derived rigorously. In the light of these methodological caveats, three sets of brief observations about three different letters in our existing sequence should now prove useful.

(i) The opponents in the Previous Letter to Philippi. In this subsection, we can affirm certain things about the figures evident in the Previous Letter (i.e., Phil 3:2–4:3), noting two further historical details within the broader situation in §§ii and iii following. We should begin by affirming the probability first that the Previous Letter treats one set of opponents and not two separate groups, as has sometimes been suggested.

The passage comprises three subsections and a short coda. In the first subsection, Paul begins by identifying certain "dogs" in 3:2, apparently responding to their agenda with a set of integrated claims that runs through v. 11. He then describes, in a second, distinguishable argumentative move, the relationship between perfection and current imperfect reality by drawing an analogy in terms of Greco-Roman athletics, known as "the *agōn* motif" in dependence on the classic treatment by Pfitzner (1967). This discussion runs through v. 16. And this last verse also introduces the motif of "stepping" or "walking," which is then elaborated as Paul begins another caustic contrast in v. 17 that runs through 4:1. In this third subsection, he urges careful observation and imitation of both himself and those walking as he does, as against those "who walk . . . as enemies of the cross of Christ." Paul describes those figures in deeply unflattering terms: "their stomach is their god" (v. 19).[15] But the subsection ends largely positively, with exhortations to the Philippians to stand firm and to wait for their savior from heaven, who will effect a dramatic and glorious transformation of their humble bodies. The passage then concludes with a brief exhortation to Euodia and Syntyche to mend their differences, since any disunity threatens the united front that Paul is clearly hoping the Philippians will present to the dangerous figures just mentioned.

Although the argumentation of the passage unfolds through these distinguishable steps, it is difficult to detect any pivot away from the same basic concerns. The second subsection progresses smoothly into the third with the exhortation of v. 16, which effects a skillful transition. There Paul says, πλὴν εἰς ὃ ἐφθάσαμεν, τῷ αὐτῷ στοιχεῖν. This rounds off the athletic imagery just used in vv. 12-15 but also inaugurates the discussions of "stepping" and "walking" that are central to what follows (see esp. στοιχέω in v. 16; περιπατέω in v. 17 and v. 18). And in just the same way, the motif of "walking" almost certainly resumes the set of Jewish practices named or alluded to — sometimes rather polemically — from v. 2 onward: "good works," circumcision, Jewish ancestry, and mastery of the Hebrew language, along with, climactically, a Torah observance that is both zealous and faultless, "walking" being a standard designation, drawn ultimately from Scripture, for Jewish ethics. These practices would denote in broadly Jewish terms membership in the "polity of Israel" (see 3:20). And the very proximity of the two direct discussions of opposition should be borne in mind as well. They are separated by just five verses of closely related material.

In the light of all these connections, it seems that the burden of proof rests on the denial of an identification of the figures Paul denounces in vv. 2 and 18-19. And in view of this, it seems most likely that these figures were some group of rival "Christian" leaders.

Admittedly, they seem to have advocated various Jewish practices and traditional Jewish identity markers, such as circumcision.[16] But their teaching is not necessarily reducible to these matters; they are merely the ones that Paul initially identifies. Most of the early Christian leaders were Jews, and most early Christian ethics is recognizably Jewish, including much of Paul's, so this

15. On this see Sandnes (2002); and, more briefly, my 2009 (497, in the broader context of 69-518).

16. See esp. an insightful treatment by Thiessen (2011); earlier and briefer is Marcus (1989); more general background information on perceptions of circumcision in Judaism in the late Second Temple period can be found in Cohen (1999).

is not necessarily surprising or especially delimiting. It is doubtful, of course, that they would have used the name Christian, which may not yet have been invented, and even if it had been, was not in widespread emic use.[17] But these figures do seem to have belonged to the distinctive movement of Jews and pagans loyal in some sense to Jesus that was later identified as the church. It is rather easier to understand Paul's polemic with this supposition, as against without it.

The Philippians were apparently loyal Christians and fairly obedient followers of Paul. Indeed, arguably they were his most devoted church. It is hard to understand, then, how leaders could have gained entrance into their community with any sort of teaching legitimacy without making basic Christian claims. Complementing this suspicion, it is hard to understand how figures as overtly wicked as those depicted in Paul's quotation could have been accepted by the Philippians. It seems more likely, then, that Paul is polemically characterizing these figures as more overtly dangerous than they may appear — in sharply negative terms — to elicit this judgment from the Philippians concerning them. Paul *wants* the Philippians to view this set of figures as enemies of the cross of Christ, because, quite simply, there is a good chance that they will not do so, and that the Jewish practices enumerated or alluded to in 3:3-6 will be seen as complementing or — *quelle horreur* — *completing* a gospel centered on the cross as he has taught it. Overtly dangerous foes or oppositional groups, we might say, do not need to be polemically characterized, or even widely polemicized against, because their unacceptability is obvious. They could be "racialized," but that is a slightly different rhetorical operation. But it is deceptively similar opposition that tends to receive the most vituperative rhetorical treatment. Hence, the function of Paul's polemic in Philippians 3 as an overtly delegitimizing strategy reinforces the suspicion that Paul's opposition was Christian.

We should now note that a *specific* group of rival Jewish Christian leaders is most probably in view.

We have just seen that Paul is exhorting the Philippians to be vigilant concerning an alternative account of the Christian gospel, which we can now see, in addition, included various Jewish practices that Paul considered unacceptable. It follows that this version of the gospel was being advocated by

---

17. See the judicious discussions in Horrell (2007); and Rowe (2009, 126-35). A more relevant but dated essay is J. Taylor (1994). I would press the date for the assignment of the name rather earlier than their estimates, on the basis in part of this unfolding discussion concerning Pauline chronology, in combination with the evidence, suitably interpreted, of Acts 11:26c.

someone, so presumably a small group of advocates was involved. Paul regards this advocacy in both the Previous Letter and Philippians as a fatal compromise of Christ's work on the cross and urges his auditors to reject it completely, presenting a united front to it, like the first ranks of a legion moving into combat — although this rank apparently includes some women. More practically, this tactic will play out in terms of a particular imitation. Just as the Philippians are urged to copy Paul and those like him, they are to "stand firm against" and reject another group of people, that is, to not copy them. But these warnings in terms of imitation make little sense unless they refer to particular persons who are being imitated, or not. Hence, the advocacy at Philippi of an alternative gospel involving a number of Jewish practices unacceptable to Paul, together with the presence of rival programs of imitation, suggests that groups of real people are involved on both sides of the situation. Paul and his followers, with their key practices, are being deployed over against another group whom Paul regards as dangerous in their advocacy of certain additional traditional Jewish practices.

Accordingly, we will assume from this point onward that particular persons were involved within the broader situation addressed by the Previous Letter and Philippians, and that the burden of proof will rest on those who claim otherwise — whether that Paul is laying theological groundwork in part of this passage, as against refuting someone's position throughout, or, alternatively, that he is articulating a broader "religious" position, such as an account of "Judaism" in general. I suspect that these types of interpretation will struggle to explain the concerns of the text that seem focused on specific issues and particular people who are competing with Paul for the loyalty of his Christian converts at Philippi. And with this judgment about the opposition made, we should now note a further concrete detail of the situation that has become apparent from the Previous Letter and from Philippians.

Paul's Previous Letter to Philippi suggests that he actually knew of this opposition in some sense while he was last with the Philippians, because he speaks in v. 18 of warning them verbally "many times" of these "enemies of the cross of Christ" (πολλοὶ γὰρ περιπατοῦσιν οὓς πολλάκις ἔλεγον ὑμῖν, νῦν δὲ καὶ κλαίων λέγω, τοὺς ἐχθροὺς τοῦ σταυροῦ τοῦ Χριστοῦ). We have already determined that a generic warning here is unlikely. (This statement is linked with the preceding statement and subsection by the motif of "walking," and thereby gestures toward the Jewish practices enumerated negatively in vv. 2-6. And other hints in the data seem to confirm this specificity.) So it seems that Paul already knew of the existence and danger of this group when he was last in Macedonia, and he warned the Philippians against them in terms not dissimilar to the polemical injunctions found in 3:18-19 and 21. But the details in the Previous Letter suggest that Paul did not engage in detailed instructions about this group at that time — a reconstruction of their specific agenda, of its rationale, and of various reasons why he finds it unacceptable. If he had, the detailed instructions in the Previous Letter, repeated in turn in Philippians 3, would have been redundant, as would any further future visits; Paul would have said all that he wanted to say about this threat to the Philippians in person already. So something has happened in the interim. And this shift seems to be confirmed by the travel plan that the letter to the Philippians announces. After his anticipated release from prison "soon," Paul intends to visit the Philippians (see 2:24), and we can infer with some confidence that it was probably the threat of the opponents, at least in part, that led to this, as well as to the intervening visit by Timothy (2:19). Paul presumably felt when writing Philippians that it was import-ant to visit his Macedonian congregations and to check personally on their loyalty and stability. It follows, however, that the opponents have become a direct threat to the Macedonians since he left them just previously. He knew about these opponents then, and apparently warned the Philippians repeat-edly concerning them. But he has since followed up these warnings with a polemical writing, the Previous Letter, which has been partly reiterated in Philippians, and with a set of promised and scheduled visits. Hence, it seems that the "threat level," so to speak, from these figures has escalated during this short period of time to the point that Paul now feels compelled to make a return journey to Philippi, even following his more detailed epistolary in-structions. So we should posit the arrival of these figures on the immediate scene in a way that can directly threaten the Philippian congregation after Paul's departure from Philippi, and probably from Macedonia as a whole, but just prior to the composition and dispatch of the Previous Letter, and so prior to the later composition and dispatch of the extant Philippians. Paul's announced intention to revisit the Philippians after Timothy's visit suggests this reconstruction of events.

These are all important realizations: that the opposition at Philippi was a particular single group of rival Jewish Christian leaders, and that Paul knew of them from somewhere previously but only perceived them as a direct threat to the Philippians after his departure from Macedonia — a claim that will be corroborated by our investigation of 2 Corinthians that follows.

With these insights in place, we can now turn to some of Paul's other letters and try to detect the imprint of these figures and their developing tra-jectory there. We will first consider Romans.

(ii) The opponents in Romans. It is highly significant that many of the features evident in Philippians 3:2–4:3 seem evident as well in Romans. Two similarities seem especially important, and these match the steps we have already observed within Paul's critique in the Previous Letter quite closely.

First, we should note briefly that the substantive agenda Paul delineates for the opponents in Philippians 3:2-6 seems like a compact version of an agenda that is delineated at length in Romans, especially in 1:16–5:1 and 9:30–10:17. We have not yet looked at this agenda closely, and we do not need to reconstruct it exhaustively given our present purposes. But what we can say with some confidence is that this material is distinctive within Paul's texts and hence easily identified. It contains two principal components that are interwoven.

Certain Jewish practices are in view, which Paul bitterly opposes being foisted on his pagan converts — notably, circumcision and comprehensive Torah observance. That both of these seem to be advocated by the opponents at Philippi is suggested by vv. 2b-3a ([2b] βλέπετε τοὺς κακοὺς ἐργάτας, βλέπετε τὴν κατατομήν. [3a] ἡμεῖς γάρ ἐσμεν ἡ περιτομή . . .), v. 5a (περιτομῇ ὀκταήμερος), v. 6 (κατὰ ζῆλος διώκων τὴν ἐκκλησίαν, κατὰ δικαιοσύνην τὴν ἐν νόμῳ γενόμενος ἄμεμπτος), and v. 9a (καὶ εὑρεθῶ ἐν αὐτῷ, μὴ ἔχων ἐμὴν δικαιοσύνην τὴν ἐκ νόμου . . .). And it is therefore significant that the advocacy of these practices for Christians is considered at length and rejected in Romans, especially in 1:18–5:1 and 7:1–8:14. (Circumcision is addressed directly in Rom 2:25-29; 3:30; 4:9-12).

Paul's articulations of this dangerous nomistic advocacy, along with his own Torah-flexible response, are mediated by a distinctive vocabulary — the second principal component within the broader agenda. He speaks of "works of Torah" — usually ἔργων νόμου, although signaled in Philippians by the parallel phraseology just noted in vv. 2, 6, and 9a; of "righteous activity," to adopt an uncontroversial if somewhat bland translation of δικαιοσύνη here, and this is frequently coupled with other δικαιο- terms like δικαιόω, usually rendered as "justify"; and of "faith," whether in or of Christ, and expressed in nominal or verbal form (see πίστις [Χριστοῦ] and πιστεύω). Distinctive clusters of νόμος, πίστ-, and δικαιο- terms therefore identify these texts, along with associated motifs such as [un]circumcision (see περιτομή and ἀκροβυστία). Indeed, because of the prevalence of πίστ- and δικαιο- terms, which are frequently translated in terms of "faith" and "justification," it is possible to speak simply of the "justification" texts and arguments. We learn from Romans, moreover, that these lexical and phraseological markers were derived ultimately from certain scriptural texts. Elsewhere in Paul, the citations of these texts and motifs correlate perfectly (i.e., in Rom and Gal).[18] But we do not need to resolve the complex issues surrounding the correct construal of these terms, texts, and arguments in order to draw the obvious point for framing. Irrespective of its actual meaning, the same basic agenda is clearly in play in both Philippians and Romans, and distinctively so. Only one other Pauline letter has a matching correlation of these three clusters of terms and scriptural texts, in relation to these particular practices, and we will turn to consider it shortly. Paul's letter to Rome is clearly spelling matters out much more fully, while the Previous Letter is alluding to the same argumentation more cryptically and aggressively. But these differences in depth do not obscure the fundamental substantive agreement.

We can now note, second, that, as in Philippians 3:12-15, an athletic discourse — the ἀγών motif — is subtly interwoven with much of this material in Romans. This is especially apparent in Romans 9–11. The discourse is introduced in 9:16; is developed overtly through 9:30–10:4, four references to athletics being strung through just this short subsection; and is reiterated in 11:11. That six athletic tropes are worked into the distinctive discussion of Romans 9–11, which also extensively resumes the distinctive justification terminology from 1:16–5:1 (i.e., "works of Torah," "faith," and "righteous activity"; see esp. 9:33–10:17), seems significant.[19] Again, the concerns of the Previous Letter seem resumed in Romans, although writ large in the later letter.

18. The terminology of "work of Torah" seems to derive primarily from Lev. 18:5 (καὶ φυλάξεσθε πάντα τὰ προστάγματά μου καὶ πάντα τὰ κρίματά μου καὶ ποιήσετε αὐτά, ἃ ποιήσας ἄνθρωπος ζήσεται ἐν αὐτοῖς· ἐγὼ κύριος ὁ θεὸς ὑμῶν); that of the righteousness of God from Ps 98:2 [97:2 LXX] (ἐγνώρισεν κύριος τὸ σωτήριον αὐτοῦ, ἐναντίον τῶν ἐθνῶν ἀπεκάλυψεν τὴν δικαιοσύνην αὐτοῦ) and Ps 143:1-2b [142:1-2b LXX] (καὶ μὴ εἰσέλθῃς εἰς κρίσιν μετὰ τοῦ δούλου σου, ὅτι οὐ δικαιωθήσεται ἐνώπιόν σου πᾶς ζῶν); and that of "faith" from Gen 15:6 (καὶ ἐπίστευσεν Αβραμ τῷ θεῷ, καὶ ἐλογίσθη αὐτῷ εἰς δικαιοσύνην); Hab 2:4b (ὁ δὲ δίκαιος ἐκ πίστεώς μου ζήσεται); and Isa 28:16b ([διὰ τοῦτο οὕτως λέγει κύριος Ἰδοὺ ἐγὼ ἐμβαλῶ εἰς τὰ θεμέλια Σιων λίθον πολυτελῆ ἐκλεκτὸν ἀκρογωνιαῖον ἔντιμον εἰς τὰ θεμέλια αὐτῆς] καὶ ὁ πιστεύων ἐπ' αὐτῷ οὐ μὴ καταισχυνθῇ). Other texts are involved, e.g., Joel 2:32 [3:5a LXX], but need not be mentioned here (see καὶ ἔσται ὃς, ὃς ἂν ἐπικαλέσηται τὸ ὄνομα κυρίου, σωθήσεται). These texts are not cited explicitly in Phil 3:2–4:3, but their distinctive vocabulary is present there.

19. That is, Paul uses such athletic imagery elsewhere as well (see 1 Cor 9), but not in combination with justification terminology and argumentation. The overlap between these two data sets therefore increases the likelihood that this shared use of athletic imagery is significant evidence for the presence of the same basic concerns on Paul's part here in Rom as in Phil/PLP. This material is discussed in my 2009 (esp. 789-92, where I add the important qualification that Paul seems to be trying to *subvert* this discourse in Rom, as against deploy it in a straightforward fashion as he does in Phil and elsewhere).

The third subsection in the Previous Letter is more directly aggressive concerning the advocates of Jewish Christian practices than the preceding clusters of material (see esp. 3:18-19), stating at one point that "their stomach is their god" (ὧν ὁ θεὸς ἡ κοιλία). This is a stock phrase in Greco-Roman abuse, although in this context, where Jewish practices are in view alongside Paul's distinctive pneumatological and eschatological gospel, a more delimited meaning seems possible. Nevertheless, it is true on any reading that Paul is using harsh rhetoric or invective. A phrase in v. 21 is also worth noting carefully in this relation: at the glorious return of Christ, "everything will be submitted to him" (see ὑποτάξαι αὐτῷ τὰ πάντα). Hence, the Philippians are to stand firm against these "enemies of the cross of Christ," assured of final victory.

It seems significant that the closest parallel to this directly polemical material within the Pauline corpus is Romans 16:17-20, an equally fiery passage that at one point uses almost the same descriptor. The figures being warned against there (see σκοπεῖτε in 16:17; the same verb is used on the other side of the comparison in Phil 3:17) "do not serve *the Lord Jesus but their own stomachs*" (οἱ γὰρ τοιοῦτοι τῷ κυρίῳ ἡμῶν Χριστῷ οὐ δουλεύουσιν ἀλλὰ τῇ ἑαυτῶν κοιλίᾳ). They present teaching contrary to what the Romans have learned, and have been reminded of at length by Paul (see Rom 15:15). Further, as in Philippians 3:21, victory over them is assured (Rom 16:20): "the God of peace will crush Satan under your feet shortly" (ὁ δὲ θεὸς τῆς εἰρήνης συντρίψει τὸν σατανᾶν ὑπὸ τοὺς πόδας ὑμῶν ἐν τάχει), an allusion to God's promise to Eve that her offspring would in due course crush the serpent's head (see Gen 3:15: αὐτός σου τηρήσει κεφαλήν), as well as to Pss 8:6 and 110:1.[20]

Many scholars have struggled with the aggression of Romans 16:17-20, some going so far as to suggest that it is an interpolation.[21] But there is a simpler, not to mention better attested solution. Here at the end of the letter, where critical matters were often positioned, the main reason for Paul's composition of Romans breaks through overtly in this patch of invective that parallels Philippians 3:15-21 so closely. The same figures that concerned Paul in the Previous Letter and Philippians 3:2–4:3, Jewish Christian rivals whom Paul views as "enemies of the cross of Christ," lie behind the fulsome refutations of Romans as well. Moreover, with this parallel, it can now be seen that each of the three subsections in the Previous Letter has received an equivalent development in Romans. The distinctive substantive concerns developed by way of justification

20. See my 2009 (697 and nn. 63-64). This material was also briefly noted in ch. 2, as part of a possible doublet of peace wishes at the end of Rom; see also 15:33.
21. I provide some rebuttal for this suggestion in 2009 (513-15).

terminology and argumentation, the interwoven athletic discourse, *and* the direct polemic against dangerous satanic adversaries are all held in common between Philippians and Romans. And in the light of these parallels, we have reason to believe that the same opponents are circulating at this time through Paul's mission field, and that he fears their arrival in Rome as much as he fears their arrival in Macedonia. But we also have reason to suspect that although Paul knew of them himself before he last visited Macedonia, they did not become a direct local threat to his communities until after he had left Macedonia with the Macedonians' contributions to the collection and arrived in Corinth. This suspicion is confirmed by a brief reconsideration of 2 Corinthians.

(iii) The opponents in 2 Corinthians. It needs to be emphasized again at the outset of this brief discussion that we do not need to provide a comprehensive account of "the super-apostles" here (the name we will use to designate the opposition Paul is engaging in much of 2 Cor, following the apostle's own lead in 11:5 and 12:11; we will call Paul's opponents in the Previous Letter to Philippi, Phil, and Rom his "enemies," following his lead in Phil 3:18). We need only to determine whether they are the same as the group of opponents just identified in the Previous Letter, Philippians, and Romans. Were the "super-apostles" also the "enemies"? And as far as I can tell, three simple and obvious contentions stand against an identification, while the one argument apparently in favor of it turns out on closer examination to be weaker than it first appears.

We must of course resist needlessly multiplying the opponents — a road to reconstructive perdition. But we must also resist oversimplifying the data and flattening out important distinctions in the interest of explanatory economy. As Einstein is said to have urged, *everything should be as simple as possible, but not simpler.* So here we will open up the frame to the possibility that through his Aegean period, as Käsemann famously asserted, Paul had to fight a war on two fronts — against the super-apostles and against the enemies.[22] We will refrain, as we go forward, from complicating things further.

---

22. Käsemann's classic account of this war is rather more Lutheran than mine. See esp. his essay entitled "Justification and Salvation History in the Epistle to the Romans" (1971, 60-78); in his opinion, in broad terms, Paul fought, on the one hand, against the "enthusiasts," i.e., the charismatic radicals presaging Münster, not to mention later Pietists, and on the other, against the "legalists," i.e., proto-Catholics. I do not see the data aligning in quite this fashion, although Käsemann's view by no means lacks insights. Käsemann *himself* fought a war on two fronts — against Rudolf Bultmann's overly individualistic interpretation of Paul's gospel, and against overly salvation-historical interpretations as found in (i.a.) Krister Stendahl and Oscar Cullmann.

Nevertheless, for the purposes of framing, it seems necessary to make this basic preliminary distinction.

First, there seems to be little or no match between the substantive concerns of 2 Corinthians and the substantive agenda Paul debates in the Previous Letter, Philippians, and Romans in relation to the enemies. Although justification terminology occurs occasionally in 2 Corinthians, it never functions in the distinctive collocation in which it is found in the letters engaging with the enemies, and it is vestigial. Indeed, Torah observance is never addressed in 2 Corinthians — except, that is, as a hermeneutical phenomenon, as in 2 Corinthians 3, but this concern is rather different from the ethical anxieties informing Paul's treatment of Torah in relation to the enemies. Faith occurs sporadically, as it does in all of Paul's letters, but never in relation to righteous activity or in opposition to Torah observance (see the occurrence of the noun in 1:24 [2x]; 4:13; 5:7; 8:7; 10:15; 13:5; and of the verb only in 4:13, although there twice; this text cites Ps 115:10 LXX, which uses the verb). Meanwhile, righteousness terminology occurs sporadically — once rather famously if opaquely in 5:21 (see, in addition, 3:9; 6:7, 14; 9:9-10 [2x, the first instance here being a citation of Ps 111:9 LXX]; 11:15; the cognate verb does not occur) — and again, in splendid isolation from other justification concerns. There is then little or no match between justification material and 2 Corinthians, suggesting that the substantive agenda of the enemies is not in play in 2 Corinthians.

Second, matching this aporia in terms of justification material, the dominant substantive concerns of 2 Corinthians find little or no match in the concerns of the Previous Letter, Philippians, and Romans. We can draw here on our earlier investigations in chapter 2 concerning questions of partition in 2 Corinthians and recall that the letter is largely concerned with ethical lapses, disloyalty, and partisanship among the Corinthian Christians. Paul's leadership is clearly being hotly debated, and this raises important theological matters, but the letter is concerned (to put things summarily) with matters of apostolic style rather than soteriological substance, and this does not seem to have been in contention in the same way in the Previous Letter, Philippians, and Romans. (We will broaden this distinction considerably in a moment when we turn to Galatians.) Moreover, the main substantive concerns in relation to the enemies are focused on rejecting certain Jewish practices. Paul seems to be strenuously opposing his auditors' adoption of Jewish practices such as circumcision, and in Romans, especially chapter 14, he is nuancing any adoption of temporal or dietary observances as well. But much of 2 Corinthians, like 1 Corinthians, is actually urging the Corinthians to *embrace* certain Jewish practices more enthusiastically, notably in relation to sexual behavior. So here Paul's argument is running in the opposite direction.

Third, just as there is little or no presence of the agenda of the enemies in 2 Corinthians, and of the agenda of the super-apostles in the Previous Letter, Philippians, and Romans, athletic imagery is absent from 2 Corinthians. First Corinthians uses athletic imagery, but this is hardly surprising in and of itself. As we have already intimated, the discourse was widespread in Greco-Roman antiquity. However, it does seem significant that this discourse is never interwoven with justification material there, the location it occupies distinctively in the Previous Letter, Philippians, and Romans, and hence, by implication, in the teaching of the enemies. Meanwhile, 2 Corinthians is utterly silent concerning this discourse.

By this point, then, we can see that neither of the concerns of the first two subsections in the Previous Letter — the material concerns of Paul with the enemies couched in terms of justification; and the careful appeal, in the right terms, to athletic imagery — are present in 2 Corinthians, nor are the main concerns of 2 Corinthians present in the Previous Letter. So a match between the two groups of opponents looks highly unlikely.

It might be replied that at least one element within Paul's critique of the enemies in the Previous Letter is present in 2 Corinthians, namely, invective. The super-apostles are certainly described in 2 Corinthians in terms as harsh as those used in Philippians 3:18-19 and Romans 16:17-20, and terminology and phraseology seems at times to overlap quite directly. The super-apostles too are servants of Satan (see 2 Cor 11:13-15 and Rom 16:20), and "deceitful workers" (cf. ἐργάται δόλιοι in 2 Cor 11:13 with "the evil workers" in Phil 3:2: τοὺς κακοὺς ἐργάτας). At first glance, this might suggest a degree of overlap, the substantive differences between Paul's other treatments perhaps then being explicable on grounds of development or increasing information or some similar factor. But similarity in invective and related linguistic terminology is hardly a strong ground for an identification of reference; for terminology devoted to the vilification of powerful opponents to be held in common across different particular figures seems unsurprising (and a further plausible explanation for this phenomenon will be suggested in any case in due course). So the judgment that the super-apostles treated in 2 Corinthians were distinct from the enemies of the Previous Letter, Philippians, and Romans still holds, and this fits in with our gathering suspicions that the arrival of the enemies in Paul's immediate locale postdated his departure from Macedonia, where we know that he wrote 2 Corinthians. Second Corinthians suggests that the enemies were not in direct view at its time of writing. In Corinth, however, they were — which allows us to make an important sequencing suggestion.

We are already aware of a sequence of letters written by Paul to Philippi: the Previous Letter, part of which was quoted again in Philippians 3:2–4:3, and the letter preserved in full and known to us as "Philippians," which was the second communication historically within the series. Moreover, these letters seem to have been written after Paul had left the Macedonian communities. An urgent exigence had arisen since then, to which he was now responding by writing letters, and by promising a future visit. The urgency of the situation is suggested by the polemical tone of the Previous Letter; by the composition and dispatch of a second letter, part of which quoted the Previous Letter; and by Paul's dispatch of Timothy to Macedonia on an imminent visit (although subsequent to Epaphroditus's departure), despite Paul's expectation that he would soon be released from imprisonment and able to travel to Philippi himself. This generates the following short sequence.

— Visit to Macedonia —
arrival of the enemies / [PLP] — Phil —
Timothy VM — Paul VM —

And it should be fairly clear by now that this sequence fits neatly into our developing "epistolary backbone" after 2 Corinthians and near to Romans, which would suggest locating Paul's imprisonment and the composition of these letters to Philippi at Corinth. In 2 Corinthians, written from Macedonia, the enemies are not yet in view — although the super-apostles certainly are (and this is a significant problem for the main alternative location to Corinth at this time, namely, Ephesus).[23] But by the time Paul writes Romans from

23. That is, Ephesus has been the most popular candidate for those attuned to the possibility of Paul writing letters from an incarceration in the middle of his Aegean period. This was suggested some time ago by one of the great Pauline interpreters, G. Adolf Deissmann (1923), and argued in English-speaking circles by those influenced by him. In fact, Deissmann's advocacy of the view considerably preceded his published opinion in 1923; by this time, he had already influenced B. Robinson (1910). The view is most closely associated in English-speaking scholarship with another figure influenced by Deissmann, George Duncan (1929), who published the first monograph-length treatment — and suggested that it was first proposed by Origen! See also Duncan (1931-32); and subsequently (i.a.) Riddle (1940); Koester (1995). This hypothesis tends to lean on Acts' assertions that Paul spent as many as three years based in Ephesus (see 19:8, 10, 22; 20:31), which offers enough time for the imprisonment and journeys that we see in Phil. But we have no way of knowing yet whether Acts' data is reliable, so that to follow this suggestion would be to work inappropriately in terms of that source's frame. We must

Corinth, the enemies themselves are receiving a subtle and powerful response from the apostle, along with one or two barbed rejoinders. So the Philippian correspondence and sequence maps very nicely into this interval, which is oriented by Corinth.[24]

(3) Corinthian Nebenadressat in Philippians

In an almost disturbingly optimistic passage in Philippians, Paul describes his imprisonment in highly positive terms (so 1:12: Γινώσκειν δὲ ὑμᾶς βούλομαι, ἀδελφοί, ὅτι τὰ κατ᾽ ἐμὲ μᾶλλον εἰς προκοπὴν τοῦ εὐαγγελίου ἐλήλυθεν). First, news of Christ has spread through the governor's residence by means of his imprisonment (v. 13: ὥστε τοὺς δεσμούς μου φανεροὺς ἐν Χριστῷ γενέσθαι ἐν ὅλῳ τῷ πραιτωρίῳ καὶ τοῖς λοιποῖς πάσιν). Second, the majority of the local Christians have been emboldened to proclaim the Christian position without fear (see esp. v. 14: καὶ τοὺς πλείονας τῶν ἀδελφῶν ἐν κυρίῳ πεποιθότας τοῖς δεσμοῖς μου περισσοτέρως τολμᾶν ἀφόβως τὸν λόγον λαλεῖν). But third, Paul turns in v. 15 to describe a situation whose familiarity to later readers should not be allowed to override its extraordinary information about the local church.

[1:15] τινὲς μὲν καὶ διὰ φθόνον καὶ ἔριν, τινὲς δὲ καὶ δι᾽ εὐδοκίαν τὸν Χριστὸν κηρύσσουσιν· [16] οἱ μὲν ἐξ ἀγάπης, εἰδότες ὅτι εἰς ἀπολογίαν τοῦ εὐαγγελίου κεῖμαι, [17] οἱ δὲ ἐξ ἐριθείας τὸν Χριστὸν καταγγέλλουσιν, οὐχ ἁγνῶς, οἰόμενοι θλῖψιν ἐγείρειν τοῖς δεσμοῖς μου. [18a] Τί γάρ; πλὴν ὅτι παντὶ τρόπῳ, εἴτε προφάσει εἴτε ἀληθείᾳ, Χριστὸς καταγγέλλεται, καὶ ἐν τούτῳ χαίρω.

---

therefore evaluate the claim solely in terms of the epistolary evidence, which is not especially convincing. Ephesus (or, alternatively perhaps, Pergamum) seems an unlikely if not impossible option because of the need for a preceding and largely innocuous Macedonian visit to be reflected in Phil. Phil would also then be puzzlingly silent about the collection, and its optimistic account of Paul's imprisonment would seem incommensurate with the 2 Cor account of Paul's crisis in Asia (see 2 Cor 1:8-10).

24. Rome seems unlikely because of its temporal distance from any Macedonian visit in the past; it could not explain the urgency of the situation. It would also require that the crisis caused by the enemies unfolded suddenly during Paul's incarceration at Rome, which seems unlikely if not impossible — either this, or a long period of time would need to be interposed between PLP and Phil, which seems implausible. In fact, Thessalonica is the most plausible alternative at this point, but it will be excluded by the evidence adduced in the subsection that follows, which rather nicely corroborates Corinth — in terms of Nebenadressat.

Some local Christians, Paul states here, are proclaiming Christ out of a partisan spirit. Indeed, they are proclaiming him insincerely (οὐχ ἁγνῶς), apparently in the hope of making Paul's imprisonment and trial more difficult (see οἰόμενοι θλῖψιν ἐγείρειν τοῖς δεσμοῖς μου). Paul uses a particular lexicon to describe these hostile evangelists. They are characterized by φθόνος,[25] ἔρις,[26] and προφάσις.[27] It seems reasonably significant, then, that we find some of these terms occurring elsewhere in direct description of the Corinthians. In 1 Corinthians 1:11 Paul says, ἐδηλώθη γάρ μοι περὶ ὑμῶν, ἀδελφοί μου, ὑπὸ τῶν Χλόης ὅτι ἔριδες ἐν ὑμῖν εἰσιν. And in 2 Corinthians 12:20 he reuses this word, adding ζῆλος, θυμοί, ἐριθείαί, καταλαλιαί, ψιθυρισμοί, φυσιώσεις [καί] ἀκαταστασίαι for good measure, to describe what he fears he will find upon arrival in Corinth for his third visit.

This evidence is so overt that there is no need to labor the point. The deeply divided local church that Paul articulates explicitly in Philippians looks very much like Corinth. The use of the same terminology alone would not be enough to establish the same referent, as just noted above in relation to Paul's polemics with similar words referencing different opponents, but it is coordinated here with a particular concrete situation in the community. A majority of the local community seems tentatively pro-Paul (see τοὺς πλείονας τῶν ἀδελφῶν). But a minority seems partisan and profoundly hostile. We have no extant evidence of any other Pauline church with this level of division and a minority faction this hostile to Paul. Paul never uses these negative terms to describe another one of his communities directly. And in the light of this explicit evidence in terms of the encoded audience, further hints in Philippians in terms of *Nebenadressat* now take on more weight than might otherwise be the case, corroborating the developing suspicion that the community surrounding Paul when he wrote Philippians was Corinthian.

One of the overriding concerns of Philippians is unity. This is a sustained theme in the letter, receiving multiple developments, and it grounds one of the most famous christological paragraphs that Paul ever penned (2:5-11). But it is arguably underdetermined by the actual situation that Philippians addresses at Philippi — two women in conflict over an unspecified issue (4:2-3) and the possibility of external opposition (see esp. 1:28 and 3:2). Paul's rhetoric does not seem entirely in keeping with these contingent realities at

---

25. See elsewhere in the Pauline canon Rom 1:29; Gal 5:21; 1 Tim 6:4; Titus 3:3.

26. See Rom 1:29; 13:13; 1 Cor 1:11; 3:3; 2 Cor 12:20; Gal 5:20; 1 Tim 6:4; Titus 3:9; see also the closely related ἐριθεία in Rom 2:8; 2 Cor 12:20; Gal 5:20; Phil 2:3.

27. See 1 Thess 2:5.

Philippi, although he may of course just be demonstrating a degree of heavy-handedness or incompetence in this. However, once we recall the location of the letter's composition, the emphasis seems plausibly explained. In this sustained emphasis on unity, Paul is speaking not just to the Philippians but to the letter's *Nebenadressat,* the Corinthians, a community riven by conflicts revolving around status differentials and assertions. They clearly *do* need to continue to hear this sort of admonition. A brief rehearsal here of the relevant data should suffice to make this point firmly.

Paul's explication of unity begins in 1:27; worthy political contention on behalf of the proclamation of Christ entails standing firm in one spirit and contending with one mind so that in no way are the Philippians dismayed by those who oppose them. Paul's exhortations to unity in the face of pressure and suffering then continue essentially uninterrupted through to his famous account of the incarnate and suffering Christ in 2:5-11. But he prefaces this Christology with an exhortation to the Philippians to renounce any claim to status in behalf of unity: [2:2] πληρώσατέ μου τὴν χαρὰν ἵνα τὸ αὐτὸ φρονῆτε, τὴν αὐτὴν ἀγάπην ἔχοντες, σύμψυχοι, τὸ ἓν φρονοῦντες [3] μηδὲν κατ᾽ ἐριθείαν μηδὲ κατὰ κενοδοξίαν ἀλλὰ τῇ ταπεινοφροσύνῃ ἀλλήλους ἡγούμενοι ὑπερέχοντας ἑαυτῶν, [4] μὴ τὰ ἑαυτῶν ἕκαστος σκοποῦντες ἀλλὰ καὶ τὰ ἑτέρων ἕκαστοι. This exhortation then undergirds the introduction in v. 5 to the powerful christological material that follows: [5] Τοῦτο φρονεῖτε ἐν ὑμῖν ὃ καὶ ἐν Χριστῷ Ἰησοῦ. . . . But Paul's concern with unity is evident through much of the rest of the letter as well.

Timothy is an example of someone who does not seek his own interests (2:19-23). Epaphroditus exemplifies the same with his concern for the Philippians in the midst of his own illness and his preparedness to die on behalf of Christ (2:25-30). Paul then names names in chapter 4: he pleads with Euodia and Syntyche to be of one mind with one another (4:2), assisted by their "loyal comrade" and Clement, although he supplies no details concerning the dispute between these two women, which makes evaluating its significance difficult. After this, the letter characteristically moves on to positive exhortations in terms of joy and peace — a peace now understood to lie, not only in participation, beyond the flesh, in the mind of Christ, but also in constant striving for a unified community.

When this evidence is introduced alongside the direct evidence already adduced in Philippians in relation to Corinth, the suspicion is reinforced that Paul's sustained emphasis on unity in the letter, along with its elaborate theological basis and repeated references to concrete exemplars, has more in view than two women at Philippi, although clearly it does place their conflict in the foreground. Paul's repeated appeals to abdicate status and to place others first are intended for Corinth as well. But this consideration of the rhetoric of unity does not exhaust the text's pointed inferences in terms of *Nebenadressat*. Two more indications in Philippians are noteworthy.

In the last major section in the letter — or, alternatively, in a major and somewhat distinct subsection within the letter ending — Paul responds to a gift of money that Epaphroditus has brought from Philippi (see 4:11-19). Paul spends nine verses dancing around his receipt of this offering, beginning in a way that can seem positively churlish. For three verses he describes how this was largely unnecessary — and this in response to a visit that almost cost the messenger his life — because he has learned the secret of living in all circumstances, whether impoverished or abundant. In v. 14 he seems to concede that the Philippians nevertheless "did well to join together with him in his suffering" (see πλὴν καλῶς ἐποιήσατε συγκοινωνήσαντές μου τῇ θλίψει). In the next two verses, Paul then tells a short story about how they supported his original mission in Thessalonica, and then beyond, in material terms, although he seems again to qualify the narrative immediately by claiming that he was never seeking a gift in this but a harvest that would accrue to the givers' heavenly account (see 4:17, read as a historical present, although not much rides on this: οὐχ ὅτι ἐπιζητῶ τὸ δόμα, ἀλλὰ ἐπιζητῶ τὸν καρπὸν τὸν πλεονάζοντα εἰς λόγον ὑμῶν).[28]

Only after these two extended qualifications do we come to the point where Paul acknowledges fulsomely receiving this gift from the Philippians (v. 18), although even here he never actually says "thank you." And he immediately adds the further qualification that his God will respond by filling all the Philippians' needs out of the riches found "in glory" and "in Christ Jesus" (v. 19), rounding off the entire paragraph doxologically.

What are we to make of this oddly convoluted response to the Philippians' generosity, this "thankless thanks" that is carefully qualified no less than three times — by strong affirmations of Paul's autarky, by a narrative of missionary support that is not a gift per se but an addition to the account of the givers, and by a strong affirmation of God's reciprocal enrichment in return? We could posit in the first instance a fraught relationship with the Philippians.

28. Briones (2011, esp. 47-50) gives a succinct summary of recent debate, noting the prevalence of the view of Peterman (1991; 1997), which seeks to explain the absence of thanks in terms of evidence from certain papyri that close friends did not need to offer thanks in words (despite, that is, doing so by way of such disavowals); Briones appeals instead to a brokerage analysis. My suggestion is that these notions should be supplemented by the more contingent and less convoluted explanation of Paul's rhetoric that follows here.

But there is no evidence of that; rather, the Philippians seem to have been the most loyal and committed of all of Paul's communities. Moreover, this narrative would seem to undermine rather than to affirm the relationship, in its studied avoidance of sheer gratitude. But we can explain Paul's careful qualifications in the light of the situation at Corinth, where money was a deeply sensitive issue.

It is not necessary to reconstruct completely here the Corinthian critique of Paul in relation to money. It will suffice to note three issues. First, Paul seems to have refused to accept money from the Corinthians when evangelizing them, although he did accept money at the time from other communities who seem to be identified here specifically as the Philippians (see Phil 4:15, where Paul speaks of support after leaving Macedonia; see also 2 Cor 11:9). This may well have been in part an attempt to avoid characterization as a client.[29] But it caused ongoing difficulties at Corinth (see esp. 1 Cor 9; 2 Cor 11:7-11; 12:13-16). Second, as we have already seen at some length, Paul nevertheless went on to ask for the collection of a large sum of money that he said was destined for Jerusalem (1 Cor 16:1-4; 2 Cor 8 and 9), and one suspects that the Corinthians were among the key donors to that project, the congregation containing wealthy members (see 1 Cor 1:26). And third, this project created a further vulnerability for Paul. It seems to have given rise to accusations of fraud — specifically, that although nobly (or arrogantly) eschewing direct personal support from the Corinthians, he nevertheless intended to abscond with this even larger sum that he was raising ostensibly for the Christian community in Jerusalem (see arguably 2 Cor 12:17-18). Thus, in the light of these criticisms circulating at Corinth, Paul's convoluted response to the gift of money from the Philippians makes perfect sense. Indeed, the arrival *of* a gift of money from the Philippians during his imprisonment at Corinth put him in a difficult situation!

Paul has no actual need of such direct support, he says. As he claims famously, "I can do everything that I need to do [and presumably survive it] through Christ, the one who strengthens me" (see 4:13: πάντα ἰσχύω ἐν τῷ ἐνδυναμοῦντί με). He will not necessarily look very impressive as a result, perhaps as he labors with his hands night and day (see 2 Cor 10:10b; 1 Thess 2:9). But at least he will thereby avoid a charge of charlatanism — and also avoid accepting the obligations of a client. Paul does accept aid if it is in support of mission in *another* place, in this case from another previously established community, although again this functions primarily to bless the givers, in their

29. The thesis of (i.a.) P. Marshall (1987), and there seems to be at least some truth in it.

heavenly accounts, and not the recipient. Moreover, such giving is therefore primarily to God — a fragrant sacrifice and pleasing and appropriate offering (so v. 18b) — which will entail obligations of reciprocity, insofar as they are activated, *from* God, and not primarily from Paul himself.

We see, then, that in crafting this response to the Philippians' gift, Paul has ingeniously threaded the financial needle at Corinth. He has preserved his original financial posture of autarky at Corinth. But since this can clearly cause fund-raising difficulties for further projects in terms of mission and benefaction, not to mention vulnerabilities, he has emphasized alternative rationales for giving that reinforce what the Corinthians have already heard (see esp. 2 Cor 8 and 9). Giving is a good idea, on numerous grounds, but entails no reciprocal obligation on Paul's part.

If these brief characterizations hold good, then once again a carefully nuanced discussion in Philippians that seems underdetermined on strictly contingent grounds, in terms of the Philippians themselves, seems fully comprehensible once the Corinthian *Nebenadressat* have been taken into account. (Nowhere else do we read in Paul's letters of the financial complexities and criticisms that we find associated with Corinth, which seem to be in play in Phil 4:11-19.) And with this second aspect of the Corinthian *Nebenadressat* identified, we can turn to consider a third.

In Philippians 2:19-23, as we have already seen, Paul announces a pending visit from Timothy, who is one of the co-senders of the letter (see 1:1). But Paul's characterization of Timothy, who is already known to the Philippians (see 2:22a: τὴν δὲ δοκιμὴν αὐτοῦ γινώσκετε), is strangely extended and even defensive. He writes, in hyperbolic terms, "I have no one else who is so equivalent to me in soul — who is sincerely concerned about everything to do with you" (2:20: οὐδένα γὰρ ἔχω ἰσόψυχον, ὅστις γνησίως τὰ περὶ ὑμῶν μεριμνήσει). Indeed, "everyone else," presumably by way of comparison, "seeks their own concerns and not those of Jesus Christ" (v. 21), while Timothy has served the gospel with the devotion of a valued slave and the dedication of a son (v. 22).

Such comments are, strictly speaking, unnecessary vis-à-vis the Philippians, who seem loyal to Paul and already know Timothy. That is, Paul's hyperbolic insistence on Timothy's character and importance seem to be underdetermined by the Philippian situation. But they are again readily explained by Corinthian *Nebenadressat*.

Timothy appears in most of Paul's letters. But only in the Corinthian correspondence and here does Paul engage in extended defense of his importance and character. In 1 Corinthians Paul already seems worried about Timothy's reception at Corinth (see esp. 16:10-11); his instructions there are filled with foreboding: [10] Ἐὰν δὲ ἔλθῃ Τιμόθεος, βλέπετε ἵνα ἀφόβως γένηται πρὸς ὑμᾶς· τὸ γὰρ ἔργον κυρίου ἐργάζεται ὡς κἀγώ· [11] μή τις οὖν αὐτὸν ἐξουθενήσῃ. προπέμψατε δὲ αὐτὸν ἐν εἰρήνῃ, ἵνα ἔλθῃ πρός με· ἐκδέχομαι γὰρ αὐτὸν μετὰ τῶν ἀδελφῶν. And in 2 Corinthians Timothy's place at Corinth has been taken by Titus. It seems that the Corinthians do not respect Timothy — who is apparently a deeply unimpressive and even underconfident figure — even as some of them have little time for Paul. And this explains Paul's remarks concerning Timothy in Philippians 2:19-23. While the apostle's hyperbolic introduction there makes little sense given what we know of the Philippians, it makes perfect sense given what we know of the Corinthians.

In short, the Corinthians seem to be the most plausible *Nebenadressat* of the letter to the Philippians. Paul articulates a bitterly divided church in his immediate locale using terms that he deploys elsewhere to describe the Corinthians but no one else. The letter then contains a sustained emphasis on unity effected especially by an abdication of status, provides a nuanced account of financial giving, and affirms the character and importance of Timothy, all of which make little sense at Philippi in these emphatic and extended forms but would certainly have resonated appropriately at Corinth. These considerations all function to reinforce our confidence in the earlier judgment that Corinth is the most plausible location for both the Previous Letter to Philippi and Philippians within our existing frame. Indeed, in view of the accumulated evidence, I suggest that the case turns out to be surprisingly strong for the location of Philippians at Corinth.

This provenance is certainly not often suggested by Paul's modern interpreters, but arguably this only demonstrates the widespread hold that Acts data has (illegitimately) on initial framing decisions for Paul's letters. Clearly, there is quite a bit to be said for Corinth as the location of Philippians in epistolary terms, so we will proceed in these terms until persuaded otherwise (and it is worth noting that later data will "lock in" this location strongly, and from multiple angles). We should now ask where Philippians fits specifically within our existing frame.

We have established that Philippians should be positioned in Corinth. However, we do not yet know whether Philippians was written before or after Romans. Either alternative seems possible — and I suspect that a definitive answer to this question is impossible, certainly at this point. But fortunately, not a lot turns on an exact judgment here just yet (and additional data later might help generate further precision). If we take the endings of the two extant letters at their word, then it makes *marginally* more sense to sequence both the Previous Letter to Philippi and Philippians prior to Romans.

Romans anticipates in sweeping terms a journey by Paul to Jerusalem, followed by a journey to Spain by way of Rome (15:23-25, 28-29), and apparently fairly immediately. It is as if Paul is dispatching Romans in one direction, to the west, just as he embarks in the other direction, to the east, with a party of companions guarding the collection. It is, however, entirely possible that a visit to Macedonia led off this journey to Jerusalem — the visit, that is, that the letter to the Philippians promises the Philippians themselves.[30] The imprisonment implied by Philippians would then have taken place prior to the composition of Romans, at some time during the previous winter. After the release anticipated in Philippians, Paul would have crafted Romans and departed on his promised visits — and perhaps Romans was itself conceptualized to a significant extent during this Corinthian incarceration.

If Philippians follows Romans, however, we have to posit an important change in expectations. A charge, arrest, imprisonment, and trial must unfold — and presumably rather rapidly — after the dispatch of Romans but before Paul's actual departure for Jerusalem. So Paul's expectations in Romans are not immediately realized.

Now, this is certainly not impossible. But we have no explicit data yet that might suggest this shift. So we will simply endorse the most straightforward scenario for now, aware that it will be helpfully reassessed in due course. These decisions generate the following sequence.

$$\ldots [PLC] - 1\ Cor - 2\ Cor -$$
$$[PLP]^{Phil\ 3:2-4:3} - \mathbf{Phil} - Rom \ldots^{31}$$

The more extended account of the frame, including the arrival of the enemies spoken of in the Previous Letter to Philippi, Philippians, and Romans — that is, the enemies' visit to Corinth — is then as follows, assuming that the composition and dispatch of the Previous Letter followed so quickly after the arrival of the enemies that these events can be treated within the same basic interval.

$$\ldots Paul\ VC2 \ldots$$
$$//\ year\ change(s)\ //$$
$$\ldots Apollos\ VC1\ /\ [PLC] - Corinthian\ VEs\ /\ [Corinthian\ reply] -$$
$$//\ year\ change\ //$$

---

30. This is an important datum I will return to consider in due course, although in another study, since Acts data needs to be involved.

31. The alternative would be: . . . [PLC] — 1 Cor — 2 Cor — [PLP]^{Phil 3:2-4:3} / Rom — Phil . . . ; not much changes either way.

— 1 Cor (LT) — Apollos VC2 / super-apostles VC — Titus VC1 —
Asian crisis
— 2 Cor / Titus VC2 — Paul VC3 — enemies VC / [PLP]Phil 3:2–4:3 — **Phil** —
// year change //
... Rom — Paul VJ ...

And with all these realizations in place, we are as ready as we can be for the crucial framing discussion concerning the location of Galatians in relation to our developing sequence.

2. Locating Galatians

2.1 Preliminary Methodological Considerations

Debate of this critical question is highly confused. A great deal of data seemingly needs to be mutually coordinated, on which it is difficult to achieve any clarity, let alone some point of decisive purchase. Modern interpreters customarily debate whether the Galatians were "northern," that is, ethnic Gauls from the center of the Roman province, or "southern," that is, mere provincials inhabiting colonies along the Via Sebaste in the southern part of the province. They have to weigh simultaneously the number of visits Paul has made to Jerusalem from competing claims in different data sets. The letter itself knows of only two (1:18-19; 2:1-10), but Acts has at least three viable candidates in play, and possibly four (9:26-30; 11:30; 15:2-29; 18:22b). And there is the obvious resonance between Galatians and Romans to take into account.

Much of this initial complexity and even confusion can be clarified, however, by the introduction of the correct attitude to the sources. The questions of the precise geographical location of the letter's recipients and of the number of visits Paul has made to Jerusalem arise in earnest only once data from Acts is introduced. That data is important and will be considered carefully in due course, but this is not the right point for that consideration. If we bracket Acts out for the moment, then many of our initial questions subside, along with much of the initial confusion within the discussion. This will allow us to focus on the key issues apparent in the data at this stage of the broader discussion. But our principal question does remain, along with some awkward secondary puzzles. We need to find a reason to place Galatians either within or in relation to our developing frame decisively. And we encounter some puzzling blanks in the data of Galatians itself as we approach these questions.

Unusually, Paul does not mention the source of his information about the evident crisis in Galatia. Nor does he provide a detailed travelogue. If ever one expected the announcement of a pending and urgent visit, it would be in this letter, and yet the only thing we have approaching such a plan is an expression of frustration that he wants to visit but cannot, a wish that is left completely unexplained (see 4:20: ἤθελον δὲ παρεῖναι πρὸς ὑμᾶς ἄρτι καὶ ἀλλάξαι τὴν φωνήν μου, ὅτι ἀποροῦμαι ἐν ὑμῖν). But this lack of the usual data concerning Paul's sources and plans does not just handicap the later interpreter in answering the basic questions; it is part of the letter's rhetorical dynamic and so ought to be explained plausibly as its provenance is interpreted, if it can be. Hence, plenty of difficulties remain to confront at this stage in our overarching analysis, even without the complications generated by the premature insertion of Acts into the discussion.

Having grappled with all of this for some time now, I have come to the conclusion that at this preliminary and provisional stage in analysis, working with epistolary data alone, there is one principal contention that locates Galatians fairly decisively and explains its puzzling aporia. But it is not Knox's contention that 2:10 obviously concerns the collection, because this is simply not the case. Galatians 2:10 *might* refer to the collection, but this claim must be developed in relation to other data and can only ever achieve the status of a corroborative argument. In my view, it is the opposition that is the key to the location of Galatians; hence, the prior locations of Philippians and of the Previous Letter to Philippi within the epistolary "spine" are the critical preliminaries for a satisfactory case in relation to Galatians. Accordingly, if the judgments just made with respect to those texts are reliable, then Galatians can be placed with a high degree of confidence within our developing sequence. This location can be corroborated by two further arguments concerning the collection for Jerusalem and the most likely *Nebenadressat*. Galatians resonates strongly with a Corinthian locale, and grasping this aspect of the letter's provenance will resolve another long-standing question in Galatian studies, namely, the apparent shift in direction within the letter as Paul turns to address certain ethical concerns at 5:13.

We will thus try to position Galatians within our developing frame principally by way of a consideration of the opposition in view, and then try to support this judgment with the two arguments just noted — in terms of the collection and of the appropriateness of a Corinthian point of origin for many of the letter's concerns. After this set of moves, by virtue of the wealth of further biographical information that Galatians introduces, we will have generated a workable extended biographical frame for Paul, at which moment we can pivot to address a possible external reference and date, in this chapter's final section.

2.2 The Opponents

We have already seen in the previous section, which addressed the opponents in Philippians, that a group of "enemies" seems to have elicited a cluster of letters by Paul while he was in Corinth: the Previous Letter to Philippi, Philippians, and Romans. Three aspects of Paul's engagement with these figures enabled a basic identification of the same figures in each of these letters sufficient to link them within the same broad situation: (1) the presence of a substantive agenda advocating circumcision and comprehensive Torah observance, which Paul counters using scriptural language, thereby generating (2) a distinctive accompanying discourse that correlates "works," "faith," and "righteousness," and (3) the presence of interlaced athletic metaphors. We will note in what follows that Galatians too contains all the hallmarks of Paul's rhetoric vis-à-vis the "enemies," suggesting its location within this short letter sequence.

That Paul's letter to the Galatians contains the justification discourse hardly needs to be demonstrated. It famously discusses righteousness, justification, faith, and works of Torah, intensively. These terms are especially concentrated from 2:15 through much of chapter 3, recurring in small subsections later in the letter, most notably in 5:5-6. As in Romans, moreover, the close relationship between these terms and phrases and Scripture is readily apparent, Galatians citing key scriptural texts in an especially concentrated fashion in 3:6-14 (Gen 15:6; 12:3/18:18; Deut 27:26; Hab 2:4; Lev 18:5; Deut 21:23). Equally significantly, however, Galatians is overtly concerned to counter the suggestion that Paul's Galatian pagan converts be circumcised, one of the key Jewish practices apparently advocated by the enemies to which Paul is deeply opposed (see 2:3; 5:2-3; 6:12-13, 15). But broader Torah observance is clearly also being advocated (see 2:15-21; 3:3; 4:5-12, 21; 5:1-4). In short, that the substantive agenda of the enemies as attested by the Previous Letter to Philippi / Philippians 3 and Romans is being engaged by Galatians, along with its distinctive scriptural discourse, is obvious.

Galatians is not as overtly committed to athletic metaphors as is the Previous Letter / Philippians 3. However, the use of these in Romans is subtle, and much the same situation holds for Galatians. The discourse comes to the surface overtly in 5:7-8, where Paul applies it pejoratively to the enemies. The Galatians were running a good race. Hence, those who have "cut in on you" are not being persuasive in a truthful way, Paul suggests (and one wonders whether this is not also a cunning pun on the "cutting" involved with circumcision; see [5:7] Ἐτρέχετε καλῶς· τίς ὑμᾶς ἐνέκοψεν τῇ ἀληθείᾳ μὴ πείθεσθαι; [8] ἡ πεισμονὴ οὐκ ἐκ τοῦ καλοῦντος ὑμᾶς). But Paul also applies the discourse to himself in 2:2b (ἀνέβην δὲ κατὰ ἀποκάλυψιν· καὶ ἀνεθέμην αὐτοῖς τὸ εὐαγγέλιον ὃ κηρύσσω ἐν τοῖς ἔθνεσιν, κατ᾽ ἰδίαν δὲ τοῖς δοκοῦσιν, μή πως εἰς κενὸν τρέχω ἢ ἔδραμον). So it is present in two places, and Philippians 3:12-16 in effect develops the comment in Galatians 2:2b, where athletic imagery is used by Paul self-referentially.

The point does not need to be labored further. The opponents in Galatians are a perfect match for the problematic figures already identified in the Previous Letter to Philippi, Philippians, and Romans. Paul is engaging in this letter as well with "the enemies of the cross of Christ" (see the centrality of the cross in Gal 5:11; 6:12-15), and so Galatians clearly belongs in the letter sequence oriented toward these figures — either this, or powerful arguments to the contrary will need to be produced.

We can now support this vital initial judgment with two further arguments that are too weak to function as decisive considerations in their own right but are striking corroborations of the claim just established.

2.3 First Corroborative Consideration — the Collection

This corroborative argument needs to proceed through two partly independent steps. The first is the realization that Galatians reveals a further significant element within the discourse of the enemies, one that will resolve some of the key remaining puzzles surrounding Galatians in its own right.

The enemies seem to have made various claims about Jerusalem, and so seem, at least in some sense, to have come from the holy city. They also seem to have made a series of particular claims about Paul in this relation. And in the light of this, in the argument's second step, we can see that Paul does refer to the collection in Galatians 2:10, but in carefully nuanced terms, because he is constrained by this countervailing discourse and does not want to appear to be subservient to the early church's senior figures, who are based in Jerusalem. That is, he does not want to corroborate a key part of his opponents' discourse. Nevertheless, in suitably subtle terms, it can be seen that Galatians does attest to the ongoing collection project with which Paul was involved at this time, corroborating the placement of Galatians close by 1 Corinthians, 2 Corinthians, and Romans, as Knox suspected. Our understanding of this project will be considerably deepened by the information that Galatians provides. But in order to appreciate this, we must first reconstruct a discourse concerning Jerusalem that Galatians attests within the broader debate between Paul and the enemies.

(1) Jerusalem

I will follow here in the footsteps of one of the great forerunners of the modern historical-critical analysis of Paul, F. C. Baur, as well as those of one of his most brilliant modern advocates, at least in biographical terms, J. L. (Lou) Martyn, and suggest that Paul's apostolic status is being questioned in certain respects by other "Christians" within the Galatian situation.[32]

Paul breaks off from the first element within the epistolary prescript, as he appends a title to his name, to deny a doublet of misunderstandings and to affirm a complementary pair of divine authorizations: "Paul, a divine delegate — not [delegated] from men or by means of men but by means of Jesus Christ and from God the Father, who raised him from the dead — " ([1:1] Παῦλος ἀπόστολος οὐκ ἀπ᾽ ἀνθρώπων οὐδὲ δι᾽ ἀνθρώπου ἀλλὰ διὰ Ἰησοῦ Χριστοῦ καὶ θεοῦ πατρὸς τοῦ ἐγείραντος αὐτὸν ἐκ νεκρῶν). This is a strong signal of one of his main concerns in writing to the Galatians.

He then returns to the first customary element in the prescript, the addressers, stating that all the brothers with him are also in effect the authors of the letter (see 1:2), although this is doubtless hyperbolic. After an unusual "astonishment" paragraph effects a transition from the letter opening to the body (1:6-10), he then resumes the two denials just made within the prescript: "I want you to know, brothers, that the declaration declared by me is not in accordance with men, for neither did I receive it from men nor was I taught it [from men] but [I received it / was taught it] through a revelation of and from Jesus Christ" ([1:11] Γνωρίζω γὰρ ὑμῖν, ἀδελφοί, τὸ εὐαγγέλιον τὸ εὐαγγελισθὲν ὑπ᾽ ἐμοῦ ὅτι οὐκ ἔστιν κατὰ ἄνθρωπον· [12] οὐδὲ γὰρ ἐγὼ παρὰ ἀνθρώπου παρέλαβον αὐτὸ οὔτε ἐδιδάχθην ἀλλὰ δι᾽ ἀποκαλύψεως Ἰησοῦ Χριστοῦ). After an account of his unexpected commission (1:13-17), in which he explicitly denies going to Jerusalem ([1:16b] εὐθέως οὐ προσανεθέμην σαρκὶ καὶ αἵματι [17a] οὐδὲ ἀνῆλθον εἰς Ἰεροσόλυμα πρὸς τοὺς πρὸ ἐμοῦ ἀποστόλους), Paul then supplies an account of his relationship with Jerusalem and the apostles, who seem to have been based in that city, describing a first, rather short visit

---

32. Martyn's theological framework is very different from Baur's (see Martyn 1997b), but his biographical perceptions in relation to Paul and the broader development of the early church are similar, being sensitive to the critical role of Jewish Christianity, and to the conflict that seems to have unfolded between that "discourse" and the Pauline mission; see his magisterial 1997a. In endorsing the interpretative tradition within the modern period that originates with Baur and flows through Martyn, I am also repudiating the brilliant but ultimately unwarranted exemplary and ethical construal of the biographical material in this epistle urged by (i.a.) Lyons (1985, restated in 2012).

three years after his commission (1:18-19), and a second, consultative visit some "fourteen years" after this (2:1-10). In view of these textual developments, it seems difficult to avoid the inference that Paul's apostleship is being defined unhelpfully by his opponents in relation to the early church's Jerusalem leadership, and hence that the apostolic concerns are rather different from those being debated by the Corinthians. Paul is apparently being presented as the subordinate of Cephas, James, and the other leaders of the early church, having been authorized and catechized by them during his various visits to the holy city — some of which he was presumably summoned to make (see 2:2a). The first third of Galatians is largely devoted to negating this narrative in suitably nuanced terms, shifting to other concerns only in 2:15.

Jerusalem does not drop entirely out of sight after this, however. In 4:21-31 Paul contrasts, somewhat infamously, a present Jerusalem with a Jerusalem "above" (4:25b-26a). The present Jerusalem is correlated with what we would call historical Jerusalem — the city located in Judea filled with flesh-and-blood inhabitants. Paul polemically suggests that this city is nevertheless a fleshly community begotten in slavery, like the son of Hagar, and that the city above is the key to the Galatians' future. That city, promised in Scripture (here Isa 54:1), is born as Isaac was — as the result of a divine promise, in freedom, and by means of the Spirit.

Setting aside the plausibility of Paul's argument here, which is much debated, the important point for framing is simply the emphatic resumption of historical Jerusalem in polemical terms within the argument of the letter, one that is probably briefly reprised in a certain sense by Paul's final prayer in 6:16b for God's mercy to fall on Israel. Despite its frequent spiritualization, the most likely reading of this text is, as in Romans 11, in terms of Paul's hope that historical Israel would respond to God's mercy and embrace Jesus as Messiah and Lord.[33]

We do not need to tease out the details of these texts and arguments further. It suffices here to grasp the most basic aspects of the situation. Paul's encoded opposition in Galatians seems to have deployed a narrative of his apostolic subordination to the mother church in Jerusalem, which contained the original disciples of Jesus and his family members and was based in the holy city that lay at the heart of Judaism. These figures seem, moreover, to have been typically Jewish and Torah-observant. It seems likely, then, that Paul's radical gospel is being portrayed by his enemies as the teaching of a renegade who has, at the least, exceeded his authorization. Irrespective of the exact details, appeals to Jerusalem are being made by Paul's opponents on a number of levels,

---

33. So, entirely correctly in my view, Eastman (2010).

which seem entirely plausible in the context of early Jewish Christianity.[34] And
we learn something rather helpful from this for our framing project.

Paul's opposition has a significant relationship *with* Jerusalem. And this
opposition seems to be something approaching a wave that is flowing across
his mission fields, moving from east to west. Beginning in Jerusalem, this wave
of hostile opposition has affected Syrian Antioch at some point (see 2:11-14). It
then probably traveled through Galatia and Asia until it arrived on the shores
of the Aegean. Paul is now experiencing this wave in some sense in Corinth, in
Achaia, and he fears its presence in Philippi, in Macedonia, and in due course
in Rome, in Italy. We could explore this wave further, but it will be most helpful
for now to turn and consider the possible presence of the collection within
Paul's countervailing discourse in Galatians, resuming an important line of
discussion from chapter 2.

(2) The Collection in Galatians 2:10

Any discourse of subordination in relation to Jerusalem boxes Paul in with
respect to certain issues very cleverly. We know that Paul is currently involved
in raising a large sum of money for the poor within the Jerusalem church.[35]
But this can now be portrayed by his enemies as the action of a client busily
carrying out his patrons' instructions — a client who in other respects is dis-
obedient, and so is with all this frantic financial activity perhaps involved in

34. I suggest that Gal 5:11, properly understood, also functions cleverly within this
broader polemic (2011).

35. It is vital to appreciate that this part of the frame is now in place around Gal on
independent grounds. The collection has been spoken of prior to the composition of Gal by
1 and 2 Cor, and will be spoken of after its dispatch by Rom. These realizations speak to many
of the concerns raised by current critics of this narrative — see, e.g., B. Longenecker (2010,
157-89). Clearly there is no dependence here on the dubious equation between the poor of Gal
2:10 and the early church in Jerusalem as a whole by way of appeal to the designation of the
latter as Ebionites. Rather, Rom 15:26 suggests fairly directly that Paul is referring in Gal 2:10
to the poor within the Jerusalem church. It follows from this that the socioeconomic connotation of the signifier "poor" that Longenecker is so concerned to emphasize in 2:10 must not
be avoided. The Galatians would have been well aware of its limited reference here, however,
to poor "Christians" in Jerusalem since Paul had — given our developing frame — just visited
them with a report about Antioch and Jerusalem, and with instructions (1 Cor 16:1; see also Gal
4:13), although these clarifications are, to repeat, not apparent without the existing frame. This
local decision does not in my view undermine the broader importance of alleviating poverty
within Paul's general Christian ethic that Longenecker has helpfully recovered.

dishonesty, or currying favor, or readying a large bribe to buy his way out of trouble (see 1:10). Moreover, if Paul travels to Jerusalem himself in due course, it could be said that he is merely returning as commanded at the conclusion of his errand. Paul's actions thereby confirm his subordinate status, and his enemies' claim to override his anomalous ethical instructions would seem to be vindicated. What is Paul to do?

Clearly, he must counter this narrative by providing an alternative story of his actions. The collection — if it is not to be abandoned — must be represented as an agreement between equals rather than an obligation enjoined on a subordinate, although given that Paul is the only one apparently involved directly in money raising, this will involve some sophisticated narrative footwork. His relationship with Jerusalem will have to be nuanced as well, and presumably during the same story, since the collection is closely related to dynamics unfolding at Jerusalem. The relationship itself can hardly be abandoned. The mother city of Judaism and the center of the early church deserve respect, so responsible contact with it should be maintained. Moreover, not to do so would presumably reinforce any narrative of Paul as a renegade. But by the same token, any travel to the holy city cannot be a matter of Cephan command. It must somehow be an appropriate meeting between peers.

These are the narrative needles that Paul threads so skillfully in Galatians 2:1-10, but one result is a subtle displacement of any overt references to the collection. Indeed, Paul's extraordinary syntax testifies to the rhetorical challenges operative through 2:1-10, although the first three verses proceed smoothly enough.[36]

Paul states first that the cause of this visit was a "revelation" (κατὰ ἀποκάλυψιν); thus, he was not summoned, nor apparently were his companions, Barnabas and Titus. He then privately consulted with "those who 'seemed to be [something]' lest he was running or had run in futility" (see 2:2b: τοῖς δοκοῦσιν, μή πως εἰς κενὸν τρέχω ἢ ἔδραμον). And, he says, Titus was not compelled to be circumcised, although he was a pagan (lit. "Hellene," i.e., uncircumcised) — the agenda of the enemies in Philippians and Romans being clearly recognizable here. After this, Paul breaks off into the first of several short parenthetical observations.

Verses 4-6a supply further information about the situation, apparently at-

---

36. The commentators are not always as helpful as they could be; however, see esp. de Boer (2011, 104-28); Martyn (1997a, 187-228, esp. 222-28); and R. Longenecker (1990, 43-63). Luedemann's seminal treatment is especially sensitive to framing questions and their relationships with the collection here (1984, esp. 64-100). Some key syntactical and semantic issues are also scrutinized helpfully by B. Longenecker (2010, 195-97).

tributing the cause of the discussion concerning Titus's circumcision to a group of slithering false brothers (διὰ δὲ τοὺς παρεισάκτους ψευδαδέλφους), *but also,* shortly after this, to the Jerusalem apostles themselves. Titus, despite being a pagan, was not compelled to be circumcised — this "because of the covert false brothers . . . *and* [pressure] from those who appeared to be something" ([2:3] ἀλλ' οὐδὲ Τίτος ὁ σὺν ἐμοί, Ἕλλην ὤν, ἠναγκάσθη περιτμηθῆναι; [4] διὰ δὲ τοὺς παρεισάκτους ψευδαδέλφους . . . [6] ἀπὸ δὲ τῶν δοκούντων εἶναί τι). Paul narrates his responses to these two constituencies in different ways, however. He claims in v. 5 that he did not give in to the demands of the false brothers for a moment, thereby maintaining the truth of the gospel for his auditors. And in v. 6 he throws a useful scriptural proverb against the superficially impressive apostles: "And [as for] those who seemed to be something: what they were makes no difference to me; 'God is no respecter of personal appearance' [Deut 10:17]."

After this comment, Paul resumes the discussion of their role in the situation when v. 6b resumes the subject of v. 2, namely, "those who seemed to be something" (τοῖς δοκοῦσιν). But the narrative has moved on from the "Titus incident." Paul now claims that "those who seemed to be something *added nothing to me*" (ἐμοὶ γὰρ οἱ δοκοῦντες οὐδὲν προσανέθεντο). Rather, an act of recognition took place that will dominate the narration through v. 9.

These figures saw that the gospel for the uncircumcised had been entrusted by God to Paul, just as the gospel for the circumcised had been entrusted to Cephas, here called Peter — a claim that prompts another parenthetical explanation: "for the one who was working through Peter in his delegation [lit. apostleship] to the circumcision was working also through me in [my delegation] to the pagan nations" (ὁ γὰρ ἐνεργήσας Πέτρῳ εἰς ἀποστολὴν τῆς περιτομῆς ἐνήργησεν καὶ ἐμοὶ εἰς τὰ ἔθνη). This acknowledgment of parallel divine activity underlies the recognition first voiced in v. 7 and now resumed in v. 9 that a particular divine benefaction, a "grace," has been given to Paul. As a consequence, a larger group of workers now enters into a partnership, confirming it with a shake of the right hand, as was customary.[37]

This partnership turns out to involve a division of labor. James, Cephas, and John, whom we now finally learn "seemed to be . . . *pillars*" (στῦλοι), will go to the Jews or Judeans, and Paul and Barnabas will go to the pagans. Hence, by the end of v. 9 a partnership has been formed between missionary equals in recognition of the same but complementary activity of God within the respective primary ministries of Peter and Paul.

However, one last verse in the subsection remains that is not grammati-

---

37. See Ogereau (2012).

cally self-sufficient — v. 10. It begins μόνον τῶν πτωχῶν ἵνα μνημονεύωμεν . . . , which seems to introduce a condition into what has already been said: ". . . only that we should continue to remember the poor, the very thing that I was also eager to do" (μόνον τῶν πτωχῶν ἵνα μνημονεύωμεν, ὃ καὶ ἐσπούδασα αὐτὸ τοῦτο ποιῆσαι). As in v. 6, this statement seems to resume an earlier sentence after a parenthetical interruption (v. 6a resuming v. 3, anaphorically complementing vv. 4a-5). But v. 8 is a parenthetical explanation of v. 7, so we can set that to one side for the moment, leaving a complex sentence leading up to v. 10 that really begins in v. 6b:

> [2:6b] ἐμοὶ γὰρ οἱ δοκοῦντες οὐδὲν προσανέθεντο
>   [7] ἀλλὰ τοὐναντίον ἰδόντες ὅτι πεπίστευμαι τὸ εὐαγγέλιον τῆς
>   ἀκροβυστίας καθὼς Πέτρος τῆς περιτομῆς . . .³⁸
>   [9] καὶ γνόντες τὴν χάριν τὴν δοθεῖσάν μοι, Ἰάκωβος καὶ Κηφᾶς καὶ
>   Ἰωάννης, οἱ δοκοῦντες στῦλοι εἶναι, δεξιὰς ἔδωκαν ἐμοὶ καὶ Βαρναβᾷ
>   κοινωνίας, ἵνα ἡμεῖς εἰς τὰ ἔθνη, αὐτοὶ δὲ εἰς τὴν περιτομήν·
> [10] μόνον τῶν πτωχῶν ἵνα μνημονεύωμεν, ὃ καὶ ἐσπούδασα αὐτὸ τοῦτο
> ποιῆσαι.

If this reconstruction is correct — and it does not involve flagrant grammatical violations or anacolutha — then we can now see that the pillars did not add anything to Paul . . . *except*, v. 10 finally tells us, that he remember, or continue to remember, the poor — which very thing, he hastens to add, he was eager to do.³⁹ So they *did* "add something," at least by way of a request. But Paul's com-

---

38. [8] ὁ γὰρ ἐνεργήσας Πέτρῳ εἰς ἀποστολὴν τῆς περιτομῆς ἐνήργησεν καὶ ἐμοὶ εἰς τὰ ἔθνη.

39. Some further questions within the verse remain, namely, the precise meanings of the present subjunctive verb μνημονεύωμεν and the aorist ἐσπούδασα. (B. Longecker provides a useful analysis [2010, 190-93].) The former could be continuative or inceptive; and the latter could be a past temporal reference, to an activity prior to the time being reported, *or* emphasizing aspect, hence possibly referring to an inceptive activity again. This yields three possible readings: (1) an exhortation by the Jerusalem leadership to continue an activity of "remembrance of the poor" (i.e., with gifts of money), which Paul had previously been vigorously committed to/engaged with; (2) an exhortation to continue this activity, which Paul *then* became vigorously committed to/engaged with zealously, i.e., at its time of suggestion; or (3) an exhortation to begin or undertake an act of financial remembrance, which Paul was vigorously committed to at the time of asking. However, for framing purposes these grammatical options reduce to two: was Paul speaking of a continuation of giving, implying that previous giving had taken place; or, was Paul merely speaking of the beginning of an act of fundraising and giving? The confidences of various scholars notwithstanding, it seems to me that no firm judg-

plicated sentence introduces a great deal of material that carefully frames this suggestion. It effects this largely by way of two participial constructions built from ἰδόντες and γνόντες, the second construction also containing a complete subordinate sentence. (These could be circumstantial constructions but seem best read conditionally or even causally: "but *because* they had seen . . .") And vv. 6-10 can now be seen as something of a rhetorical masterpiece.

The intervening material in vv. 7-9 drags an alternative narrative across the trail of an exception to the claim that Paul's gospel was not conditioned in any way by the Jerusalem leadership, and frames that condition so that it is neither a patron-client arrangement nor even a condition of participation within a mutual agreement. The intervening narrative suggests that the mutual agreement and partnership between Paul and his colleagues and the Jerusalem leadership derived from the recognition of the work of God, which took place *prior* to the mention of money. Indeed, the handshake of mutual agreement between them, noted by v. 9, is framed by this narrative that recognizes the underlying and more fundamental work of God. The participation itself is therefore *in God's work of mission among Jews and pagans*. Hence, the provision of money is merely the mutual sharing of resources in which those *already* in a partnership would engage. But because Paul's pagans seem to have had rich resources (although presumably this was true of only some of them), any gifts of money within the partnership could plausibly take place initially from the pagans to the poor among the saints in Jerusalem. This explains any apparent one-sidedness in the present flow, defusing the counternarrative that it is an obligation from one party to another. Paul is, moreover, clearly not a client of Jerusalem in this but a partner within the divine mission, and so he also journeys there for the meeting at the divine behest. He respects Jerusalem and is in contact with them, as a good partner should be, but is not beholden to them.

If this construal of the difficult and sophisticated narration in 2:1-10 is correct, then I suggest that we do find here a subtle confirmation of the collection. Because of the rhetorical constraints within which he is operating,

---

ment is possible on the basis of this text alone, or on the basis of the rest of Gal. The text shifts a little strangely from a plural exhortation to a singular affirmation, but there is no difficulty imagining a request being made to both Paul and Barnabas, whether to continue or to begin their charitable work, followed by Paul's affirmation of his own particular zeal here in some way, whether past or present. Therefore it simply cannot be claimed confidently that a previous collection is in view here, although it might be. The important judgment for our developing frame, however, is that this does seem to be a clear reference to the origins of Paul's current fundraising project. And, as our frame develops, we may yet be able to return to make a stronger judgment about the precise implications of Gal 2:10.

Paul does not reference it especially overtly. But it does seem to be there. Moreover, I suggest that the potential embarrassment caused to him by the collection seems to provide the best explanation of his unusually difficult syntax. The graceless syntactical complexity of Paul's account is well explained as a deliberate rhetorical ploy designed both to distract from and to reframe the collection. It is not the work of a client, or even the condition of participation in a partnership with the Jerusalem leaders. It is an appropriate material response within a prior partnership that is generated in turn by the recognition of divine activity. In further support of this suggestion, we should note that we learn from this reading why Paul offers no travel plan in Galatians.

He is occupied with the collection, with which he will soon travel to Jerusalem. There is no need to reinforce the narrative of his enemies here by stating that his obligations to Jerusalem must currently override his affection for his friends in Galatia. This would make Paul again seem very like a client, rushing to do as he is told — at least in this respect. And with this realization, we can resolve one of the secondary puzzles in Galatians — its lack of a travelogue. We also shed light on several other places in the frame.

We learn, in all probability, why Paul's diffidence about accompanying the collection as probably expressed in 1 Corinthians 16 has been replaced by the agenda of Romans 15. Paul is determined in the latter to go to Jerusalem to engage again with the Jerusalem leadership concerning his mission, rather as he has done in Galatians 2:1-10. With the arrival of the enemies, the seriousness of the situation in Jerusalem has become apparent; it will need to be personally addressed. We also get a sense of the deep hostility harbored toward Paul by other Judeans; he prays in Romans 15:30-32 for safety from a threat of death. We learn, moreover, in all probability, why Galatia is absent from the final roll call of participants in the collection in Romans 15:26. It seems that Paul's letter did not succeed in retrieving the situation there, although this is not particularly surprising given its gravity; a mere text would have little hope of regathering a community that had been taken over and catechized by another group of leaders. And I suggest that we are also entitled to infer that Jerusalem, the enemies, and the collection are all connected in some way. But there is no need to tease these connections out further given our present focus on basic framing.[40]

---

40. These particular connections are not yet explicit. But we know that Paul seems determined to return to Jerusalem with a large sum of money. We learned earlier from Gal that Paul's enemies seem to have had some significant connection with Jerusalem. And we have just learned that the origins of the collection lay in a meeting in Jerusalem during which the agenda of the enemies also seems to have been in play (2:3b-5). The apostles themselves

This explanatory power waxing through the frame should increase our confidence in the plausibility of the reading of 2:1-10 that underlies it, and strengthen the likelihood in turn that Galatians belongs in the letter sequence that is oriented in part by the collection, as 2:10 subtly suggests. The collection is, as Knox argued, present in Galatians, although the case is not as simple or decisive as he suggested. But this observation can function as a useful corroboration of the judgment that we have already made concerning the letter's location on the basis of the opponents' basic identity. And still more can be said in favor of locating Galatians at this general point in the frame. Its encoded *Nebenadressat* point toward its composition at Corinth.

2.4 Second Corroborative Consideration — Corinthian Nebenadressat

Much of the content and rhetoric of Galatians has now been plausibly explained, at least in preliminary and provisional terms, in relation to the enemies. We have analyzed the letter opening and much of the initial biographical material, probing it for information about the origin of the collection at Jerusalem. We have briefly noted how the substantive agenda of the enemies was apparent from 2:15, extending through chapter 3 and into chapter 4, frequently infused with the distinctive cluster of scriptural terms and phrases that Paul employs to refute it. Chapter 4 then makes a cluster of entirely understandable personal appeals, pivoting after this to address an element newly apparent in the enemies' agenda from Galatians, namely, certain claims vis-à-vis Jerusalem. Highly recognizable summary material occurs at the start of chapter 5 — that is, justification material, followed by invective, which is another standard feature of Paul's engagement with opponents. Jumping ahead a little, we can note that a distinctive letter ending begins in 6:11. And just before this is a stern admonition in future eschatological terms, which seems quite understandable in view of the broader Galatian situation. There, Paul in effect contrasts a present investment in a life oriented by the flesh with one oriented by the Spirit. But this summary has left one significant section in Galatians out of our basic reading in terms of the enemies, namely, 5:13–6:5, a section that has puzzled some commentators.[41]

It will assist our interpretation of this material to recognize first that Paul

---

seem to have been involved in some way with that agenda (see 2:6), and they were also clearly involved with the origins of the collection (see 2:6b and 10). So it seems apparent that all these figures and events were connected.

41. As always, Martyn (1997a, 479-558) is exemplary; see also de Boer (2011, 329-92).

has crafted a chiasm of ethical material in the bulk of this section, allowing us to compress the material into a set of five concerns (A/A'-E/E').[42]

A [5:13] Ὑμεῖς γὰρ ἐπ' ἐλευθερίᾳ ἐκλήθητε, ἀδελφοί· μόνον μὴ τὴν ἐλευθερίαν εἰς ἀφορμὴν τῇ σαρκί, ἀλλὰ διὰ τῆς ἀγάπης δουλεύετε ἀλλήλοις. [14] ὁ γὰρ πᾶς νόμος ἐν ἑνὶ λόγῳ πεπλήρωται, ἐν τῷ· *ἀγαπήσεις τὸν πλησίον σου ὡς σεαυτόν.*

B [15] εἰ δὲ ἀλλήλους δάκνετε καὶ κατεσθίετε, βλέπετε μὴ ὑπ' ἀλλήλων ἀναλωθῆτε.

C [16] Λέγω δέ, πνεύματι περιπατεῖτε καὶ ἐπιθυμίαν σαρκὸς οὐ μὴ τελέσητε. [17] ἡ γὰρ σὰρξ ἐπιθυμεῖ κατὰ τοῦ πνεύματος, τὸ δὲ πνεῦμα κατὰ τῆς σαρκός, ταῦτα γὰρ ἀλλήλοις ἀντίκειται, ἵνα μὴ ἃ ἐὰν θέλητε ταῦτα ποιῆτε.

D [18] εἰ δὲ πνεύματι ἄγεσθε, οὐκ ἐστὲ ὑπὸ νόμον.

E [19] φανερὰ δέ ἐστιν τὰ ἔργα τῆς σαρκός, ἅτινά ἐστιν πορνεία, ἀκαθαρσία, ἀσέλγεια, [20] εἰδωλολατρία, φαρμακεία, ἔχθραι, ἔρις, ζῆλος, θυμοί, ἐριθεῖαι, διχοστασίαι, αἱρέσεις, [21] φθόνοι, μέθαι, κῶμοι καὶ τὰ ὅμοια τούτοις, ἃ προλέγω ὑμῖν, καθὼς προεῖπον ὅτι οἱ τὰ τοιαῦτα πράσσοντες βασιλείαν θεοῦ οὐ κληρονομήσουσιν.

E' [22] ὁ δὲ καρπὸς τοῦ πνεύματός ἐστιν ἀγάπη χαρὰ εἰρήνη, μακροθυμία χρηστότης ἀγαθωσύνη, πίστις [23] πραΰτης ἐγκράτεια·

D' κατὰ τῶν τοιούτων οὐκ ἔστιν νόμος.

C' [24] οἱ δὲ τοῦ Χριστοῦ Ἰησοῦ τὴν σάρκα ἐσταύρωσαν σὺν τοῖς παθήμασιν καὶ ταῖς ἐπιθυμίαις. [25] Εἰ ζῶμεν πνεύματι, πνεύματι καὶ στοιχῶμεν.

B' [26] μὴ γινώμεθα κενόδοξοι, ἀλλήλους προκαλούμενοι, ἀλλήλοις φθονοῦντες.

A' [6:1] Ἀδελφοί, ἐὰν καὶ προλημφθῇ ἄνθρωπος ἔν τινι παραπτώματι, ὑμεῖς οἱ πνευματικοὶ καταρτίζετε τὸν τοιοῦτον ἐν πνεύματι πραΰτητος, σκοπῶν σεαυτὸν μὴ καὶ σὺ πειρασθῇς. [2] Ἀλλήλων τὰ βάρη βαστάζετε καὶ οὕτως ἀναπληρώσετε τὸν νόμον τοῦ Χριστοῦ.

The chiasm pivots at its center around contrasting vice and virtue lists (E: vv. 19-21; E': vv. 22-23). And in the middle subsections of the two series,

---

42. A variation on this arrangement can be found in Thomson (1995).

C/C', we learn that these lists are generated by fundamentally different ontologies. Vice is generated by those living in the flesh; virtue, by those living in the Spirit, who have also crucified the fleshly life through Christ and his cross. (A participatory understanding of Christian ethics must be presupposed here.) Subsections D/D' then suggest that this sort of life in the Spirit takes its participants beyond a world ordered by Torah, which is an important point for the Galatians to appreciate; they are not "under Torah." But subsections A/A' state clearly that this does *not* take them beyond a world that is ethically ordered. The Galatians are still shaped by the Torah that is Christ (or something similar), and live in him in a world ordered by love. Hence, they are in a certain sense living in a world ordered in fulfillment of the older written Torah, because it can now be seen that all of the Torah's teachings have been fulfilled by love of neighbor.

Most of this chiasm seems to make sense within the broader engagement with the agenda of the enemies that explains the rest of the letter so economically. It is in fact an excellent summary of the radical Torah-free ethic that Paul is urging his Galatian auditors not to abandon in favor of any countervailing, nomistic approach, which Paul takes to be rooted in the flesh. But a few elements in the chiasm have not yet been explained.

In subsections A/A' Paul's affirmation that when the Galatians live by the Spirit they are fulfilling the love command is interwoven with complementary narratives. In A his auditors are to love their neighbors as themselves and thereby to serve one another. And this will apparently preclude their freedom's degeneration into an opportunity for the flesh. Their freedom will not lack content, or develop deceptively into another ethical opportunity for fleshly living (see subsection E). In A' Paul takes this mutual service one step further, urging his auditors to restore a person caught in a transgression gently — although remaining vigilant lest they themselves be tempted. These somewhat distinctive exhortations are then further offset by subsections B/B', which we have not yet addressed.

Subsection B urges the letter's auditors not to "eat one another" lest they be destroyed. And subsection B' warns against similarly self-destructive behavior within a community, although in less dramatic terms. The letter's auditors are not to be "conceited," "provocative," or "envious" of one another. But this set of concerns is no mere passing fancy on Paul's part. It is resumed in the coda supplied to the chiasm by 6:3-5. (An obvious transition to different ethical concerns takes place in v. 6, flowing through v. 10, which we have just noted fits the broader reading in relation to the agenda of the enemies that we have already developed.) But vv. 3-5 are different.

[6:3] εἰ γὰρ δοκεῖ τις εἶναί τι μηδὲν ὤν, φρεναπατᾷ ἑαυτόν.
[4] τὸ δὲ ἔργον ἑαυτοῦ δοκιμαζέτω ἕκαστος, καὶ τότε εἰς ἑαυτὸν μόνον
τὸ καύχημα ἕξει καὶ οὐκ εἰς τὸν ἕτερον·
[5] ἕκαστος γὰρ τὸ ἴδιον φορτίον βαστάσει.

This material focuses again on the single corrosive dynamic of invidious comparison within a community, urging sober self-estimation (v. 3) and critique only of one's own work (vv. 4-5). It is clear that Paul has deliberately taken some time in the midst of his careful chiastic exhortations to inveigh in Galatians against internal community strife.

This concern is introduced in subsection A, being implicit in v. 13b and v. 14; is emphasized in B (v. 15); is reiterated strongly in the vice list in E (see vv. 20-21: [20] ἔχθραι, ἔρις, ζῆλος, θυμοί, ἐριθεῖαι, διχοστασίαι, αἱρέσεις [21] φθόνοι), referenced by *eight* of the fifteen named sins; is resumed explicitly in B′ (v. 26); and, following the chiasm proper, is expanded in a coda (6:3-5). But this predominant concern is linked with other sins that occur here distinctively within the letter, although not with this degree of emphasis.

The opportunity for the flesh announced portentously in v. 13 is linked by the vice list with sexual immorality, idolatry, and drunkenness. Moreover, there is the mysterious matter of the transgressor in 6:1, for whom Paul urges gentle restoration, although with care too that the restorers do not fall into the same transgression. And these concerns are initially somewhat puzzling.

There have been no hints in the letter thus far that the Galatians are sexually immoral, idolatrous, or drunken. Worse than this, however, one would hardly expect a community being tempted primarily by Judaizing to be suffering from these sins. They seem to be characterized, rather, by an enthusiasm for ethical rigor. It is understandable that Paul would wish to tamp down intracommunal conflict in the face of a hostile takeover bid by outsiders; any disunity could be exploited by such figures — although, it must be said, the Galatians have not evidenced such disunity to this point. But comprehensive Torah observance must surely lead the Galatians directly away from immorality, idolatry, and carousing. So Paul's exhortations in these terms seem redundant.

Various explanations have been offered to try to comprehend these exhortations, which are a minor but overt set of concerns in the letter. So, rather famously, Lütgert (1919) even proposed a "two-front" theory for the Galatian situation, suggesting that the congregation was divided into Judaizing and antinomian groups.[43] But these explanations have generally struggled

---

43. The theory was popularized in English-speaking scholarship by Ropes (1929).

to convince. There is little or no evidence in Galatians suggesting deep divisions in the congregation in the way that much evidence suggests the Corinthians were so divided. However, I would propose that a simple explanation of these textual dynamics lies to hand that has the added virtue of assisting our broader framing project — a reading sensitive to the phenomenon of *Nebenadressat*.

These minor but overt concerns are all redolent of the Corinthian situation, which they fit like the proverbial hand in a glove. We know well by now that the Corinthians were a deeply and destructively divided community, thereby explaining the main concern evident in these secondary remarks by Paul. But they also faced ongoing challenges in terms of sexual immorality and idolatry, and drunkenness would have been a standard association for both of these practices. It might be replied that most congregations are divided; it is not implausible to expect Paul's pagan converts in Galatia to have had struggles in these terms — and therefore not necessary to posit Corinthian *Nebenadressat*. However, one piece of evidence tips me away from a "generic" reading and toward the more specific, Corinthian hypothesis fairly decisively. We seem to have a touching reference in Galatians 6:1 to the distinctive process of restoration that was central to the rhetorical strategy of 2 Corinthians. As we have already seen in chapter 2, in 2 Corinthians 2:5-11 Paul counsels the Corinthians to forgive and reintegrate a transgressor rather than to visit continuing dishonor on him. And this process looks very much like the narrative presented more briefly in Galatians 6:1, which is otherwise largely unparalleled within Pauline exhortation. Galatians 6:1 seems to reference the Corinthian situation *directly*. And this encourages us to see deliberate evocations of Corinthian challenges in the other ethical material just noted as well.

I would suggest, by way of summary, that Corinthian *Nebenadressat* explain neatly all the secondary concerns present in Galatians that we have just tabulated and that seem incongruous within that primary situation, which we have explained in broad terms vis-à-vis the agenda of the enemies. These concerns are an excellent match for Corinth, speaking to all the main Corinthian problems (see esp. 2 Cor 12:20-21). And this suggests in turn that the Corinthians were the letter's first auditors, although they were not its actual addressees. They "overheard" this powerful and frequently polemical communication, and thus received the further benefit of some oblique ethical reinforcement from Paul in relation to their own ongoing problems. And this further strengthens our earlier judgment that Galatians belongs in the epistolary spine, during Paul's third visit to Corinth.

2.5 Summary and Sequence

(1) Inserting Galatians

We have concluded that Galatians should be located within the epistolary frame that we have already developed. The principal reason for this judgment is that the opposition in view is the same as the group in view in the Previous Letter to Philippi, Philippians, and Romans — the enemies. So Galatians belongs somewhere within this short sequence. This ground then depends on the placement of Philippians at Corinth during Paul's third visit to that city, a more distinctive feature of our developing frame, although it seems strongly established. And that conclusion has been strengthened by two corroborative considerations, neither of which depends on the Corinthian placement of Philippians. First, we noted how the collection for Jerusalem is arguably present — suitably narrated — in Galatians 2:10. This confirms the location of Galatians within this broader letter sequence at some point, although, strictly speaking, it could suggest a location anywhere between the inception of the collection, in the Previous Letter to Corinth, and its completion, presumed at present to be just after Romans. Second, there is good evidence in the letter for Corinthian *Nebenadressat* (see esp. 5:13-14, 15, 20-21a, 26; 6:1-5), suggesting its location during Paul's third visit to Corinth, which is right where the analysis of the opposition placed the letter in any case. So we need now only to ask where exactly Galatians fits into this sequence in relation to Paul's third visit to Corinth, the Previous Letter to Philippi, Philippians, and Romans — although there is a fairly obvious answer to this query.

Paul is not in prison or on trial in Galatians. At least, this seems the more likely reading of the evidence in the letter than one supposing that he is but is concealing it; Paul seems elsewhere to make much rhetorical use of imprisonment. Hence, a position alongside the Previous Letter to Philippi, at the front end of the breaking controversy, seems likely. The Previous Letter to Philippi and Galatians were most likely companion letters, born together when a dreadful crisis for Paul's mission suddenly became apparent at Corinth — the moment when a particular wave of Jewish Christian opposition in effect crashed ashore at his own feet for the first time. Paul realized with alarm that it had run all the way from Jerusalem, east to west, and through many if not all of the communities to the east that had been founded by him and his allies. There was no telling yet how much farther it would reach — hence Romans. But the situation as it stood indicated the sad possibility that Jerusalem itself was hostile to his work. It is worth noting now that this location for Galatians makes good sense tactically on Paul's part.

When the crisis first broke in his area — when the wave of enemies arrived — it seems likely, as we just suggested, that Paul composed and dispatched a volley of letters from Corinth to his communities that were under direct threat. Hence, Galatians would almost certainly have traveled to Galatia by way of Ephesus and would consequently have been "overheard" by the Asian Christians as well. Unfortunately, we know too little about Pauline Christianity in Ephesus at this time to posit *Nebenadressat* with any confidence other than to make the bland observation that any Asian Christians would have benefited — at least, from Paul's point of view — from this tirade against the enemies (although our understanding of this region will be expanded by our discoveries in ch. 5). But we can fill in here one further gap in our data in Galatians with this supposition.

It seems most likely that Paul did not include specific information about his sources for the Galatian crisis in Galatians because he learned about it when the enemies themselves arrived in Corinth, so the second puzzling lacuna in this letter is now potentially explained. (The first was Paul's refusal to travel directly to Galatia, and to explain why.) No member of his circle or Galatian congregant brought him news from Galatia directly of the region's challenges; this information probably arrived entirely unpleasantly and somewhat indirectly with the arrival of the enemies themselves, perhaps as one element within their boasting, and this would have limited Paul's knowledge of the situation quite sharply. With this further realization, we can now see that the basic Pauline letter sequence is:

$$\ldots \text{[PLC]} - 1 \text{ Cor} - 2 \text{ Cor} - \text{[PLP]}^{\text{Phil 3:2-4:3}} / \textbf{Gal} - \text{Phil} - \text{Rom} \ldots$$

The more extended account of the frame — running through what we can now appropriately call Paul's "year of crisis" — is:

$$\ldots \text{Paul VC2} \ldots$$
$$// \text{ year change(s) } //$$
$$\ldots \text{Apollos VC1 / [PLC]} - \text{Corinthian VEs / [Corinthian reply]} -$$
$$// \text{ year change } //$$
$$- 1 \text{ Cor (LT)} - \text{Apollos VC2 / super-apostles VC} - \text{Titus VC1} -$$
$$\text{Asian crisis}$$
$$- 2 \text{ Cor / Titus VC2} - \text{Paul VC3} - \text{enemies VC / [PLP]}^{\text{Phil 3:2-4:3}} / \textbf{Gal} - \text{Phil} -$$
$$// \text{ year change } //$$
$$\ldots \text{Rom} - \text{Paul VJ} \ldots$$

We could go on at this point to consider two further biographical questions, namely, the area and the timing of Paul's "Galatian" mission. But since both concern what we will call "founding visits," we will postpone them until the next chapter when they begin to be raised in earnest by our consideration of the Thessalonian correspondence. We should turn now instead to the first major dividend accruing to our overarching framing project from the sequencing of Galatians we have posited — although more than one bonus payment lies just ahead.

(2) The Resulting Extended Sequence

Galatians contains a wealth of information — albeit carefully nuanced — about some of Paul's most important activities prior to this dense letter sequence, information reaching all the way back to his life prior to his apostolic commission. This information comes almost entirely from 1:12–2:14:

> Previous life (1:13-14): zeal for the Torah, and persecution of the early church
> Apostolic commission (1:15-17)
> Missionary activity in the region of Damascus (1:17b)
> Activity in "Arabia" (1:17b)
> Activity having "returned" to Damascus (1:17b)
> Duration of "three years" (μετὰ ἔτη τρία; 1:18)
> Visit to Jerusalem — Paul's first as an apostle (1:18-20)
> Activity in the regions of Syria and Cilicia, not Judea (1:21-24)
> Duration of "fourteen years" (διὰ δεκατεσσάρων ἐτῶν; 2:1)
> Visit to Jerusalem — his second (2:1-10); collection inaugurated (2:10)
> An "incident," that is, dispute, at Syrian Antioch (2:11-14)
> > [Strictly speaking, Paul does not order VJ2 and what we will call the "Antioch incident" chronologically in Galatians, so we will simply juxtapose them in our developing frame for the moment.]

We need to make three observations concerning this extended sequence before we try to coordinate it with our existing letter sequence.

First, it seems most likely that, in typical ancient fashion, Paul is including a fraction of an entire year within his references in Galatians 1:18 and 2:1 to durations of time. It is unlikely that his visits to Jerusalem were after intervals of *exactly* three and fourteen years respectively — to the day, so to speak. So when he writes "three" and "fourteen" years, we should think in modern terms of 2.x and 13.x years; translating it "within three/fourteen years" might capture his ancient meaning more accurately.

Second, it might be asked whether these durations should be calculated consecutively or concurrently. Is Paul adding the intervals to one another, giving a possible combined chronological total of 15.x + .x years? Or is he starting again from the same marker in 2:1 and supplying only a chronological total of 13.x years overall? Or is he not supplying contiguous temporal intervals at all? A consecutive reckoning of Paul's intervals, leading to a space of 15.x + .x years, tends to break the biographical frame that is derivable from Acts. A concurrent approach can be used as a response to this difficulty. But there is nothing decisive in Paul's text suggesting that we should add up his numbers in a concurrent fashion — for example, a dative construction stating that something happened "in the third year [after X]," and then "in the fourteenth year [so implicitly after X again]."[44] Paul's language in 1:18 and 2:1 is accusative and so most likely simply denotes periods of temporal extent, using the metaphor of space for time; hence, the intervals in question extended for 2.x and 13.x years respectively. The surrounding narrative then orients their placement, although Paul's language is not as precise as his modern chronographers might wish[45] — a feature shared with most ancient chronological material (see Bickerman

44. This would presuppose that Paul's commission functioned like a regnal accession year or something similar, that is, as an event of universal calendrical importance in relation to which all other events could be positioned. This would not be an uncommon way for ancient people to think about time in certain contexts. But it seems more like a retrospective ecclesial valuation of Paul's apostolic role than a reading of his own accounts of his call and of subsequent events.

45. Although it is often overlooked, Luedemann (1984 [1980], 61-64) points out correctly that the temporal intervals Paul supplies do not necessarily have to be added together neatly in relation to visits to Jerusalem. Paul's repeated use of ἔπειτα might simply link preceding and following events in 1:18, 21, and 2:1. Temporal spans are supplied for only two of these statements; hence, other incidents and activity should arguably be inserted between them. The span of 2.x years in 1:18 might then begin after the activity of 1:17, namely, work in "Arabia" and a return to Damascus, suggesting further work in Damascus for 2.x years. And the span of 13.x years in 2:1 might begin after Paul's first visit to Jerusalem, which lasted for a fortnight in addition to travel time, and more importantly, also after his work in Syria and Cilicia (in v. 21) had begun. We should note, however, that Luedemann's reading might have perplexed Paul's Galatian auditors more than the simple approach. (Luedemann also rehearses and rebuts Suhl's case effectively — that the shift between the prepositions μετά and διά in 1:18 and 2:1, and rhetorical needs of the situation, i.e., length of time away from Jerusalem, suggest a concurrent reckoning. The prepositional shift is dubious grounds for a significant shift in meaning, and Paul's rhetorical needs would hardly be served much better by the addition of three to eleven years' absence.)

1980 [1968]). But since we are under no pressure at this moment to adopt a concurrent calculation to accommodate other dates and time intervals, we will employ for now the most straightforward approach, adding the two spans in a basic relationship with Paul's commission and his contact with Jerusalem, and simply see where this takes us. Other approaches are not being excluded, but merely set aside to be evaluated at the appropriate moment.

Third, it might be asked whether Paul is working with Roman or Jewish calendars — although fortunately, this is largely irrelevant. Second Corinthians makes two important references to a previous year, when the collection began. But both are references to some of the information conveyed to the Corinthians by the Previous Letter to Corinth, which was likely written prior to the start of both the Roman and the Jewish year; the closing of the popular travel season was effectively coterminous with the Jewish New Year, and the Roman New Year began in the middle of the winter, long after the sea lanes had tapered off to sparse winter traffic. Hence, Paul's previous letter to Corinth probably reached Corinth from Ephesus prior to both of the likely New Years in view. Our sequence has already indicated, moreover, that 2 Corinthians was written after Paul's journey from Asia to Macedonia, which began after Pentecost (see 1 Cor 16:8). Paul wrote 2 Corinthians in response to a coordinated rendezvous there with Titus. But this takes us either into the middle or toward the end of the summer, which is still prior to either the Jewish or the Roman New Year ending the year in question and beginning the next.[46]

In any case, our main concerns in what follows are with seasons, traveling times, and absolute intervals, for which we will supply a modern dating system. This is of course fortuitously Julian, that is, Roman, in its monthly references and basic account of the calendar year (and hence also a little deceptive), but it is post-Christian in absolute chronological or annual terms, that is, Gregorian. Whether Paul thought in Roman or Jewish terms, or in both,

---

46. My suspicion is, furthermore, that 2 Cor belongs toward the middle of the summer. Paul planned a fairly long stay with the Corinthians, as suggested by 1 Cor 16:6, but was unsure whether he would winter there. So he expected to be able to travel on either toward Jerusalem or to another mission if he chose, suggesting a planned arrival in Corinth in the late summer. The composition of 2 Cor would interrupt this plan, but at a relatively early stage. And the events we know of — the crisis in Asia and the sending of Titus with a Macedonian delegation to Corinth prior to Paul — do not suggest delaying this timetable by many months, as we have already seen. In addition, the composition after this of Gal, PLP, and Phil in Corinth suggests that the crisis with the enemies and the imprisonment and trial in Corinth could well have delayed him there, resulting in a departure after his release in the following spring. It was then this new crisis that took Paul's third visit to Corinth into both of the new years in question, in all probability.

does not matter that much for the dates of our biographical reconstruction as long as we realize that it is, in effect, an accurate anachronism.

With these clarifications in mind, we now come to the moment when we try to coordinate this extended sequence concerning Paul's previous life provided by Galatians with the detailed sequence of letters and events during Paul's year of crisis that is already in place. But how do we actually do this?

Most of the heavy lifting has already been done. That is, we know that Galatians belongs between 2 Corinthians and Romans, and hence in the middle of the collection project. Moreover, we know that the collection was announced to the Corinthians in the preceding year by the Previous Letter to Corinth. But we now also know that the collection was affirmed by Paul personally in Jerusalem, on his second (apostolic) visit to Jerusalem, as narrated subtly by Galatians 2:1-10. And it seems most likely that these last two events fell reasonably close to one another. Paul probably announced the collection to the Corinthians in the Previous Letter to Corinth on his return to the Aegean area from Jerusalem. If he traveled by way of Syrian Antioch and Galatia, as seems likely from Galatians 2:11-14 and 1 Corinthians 16:1, then this somewhat indirect journey would still have taken only — in sheer travel time — between 36.8 and 43.5 days (ORBIS July 31, 2013). So this is the lower limit to the temporal interval separating Paul's second visit to Jerusalem (and his affirmation of the collection to the Jerusalem leadership) and his composition of the Previous Letter to Corinth, upon his arrival in the Aegean, in Ephesus. Chapter 5 will insert some dramatic events into this journey, but these unfold in terms of months, not years, so our basic coordination between Paul's second Jerusalem visit and the Previous Letter to Corinth, and then with the rest of the letters that mention the collection, will hold good.

We will of course look as the frame develops for further precision concerning this configuration, but we certainly have enough now to be getting on with, namely, a basic outline for Paul's entire missionary career up through Romans — a comprehensive relative chronology. We will not include in the following synthesis all the information that we have sequenced concerning Paul's year of crisis, just the most salient items. But perhaps most importantly, we must from this point on speak of three visits by Paul to Jerusalem.

Previous life as a Pharisee
Apostolic commission
Activity in the region of Damascus
Activity in "Arabia"
Activity in Damascus

First visit to Jerusalem, 2.x years after commission
Activity in Syria and Cilicia
. . . Second visit to Corinth . . .
// implicit year change in modern terms //
Second visit to Jerusalem / Antioch incident, 13.x years after first visit
[Previous Letter to Corinth] / activity in Asia
[Corinthian reply]
// year change //
1 Corinthians — 2 Corinthians
Third visit to Corinth
[Previous Letter to Philippi] / Galatians — Philippians
// year change //
Romans
Third visit to Jerusalem . . .

And with this sequence realized, we can now turn and rapidly cut a veritable Gordian knot in Pauline biography: the relationship between Paul's second visit to Jerusalem, recounted in Galatians 2:1-10, and the incident at Syrian Antioch, recounted in 2:11-14.

(3) The Relationship Between Paul's Second Visit to Jerusalem and the Antioch Incident

Although many scholars assume that the order between these events as narrated in Galatians is their original historical order, nothing in the text necessitates this, and much later historical and theological reconstruction rests on the decision, so it is worth scrutinizing carefully. As Luedemann (esp. 1984 [1980]) has pointed out, rhetors in Paul's day could arrange the events in their narratives in order to achieve maximum rhetorical advantage, and so could abandon strict historical sequencing when necessary, although ideally without causing confusion. Much modern literary analysis of texts also exposes the jumbled chronologies operative within them. Put more positively, texts arrange their material with rather different goals in mind than sheer temporal sequence, and do so frequently. Plots are seldom strictly historical. And a careful reading attuned to this issue reveals that Galatians itself jumps around overtly in strictly chronological and historical terms.

The letter begins with Paul's present apostleship, although this is grounded in God's past resurrection of Jesus from the dead (v. 1). The text returns to the brothers presently with Paul at the time of the letter's composition (v. 2a) but then speaks again of the past moment of Christ's redeeming death (v. 4), doxologically pivoting after this to a brief focus on eternity, or the present extending into the age to come (v. 5). The letter's distinctive opening paragraph then begins by expressing astonishment at the Galatians' recent desertion "from the one who called you" (v. 6) precipitated by the arrival of certain "troublers" (v. 7) — two separate events in the past — and going on to posit a hypothetical future: if Paul's group or even heavenly messengers should come and preach a different proclamation from the one they first received, they should be accursed (vv. 8-9). The text then returns to the matter of Paul's proclamation, stating that it was received by way of revelation, here referencing Paul's commission (vv. 11-12). And from this earlier point, it pushes still further into the past as it begins to speak of Paul's previous way of life (v. 13). A more sequential (albeit selective) account then begins, which we have studied in some detail.

After this more obviously biographical material, the text returns to the present in 2:15-16, presumably folding various Jewish Christians into Paul's presuppositions, and thereby referencing their past conversions, before finishing the sentence with a future reference: "through works of Torah all flesh will not be declared righteous."

We could go on, but enough has surely been said to make the point that the temporal references within Galatians are rhetorically deployed and extremely dynamic. They oscillate between various events in the past, the present, and the future, often within the same sentences. There is no basis, then, for insisting on strict temporal continuity within the biographical enumeration unless that is explicitly signaled. And in the case of 2:11-14, it is not. This subsection begins by saying simply, "[And] *when* Cephas came to Antioch . . ." (Ὅτε δὲ ἦλθεν Κηφᾶς εἰς Ἀντιόχειαν). So Luedemann is right to pose the question whether this incident followed the meeting just described in 2:1-10 — the majority position — or preceded it. Deciding this question is difficult, however, and especially given the methodological constraints of proper framing. Nevertheless, our developing frame provides some relatively simple pieces of evidence that avoid circularity, and point quite strongly in the direction of one solution. In order to grasp these, however, certain further features in the data must be appreciated.

Galatians 2:1-10 describes a meeting dedicated — at least in large measure — to resolving a particular issue that was clearly quite contentious. The issue related to whether Titus, a convert to Paul's movement, needed to be circumcised. Paul presents this meeting as a successful deliberation that parted on good terms with the key parties all shaking hands, and Paul apparently committing to a gift of a large sum of money — the nature of this commitment being suitably defined. Experts in modern conflict resolution, most notably in restorative justice, would recognize here immediately a traditional process designed to resolve conflict.[47] Paul's second visit to Jerusalem was a process of conflict resolution that ended well but clearly presupposed a prior problem.

The incident that took place at Syrian Antioch, recounted in Galatians 2:11-14, is in many respects the opposite of this. It describes public confrontations between Paul and other key leaders in the early church, most notably, Barnabas and Cephas, and conflict with James is also indirectly present. In particular, Paul challenged Cephas, apparently unanswerably, but the situation is left narratively and biographically unresolved. Paul never tells us what came next. We are left with his pungent denunciation of Cephas's playacting, not knowing what Cephas did after this, or what Paul did. In short, the account of an incident at Antioch in Galatians 2:11-14 describes a situation of conflict that is left unresolved.

We should now try to sequence the two events, recalling that Paul's second Jerusalem visit implies a prior conflict followed by its resolution, while the incident at Antioch is itself a conflict that may or may not have eventually reached resolution. There are only two basic possibilities:

1. [implied conflict] — resolution at Jerusalem — conflict at Antioch . . .
2. conflict at Antioch — resolution at Jerusalem . . .

The first possibility suggests that the rhetorical order was the original historical order, and it leaves its slightly more extended historical sequence with an unresolved conflict in place between Paul and the Jerusalem leaders. The second possibility suggests that the rhetorical order of the events is precisely rhetorical and not historical; it generates a simpler historical narrative of two main phases that leaves the conflict between Paul and the Jerusalem leaders resolved. And we need now to ask which sequence fits best into our existing frame, recalling that Galatians itself has already been located after 1 and 2 Corinthians and before Philippians and Romans, alongside the Previous Letter to Philippi.

47. See in particular Moore and McDonald (2000); Zehr (2002); Pranis (2005). C. Marshall (2012) traces these processes out superbly in relation to Lk 10:30-37 and 15:11-32, i.e., the parables of the Good Samaritan and the Two Brothers, which are treated as instances of victim reintegration and offender reintegration respectively. A charming overview of traditional approaches to conflict resolution in dialogue with modern practices is provided by Diamond (2012, 79-170 [pt. 2, "Peace and War"]).

There is a fairly obvious answer to this question. Sequence 1, which equates rhetorical order with historical order, is highly implausible when placed within the existing letter sequence. Sequence 2, however, fits neatly when we recognize that 1 Corinthians — a letter penned in the spring of Paul's year of crisis, after which Paul wrote Galatians — speaks strongly of unity between Paul and Jerusalem in 15:1-11.

This text is one of Paul's most ecumenical passages, affirming in the strongest possible terms that his gospel and the gospel of the apostles and the Twelve are part of the same tradition. It therefore presupposes a fundamentally resolved relationship between Paul and Jerusalem. And sequence 1 struggles to make sense of this, while sequence 2 can integrate it with ease.

Sequence 1 rapidly gets into all sorts of difficulties. It leaves Paul's relationship with Jerusalem fundamentally unresolved; his relationships with James, Cephas, and Barnabas confrontational, divided, and presumably in jeopardy. Its advocates now have two equally unworkable choices when trying to explain the ecumenical equanimity displayed by 1 Corinthians shortly after Paul's second Jerusalem visit and just a few months before Galatians. What can they do with the disruption left trailing historically by the nasty dispute at Antioch?

They can try to resolve the aftermath of the Antioch incident before the Previous Letter to Corinth and the year of crisis begins. However, any such resolution would seem to be unlikely without a further visit to the key parties involved, as in Galatians 2:1-10, and this would be a visit most plausibly to Jerusalem. But a visit to Jerusalem is excluded by the silence in Galatians concerning one. Moreover, the sources are silent concerning any dramatic events at Antioch that took place between Paul's second Jerusalem visit and the composition of 1 Corinthians (not to mention the Previous Letter to Corinth, which inaugurated the conciliatory gesture of the collection), during which we would have to posit both a breakdown in all these key relationships *and* their restoration. So this attempted solution falters.

Alternatively, they could try to resolve the difficulties by placing the Antioch incident after 1 Corinthians. First Corinthians could thereby bask in the lingering glow of the Jerusalem meeting recounted in Galatians 2:1-10, and the disruptions apparent at Antioch could follow in the broader sequence just prior to Galatians. However, there is of course absolutely no evidence that Paul made a dash back to Syria at this time to confront a series of Jewish Christian leaders, and we know more about this period in his life than any other. He had his hands full right where he was! So this attempted solution collapses as well.

Sequence 2, however, leaves Paul's relationship with Jerusalem funda-mentally *resolved*, and hence the broader narrative flows on plausibly from his second visit to the holy city through the affirmations of 1 Corinthians 15 in the spring of the next year. The further disturbance to that relationship then arrives after 1 Corinthians with the appearance of the enemies, in response to which Galatians was written. And this sequence arguably explains Paul's rhetorical reversal of these incidents, at least in part. The reversal leaves Paul courageously standing firm for the gospel — if necessary, *contra mundum* — just the impression the Galatians need to gather. Moreover, this sequence explains why Paul went to Jerusalem in the first place. The Antioch incident and its immediate precursors *were* the conflict that had to be resolved per-sonally in Jerusalem (although this is not a contention in direct support of the sequence; it is merely helpful).[48] And we also learn how the dispute ended, that is, reasonably well, at least in the short term.[49]

In short, sequence 2, taking the Galatian events in reverse order, explains what is going on through the year of crisis perfectly, especially in relation to 1 Corinthians 15, and without complication or multiplication, whereas se-quence 1, in either of its two variations, seems unworkable. So we will proceed on the assumption that the Antioch incident preceded, and in effect caused, Paul's second visit to Jerusalem, and will adjust our developing frame accord-ingly.[50] With this realization in place, we can turn to the matter of possible external references and dating — something that, if successful, would anchor our relative sequence firmly to external events, which would in turn generate further important chronological predictions.

48. It also explains Paul's later ambiguity about the reception of the collection in Je-rusalem in Rom 15:30-32. After the arrival of the enemies, along with their counter-narrative concerning Jerusalem, Paul is no longer sure of the disposition *of* the Jerusalem leadership toward him. However, that he is still traveling there with a large sum of money and under threat of death speaks volumes concerning his ecumenical commitment.

49. And this means that we can dispense in turn with those biographical extrapolations that know what happened after this dispute on the basis of Gal 2:11-14 alone, a text which says absolutely nothing about its aftermath but ends in the middle of the argument, with Paul rebuking Cephas.

50. And this realization lends further, albeit marginal, support to the suspicion that Paul and Barnabas arrived in Jerusalem from Antioch for the conference with a sum of money — a clever stratagem! This would also explain the shift from plural to singular in the verbs of Gal 2:10; Barnabas is not primarily involved in Paul's current collection, as he was, presumably, in the collection from Antioch. Clearly, however, Acts data will be necessary to confirm the existence of an Antioch collection solidly, notably 11:27-30.

3. Dating the Sequence

In view of the following chronological anchor, we should firmly resist any suggestion that Paul's letters provide insufficient data in and of themselves to generate an absolute chronology. This assertion — made distressingly frequently — is simply mistaken (and after the following chapter, we will have doubled the evidence for its rejection).[51] There is a firm absolute date lurking within Paul's epistolary data.

3.1 The Aretas Datum

In 2 Corinthians 11:32-33, Paul tells a strange little story to the Corinthians, although its puzzling rhetorical role need not detain us here.[52] Usefully, he even swears on oath in the preceding verse that, however improbable its content, it is the truth. At some point, he escaped from an "ethnarch" who had been appointed by King Aretas to oversee the city of Damascus. He apparently avoided armed guards and patrols blocking his exit from the city through one of its famous seven gates — the ancient equivalent of a lockdown — by slipping out over the walls. (This involved being lowered in a basket from a window

---

51. Riesner's "Pauline Chronology" in Westerholm's (2011) introduction to Paul says almost immediately: "No statement in Paul's letters allows a clear connection to a concrete date from contemporary history, rendering the establishment of an absolute chronology effectively impossible" (Riesner 2011, 9). Haacker's entry in Dunn's (2003b) introduction does not explicitly repudiate the possibility of deriving a date from Paul's letters but does do so implicitly: "The only sure basis for the chronology of Paul's missionary career is his encounter with the proconsul L. A. Gallio in Corinth according to Acts 18:12-17" (Haacker 2003, 20). Betz concurs: "While scholars agree that priority of credibility should be given to Paul's own letters, without Acts no extended sequence of events can be determined" (1992/*ABD* 5:190). Donfried's statement in the same resource is more explicit and accurate in methodological terms than Betz's but contains serious lapses: "When all is said and done, Paul gives us not one specific date. Inevitably, if one is to establish a possible chronology of this period, there will have to be some dependence on Acts. Recognizing this, one should be cautious to use Acts in a way which is both critical and plausible. Yet it must be acknowledged that no matter from what perspective one views the data, *there can be no absolutely definite chronology of this period;* all attempts must be tentative and subject to correction and revision" (1992/*ABD* 1:1017).

52. Welborn (1999) provides a useful suggestion, although I am not entirely convinced by it. I suspect that Paul is developing an Odyssean narrative, rooted in the *Odyssey*, in which cunning and dangerous escapes demonstrate a certain sort of wisdom and strength. The importance of Odyssean themes to 2 Cor 10–13 has been noted briefly by Malherbe (1983a), although Malherbe's principal focus is on 2 Cor 10:3-6.

in the wall; present-day inhabitants of Damascus living on the walls still use similar contraptions to avoid the long walk, carrying goods and so on, to and from the city gates.)

[11:31] ὁ θεὸς καὶ πατὴρ τοῦ κυρίου Ἰησοῦ οἶδεν, ὁ ὢν εὐλογητὸς εἰς τοὺς αἰῶνας, ὅτι οὐ ψεύδομαι. [32] ἐν Δαμασκῷ ὁ ἐθνάρχης Ἀρέτα τοῦ βασιλέως ἐφρούρει τὴν πόλιν Δαμασκηνῶν πιάσαι με, [33] καὶ διὰ θυρίδος ἐν σαργάνῃ ἐχαλάσθην διὰ τοῦ τείχους καὶ ἐξέφυγον τὰς χεῖρας αὐτοῦ.

The reason this odd episode generates an absolute date is fairly simple. We have no record other than Paul's comment here of the city of Damascus being under the direct control of King Aretas — this necessarily being a reference to King Aretas IV of Nabataea (b. ca. 8 BCE). And when we are forced to determine when this must have been — since Paul attests on oath that it was the case — there is only one, relatively small historical window for this control, although on reflection it seems to be a plausible one.[53] We can thus date the episode reasonably precisely.

Damascus was part of a group of autonomous cities located broadly to the east of Galilee and Judea known as the Decapolis. However, it lay some distance away from the other cities that enjoyed independent status, although within territory that Aretas IV's great forebear, Aretas III, had controlled. Rather significantly for the following argument, it lay immediately to the north of the tetrarch Philip's territory, the rest of the Decapolis lying to the south. Josephus provides details of Philip's territory. It comprised various areas to the north and east of the Sea of Galilee known as Gaulanitis, Batanaea, and Trachonitis.[54]

Philip himself died in 34 CE. His tetrarchy was then administered "in trust," Josephus tells us, by the governor of Syria (*Jewish Antiquities* 18.108; Josephus is our principal source for these events). However, that post was empty

---

53. Significantly, all the other options offered to explain this story are fundamentally implausible. The main alternatives are: (1) that the city was actually being guarded from the outside; (2) that the ethnarch of King Aretas was in charge of only part of the city, as an important trade representative or local community leader on analogy to the ruler of the Jewish community in Alexandria; and (3) that King Aretas was gifted the city on the accession of Gaius in 37 CE. But options 1 and 2 cannot explain why Paul had to leave the city. If option 1 were the case, he would have been safer staying inside; if option 2 were the case, he would have needed only to stay in the appropriate quarters of the city and/or to appeal to the governor. And option 3 is unattested and highly unlikely. Aretas was not a client of Gaius, or even a client king within the empire. These options are catalogued and refuted in more detail in my 2002.

54. See *Jewish Antiquities* 15.343-46; 18.27-28, 106-8, 114; 20.138; *Jewish War* 2.247.

from shortly after Philip's death as well, so it seems that Antipas, the governor of Galilee and Perea, and a devoted client of the aging emperor Tiberius, administered Philip's former territories on Rome's behalf — and presumably taking a suitable cut for his troubles (18.113).

At roughly this time, Josephus reports that Antipas was attacked by King Aretas of Nabataea, suffering a serious military reverse (18.113-14). The flash point seems to have been a border dispute around Gamala, a town that lay on the eastern side of the Sea of Galilee, in Philip's territory of Gaulanitis, but near to the Decapolis (18.113). It is this event that plausibly led to King Aretas's control over the city of Damascus.[55]

Aretas, as evidenced directly by Paul, seems to have extended his conquest of Philip's former territory at this time to include the northernmost member of the Decapolis. (Damascus would have been a great prize for dynastic, agricultural, and commercial reasons.) We cannot say whether Aretas already controlled the rest of the Decapolis, to the south of Gaulanitis, before his defeat of Antipas, although it seems likely that this powerful and aggressive ruler had been systematically extending his territory for some time at the expense of these independent cities. Their annexation would not have caused the same tensions between Aretas and the Roman emperor that conquests of the territory of imperial clients could. But we can say with confidence that Aretas nevertheless could not realistically have controlled distant Damascus without first taking control over the intervening territory of Gaulanitis, Batanea, and Trachonitis, which had formerly been ruled by Philip and was now being administered by Antipas.[56] Nevertheless, Josephus attests that at some point Aretas did succeed in defeating Antipas, thereby extending his reach over the former tetrarchy, and it is plausible to suppose on the basis of Paul's evidence that Aretas took this opportunity to grasp Damascus as well.

After this victory, Aretas would no doubt have appointed his own governors over the cities he had just conquered, and this would have allowed a situation to develop in which his governor, seeking to arrest Paul, might have guarded the city to try to apprehend him, since Paul's exact whereabouts were presumably unknown. Hence, the date of the successful attack by Aretas on Antipas and his territories opens the chronological window, so to speak, within which Paul's escape from Damascus can be anchored.

Several considerations allow us to date the invasion, and the opening of the window, with reasonable precision to the year 36 CE.

55. This historical narrative was first realized in Bowersock (1983, 65-69).
56. My argument in 2002 is insufficiently precise concerning this point.

(i) Antipas had appealed to the emperor Tiberius for help after his military humiliation (*Jewish Antiquities* 18.115). Vitellius, the governor of Syria, failed to respond immediately to the invasion, however, for reasons to be noted shortly. He marched south to assist the emperor's client only after a direct order to do so (18.115). But when he arrived in Ptolemais he received news of the emperor's death, at which point he declined to press his military expedition any further (18.90-95, 120-24). The emperor's death is well documented as occurring in March 16, 37 CE, news of this possibly arriving in Ptolemais as early as 30 March, or just over thirteen days later.[57] And this suggests that Aretas's original military strike and Antipas's defeat took place in the preceding fall of 36, since it is likely that Antipas was defeated by Aretas during the campaigning season and consequently at some point from the spring of 36 onward.

(ii) Vitellius's strange behavior is explicable in terms of another set of events that can also be dated to 36, and that suggest the defeat of Antipas by Aretas later rather than earlier in the campaigning season.

In the same year as the invasion, Vitellius had presided over a great diplomatic triumph — a successful negotiation of peace with the dreaded Parthian Empire currently gathering in strength under the leadership of the formidable Artabanus. Antipas had played a minor role in these negotiations, having been charged with managing and financing them. However, he had also taken the liberty of writing to the imperial court with a glowing account of their success prior to Vitellius's own report being written and dispatched, and had thereby upstaged Vitellius at the moment of his greatest political triumph (*Jewish Antiquities* 18.96-105).[58] This offense explains Vitellius's later reluctance to intervene on Antipas's

---

57. ORBIS (April 23, 2014). Incidentally, this dating corroborates the suggestion of Josephus that Vitellius dismissed his troops at this time to their winter quarters (*Jewish Antiquities* 18.124). Pilate's tenure as ruler of Judea also ended during this period with his dispatch to Rome to answer for his massacre of members of a gathering of Samaritans on Mount Gerizim (18.85-89; see also 15.405). There is possibly some confusion in Josephus concerning these events, but they do not need to be untangled completely given our present concern.

58. This important negotiation is also noted by Tacitus, *Ann.* 2.58 (although the year is far too early — 18 CE); Suetonius, *Gaius Caligula* 14.3 and *Vitellius* 2.4 (who locates the negotiation slightly more accurately during the reign of Gaius); and Cassius Dio 59.27.3-4 (who also locates it during the reign of Gaius). Josephus is certainly correct, however, in placing it where he does, in 36 CE, the last year of Tiberius's reign. His intertwined chronologies of Pilate, Vitellius, and Antipas only make sense here, and yet here they make perfect sense. More detail concerning this claim is provided by my 2002, esp. 293.

behalf after his humiliation by Aretas, along with key aspects of Aretas's political calculations. Vitellius was apparently only too happy to turn a blind eye to Antipas's reversal. Moreover, the strike by Aretas was also in part a matter of his honor and revenge. The wife famously thrown over by Antipas for Herodias was Aretas's daughter, who narrowly escaped being murdered.[59] So both local leaders had good reason to see Antipas humiliated.

These events suggest in turn that the chronological window for Paul's escape was later rather than earlier in the year. The negotiations with the Parthians had to take place, and the ensuing exchanges of news, before Aretas's invasion. And it would have taken a further short period of time for Aretas's new appointees to take over administration of the former tetrarchy and Damascus after his victory, and then to respond to local requests for the capture of troublemakers like Paul.

It follows from these considerations that Paul must have escaped Damascus from sometime in the fall of 36 CE onward. But we should note that this chronological window for Paul's escape then closed fairly quickly.

The emperor Tiberius died in early 37 CE, and his successor, Gaius, gifted a great deal of land in and around Judea to his friend and client Herod Agrippa, notably the former territories of Philip and Lysanias (*Jewish Antiquities* 18.237; see also 15.344; 20.138), hence Trachonitis, Batanea, and Gaulanitis, along with Chalchis in the Lebanon. This grant would inevitably have removed control of Damascus from the hands of Aretas since it lay beyond the northern borders of these territories, and the rest of Aretas's domains lay to their south. If Aretas ignored this new arrangement, moreover, he risked a military confrontation directly with a new emperor and his favorite as opposed to an elderly emperor and his hated client — and even the latter calculation had proved unwise, only Tiberius's fortuitous death protecting Nabataea from invasion by upward of twenty thousand Roman troops. And this all suggests that Paul's escape from a governor of Damascus appointed by King Aretas must have taken place before the king's retreat from his recently acquired territory in the spring of 37. It follows, furthermore, that we now have an absolute date for an event in Paul's life that is derived from his own letters — and, in this case, completely inadvertently, which increases its value. It remains only to trace through its implications.

---

59. See *Jewish Antiquities* 18.109-15. Josephus recounts further that many Jews viewed this defeat as divine punishment for Antipas's execution of John the Baptizer (18.116-19).

3.2 Dating the Sequence, and Its Implications

The escape almost certainly took place on the eve of Paul's first apostolic visit to Jerusalem (see Gal 1:18). It is highly unlikely, that is, that it coincided with his first arrival in Damascus, immediately after his divine commission, since Galatians tells us that he went after this into "Arabia" (1:17b). If the escape belonged at this time, then he would have begun to evangelize the territory of the governor and the monarch whom he was trying to escape. Much more probable is the supposition that the hostility drew his work in Arabia/Nabataea and the Decapolis to a close. Paul escaped out of the area to Jerusalem, and he subsequently went on to missionary work in different regions, namely, Syria and Cilicia (1:21). And this suggests coordinating the date of Paul's dramatic escape with his first visit to Jerusalem.

For simplicity's sake, we will place the escape for now at the front end of the chronological window, in the fall of 36 CE, aware that our absolute dates could well shift six months or so. However, later data will enable us to narrow our options down here appropriately and to affirm this location with reasonable confidence (although some of that data is supplied by Acts).

Reckoning backward and forward from the Aretas datum in the fall of 36 CE and its coordination with Paul's first Jerusalem visit, the following absolute chronology is generated for Paul's career:

Prior to 34 CE:	Previous life as a Pharisee
Early/mid-34:	Apostolic commission
Early 34-mid-36:	Activity in the region of Damascus
	Activity in "Arabia"
	Return to Damascus
Late 36:	Escape from Damascus
	First visit to Jerusalem, 2.x years after commission
37:	Activity in Syria and Cilicia
	. . . Second visit to Corinth . . .
Late 49/early 50:	Antioch incident
	Second visit to Jerusalem, 13.x years after first
Late 50:	[Previous Letter to Corinth] / activity in Asia
	[Corinthian reply]
51:	**1 Corinthians, 2 Corinthians**
	Third visit to Corinth
	[Previous Letter to Philippi], **Galatians, Philippians**
52:	**Romans**
	Third visit to Jerusalem

Absolute chronologies allow greater precision and occasional correlation with external events. They generate precise expectations, which can be either strikingly confirmed or disconfirmed. In other words, they can be checked. What important expectations and potential dis/confirmations are generated by this schema? Two clusters of implications should be noted carefully — first, surrounding Paul's "year of crisis," and second, surrounding the early part of his career.

First, we can now see that Paul's year of crisis extended principally from the spring of 51 CE, when he began to deal directly with the deterioration in the situation at Corinth with 1 Corinthians / the Letter of Tears, to the spring of 52, with the enemies arriving about halfway through this calendar year. Hence, very significantly, we now expect an imprisonment and capital trial of Paul in Corinth at some point in the second half of this period, and so in the winter that extended from 51 to 52. Paul's letter to the Philippians in particular seems to suggest a period of trouble here extending through several months. Moreover, we expect Paul to depart on his third Jerusalem visit, with the collection, in the spring of 52 CE. A considerable amount of data can be brought to bear on these expectations in due course, and I suggest that the underlying dates will be vindicated convincingly.[60]

Second, a large window has been opened for missionary work by Paul, beginning from his first visit to Jerusalem in late 36 CE, and closing only in or just before 50 CE, by which time he is evidently at work in Asia. In the intervening period, he must at some point have evangelized the areas to which he later sent letters, namely, Galatia, Macedonia, and Achaia. These are the only places for which we currently have extant letters; we have no letters addressed to communities in Arabia, the Decapolis, Syria, or Cilicia, although we do have epistolary data attesting to a church in Syrian Antioch — principally, Galatians 2:11-14. There is no reason to suppose that the evangelizing of these areas took place late in the period, although it might have. Nor do we yet know in what order it took place. But we can now search for evidence that Paul founded

60. It would be interesting if an imperial triumph occurred just prior to the middle of 51 CE, thereby explaining the allusion in 2 Cor 2:14-16. And arguably, one did. Claudius celebrated the final capture of Cara[c]tacus, the guerrilla leader of British opposition to Roman rule, who was apprehended around 51 CE. The emperor famously pardoned him: see Tacitus, *Annals* 12.37-38. See also Tacitus, *History* 3.45; Cassius Dio 60.19-22; Josephus, *Jewish War* 3.6; Eutropius, *Roman History* 7, 13; Suetonius, *Claudius* 17; *Vespasian* 4; Zonara, *Chronikon* 186. However, it is important to appreciate that Claudius celebrated triumphs in relation to the conquest of Britain repeatedly. The first probably took place shortly after the campaign in 43 CE. The Arch of Claudius at Rome, voted in his honor in 43, was dedicated in 51 CE, or perhaps early in 52.

Christian communities in the northeast quadrant of the Mediterranean in the late 30s and the 40s — the reign of Gaius followed by the first two-thirds of the reign of Claudius — and this is an impressively early date for vigorous Christian proselytization of this nature, given that the founding events underlying the movement had in all probability taken place in Judea only around 30 CE. Paul has been evangelizing local territories since 34, and more distant regions since late 36, and he has not been alone in doing so. We should therefore remain open to the imprint of external events between 37 and 50 CE on any of his letters written at this time, an expectation that leads directly to our next chapter and its detailed considerations of 1 and 2 Thessalonians.

CHAPTER FOUR

Locating the Thessalonian Correspondence

1. Locating 1 Thessalonians

1.1 The Surrounding Sequence and the Immediate Implied Exigence

The texts already in play supply enough evidence for the articulation of a basic sequence of missions in what we would call Europe, the events of which should now be teased out as fully as the epistolary evidence allows.

In Paul's parlance, the missions took place in the regions of Macedonia and Achaia, and apparently in that order (see 1 Thess 1:7-9a;[1] 3:1). The founding visit to Philippi preceded the founding visit to Thessalonica (1 Thess 2:2a; Phil 4:15-16),[2] these being the two successful local missions that we know of at this time in Macedonia. Paul, Silvanus, and Timothy seem to have been directly involved. The Philippian mission involved suffering and insult (1 Thess 2:2a) and was followed by further struggle in Thessalonica (1 Thess 1:6; 2:2b, 14; 3:3, 4, 7; this is addressed in more detail momentarily). Paul, along with Silvanus and Timothy, wrote 1 Thessalonians from Athens at some point after these founding visits (1 Thess 1:1; 3:1),[3] hence from the neighboring region

1. 1:7: ὥστε γενέσθαι ὑμᾶς τύπον πᾶσιν τοῖς πιστεύουσιν ἐν τῇ Μακεδονίᾳ καὶ ἐν τῇ Ἀχαΐᾳ κ.τ.λ.

2. 1 Thess 2:2: ἀλλὰ προπαθόντες καὶ ὑβρισθέντες, καθὼς οἴδατε, ἐν Φιλίπποις ἐπαρρησιασάμεθα ἐν τῷ θεῷ ἡμῶν λαλῆσαι πρὸς ὑμᾶς τὸ εὐαγγέλιον τοῦ θεοῦ; Phil 4:15: οἴδατε δὲ καὶ ὑμεῖς, Φιλιππήσιοι, ὅτι ἐν ἀρχῇ τοῦ εὐαγγελίου, ὅτε ἐξῆλθον ἀπὸ Μακεδονίας, οὐδεμία μοι ἐκκλησία ἐκοινώνησεν εἰς λόγον δόσεως καὶ λήμψεως εἰ μὴ ὑμεῖς μόνοι, [16] ὅτι καὶ ἐν Θεσσαλονίκῃ καὶ ἅπαξ καὶ δὶς εἰς τὴν χρείαν μοι ἐπέμψατε.

3. 1 Thess 1:1: Παῦλος καὶ Σιλουανὸς καὶ Τιμόθεος τῇ ἐκκλησίᾳ Θεσσαλονικέων. . . . [3:1] Διὸ μηκέτι στέγοντες εὐδοκήσαμεν καταλειφθῆναι ἐν Ἀθήναις μόνοι [2] καὶ ἐπέμψαμεν

of Achaia.[4] And the same three figures were responsible for the mission in Corinth (2 Cor 1:19).[5] We are, however, unsure at this point whether all these events followed immediately upon one another, so that the time intervals between them were relatively short, or whether they were more dispersed. The data just noted suggest only that the founding missionary visit to Thessalonica (FVT) followed straightaway the founding visit to Philippi (FVP), so it is conceivable that the founding visit to Corinth (FVC) might have preceded the later founding visit to Athens (FVA). More significantly, the Achaian mission could have been separated from the Macedonian mission by a period of time (assisted here by a possible reading of 1 Thess 1:8-10). All the events seem to belong to the same broad missionary trajectory, because the missionaries are the same — most notably, including Silvanus only here within Paul's broader activities. But we do not know exactly how long this missionary group operated together or what other regions it may have visited. If it was effective and harmonious, it presumably could have worked and traveled together for years. Most scholars probably have strong initial preferences for the temporal priority of the Athenian over the Corinthian mission and for their immediate contiguity, but this is almost certainly because of the Acts narrative, and we are not yet able to control that source's contributions precisely. So before moving on, we must try to answer the question of immediate versus loose sequencing for the missions in Macedonia and Achaia that involved Paul, Silvanus, and Timothy. And a plausible epistolary response to this question will turn largely on the provenance of 1 Thessalonians. Does this letter follow immediately the missions to Philippi and Thessalonica, bolting the missions to the two neighboring regions closely together (i.e., at least with Paul's founding visit to Athens), or is a significant interval of time discernible between the original events in Macedonia and the composition of 1 Thessalonians in Achaia? Compare the sequence

$$... FVP — FVT ... FVA — 1\ Thess ... FVC ...$$
or even

Τιμόθεον, τὸν ἀδελφὸν ἡμῶν καὶ συνεργὸν τοῦ θεοῦ ἐν τῷ εὐαγγελίῳ τοῦ Χριστοῦ, εἰς τὸ στηρίξαι ὑμᾶς καὶ παρακαλέσαι ὑπὲρ τῆς πίστεως ὑμῶν κ.τ.λ.

4. Scholars sometimes forget that Athens was in Achaia; hence, the Athenian mission, attested in 3:1 indirectly, was the first Pauline mission in Achaia (see also 1 Cor 1:16; 16:15). The putative Corinthian location of 1 Thess will be addressed in more detail shortly but has little to recommend it on epistolary grounds.

5. 2 Cor 1:19: ὁ τοῦ θεοῦ γὰρ υἱὸς Ἰησοῦς Χριστὸς ὁ ἐν ὑμῖν δι᾽ ἡμῶν κηρυχθείς, δι᾽ ἐμοῦ καὶ Σιλουανοῦ καὶ Τιμοθέου κ.τ.λ.

... FVP — FVT ... FVC ... FVA — 1 Thess ...

with the rather tighter sequence

... FVP — FVT — FVA — 1 Thess — FVC ...

The exact exigence and corresponding composition and rhetorical strategy of 1 Thessalonians are much debated.[6] But framing can rest on basic and largely incontestable claims here.[7]

The letter contains a distinctive implied narrative about its prehistory. Paul and Silvanus had intended to visit the Thessalonians but had been prevented from doing so (2:18), and Paul attributes the failure to evil countervailing forces. So they had resolved to stay in Athens but send Timothy to visit (his movements apparently not being constrained by evil forces). Timothy had been sent to "strengthen" and "encourage" the Thessalonians' fidelity (3:2) so that they

---

6. The useful language and definition of exigence come from Bitzer (see esp. 1968). Jasinski (2001, accessed June 7, 2013) provides a helpful explanation of exigence, concluding that "situational analysis is at the center of any effort to understand and assess the instrumental function of rhetorical practice" — a Pauline letter being a complex ancient rhetorical practice and act. Bitzer's much criticized "objectivism" (by Vatz and others) in relation to exigence should be augmented with elements of "constructivism," but his fundamental insight remains valid. And this was in certain respects just a recovery of the ancient insight that rhetorical acts are deeply shaped by their occasion. R. Longenecker (1990) utilizes Bitzer in the analysis of Gal.

7. Debate has unfolded over several issues in relation to 1 Thess, in addition to distinctive questions surrounding provenance — in particular, over the contributions of epistolary and rhetorical analysis to interpretation, the function of 2:1-11, and the role of Hellenistic philosophical discourse (SNTS focusing on these questions); and over the structure of the letter, with particular reference to its multiple acts of thanks, the definition of its "body," and the balance between the rhetoric (broadly speaking) of chs. 1-3 and the paranesis of chs. 4-5. There are many minor interpretative points of contention as well — the notorious text-critical crux of 2:7, the status of the virulently anti-Jewish (or anti-Judean) 2:14-16, the broader cultural resonances of the slogan "peace and safety" in 5:3 (i.e., whether this echoed the imperial cult), and so on. But most of these questions need not occupy us here, although some will be touched on in passing. Useful orientations to these debates are provided by the collections of studies in R. Collins (1990); and Donfried and Beutler (2000); and by the annotated bibliography by Weima and Porter (1998).

Among the commentators from whom I have learned the most are Best (1972), Wanamaker (1990), and Malherbe (2000). Jewett's (1986) contributions, although not in strict commentary form, have been deeply informative as well. What I suspect will be highly significant commentaries are forthcoming from Donfried (ICC) and Weima (BECNT). Among the more detailed secondary studies, Nicholl's (2004) superb doctoral thesis, published in the SNTSMS series, deserves special mention — and perhaps also more sustained attention. My rare demurrals from Nicholl's readings will be clearly noted in what follows.

would not be unsettled by certain sufferings (3:3).[8] He had duly visited and returned — a journey from Athens to Thessalonica taking between four days and a fortnight depending on mode,[9] and a return journey roughly the same.[10] And he had brought good news concerning the Thessalonians. They remained loyal and faithful, as well as loving and affectionate toward the missionaries (3:6).[11] The missionary party, apparently dominated by Paul (5:27-28), then wrote a letter in response that positively overflowed with thankfulness. The missionaries stated that they were encouraged by the Thessalonians' steadfastness (3:7-8),[12] although the letter went on to address other ethical situations that Timothy had communicated to Paul (see especially 4:1-8 and 5:4-11), and they responded to two direct inquiries from the community (see 4:9; 5:1).[13]

Especially significant within this narrative for our current purposes is one of the major stated causes of Paul's writing. The Thessalonians were suffering, and he was worried that this had weakened their resolve and their loyalty. Moreover, in the point crucial for any sequencing judgments, it seems that this suffering was closely connected to the suffering that they had all experienced during the original founding of the community. If the same basic period of suffering was in view, then it follows that 1 Thessalonians was composed not

---

8. [3:2] καὶ ἐπέμψαμεν Τιμόθεον, τὸν ἀδελφὸν ἡμῶν καὶ συνεργὸν τοῦ θεοῦ ἐν τῷ εὐαγγελίῳ τοῦ Χριστοῦ, εἰς τὸ στηρίξαι ὑμᾶς καὶ παρακαλέσαι ὑπὲρ τῆς πίστεως ὑμῶν [3] τὸ μηδένα σαίνεσθαι ἐν ταῖς θλίψεσιν ταύταις.

9. In January, representing winter possibilities, a rapid, direct journey by sea from Athens to Thessalonica would have averaged 3.3-3.5 days; a coastal sea journey taking care to travel only by day, 7.8-8.3 days; an overland journey at the typical speed for private travel, 13.3 days; an accelerated private journey (i.e., vehicular or on horseback), 9.6 days. In May, representing spring and summer possibilities, a rapid, direct journey by sea from Athens to Thessalonica would have averaged 3.8-4.4 days; a coastal sea journey taking care to travel only by day, 6.8-7.5 days; and the land averages are basically the same. Counterintuitively, then, sea travel would most probably have been slower in the spring, because of less favorable wind conditions (ORBIS May 7, 2013).

10. In January, a rapid, direct journey by sea from Thessalonica to Athens would have averaged 3-3.2 days; a coastal sea journey taking care to travel only by day, 7-7.5 days; and the land averages suggested are the same as above. In May, a direct journey would have averaged 3.6-4.3 days, and a coastal, more cautious journey, 6.2-7.3 days (ORBIS May 7, 2013).

11. [3:6] Ἄρτι δὲ ἐλθόντος Τιμοθέου πρὸς ἡμᾶς ἀφ' ὑμῶν καὶ εὐαγγελισαμένου ἡμῖν τὴν πίστιν καὶ τὴν ἀγάπην ὑμῶν καὶ ὅτι ἔχετε μνείαν ἡμῶν ἀγαθὴν πάντοτε κ. τ. λ.

12. [3:7] διὰ τοῦτο παρεκλήθημεν, ἀδελφοί, ἐφ' ὑμῖν ἐπὶ πάσῃ τῇ ἀνάγκῃ καὶ θλίψει ἡμῶν διὰ τῆς ὑμῶν πίστεως, [8] ὅτι νῦν ζῶμεν ἐὰν ὑμεῖς στήκετε ἐν κυρίῳ κ. τ. λ.

13. Some type of sexual immorality was addressed, then drunkenness; and the Thessalonians seem to have been concerned about the death of one or more of their community, as well as "times and seasons" in relation to the Lord Jesus' *parousia*.

long after the community's establishment and largely contiguous to it, and almost certainly prior to the Corinthian mission as well. (This would also make sense of the letter's composition in Athens.)

Paul first states in 1:6 that the Thessalonians received the word with suffering along with great joy (καὶ ὑμεῖς μιμηταὶ ἡμῶν ἐγενήθητε καὶ τοῦ κυρίου, δεξάμενοι τὸν λόγον ἐν θλίψει πολλῇ). He goes on to say in 2:2 that the original missionaries experienced suffering as well (ἐπαρρησιασάμεθα ἐν τῷ θεῷ ἡμῶν λαλῆσαι πρὸς ὑμᾶς τὸ εὐαγγέλιον τοῦ θεοῦ ἐν πολλῷ ἀγῶνι κ.τ.λ.), although this could be construed merely as "struggle." The narrative of suffering is amplified, however, when 2:14 states that the Thessalonians were persecuted, like the Judeans, by their own countrypeople (ὅτι τὰ αὐτὰ ἐπάθετε καὶ ὑμεῖς ὑπὸ τῶν ἰδίων συμφυλετῶν καθὼς καὶ αὐτοὶ ὑπὸ τῶν Ἰουδαίων); some would remove this last evidence as part of an interpolation — expanding Rudolf Knopf's (1905) suggestion that 2:16c was a marginal gloss — but this hypothesis is unnecessary and ultimately implausible, regardless of how much more palatable we might find it morally.[14] Following this third reference to difficulties, Paul moves to expressions of regret that he cannot be present (2:17-20). His account of Timothy's visit follows, in the aftermath of which the composition of the letter took place. And here he writes that a key cause of the missionaries' concern was the possibility that the Thessalonians had been unsettled by their suffering, and specifically by "*these* sufferings" (see τὸ μηδένα σαίνεσθαι ἐν ταῖς θλίψεσιν ταύταις in 3:3), this being the letter's fourth reference to suffering.[15] Hence, what is effectively a narrative of suffering runs through the letter to the midpoint of chapter 3. And it simply makes the most sense if the sufferings spoken of all refer to the same basic period of struggle that began when the community was founded. One continuous period of struggle is in view that was inaugurated when the missionaries came to Thessalonica and founded the community and has continued during their recent absence.

The first two instances of suffering specifically reference difficulties associated with the founding visit (1:6; 2:2). The third instance does not. It gives

14. Key advocates of the interpolation of 2:13-16 include Pearson (1971); Boers (1976); Koester (1982, 113). And, as we have just seen, Knopf (1905) suggested a variation on this proposal, a hypothesis expanded by Goguel (1925) to include vv. 14-16. The modern advocacy of interpolation tends to depart from Pearson's essay. Useful discussions of 2:14-16 include Jewett (1986, 36-42); Broer (1990); Holz (1990); Wanamaker (1990, 29-33); and Bockmuehl (2001); although I find Best (1972, 112-23, esp. 123) particularly crisp and persuasive. These scholars all reject the suggestion of an interpolation, largely on grounds of insufficient evidence.

15. I am grateful to my then doctoral student Colin Miller for forcing me to reckon appropriately with the implications of this phrase.

a more specific account of the suffering's agency — the Thessalonians' own fellow countrypeople. But it does not characterize that suffering differently, so listeners would have carried through the two markers already noted. Moreover, this identification would have been corroborated by the similarities in language between 1:6 and 2:14, both short accounts beginning with the same clause: ὑμεῖς μιμηταὶ . . . ἐγενήθητε.[16] Assisting this stylistic resumption, the substantive claim in both texts is the same as well — that the Thessalonian suffering was an imitation of Christ, of the missionaries, and, in due course, of the early church in Judea, in that it was inflicted by fellow countrypeople. Hence, not only does Paul give no indication of a shift in reference for these three accounts of suffering, but the text resists any such differentiation. It is therefore hard to avoid the conclusion that 3:3, with the phrase "these sufferings," is overtly resuming this narrative that is carefully threaded through the earlier parts of the letter.[17]

In sum, the relevant data combine to suggest that the sequence of events detailed in the letter is reasonably immediate: suffering took place at Thessalonica as some Thessalonians converted to Christ and a loyal community was constituted; the missionaries left, ending up at Athens; they badly wanted to return, given the pressure that the Thessalonians were under, but were constrained; fearing damage to the community, they sent Timothy, who was apparently not so constrained; and upon Timothy's return and report of his visit,

16. Cf. καὶ ὑμεῖς μιμηταὶ ἡμῶν ἐγενήθητε καὶ τοῦ κυρίου, δεξάμενοι τὸν λόγον ἐν θλίψει πολλῇ μετὰ χαρᾶς πνεύματος ἁγίου; and ὑμεῖς γὰρ μιμηταὶ ἐγενήθητε, ἀδελφοί, τῶν ἐκκλησιῶν τοῦ θεοῦ τῶν οὐσῶν ἐν τῇ Ἰουδαίᾳ ἐν Χριστῷ Ἰησοῦ, ὅτι τὰ αὐτὰ ἐπάθετε καὶ ὑμεῖς ὑπὸ τῶν ἰδίων συμφυλετῶν καθὼς καὶ αὐτοὶ ὑπὸ τῶν Ἰουδαίων.

17. Malherbe (2000, 193) resists this conclusion, ingeniously but ultimately unpersuasively, suggesting that Paul portrays his own suffering as his separation from the Thessalonians in 2:17-20, and that his θλίψις, according to 3:7, is relieved by the coming of Timothy, so that "*thlipsis* in this chapter does not refer to external pressures but to internal distress." But Paul does not characterize his separation from the Thessalonians in 2:17-20 with the signifier θλίψις. This is not fatal to Malherbe's reading, but it entails that it rests on evidence from adjacent material. Yet Paul does not then explicitly state that his sufferings in 3:7 were caused by his separation from the Thessalonians. Rather, he references warnings he supplied when he was present with the Thessalonians during the founding mission about their coming suffering (3:4). And this cluster of explicit references explains plausibly the language of emotional burden that Paul deploys through the passage so saliently. He cannot "bear" the situation further and so dispatches Timothy to Thessalonica, according to 3:1 (Διὸ μηκέτι στέγοντες εὐδοκήσαμεν καταλειφθῆναι ἐν Ἀθήναις μόνοι [2] καὶ ἐπέμψαμεν Τιμόθεον . . .), language that is repeated in 3:5 (διὰ τοῦτο κἀγὼ μηκέτι στέγων ἔπεμψα εἰς τὸ γνῶναι τὴν πίστιν ὑμῶν). The characterizations of Timothy's visit and its results then only reinforce the developing reading in terms of Paul's anxiety about the Thessalonians' state under duress. His concern for the community is palpable (see also ἀνάγκη in v. 7).

they wrote a joyful and grateful letter seeking to affirm the Thessalonians' resolve and loyalty, as well as to correct some of the community's problematic developments and to respond to some of its concerns. And there are no reasons or overt pieces of evidence — at least yet — that suggest complicating this account. Various countervailing arguments suggesting a significantly longer time lapse between Paul's mission to Thessalonica and 1 Thessalonians collapse on closer examination,[18] as do any suggestions that the missionaries were writing from Corinth.[19] And this judgment yields the following, largely contiguous, sequence.

FVP — FVT — FVA — Timothy VT —
Thessalonian reply — 1 Thess
. . . FVC

However, some qualifications to our developing frame are worth bearing in mind.

We do not yet know how close the founding visit to Corinth was to the events surrounding 1 Thessalonians in Athens. We have no reason to posit a long period of time or major episodes between the missions in Athens and Corinth, but we will leave things unspecified at present, because they cannot be definitively excluded. In particular, we will need to consider shortly whether the missionaries did return to Thessalonica in person before moving on, either to Corinth or somewhere else. Moreover, we do not need the missions to Thessalonica and

---

18. Putative indications of a significant time lapse between the founding visits to Thessalonica and Athens seem indecisive: (1) the possible death of some Thessalonians (see 4:13); and (2) Paul's encounter with people from outside both Macedonia and Achaia who know of the Thessalonians' new loyalty (see 1:6-7; I used to be enthusiastic about the implications of this data but have reluctantly abandoned it). With regard to (1), ancient death rates were so high that this contention is completely indecisive. One factor complicating it is the possibility that the Thessalonians became concerned about those who had already died, as some Corinthians seem to have done (1 Cor 15:29), although we have no evidence for this concern in a Pauline church outside Corinth. With regard to (2), visitors from outside the two regions who had heard of the Thessalonians' conversion *could* have traveled to Athens, which was not a major commercial center at this time but was prestigious and in effect a tourist destination, where Paul heard *their* report. Alternatively, the syntax could contain a parenthesis (and on closer examination most probably does), suggesting only that news of the Thessalonians' fidelity has "sounded out" beyond Macedonia and Achaia (see Rom 1:8; 16:19; 1 Cor 1:2).

19. This suggestion must appeal to Acts, and that data is not yet in play; a more detailed examination of the Corinthian possibility will consequently have to wait until the relevant Acts data is introduced.

Athens to be absolutely contiguous. They occupy the same basic period of duress in Thessalonica, but this could have extended for some weeks or months.

The evidence is insufficient to establish the presence within this sequence of a Thessalonian letter brought to Paul by Timothy containing questions (see esp. 4:9 and 5:1). Fortunately, not much turns on this judgment. That a *text* from the Thessalonians to Paul existed — the "Thessalonian reply" — is clear. Whether it was oral and written or entirely oral is harder to say but ultimately not that significant. And even larger doubts surround the question whether a letter from Paul to the Thessalonians accompanied Timothy on his prior visit. There seems little to suggest that one did, although this scenario will be revisited when 2 Thessalonians is assessed shortly, because some scholars would introduce that letter in this location.[20]

But beyond mere qualifications, possible objections to this scenario should now be addressed. First, it could be argued that 1 Thessalonians is a composite and so cannot be used in the straightforward way that it has been here to reconstruct this contiguous sequence. But an examination of the relevant literature and arguments suggests that this challenge to the integrity of the letter and the related frame is not especially powerful.[21] An alternative

---

20. Malherbe's (2000, 75-78) judgments here are convincing, although under the impress of Acts, he locates the letters in Corinth. Much turns on the force of the epistolary formula περὶ δέ (4:9; 5:1). This does indicate a previous letter from the addressees in 1 Cor, but largely because that letter references a previous letter explicitly (see 7:1, 25; 8:1; 12:1; 16:1, 12). In other epistolary literature, the formula does not necessarily imply a previous written communication but merely introduces a new subject. Indeed, even whether each specific instance in 1 Cor denotes something in the Corinthians' previous letter is debated; see M. Mitchell (1989). The hypothesis of a preceding letter to the Thessalonians distinguishable from 2 Thess is attributed by Malherbe to J. Harris (1898). Note also that, strictly speaking, three variations on this theory need to be addressed — those advocating the sending of a previous letter to the Thessalonians with Timothy, those advocating the sending of a previous letter to the Thessalonians independently of Timothy, and those advocating the sending of 2 Thess as that previous letter in one of these two locations.

21. See Schmithals (1972 [1965]; 1984). Murphy-O'Connor (1995; 1996, 102-29, esp. 104-14) is another strong advocate of the partition of these letters. This argument appeals in the main to the unusually replicated and/or extensive thanksgivings already noted. But few would seriously entertain this case today. Its primary difficulty is an overly inflexible account of the thanksgiving paragraph in Paul; if this is a flexible epistolary structure, then it might plausibly if distinctively have been deployed in relation to the broader rhetorical situation apparent in 1 Thess (and the very judgment of distinctiveness is anachronistic if 1 Thess was Paul's first letter, although 2 Thess 3:17 *might* stand against this). Good surveys of the claims of partition, and judicious refutations, can be found in R. Collins (1979/1984, 96-135); Koester (1979, 38); Jewett (1986, 31-36); Wanamaker (1990, 34-37). Paul's thanksgivings have been much discussed:

and rather more fatal objection would be that 1 Thessalonians is simply a fake and so cannot be used at all, resulting in the collapse of this and dependent parts of the frame. (We would end up in this case with just FVP — FVT . . . FVC.) So before moving on positively, this challenge will need to be laid to rest — or accepted. As we engage it, an important new explanatory dimension will be introduced into our discussion, namely, authorial authenticity versus pseudepigraphy. This will be explored fully from the discussion of 2 Thessalonians onward, which takes place shortly. But it has a preliminary role to play in relation to 1 Thessalonians and so is usefully introduced here.

1.2 The Question of Dependence

There are a number of striking similarities between 1 Thessalonians and 1 Corinthians, and we need to consider the significance of this phenomenon, which will arise again elsewhere — notably, between Ephesians and Colossians, and 1 Timothy and Titus, not to mention immediately between 1 and 2 Thessalonians. Close correlations in structure and/or linguistic texture between Pauline letters are evidence of some sort of dependence, and it must be asked whether plausible explanations of this dependence lie to hand in terms of Pauline authorship, or whether pseudepigraphy is a superior explanation, leading to the discard of all dependent letters from preliminary framing.[22]

(1) Evidence of Dependence

Although similarities between 1 and 2 Thessalonians have dominated most discussion in this relation, the similarities between 1 Thessalonians and 1 Corinthians are worth noting here, and are too extensive to be mere coincidence.

---

see in particular Schubert (1939); O'Brien (1977); Jervis (1991); Lambrecht (1990). Any deeper engagement with the letter's exigence requires a careful account of the thanksgivings in the first three chapters; however, that task lies beyond preliminary framing.

22. It is worth emphasizing in passing that a methodological parting of ways takes place at this juncture. If the reasons adduced here for authorial dependence turn out to be flawed, and the only plausible explanation for dependence turns out to be the function of the quoted material effectively as Scripture, then one can simply press this criterion alone for all initial questions of authenticity. This leads us very quickly to a "seven-letter canon" (i.e., Rom, 1 Cor, 2 Cor, Gal, Phil, 2 Thess [in my view], and Phlm), although further critical questions would have to be asked about the relationship between Rom and Gal, and some would argue for a return to the *Hauptbriefe*.

Certainly, they seem at first glance to reinforce the judgment of F. C. Baur and those of like mind that 1 Thessalonians is too wooden to be authentic.[23] A more detailed consideration of the whole issue needs to start with a brief rehearsal of the relevant data.

Both letters begin with accounts of the communities' initial conversions (1 Thess 1:5-10; 2:13-16; and see esp. 1 Cor 1:14-17) that are interwoven with relatively extended accounts of apostolic integrity (1 Thess 2:1-12; 1 Cor 2:1–4:13). Thanksgivings are present here as well, although, unsurprisingly, the instance in 1 Corinthians (1:4-9) is rather briefer than the distinctively developed acts of thanks in 1 Thessalonians. Travelogues, both involving Timothy, immediately follow, closing off these major subordinate discussions (1 Thess 2:17–3:11; 1 Cor 4:16-21). There is then a marked transition to a more topical approach to distinctive ethical matters (1 Thess 4:1; 1 Cor 5:1), in which questions of sexual ethics and future eschatology are prominent. To connect these loosely related discussions, the letters use either disclosure formulae (e.g., Οὐ θέλομεν δὲ ὑμᾶς ἀγνοεῖν, ἀδελφοί, περί κ.τ.λ.) or the standard epistolary formula περὶ δέ. Several final vestigial exhortations in 1 Thessalonians also find echoes in 1 Corinthians — a reference to pneumatological gifts, especially prophecy (see 1 Thess 5:19-20), to the "weak" (1 Thess 5:14b), and to respect for local leadership (see 1 Thess 5:12-13a). And the distinctive triad of faith, hope, and love so prominent in 1 Corinthians (esp. ch. 13) is also present in 1 Thessalonians (1:3 and 5:8).

This is an impressive list of initial similarities, but closer scrutiny reveals that many of its items receive different specific development within the respective letters. Paul's account of the first conversions at Corinth is ancillary to his apostolic discussion, and this in turn is fundamentally comparative, emphasizing (i.a.) the motif of weakness over against a rhetorically trained rival. The apostolic account in 1 Thessalonians is ancillary to the extended account of the Thessalonians' conversions, and the argument seems fundamentally exhortative (at least in broad terms). Insofar as it is apologetic — a function much discussed — it does not reflect a countervailing discourse with the same sharpness as the material in 1 Corinthians. The later topics in the letter also seem directed to overlapping but different situations.

Paul's concern with sexual behavior at Thessalonica does not seem especially urgent (4:3-8). It may have been prompted — at least in part — by an inquiry from the Thessalonians about "brotherly love" (see περὶ δὲ τῆς φιλαδελφίας in 4:9), which could have been understood by pagan converts

---

23. "A closer view of the Epistle betrays such dependence and such want of originality as is not to be found in any of the genuine Pauline writings" (Baur 2003 [1845], 2:85).

as involving sexual relations between men. The situation at Corinth, however, seems more complex. Paul addresses incest, the regular use of prostitutes, and a contrasting troublesome abstinence, and goes on to provide instructions about betrothals (1 Cor 5:1-13; 6:6–7:40). There is an interesting verbal parallel between the two letters — the use in these contexts of the relatively unusual πρᾶγμα (see Rom 16:2; 1 Cor 6:1; 2 Cor 7:11; 1 Thess 4:6).

The situation is similar with respect to eschatology. Paul apparently does not want the Thessalonians to be unduly grieved over those who have died (1 Thess 4:13-18); they will certainly not be left behind when the Lord Jesus returns. Hence, this discussion includes a brief account of expected future eschatological events. But it goes on to develop into an affirmation of a fundamentally agnostic position toward the precise time-tabling of the *parousia*, which will come like "a thief in the night" (1 Thess 5:2b — note, this material will be analyzed in more detail shortly). And this entails a sober and watchful posture by those associated ultimately with the day, over against one of inattention and drunkenness by those who are creatures of the night.

The concerns in 1 Corinthians again seem related but distinct. Some Corinthians seem to have denied the resurrection of the dead and hence the possibility of any future events (see 1 Cor 15:12). The dead are mentioned, but grief for them is not central to the text's concerns (see 15:20, 22-23, 29). Instead, the Corinthian debate seems to have been related to concerns about bodiliness, which Paul addresses at length (15:35-57), concerns not at all apparent at Thessalonica.

The principal similarity between the two letters reduces, then, to one of broad structure. Both letters begin, to a degree, with questions of apostolic integrity, although the specific accounts of that integrity differ. Context-appropriate and hence slightly divergent travelogues conclude these discussions. The letters then both move on to questions of local community ethics, arranged by topic, which in both locations include questions of sexual behavior and eschatology. Moreover, sexual behavior is addressed prior to eschatology, with a possible verbal echo in context. There is then one final echo within the letters' endings in terms of respect for local leadership.

It must be conceded that this is a notable set of parallelisms, largely in broad compositional terms. What explains it best?

(2) Possible Explanation in Authorial Terms

One explanation often favored by interpreters, whether explicitly or implicitly, appeals to temporal proximity, although presumably buttressed by appeals to memorization and orality. This explanation would suggest that a recently composed letter, much spoken and spoken of during the process of composition, could resonate through the composition of a subsequent letter, perhaps largely subliminally. That entire linguistic units were remembered or simply internalized and then reproduced in this way is unremarkable in a fundamentally oral culture, within which people like Paul possessed highly trained memories.

I am not entirely persuaded by this reasoning, however. I concede the general claims concerning orality and memory — and they will be apposite to our consideration of dependence between Ephesians and Colossians — but this appeal does not explain the apparently deliberate reproduction specifically of the broad outline of 1 Thessalonians within 1 Corinthians, along with occasional specific motifs. (It has already been established that 1 Thessalonians occupies a missionary space prior to Paul's year of crisis in 51, at the beginning of which 1 Corinthians was composed.) We see no such architectonic reproductions in the letters subsequent to 1 Corinthians, that is, 2 Corinthians, Galatians, Philippians, or Romans, nor between any of those letters, which were written close to one another and so presumably equally affected by orality and memory. Vestigial remnants are another matter, but they are not present here (i.e., occurring in 1 Corinthians after and from 1 Thessalonians).[24] The relationship between 1 Thessalonians and 1 Corinthians is both broader and more distinct than anything else we have yet found within the developing Pauline letter collection (which presently comprises six letters). And this, it seems to me, denotes deliberate dependence at a broad level, something better explained in this instance by pseudonymity than by mere temporal proximity. But there is another possible explanation in terms of original authorship that ought to be considered before endorsing pseudonymity.

New Testament scholars are becoming increasingly aware of the likelihood that Paul and his circle of coworkers retained copies of letters. Unfortunately, this seems to have been such a common practice in the ancient world, especially in elite circles, that it is almost entirely unremarked upon. However, telltale remarks — as usual, primarily from Cicero — reveal this apparently ubiquitous practice.[25] It is not coterminous with the practice of

---

24. Tatum's (2006) work is especially important here. Note that we did tabulate some motifs in 1 Thess that seem to be developed rather more significantly in 1 Cor, but this is not, strictly speaking, a vestigial continuation so much as its converse.

25. See (i.a.) *Atticus* 1.17; 3.9; *Fam.* 7.25.1; 9.26.1; *QFr* 1.2.6; 2.12.4; *PZen* 10; 43; *PTebt* 32; "*P.Mich.Inv. 855:* Letter from Herakleides to Nemesion," *ZPE* 27 (1977): 147-50; Plutarch, *Eum.* 2.2-3; Ignatius. See the fuller discussion in Richards (2004, esp. 156-61, 214-15, 217-18). Stirewalt

sending multiple letters to ensure their safe arrival.²⁶ Nor is it the same as simply sharing a copy with other interested parties (and these were not always authored by the sharer), although these practices presuppose the existence of copies.²⁷ But there were good reasons for authors to make copies of their letters in addition to those just noted. Given the vagaries of ancient travel and weather and the fragility of letters, they were frequently lost completely. Creating copies was therefore a simple expedient, and was cheap and easy to do — the ancient equivalent of making a backup file on a computer. But copies could also then be used as evidence if necessary, as well as, a little less threateningly, as resources for further correspondence. And these overlapping epistolary practices can explain the similarity between 1 Thessalonians and 1 Corinthians neatly.

The founding visit to Corinth took place sometime after the founding visit to Athens. If the missionary party retained copies of its letters, then it arrived in Corinth with a copy of 1 Thessalonians, and it is likely that the Corinthians were interested in this letter and heard it. (As a result, the Corinthians' first apostolic letter from Paul was actually 1 Thess.) And they probably went on to produce their own copies of it, if Paul and his circle did not simply supply those. So when Paul wrote 1 Corinthians later, coauthoring this time with Sosthenes, it seems quite plausible that he would evoke an earlier piece of correspondence that the Corinthians knew well, in effect building on its structure and cadences. Moreover, 2 Corinthians reveals a problem at Corinth for Paul of inconsistency (2 Cor 1:12-22), a perception generated, at least in part, by the shift in travel plans announced in 1 Corinthians 16:5-9. If Paul anticipated this problem at all, then it makes further sense for him to graft 1 Corinthians in general terms onto 1 Thessalonians in an act of demonstrable consistency. Given the apparent flexibility of some of the advice that Paul was articulating through 1 Corinthians, such consistency might have been rhetorically prudent in any case.²⁸ But a further explanatory layer should probably be added to

---

provides appropriate background evidence for this view, arguing that Paul's letters were modeled significantly on official letters, which were copied and archived (2003, esp. 1-55). However, he ultimately argues himself — perhaps a little inconsistently here — for the ephemeral nature of Pauline letters.

26. Cicero, *Fam.* 7.18.2; 9.16.1; 10.5.1; 11.11.1; 12.12.1; *PMich* 8.500.

27. Cicero, *Fam.* 9.12.2; 10.32.5; *Brutus* 1.16.1; *Atticus* 1.17; 3.9; 4.6; 8.9; see 13.21a; *PZen* 10; 43.

28. It might be asked why Paul did not model 1 Cor on 2 Thess, at least in addition to 1 Thess (assuming the authenticity of 2 Thess for the moment). However, 2 Thess is very brief, and the structure of 1 Thess is more apposite, with apostolic information following the letter

the mere existence of this possibility by way of letter copies, along with the rhetorical utility of allusion and recapitulation at Corinth.

The preservation and repetition of Paul's letters, both by his circle and by his recipients, to the point that these could be repeatedly invoked later on, suggests that they carried an authoritative weight that modern interpreters can overlook when they are viewed as *merely* occasional. They are clearly occasional documents. But apparently, they spoke into their particular occasions with deeply considered authority that was expected to be attended to carefully and applied. They were pedagogical templates, analogous to philosophical letters, elicited by circumstance but dispatched to be learned and internalized. Alternatively — or perhaps complementarily — they were official epistles.[29] Within this circle of expectations and practices, evidence of dependence between the different letters is really no surprise.

We should therefore reject pseudonymity as necessarily the most plausible explanation of dependence. And with this realization, a critical insight has been introduced into the evaluation of Pauline letters at the level of preliminary framing. We must take constantly into account Paul's ongoing possession of copies of his letters, along with the possibility that his recipients might have possessed particular copies as well. And the existence of something of an early archive of Pauline epistolary material at Corinth will also be worth bearing in mind. Pauline letters circulated within a more heavily intertextual Pauline universe than we might previously have suspected. Both their sender and their recipients seem to have "read, marked, learned, and inwardly digested" them. And since the phenomenon of dependence possesses a ready explanation in authorial terms in this way, it will not feature significantly in what follows as an argument for pseudepigraphy, although it will still require careful investigation in due course with respect to its important contributions to the articulation of contingency.

With this decision made, we can turn to consider the preliminary issues surrounding 2 Thessalonians.

---

opening and then a topical account of various matters, including sexual ethics, taking place. So this arrangement seems quite comprehensible.

29. See, most recently, an exaggerated but provocative case in roughly these terms by Hanges (2012). Background for the similarity with official letters is, as already noted, provided by Stirewalt, although he does not pursue this particular claim (2003, esp. 1-55). Note also that the Thessalonian letters are among the clearest in the entire Pauline collection in this relation, repeatedly utilizing the terminology of tradition and pedagogy. 2 Thess 2:15 puts the points especially well (although it is yet to be decided whether this text is authentic): ἀδελφοί, στήκετε καὶ κρατεῖτε τὰς παραδόσεις ἃς ἐδιδάχθητε εἴτε διὰ λόγου εἴτε δι᾽ ἐπιστολῆς ἡμῶν. Malherbe's (2000) commentary is especially sensitive to this dynamic.

2. Locating 2 Thessalonians

2.1 Preliminary Methodological Considerations

When we begin to assess 2 Thessalonians, we encounter the first letter in the Pauline corpus during our unfolding reconstruction whose authenticity has been widely doubted. Ideally, our analysis should still move from inclusion to exclusion, beginning with a careful analysis of the letter's possible authentic contingency in its own terms and in relation to the developing biographical frame, and then moving on to an assessment of considerations questioning its authenticity. But the arguments concerning pseudepigraphy for 2 Thessalonians are so prominent that this is rhetorically unrealistic. So we must first articulate why so many of these arguments have to be set to one side. After this digression, with the ground suitably cleared, we will return to an initial assessment of the letter in terms assuming authenticity, following this with a further consideration of pseudepigraphy that will be couched in slightly different, and presumably rather sounder, methodological terms.

Arguments for the pseudepigraphy of 2 Thessalonians have a long history within the modern academic period. They are traced back usually to J. E. Christian Schmidt's concern voiced in 1801 with the eschatological portrayal in 2 Thessalonians 2:1-12, arguments taken a step further by Kern in 1839. Further weighty objections were made by Wrede in 1903, on the heels of Holtzmann in 1901, principally concerning the structural and linguistic dependencies evident between the two Thessalonian letters. More idiosyncratic contributions were then made in the twentieth century by Braun (1952-53) and Marxsen (1968; 1969), before the powerful case by Trilling (1972) appeared. These contributions have interwoven subsequently with others,[30] generating a discourse of pseudonymous advocacy that can be traced through much late-twentieth-century scholarship on 2 Thessalonians and beyond.[31] But all of these scholarly cases generally invoke differences in one or more of the following data sets: (1) style (including vocabulary and syntactical data together under this rubric); (2) substance, at least in relation to some specific theological *topos*, such as eschatology. (Differences in letter form are largely absent from the

---

30. See esp. Vielhauer (1978, 89-102); Koester (1982, 241-46); Friedrich (1981, 252-57); Holland (1986; 1990); F. Hughes (1989); Richard (1995); Esler (2000b); Leppä (2006); Pervo (2010).

31. Useful recent surveys and assessments of this debate include Jewett (1986, 3-18); Wanamaker (1990, 17-28); Nicholl (2004, 198-221); Foster (2012, 154-59); all of whom reject the case for pseudonymity firmly. (See also Rigaux 1956.)

debate over 2 Thessalonians and so not tabulated and/or introduced here.)[32] And arguments running in the opposite direction, in terms of (3) dependence, are also standard, as we have just seen.

An important recent example of a case for 2 Thessalonians' pseudepigraphy can be found in Bart Ehrman's *Forgery and Counterforgery* (2013), and we will concentrate momentarily on this as representative of the broader discussion (although supplementing it where appropriate).

Ehrman bundles the foregoing arguments into a combined case against authenticity. It begins with considerations in terms of similarity, which are held — presumably correctly — to denote some form of dependence (158-60).[33] But we can safely set these to one side in the light of our previous discussion of 1 Thessalonians and 1 Corinthians. We have no way of knowing whether the dependence evident between 1 Thessalonians and 2 Thessalonians is a product of authorial or pseudepigraphic copying, and even assessing its direction seems to be — rather unfortunately — next to impossible.[34] Ehrman's case continues, however, with two further contentions in terms of difference, specifically, in terms of style and eschatology.

Ehrman suggests that the letter's style is demonstrably different from other authentic Pauline letters (160-62), resting here especially on a study by Darryl Schmidt (1990) that documented syntactical complexity in Pauline

---

32. That is, this feature of the situation has to be argued differently in relation to 1 Thess and 2 Thess, because of the similarities, not the perceived differences, between the two letters. But in these terms it is indecisive. Either Paul arguably deliberately reproduced to a degree either an early letter form or his preceding letter, or a pseudepigrapher reproduced 1 Thess. So the situation is no different here in formal methodological terms from the argument from phraseological dependence. Arguments from letter form are more significant when assessing the authenticity of other Pauline letters and tend to be argued there in terms of unique differences.

33. The letter openings are almost, if not completely, identical: see 1 Thess 1:1 and 2 Thess 1:1 (2 Thess adds ἡμῶν: Παῦλος καὶ Σιλουανὸς καὶ Τιμόθεος τῇ ἐκκλησίᾳ Θεσσαλονικέων ἐν θεῷ πατρὶ ἡμῶν καὶ κυρίῳ Ἰησοῦ Χριστῷ κ.τ.λ.). The concluding grace wishes are also almost identical: see 1 Thess 5:28 and 2 Thess 3:18 (2 Thess adds πάντων: Ἡ χάρις τοῦ κυρίου ἡμῶν Ἰησοῦ Χριστοῦ μετὰ πάντων ὑμῶν), although Rom 16:20 is identical in the best reading to the form in 1 Thess, and the suspect Rom 16:24 is identical to 2 Thess; 1 Cor 16:23 is very close as well. There are numerous other moments of verbatim agreement in the letter bodies. The most striking will be discussed shortly, namely, between 1 Thess 2:9 and 2 Thess 3:8 ([τὸν κόπον ἡμῶν καὶ τὸν μόχθον·] νυκτὸς καὶ ἡμέρας ἐργαζόμενοι πρὸς τὸ μὴ ἐπιβαρῆσαί τινα ὑμῶν κ.τ.λ.). Ehrman lists nine other short phrases or lexical juxtapositions that the two letters share uniquely (159).

34. I will venture a tentative suggestion here shortly in relation to 1 Thess 2:9 and 2 Thess 3:8.

thanksgiving paragraphs, the use of genitive phrases in non-phrase strings, and the ratio between coordinating and subordinating constructions. (This type of argument has a long prehistory in the debate, and many other stylistic differences could have been cited, but the case by Ehrman and Schmidt may be taken as representative.)

	Complexity *embedded clauses +* *layers of embeddedness*	Genitives *non-phrase strings/* *1,000 words*	Coordinate vs. Subordinate Constructions *relative frequency/* *100 words*
Rom	5+4	12.8	68:34
1 Cor	6+4	8.8	77:47
2 Cor	5+3	13.2*	59:42
Gal	n/a	15.2	65:44
Phil	7+6†	7.4	53:36
1 Thess	10+5	10.8	49:38
Phlm	n/a	11.9	50:38
2 Thess	22+15	26.7	41:38*
Eph	18+13	31.8*	27:26
Col	12+8	29.7	19*:26*

* Ehrman should have rounded Schmidt's figures up to the figures shown.
† Ehrman misreports Schmidt's figure here.

Ehrman concedes at one point that "in isolation this kind of stylistic demonstration can carry little weight" but suggests quickly that its combination with the evidence of dependence adds that weight. When the texts of 1 Thessalonians and 2 Thessalonians are dependent, they do not evidence divergences, he observes, but when the texts are independent, these stylistic differences appear. However, this risks being a merely tautologous observation. Clearly, when the two texts are dependent, they would not evidence any divergence. Ehrman's claim seems to be, then, that the style of 2 Thessalonians is even more different from 1 Thessalonians than it first appears, once dependence is controlled for (162). But this entails not so much the combination of two different types of argument as the intensification of one, namely, the evidence of stylistic difference.

Ehrman goes on to appeal to substantive differences between the two letters in terms of eschatology. Again, this contention has a long prehistory — indeed, arguably the longest in the modern period, reaching back to J. Schmidt in 1801 — and its underlying exegetical claims will be scrutinized carefully in due course. But I will set aside for the moment any objections to Ehrman's particular construals (and those reading like him). He argues that "the image [of the end in 1 Thessalonians] is at odds with the view set forth by the author of 2 Thessalonians." The author of the former (which is also representative of Paul's other authentic letters on the basis of Rom 13:12 and Phil 4:5) expects that "the end is to come suddenly and expectedly, 'like a thief in the night'" (5:2). The author of the latter thinks that, conversely, "there will in fact be plenty of warning, a whole sequence of events that must transpire." Ehrman then asks pointedly: "How would Paul change his eschatological views so suddenly and decisively?" He goes on to conclude that "coupled with the problems posed by the parallels themselves, and the differences of style, the case for inauthenticity is very strong" (165-66).

It is hard not to be swayed by Ehrman's case, which rests on scholarly studies and sharp observations and is prosecuted with characteristic clarity and vigor. And it represents well an entire tradition within the field. But we now need to scrutinize these arguments more closely. And I would suggest that certain major problems emerge that deeply problematize this and every similar type of argument for pseudonymity. There are three clusters of methodological subterfuge present in this sort of case.

(1) The Significance of Difference Per Se

The basic initial problem with this argument, irrespective of its data set (i.e., vocabulary, style, letter form, or substantive observations), is that without the establishment of the authentic Pauline sample — that is, with what we might call the universe of relevant Pauline possibilities, along with its mean in the sense of its typical elements — demonstrations of difference per se are merely tautologous or "empty." They point only to the limits of that sample, given that, in order to avoid question begging, all our items, contested and uncontested, are being initially included within it. So we must ask what the significance of the tabulation of differences offered by D. Schmidt and Ehrman really is when they are presented baldly, without further interpretation or contextualization.

Schmidt and Ehrman suggest that a 10+5 level of complexity in a thanksgiving is authentic (1 Thess), but a 12+8 (Col) or a 22+15 (2 Thess) is too extended. Similarly, 12.8 strings of genitives per thousand words are authentic (Rom) but 29.7 are not (Col). And a ratio of 59:42 in coordinating and subordinating constructions is authentic (2 Cor), but one of 41:37 (or 38) is not

(2 Thess). But we do not yet know whether the Pauline epistolary possibilities for complexity in thanksgivings would have extended to, say, 25+18, or not. We learn from a comparison made in these terms only that the level of complexity in the thanksgiving in 1 Thessalonians is lower than it is in Colossians and 2 Thessalonians. Similarly, Paul's possibilities for genitive strings might have included 30 or 35 per thousand words, and Colossians might then lie closer to the mean of Pauline possibilities than Romans. We do not know. At first glance, we learn from this data only that Romans has around 13 genitive strings per thousand words and Colossians 30. In florid circumstances, perhaps Paul might have crafted a 1:2 ratio of coordinating to subordinating constructions. Indeed, perhaps his default position stylistically was somewhat convoluted (at least by modern standards). We have no way yet of telling. So the tabulations of Schmidt and Ehrman are actually meaningless in the first instance as evidence for pseudepigraphy. Since all of Paul's extant canonical letters are in play at this point, when differences are being initially assessed, any observable differences between them are automatically indicative only of the limits of authenticity and therefore collapse into empty tautologies: "the grammar in Romans in certain respects is not like the grammar in Colossians," and so on. This does not tell us much.

But I suspect that this fairly obvious problem has been frequently overlooked, in part, because it feels intuitively embarrassing to Pauline analysts when it is argued in relation to substantive concerns. A quick appraisal of the tabulation of substantive difference might prove helpful.

Tabulations of substantive differences between the Pauline letters are often presented as "contradictions." (A less inflammatory characterization is "tensions.") And many scholars recoil from such tabulations because they want to argue ultimately that Paul's theological position was fundamentally consistent. Only this would seem to allow his authoritative deployment in any ecclesial setting or, less tendentiously, a comprehensible discussion of his thought in academic terms as it stretches across more than one letter and situation. If these positions are to be maintained, then it is better to consign observable differences in theological substance to a pseudepigrapher than to concede that Paul changed his mind about some significant question or was simply confused. So, for example, it seems intuitively more palatable for an interpreter to assign the eschatology of (say) 2 Thessalonians to a pseudepigraphic corrector than to believe, at least initially, that Paul wrote one thing about the end time in 2 Thessalonians and something rather different in 1 Thessalonians, or vice versa. Consequently, the tabulation of theological difference can play on an underlying commitment, on the part of most Pauline interpreters, to Paul's substantive consistency and systematic rigor, which rests in turn on his ecclesial authority or discursive comprehensibility. But we need to register a caveat in terms of contingency and an objection in terms of coherence against this entire argumentative dynamic.

Tabulations of these sorts of potentially embarrassing substantive differences depend on an exhaustive account of the relevant texts "all the way down." We must know that the different positions articulated in different letters represent Paul's fundamental and comprehensive theological views on a given question — in Beker's terminology, his coherence — and these claims are plainly apparent in Ehrman's argument. But such claimants must first run the contingent gauntlet. That is, demonstrations of substantive contradiction must first show that Paul's contradictory statements are not comprehensible under any circumstantial terms. And Ehrman never demonstrates this. (A preexisting preference for pseudepigraphy can obscure the need to do so, since later pseudepigrapha presumably lacked a highly specific contingency; they were fundamentally coherent texts. But this approach begs the question.) And a careful contingent analysis of the Thessalonian letters might suggest that both eschatological presentations fit together within a particular coherence that is obscured by their circumstantial and consequently allusive, partial, and/or particular deployments. If a contingent resolution of any apparent contradictions proves possible, then any charges of substantive incoherence and attendant judgment of pseudepigraphy must falter. Ehrman, and those arguing like him, have left themselves vulnerable here.

But he might be able to meet this challenge if he supplies more detailed and historically sensitive exegesis in due course (i.e., sensitive to possible original Pauline situations), so this observation operates as a caveat — albeit a fairly stringent one. An objection in terms of straightforward contingency is still more powerful, however.

We observed in chapter 1 that prior to the construction of a preliminary narrative frame that can control for contingency, the very nature of Paul's underlying theology is unknown. Hence, it simply needs to be recalled here that when differences in substantive terms are tabulated, they do not necessarily entail different authorship. They do so only on the assumption that Paul was an utterly consistent thinker in systematic terms, on the level of his coherence, and we do not yet know this. So the tabulation of substantive differences again tells us nothing initially in terms of authorship. It might merely be evidence that Paul was a thinker who changed his mind, and we consequently have no way of knowing whether Ehrman's critical inference in this relation is correct. Could Paul have changed his mind fundamentally in relation to future eschatology between the writing of 1 and 2 Thessalonians (or 2 Thess and 1 Thess)? The answer might well be yes. His thinking might have "developed." He might have shifted his position for powerful circumstantial reasons. He might simply have been saying whatever he thought he had to in order to affirm the Thessalonians. He might have been confused. We just do not yet know. And in view of this uncertainty, it can be seen that a critical non sequitur underlies Ehrman's argument and vitiates his conclusion. The perception of a set of substantive tensions leads us only to a set of options, just one of which suggests pseudepigraphy, but all of which are equally plausible during preliminary framing.

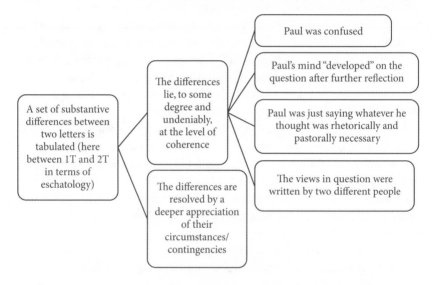

(2) The Attempt to Establish a Centroid through Stylometrics

One way of dealing with the key difficulty apparent in the foregoing situation — that is, the mere tabulation of differences — is to establish what some statisticians call a "centroid" within the initial sample, a task that most scholars in fact sense and attempt.[35] If a typical or mean position can be determined, then some sense of outlying data samples might be achievable. But most attempts to do so beg the key questions — often quite spectacularly — and so should

35. This is Neumann's term (see his 1990), used to denote a cluster of demonstrably authentic data within the entire extant sample that lies close to the Pauline means on all key markers of style and is also large enough to allow some sense of the appropriate degrees of deviation from the means to be assessed for their significance as they occur in any remaining data.

be abandoned as quickly and comprehensively as claims based on differences per se. Scholars simply nominate a theme or letter as typical and work from that place, generally failing to recognize the academic and/or denominational biases that underlie the nomination, and/or its utter arbitrariness. That is, the error that advocates of pseudepigraphy in terms of difference tend now to fall into is the prejudicial establishment of a centroid that is then merely circularly self-confirming and so proof again of nothing. (And unfortunately, this can then create a deceptive scholarly dynamic — an appearance of demonstration that is actually invalid and that tends to block further progress in more valid terms.)[36] The establishment of a centroid in neutral terms must appeal to the somewhat forbidding but potentially significant discipline of stylometrics.

Stylometrics, or "nontraditional authorship attribution," might appear at first glance to offer some hope of resolving the dilemmas apparent in the assessment of the authenticity of the extant Pauline data. By applying statistical analysis to arrays of stylistic data, stylometrics attempts to avoid just the arbitrariness and prejudices that dog the positing of a centroid in substantive terms. The analysis of the data is diverse and technically neutral. So the question here is not so much whether its results are merely arbitrarily or even invidiously self-confirming as whether it can do what we need it to do — that is, identify possible pseudepigrapha within the extant Pauline sample demonstrably.

It is a little disconcerting, then, to learn that stylometric analysis has had a long and at times checkered history.[37] Its roots lie in certain extraordinarily

36. For example, many modern scholars posit "justification" as a key marker of authentic Pauline material, thereby — setting aside some basic definitional issues — privileging Rom, Gal, and Phil as the Pauline centroid in substantive terms (and we noted Schnelle's use of this "argument" in ch. 1). Running this assumption through the rest of the Pauline data, tabulating differences, then usually problematizes the authenticity of Eph and Col, since the former is only vestigially committed to justification (see 2:8-10) and the latter not at all. So frequently these letters are excluded as, at best, disputed and, at worst, pseudepigraphic. But all the key questions in terms of both contingency and coherence are begged by this approach. We have not yet ascertained whether justification language is affected significantly by certain circumstances. And we have not ascertained whether Paul's coherence includes justification centrally, includes it as an aspect of his systematic thinking, or does not contain it — i.e., as a discrete doctrine — at all. So our key results are simply invalid in view of their question-begging circularity. Worse than this, however, we have created a semblance of scholarliness with this argument, which can be elaborated in impressive terms, *and* we have corrupted the possibility of any further investigations into these questions. Our frame has been contaminated by circularity, and we now have no valid control over the later assessment of contingency or of the nature of Paul's coherence.

37. Useful surveys can be found in D. Holmes (1994; 1998); Rudman (1998); Juola (2006); Stamatatos (2009). Note how these postdate the key NT contributions.

learned and diligent studies in the nineteenth century.[38] But its rise to real significance took place in the 1960s, when stylometric analysis largely succeeded
in identifying the disputed authorship of some of the Federalist Papers.[39] Since
then, it has gone through a number of disciplinary scandals,[40] but, critical to
our concerns, something of a great leap forward took place in the late 1980s
and early 1990s with a shift to the creation of multivariate data arrays and
their powerful computer-assisted evaluations[41] — most significant here being
principal component, linear discriminant, and correspondence analysis. (This
step is associated primarily with the Australian scholar John Burrows; see his
1987; 1989; 1992a; 1992b; and his further important methodological contribution to the discipline in 2002.)[42] Since this development, stylometrics has
shifted its primary attention from classic literary questions to the analysis of
short e-texts, partly because of their importance to the detection of fraud and
terrorism, along with their abundance in machine-readable form, but attention
to classical questions has not died out. Moreover, it is still widely acknowledged within the discipline that the "holy grail" of nontraditional authorship
ascription, that is, a universally acknowledged and successful method, has yet
to be found.[43] Nevertheless, progress is burgeoning and impressive, as a quick
sweep through the contributions to the flagship journal *Literary and Linguistic
Computing* indicates. Suffice it to say that the discipline in its current state
leaves the Pauline interpreter with some challenges, although their force will
not be felt fully until the discussions of the next chapter.

Most Pauline interpreters not only lack advanced mathematical and sta-

---

38. See Mendenhall (1887); also Mascoll (1888a; 1888b). Kenny (1986, 1-2) notes that the
earliest study in these terms was arguably in 1851 by Augustus De Morgan, the brilliant non-
conformist mathematician, who ventured some systematic stylistic observations in a letter to
a friend from Trinity College, Cambridge, the Rev. William Heald (De Morgan 1882, 214-16).

39. See Mosteller and Wallace (1964; 1984).

40. Over "Morton's method" (see Morton 1978); the application of Fischer's statistical
model to authorship, developed to predict the probabilities of catching new butterfly species
in Indonesia (Thisted and Efron 1987); the "cusum" or "Qsum" controversy; and Foster's al-
leged Shakespearean identification of the author of "A Funeral Elegy" by "W.S." (Juola 2006,
244-45). Incidentally, the problems with the Qsum approach undercut most of Barr's (2004)
contributions to Pauline stylistics in these terms, and Walters's (2009) recent contribution to
the authorship of Lk and Acts suffers from similar problems.

41. Juola (2006, 239-40) explains that multivariate analyses can look at the distributions
of features and properties — e.g., word length and/or vocabulary richness — whereas univariate analyses look at the mere presence or absence of a feature.

42. I am grateful to Prof. Burrows for his personal help and guidance here.

43. So Juola (2006, 235).

tistical training but tend to dislike and to avoid it.[44] Hence, very few possess the diverse competencies necessary to evaluate the contributions from the stylometric analysis of the Pauline corpus, let alone to make them. The field is therefore dominated locally by a number of scholars that can be counted on the fingers of the proverbial single hand, along with a marginally larger number of key studies: Anthony Kenny's elegant monograph *A Stylometric Study of the New Testament*, published in 1986; Kenneth J. Neumann's *The Authenticity of the Pauline Epistles in the Light of Stylostatistical Analysis*, published in 1990; a set of sophisticated essays by David Mealand published from the late '80s through the '90s (1988; 1989; 1995; 1997; 1999); and an isolated but important study by Gerard Ledger (1995). Kenny's work predates the great leap forward that took place through the early '90s after Burrows, but it remains a critical contribution in my view, because it walks its readers through the key differences for stylometric purposes between English and Greek grammar.[45] The vast majority of authorship ascription techniques presuppose English grammar. The three remaining scholars are then post-Burrows (i.e., at least Burrows phase one), using multivariate data arrays and sophisticated subsequent statistical analysis. They thereby take the analysis of Paul's style beyond the mere tabulations of selected stylistic differences still offered by other traditional NT analysts like Ehrman and Schmidt.[46] But even their contributions would still be viewed as dated by the cutting edge of stylometric analysis.[47] For example, they lack any reference to or use of "support vector machines" (SVM),

44. As noted by Foster (2012). I studied computer-assisted analyses of voting intensively as an undergraduate and so possibly have a slight advantage here.

45. Kenny prefers serial univariate to multivariate analysis. He treats 96 measurements.

46. Neumann seems not to know of Burrows's work but uses the same basic approach — specifically, the application of linear discriminant analysis (LDA) to the multivariate data array. Mealand is aware of it; he uses principal component analysis (PCA) first, and also uses correspondence analysis (CA). I am grateful to the Rev. Dr. Mealand for his personal help and guidance here.

47. An interesting disciplinary benchmark was provided in 2004 by a large "ad-hoc authorship attribution competition" (AAAC); see Juola (2004). From thirteen sample sets in Romance languages, the winners successfully identified 71 percent of the items, using a machine learning approach, specifically, SVM (support vector machines) with a linear kernel function (Juola 2006, 288-98). Juola notes that the four best-performing methods, both in the competition and more widely, have been SVM, linear discriminant analysis, and *k*-nearest neighbor in a suitably chosen space (either by cross-entropy or by *n*-gram distance). The most successful methods tend to use a large number of features. Intriguingly, Juola also suggests on the basis of the AAAC that principal component analysis is especially problematized and not always reliable, being useful in large measure because of its capacity to be easily explained and to produce easy-to-understand (if only modestly effective) results.

which are now central in the field, largely because the technique had not been invented at the time when they wrote, nor do they employ Burrows's popular Delta method of analysis, introduced in 2002.[48] (An important exception here is Andris Abakuks, but he is — at least to this point — focused on the Synoptic Problem; see his 2006a; 2006b; 2007; 2012.)[49]

Nevertheless, in the observation crucial for our current question, although Neumann, Mealand, and Ledger disagree on some points, they are all extremely confident that 2 Thessalonians exhibits no significant stylistic variation from the other most plausibly authentic Pauline letters, a judgment with which the more cautious Kenny unsurprisingly concurs. (Ledger in fact views 2 Thess as more Pauline than 1 Thess, with doubts about the latter rather than the former on stylistic grounds.) And this observation should not date.[50] That is, the three best currently available computer-assisted analyses of variation at the stylistic level of 2 Thessalonians in the broader setting of the Pauline corpus and beyond, employing multivariate data arrays — Neumann using linear discriminant analysis; Ledger, principal component analysis; and Mealand, linear discriminant prefaced by principal component analysis, as well as, increasingly, correspondence analysis — suggest that its variation is not in fact significant; and Kenny, using univariate data arrays, concurs. Consequently, this stylometric material suggests that arguments in favor of 2 Thessalonians' pseudepigraphy on the basis of unacceptable stylistic variation are simply false. Those arguments have "cherry-picked" the data, that is, highlighted the tabulations of difference that support their case and ignored the vast numbers of variations that do not, thereby creating a false account of the situation.[51]

48. See Burrows (2002; 2003); refined by Hoover (2004a; 2004b); and assessed later by Smith and Aldridge (2011). The method is based on the frequencies of the most frequent words in disputed texts. Burrows worked originally with a known corpus, tabulating the occurrences of the most frequent 150 words — the Delta. Z-scores were then calculated for each author and text, expressing the extent to which a given word's occurrence varied from the mean. (The score is derived by subtracting the word's occurrence in the disputed text from the mean, and then dividing the result by the standard deviation of the word in the primary set of data.) The z-scores were graphed and the resulting lines for different texts compared. The test works best identifying unknown texts against a group of texts whose authors are already known and for whom samples of 500-1,500 words are available. This limits — but does not eliminate — its usefulness in relation to Pauline questions.

49. I am grateful to Prof. Abakuks for his personal help and guidance here.

50. Whether stylistics can take us beyond this largely negative result into a trustworthy positive analysis is a question we must consider carefully in the next chapter.

51. See, in particular, Rudman's (1998, 358-59) concerns. I am grateful for Prof. Rudman's personal help and guidance here. It might be worth noting that vocabulary lists can be

Ehrman relied on Schmidt, who tabulated 3 sets of differences, but Ledger isolated 29, Kenny assessed 96, and Neumann initially considered 617. (Linear discriminant and principal component analyses allow tabulations of this complexity to be managed.)

Advocates of nontraditional authorship ascription insist that the discipline's contributions are complementary to traditional techniques of ascription based on external attestation of transmission and close reading. But they are especially significant here, because they are not being deployed in primary support of a claim of authorship ascription but focused negatively on a more limited question, in relation to which they can pronounce more definitively. These highly specialized studies suggest, effectively in passing, that perceived differences in style between 2 Thessalonians and certain other authentic Pauline letters are not indicative of different authorship, because in terms of its overall stylistic fingerprint, 2 Thessalonians is not anomalous. And with this realization, it can be seen that Ehrman's representative case for 2 Thessalonians' pseudepigraphy has faltered in every respect. His contentions in terms of dependence, and of substantive and stylistic differences, are ultimately unpersuasive — a judgment applying, as far as I can tell, to the vast majority of the rest of the debate in this relation, at which point we need to pause to consider where we are now positioned in broad methodological terms.

The possibility remains that some of the Pauline letters in the canon are pseudepigraphic, and ideally, we would like to exclude them from further historical reconstruction. So, for example, Kenny, Neumann, Mealand, and Ledger all raise doubts on stylometric grounds about at least one letter, and frequently about more than one. Hence, just as we do not want to exclude authentic material from the frame's construction arbitrarily, we do not want to insert fake material, in strictly historical terms, and allow it to do key work (although the latter scenario is easier to correct than the former, which is essentially irresolvable). So how might we go about doing this in our more methodologically straitened situation?

The following discussion of 2 Thessalonians will be an initial case study in terms of these constraints, and it must begin, as we noted earlier, with a presumption of authenticity. So §2.2 will try to develop a rigorous contingent account of 2 Thessalonians that explores the letter's own account of its circumstances, probing its plausibility; §2.3 will then try to generate a plausible account of the letter's date; and §2.4 will investigate the plausibility of the letter's

---

similarly unreliable, especially where differences in genre are concerned, although Burrows's Delta method speaks to this issue; see Juola (2006, 240; citing in particular Hoover 2003).

location in relation to the rest of our developing biographical frame, assessing the difficult question of sequence. Finally, §2.5 will return to the question of pseudepigraphy, trying to articulate and to assess appropriate reasons for exclusion in the light of these positive considerations. (It will differ here from cases that lie ahead of us in that the stylometric situation has already been settled unanimously and positively with respect to 2 Thessalonians; future cases will require a careful stylometric consideration at this moment in slightly different terms.) In this way, vicious broader explanatory circularity should be avoided, and the appropriate historical sensitivity simultaneously achieved.[52]

2.2 The Immediate Implied Exigence

Can a plausible account of the contingency of 2 Thessalonians be supplied even if some of the details must remain frustratingly vague (a not uncommon problem for the Pauline scholar)? The letter provides enough information to sketch out a possible original scenario whose plausibility will then need to be weighed.

The missionary party of Paul, Silvanus, and Timothy has "heard" that the Thessalonians have been unsettled by the suggestion "that the day of the Lord has come" or ". . . is imminent" (see 3:11: Ἀκούομεν γάρ τινας περιπατοῦντας ἐν ὑμῖν ἀτάκτως κ. τ. λ.; and 2:2b: ὅτι ἐνέστηκεν ἡ ἡμέρα τοῦ κυρίου). To make matters worse, this suggestion might even have been said to have come from the missionaries themselves (2:2b: μήτε διὰ πνεύματος μήτε διὰ λόγου μήτε δι' ἐπιστολῆς ὡς δι' ἡμῶν). The disquiet caused by this intervention (see τὸ . . . σαλευθῆναι ὑμᾶς in 2:2a) seems to be the letter's primary exigence, dominating most of its content (specifically, 1:4–3:3). The fidelity of the Thessalonians has been shaken. Like nervous troops in combat under heavy fire, they are wavering and possibly about to break and flee. But a second situation is also apparent in the letter. Some of the Thessalonians are acting lazily, refusing to work and consequently to contribute to what seems to be a common pot in the community, although they are still eating from it (3:10-13).[53] Paul seems to be concerned about this laziness and its consequences as well.

---

52. As our frame develops, we can expect that our judgments may be cumulatively corroborated as well. If so, with these judgments in place and a frame firmly established, we will be able to return to make coherent judgments about other features of the Pauline data in the appropriate manner. That is, we will be in a position to reach valid assessments of Paul's theological consistency, his use of letter forms, and his stylistic possibilities in retrospect, reversing the usual flow of analysis but thereby reaching more cogent conclusions.

53. There is no indication in the text that these two problems should be linked, although

The double exigence is nicely confirmed by the emphases in the letter's first thanksgiving on the key virtues of fidelity and love. Paul clearly wants the Thessalonians to stand firm faithfully despite the pressures they are under as they await the Lord Jesus' *parousia* (1:3, 4-12; 2:13-16; 3:1-3); and he wants them all to love one another concretely (1:3), with good intentions, thereby walking worthily of their calling (1:11) and not bringing it into disrepute — not to mention undermining the community — by the laziness of some.

Two details within this broad scenario now need to be addressed more specifically. Scholars puzzle over the precise vehicle, so to speak, whereby the unsettling news concerning the Lord Jesus' *parousia* has entered the community. And they puzzle over the exact content of this news.

Unfortunately, we do not know precisely how the Thessalonians were unsettled by the eschatological suggestion that was so troubling them, possibly because Paul himself was unsure. It is difficult if not impossible to determine from his convoluted and ambiguous account in 2:2 whether the unsettling information was introduced by way of a prophecy or some other spiritual communication (literally, "a spirit"), by some teaching, or by a letter falsely attributed to Paul.[54] Paul certainly wants to prevent this last scenario from occurring again, if it has once already, giving detailed instructions at the end of 2 Thessalonians about his authenticating autograph. *All* his letters are signed with at least a grace wish in his distinctive hand (3:17-18; see esp. ὅ ἐστιν σημεῖον ἐν πάσῃ ἐπιστολῇ). But we cannot tell whether this was how the original alarm was caused — only that it seems to have been a strong

---

they frequently are. A fascinating account in these terms is Jewett (1986). This linkage does not need to be assessed during preliminary framing.

54. See [2:1]Ἐρωτῶμεν δὲ ὑμᾶς, ἀδελφοί, ὑπὲρ τῆς παρουσίας τοῦ κυρίου ἡμῶν Ἰησοῦ Χριστοῦ καὶ ἡμῶν ἐπισυναγωγῆς ἐπ᾽ αὐτὸν [2] εἰς τὸ μὴ ταχέως σαλευθῆναι ὑμᾶς ἀπὸ τοῦ νοὸς μηδὲ θροεῖσθαι μήτε διὰ πνεύματος μήτε διὰ λόγου μήτε δι᾽ ἐπιστολῆς ὡς δι᾽ ἡμῶν, ὡς ὅτι ἐνέστηκεν ἡ ἡμέρα τοῦ κυρίου. Good discussions of this material's ambiguity can be found in Holland (1990); E.-M. Becker (2009); Ehrman (2013, 167-68). Roose (2006) is probably, as Ehrman suggests, oversubtle. Ehrman posits that 2 Thess 2:15 points to the normal modes of Pauline teaching, by word and by letter, leaving out "a spirit" and thereby indicating that this was not a Pauline mode. If this was the case, then the final modification in 2:2 does not apply to the "spirit" and so must apply grammatically only to the last item in the series, namely, the letter. (It cannot apply to the last two and not the first without clarification.) However, 1 Cor 5:3-4 problematizes this case. Moreover, pagan religiosity is steeped in possibilities here. That the *daemon* or "spirit" of a founding figure would be present with his community from a distance would be an entirely plausible pagan expectation, although doubtless Paul did not want to be worshipped, and he might have been embarrassed to be linked to a statue. But the Corinthian data suggests that he did not gainsay this phenomenon in broad terms, apparently on pneumatological grounds.

possibility. The information might have been falsely attributed to Paul and the other missionaries, but it might simply have arisen by way of a false prophecy or some such. It does seem most probable that the Thessalonians thought they had received information in some way from Paul. And fortunately, the exact mode by which the disquiet was caused is not vital to our present reconstruction. It is the fact of the Thessalonians' disquiet that elicits 2 Thessalonians, irrespective of its precise causality. That is, we can be sure that a *text* of some sort has arrived with a particular piece of information that has deeply troubled them, a situation that is plausible. We turn, then, to the rather more important question concerning what exactly that text contained.

The answer to this question arises initially and primarily in relation to the force of the verb ἐνέστηκεν in 2:2b. At first glance, the use of the perfect tense here suggests that the day of the Lord is past, with ongoing force (at least in some sense). This is the invariable sense of the verb in this tense elsewhere in Paul (see Rom 8:38; 1 Cor 3:22; 7:26; Gal 1:4; see also a future in 2 Tim 3:1; the only other NT occurrence is Heb 9:9). Furthermore, this construal could plausibly explain the Thessalonians' alarm.

If the Thessalonians had become concerned that the *parousia* of Jesus had taken place, then they had grounds for considerable anxiety. Putting things at their simplest, they would now have to ask whether they had been left behind. If Jesus had returned and gone again, then their endurance through frightful pressure had been in vain. They were deceived, pathetic, and ridiculous, as well as — worse still — not saved at all. Few suggestions could presumably have unsettled them more than this one. And in the light of its effectiveness, one wonders what solid grounds exist for endorsing an unusual future reading of the verb and some other scenario.[55] So we will carry on assuming

---

55. So, e.g., Ehrman (2013, 164-66), building on earlier suggestions by (i.a.) Stephenson (1968) and Lindemann (1977), argues that the letter envisages an imminent *parousia* analogous to Mk 1:15: "the kingdom of God is at hand." But in addition to overriding the simpler reading that seems unambiguously effective, a future reading seems fatally flawed. It is hard to envisage quite why it would have been so unnerving to suggest to the Thessalonians that Jesus was about to return when apparently this was exactly what they were waiting for. They would have been delighted and affirmed by such news, not troubled and alarmed. Ehrman's account of the letter's contingency is hampered by the fact that he does not believe that the letter was original to Paul, i.e., his argument against the construal of the perfect tense with respect to past events rests on a reconstruction of the original Pauline situation that he later goes on to repudiate. If an interpreter has already decided that the letter is pseudepigraphic, then a modified perfect reading, with reference to an imminent *parousia*, makes rather more sense. (Indeed, arguably this is the only reading that makes sense. A later pseudepigrapher would presumably have little interest in correcting a general expectation in the church that the *parousia* had already

this reconstruction of the initial Thessalonian turmoil. It had been suggested to the Thessalonians in some convincing way, perhaps with fake apostolic authority, that the *parousia* of the Lord Jesus had already taken place. And this had all come to Paul's attention through some unnamed oral report.

To defuse this concern, Paul makes a particular argument. He reprises something of a grand eschatological timetable pointing out that certain key events must still take place before Christ returns. The timetable revolves around the revelation of a "Man of Lawlessness" (ὁ ἄνθρωπος τῆς ἀνομίας, ὁ υἱὸς τῆς ἀπωλείας — although he is not glossed with lawlessness so much as associated with it). This figure will enthrone himself in God's temple blasphemously in a false *parousia* accompanied by all kinds of ostensible wonders. Many will be deceived by this, thereby generating a widespread apostasy (2:3, 10-12), and they will receive harsh punishment — this group clearly including those currently troubling the Thessalonians (1:6, 8-10). The judgment will take place when the Lord Jesus overthrows the Man of Lawlessness and his minions during his own glorious and vastly more powerful *parousia*. The Lord Jesus will strike then with a breath (2:8), a tongue of fire, and a multitude of angels (1:7-9). In short, Paul suggests in 2 Thessalonians that the real *parousia* cannot come until the false *parousia* of the Man of Lawlessness has taken place, an event that should be utterly unmistakable, although it is for now hidden and restrained (2:6-7). So the Thessalonians can rest assured that the Lord Jesus' *parousia* has *not* yet taken place.

Rather significantly, the letter suggests that Paul is merely reminding the Thessalonians here of something he had already taught them in person (see 2:5: Οὐ μνημονεύετε ὅτι ἔτι ὢν πρὸς ὑμᾶς ταῦτα ἔλεγον ὑμῖν?). Nevertheless, encouraged and strengthened by this proof that the Lord Jesus is yet to return, deployed partly by way of reminder in the letter, the Thessalonians can now respond to their election by standing firm in word and deed, loving God and persevering as Christ did, with a firmness that should extend to an ongoing commitment to the teachings and traditions transmitted by their founding missionaries. And with this whole issue settled, Paul turns in the letter to the secondary but still significant matter of laziness on the part of some within the community.

What are we to make of this immediate implied exigence? Is it plausible? It seems to me that this is a plausible account of the letter's immediate exigence in terms of an original Pauline mission. Some details are irritatingly

---

taken place.) But to make that claim at this stage in the discussion begs the question and risks inaugurating a vicious argumentative circle.

vague. We would dearly like to know how Paul actually found out about these difficulties in the Thessalonian community, not to mention exactly where he is and who is taking 2 Thessalonians back to Thessalonica. But these are the characteristic frustrations of the modern historian interested in ancient events. We lack answers to these questions for other letters long deemed authentic.[56] That the Thessalonians would have been troubled in this way seems believable, as does the laziness of some. (They were a community of ancient artisans.)[57] Their persecutions by their neighbors are well attested elsewhere. And the widespread ancient phenomenon of pseudepigraphy attests — somewhat ironically — to the plausibility of the original scenario that some of those neighbors might have been maliciously trying to deceive and upset the fledgling community with a fake communication. Moreover, that Paul would write in response to steady and to correct them seems equally believable. We ought to conclude, then, that the letter is fundamentally plausible in terms of its own account of its genesis. Nothing here is objectionable, let alone especially fatal to authenticity.

If the letter has hereby received a plausible explanation of its immediate exigence, we can turn to consider the remarkable information it offers with respect to external events and thereby to the question of absolute chronology. (It is best to approach this question before considering the question of sequence.)

2.3 Dating

I suggest that the eschatological scenario just sketched resonates quite strongly with a particular historical episode in the first century CE, allowing the fairly confident establishment of a *terminus a quo* for the letter's composition, and consequently for Paul's Thessalonian mission, to which he refers briefly (2:5). Unfortunately, we cannot reach a *terminus ad quem* with equal confidence, because the events Paul enumerates are presently somewhat concealed — the word he uses is "restrained" or "delayed," in combination with an implicit hiddenness — and some of the texts written later in the NT seem still to have an open mind about their arrival. But to have an absolute marker after which this letter was written and the preceding founding visit took place is itself a rare

---

56. Most notably, we do not know the source of Paul's information about the Galatian communities with certainty, or who conveyed Gal to them.

57. That is, they were probably adept at the forms of resistance typical of a deeply hierarchical society — slow work, avoidance of set tasks, etc. — as documented brilliantly by Scott (1990).

chronological prize. And perhaps there are hints about how close 2 Thessalonians lies to the events in question.

The underlying episode is, as Hugo Grotius (1679 [1640]; 1829 [1641]) suggested some time ago, "the Gaian crisis," meaning specifically the plan of Gaius to erect a statue of himself as Jupiter in the temple at Jerusalem, along with the plan's consequences.[58] Scholars often resist this suggestion, but invariably for weak reasons.[59] The episode caused enormous turmoil to Jews, especially in Galilee and its environs, and left an indelible mark on various ancient sources.[60] (We are not so well provided with sources on Gaius's reign in general.) The progress of this plan can be dated reasonably precisely, largely because its accomplishment rested on the governor of Syria, Publius Petronius, appointed to achieve it. (He replaced Lucius Vitellius, who was involved with the broader events that led to Paul's dramatic escape from Damascus late in 36 CE.)

Petronius marched to Ptolemaus during a campaign season — that is, between spring and autumn — with three legions and complementary auxiliaries (so presumably, some thirty to fifty thousand men) to install the statue by force, if necessary, in the following year (Philo, *Embassy to Gaius* 31.207). The enormous statue was being constructed at this time in Sidon (31.222). This placed Petronius on the coast not far away from the northern Jewish

58. Grotius's discussion is astonishingly learned. He cites Josephus, Philo, Suetonius, and Tacitus while building his historical case for an identification between the Man of Lawlessness and Gaius, going on to consider the identification of "the delayer" in relation to the Syrian governorships of L. Vitellius and Petronius. This position is quite well represented in modern NT scholarship, although perhaps not as well as it should be. N. Taylor (1996, 104 n. 15) lists the commentators Best, Dibelius, Frame, Marshall, and Wanamaker. Nicholl (2004, 121) lists the further support for this reading, in some sense, of Trilling, Friedrich, Richard, Peerbolte, and Légasse. Nicholl is himself opposed to the identification — a rare mistake.

59. A principal difficulty seems to be the supposition that 2 Thess was written well after the Gaian crisis; see, e.g., Best (1972, 288). But this is mistaken on two grounds. First, the eschatological modification introduced earlier may well have still been in effect, as it were, and the later references in Mk and Mt confirm this; and second, the late dating is likely to be wrong. Here of course we are using the episode precisely to date 2 Thess; that is, we are letting the letter tell us in the first instance where it should be located chronologically. So this historical echo is a benefit and not an embarrassment.

60. See Josephus, *Jewish War* 2.184-203; *Jewish Antiquities* 18.256-309; 19.15-114; Philo, *Embassy to Gaius* 29.188; 31.207-8; Tacitus, *Annals* 5.9.2; 3 Macc (in my view); see also Mk 13, esp. v. 14 (and see Mt 24:15-22; Lk 21:20-24; Dan 9:27; 11:31; 12:11); also 1 Macc 1:36-40; 2 Macc 6:2. It is arguably noted in some rabbinic texts as well (see N. Taylor 1996, 102 n. 5). Pompey's blasphemy in the temple — which did not amount to the introduction of idolatry — is probably reflected in *Pss. Sol.* 17:11-15.

territories, especially Galilee. And he consequently encountered on his arrival what was in effect a massive campaign of passive resistance by regional Jews, one so extensive that the autumnal harvest was jeopardized (and this confirms the earlier seasonal sequence).[61] Petronius responded to this campaign rather remarkably, undertaking to petition Gaius to ameliorate the plan, doubtless thereby risking his office and also possibly his life. So the plan was delayed over the winter (see esp. 31.217; 32.239; 33.248, 253; 34.258), delay also being caused by a petition to Gaius in Rome at the same time by his client Agrippa (35.261-42.337). This interference stalled the plan through the winter, and Philo even suggests that the goal of making a statue publicly in Sidon was abandoned, being replaced by a scheme to make one secretly in Rome (42.337; 43.338). This was to be installed personally in the course of a coastal voyage by the emperor to Alexandria. But Gaius was assassinated in January of the following year — in time for this news to overtake his instructions to Petronius to commit suicide for his disobedience. He was killed on January 24, 41 CE, and the vagaries of winter travel in relation to the contrasting instructions to Petronius further confirm this account. So a firm date can be derived for the events of the preceding year, that is, 40 CE.

The actual inception of the plan is harder to determine but seems to have become public knowledge during the previous winter. We know this in particular because Philo was present in Rome on a perilous midwinter journey at this time (*Embassy* 29.190), petitioning the emperor on behalf of the Jewish community in Alexandria in the wake of that community's troubles (see also *Flaccus*). (The extent to which those troubles caused the crisis in Judea is difficult to determine but unnecessary to work out here.)

Grotius suggested some time ago that the eschatological timetable in 2 Thessalonians 2:3-12 reflects these particular events in certain indelible ways. And in my view, this suggestion is hard to improve upon.

Jewish tradition was familiar with the threatened desecration of the Jerusalem temple with a pagan cult by an evil foreign ruler because of the Maccabean crisis in the second century BCE, a narrative imprinted especially on the book of Daniel. This bequeathed a discourse of eschatological temple violation to both Jews and Christians, one that involved the blasphemous as-

---

61. It is difficult to tell whether the reaping of the spring and summer harvest was being jeopardized or the sowing of the winter harvest. Josephus suggests the latter, because Petronius's courage was confirmed by miraculous rainfall, the necessary prerequisite for successful sowing and germination (*Jewish Antiquities* 18.286). But this story seems a little too convenient, not to mention biblically resonant. Other sources suggest more a failure to harvest the summer crop.

cription of deity to pagan kings. But the text of Daniel is principally concerned with the destruction of Jerusalem and the pollution of the temple's altar. Famously, the book speaks in this regard of "the abomination that desolates" (see τὸ βδέλυγμα τῆς ἐρημώσεως in Dan 9:27; 11:31; 12:11; see also 8:13), the phrase reprised by two of the Gospels (Mk 13:14; Mt 24:15-16; it is conspicuously dropped by Lk; see 21:20-21). It is possible that this phrase refers to the idolatrous statue of Zeus erected in the temple by Antiochus Epiphanes. But 1 Maccabees understands it more plausibly to be an altar dedicated to Zeus that was placed on top of the original altar of burnt offerings, thereby polluting the Jewish altar underneath with sacrifices of unclean food, most notably of pork (see 1:54, 59). That the lifeblood of unclean animals ran down regularly over the site at which daily libation was undertaken with holy lifeblood from clean animals was a terrible desecration for Jews, eliciting strong language. And this arrangement accords with typical pagan temple practice. The cult statue would normally have been placed inside the building, which housed what was effectively the god in suitable comfort and splendor. Sacrifices took place outside, in front of this structure. So "the abomination that desolates" in Daniel seems to have been the desecrating altar to Zeus, erected outside the holy of holies, on top of the altar of burnt offering.

It is significant, then, that 2 Thessalonians, unlike other texts in the NT, does not reprise this phrase exactly but introduces its own terminology and an adjusted scenario. It focuses, not on a desecrating altar, but on "the Man of Lawlessness," who will be enthroned in the temple and demonstrate thereby that he is God (see *Embassy* 44.343). The same verse also describes this figure in language that resonates with worship, stating that he will "oppose and lord it over everything [else] called 'God' or 'worshipped'" (4a: ὁ ἀντικείμενος καὶ ὑπεραιρόμενος ἐπὶ πάντα λεγόμενον θεὸν ἢ σέβασμα).

This placement of an enthroned figure at the center of the cult and the consequent emphasis on the worshipful confession of his divinity were distinctive to Hellenistic and, later, to Roman imperial worship, although the Roman variation had no extensive sacrificial practices. However, it was certainly sufficient to offend aniconic transcendental Jewish monotheists deeply, and just the same outrage is apparent in the text of 2 Thessalonians.[62] But the

---

62. A standard introduction to the imperial cult is Price (1984). The cult's relevance specifically to Pauline texts is explored in Horsley (1997; 2000; 2004); although these compilations must be used with caution. A more nuanced discussion of the cult in relation to NT concerns, although revolving around Lk and Acts, is the exchange between Barclay and Rowe: see Rowe (2005; 2009); Barclay (2011b); Rowe (2011); see also Barclay (2011a). Jewish aniconic sensibilities are nicely explicated by Barclay (2004); see also Marcus (2006).

focus by 2 Thessalonians on the enthronement of a figure in the temple and his blasphemous acclamation as divine are distinctive additions to the preceding Jewish discourse of eschatological temple violation, which was principally concerned with the city's destruction and the altar's desecration. We must ask, then, why the eschatological discourse in 2 Thessalonians ignores both of those last events, which were unambiguously public, and focuses instead on the events of the blasphemous enthronement. These emphases are new. But of course they are readily explained by Gaius's plan to install a bust establishing his own divinity in the precise form of Jupiter in the Jerusalem temple, a plan inaugurated, at the latest, during the winter of 39-40 CE. Moreover, only at this time in the Common Era was the Jerusalem temple specifically threatened with the installation of a cult statue celebrating a mortal man's divinity and, in effect, only with this — that is, not also with the destruction of the city or the desecration of the altar. Pompey simply entered the holy of holies; and during the first revolt, the city and the temple were destroyed. This particular desecration was not repeated until the second destruction of Jerusalem after the second revolt and the reestablishment of the city as Jupiter Capitolinus in the 130s CE, although the temple had been destroyed for decades by this time, and this is too late a date to affect the composition of 2 Thessalonians in any case.

A final detail seems to support this underlying reference to Gaius. The book of Daniel suggests that the abomination of desolation was "established" in God's temple (9:27: ἔσται . . . ; 11:31: στήσονται καὶ μιανοῦσι . . . δώσουσι; 12:11: ἐτοιμασθῇ δοθῆναι . . .), and this seems, as we just noted, to have referred to a polluting altar. However, 2 Thessalonians speaks, rather, of the Man of Lawlessness *sitting down* in the temple: ὥστε αὐτὸν εἰς τὸν ναὸν τοῦ θεοῦ *καθίσαι* ἀποδεικνύντα ἑαυτὸν ὅτι ἔστιν θεός (2:4).

The verb καθίσαι appears only five times in the Pauline corpus (see also 1 Cor 6:4; 10:7; Eph 1:20; 2:6), but in the active and intransitive in its fifty-odd occurrences throughout the NT, it almost invariably means "[to] sit down." Only Luke 24:49 and Acts 18:11 use it metaphorically to denote "settle" or "stay," this usage being signaled by a clear reference in the immediate context to time. Hence, the instance in 2 Thessalonians is indubitably to seating, which in this cultic context denotes enthronement. It is precisely this act that "demonstrates that he is 'God,'" namely, the figure's blasphemous enthronement as king in the temple of the true divine King who cannot be imaged, and his acclamation as such by foolish and deceived pagans and apostates.

The imperial cult statues were generally standing figures in militaristic poses, so this textual detail might seem at first glance to count against the suggestion that the Gaian crisis lay behind the language of 2 Thessalonians.[63] However, the sources note that Gaius's divine identifications were especially profligate and bold. He linked himself to many gods, and portrayed himself not infrequently as Jupiter, the king of the gods. Hence, it was apparently his intention to install a statue celebrating his divinity as Jupiter in the Jerusalem temple. Cassius Dio notes, moreover, that this magnificent statue was to be modeled on the famous chryselephantine image of Zeus crafted by Phidias at Olympia — one of the seven wonders of the world (59.28.3).[64] Suetonius indirectly confirms this when he records that Gaius tried to remove the original statue from Olympia to Rome, intending to replace its head with his own image (*Gaius* 2.2). And this statue, unusually, was enthroned and seated. (The anomaly was entirely deliberate; this feature, combined with the cramped temple design at Olympia, created an atmosphere of overwhelming power. As Strabo notes, "If Zeus were to stand up he would unroof the temple" [8.3.30]. The statue is also described in detail in Pausanias: 5.11.1-9.) So this detail in the text of 2 Thessalonians seems to confirm nicely the specific contours of the Gaian plan and, consequently, to corroborate the influence of that specific event on the eschatological scenario to which it alludes. And it follows, if this association holds good, that the eschatological scenario presupposed by 2 Thessalonians had to be constructed sometime after late 39 CE, with the founding visit to Thessalonica necessarily taking place after this temporal marker as well, since the letter is reminding the Thessalonians of a specific timetable and scenario that they were taught personally by Paul during the community's establishment (2:5).

Somewhat unfortunately for chronographers, the presence of this specific set of motifs within early Christian eschatological discourses in later texts, most notably in Mark and Matthew, suggests that the expectation of an analogous blasphemous defilement of the temple persisted long after Gaius's specific plan was halted. So we know only when these specific expectations entered the early church's eschatological discourse. Luke possibly points toward the gradual abandonment of this expectation by one tradition after the destruc-

---

63. Nicholl (2004, 121) presses this argument and is thereby led astray on this point.

64. "It seems that he had constructed a sort of lodge on the Capitoline, in order, as he said, that he might dwell with Jupiter; [3] but disdaining to take second place in this union of households, and blaming the god for occupying the Capitoline ahead of him, he hastened to erect another temple on the Palatine, and wished to transfer to it the statue of the Olympian Zeus after remodelling it to resemble himself. [4] But he found this to be impossible, for the ship built to bring it was shattered by thunderbolts, and loud laughter was heard every time that anybody approached as if to take hold of the pedestal; accordingly, after uttering threats against the statue, he set up a new one of himself."

tion of the temple.[65] But hopes that the temple would be rebuilt, and hence that the architecture necessary for the antichrist's penultimate eschatological blasphemy would be present, persisted in some circles well into the second century (and have not necessarily died out even today); certainly, much Jewish discourse at the same time seems confident of this restoration. Moreover, the emphasis on the Man of Lawlessness's present hiddenness in 2 Thessalonians creates an interpretative space — probably unwittingly — that allowed these continuing expectations. So we cannot say exactly when such expectations faded, providing a firm *terminus ad quem* for this text.

The text speaks in addition of delay, the precise identification of which has greatly vexed later interpreters. There are good historical candidates for this role in terms of the original episode, notably Petronius or Agrippa, with Petronius specifically being said several times by Philo to have caused "delay."[66] But it seems unlikely that these specific identifications are correct. If so, we would expect some adjustment to the scenario after the collapse of the plan in early 41 CE, and there is no trace of this in our Pauline sources. More likely is an original reference to the activities of a heavenly angel or cosmic power, a staple feature of apocalyptic discourses.[67] Such an actor could have been interpreted with respect to historical actors like Petronius,[68] who may well have originated the actual motif of delay within the story by his heroic actions in the later months of 40 CE. But a heavenly power and its delaying actions could have then shifted smoothly to other historical figures without apology,

65. His Gospel still attests to expectations that the *parousia* of the Lord Jesus would be sudden; see esp. 17:22-35.

66. See above. See also, for the results of Agrippa's petition, *Embassy* 42.333-34; however, the word "delay" is not used here, and strictly speaking, the plan was cancelled and then replaced almost immediately by another equally sacrilegious scheme. So Petronius seems a better candidate for "the delayer" in historical terms.

67. This reading is canvassed well by Nicholl (2004, 123; 225-49). Nicholl urges the identification of "the restrainer" with the archangel Michael, introducing data esp. from Dan 10:13, 20-21 in support. But — like most — he then struggles to explain the neuter grammar of the phrase τὸ κατέχον in 2:6. He points to places elsewhere in the NT where neuter constructions arguably emphasize a quality rather than an antecedent person (1 Cor 1:27-28; 11:5; Gal 3:22; see also Mt 12:6; Jn 3:6; 17:24; 1 Jn 5:1-4), but this sample is not impressive. Perhaps worth considering is the possibility that the underlying actor is, strictly speaking, not an angel but a στοιχεῖον, which would take the neuter (see Gal 4:3, 9; Col 2:8, 20; elsewhere, probably in a different sense, see only Heb 5:12; 2 Pet 3:10, 12); alternatively, but in the same vein, the presupposed notion could be μυστήριον.

68. Robert Moses has recently shown how just this interaction between cosmic powers and human actors corrupted and misled by them into evil practices characterizes Paul's thinking (2014).

just as the precise identification of the hidden Man of Lawlessness seems to have shifted easily from Gaius after January 41 CE to someone else who would be revealed plainly in due course. Nero was enthusiastically identified by many with the beast in Revelation, and so as the antichrist,[69] and this identification was then sometimes linked with the Man of Lawlessness in 2 Thessalonians,[70] a reassignment that took place from the 60s CE and hence just two to three decades after the narrative initiated by Gaius. As if to confirm this suspicion, the Man of Lawlessness was then happily identified with a plethora of further candidates through later church history, Grotius introducing his perspicacious historical suggestion in the sixteenth century to counteract the Protestant correlation of the Man of Lawlessness with the pope.[71]

These considerations all entail that it is difficult to judge whether the eschatological scenario in 2 Thessalonians is best construed as being composed as the Gaian crisis was unfolding — and not so appropriately after its collapse — allowing us to date both the mission at Thessalonica and 2 Thessalonians in or immediately around 40. It is certainly helpful to learn that this mission has to have taken place sometime after late 39 CE, although possibly as early as this date. But some hints from other data tilt me toward the judgment that the Macedonian and Achaian missions fell toward the front end of the relevant chronological window that extended from Paul's work in Syria and Cilicia from late 36 CE, "three years" after his call, to his year of crisis in 51. (By 51 the Macedonian and Achaian communities are clearly established.) These hints would place the Macedonian and Achaian missions in the early 40s, although more than this is hard to say.

---

69. See esp. Rev. 13:1-8, 11-18. This was also the view of (i.a.) the *Sibylline Oracles*, esp. 17:11-22; Victorinus (CSEL 49:118-20; *ANF* 7:358); Commodianus (*Instructions* 41; *ANF* 4:211 — combining the Nero *redivivus* view with the main alternative, that the antichrist would be a Jew descended from the tribe of Dan); the fifth-century *Liber genealogus* (614-20); and Sulpicius Severus (*Hist. sac.* 2.29). (I have found Gumerlock 2006 esp. helpful for this question; see also Thiselton 2011, 213-23.)

70. Several of the patristics talked about the antichrist in terms of 2 Thess 2 — (i.a.) Justin (*Dialogue with Trypho* 110; *ANF* 1:253-54); Tertullian (*On the Resurrection of the Flesh* 24; *ANF* 3:563; see Thiselton 2011, 215); Origen (*Against Celsus* 6.46; Thiselton 2011, 215); Chrysostom (*Hom. 2 Thess* 4; *NPNF*¹ 13:389); Cyril of Jerusalem (*Catechetical Lectures* 15.14, 17; *NPNF*² 7:108; Thiselton 2011, 215); Theodoret (*Commentary on the Letters of St. Paul*, trans. R. C. Hill, 2 vols. [Brookline, Mass.: Holy Cross Orthodox Press, 2001], 2:129). Some noted an earlier connection with Nero.

71. Thiselton (2011, 217) traces this view back to Joachim of Fiore (1135-1202), predating Grotius's struggles by over four hundred years. Other later historical candidates include Muhammad, the French Revolution, and the German Empire (Thiselton 2011, 231).

The only temporal spans that we have at this stage from Paul's writings for his missionary work in a given area are supplied by Galatians 1:17, where he speaks of work immediately after his call near Damascus in "Arabia." But we have learned that this designation encompassed two quite distinct regions, namely, the Decapolis and the kingdom of Nabataea (see 2 Cor 11:32-33). Paul tells us that this work lasted for two to three years. And we can make some extrapolations on this basis, although they need to be treated with the appropriate caution.

The data might be somewhat anomalous, since it derives from the years immediately following Paul's call, and we might suspect some significant shifts in his praxis after his arrival in Antioch (Gal 1:21). However, it is all the data that we have and may still be roughly indicative. It suggests that Paul spent between one and one and a half years evangelizing a given region. And this implies that Paul spent from late 36 CE through late 38 or 39 evangelizing Syria and Cilicia, and then moved on. A mission in Macedonia around 40 CE would fit neatly with this early temporal suggestion (which will be both adjusted and confirmed in due course).

This timing would help explain some of the eschatological anxieties that the Thessalonians were dealing with. As we will see in more detail shortly, they questioned Paul about the timing of the Lord Jesus' *parousia* (or something similar). They became unsettled by the notion that this *parousia* had already taken place, but were recalled by Paul to the parallel suggestion that the *parousia* of the Man of Lawlessness was still outstanding. The suitability of these questions to the immediate aftermath of the Gaian crisis is not incontestable proof that 1 and 2 Thessalonians were composed then, but they certainly fit well with that period. If the initial explicit historical candidate for the Man of Lawlessness had been assassinated, and the associated explicit plan to desecrate the Jerusalem temple had collapsed, then it seems understandable that the Thessalonians would want information about the timing of the *parousia* of the Lord Jesus, and that they could be troubled further by a persuasive suggestion that that day had already come. So the suitability of the early location for the Thessalonians' eschatological concerns seems marginally to confirm the implications of the time intervals implicit in Galatians 1:17 for the dating of this correspondence.[72]

In sum, it seems certain that 1 and 2 Thessalonians were composed after the Gaian crisis and, furthermore, since they presuppose teaching in those

---

72. I am not convinced by Luedemann's (1984 [1980], 201-61) ingenious argument at this point in terms of the deaths of Christians; see more in this relation shortly.

terms during the mission to Thessalonica, that the mission took place either during or after that crisis, hence sometime from 40 CE onward. Certain hints in the data then suggest placing this mission and the resulting correspondence — and consequently the Athenian mission as well — quite close to this *terminus a quo* rather than at the other end of the chronological window. We suspect, that is, that the Macedonian and Achaian missions took place in the early 40s CE, but this is a rather more tentative judgment.[73]

With the question of dating settled, at least to some degree, we can turn to the final question remaining in contingent terms, namely, the sequencing of 1 and 2 Thessalonians.

2.4 Sequencing

The sequencing of 1 and 2 Thessalonians is a very difficult question. Precious little evidence of real validity seems to be present in the sources, necessitating another rather tentative conclusion.[74] Nevertheless, so much dubious reasoning is present, clouding the issue, that we will have to begin again by doing some clearing. Only then will we be able to address the material evidence, such as it is, and to generate the most plausible judgment.

The main indecisive contentions generally fall into one of four groups: most famously and complexly, related to (1) the instructions concerning eschatology in the two letters; and, more prosaically, related to (2) the letter endings; (3) the issue of laziness; and (4) the nature of the implied sufferings. I will suggest here, however, that all of these arguments are dogged by a single basic difficulty: that the data is susceptible to plausible reconstructions in terms of both key possibilities (and often of more besides), whether with 2 Thessalonians preceding 1 Thessalonians or following it (FVT — 2 Thess — 1 Thess . . . or FVT — 1 Thess — 2 Thess . . .). That is, scholars frequently seem to think that because they have explained the data plausibly in terms of one sequence, it is decisive. However, this is the case only if plausible alternative configurations are lacking or can be confidently eliminated, and generally they are not and cannot be. In the presence of two different but equally plausible scenarios

73. Ultimately, data from Acts will contribute helpfully here.

74. This was all something of a surprise to me. I had long argued that reversing the canonical sequence solved all our problems in this relation, and fairly obviously so. But on returning to consider the question in detail, I experienced — not for the first time in this study — the collapse of a cherished hypothesis. It was at least reassuring to find that the great majority of the argumentation surrounding this question seemed to suffer a similar fate.

running in reverse directions, we must set aside the data being appealed to as unhelpful, however much we might favor one scenario. I call this situation one of "multiple plausible narrativity." Any data characterized by multiple plausible narrativity is unhelpful for sequencing questions, not to mention for many other judgments during preliminary framing.

This difficulty is further complicated by the recognition of a set of caveats. On the one hand, we must recognize the distance between modern interpreters and the ancient situation, both temporally and culturally. And on the other, we must acknowledge the paucity of our data and our consequent lack of any comprehensive knowledge of that situation. These powerful constraints further limit the weight that we should place on our reconstructions of the original situation.

Bearing these challenges and constraints in mind, we can turn to assess the four types of arguments usually made in relation to sequencing 1 and 2 Thessalonians, arguments that overlap with pseudepigraphy as an alternative explanation of some of the difficulties ostensibly apparent in the data.

(1) The Instructions Concerning Eschatology

We have already briefly explored the eschatological scenario in 2 Thessalonians; however, we have yet to direct a similar level of attention to the scenario in 1 Thessalonians.

Future eschatology is clearly an important thread running through 1 Thessalonians, as it is in 2 Thessalonians. The principal concern in 1 Thessalonians as a whole seems to involve slightly defensive exhortation on Paul's part, rhetoric to this end dominating the letter from the first thanksgiving through to the end of chapter 3. Eschatology surfaces within this discussion in 1:10, 2:19-20, and 3:13, but it comes into more sustained focus only in 4:13–5:9, with a final flourish occurring in 5:23-24. Three subsections are discernible within the longer principal treatment. First, Paul argues in 4:13-18 on the basis of Jesus' resurrection that those who have died will be resurrected and included within the joyful reunion occurring at the Lord Jesus' *parousia*. He then seems to respond, second, to a query from the Thessalonians that is reprised (at least in part) in 5:1 "concerning times and seasons" (περὶ . . . τῶν χρόνων καὶ τῶν καιρῶν). He replies to this somewhat cryptically that the day of the Lord will come "like a thief in the night . . . [when] destruction will fall on them [i.e., on those saying 'peace and safety'] like birth pangs on a pregnant [and presumably full-term] woman" ([2] . . . ἡμέρα κυρίου ὡς κλέπτης ἐν νυκτὶ οὕτως ἔρχεται . . . [3] . . . αἰφνίδιος αὐτοῖς ἐφίσταται ὄλεθρος ὥσπερ ἡ ὠδὶν τῇ ἐν γαστρὶ ἐχούσῃ). Paul then segues in v. 4, in a third development, to place ethical pressure on the Thessalonians through v. 11. They do not in fact belong to the night, during which this thief might come unexpectedly and overwhelm them; they belong to the day, and so should not engage in drunken nocturnal revels but in lives of fidelity, affection, and hope.

It is critical now to be as precise as possible about the eschatological claims made in these three subsections.

The first subsection suggests that some Thessalonians were concerned about the deaths of community members. In his response, Paul supplies details concerning the *parousia*. It will be signaled by the shout of an archangel and a divine trumpet blast. The dead will then rise and will be caught up with the remaining living believers to meet the Lord "in the clouds" and, ultimately, "to be with him forever" (. . . ἐν νεφέλαις εἰς ἀπάντησιν τοῦ κυρίου εἰς ἀέρα· καὶ οὕτως πάντοτε σὺν κυρίῳ ἐσόμεθα). Most importantly, then, any dead within the community will certainly not be left behind or miss out on the reunion inaugurated by the *parousia;* they will, rather, be summoned, effectively from the ground, to join it.[75]

The second subsection is critical for our discussion. Paul is responding to a Thessalonian query that is frustratingly bland ("concerning times and seasons"; see Dan 2:21 and, more distantly, Wis 8:8).[76] He suggests initially that it is superfluous for him to write anything, since they already know well, or "accurately" (ἀκριβῶς), that the *parousia* will come like a thief in the night.[77] Hence, there seems to be an appeal here to preceding teaching (see 4:1-2), which was probably originally dominical, and Paul's affirmations are consequently not new. That is, the use of the intensifying adverb suggests that this

75. As Nicholl (2004, 26-32) notes, a tension in Paul's argument has puzzled some scholars. Resolving this need not detain us; however, it is worth noting. In 4:14b God "brings" those who sleep with and through Jesus. In the later sequence, however, those who sleep are resurrected by various heavenly commands, form something of a reception committee for the coming Lord Jesus in the clouds, and stay with him forever. So the movement in the meeting seems to be in the opposite direction. But as Nicholl suggests, probably Paul is simply narrating elliptically. After meeting the Lord Jesus in the clouds, rather as a city's leading citizens would process out to meet a visiting official or emperor, the group returns to earth, just as the citizens and the official would return to a city ceremoniously if not triumphantly. In a renewed cosmos, God [the Father], the Lord Jesus, and the community then live together forever.

76. It might be significant that this phrase in Dan occurs alongside reference to the dethroning and enthroning (lit. "seating") of kings; καὶ αὐτὸς ἀλλοιοῖ καιροὺς καὶ χρόνους, μεθιστῶν βασιλεῖς καὶ καθιστῶν.

77. Cf. Mt 24:43-44; Lk 12:39-40; also Rev. 3:3; 16:15.

is not merely a disclosure formula smoothing the way rhetorically to the disclosure of something that is new.[78]

The narrative of a thief coming in the night is expanded in v. 3 by the narrative of a pregnant woman suddenly going into labor.[79] This rush of events is then applied to surrounding non-Christians who are uttering what might be an idolatrous slogan from the imperial cult.[80] They will not escape the sudden arrival of God's anger at their wickedness. And after this, as we have already seen, Paul pivots in a third subsection into exhortation principally to avoid drunkenness based on the identification of the Thessalonians with the day, not the night, a discussion that supplies little further concrete information about eschatology per se.

I would suggest at this point that it is important not to overinterpret the material supplied in the second, briefest and most controversial eschatological subsection. Paul's point appears to be principally that the Thessalonians already know that, despite its drama, the actual *parousia* of the Lord Jesus will be sudden (αἰφνίδιος) and, in and of itself, unexpected, although principally for those outside the community. It seems possible, then, that he is simply resisting time-tabling this event.[81] The stupendous happenings enumerated in the first

78. See, on the formula in general and in Paul, Mullins (1964); O'Brien (1977, 201-2); J. White (1984, 207-8); Porter and Pitts (2008; 2013).

79. This is certainly biblical and may also have been dominical; see Isa 13:8; Jer 6:24; Hos 13:13.

80. The presence of the imperial cult in this slogan is argued by Weima (2012); and, more generally, by Koester (1990; 1997). Some, conversely, hear an echo of Jer 6:14 (see 8:11; Ezek 13:10) — so Nicholl (2004, 54). The latter reading seems initially to fail to account for the use of εἰρήνη καὶ ἀσφάλεια in v. 3 instead of the LXX's double use of εἰρήνη. However, there are compelling echoes of Jer 6 (LXX) in the context of 1 Thess 5:3: for God's wrath in Jer 6:11, being felt inside Jeremiah (τὸν θυμόν μου), see 1 Thess 5:9; for labor pains in Jer 6:24 (ὠδῖνες ὡς τικτούσης), see 1 Thess 5:3b; for the end's suddenness in Jer 6:26 (ὅτι ἐξαίφνης ἥξει ταλαιπωρία ἐφ᾽ ὑμᾶς), see 1 Thess 5:3b. This accumulation of allusions is difficult to deny. (The subtle linguistic differences between the LXX and Paul's Greek might then combine to suggest the presence of an Aramaic Urtext.) Ultimately, it may not be necessary to decide between the influences on Paul's text from these two discourses. Both may have been operative in a hybridized discussion.

81. An influence from Jer 6:14 might reinforce this reading marginally. As we just saw above, that text refers to the deposition and enthronement of kings, possibly suggesting that the Thessalonian query is related to these divine actions as well. This would suggest that they are interested in when the Roman emperor, soon to be revealed as the Man of Lawlessness, will be deposed and the rightful cosmic ruler, the Lord Jesus, arrive and be enthroned alongside his Father. Paul's answer, however, is that this climactic event will be unanticipated and sudden. It will also *surprise* those who have not converted.

subsection that will inaugurate the resurrection of at least the Christian dead, namely, shouting archangels and sounding heavenly trumpets, will erupt at the appropriate time, catching many non-Christians off guard. At that moment, the pagan opportunity to convert and turn away from idolatry, sexual immorality, and drunkenness will be over (1:9-10).[82]

From all of this, we can surmise the following situation. The Thessalonians seem to have been concerned about two things, and Paul with a third by way of further response. They were concerned about the fate of their dead in relation to Christ's *parousia*. And they might also have wanted more specific information about its timing. Paul responds to these concerns directly, although more charitably to the first than to the second. The dead in Christ will certainly not miss out on the *parousia* but will be resurrected. However, the Thessalonians already know that the *parousia* of Christ will be sudden and unexpected. Moreover, Paul clearly remains concerned about certain aspects of their behavior, here especially with (in more modern parlance) the issue of substance abuse over against the positive practices of fidelity, affection, and hope.

With these clarifications in place, we need to consider the key question of sequencing in relation to this particular data set. How does this eschatological scenario fit together with the scenario articulated by 2 Thessalonians?

82. Nicholl (2004, esp. 49-79) argues powerfully for a tighter integration within this material than I do. He integrates the third subsection that I have identified here as ethical and somewhat discrete (5:4-11) with the second (i.e., 5:1-3), suggesting that the Thessalonians themselves feared the arrival of the day of the Lord and its wrath, in large measure *because* some of their members had died (so subsection one, 4:13-18). For pagans, this might have seemed like a *prodigia*, indicating that they had fallen under the wrath of God. And this could well have led in turn to fear concerning the *parousia* of the Lord Jesus that Paul counters through much of 5:1-11. I am almost persuaded by this reading, and concede its plausible construals of vv. 4b and 9a in particular ([5:4] ὑμεῖς δέ, ἀδελφοί, οὐκ ἐστὲ ἐν σκότει, ἵνα ἡ ἡμέρα ὑμᾶς ὡς κλέπτης καταλάβῃ. . . . [9] . . . ὅτι οὐκ ἔθετο ἡμᾶς ὁ θεὸς εἰς ὀργὴν). But Nicholl underplays the ethical thrust in vv. 4-11, which is unavoidable in vv. 6-8. This material then seems to draw Paul's strong reorientation of the imagery of day and night in the preceding vv. 4 and 5 into its concerns, as signaled especially by the emphatic ἄρα οὖν that opens v. 6. The negative statements concerning the Thessalonians' location — that they are *not* in darkness and at risk of being overwhelmed (v. 4) or destined for wrath (v. 9a) — then function perfectly comprehensibly as rhetorical reinforcements in negative terms of the Thessalonians' positive location within the community over against its evil surrounding detractors, and thereby within the practices of that illuminated group. That is, the statements do not necessarily need to be mirror read, as directly reflective of Thessalonian anxieties. These comments are not sufficient to undermine Nicholl's comprehensive and careful case, but they do indicate grounds for caution in terms of its full acceptance.

Scholars have argued persuasively on almost all sides of this question: that the scenario in 1 Thessalonians must precede 2 Thessalonians, with the sequence being quite plausible in these and only these terms; that the scenario in 2 Thessalonians must precede 1 Thessalonians, being plausible in only these terms; and that the scenario in 2 Thessalonians is implausible in relation to 1 Thessalonians whether before or after it, and so 2 Thessalonians must be pseudepigraphic (or, strictly speaking, Paul is contradicting himself again). (The missing explanatory option is that the scenario in 1 Thessalonians is implausible both before and after 2 Thessalonians, and so 1 Thessalonians must be pseudepigraphic; the suggestion that both letters are pseudepigraphic clearly cannot be made in these terms.) We will of course be particularly concerned with the first two options here, although open to the third.

The strong views I used to hold on this issue have collapsed on closer examination. The critical question to ask initially is whether the two eschatological scenarios explicated by the two letters are compatible. If they are, then many other questions and implications evaporate. From this point, the sequencing could go in both directions on eschatological grounds, since 1 and 2 Thessalonians would be filling out different (compatible) aspects of one basic scenario as elicited by local contingent factors. Further claims on the basis of the eschatologies advocated by the two letters would then be indecisive. Suggestions of development and/or of contradiction entailing pseudepigraphy on these grounds would clearly be undermined, and we would in fact know little more than we already do about framing, at least on grounds of eschatology. So we need to focus on this question of compatibility for a moment.[83]

The eschatological scenario in 1 Thessalonians assumes genuine anxiety on the part of some Thessalonians about their dead, but in the ancient world this would have been ubiquitous and could have arisen very quickly after the missionaries' departure, or anytime thereafter. In 1 Thessalonians 4:13-18 Paul presumably fills in something of a gap in their knowledge. That converts from paganism were not familiar with the resurrection of the dead in this early Christian variation seems quite understandable. He then seems to resist time-tabling the *parousia* of Jesus, appealing to an existing teaching about the suddenness of this event that evokes a standard Jewish metaphor for the end time, namely, labor pangs, in a story glossing the more dominical narra-

---

83. Nicholl (2004, 8-9, 12) briefly canvasses the position's supporters and detractors, including, somewhat strangely, advocates of the pseudonymity of 2 Thess who nevertheless view the eschatologies in the two letters as complementary (Wrede, Hollmann, Trilling, Bailey, R. Collins, Holland, F. Hughes, Giblin, Menken, Richard).

tive of a thief or brigand robbing someone in the night. The unexpectedness of this event is oriented principally toward non-Christians, however ([5:3] ὅταν λέγωσιν· εἰρήνη καὶ ἀσφάλεια, τότε αἰφνίδιος αὐτοῖς ἐφίσταται ὄλεθρος … [4] ὑμεῖς δέ, ἀδελφοί, οὐκ ἐστὲ ἐν σκότει, ἵνα ἡ ἡμέρα ὑμᾶς ὡς κλέπτης καταλάβῃ). At no point does the text state that the Thessalonians themselves were to be taken by surprise, although the *parousia* of the Lord Jesus would be dramatic and sudden: "You brothers are *not* in darkness with the result that that day will overwhelm you like a brigand['s attack]."

The eschatological scenario in 2 Thessalonians responds to an anxiety on the part of the Thessalonians that the *parousia* of Jesus had already come. Paul disproves this supposition by appealing to an eschatological timetable oriented by the Man of Lawlessness. Displaying the imprint of Jewish eschatological expectations tempered by the Maccabean era and, more recently, the Gaian crisis, Paul argues that this figure must be enthroned in the Jerusalem temple and blasphemously acclaimed as God, in the midst of a general apostasy, before the *parousia* of Christ can take place; in essence, this false *parousia* must precede the real one. Since it has not, Jesus' *parousia* has not yet taken place; and Paul appeals again to earlier oral teaching.

It seems to me, after careful consideration, that these two scenarios are plausibly compatible. They can fit together. This is not to say ultimately that they did, but the possibility that they did cannot be decisively excluded here. The key observations allowing this judgment are the realization that 2 Thessalonians time-tables future events broadly, but specifically in relation to the *parousia* of the Man of Lawlessness, and that 1 Thessalonians explicitly asserts temporal agnosticism only in relation to the Lord Jesus' *parousia*. His arrival will be dramatic and sudden. But there is no explicit evidence that 1 Thessalonians is making a blanket claim about all eschatological events in terms of their unanticipated suddenness. Only the Lord Jesus' arrival is said to be sudden, here in accordance with original teaching, and it will actually surprise only outsiders. Nor does 2 Thessalonians exclude a sudden *parousia* by the Lord Jesus, and its focus on the time-tabling of the Man of Lawlessness might even be said to support this point. Consequently, the situations in Thessalonica that seem to have caused these epistolary responses with their fragmentary eschatological reminders are necessarily plausible in any sequence or arrangement as well.

In support of this basic judgment, it needs to be appreciated that this narrative of perceptible historical crises effected by evil historical figures, combined with agnosticism about the actual irruption of the heavenly kingdom from beyond history, accords with certain Jewish eschatological expectations from Paul's day. The book of Daniel carefully time-tables the final woes of Judea — but not the actual arrival of the end. So Paul may well have taught the Thessalonian community during his founding visit that certain key woes had to fall on the world before the *parousia* of the Lord Jesus, namely, the desecration of the temple by the Man of Lawlessness, who seems to have been narrated, at least initially, with respect to the evil emperor Gaius, and that after this set of dramatic and palpable events, the Lord Jesus would return suddenly and dramatically, catching up his community to meet him in the clouds and ultimately to be with him forever. Paul's later letters to the community then pick up aspects of this underlying scenario when prompted by quite specific situational exigencies. But it follows that either 1 Thessalonians or 2 Thessalonians could plausibly have preceded the other. The order would simply have depended on the order in which the specific circumstances arose at Thessalonica eliciting the particular questions and responses in view, and there is no obvious or necessary order to those communal crises.

The Thessalonians could first have been unsettled by a deceptive suggestion from a spiteful neighbor that the Lord Jesus had already returned. Paul would then have reiterated in 2 Thessalonians his original eschatological timetable in relation to the Man of Lawlessness to reassure them, perhaps with a degree of exasperation. Obviously, the Lord Jesus had not yet returned, because the temple desecration had not yet taken place. Some Thessalonians might then have become concerned about the dead, possibly because a child had died or was dying, or in view of some illness. They also seem to have thought at this time that a degree of time-tabling for the Lord Jesus' *parousia* similar to the events scheduled for the Man of Lawlessness would be desirable — and they were not the last Christians to want this information. Hence, the eschatological concerns of 1 Thessalonians are readily understandable at this juncture, as is Paul's redirection of the Thessalonian interest in future eschatology into present ethics (1 Thess 5:4-11). But this order can be plausibly reversed.

The Thessalonians could have become concerned about their dead and, after reflection on Paul's original eschatological teaching concerning the Man of Lawlessness, have wanted more specific information about the *parousia* of the Lord Jesus. So Paul could have addressed their concerns in the manner just enumerated in the context of another principal communication. Then, at some later moment, false information could have been introduced into the community suggesting that the Lord Jesus had already come — perhaps even playing upon the temporal agnosticism asserted by Paul in 1 Thessalonians. Someone might have suggested that the Lord Jesus had indeed come back like a thief in the night, perhaps near Jerusalem, and his followers had been gathered and had departed, leaving the Thessalonians behind. To correct this anxiety, Paul would then have reaffirmed in 2 Thessalonians the explicit timetable within his earlier eschatological schema that invoked the Man of Lawlessness and the desecration of the temple, thereby proving that the critical day had not in fact come.

Both sequences seem basically plausible, especially when we recall that our judgments are limited here by considerable temporal and cultural distances and by a distinctly partial data set. Hence, the compatibility between the eschatological instructions in the two letters entails that they provide us with no decisive information about sequencing. But this realization does at least entail the rejection of any suggestions that development had to have taken place between the letters on the grounds of eschatology, whether in one direction or the other, or — putting the same case more strongly — that the scenarios are so incompatible that one letter has to be inauthentic. (As we saw earlier, this last contention is flawed in any case, since we have at this point no gauge of Paul's consistency.) At bottom, in response to this entire area of debate, we simply need to appreciate the possibility of an ongoing commitment by Paul through this part of his missionary work — that is, from the founding visit to Thessalonica and beyond — to a broadly Jewish eschatological timetable revolving around the desecration of the Jerusalem temple by the Man of Lawlessness, although envisaged after Gaius in the garb of a blasphemous Roman emperor, which would be followed by the sudden *parousia* of the Lord Jesus and his kingdom (this being a departure in certain key respects from standard Jewish expectations). But none of Paul's later letters gainsay this commitment, however much we might want them to (i.e., he never explicitly repudiates a timetable for the end revolving around the Man of Lawlessness, nor are any of his expectations incompatible with that). And with this realization, we can set the eschatological material in these letters to one side for the moment. It makes no useful contribution to the sequencing of 1 and 2 Thessalonians or, ultimately, to the question of pseudepigraphy.

Our evaluation of the evidence contributed by the letter endings can be briefer.

(2) Clues in the Letter Endings

Both letters have distinctive conclusions that seem at first glance to convey helpful information about sequencing. But on closer examination, both pieces of data collapse into unhelpful ambiguity.

Somewhat distinctively in the Pauline corpus, 1 Thessalonians charges
its recipients to have the letter read out to all the community: [5:27] Ἐνορκίζω
ὑμᾶς τὸν κύριον ἀναγνωσθῆναι τὴν ἐπιστολὴν πᾶσιν τοῖς ἀδελφοῖς. This could
suggest the correction of their reception of a previous letter that was *not* read
out to all the *adelphoi* — presumably 2 Thessalonians. However, it might be
no more than an instruction not to treat 1 Thessalonians as a private letter so
much as a public one, the genre of an apostolic letter from Paul apparently
being a little difficult to comprehend even in the first century (see Richards
2004, 126, 202, 221). And this would have been a particular difficulty if 1 Thessalonians was the *first* letter that the Thessalonians received from Paul. So this
datum is ambiguous.

More promisingly, 2 Thessalonians takes pains to affirm its personally
signed autograph as a marker of authenticity:

[3:17] Ὁ ἀσπασμὸς τῇ ἐμῇ χειρὶ Παύλου, ὅ ἐστιν σημεῖον ἐν πάσῃ ἐπιστολῇ·
οὕτως γράφω. [18] ἡ χάρις τοῦ κυρίου ἡμῶν Ἰησοῦ Χριστοῦ μετὰ πάντων
ὑμῶν.[84]

It has been suggested plausibly that the Thessalonians would already know
that Paul authenticated his letters with a personally written autograph if
they had already received 1 Thessalonians. So the information in 2 Thessalonians 3:17-18 belongs rather more plausibly at the front end of an epistolary
sequence, as the first letter the Thessalonians received — if, that is, this is
not evidence of a brazen forger.[85] However, Paul writes here that his auto-
graphed grace wish is the key authenticating sign in *every* letter, and this
opens the door to a possible scenario within which the Thessalonians have
been confused by letters arriving in two forms. They might have known
that a letter authenticated by a signed grace wish was Pauline, but they
did not necessarily know from 1 Thessalonians that this was *invariable,* a
gap in their knowledge that a clever and malicious pseudepigrapher might
have chosen to exploit. Second Thessalonians indicates clearly, moreover,
that this is a scenario of which Paul is well aware (2:2). In response to this
possibility, then, Paul could well have written in a second genuine letter
that "this [signature] is the sign [of authenticity] in *all* my letters." So this
initially promising data is unhelpful for our present question; it is undermined by multiple plausible narrativity.

84. Cf. also esp. 1 Cor 16:21-22; Gal 6:11(-17); Col 4:18; also Phlm 19.
85. So Ehrman (2013, 170-71), on the heels of many others.

(3) The Issue of Community Laziness

It has been argued that the problem of community laziness and consequent ex-
ploitation of the communal meal evident especially in 2 Thessalonians suggests
that it preceded 1 Thessalonians. As we have seen, this problem is addressed
fairly directly and sternly in 2 Thessalonians 3:6-15, but it is rather less prominent in 1 Thessalonians if visible at all. Admonishment of the lazy occurs in one
rather generic line of exhortation — νουθετεῖτε τοὺς ἀτάκτους (5:14) — in the
midst of a set of similarly generic instructions at the end of the letter in 5:14-
22. Intriguingly — as we have already seen — an identical characterization of
the missionaries' original labor is used in both letters, although this material
is developed locally in distinctly different directions:

[1 Thess 2:9] Μνημονεύετε γάρ, ἀδελφοί, τὸν κόπον ἡμῶν καὶ τὸν μόχθον·
νυκτὸς καὶ ἡμέρας ἐργαζόμενοι πρὸς τὸ μὴ ἐπιβαρῆσαί τινα ὑμῶν
ἐκηρύξαμεν εἰς ὑμᾶς τὸ εὐαγγέλιον τοῦ θεοῦ.

[2 Thess 3:7] Αὐτοὶ γὰρ οἴδατε πῶς δεῖ μιμεῖσθαι ἡμᾶς, ὅτι οὐκ ἠτακτήσαμεν
ἐν ὑμῖν [8] οὐδὲ δωρεὰν ἄρτον ἐφάγομεν παρά τινος, ἀλλ᾽ ἐν κόπῳ καὶ
μόχθῳ νυκτὸς καὶ ἡμέρας ἐργαζόμενοι πρὸς τὸ μὴ ἐπιβαρῆσαί τινα ὑμῶν·

When one steps back and looks at this material, however, it is again hard to avoid
the conclusion that a plausible narrative of the underlying problem is possible
in terms of either sequence. The vaguest hint of an issue is evident in 1 Thessalonians, and a considerable concern is evident in 2 Thessalonians. But presumably, there could have been a whiff of trouble present when 1 Thessalonians was
written in response to the report of Timothy that then developed into more of a
congregational crisis by the time 2 Thessalonians was written, or, equally plausibly, a congregational crisis evident first in 2 Thessalonians could have subsided,
having been effectively addressed by that letter and the community's leadership
(see 1 Thess 5:12-13), so that only the vaguest of references was necessary by the
time 1 Thessalonians was written. Plausible scenarios can be constructed for
either sequence, and this is precisely the problem.[86] Any judgment on the basis
of this data is undermined as well, then, by multiple plausible narrativity.

86. Some scholars attach this evidence to the eschatological material, suggesting that
some of the Thessalonians had stopped working *because* they were expecting the Lord Jesus'
parousia imminently. But there is no evidence for this connection in the letter, and again, it
does not help us with sequencing in any case, because both letters were plausibly written in a
strong eschatological shadow.

(4) The Nature of the Thessalonians' Sufferings

Manson (1953) reprised an interesting argument by Weiss (1959 [1917]) that the sufferings evident in both letters fall onto a discernible continuum.[87] The sufferings at Thessalonica recounted by 2 Thessalonians are, he suggests, present; the verbs in 1:4 and 5 are in the present tense (ἀνέχεσθε ... πάσχετε ...), as are the participles in vv. 6 and 7 (τοῖς θλίβουσιν ὑμᾶς ... καὶ ὑμῖν τοῖς θλιβομένοις ...). The entire posture of much of the letter subsequently — as signaled strongly by the thanksgiving (1:3-12) — is then future.[88] Conversely, the sufferings articulated by 1 Thessalonians are just past. As we have already seen in §1, Paul crafts a sophisticated apologetic and paranesis through that letter's first three chapters, in part by linking the sufferings of the missionaries with the sufferings that the Thessalonians originally endured during their conversions. It seems plausible to suggest, then, that 2 Thessalonians was dispatched into the midst of those sufferings, as they were currently unfolding, and 1 Thessalonians was sent just after they had subsided, when their immediate history could be recalled to strengthen the ties between the Thessalonians and Paul.

However, in order for this promising argument to hold, we must assume that the Thessalonians endured just one phase of suffering, which took place around their conversion, and that the hostility of their neighbors then subsided permanently. And this seems implausible. Many conflicts run for long periods of time and are often studded with distinct disputes (see Moore and McDonald 2000, esp. 15-24). Hence, it can be objected against Weiss and Manson that 1 Thessalonians does indeed look back on a period of original suffering but that 2 Thessalonians might attest to a later eruption of difficulty caused by the same group of protagonists who had been irritated by the unresolved situation, by the Thessalonians' persistence — possibly strengthened by Timothy's visit and 1 Thessalonians — and perhaps even by further conversions; and subsequent church history attests richly to the plausibility of this countersuggestion. (First Thessalonians will need to hold its place reasonably close to the original suffer-

---

87. Manson's own arguments designed to supplement Weiss are weak, being more susceptible than most to multiple plausible narrativity (see Manson 1953, 443-46).

88. That is, certain concrete expectations vis-à-vis the immediate future will, on the one hand, remove any uncertainty from the Thessalonians concerning the Lord Jesus' *parousia* (see 2:1-2) and, on the other, strengthen them in their endurance as they anticipate the dramatic reversal of roles that this event will inaugurate. Those currently oppressing them will be crushed, and they will be gloriously relieved and vindicated. But they must endure *the present* in order to benefit from *the future*. And this entire temporal and historical orientation is different from 1 Thess, which builds from the (immediate) past into the present.

ings endured during the founding of the community, but 2 Thess could conceivably be inserted into the space just before its composition, or fall well after it.)

It can be objected further that this argument places too much weight on a modern reception of the tenses in question. The use of the aorist in 1 Thessalonians, Porter (1989) would remind us, does not necessarily denote past action primarily but rather aspect. So Paul could be doing little more than suggesting a discrete view of the Thessalonian sufferings in 1 Thessalonians, which would be understandable, as he weaves that specific story into his broader rhetorical concerns (i.e., he would have to use the aorist for this even if the sufferings were ongoing, since Koiné lacks a present finite tense). So there is no fixed implication flowing from Paul's grammar in 1 Thessalonians that these sufferings were discontinuous, past, or over, and the situation is not therefore necessarily discontinuous with 2 Thessalonians. In short, once again, the contention seems indecisive. Plausible narratives encompassing the data of suffering can be constructed for either sequence — the precedence of 2 Thessalonians or the precedence of 1 Thessalonians — even conceding that the suffering has modulated significantly between the two letters, which it probably has not.

By this point in our analysis, it can be seen that all the main contentions offered in the literature with respect to sequencing have foundered. But we do have some data yet to consider, on the basis of which I suggest we can reach a judgment, albeit a tentative one. A small cluster of limited contentions, in combination, marginally suggests that 1 Thessalonians preceded 2 Thessalonians — a surprise to me, a vociferous supporter of the priority of 2 Thessalonians for many years. So the canonical order is, probably entirely fortuitously, the correct original historical order.

We should consider first which sequence is most likely in terms of immediate contiguity — a slightly easier question to resolve — and then ask whether it is more plausible to separate the two letters significantly in terms of time or to hold them together. We know already that 1 Thessalonians was composed at Athens, shortly after the Thessalonian mission. Is it plausible, then, to suggest that 2 Thessalonians preceded 1 Thessalonians at Athens? Or is the reverse sequence more likely, at which point we would have to consider the probable lapse of time that took place between the two letters, and the possibility of 2 Thessalonians coming from another location altogether?

In this specific situation, at Athens, it seems more likely on balance that 1 Thessalonians came first. That letter gives a fulsome account of Paul's previous relationship with the Thessalonians, emphasizing every available evidence of affection. It details various aspects of the original visit, Paul's ongoing emotional concern, and his dispatch of Timothy. The narrative culminates in Paul's overflowing thankfulness upon Timothy's return that then finds expression in the composition of 1 Thessalonians. (Paul's affection is so articulated that one almost overlooks the fact that he is not visiting in person.) And given the presence of such a narrative, Paul's silence concerning a previous letter would be puzzling. This act too would presumably demonstrate affection and concern. But 1 Thessalonians never mentions this additional evidence of affection and loyalty on Paul's part.

It might be objected that 2 Thessalonians is rather too abrasive to inhabit such a narrative. However, 2 Thessalonians is dominated by Paul's pastoral concern to alleviate the anxiety at Thessalonica that the day of the Lord might already have come and have left the Thessalonians behind (or some such). It is extended evidence — suitably interpreted — that he cares. So we would expect it to be mentioned as further evidence of his concerned posture. Conversely, if that letter had damaged his relationship with the Thessalonians, then we would expect a detailed account from Paul concerning how to read it "correctly" — affectionately — as we find in 2 Corinthians concerning the reception of 1 Corinthians.[89]

Arguments from silence are seldom sufficient in their own right to establish a hypothesis. But we are not establishing something here so much as trying to detect on balance whether 1 Thessalonians or 2 Thessalonians came first, knowing that one did. And on balance, the silence of 1 Thessalonians concerning a previous letter, when the rhetoric of chapters 1-3 would suggest its acknowledgment, counts against 2 Thessalonians' existence at the time of 1 Thessalonians' composition. That is, when trying to settle this question, we must ask ourselves which letter most plausibly came first, with no preceding communication, and which letter most plausibly came second, with a possible preceding communication. And 1 Thessalonians seems most plausibly to have come first.[90]

Moreover, 2 Thessalonians most plausibly comes second. In 2:15 Paul writes, "Therefore, *adelphoi,* stand and grasp on to the traditions which you

89. A question discussed extensively in ch. 2.

90. It might also be worth noting here that it seems unlikely, if 2 Thess preceded 1 Thess, that 2 Thess accompanied Timothy on his previous visit. Timothy is a coauthor in that letter. Paul elsewhere praises Timothy as his letter bearer, yet 2 Thess is silent in this respect. We would really need, then, to posit another communication in addition to this one, which is of course somewhat problematic. Paul is silent about it. It would seem redundant in the light of Timothy's visit. And there is probably not a lot of time to squeeze this extra communication in during the Athenian mission prior to the composition and dispatch of 1 Thess.

were taught, whether through verbal teaching or through a letter from us" (Ἄρα οὖν, ἀδελφοί, στήκετε καὶ κρατεῖτε τὰς παραδόσεις ἃς ἐδιδάχθητε εἴτε διὰ λόγου εἴτε δι᾽ ἐπιστολῆς ἡμῶν). The evidence of this verse is not decisive, as some have argued unpersuasively.[91] It cannot be said with certainty that this verse denotes a letter previous to 2 Thessalonians, because the aorist — although an unusual passive — might simply be an epistolary aorist and so denote the present letter, that is, 2 Thessalonians itself.[92] However, this verse is certainly compatible with a reference to a preceding letter, and might, given this inclusive reference, subtly begin to anticipate the turn in the letter body to the distinctive paranetic concern of 2 Thessalonians 3:6-13 with laziness, drafting in the reinforcement of the relevant parts of 1 Thessalonians. As we have seen — granting the surrounding reconstruction — 2 Thessalonians even quotes a useful phrase from that letter, in 3:8 (ἐν κόπῳ καὶ μόχθῳ νυκτὸς καὶ ἡμέρας ἐργαζόμενοι πρὸς τὸ μὴ ἐπιβαρῆσαί τινα ὑμῶν). Hence, just as 1 Thessalonians belongs best first, on grounds of a pregnant silence, 2 Thessalonians belongs best second, on grounds of its plausible possible reference to a previous letter, along with its many echoes of that letter, including one especially strategic quotation.[93]

For these reasons, I incline toward the judgment that 1 Thessalonians preceded 2 Thessalonians. But can we say more than this, in particular, about the probable lapse in time that took place between the composition of 1 Thessalonians and 2 Thessalonians? Certainly, not confidently. However, some considerations are indicative.

A judgment concerning this further question turns initially on whether Paul had visited the Thessalonians after the dispatch of 1 Thessalonians but before the composition of 2 Thessalonians, as might be suggested by 1 Thessalonians 2:17-18 and the poignant prayerful promise of 1 Thessalonians 3:10 and 11 ([10] . . . νυκτὸς καὶ ἡμέρας ὑπερεκπερισσοῦ δεόμενοι εἰς τὸ ἰδεῖν ὑμῶν τὸ πρόσωπον καὶ καταρτίσαι τὰ ὑστερήματα τῆς πίστεως ὑμῶν; [11] Αὐτὸς δὲ ὁ θεὸς καὶ πατὴρ ἡμῶν καὶ ὁ κύριος ἡμῶν Ἰησοῦς κατευθύναι τὴν ὁδὸν ἡμῶν πρὸς ὑμᾶς· κ.τ.λ.). Admittedly, such statements were epistolary stereotypes. Nevertheless, a little more than a stereotypical expression of longing seems to be involved here. There are good reasons pastorally — to put things a little anachronistically — for Paul to have wanted to visit the Thessalonian

91. See Wanamaker (1990, 40-41).

92. So, correctly on this point, Wanamaker (1990, 41).

93. It might be objected that 1 Thess could refer to a previous letter's incorrect reception with 5:27, and that is a possibility. But this remains a fundamentally ambiguous datum, and it does not directly overthrow the two contentions just noted.

community in order to strengthen them, as he says he does. They were suffer-ing and, in certain respects, confused and unethical, although they remained affectionate and loyal. Yet Paul did not visit at the time of 1 Thessalonians' composition, presumably because, at least to a certain extent, he could not, and so 1 Thessalonians took his place. One suspects, nevertheless, that he would have visited as soon as circumstances, and the broader needs of his missionary work, permitted. And these expectations flowing from 1 Thessalonians create certain implications for the most appropriate location for 2 Thessalonians. It seems that this promised second visit had not taken place at that letter's time of writing.

A visit to the Thessalonians is mentioned in 2 Thessalonians twice. Sec-ond Thessalonians 2:5 looks back on a stay with the Thessalonians, with Paul revealing (as we have already seen) that his current eschatological teaching concerning the end time is a reiteration of things he taught when he was with them personally (Οὐ μνημονεύετε ὅτι ἔτι ὢν πρὸς ὑμᾶς ταῦτα ἔλεγον ὑμῖν;). But this data does not tell us that this stay was the founding visit. It could conceivably refer to the visit promised in 1 Thessalonians.

Second Thessalonians 3:7-10 speaks of a visit as well, emphasizing at this later stage in the letter the missionaries' labors among the Thessalonians ([7] Αὐτοὶ γὰρ οἴδατε πῶς δεῖ μιμεῖσθαι ἡμᾶς, ὅτι οὐκ ἠτακτήσαμεν ἐν ὑμῖν [8] οὐδὲ δωρεὰν ἄρτον ἐφάγομεν παρά τινος, ἀλλ᾽ ἐν κόπῳ καὶ μόχθῳ νυκτὸς καὶ ἡμέρας ἐργαζόμενοι πρὸς τὸ μὴ ἐπιβαρῆσαί τινα ὑμῶν). There is no hint that this was a different visit from the stay referenced earlier by 2:5. But this second reference famously echoes language from 1 Thessalonians (specifically, 2:9: Μνημονεύετε γάρ, ἀδελφοί, τὸν κόπον ἡμῶν καὶ τὸν μόχθον· νυκτὸς καὶ ἡμέρας ἐργαζόμενοι πρὸς τὸ μὴ ἐπιβαρῆσαί τινα ὑμῶν ἐκηρύξαμεν εἰς ὑμᾶς τὸ εὐαγγέλιον τοῦ θεοῦ). And in 1 Thessalonians Paul is clearly referencing the founding visit with this material.

It has already been emphasized that 2 Thessalonians is dependent on 1 Thessalonians to a degree, and never more so than here. But in this particular instance, it is now comprehensible as part of a rhetorical strategy in 2 Thessalo-nians designed to encourage the lazy Thessalonians to work and to contribute to the community materially by recalling the missionaries' exemplification of hard labor. First Thessalonians uses the same data to emphasize the apostles' dedication and affection. The quotation in 2 Thessalonians is still an appeal to tradition and exemplification, but it is developed rather differently in con-tingent terms (see 2 Thess 2:15; 3:4, 6-12). The hard work of the missionaries is an example simply of work for the lazy Thessalonians to follow. In the light of these connections, it is hard to avoid the conclusion that the recollections of

Paul's presence with the Thessalonians made at two points in 2 Thessalonians — and woven into the rhetorical warp and woof of the letter — reference the founding visit, as they do overtly in 1 Thessalonians. To use a quotation of earlier material referencing the original founding visit to speak of a second visit in an exemplary manner later in 2 Thessalonians would be decidedly awkward. So we may conclude with some confidence that the visit promised in 1 Thessalonians had not yet taken place when 2 Thessalonians was written. Second Thessalonians reaches back for many of its rhetorical resources to the same stay that 1 Thessalonians recalls — the original mission. And this generates certain implications for the location of 2 Thessalonians.

It seems likely, given this conclusion, that 2 Thessalonians was written soon after 1 Thessalonians. Only a short time interval explains plausibly the silence in 2 Thessalonians concerning the promised visit, which is badly needed and has yet to take place, and the brusque breach of other key features of ancient relationality and epistolary etiquette. In this location, effectively right after 1 Thessalonians, there is no need to reiterate the statements of longing or requests for prayer made in 1 Thessalonians — they still stand — or to explain that circumstances preventing this visit have not changed. Indeed, with a short lapse of time, the probability that the same obstructive circumstances are still in place is high. Thus, the silence of 2 Thessalonians concerning the promised and expected second visit of Paul to Thessalonica is explicable if 2 Thessalonians follows quite hard on the heels of 1 Thessalonians. Conversely, as time lengthens between the composition of the two letters, the silence of 2 Thessalonians concerning this visit becomes increasingly difficult to explain. If some time has elapsed before the composition of 2 Thessalonians, then we would expect Paul at least to mention the frustrating fact that the same forces still obstruct his short journey to the north as obstructed it in 1 Thessalonians. Moreover, as time passes, we would expect those circumstances to fade. But if they have, then there is no explanation in 2 Thessalonians of his ongoing failure to visit. Nor are there any expressions of longing in 2 Thessalonians, which are expected epistolary expressions even in the absence of genuine deep affection. Their absence in a letter written after some time would have been positively insulting, and would give the lie to the elaborate rhetoric of affection that Paul crafted in 1 Thessalonians.

But these difficulties — some of which plausibly underlie scholarly suspicions of pseudepigraphy[94] — are ameliorated if 2 Thessalonians was written

---

94. Bercovitz (May 25, 2013) lists the appearance of this argument in Holtzmann, Wrede, von Dobschütz, and Lindemann.

soon after 1 Thessalonians, and there is nothing to prevent this. First Thessalonians was sent to Thessalonica by way of an unnamed sender — possibly
simply a hired figure. Second Thessalonians then responded to an anonymous
and somewhat inchoate oral report received soon after this (2:2; 3:11). It is a
less overtly affectionate letter than 1 Thessalonians, although the claim that it
lacks all affection is exaggerated. But Paul might well have been a little frustrated at this juncture to hear that the community had become unsettled, in
part by failing to recall and apply an obvious piece of original eschatological
instruction, and that some members had stopped working altogether — and
this apparently in the immediate aftermath of the carefully crafted teaching in
1 Thessalonians about affection and other key aspects of ethics and eschatology. The rougher and somewhat brusquer 2 Thessalonians fell into this space,
and this all makes good sense. However, any later location for the letter leads
to various unanswered questions. We can conclude, then, that 2 Thessalonians
is best located quite soon after 1 Thessalonians, and hence at Athens as well.[95]
Our resulting sequence is

$$\text{FVP — FVT — FVA — Timothy VT}^{96}\text{ —}$$
$$\textbf{1 Thess — 2 Thess}$$
$$\dots \text{FVC}^{97} \dots$$

95. I have not emphasized here a datum that used to excite me, namely, Paul's statement
in 2 Thess 1:4 that he has boasted about the Thessalonians' endurance "in the assemblies of
God" (ὥστε αὐτοὺς ἡμᾶς ἐν ὑμῖν ἐγκαυχᾶσθαι ἐν ταῖς ἐκκλησίαις τοῦ θεοῦ ὑπὲρ τῆς ὑπομονῆς
ὑμῶν καὶ πίστεως ἐν πᾶσιν τοῖς διωγμοῖς ὑμῶν καὶ ταῖς θλίψεσιν αἷς ἀνέχεσθε). His plural
grammar almost certainly implies that Paul has established at least one community in addition
to his current location by the time he writes 2 Thess. On bald epistolary grounds, we might
therefore infer that he cannot be at Athens when writing 2 Thess, the first community we know
of explicitly after the mission in Thessalonica, but is most likely in Corinth, or perhaps even
beyond that community. However, the risk we run if we emphasize this datum is the later discovery that a mission intervened between Thessalonica and Athens (as Acts of course suggests).
If this seems plausible (and Rom 16:21 in conjunction with Acts 20:4 arguably confirms it), then
we would not only have to reintroduce a possible Athenian provenance but *then* consider in
detail whether 1 Thess or 2 Thess came first in Athens (and so on). Thus, it just seems best on
practical grounds to be open to the possibility that a mission might have taken place between
the Thessalonian and Athenian missions, with the silence on this in Paul's Thessalonian letters not necessarily indicating inactivity (see Gal 1:21!), and to have the detailed comparative
discussion of the epistolary data here.
       96. A visit by Timothy from Athens to Thessalonica and back, bringing a "text" from
the Thessalonians, including some questions.
       97. We are still not yet absolutely sure whether the founding visit to Corinth took place
immediately after the founding visit to Athens, although we have no good reasons for thinking

First Thessalonians is at present our earliest extant letter from Paul, as many scholars have supposed, although it was followed fairly quickly by 2 Thessalonians, with various hints in the data tentatively suggesting the composition of both shortly after 40 CE, by which time the Thessalonian community itself had been founded. And with these judgments made, we need to return to consider in this chapter's final subsection whether 2 Thessalonians and/or, to a lesser extent, 1 Thessalonians belong in the sequence of authentic Pauline letters at all.

2.5 Contentions in Favor of Pseudepigraphy

I have set the bar high for any judgment of pseudepigraphy but have done so entirely deliberately. If we do not reject invalid argumentation at this stage, during our construction of the preliminary frame, then all of our historical results risk being vitiated. It is better to make our lives difficult when considering the authenticity of letters individually than to embrace corrupted conclusions concerning all of them, both authentic and inauthentic. To this end, uncontrolled circular arguments from style, letter form, and substance have been excluded, as have indecisive arguments from dependence.[98] So we need now to ask what arguments are left. We do still want to exclude pseudepigraphic texts from our developing historical reconstruction of Paul if we can.

Traditional approaches to the evaluation of authenticity in general revolve around two principal and distinguishable processes: a close examination of the artifact in question by some expert in related historical artifacts; and a careful investigation of the artifact's historical provenance or pedigree. Both must tally — at the least — for the artifact to be pronounced authentic.

So, for example, in December 1983, an art dealer, Gianfranco Becchina, approached the J. Paul Getty Museum in California with a marble statue *kouros*

---

otherwise. We do have strong evidence that these two missions took place during the same broad mission by Paul, Silvanus, and Timothy.

98. If the roles of secretaries and/or co-authors in some of the letters are emphasized, as urged by Richards (1991; 2004, 32-46, 59-93) and Murphy-O'Connor (1995, esp. 6-37), then parsing authorial differences in relation to style is even more problematic. It is clear that Paul used scribes at times, most obviously in Rom 16:22, but see also the emphatic shifts to his handwriting denoted in 1 Cor 16:21; Gal 6:11; Col 4:18; 2 Thess 3:17; and Phlm 19. And he is the sole author only of Rom, Eph, 1 and 2 Tim, and Tit, and probably also of Gal (because it is unlikely that "all the *adelphoi*" at Galatia co-wrote that letter). All the other letters possess other explicit authors—1 and 2 Cor, Phil, Col, 1 and 2 Thess, and Phlm.

ostensibly dating from the sixth century BCE.[99] The price of the beautifully preserved specimen was $10 million. The Getty called in its experts. Some analyzed the statue itself. It was compared with other extant *kouroi* and determined to be in the style of the Anavyssos *kouros* in the National Archaeological Museum of Athens. Its composition and surface were analyzed, the initial conclusions being that it was carved from ancient dolomite marble from a quarry at Cape Vathy on the island of Thasos, and that the surface was calcified consistent with centuries of exposure. Other experts analyzed the statue's pedigree. It was accompanied by numerous letters, which seemed to document a reputable provenance. It had been in the private collection of a Swiss physician, Lauffenberger, who had acquired it from a famous Greek art dealer in the 1930s, a certain Roussos. The Getty's legal department was persuaded by this provenance, as was the museum by the broader case. It purchased the statue amidst much fanfare.

Unfortunately for the Getty, the case soon fell apart. Further experts detected anomalies in the style of the *kouros*. It was actually a pastiche of all the known styles, and possessed unaccountably modern feet and a unique feature — fingernails. And the surface of the *kouros* was too pristine. Experienced archaeologists doubted immediately upon seeing it that it had ever been buried. Indeed, a geologist eventually concluded that the statue's surface could have been "aged" by the application of potato mold in a matter of weeks. (That the marble was from the ancient quarry was true.) Moreover, the letters were investigated further and found to be fakes as well. One letter dated 1952 bore a postal code that did not exist until some twenty years later. Another referenced a bank account in 1955 that was not opened until 1963.

This famous story is an object lesson in the authentication of items of doubtful provenance and the detection of fakes. I would suggest that when interpreters have doubts about letters bearing the name of the apostle Paul, the same two broad processes should be applied.

(1) Examination of the Item

It is possible to scrutinize the item in question — in our earlier example, the putative *kouros*, but in this study, putative letters by the apostle Paul — in a number of different ways. Three in particular are important.

---

99. An entertaining version of this story can be found in Gladwell (2005, 3-17: "The Statue That Didn't Look Right").

We are rapidly developing a sensitivity to the plausibility of an account that a Pauline letter gives of itself — its immediate implied exigence. Authentic letters to date seem to supply a fundamentally believable account themselves of the reasons why they were written. (Several of the letters already treated are of course unquestioned in this regard, notably, Rom, 1 Cor, 2 Cor, Gal, Phil, and, to a certain extent, 1 Thess. The difficulties thus far in this regard have been associated with 2 Thess.) Their accounts of the underlying issues, which are usually closely related to various difficulties in a congregation that Paul had a part in founding, are plausible, as is the epistolary response itself, along with any other responses taking place in their immediate setting (i.e., visits and similar communications). False letters would presumably lack any grounding in detailed original circumstances and so be vulnerable to careful probing on this front. We must continue to pay due attention to the historical caveats necessitated by interpretative distance and poverty of information, thereby once again tilting analysis in favor of authenticity. But much can still be done in this regard.

As in the case of the fake *kouros,* Pauline letters should be judged pseudepigraphic when they evidence mistakes (e.g., the *kouros* unaccountably possessing fingernails), although errors can fall into different subcategories.

We are carefully developing here an account of Paul's missionary activity, and although it is patchy (and will remain so), parts are quite detailed. It is as if we are assembling a very complex jigsaw puzzle. Admittedly, not all of it will ever be completed. But we can still ask whether the remaining pieces fit smoothly into those that have already been placed or whether they have to fit somewhere else entirely. Or, still more significantly, we can examine whether pieces purported to sit contiguous with a piece already placed fit accurately the edge they are being laid against. In this sense, without begging the question, we can ask whether a letter fits into the existing details of our developing biographical frame, fits somewhere else, or does not really fit at all. In this last case, we are dealing with a biographical mistake and hence almost certainly with a pseudepigraphon. So we must scrutinize the contested letters carefully for mistakes vis-à-vis the developing frame, which are distinguishable from their internal accounts of provenance although clearly not separable from them. But mistakes in these types of compositions can occur in another way.

Most significant for the judgment of pseudepigraphy is the presence of anachronisms, that is, of small fragmentary allusions to events much later in church history that we can confidently discount from the time of Paul. The detection of an incontrovertible anachronism is the closest thing we have to an instantly decisive case for pseudepigraphy, although its credibility rests on the definitive exclusion of the evidence in question from the time of Paul. The presence of an anachronism is nothing less than a smoking gun at the scene of the crime for any scholars suspecting a particular letter of being faked.

In sum, we must examine carefully the item in question in broadly comparative and historical terms, here scrutinizing it for mistakes, whether in terms of immediate implied exigence, broader fit with the developing biographical frame, or small but incontrovertible anachronisms, and especially any references to a time when Paul was long dead.

(2) Investigation of the Provenance

The second line of investigation concerns an item's provenance — in the case of the *kouros* offered to the Getty, the scrutiny of its bundle of letters of supposed authentication. In the case of the Pauline letters, unfortunately, we have lost the decisive marks of authentic transmission that 2 Thessalonians emphasizes so clearly — a concluding grace wish in Paul's own hand, which was sometimes accompanied by longer sections of material in the same distinctive handwriting. As soon as Paul's originals were copied, this marker was erased. And mere claims that the marker is present, in and of themselves, are untrustworthy.[100] We can still investigate various other aspects of these letters' transmission, although the distance of the originals from our present location limits this sort of investigation sharply. Three distinguishable types of investigation again seem useful.

It will be helpful to note whether any ancient figures relatively close to the time of Paul questioned the authenticity of any letters. Some did. But this observation is rather more powerful if it can be combined with a determination of which letters were included in the original Pauline collection. If this can be ascertained, the case against any letters not so included — and some seem not to have been — is strengthened. Mere inclusion will not automatically entail authenticity, nor exclusion pseudepigraphy. But it will count for something. And knowing this will be especially helpful if its implications correlate with our judgments reached on internal grounds.

In addition, we should utilize a third major methodological approach to the detection of pseudepigraphy, namely, nontraditional authorship ascription, or stylometrics, although I would suggest again that this evidence functions best as a complementary set of considerations and not as a primary argument.

---

100. Ehrman (2013) makes this point well.

Moreover, the negative judgments of stylometrics — that is, when ostensibly offensive differences in terms of some parameter are not detected statistically — are more reliable than its positive assertions, although the latter might still make a useful contribution.

With these clarifications in place concerning the detection of pseudepigraphy, we can turn back to 1 and 2 Thessalonians and reach some preliminary judgments about their status fairly quickly, recalling that contentions in nontraditional terms, that is, from stylometrics, have already had their contributions assessed.

The preceding analysis in this chapter has given us no grounds to suspect the basic plausibility of the contingencies enumerated in each letter; indeed, this was one reason for probing those so carefully. Both made sense in immediate historical terms. First Thessalonians was entirely comprehensible as a response to good news from Timothy, who had been sent to Thessalonica to check up on the community that was under considerable pressure. The letter also responded to plausible inquiries from the Thessalonians and to information about them — and it is not much doubted in any case. Second Thessalonians too was plausibly comprehensible as a response to disturbing news about the community. They had been upset by the introduction of false information about the Lord Jesus' *parousia,* and some of the members were being lazy and exploitative of the community's common meal. That some hostile external party might have tried to undermine the community through this sort of deception is entirely believable, given the narrative of suffering for the community that is already attested. We do not know whether this was attempted by a pseudepigraphon (2 Thess 2:2). This was a possibility in general cultural terms, but a false oral report seems equally likely, not to mention a false "spirit," whether a false prophecy (so that the Thessalonians might have partly just upset themselves) or a false spiritual "channeling" of Paul. And that some ancient Thessalonians proved to be lazy is hardly a problem! In short, then, Paul's desire to write and what he actually wrote are plausibly explained in both cases by the information provided. So we have no reason to doubt the authenticity of 1 Thessalonians or 2 Thessalonians at this preliminary stage of our broader reconstruction on grounds of implausible immediate implied exigence.

Similarly, both letters evidence no obvious mistakes. Rather, both fit neatly into our broader developing biographical frame. We already know that a missionary party composed of Paul, Silvanus, and Timothy arrived in Corinth, and that the Corinthian mission was plausibly preceded by missions to Philippi and Thessalonica (in that order). The existence of a mission in the intervening city of Athens is plausible, given a straightforward geographical trajectory for the broader mission. The named missionary party is exactly right. The one broader chronological allusion supplied by the letters, principally by 2 Thessalonians, also falls into the broader window that has already been established. Paul must have founded the churches in question between 37 or 38 and 50 CE, and the Gaian crisis unfolded principally through 40. Indeed, the shocking nature and earliness of this eschatological scenario speak in favor of authenticity. It is hard to understand how this adjustment could have entered the tradition later, that is, after January 41 CE, when it was no longer so relevant or even meaningful.

It has been objected in this relation that 1 Thessalonians 2:16b is an anachronistic reference to the destruction of Jerusalem (ἔφθασεν δὲ ἐπ᾽ αὐτοὺς ἡ ὀργὴ εἰς τέλος) — although the particular concern usually functions, somewhat curiously, as an argument for interpolation into 1 Thessalonians and not its pseudonymity. But while this might be a plausible reference to the destruction of the first Jewish revolt, it could also be a reference to one of many instances of gubernatorial brutality in Judea at the time, perhaps associated with the revolt of Theudas, or to the famine that is chronicled elsewhere as taking place during this period. (Its precise date is difficult to determine.) Even more decisively, however, we can see now that this statement plausibly referred to the Gaian crisis and/or its immediate aftermath. This would have looked very much like the wrath of God falling on Judea, both finally and fully.

In short, the letters fit convincingly into our developing biographical frame, and they evidence no obvious mistakes or anachronism. Rather, the one date they allude to is embarrassingly early, and it even allows something of an interpretative crux in its companion letter to be plausibly explained.[101]

The letters also evidence no obvious problems of transmission. But the

---

101. The evocation of Judean events and discourses by both letters is also intriguing; this might corroborate their earliness and consequent closeness to the Judean mission, so that they might offer priceless insight into teaching by the early church about Jesus in Judea in the 30s.

Note also that if 1 Thess 2:16b is most plausibly explained by the Gaian crisis, then this suggests that the two letters were composed during that crisis in 40 or early 41 CE. Paul could hardly reference this situation as the wrath of God falling on Judea "finally" and/or "fully" after the plan had collapsed. But this makes perfect sense while it was unfolding, primarily during 40. And although an identification of 2:16b with this crisis is not certain, this does seem to be probable; certainly it is the best explanation, and especially when the concerns of 2 Thess are taken into account, along with its proximity to 1 Thess. These (belated) realizations make the tentative location of 1 and 2 Thess in 40 to early 41 CE that much more likely.

argument from the probable shape of the earliest Pauline letter collection is best attempted after several more internal judgments have been made. Suffice it to say here that later discussion will only confirm the probable authenticity of both 1 Thessalonians and 2 Thessalonians on those grounds. And stylometric analysis, whether pursued with caution or with vigor, provides nothing that would trouble these judgments decisively.

We conclude, then, that there are no good grounds at this point for disqualifying either 1 Thessalonians or 2 Thessalonians from authenticity. And so the parts of the frame to which they contribute will remain in place for now. It needs to be emphasized that inclusion can later be revised in favor of exclusion; our decisions here are provisional. But the burden of proof is established by these framing decisions.

And we have now completed a "seven-letter canon," although it differs from the usual version by including 2 Thessalonians and not including Philemon, at least yet. The inclusion of 1 Thessalonians will of course not surprise many scholars. But the firmness of our judgment concerning 2 Thessalonians might. I would suggest, however, that this conclusion can be held with considerable confidence. I know of no good arguments against the authenticity of this letter and several strong considerations in favor of it. To the best of our knowledge, Paul wrote 2 Thessalonians.

In the next phase of our investigation, we will turn to the intriguing short letter by Paul addressed principally to Philemon, along with two other letters that, if authentic, cluster around this text — Colossians and Ephesians. This discussion will be a critical test of both our programmatic methodology and our steadily developing biographical frame.

CHAPTER FIVE

Locating Philemon, Colossians, and "Ephesians"

1. Locating Philemon

This chapter's deliberations begin with a consideration of Paul's "short, attractive, graceful and friendly" letter to Philemon.[1] Philemon is usually included without demurral in the group of authentic Pauline letters, but determining its exigence opens up a useful area of further interpretative possibility within our developing frame. So its data merits careful scrutiny.

The letter describes an intriguing scenario as its immediate exigence. Like 2 Thessalonians 1:4, Philemon 2 lacks a particular geographical association for its reference to an "assembly," but its addressees are nevertheless quite specific. Although usually referred to as "Philemon," the letter was addressed to a community. Paul was sending an unhappy slave, Onesimus, or (from the Latin) "Useful," back to his master, Philemon. We know this because after the prescript, the letter's address shifts consistently into a first-person masculine mode. However, the letter begins with a communal focus. Philemon was apparently married to Apphia (she is less probably his sister), and they belonged to an assembly that met in the house of a veteran, Archippus.[2] So three figures are named initially, along with a house

1. Baur (2003 [1845], 2:80).
2. Somewhat strangely, this feature of the data is much overlooked. The leadership of the house church is usually attributed to Philemon. However, the syntax of v. 1 makes the most sense if the church meets in Archippus's house, and his presence in the prescript is otherwise inexplicable. (Col, if authentic, supports this identification as well; see 4:17.) Apphia is explicable as Philemon's wife or, less likely, his sister. The only reasonably extensive analysis of Archippus is by John Knox (1959). He theorizes that Archippus was Onesimus's owner as well as the host of the church addressed by the letter known as Philemon. But this reading leaves the first

church. Paul was himself in prison at the time of writing — a state he makes much of (1, 9, 13, 23) — and Epaphras is said to be a "fellow prisoner" (ὁ συναιχμάλωτός μου; 23). Paul is also accompanied by a substantial group of "fellow workers" — Mark, Aristarchus, Demas, and Luke, at the least, along with his co-sender, Timothy.

Scholars have pondered the exact situation that underlay Onesimus's meeting with Paul. I still find Lampe's (1985a) suggestion persuasive — that Onesimus was not a runaway *(fugitivus)* but rather a "truant" slave *(erro),* appealing to a "friend of the master" *(amicus domini)* for an intervention into a difficult situation. That a runaway slave would contact anyone associated with his master defies all reason (and that Onesimus would just happen to have been arrested and imprisoned in the same cell as Paul, so to speak, seems highly improbable, not to mention that the letter itself is silent concerning an utterly desperate legal situation). But a deliberate if unofficial appeal by an unhappy slave to an authority figure in relation to his master, a slave therefore operating at the time effectively AWOL as an *erro,* explains the situation in the prison plausibly.[3]

As we turn from the letter's immediate implied exigence to consider its location in relation to our frame, it is helpful to note that Paul's complex strategy on Onesimus's behalf vis-à-vis Philemon extends beyond the mere dispatch of a helpful letter, to the somewhat intimidating promise of a visit — apparent in his request for the preparation of a guest room (ξενία). And this data, combined with the immediate exigence of a slave operating as an *erro,* suggests that Paul was imprisoned relatively close by Philemon's location and hence most probably in the same region or province, and even the same area.

Paul's pointed request for the preparation of a guest room would seem to suggest a visit rather soon, perhaps within days. And if Onesimus had been away on his unauthorized visit for much more than a few days, he would probably have been declared a runaway or *fugitivus,* a fearful status that he evidently wished to avoid by contacting Paul. So the letter implies at the least that Paul's imprisonment was not very far from Philemon's community, that is, not too

---

two names in the prescript opaque and hence is as unsatisfactory in immediate terms as the traditional reading that it seeks to supplant.

3. Bellen (1971, 18, 78) arguably made this suggestion earlier. Its subsequent qualification does not affect our case here. Having said this, I have not found its attempted refutation plausible: see Harrill (1999); Wengst (2006, 31-32). For its subsequent — learned — endorsement, see Arzt-Grabner (2003; 2010). Useful general treatments of slavery during the Roman era may be found in Bradley (1987 [1984]; 1994); more controversial is Patterson (1982). An important work treating slavery in relation to the NT is Glancy (2006 [2002]).

many days' walk in any direction. (This reasoning seems to exclude the Acts-based locations of Caesarea and Rome,[4] by way of anticipation.)[5] Unfortunately, the letter does not go on to tell us explicitly where either Paul's prison or the community in question lay. However, some hints in the data are suggestive.

Philemon's wife, Apphia, possesses a name frequently found in the province of Asia and attested specifically at Colossae.[6] And later tradition associated the letter with Colossae, which was located on the border between Lydia and Phrygia, since this was (at the least) the destination of a letter bearing Paul's name that is strongly associated with his letter to Philemon. So there are hints that the community lay in Asia. And both hints corroborate one another, essentially independently.

Moreover, the letter presupposes an effective founding visit from some member of the Pauline mission. But Paul himself sends no greetings from the local "brothers" at his location, so he does not seem himself to be imprisoned at the site of a successful mission; no local Christian seems to be named besides itinerant members of his circle of coworkers. And this oddly asymmetrical scenario along with the figures specifically named do not obviously resonate with any of the communities that we already know about from the other au-

4. For some useful points of comparison, ORBIS (May 24, 2013) suggests that a fast journey between Ephesus and Laodicea (ad Lycum) would have taken just under 5 days (4.8) at roughly any time of year (winter barring travel rather than slowing it in these terms), and from (Asian) Apamea or Pisidia to Laodicea, just under 3 (2.9).

5. It might be suggested in support of a more "traditional" location at Caesarea or Rome that Paul is writing as an "old man" (πρεσβύτης; 9). This is the only ostensible reference to Paul's age that we have from his writings and so is worth considering carefully. But (1) it is indecisive for dating purposes, since we do not know from the letters how old Paul was when he began his ministry, and he could have been an "old man" in 50 CE, albeit an active one (Acts data *might* stand against this but should not be appealed to yet; see νεανίας, "youth" in 7:58); (2) it is not necessarily a reference to old age in any case, referring in some instances, like πρεσβευτής, to ambassadorial status and functions (Polyaenus 8.9.1; BDAG) and in others, as a technical term, to status in a group so designated (i.e., one of "the elders" is not necessarily old); and (3) this last reading is possible in place of πρεσβύτης in v. 9 (Bentley's conjectural emendation; see BDAG). Ambassadorial references occur elsewhere in Paul (see esp. 2 Cor 5:20; see also Eph 6:20), whereas πρεσβύτης is unattested elsewhere. Scribal confusion between the two signifiers would have been understandable, and the diplomatic reading makes excellent sense in the immediate context. That this important ambassadorial figure, who is enduring such humiliation, nevertheless implores Philemon on Onesimus's behalf is a powerful rhetorical appeal in terms of both *ethos* and *pathos*. (This is not to discount the appeal of an imprisoned old man petitioning Philemon.)

6. BDAG citing *CIG* 3:1168, 4380k, 3; this is helpfully discussed by Barth and Blanke (2000, 254).

thentic letters considered thus far, that is, with Paul's communities in Galatia, Macedonia, and Achaia, in relation to which we have already treated Romans, 1 and 2 Corinthians, Galatians, Philippians, and 1 and 2 Thessalonians. However, if this seems implausible, we know of successful Pauline communities outside of these regions only in Asia, although even in this region, the letter does not resonate with what we know of Paul's mission in Ephesus (see 1 Cor and, to a lesser extent, 2 Cor), where Prisca and Aquila were present. So we end up, after tracing through these implications — at least in probabilistic terms — with a location prior to the successful Ephesian mission in Asia.

Clearly, this case is far from decisive. Too many figures traveled too far during the Principate for us to place much reliance on the implications of Apphia's name (and Lydia springs immediately to mind, to nod in the direction of Acts once more); the letter to the Colossians might have been concocted; and the conjunction of evidence here might have been coincidental. Moreover, Archippus's house church might have been in Lystra or some similar location, with Paul imprisoned nearby (although later data will speak against this). However, I doubt that all these objections can hold good simultaneously, and any counterproposals are utterly unattested. So we will tentatively locate both Philemon and Archippus's house church in Asia — more specifically, in the regions of Lydia or Phrygia (although the latter might take us into the western reaches of the province of Galatia) — but will refrain for now from building too much on this judgment.[7]

If Philemon was written in Asia (or western Galatia) prior to the Ephesian mission, then it would predate 1 Corinthians, which we have already determined in chapter 2 was sent from Ephesus to Corinth in the spring of 51 CE. Moreover, in the spring of 51 Paul is in Ephesus looking back on a communication with Corinth (the Previous Letter to Corinth), as well as on other events that had unfolded in relation to that congregation (i.e., Apollos's first visit to Corinth). He has been evangelizing Ephesus, and apparently a great but challenging opportunity has just arisen for him there (see 1 Cor 16:9: θύρα γάρ μοι ἀνέῳγεν μεγάλη καὶ ἐνεργής, καὶ ἀντικείμενοι πολλοί). So we may extend his ministry and presence in Ephesus back through at least part of the previous winter. And we can chart Paul's activities through the calendar year beginning in 51 with considerable precision. The letter to the Roman Chris-

---

7. This takes our developing frame close to Riddle's (1940) position, as well as, to a degree, to Duncan's (1929), and to some of Knox's (1990) comments made late in life. But most scholars sensitive to the importance of Paul's Asian mission for the letters are preoccupied with his activities in Ephesus, presumably being influenced here — somewhat inconsistently — by the Acts narrative. And I see no decisive epistolary evidence for this preoccupation, at least yet.

tians closes this period, leaving him in the spring of 52 contemplating journeys out of the entire area — to Jerusalem, to Rome, and then on to Spain. So it is unlikely that the events eliciting Philemon unfolded after 52. However, we have a considerable chronological window between the Macedonian and Achaian missions undertaken as early as 40-41 CE and the beginning of Paul's Ephesian ministry late in 50, within which this letter could fall.

We know, moreover, that Paul traveled to Syrian Antioch and to Jerusalem just before the composition of 1 Corinthians, and presumably before the Previous Letter, hence toward the end of this interval (i.e., somewhere from late 49 through mid-50 CE, 13.x years after his first visit to Jerusalem, in late 36 CE). He seems to have visited the Galatians during his return journey, giving them instructions about the collection (1 Cor 16:1). We have not yet determined decisively whether these were "ethnic" or "provincial" Galatians, but the northern route between Syrian Antioch and Ephesus on the journey back from Antioch and Jerusalem could have taken Paul past the Lycus valley and so through Lydia and western Phrygia, and the southern route almost certainly would have.[8] Hence, this seems a plausible if tentative location for Philemon and its particular exigence temporally. If Paul was imprisoned during his return journey to the Aegean from Syrian Antioch and Jerusalem, then the data evident in Philemon would be plausibly explained. And this would locate these events in 50 CE, with the incident in Syrian Antioch and Paul's second visit to Jerusalem (see Gal 2:11-14, 1-10) taking place just before them.[9]

8. ORBIS suggests that even a northern east-west route across "Turkey," passing through Ancyra, could have gone through Pisidian Antioch/Apamea if a southerly route from Dorylaeum to Ephesus was taken, via Pisidian Antioch and the mouth of the Lycus valley, as against a more westerly route through Sardis and Smyrna. A more southerly east-west route across Turkey would almost certainly have gone past the Lycus valley. Having said this, a north Galatian provenance for that letter might open up the possibility of an imprisonment in the Hermus River valley to the north, somewhere in the vicinity of Sardis — the outlet for the second major (more northern) east-west route through Anatolia (the Lycus valley being on the major southern east-west route). A third alternative might be some location farther west from the Lycus valley, in the valley of the Maeander River, hence closer to Miletus and Ephesus. But later data will confirm the likelihood of a provenance to the east of the Lycus valley location, at which point composition prior to the visits to Antioch and Jerusalem seems highly unlikely as well. (And even if Acts data is introduced, we still cannot suppose with any confidence that Paul took an inland route from Ephesus to either Antioch or Jerusalem; a sea route seems much more probable. ORBIS (March 27, 2013) estimates for a journey to Antioch in October a cautious sea voyage of 12-15 days (12.3-15.1; i.e., traveling only by day and along the coast) but a journey overland, on foot, of around 37.

9. Their specific window extended, according to previous data, from late 49 CE through mid-50. But a cutoff date of early 50 for this window looks likely if our suppositions here about

In sum, the epistolary evidence locates Paul in this general area at this time — in Asia in 50 CE. There seem to be no obvious difficulties with these judgments (at least yet), although some have been made only tentatively, as the evidence allows.

Stylometric data can get little purchase on Philemon, in part because the letter is so short. Meaningful samples usually require around 500 words, and arguably more, and Philemon contains only 335. (As stylometric techniques advance, the relevant word limits are dropping, so this limit may ultimately relax; however, at present it holds.) So we receive neither confirmation nor disconfirmation of the letter's authenticity in stylistic terms. But should we entertain suspicions about the letter's authenticity on more traditional grounds?

In fact, few scholars have doubted Philemon's authenticity, probably largely because of its brevity, specificity, and apparent innocuousness. Raymond Brown (1997, 502) puts the case for authenticity here succinctly: "The [question] is why would someone bother to create Phlm, a note with such a narrow goal, and attribute it to Paul." The presumption of innocuousness is not especially accurate, however. Baur managed to wring quite a bit of auspicious content from this letter.[10] Further, a case could perhaps be made that the letter addresses the issue of slavery for a later ecclesial generation — essentially conservatively, from a modern liberal vantage point. But this situation and address are not notably distinguishable from Paul's day. Arguably more decisively, Philemon might have been composed to facilitate the acceptance of a more ambitious pseudepigraphon into a Pauline letter collection, namely, Colossians, with which it is closely intertwined. Having said this, however, it seems equally likely that Colossians, if pseudepigraphic, seized the opportu-

---

Phlm are correct. Paul's letter to Philemon and its associated events need to fall in an imprisonment between the Antioch incident / second visit to Jerusalem and the composition of the Previous Letter to Corinth in the fall of 50, by which time Paul is apparently unfettered and writing from Ephesus. And this looks like too much of a squeeze if Paul is in either Jerusalem or Syrian Antioch in mid-50. But there is no pressing need for this to have been the case, i.e., for the second Jerusalem visit and/or the incident at Antioch to have taken place late in the relevant chronological window. If they fell earlier, then there is plenty of time for all the implied events to have unfolded during the broader interval.

10. Baur (2003 [1845], 2:84) argues eloquently that the letter is a Christian romance that conveys "a genuine Christian idea" expressed most clearly in v. 15 (τάχα γὰρ διὰ τοῦτο ἐχωρίσθη πρὸς ὥραν, ἵνα αἰώνιον αὐτὸν ἀπέχῃς) — "that what one loses in the world, one recovers in Christianity, and that for ever; that the world and Christianity are related to each other as separation and reunion, as time and eternity." It is an ingenious reading, but it fails to account for most of the text — illustrating nicely that with sufficient determination and imagination, a "pseudonymous" reading can be supplied for virtually any text.

nity afforded by the authentic but more innocuous Philemon. Indeed, we can surmise fairly that the presence of Philemon in any Pauline collection was probably bound up with Colossians; it seems unlikely that this short and quite specific letter would have been included without some weightier assistance.[11] But its inclusion as a companion letter to Colossians makes perfect sense (and further evidence will be cited shortly in support of this claim). However, this consideration tells us nothing about the letter's authenticity.

In sum, then, the argument from anachronistic significance is unproved, and the arguments in terms of brevity and specificity still stand. Therefore, the letter's authenticity will be affirmed in what follows. And with this judgment made, we can turn to consider Colossians — a letter whose authenticity is much more widely contested but that provides rather more data for the question's assessment. We should recall in doing so, however, that the investigation of Philemon has created an intriguing interpretative option for the location of Colossians, and perhaps thereby for Ephesians as well — namely, a captivity somewhere in Asia in the year preceding the composition of the "major" letters (i.e., 1 Cor, 2 Cor, Gal, and Rom, along with Phil).

2. Locating Colossians

Locating Colossians in relation to our developing biographical frame is a fascinating but complex task; many of its aspects are hotly debated. As usual, however, at this point in our investigation, we will work from the letter itself outward so to speak. So the key initial features of its immediate implied exigence will be explored before we consider the letter's fit with our developing frame and then the contentions that surround its authenticity in terms of its arguably distinctive style, its use of possible anachronisms, and its ostensible substantive tensions vis-à-vis other letters, especially in terms of eschatology.

2.1 The Immediate Implied Exigence

(1) Paul's Incarceration

Paul was in prison when the letter was composed. This is hardly problematic, or even surprising, given the immediate locations of Philippians and

---

11. I am grateful to Yuriy Golota for drawing this argument to my attention.

Philemon, and the claim of 2 Corinthians 11:23, supported by further references to Jewish and Roman punishments in vv. 24 and 25 (. . . ἐν φυλακαῖς περισσοτέρως. . . . ὑπὸ Ἰουδαίων πεντάκις τεσσεράκοντα παρὰ μίαν ἔλαβον . . . τρὶς ἐραβδίσθην; and if Col proves authentic, this takes the ratio of letters written by Paul during an incarceration to 3/9 or 33 percent, a percentage worth pondering — and Eph and 2 Tim could add to it).[12] As we will see in more detail momentarily, a significant sequence of events seems to have unfolded while Paul was incarcerated. But this too is scarcely difficult to comprehend. Incarceration in Paul's day primarily detained people prior to trial. Its duration depended on the speed of the local judicial process, along with its integrity, and this varied a great deal. People could spend years in confinement waiting for trial if the local organization was poor or corrupt. We cannot yet judge the length of Paul's incarceration during which Colossians was composed; that judgment must await the introduction of the surrounding frame. We can say at this point that, as suggested already by Philemon, Paul does not seem to have been imprisoned in a place that had had a successful local mission, at least yet. He sends no greetings to the letter's recipients from local brothers, only from named coworkers.

(2) A Proxy Mission in Colossae

The letter states that Paul was not personally known to the Colossians (2:1: Θέλω γὰρ ὑμᾶς εἰδέναι ἡλίκον ἀγῶνα ἔχω ὑπὲρ ὑμῶν καὶ τῶν ἐν Λαοδικείᾳ καὶ ὅσοι οὐχ ἑόρακαν τὸ πρόσωπόν μου ἐν σαρκί). Their existence as a congregation is attributed to one of their own, an apparent slave called Epaphras (1:7). Thus, quite a complex sequence of events must be posited prior to the letter's composition, which should now be probed for its details and plausibility. I

---

12. *First Clement* 5:6 suggests that Paul was imprisoned seven times, although this number is clearly quite possibly legendary. For general background on Roman law, provincial administration, and justice, see the essays of Bowman, Frier, Galsterer, and Treggiari in Bowman, Champlin, and Lintott (1996); for earlier background under the republic, the essays of Cloud, Crook, and Richardson are also useful in Crook, Lintott, and Rawson (1994). Millar (1984) provides a typically learned account of imprisonment during this period — an underresearched area. For analyses specifically of Paul in prison, see Rapske (1996 [1994]), which is focused particularly on Acts data); and Wansink (1993/1996). Brent notes the helpful remark of Lucian, *Peregrinus* 12-13 (2007, 50-51), which suggests that Christian leaders could be relatively well supported during imprisonment, although this refers to conditions in the second half of the second century CE.

suggest that the data is explicable, largely — and perhaps only — in terms of the following narrative.

As we just noted, Epaphras was apparently a Colossian and a slave (1:7 speaks of Ἐπαφρᾶ τοῦ ἀγαπητοῦ συνδούλου ἡμῶν, and *sun-* [συν-] compounds are always referentially significant for Paul;[13] in 4:12 he is denoted as "one of you" [ὁ ἐξ ὑμῶν] and, again, as "a slave of Christ" [δοῦλος Χριστοῦ]). Hence, Epaphras had to have traveled first to Paul's location, which was not Colossae, and converted there, presumably having been sent there by his owner.[14]

Excursus

An alternative scenario is the possibility that Epaphras was converted by the mysterious congregation at Laodicea, or perhaps even in Hierapolis, and then converted his household to that form of Christianity sometime before Paul's arrival in the area. He could later have made contact with Paul during a trip to Paul's location, since he was presumably a well-known Christian leader, and have fallen under Paul's influence at that point. But although it is worth considering, I do not view this reconstruction as likely.

First, Colossians depicts a set of problematic practices at Colossae that Paul views as an intrusion; the Colossians are exhorted to stand firm and not move from what they were originally taught — suggesting that the foundation of the congregation was Pauline. But this original gospel came from Epaphras. If the institution of the church was Pauline, by way of Epaphras, then it follows that Epaphras was almost certainly a Pauline convert.

In support of this principal inference, we can also note, second, that Onesimus traveled to Paul for an intervention, thereby indicating that Paul was perceived to be the key local figure of spiritual authority, and suggesting as well that he was the foundational spiritual figure for the congregation. However, he was introduced to and represented at Colossae by Epaphras. And this is most easily explained if Epaphras was Paul's convert. At the least, he would have to have been extensively catechized by the apostle. Third, it seems unlikely that Paul would have affirmed Epaphras's founding role at Colossae so firmly in Colossians if Epaphras had not been considered a trustworthy mediator of Pauline tradition, and this, again, is most easily explained if he was Paul's convert. And fourth, it would have been implausibly coincidental for Epaphras, a slave, to have founded the congregation from some other source and then to have met Paul and introduced the Pauline gospel decisively at some later point.

13. The scholarly discussion of this phenomenon is generally disappointing. A relatively recent bibliography can be found in Thiselton (2000, 59); it is indicatively short. Ellis (1971) is a classic introduction to the data, updated and summarized in 1993.

14. [1:7] καθὼς ἐμάθετε ἀπὸ Ἐπαφρᾶ τοῦ ἀγαπητοῦ συνδούλου ἡμῶν, ὅς ἐστιν πιστὸς ὑπὲρ ὑμῶν διάκονος τοῦ Χριστοῦ, [8] ὁ καὶ δηλώσας ἡμῖν τὴν ὑμῶν ἀγάπην ἐν πνεύματι.

it is well attested through human history that incarceration is a fertile space for reflection and literary work, especially by (literate) activists. This space affords them time like no other to reflect, think, and compose. The result can then be work of a truly definitive nature, provided that the material can be written down in some way and retrieved from the prison. Two famous and more recent examples of such activity are Dietrich Bonhoeffer's letters and reflections written from prison during the last stages of World War II (collected and published posthumously in Bonhoeffer 2010 [1953]) and the "Letter from Birmingham Jail" written by Martin Luther King Jr. in 1963 (see 2004 [1963], 1896-1908). But these well-known instances barely ruffle the surface of the sea that is prison literature. (A particularly interesting example in this relation is the seventeenth-century Anabaptist anthology *The Bloody Theater,* collated originally by Van Braght 1951 [1660].)

The existence of this letter to the Laodiceans immediately alongside Colossians opens up a critical interpretative possibility within our developing frame that we will have to assess carefully in due course, namely, whether the letter we now know as Ephesians should occupy this locus — whether Ephesians equals Laodiceans. If Ephesians does not fit this space or, alternatively, if it fits another space better, then we need simply to note that Paul's letter to the Laodiceans is no longer extant, like the Previous Letter to Corinth and most of the Previous Letter to Philippi, and any inquiries here in relation to Colossians will largely have to stop. But if Ephesians does equal Laodiceans, so to speak, then the implications are potentially significant. Clearly, the whole question will be best considered after Ephesians is introduced into our discussion, in this chapter's third major section. For now it suffices to note that another letter was written by Paul at the same time as the composition of Colossians and Philemon, a letter addressed to the congregation in Laodicea (2:1; 4:13, 15, 16). And this observation rounds out all the key matters of immediate implied exigence.

The situation surrounding the composition and dispatch of Colossians was clearly layered and complex. But at this stage in our discussion, it is more interesting than problematic. Nothing in the letter's immediate implied exigence indicates that it was pseudonymous, so we can now turn to consider its location within our developing frame.

2.2 *Framing Considerations*

We have already used fragments of information derived from the frame when discussing the immediate implied exigence of Colossians, but this letter is so embedded in its local situation, with its complex interwoven narratives and communications, that isolating it entirely is both impossible and undesirable. However, we have yet to engage in detail with Colossians in relation to our broader frame, a task that should begin by exploring the subtle relationship between Colossians and Philemon.

It is perhaps seldom appreciated just how tightly Paul's letters to Colossae and to Philemon fit together. Most obviously, the co-senders, principal actors, and final greeters are all almost identical. (Possible aberrations in the greetings will be addressed momentarily.) Paul and Timothy are writing to figures identified — if the two letters accompany one another — as Colossian. Archippus is the head of the house congregation of which Philemon, Apphia, and now Onesimus are evidently members (Philemon 1–2); and he is addressed directly in Colossians 4:17. Onesimus is identified as a Colossian in Colossians (4:9), and is clearly returning home in Philemon (i.e., at least in some sense). Aristarchus, Mark, Epaphras, Demas, and Luke, at the least, send their greetings in both letters. So the basic elements in the letters match almost perfectly, although this would perhaps not be surprising in a careful pseudepigraphic work. However, even more impressive is the subtle substantive interlacing of the two letters.

Paul's letter to the Colossian congregation as a whole, as we have just seen, is principally concerned with the new Colossian teaching, news of this having apparently been brought to Paul somewhat fortuitously by Onesimus. The shorter letter to Philemon (as well as to Apphia, Archippus, and his house congregation) addresses Onesimus's difficult domestic situation directly. But it is intriguing to note how the longer congregational letter, Colossians, in a secondary rhetorical dynamic, also participates subtly within a broader strategy focused on ameliorating Onesimus's plight.

The letter to Philemon addresses the situation directly with a number of specific pleas. It also promises a visit from Paul himself as soon as circumstances permit. But Colossians reveals that Tychicus might have been part of Paul's plan to manage the conflict. There is no suggestion that he was a Colossian convert, although he seems to have been a slave (see σύνδουλος in 4:7). But he was an outsider, a member of Paul's circle, and presumably literate, and so possibly he would have been able to exert more leverage on various Colossians than one of their own slaves, Epaphras.

More overtly, the letter to Colossians instructs the congregation to "tell" Archippus to complete his "ministry" (4:17: καὶ εἴπατε Ἀρχίππῳ· βλέπε τὴν διακονίαν ἣν παρέλαβες ἐν κυρίῳ, ἵνα αὐτὴν πληροῖς). And this direct address in Colossians 4:17, along with the inclusion of Archippus in the address of

Philemon, has often puzzled interpreters. But this is perfectly comprehensible as part of Paul's broader strategy designed to manage the conflict between Onesimus and his owner, Philemon. Philemon is evidently a member of Archippus's house congregation; Archippus is his minister. So Colossians and Philemon draw Archippus subtly but firmly into the domestic conflict, placing local congregational *and* rhetorical pressure on him to "complete his ministry." Indeed, by 4:17 the letter has carefully constructed an account of ministry in relation to Paul, Epaphras, and (to a lesser extent) Tychicus (see 1:7, 23-25, 28–2:7; 4:7-8, 12-13). Ministers are to be trustworthy, and to exhort, to pray, and even to struggle to present everyone perfect and complete in Christ. So Archippus is drawn remorselessly into a proper ordering of the relationship within his house church between the owner, Philemon, and his slave, Onesimus, and is instructed in how to behave as he carries this out, while the community is simultaneously reminded of his authority and called upon to ensure his faithful action.

Like many NT texts, Colossians provides instructions about community order in terms of the *Haustafeln*. But it is interesting to note that these instructions are disproportionately concerned in Colossians with the relationship between owners and slaves. The four key family relationships — wives, husbands, children, and parents — receive one brief verse of instruction each. But slaves and masters are instructed for five rather longer verses, which is almost twice as much exhortation as the rest of the *Haustafeln* combined. By way of comparison, Ephesians provides twenty-one verses of admittedly distinctively expanded exhortation, but only five are directed to owners and slaves. The disproportion is striking, but it is fully comprehensible if Colossians has one eye on the conflict between Philemon and Onesimus. The baptismal instructions in Colossians are then equally suggestive.

Colossians 3:9-11 famously echoes 1 Corinthians 12:13 and Galatians 3:26-28 (although, according to our developing frame, these last texts would not have been composed when Colossians was written). However, the binary couplets transcended in this instance are "pagan [lit. Greek] and Jew, circumcised and uncircumcised, barbarian, Scythian, slave, free."[26] And these have consis-

---

26. [Col 3:9] μὴ ψεύδεσθε εἰς ἀλλήλους, ἀπεκδυσάμενοι τὸν παλαιὸν ἄνθρωπον σὺν ταῖς πράξεσιν αὐτοῦ [10] καὶ ἐνδυσάμενοι τὸν νέον τὸν ἀνακαινούμενον εἰς ἐπίγνωσιν κατ᾽ εἰκόνα τοῦ κτίσαντος αὐτόν, [11] ὅπου οὐκ ἔνι Ἕλλην καὶ Ἰουδαῖος, περιτομὴ καὶ ἀκροβυστία, βάρβαρος, Σκύθης, δοῦλος, ἐλεύθερος, ἀλλὰ τὰ πάντα καὶ ἐν πᾶσιν Χριστός κ.τ.λ.; see 1 Cor 12:13: καὶ γὰρ ἐν ἑνὶ πνεύματι ἡμεῖς πάντες εἰς ἓν σῶμα ἐβαπτίσθημεν, εἴτε Ἰουδαῖοι εἴτε Ἕλληνες εἴτε δοῦλοι εἴτε ἐλεύθεροι, καὶ πάντες ἓν πνεῦμα ἐποτίσθημεν; Gal 3:27: ὅσοι γὰρ εἰς Χριστὸν ἐβαπτίσθητε, Χριστὸν ἐνεδύσασθε [28] οὐκ ἔνι Ἰουδαῖος οὐδὲ Ἕλλην, οὐκ ἔνι

tently puzzled interpreters. Unlike Galatians 3:28 (but like 1 Cor 12:13), Colossians 3:11 contains no mention of the transcendence of "male and female." And Colossians adds an otherwise unattested couplet, "barbarian, Scythian," which is decidedly odd. Its members are opaque, especially the category "Scythian," which refers literally to a feared nomadic people inhabiting the great Eurasian steppe (although they were, strictly speaking, long extinct by this period, their place taken by other nomadic peoples). Moreover, this does not seem to be arranged in any obvious contrasting opposition as the other couplets are (i.e., Jew versus pagan, slave versus free). Barbarians and Scythians seem to come from the same category (i.e., barbarians). However, these problems are eliminated once it is grasped that the entire series of couplets in Colossians 3:11 has been arranged chiastically, and furthermore, that it thereby speaks directly to the conflict at Colossae between Philemon and Onesimus.

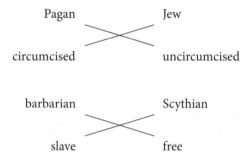

The category "Scythian" was not just a traditional Greco-Roman designation for "the nomadic barbarian other" from the steppes. It was frequently applied to those who had been enslaved from the region, presumably by means of raids along the shores of the Black Sea. Hence, "Scythian" was an attested slave name. (This was probably not just typical slave nomenclature; members of this savage race would have fetched a higher price.) And the largest local emporium for the sale of these slaves was Ephesus. It seems significant, then, that the category "Scythian" is coordinated chiastically by Colossians 3:11 with the category "slave," and the category "barbarian" with the category "owner" (technically, the word used here is "free," which would encompass more than just owners; contextually, the use of the word "free" would be especially pointed for owners).

δοῦλος οὐδὲ ἐλεύθερος, οὐκ ἔνι ἄρσεν καὶ θῆλυ· πάντες γὰρ ὑμεῖς εἷς ἐστε ἐν Χριστῷ Ἰησοῦ. For further details, see my 1996.

These coordinations map directly onto and further illuminate the situation at Colossae that is principally disclosed by Philemon. Onesimus may have been, it seems, one of the unfortunate "white Russians" enslaved by a Black Sea raid, and was very likely sold in Ephesus or one of the other great port emporiums on the western Aegean coast (although his place of acquisition does not matter overmuch). That he is now associated with Colossae is therefore plausible. His master, Philemon, is identified here as a barbarian, and his wife's (or sister's) name attests plausibly to this identification as well; he is probably a Phrygian or Lydian, something that is again not surprising for a citizen of Colossae. The carefully crafted baptismal chiasm in Colossians 3:11 thereby suggests that the difficulties between Philemon and Onesimus have an ethnic as well as a class component, a doubly difficult situation to navigate. So Colossians maps in detail here the unfolding situation addressed directly by Philemon. And it is worth noting that without this illumination, these textual details in Colossians remain opaque; they are literally uninterpretable.

Enough has probably been said by this point to suggest that the problem of slavery and its pastoral management identified by Philemon are woven into the warp and woof of Colossians (although even more material could arguably be introduced in support of this claim). The involvement of the local deacon Archippus in both Philemon and Colossians, the unusual emphasis in the *Haustafeln* on the relationship between owners and slaves, and the inordinate applicability of the unique baptismal material in 3:11 lace these two letters and their situations tightly together. We might want Paul's advice concerning slavery to be rather more radical than it is, but that is not our current concern; we need only to recognize here that the issue is writ large through the text of Colossians, if in a somewhat regrettable sense.[27] Yet unlike the overlaps between the prescripts and postscripts, this interlacement is not especially noticeable; it is easy even for modern commentators to miss these clues. And this serves to corroborate a judgment of authenticity as against pseudepigraphy concerning Colossians, at least at this stage in our discussion. As Paley put it some time ago: "This result is the effect either of truth which produces consistency without the writer's thought or care, or of a contexture of forgeries confirming and falling in with one another by a species of fortuity of which I know no example" (1790, 111).

With some confidence, then, we can turn to consider the immediate

---

27. Having said this, the implicit engagement of Col with the discourse of slavery is complex and in certain respects at least arguably subversive. Barclay (1991) is an especially interesting analysis.

implications of the interlacement of Colossians and Philemon for the rest of the frame. The first implication worth noting is the reinforcement of the letters' Asian provenance.

We learned from Philemon primarily that Paul was most probably imprisoned quite close by Onesimus's place of ownership. Onesimus had reached him as an *erro,* and part of Paul's response was to request the preparation of a guest room. There were hints that these locations were in Asia, but they were very tentative (i.e., Apphia's name; later tradition's association of Phlm with an Asian provenance by means of Col; and the general suitability of this location against what we know of Paul's situations elsewhere). We learn from Philemon, in short, something about the distance that Paul was from his recipients but not definitively where those recipients were located.

Paul's letter to the Colossians, however, clearly identifies its recipients as Colossian. And the tight connections between these two letters now allow these sets of data to be confidently combined, suggesting that Paul was somewhere in the Lycus valley when he wrote these letters, or nearby. That is, we now know with some confidence that he was not far from his recipients, and his recipients were Colossian. And this corroborates our earlier chronological estimates as well, made somewhat tentatively in relation to the hinted Asian provenance of Philemon. So we can now confirm more confidently that the imprisonment in question was during 50 CE, apparently occurring while Paul was returning from Syrian Antioch and Jerusalem by way of Galatia. But Colossians now adds further important details to this developing picture.

Paul was not imprisoned in Laodicea or Hierapolis or Colossae itself. Moreover, he seems to have been positioned *east* of Colossae and these other communities, looking west toward them, so somewhere most probably on the important route between Laodicea and Pisidian Antioch by way of Apamea, the important town located on the eastern frontier of the Roman province of Asia.

Modern people tend to think about locations and distances and to plan any travel accordingly "from above" (i.e., as if they were in a helicopter or plane), largely because of the cartographical revolution that took place from the Renaissance onward that depicts our environments in this fashion. And most modern scholars tend to think about ancient travel in the same terms — topographically, and in fairly accurate, two-dimensional and three-dimensional terms, a purview doubtless assisted by the provision of accurate maps in modern printed editions of the Bible. But this is of course anachronistic. Modern topography in these terms, based on spatially accurate cartography, became possible only after the discovery in the fifteenth century of accurate surveying techniques based on telescopes, magnetic compasses, and sextants, along with the invention and standardization of various mapping codes that modern readers take for granted — the introduction of the Mercator projection in 1569, for example. The mental landscape of ancients was very different.

It is becoming increasingly clear that Romans and other ancient peoples thought about distance and travel primarily in terms of sequences or itineraries, like beads on a string, that could lead them reliably from their current location to a destination (ironically, rather in the way that programs like Google Maps or MapQuest produce sequenced travel itineraries today, thereby returning us to ancient mental maps; see esp. Scheidel, Meeks, and Weiland 2012; Scheidel 2013). This purview is represented well by the Peutinger Table (i.e., the *Tabula Peutingeriana;* see esp. Talbert 2010), whose archetype probably dates from the fifth century CE. It is highly significant, then, that several times the postscript of Colossians suggests that Paul is thinking in terms of an underlying itinerary or sequence that runs from east to west.

In 4:13 Paul thinks of Colossae, then Laodicea, then Hierapolis (μαρτυρῶ γὰρ αὐτῷ ὅτι ἔχει πολὺν πόνον ὑπὲρ ὑμῶν καὶ τῶν ἐν Λαοδικείᾳ καὶ τῶν ἐν Ἱεραπόλει). In 4:15 he thinks of Laodicea, then of Nympha's house congregation, which seems to have been located in Hierapolis (Ἀσπάσασθε τοὺς ἐν Λαοδικείᾳ ἀδελφοὺς καὶ Νύμφαν καὶ τὴν κατ' οἶκον αὐτῆς ἐκκλησίαν). And in 4:16 he thinks first of Colossae and then of Laodicea, before reversing the sequence (καὶ ὅταν ἀναγνωσθῇ παρ' ὑμῖν ἡ ἐπιστολή, ποιήσατε ἵνα καὶ ἐν τῇ Λαοδικέων ἐκκλησίᾳ ἀναγνωσθῇ, καὶ τὴν ἐκ Λαοδικείας ἵνα καὶ ὑμεῖς ἀναγνῶτε). And the three primary sequences all run consistently in the same direction — east to west.

If Paul was thinking in terms of itinerary or sequence, then, as was most common in the ancient world, we may infer with considerable confidence that the envisaged itinerary ran west from Paul's current location to Colossae, then to Laodicea, and finally to Hierapolis, the community westernmost from him. This is not necessarily to suggest that these communities were on a straight line or direct route with respect to one another. But the most practical order in which to visit them from Paul's place of imprisonment would have been in this sequence, and this strongly suggests locating Paul's imprisonment to the east.

We should now combine this inference with the implications from Philemon concerning the relatively short distances involved and the additional suggestion that Paul is not apparently writing from a place where a successful congregation had been established. It seems likely in the light of this evidence that Paul was imprisoned somewhere between Colossae and — let us say for the moment — Pisidian Antioch, the gateway to south Galatia, where a successful congregation had been founded (although little changes here if we switch the city of origin to a gateway to north Galatia such as Dorylaion/Dorylaeum).[28]

Pisidian Antioch was around 6.4 days' journey on foot from Laodicea (utilizing ORBIS here). And Colossae was less than half a day's walk from Laodicea back toward the east (ca. 16 km; note that Colossae is too unimportant to be mapped by ORBIS, at least yet). So we may infer fairly that Paul was imprisoned somewhere to the east of Colossae and no more than six days away, and there is one particularly appealing candidate for this imprisonment: Apamea.

The strategic city of Apamea was one of the gateways to Asia from the east and was located only 2.9 days' walk from Laodicea (105 km), and even closer to Colossae (2.4 days' walk or ca. 89 km). There are no records of a successful Pauline congregation being established there, although isolated conversions were presumably possible. And it was certainly a sufficiently large administrative center to have had officials willing and able to detain someone like Paul. It seems fair to suppose, then, that Paul was imprisoned in Apamea when he wrote Colossians and Philemon; either this, or he was being held in some similar location and situation between Colossae and Pisidian Antioch (or, alternatively, Pessinus), although the other candidates do not fit the parameters in the data quite as well as Apamea. Dorylaion is a candidate, but is almost ten days' journey distant, which seems a little far. However, nothing rests on a precise location at this point, so we will with due caution suggest Apamea as the best current candidate for the locus where both Philemon and Colossians were composed, remaining open to other possibilities. We can now turn to consider potential questions within the data that might challenge our initial judgment here of authenticity concerning Colossians:

(i) Is there time during Paul's imprisonment for all the implied sequences of events to have taken place?
(ii) Is there an unacceptable disjunction between the addressees in Colossians and those in Philemon?

28. That is, not much changes if Paul is traveling at this time south, down from the main northern east-west route across Anatolia that ran through the "ethnic" Galatian communities. ORBIS suggests that this journey would have proceeded roughly from Germa through Dorylaion/Dorylaeum, then headed south, intersecting the main southern east-west route not far to the west of Pisidian Antioch. (The Antonine table lists Pessinus as sixteen Roman miles from Germa, the latter not existing in Paul's day.) A journey from Germa to Laodicea would have averaged 12.6 days (454 km); from Dorylaion, 9.8 days (351 km).

(iii) Is there contradictory information in the two letters' lists of greetings?
(iv) Does additional data concerning other figures in the Pauline mission contradict the scenario currently being advocated — that is, an early date for these letters' composition from somewhere in Asia prior to any missionary work in Ephesus taking place?
(v) And why are these letters silent about the collection for the poor in Jerusalem, which was unfolding at this time?

These could pose difficult challenges, but I suggest that there are plausible rejoinders.

(i) The duration of the incarceration during which Colossians was written is limited, at its maximum possible extent, only by the events that took place at either end. Is there time between these events for a relatively lengthy imprisonment during which the events presupposed by Colossians could have occurred? Or is there too much time compression evident here, suggesting that Colossians is a forgery?

As we have already noted briefly, this period is bound on its early end by Paul's departure from Galatia after traveling back from meetings in Syrian Antioch and Jerusalem, and those took place as early in the relevant chronological interval as late 49 CE (i.e., 13.x years after Paul's first visit to Jerusalem, which occurred in late 36 CE). The late end of the period is bound by Paul's arrival in Ephesus in time for the events presupposed by 1 Corinthians to have taken place, and these could have unfolded as late as the final months of 50 CE. This establishes the widest possible interval for the period in question — roughly December 49 through November 50 CE. We must reckon with the appropriate travel times within this interval, however.

A sea journey from Jerusalem to Antioch would have taken about a fortnight, and a journey from Syrian Antioch to Apamea by way of Galatia on foot about 21 days, or three weeks, so approximately five weeks total.[29] So if Paul left Jerusalem in January and arrived in Ephe-

---

29. ORBIS (May 29 and 31, 2013) suggests that a sea journey in November from Antioch to Jerusalem (including travel closer to these destinations on foot and river) would have taken between 8 and 13 days (7.8 and 12.6). A sea journey at that time from Ephesus to Antioch using a coastal route would have taken 7.1 days; using that route only during the day, 14.6. But the clock starts ticking (so to speak) for this marker only from Paul's arrival in Jerusalem, and his stay there may not have been that long. In January a return journey by sea to Antioch would have averaged between 8 and 14 days, depending on the precise mode (i.e., risking the

sus the following fall, around September, then he could theoretically have been incarcerated in the Lycus valley from March through August, a six-month sojourn (and this estimate is not pressing the limits of the situation). He need not have been in prison this long, but there is clearly enough time for the events implied in Colossians to have unfolded around him during an incarceration of this potential duration. Time compression is not a problem.

(ii) There is possibly a problem, however, buried in the prescripts of Colossians and Philemon. Paul's letter to Philemon is addressed to Philemon, to his wife Apphia, and to Archippus "and the assembly in your [masc. sg.] house" (Phlm 1–2). Paul's letter to the Colossians addresses the "holy and trustworthy brothers who are in Colossae" (Col 1:2). Later in the letter, as we have already seen, it also exhorts the letter's recipients to (paraphrasing) "tell Archippus to get on with his appointed spiritual task" (4:17). And this does not make a lot of sense if the addressees in the prescript of Philemon were identical with the congregation at Colossae.

Yet while this skepticism is warranted in general terms, it must give way in the face of specific data, which seems to suggest here that the entire Colossian congregation was larger than the house church addressed in Philemon. Arguably, fragments of epistolary data confirm this. Paul never addresses the recipients of Colossians as an ἐκκλησία, or assembly. Only assemblies in Laodicea and Hierapolis (the latter presumably being a single house gathering) are named as such. (The references in Col 1:18 and 24 are generalized and distinctive.) The prescript to Philemon also names a single house gathering. This suggests that the Christians in Colossae were gathering in more than one house congregation. And when this data is combined with the probable presence of a rival teacher at Colossae, it seems possible to imagine that conversions at Colossae numbered significantly more than the single household gathering named in Philemon 1b-2. This figure or group may have had some success, too, analogous to the situation at Corinth. But a further problem lurking in the two lists of greetings is more difficult to deal with.

(iii) Epaphras is characterized as a "fellow prisoner" in Philemon 23 (ὁ συναιχμάλωτός μου) but not in Colossians, while Aristarchus is characterized as a "fellow prisoner" in Colossians 4:10 but not in Philemon

---

open sea, traveling by way of the coast, or traveling coastally only during the day). A journey overland from Antioch to Ephesus (1073 km) irrespective of the season would have averaged 30.8 days, but as far as Apamea, 23.1 days (796 km), assuming the Cilician gates were open.

24. Consequently, it seems at first glance as if Aristarchus was in prison with Paul when Colossians was written, but Epaphras was in prison with Paul when Philemon was written. And this just looks like a mistake. It makes little sense in practical terms (i.e., the release of one figure and then the arrest of the other). Moreover, the explanations offered for this — where the difficulty is noted — often lack plausibility.

Rapske (1996 [1994], 238), following Kümmel and others, suggests that various figures assisted and stayed with Paul during his house arrest on different occasions and thereby merited the moniker at different times (see Acts 28:16, 30). But first, nothing suggests here that Paul is under house arrest; second, he is not in Rome (as in Acts); and third, such figures are hardly thereby actually imprisoned and so accurately described as fellow prisoners.

Some commentators have argued, rather differently, that the designation is metaphorical (so Wilson 2005, following Moule and ultimately Lightfoot), but this is an implausible reading in its own right. Paul's *sun-* compounds elsewhere are never metaphorical but fundamentally concrete. Moreover, a metaphorical meaning is somewhat opaque. In what sense is a Christian coworker a "fellow prisoner" metaphorically? Paul's gospel speaks of the very opposite, that is, of the liberation of its participants from any slavery or impediment. Nevertheless, the line of interpretation opened up by Lightfoot and Moule is ultimately helpful.

They note that the word used did not, strictly speaking, reference a prisoner in a straightforward sense; it denoted a "prisoner of war," or POW. ("Prisoner" was denoted by δέσμιος and, more rarely, by δεσμώτης, from "chain" or "bond" or "fetter" [δεσμός]; αἰχμάλωτος, however, denoted someone captured during a conflict.) Hence, Paul's use of the word αἰχμάλωτος in Colossians 4:10 and Philemon 23 did not necessarily imply a shared imprisonment, as its application in Romans to Junia and Andronicus confirms (Rom 16:7). It denoted, rather, the special status of previous imprisonment, although here described in the apocalyptic terms of a war between the gospel and the evil powers opposing it in the cosmos (this being the truth of the metaphorical reading suggested by Moule). So this signifier functions much as the designation "fellow soldier" does elsewhere for Paul (συστρατιώτης). Such a figure is no longer in the army or serving in a war but is honored by that recollection, the moniker now being interpreted additionally in terms of Christian service (and this is the characterization of Epaphroditus in Phil 2:25, and Archippus in Phlm 2). The result of this realization is that we learn rather less from the data concerning Epaphras and Aristarchus than we might first have thought we did. It seems that they both have been imprisoned at some time because of the gospel. And clearly, no contradictions are now apparent in the texts, since this is quite possible.

However, we do now have to insert an imprisonment into our previous narrative concerning Epaphras, although there are several appropriate locations for this. It is striking that he has been incarcerated already for his new piety, but this is not necessarily impossible. He could have been imprisoned when he converted at Paul's location. And he could have been detained on his return to Colossae, or on his return to Paul's location, and both scenarios would explain why he is not accompanying the letter back to his hometown (if we still need to). It seems unlikely that Aristarchus and Epaphras were both actually imprisoned at the time when Colossians and Philemon were written; we would expect Paul to be a little more consistent with his designations if this were the case, and also a little more pointed (i.e., not use the metaphorical reference; Paul never describes his own current incarcerations in these terms). Ultimately, then, I tilt toward an earlier Colossian imprisonment for Epaphras, since this helps to explain his continuing presence with Paul when Colossians was written and dispatched. So this possible inconsistency between Colossians and Philemon seems well explained. And another possible anomaly in the greetings is also worth noting in passing.

The greetings in Colossians mention in 4:11a "Jesus/Joshua who is also called Justus" (καὶ Ἰησοῦς ὁ λεγόμενος Ἰοῦστος), but he seems to have dropped from sight in Philemon (see only Μᾶρκος, Ἀρίσταρχος, Δημᾶς, Λουκᾶς, οἱ συνεργοί μου). Is this another telltale slip by a pseudepigrapher? Not necessarily, if we suppose that Paul used only this person's first name in Philemon 23b, "Jesus/Joshua," and that this was subsequently folded by reverent scribes into an extended designation for Christ, thereby erasing the reference to the figure of "Jesus/Justus" (see Ἀσπάζεταί σε Ἐπαφρᾶς ὁ συναιχμάλωτός μου ἐν Χριστῷ Ἰησοῦ). Any emendation here is conjectural, being unattested in the manuscript tradition, but seems highly plausible (i.e., Ἀσπάζεταί σε Ἐπαφρᾶς ὁ συναιχμάλωτός μου ἐν Χριστῷ, Ἰησοῦς κ.τ.λ.), a view that Raymond Brown (1997, 614 n. 31) notes in passing. This conflation would have been assisted by the μου just three words previous, which might have suggested the genitive rather than the nominative ending for Ἰησοῦς. In addition, the characterization of Epaphras in Colossians 4:12 varies, with the longer reading — "of Christ Jesus" — possibly reflecting the emendation of Philemon 23b. Alternatively, if original, it might have prompted or reinforced that emendation. So this further potential anomaly seems explicable. But other data might still cause trouble for our developing reading, which roots Colossians and Philemon in the early stages of an Asian mission.

(iv) Romans 16:5 suggests that Epaenetus was Paul's first convert — literally, "first fruits" — in Asia (see 1 Cor 16:15). Moreover, we know of Epaenetus only in conjunction with Prisca and Aquila. He seems to be part of their house gathering at Rome when Paul writes Romans in the spring of 52 CE (16:3-4). And it seems plausible to infer from this data that Epaenetus was converted through some connection with Prisca and Aquila and so most probably at Ephesus (1 Cor 16:19). But this would preclude earlier conversions of Epaphras and Tychicus in Asia, as supposed by Colossians and our developing reconstruction (later tradition identifying Tychicus with Asia, almost certainly unexceptionally; see Acts 20:4). That Paul would have been speaking in local, regional rather than broader, provincial terms about Epaenetus's Asian origin, thereby avoiding this conundrum, also seems unlikely, given his usage in 1 Corinthians 16:19.

But there is insufficient data here to build a decisive case. Epaenetus might have been part of Prisca and Aquila's house gathering in Rome and a product, earlier on, of their work in Ephesus, but he could have been living with them in Rome simply as a Pauline convert enjoying their hospitality. Or he might simply have been named in Romans immediately after them by way of association with the Asian mission and not have been staying with them at all. We should infer that he was converted prior to Epaphras in Asia, although he no longer seems to have been with Paul when Colossians was written. But Apamea was in Asia, along with any settlement to the west of it, so he could have converted in one of those locations, where Paul was imprisoned. And his presence in Rome as attested by Romans 16:5 attests directly to his mobility. Tychicus might have converted subsequent to Epaenetus in Asia as well, or he might have converted somewhere else, outside Asia. So resolving this challenge thickens our description concerning the early Asian mission helpfully, if we add the conversion of Epaenetus to Paul's current incarceration in addition to the conversion of the Colossian slave Epaphras, rather than undermining its plausibility. Similar considerations hold for Tychicus. Moreover, the existence of these congregations in the Lycus valley helps us explain Paul's otherwise somewhat opaque plural in 1 Corinthians 16:19, written the following spring: Ἀσπάζονται ὑμᾶς αἱ ἐκκλησίαι τῆς Ἀσίας. And at this point one last query remains.

(v) Both Colossians and Philemon are silent about the collection for Jerusalem, a major project that Paul is currently administering. According to
our developing scenario, he has just instructed the Galatians about its
prosecution (during a visit) and will shortly engage in a long and complex
negotiation with the Corinthians about the same, will gesture toward it
subtly in his letter to the Galatians, and will mention it at its conclusion
in Romans. Does Paul's silence about this important undertaking in Colossians and Philemon suggest that they were not written at this time?

This inference is doubtful. Paul's letter to the Philippians attests to the
fact that he does not always refer to the collection during this period. Its
mention is helpful — if not critical — for sequencing when it does take
place, but the converse does not apply. That is, it does not follow from
the silence of a letter concerning the collection that it was *not* composed
during this period. Moreover, that Paul would resist introducing a request for money into letters written to gatherings who had not yet set
eyes on him is entirely understandable. The ancient world was full of
charlatans (see Anderson 1994); hence, one of Paul's most constant struggles was the battle for perceived financial integrity, a struggle discernible
from his earliest correspondence to the Thessalonians (1 Thess 2:3, 5). So
the silence concerning the collection in Colossians and Philemon is not
only not a difficulty; in these circumstances, it is to be expected.

It seems, then, that any difficulties arising as we insert Colossians into our
developing frame alongside Philemon are more apparent than real. They are
worth exploring, and some, in their resolution, have deepened our knowledge
of the original situation, but none are fatal. And as a result, our earlier judgment
that Colossians was authentic has been strengthened; a web of overt and subtle
connections ties it into our existing frame, which should now be augmented
by its confident insertion (that is, pending the outcome of later challenges).

The existing principal sequence of letters, running through Paul's (calendar) year of crisis, can now be expanded with the addition of Philemon and
Colossians in the previous year:

$$// 50 //$$
$$\ldots \textbf{Phlm} / \textbf{Col} \ldots [\text{PLC}] —$$
$$// 51 //$$
$$1 \text{ Cor} — 2 \text{ Cor} — [\text{PLP}]^{\text{Phil } 3:2–4:3} / \text{Gal} — \text{Phil} —$$
$$// 52 //$$
$$\text{Rom} \ldots$$

With this useful expansion of the biographical frame tentatively in place, we can turn to consider some of the weightier methodological challenges to the authenticity of Colossians — in terms of dependence and style.

2.3 Questions of Dependence and Style

(1) Dependence

A specific and quite important question of dependence clearly arises here, namely, the relationship between Colossians and the prior letter to the Laodiceans (Laod). Not much turns on this if Laodiceans is simply lost; however, if Ephesians is identified with Laodiceans, then the situation waxes in importance. In fact, a matrix of possible results exists for this relationship. But only one of these can potentially alter our developing judgment here — and this presupposes that dependence in one direction can be definitively demonstrated.[30] If this option is eventually affirmed — that Ephesians demonstrably precedes Colossians and is inauthentic — then we will return and revise our judgment concerning Colossians. But in view of its unlikelihood, we can safely postpone consideration of this issue until the letter to the Ephesians is assessed in detail in §3. All the other options leave the question of Colossians' authenticity open.

	Ephesians authentic	Ephesians inauthentic
Ephesians precedes Colossians	Colossians could be authentic	*Colossians inauthentic*
Ephesians follows Colossians	Colossians authentic	Colossians could be authentic

But this still leaves other possible instances of dependence in Colossians unaccounted for.

Recently, Leppä (2003), looking back to a classic analysis by E. P. Sanders (1966), has argued that Colossians is inauthentic, because of its overt dependence on various indubitably authentic Pauline letters — a significant sugges-

---

30. I am not convinced that more complex solutions involving multiple stages are particularly plausible — for example, Holtzmann's suggestion that both Eph and Col derive from an earlier authentic proto-Colossians.

tion, because it is made independently of any judgments concerning Ephesians.[31] But we have already entered a strong objection concerning this type of
inference, and must introduce a caveat to Leppä's argument as well.

Paul evidently kept copies of his letters; the letters circulated through
multiple congregations (see Col 4:16); and copies seem to have been made
and studied in those locations. So he seems to have echoed his letters in
various ways within further correspondence when he felt the need to do so.[32]
Second Thessalonians 3:8 provides an especially good example of a small
specific echo when it quotes but also pointedly reapplies 1 Thessalonians 2:9
(2 Thess is discussed in Leppä 2006; and here in ch. 4), and we have seen
the presence of broad structural similarities between 1 Thessalonians and
1 Corinthians as well (also in ch. 4). Hence, the mere fact of dependence
has already been shown to be unremarkable, as Sanders in effect concedes.
So this aspect of Leppä's case can actually be granted, but it suggests nothing further in terms of authenticity — the false inference in her analysis
(i.e., dependence necessitates pseudonymity). Indeed, this was our principal
objection to this line of reasoning earlier. But a caveat ought to be entered
here as well.

Leppä's data is indecisive even with respect to sequencing Colossians,

---

31. Leppä (2003, 17-18) cites other advocates and endorsers of dependence, most notably, Schenk (1983; 1987); and an advocate of an alternative type of dependence, Kiley (1986).

32. Sanders makes an interesting concession in this relation: "Behind the attempt to
establish such criteria [i.e., sufficient to distinguish the parallels between a letter plausibly
written by Paul and a letter written by a later writer with access to his writings] is the assumption that Paul did not carry about with him copies of his previous letters, or, if he did, that he
did not have them memorized nor did he consult them when composing a new letter. If this
assumption is false, it would be difficult to distinguish Paul's work from that of a later imitator"
(1966, 29-30). Sanders goes on to argue that this assumption "is probably not false, however, for
there is no evidence for the literary dependence of any one of Paul's seven undisputed letters
upon another, much less upon several" (30). But this rejoinder is, in the first instance, a non
sequitur; that Paul did not quote earlier material in some cases does not prove that in others
he did not. And it is also, second, not quite accurate. A certain dependence between 1 Thess
and 1 Cor has already been noted, and many close relationships are discernible between Rom,
Phil 3:2-11, and Gal, and between 1 Thess and 2 Thess (although Sanders would probably take
this last relationship as evidence of the pseudonymity of 2 Thess). Third, Sanders actually
makes three assumptions here, not one, and all have effectively been refuted by the data. Paul
did most likely carry about copies of his letters (so Richards 1991, 165 n. 169; 2004, 156-61,
214-23; Murphy O'Connor 1995, 37), did have them memorized (and this is a strange denial
for someone like Sanders in any case — an advocate of the importance of rabbinic sources for
Pauline analysis), and did apparently consult them when composing new letters, whether to
a greater or lesser degree, as his embedded quotations suggest.

since all of the putative echoes that she assembles can be explained plausibly in the reverse direction, as the echoes of Colossians by later Pauline letters. That is, echoes of undisputed letters appearing overtly later in Colossians would break apart our existing frame, pushing Colossians later in the broader letter sequence at the least — an important result. But Leppä never demonstrates that the echoes must proceed in this single direction, from another letter *to* Colossians, thereby falsifying our frame. Indeed, demonstrating direction or causality is a common problem in the analysis of perceived dependence. Leppä assumes the inauthenticity of Colossians and so does not feel the need to address this problem of reversible dependence, but it is a critical question for our framing project.

Having said all this, it is important not to overlook the hurdle that advocates of authenticity face in this relation, namely, the supply of plausible contingent accounts of any identified echoes, something that was arguably done here on a small scale for 1 and 2 Thessalonians, and on a larger scale for the echo of 1 Thessalonians by 1 Corinthians.[33] But arguably good contingent accounts can be supplied of the echoes that Leppä and others have detected between Colossians and the undisputed Pauline letters.

So, for example, Sanders argues that

(i) Second Corinthians 4:4, Romans 1:20, 1 Corinthians 8:5-6, and Romans 11:36 are echoed in Colossians 1:15-16; but Sanders's second instance here (Rom 1:20) is forced, and the others are arguably understandable echoes of an important preexisting hymn or confession;

(ii) Second Corinthians 5:18, 1 Corinthians 8:5, and Romans 5:10 are echoed in Colossians 1:20-22a; but the front end of this set of echoes in Colossians is again explained plausibly by the hymnic origin of that material, and the second is a plausible reprise of a key Pauline theological narrative — the reconciliation of a hostile humanity (and Sanders underplays the presence of this discourse elsewhere in Paul, omitting other parallels in 2 Cor 5:16–6:1);

(iii) First Corinthians 2:7, Romans 16:25-26, and Romans 9:23-24 are echoed in

---

33. It is important to appreciate that to have demonstrated the presence of what we might call autodependence by Paul is not necessarily to have explained it plausibly in deeper terms, i.e., to have understood why he did this comprehensively. Several possibilities spring to mind, although this is not the place to analyze them: a rabbinic mind-set; a philosophical mind-set; an "oracular" mind-set; or perhaps, rather differently, what we might call GSL (the ancient equivalent of ESL). I have gestured toward some options already in ch. 4 — see perhaps most auspiciously 2 Thess 2:15.

Colossians 1:26-27; but this appeal to "the revelation schema" informed
by Jewish Wisdom traditions is again arguably unremarkable for Paul
(i.e., because it is so important substantively), and any leverage from the
doubtful Romans 16:25-26 is questionable; and

(iv) Romans 6:4, Romans 4:24, Galatians 1:1, Romans 6:11, and Romans 8:32
are echoed in Colossians 2:12-13; but Romans 8:32 is a false parallel, and
Galatians 1:1 vestigial, leaving overtly traditional verses (Rom 4:24) and
material (the Rom 6 account of baptism) in close relation to a baptismal
discussion in Colossians 2.

In sum, Sanders's echoes are less impressive than they first appear, and arguably, they combine to tell us only what theological motifs are important to Paul
— useful information in another setting, to be sure, but not here.[34] Hence, we
will set this interesting challenge to one side for now and proceed to the next
challenge to the authenticity of Colossians, namely, its much-touted difference
from the authentic letters in terms of style. Of course, some of these questions
of dependence will have to be revisited in earnest during the assessment of
Ephesians, when we will have to consider the significance of the virtual web
of intertextuality that holds between Ephesians and Colossians, and with the
undisputed letters in turn, and will have to at least try to determine the flow
of the obvious dependence in view. But that discussion can wait.

(2) Style

The stylistic challenge to the authenticity of Colossians began as early as 1838,
when it was one important aspect of Ernst Mayerhoff's case for the letter's
pseudonymity. And it reached an apparent climax with the soul-destroying
tabulations of Walter Bujard in 1973. Thus, Ehrman cites Bujard's analysis and
comments that it is "widely thought to be unanswerable" (2013, 175). But is it?

Bujard's data is impressive. However, it needs to be measured against
the statistical and (where relevant) computer-assisted evaluations of style that
were first noted in chapter 4. And we should recall the initial methodological

---

34. Sanders adds a fifth set of parallels, less persuasive by his own admission, about
which little further needs to be said except that baptismal parallels are again cited unremarked:
see, to a degree, elements of Rom 13:12b-14, 1 Thess 4:5, 1 Cor 5:11, Gal 5:19, Rom 6:6, Gal 3:27-
28, 1 Cor 12:13, and 1 Cor 15:28 in Col 3:5-11. Note that these echoes are *interesting*, and perhaps
very much so. They might shed important light on the critical matter of Paul's coherence. But
used in this way, they tell us nothing decisive about framing.

observation made there — that mere tabulations of difference are, when unin-
terpreted, largely meaningless. All of Paul's undisputed letters contain stylistic
differences from one another, and "style" itself is an immensely complicated
and largely undefined notion — a combination of dozens, if not of hundreds,
of different features of the language used in a given set of texts. So interpreters
of Paul need to be very careful, first, not to "cherry-pick" the data, tabulating
variables that indicate differences between undisputed and disputed letters,
thereby omitting those variables that either are unremarkable in a disputed
text or that suggest the oddity of an undisputed text. And second, they need to
avoid assuming blithely that an instance of difference is an automatic marker
of alternative authorship, developing pseudonymous readings in the light of
this conviction.

    Both problems are apparent in Bujard's analysis and in those like it.
Hence, we need to ask, are tabulations of difference like his helpful at all? Is
style a meaningful element in this debate? And we need to turn in response to
those who know how to evaluate the meaningfulness of differences appropriately, something that ought to take place in the standard statistical sense, that
is, in terms of distances from the mean for given variables in relation to the
measurable standard deviation of a sample. And I would suggest that Kenny's
older analysis (1986, esp. 27, and 117-18) remains helpful in this regard.

    It seems quite important that after tabulating 96 stylistic features *and
then correlating them, in order to assess their significance,* Kenny concludes that
the author of the Pauline corpus was extremely versatile stylistically. Without
this observation, his and most other tabulations simply collapse into absurdity
(i.e., the undisputed letters prove incommensurate). Once this versatility has
been acknowledged in stylistic terms, only Titus "must be under suspicion"
(1986, 95-100, quoting from 97). The sum of the coefficients (although he notes
that they are not, strictly speaking, "additive") also generates an indicative
ranking of the letters in terms of their fit with one another, that is, in terms of
cumulative differences. So, in descending order of "comfort": Romans, Philippians, 2 Timothy, 2 Corinthians, Galatians, 2 Thessalonians, 1 Thessalonians,
Colossians, Ephesians, 1 Timothy, Philemon, 1 Corinthians, Titus. In addition
to the difficulties of Titus, the relative comfort of 2 Timothy and discomfort of
1 Corinthians here are noteworthy, not to mention the locations of Colossians
and Ephesians as more "comfortable" than 1 Corinthians and Philemon.

    In short, the calculations of Kenny directly contradict the significance
(not the fact) of Bujard's tabulations, and of those like them. The latter are
unreliable indicators of *significant* differences between the style of Colossians
and the stylistic characteristics of the rest of the Pauline corpus. Can we go

further than this, however, drawing especially on the more recent computer-assisted evaluations of stylistic data in Paul to generate some more aggressive insights about authorship?

I would suggest — tentatively — that at present we cannot, although we should not rule out the possibility that more refined methods and experiments will deliver more decisive results in the future. (Indeed, I expect that they will.) But the most sophisticated analyses we currently possess — Neumann, Mealand, and Ledger — in my view lack decisiveness. Although they do seem to be able to discriminate successfully between significant blocks of material within the NT (like the Gospels, Acts, the book of Revelation, and the letters; see Ledger 1995, figs. 3 and 4, pp. 88 and 89), when they turn up the focus, so to speak, and generate plots of the Pauline letters alone, the resulting results lose plausibility (see figs. 5, 6, and 7, pp. 90, 91, and 92; also Mealand 1995, fig. 8, p. 83; and the plots below, unpublished but which Mealand kindly shared with me in personal correspondence). It becomes very difficult to detect whether the plots generated are supplying meaningful information or mere noise. So, for example, Ledger concluded rather confidently that 1 Thessalonians is doubtfully authentic, because it plots close to Ephesians, Colossians, and, to a certain degree, the Pastorals. But this is unlikely to be a meaningful result. Rather, it calls his plot into question. And the plots for Romans and 1 Corinthians are as widely spread in Mealand's analyses as the plots for Ephesians, while only the sample drawn from the first half of Ephesians tends to be an outlier.[35]

I suggest, then, that we must wait for the next generation of stylometric analyses for more decisive results at the front end of the framing process — and perhaps this is not surprising. Stylometrics has always had more success identifying an author if it already knows that one of two or more authors is respon-

---

35. An earlier statistical controversy might remain instructive. Morton (and McLeman 1966; also Morton 1978), relying in the main on data related to sentence length, concluded quite confidently that Paul wrote only Rom, 1 Cor, 2 Cor, and Gal. Kenny (1986, 101-15) placed pressure on this argument in various ways, one of which was the demonstration that according to Morton's data, 1 Cor struggles to come from the same authentic sample as any other Pauline letter except Gal and Rom (and he demonstrated the same problem in certain statistical analyses of some of Aristotle's works). This is not to suggest that the later studies of the NT noted here are anything like Morton's infamous analyses, whether in relation to the NT or to other texts and problems. But Morton illustrates the perennial problem of any statistical analysis of a given set of data — namely, whether the data collected, tabulated, and statistically analyzed reflects a real situation reliably or is either corrupted or incomplete in some way and therefore misleading. I remain hopeful that this subdiscipline will shortly yield vital insights into Pauline authorship — my hopes resting mainly on Mealand and Abakuks — but I am not convinced that corroborative results have yet been achieved entirely reliably.

sible for the text in question.[36] And this indicates the correct location for this method within framing in terms of its more positive suggestions — later on, as a corroborative contention. That is, if the pseudonymity of any Pauline letters can first be established with some confidence on traditional grounds, such as demonstrable anachronism, then stylometric analyses can be introduced under this control and potentially corroborate the judgment. But this analysis cannot be pursued yet. It is a far more difficult business to determine *whether* multiple authors are present within a given sample, especially given that the sample size is not particularly large (and this is exacerbated in the case of Paul, because he is not working in English, or even in a Romance language, the language(s) on which most computer-assisted analyses of style are premised).

However, the negative result of this brief detour into stylometrics is still significant for our current question, as it was in chapter 4. If a statistical analysis of the data like Kenny's can detect almost no meaningful variation within the extant Pauline sample, then analyses like Bujard's are revealed to be less decisive than they purport to be. Moreover, if the most sophisticated computer-assisted analyses of multivariate data arrays cannot yet achieve consensual mapping of differences beyond this, positive claims by NT scholars like Bujard on the basis of mere tabulations of particular variations are doubly judged to be insignificant. Stylometrics suggests, in short, that many arguments from style against authenticity in the past have been considerably overcooked. It seems, conversely, that we must relearn how to interpret stylistic differences in Pauline texts when framing.

Instead of allowing a mental organization of the data of difference alone to reinforce an underlying hypothesis of pseudonymity for a given text, we must learn to resist this siren's call. We must, rather, treat the differences in style apparent between Pauline texts in the first instance as possible evidence of spread within the authentic Pauline sample, and as indicative of contingency.[37] And in terms of our current question — the challenge to the authenticity of Colossians on grounds of perceived differences between its style and those of the undisputed letters — we must simply say that these differences exist (the truth of Bujard's analysis and of those like it) but that they are not

---

36. So Juola (2006); Burrows' Delta test is also apparently effective here.

37. Moreover, some cross-cultural hermeneutical humility might be called for here as well. It seems that modern Western scholars have been overestimating their ability to judge texts written in Koiné and circulated within a Greco-Roman culture that occupied the Mediterranean littoral around two thousand years ago. Indeed, perhaps many of our conclusions have been possible only because all the figures linguistically competent to judge and, if necessary, to correct them are dead.

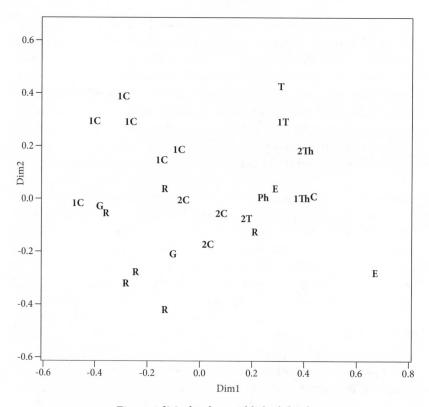

Figure 1 [Mealand, unpublished data]
*Plot showing principal component analysis of 1,000 word samples
from twelve epistles attributed to Paul*

Dimension 1 & 2 = 44.91
Dimension 1-3 = 54.76

R = Romans   C = Colossians
1C = 1 Corinthians   1Th = 1 Thessalonians
2C = 2 Corinthians   2Th = 2 Thessalonians
G = Galatians   1T = 1 Timothy
E = Ephesians   2T = 2 Timothy
Ph = Philippians   T = Titus

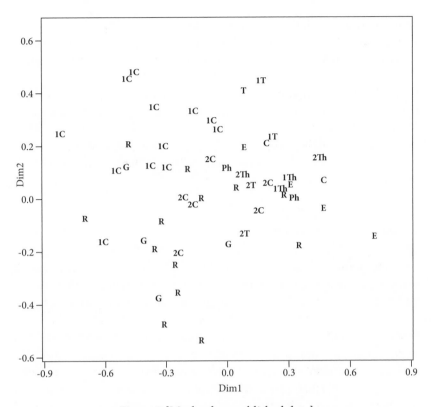

Figure 2 [Mealand, unpublished data]
*Plot showing principal component analysis of 500 word samples from
twelve epistles attributed to Paul. (The first 1,000-word sample of
Romans is divided into three subsections of ca. 333 words each.)*

Dimension 1 & 2 = 33.24
Dimension 1-3 = 41.15

R = Romans   C = Colossians
1C = 1 Corinthians   1Th = 1 Thessalonians
2C = 2 Corinthians   2Th = 2 Thessalonians
G = Galatians   1T = 1 Timothy
E = Ephesians   2T = 2 Timothy
Ph = Philippians   T = Titus

demonstrably meaningful in terms of authorship. In basic statistical terms, there is currently no evidence that these exceed the parameters of a normal single sample, lying so far from the mean in terms of the sample's standard deviations that another author has to be posited.[38] Instead, these differences should be explored vigorously in due course for what they can tell us about the situation to which Paul was specifically responding. In short, differences in style speak initially of particularity and not of pseudonymity. And with this decision made, and the stylistic challenge to authenticity abandoned — at least for the moment — we should turn to consider the challenge to the authenticity of Colossians in terms of substance.

2.4 Substantive Challenges

One of the most important indicators of pseudonymity is the presence of small mistakes in a text — telltale signs that a pseudepigrapher cannot sustain the depiction of a supposedly original contingent situation that has in fact been long lost to view. But we have already noted the most important candidates in Colossians in this respect — apparent inconsistencies between the greetings in Philemon and Colossians and so on — and found them all to be plausibly explicable in original terms. The case for pseudonymity must consequently turn to larger problems of possible anachronism if it is to prove successful. And the interpretation of Colossians has a long history in this regard. Throughout the modern period, scholars have opined that the teaching it combats is later than the time of Paul. We need now to consider the probity of this contention in a little more detail.

(1) The Problematic Teaching at Colossae

For much of the early modern period, that is, the nineteenth century, scholars viewed the teaching at Colossae as a variant on Gnosticism and hence the

---

38. Some questions will have to be asked in due course about whether a bell curve, premised on biological data and genetics, is an appropriate underlying configuration for the mapping of linguistic entities. The important companion notion of a literary "fingerprint" must also be examined. It may be that language is best mapped by another model altogether — perhaps a network that utilizes a "power law" rather than a bell curve. Statistical analyses and results would shift accordingly (and Burrows's Delta method might capture these somewhat unwittingly). Barabási (2003) introduces the broader issues lucidly.

letter's situation as necessarily later than the time of Paul. And this attack may have been abetted in the case of Protestant scholars by the perception that Colossians was overly concerned with the church and hence unacceptably close to Catholicism. Gnosticism was known during this period principally through the mirror reading of patristic figures like Irenaeus and so was thought to have flourished in the second century CE and beyond as a particular Christian heresy. But its evident fondness for the language of "emanation" and "overflow" resonated with use of the same by Colossians (see πλήρωμα in 1:19; 2:9;[39] and πληρόω in 1:9, 25; 2:10; 4:17[40]), suggesting a late and possibly even second-century date for the latter.

However, the Gnostic reading of Colossians has since been overtaken by historical events — principally, the gradual dissemination since their discovery in 1945 of the Nag Hammadi texts. Gnosticism is now viewed as a rather earlier phenomenon than was first thought and is no longer isolated within the Christian tradition, being viewed as interacting with Judaism extensively as well. This has undermined any case for the pseudonymity of Colossians on the grounds of possible resonances with Gnosticism. Indeed, it has facilitated a Gnostic reading *of* Paul (see Pagels's well-known but marginal assertions in 1992 [1975]).

The classic approach to the interpretation of the Colossian data is far from exhausting its anachronistic interpretation, however. More recently, scholars have recognized the presence of the language of emanation within the Platonic tradition, leading to readings of Colossians in terms of Middle Platonic teaching that was again often assumed to be late. This reading of Colossians has enjoyed greater prominence in recent years, thanks in large measure to the work of Eduard Schweizer (1982 [1976]; 1988), whose approach to Colossians is ably advocated by DeMaris (1994). But the importance of Philo for the development of Middle Platonism directly undermines any appeals to this reading of Colossians as evidence of Pauline anachronism.[41] (It might still be the correct construal of the data, but simply from the time of Paul.) In a similar vein, Troy Martin (1996) advocated a Cynic construal of the opponents, with no necessary implications for authorship.

However, Sappington (1991) advocated another major approach, namely,

---

39. The occurrence of πλήρωμα in the NT is dominated by Paul (see, in addition to the two references in Col just noted, Rom 11:12, 25; 13:10; 15:29; 1 Cor 10:26; Gal 4:4; Eph 1:10, 23; 3:19; 4:13) but is also usefully informed by instances in the Gospels (Mt 9:16; Mk 2:21; 6:43; 8:20; Jn 1:16).

40. The verb is much more frequent in the NT than the noun, occurring 99x, 31x in Paul (counting the cognate form ἀναπληρόω).

41. A classic analysis of Middle Platonism is Dillon (1977), where this point is obvious.

a construal in terms of Jewish apocalyptic, repristinating in his thesis the important insights of Fred Francis (1962; 1967; 1975a; 1975b; see now also esp. Stettler 2005 and I. Smith 2006). Here the rediscovery of Jewish apocalyptic texts during roughly the same period that the Gnostics were being reappraised in the wake of Nag Hammadi led to a new appreciation of the importance of angels within late Second Temple Judaism (see, i.a., Stuckenbruck 1995, summarized usefully in Hurtado 2009). And this opened up a significant new angle on the critical data in Colossians 2:18, where the text had been thought in the past to speak — rather problematically — of the "worship *of* angels" at Colossae (i.e., an objective genitive construal). It also seemed to speak of some sort of initiation or mystery rite on the basis of the text's disparaging reference to "what he has seen, by way of initiation," this being the preferred translation of the rare participle ἐμβατεύων (μηδεὶς ὑμᾶς καταβραβευέτω θέλων ἐν ταπεινοφροσύνῃ καὶ θρησκείᾳ τῶν ἀγγέλων, ἃ ἑόρακεν ἐμβατεύων, εἰκῇ φυσιούμενος ὑπὸ τοῦ νοὸς τῆς σαρκὸς αὐτοῦ). But a greater sensitivity to the concerns of Jewish apocalyptic allowed the construal of this data as a reference to "worship by [or like] the angels" (that is, a subjective or characterizing understanding of the genitive), and to "what he has seen by way of heavenly visions [i.e., after a journey or ascent, or a revelation]," both of these notions being recognizable motifs within apocalyptic strands in Judaism in Paul's day.

Furthermore, we must add to these two key modern approaches the opinion of Arnold (1996 [1995]; see also 1989; 1992), who persuasively advocated an analysis of the problem at Colossae in terms of local syncretism, at least to some degree, informed by street religion or magic.

Fortunately, we do not need to resolve this fascinating but complex debate here for the purposes of framing (although my money is on the Jewish apocalyptic reading, perhaps including traces of Judaized Middle Platonism). It suffices to note that of the four major candidates within past NT scholarship for the construction of the problematic Colossian teaching noted here, not one is necessarily post-Pauline and thereby demonstrably anachronistic.[42] Gnostic, Middle Platonic (or even Cynic), Jewish apocalyptic, and local syncretistic

---

42. T. Martin's (1996) reconstruction of the opponents as Cynics is learned and fascinating but not representative of a major tradition of interpretation — although clearly it is loosely connected to a philosophical approach. And obviously it does not exclude Pauline authorship; Cynics considerably predated Paul. The possibility of a Neo-Pythagorean resonance is worth noting as well (see Martyn 1985). I have not included here any discussion of Hooker's (1973) interesting suggestion that the opponents at Colossae did not exist in concrete terms. I think that this is highly unlikely. But more to the point, this approach will struggle to affect a judgment of authenticity.

readings of this data are all possible during the mid-first century CE. So any pressure on Pauline authorship from this teaching's infiltration to Colossae can be seen to have largely dissolved. And perhaps for this reason, a later case for the letter's pseudonymity such as Ehrman's (2013, 171-82) barely mentions this significant element within the earlier tradition in relation to claims of pseudonymity. Ehrman advocates instead the implausibility of the theological case by *the author* of Colossians, not the inappropriateness of the Colossian heretics themselves. We need now to consider the cogency of this type of argument.

(2) The Implausibility of "Paul's" Theology in Colossians

The case against the authenticity of Colossians made in substantive terms tends to appeal to its incompatible eschatology, as well as to other substantive elements that are ostensibly discordant with what Paul says elsewhere. In essence, the Paul of the undisputed letters could not have said the things that we find in Colossians. I would suggest, however, that few substantive incursions into questions of preliminary framing are more risky and less helpful than "incompatibilist" contentions in terms of Paul's eschatology. An entire series of problems is detectable within this line of argument. However, there is no need to flesh these out fully. A brief discussion should suffice.

(i) A major initial objection in methodological terms is sufficient to call the entire contention into question. Preliminary framing cannot appeal to substantive configurations of Paul's thinking, because we do not know at this early methodological stage what letters that thinking should be reconstructed from or what shape that thinking takes. We do not yet know what Paul's position on eschatology — or any other substantive matter — was in full *or* whether his position, along with his thinking and reasoning more generally, was coherent. Hence, any appeal seeking to exclude a letter from the authentic sample in terms of evident consistency begs the key questions concerning Paul's substantive concerns during framing, in terms of both content and nature. Put slightly differently: we need the data of Colossians, if it is authentic, in order to complete a full (extant) picture of Paul's thinking on any given topic. If we exclude it on the basis of a supposed reconstruction of his thinking that appeals only to other letters, we risk introducing a vicious circularity into the heart of our description — a description that it will be impossible to correct and a circularity from which it will be impossible to recover.

This alone is sufficient to rebut Ehrman's contention at this point, along with any like it. But in view of their popularity, some further objections to this line of argument are probably worth noting, although we will have to trace Ehrman's case out in a little more detail before this can be done.

Ehrman's case against the eschatology apparent in Colossians begins with the judgments that the authentic Paul was a fairly strict "futurist" and "imminentist." That is, the apostle was oriented primarily by the future coming of Christ, which he thought would be very soon, and this led to the composition of texts like 1 Thessalonians, with its strong sense of the Lord Jesus' *parousia,* and more broadly, to the urgent sense of mission apparent in its background. This eschatological reconstruction is complemented, however — as it must be — by the claim that Paul's soteriology and ethics were rooted in something of an intermediate state: Christian believers have died with Christ (so, e.g., Rom 6:1-11), thereby moving beyond the flesh, but have not yet been raised with him in any strict sense. Paul viewed believers as dead but not yet resurrected. Ehrman buttresses this claim by a reconstruction of the Corinthian situation in terms of an overenthusiastic, overrealized eschatology, which Paul corrected in 1 Corinthians 15, this last text being mirror read in this relation. Paul's resistance to overrealization at Corinth thereby seems to bear out the soteriological and ethical account of Romans in terms of an intermediate soteriological and ethical state. And Ehrman suggests that the soteriology, ethics, and eschatology in Colossians are too different to be plausibly from the same thinker.

The letter to the Colossians emphasizes the importance of the ascension of Christ for these theological *topoi,* and hence of the presence of the risen Christ in some vigorous and real sense within believers. And this incompatible emphasis on the resurrected presence of Christ is said to subtract from the futurism and imminence of Christ's *parousia;* those notions are evidently diluted. Hence, two completely different eschatological and soteriological views are apparent, one in the undisputed letters and one in Colossians, leading to a plausible judgment of pseudonymity for the latter, more developed view, and for Colossians itself.

What should we make of this case, in addition to the basic methodological problems previously noted?

(ii) I would suggest briefly that we do not need to know definitively what Paul's eschatology, soteriology, and ethic were — a full discussion of which would require respective monographs (after framing) — to be suspicious that the previous configuration of the data is too selective and somewhat oversimplified. Its omissions and simplistic assertions create a stark picture of difference and apparent incompatibility between the two sets of texts. More accurate presentations of the specific data, however, suggest a more complex set of views in Paul that overlap significantly across all the letters currently in play. A more nuanced reading of the data suggests, in short, that there is little or no evident incompatibility. The resurrected and ascended Christ is present in the lives of believers in Paul's undisputed letters (a view supported by a reasonable construal of the Corinthian data); and the future, coming Christ is present in Colossians. Any further differences between the letters can then be plausibly ascribed to contingency.

Excursus

The risen Christ is present in the two major undisputed letters to which Ehrman appeals for Paul's futurist eschatological views — Romans and 1 Corinthians. The ascended Christ, who is seated at the right hand of God, intercedes for suffering believers in Romans 8:34, a claim that develops the analysis of divine prayer for believers and creation in 8:22-23 and undergirds the famous claim in vv. 28-31 and vv. 36-39 that the divine benevolence is invincible. This location and its associated roles are noted at both the beginning and the end of the letter as well, in 1:4 and 14:10-12. And this last text reads like a cryptic summary of the ascended Christ's role in 1 Corinthians 15:24-28 — which resonates strongly in turn with Philippians 2:10-11 — in the final judgment and triumph of God (to which Rom 16:20a probably alludes as well).

But this living presence "on high" is complemented by an equally astonishing claim made throughout Romans and 1 Corinthians that Christians somehow live within this presence. Christians are, according to Paul, simply "in Christ" (a situation that can be spoken of reversibly; see Gal 2:20). So baptism, appropriately interpreted, speaks of the manner in which Christians have died and been resurrected in Christ (see Rom 6:1-11; 1 Cor 12:13; Gal 3:26-28). They are now clothed with Christ (Gal 3:27), and hence beyond the categories that might seem to structure their lives in any determinative fashion (Gal 3:28). Most importantly, it is this location that allows them to live beyond the flesh, which has been executed, and in the power of the Spirit (see also Rom 8:1-14), thereby undergirding Paul's controversial claims that the Christian ethic is beyond Torah.

Any suggestion, then, that Paul understands believers to be dead but not yet risen, and so living in some intermediate state, is misguided. This is not to suggest that everything has been resolved and Christians have been perfected. Clearly, Paul thinks that much has yet to happen. But his conceptualization of this broader situation is something we will address momentarily. Suffice it for now to note that if Christians are not presently living in some concrete sense within the resurrected and ascended Christ — most obviously, by way of the Spirit — then all of Paul's central theological claims collapse.

Complementing this realization concerning the present force of the resurrection and ascension in the undisputed letters, we ought to note that any claims concerning Paul's theology are dubiously buttressed by strong claims concerning the error at Corinth he combats in 1 Corinthians 15. The Corinthian situation was inordinately complex, and its reconstruction is fraught with difficulty — the limitations in the data, the perils of mirror reading, and so on.[43] It is rather more plausible to proceed from Paul's argument (here in 1 Cor 15) *to* the Corinthian error rather than vice versa. And that argument again seems premised significantly on the living Christ. Admittedly, some of its orientation is future. But earlier arguments in the letter suggest that the future grammar of this discussion is often argumentative, not temporal (see esp. vv. 22 and 49). So, for example, Paul's anguish over the Corinthian use of prostitutes in 6:9-19 is premised not just on future accountability but on the present unity of the Corinthians' bodies with Christ's by way of the Spirit (see also 3:16-17). This understanding of bodiliness is then extended significantly in chapters 11 and 12 when Paul addresses abuses within the worship service. In the midst of this extended and subtle set of contentions, the present unity between Christians as members of the body of Christ is entirely concrete; if it is not, Paul's arguments (again) collapse. This all suggests that 1 Corinthians is deeply committed, at least in some sense, to the presence of the resurrected Christ within the lives of believers.

And with these realizations concerning the data in Romans and 1 Corinthians (not to mention in parts of Philippians and Galatians), the arguments of Colossians no longer look so incompatible. Rather, they seem to be contingent variations on much the same set of basic convictions concerning eschatology, soteriology, and ethics.

The resurrected and ascended Christ is obviously important in Colossians (1:18; 3:1), as Ehrman notes, but equally clearly, Christians presently die and rise in him; it is this that leads to their freedom from the need for bodily circumcision in 2:11-13 (see esp. 2:12a: συνταφέντες αὐτῷ ἐν τῷ βαπτισμῷ). And this looks like (i.a.) the depiction of baptism in Romans 6:1-11 and the arguments against prostitution and liturgical disruption in 1 Corinthians 6 and 11–12. Still more significantly, the baptized are told in Colossians 3:2-4 to wait in some sense for their perfection ([2] τὰ ἄνω φρονεῖτε, μὴ τὰ ἐπὶ τῆς γῆς [3] ἀπεθάνετε γὰρ καὶ ἡ ζωὴ ὑμῶν κέκρυπται σὺν τῷ Χριστῷ ἐν τῷ θεῷ [4] ὅταν ὁ Χριστὸς φανερωθῇ, ἡ ζωὴ ὑμῶν, τότε καὶ ὑμεῖς σὺν αὐτῷ φανερωθήσεσθε ἐν δόξῃ). So Colossians is still to some degree "futurist." And it is only fair to note that the question of imminence is never addressed in Colossians — the Colossians apparently never having asked Paul for instructions concerning the timing of the *parousia*. So we might ask whether the eschatological scenario adumbrated in part by 1 and 2 Thessalo-

---

43. The hypothesis that a principal problem facing Paul at Corinth was "overrealized eschatology" is increasingly unpopular currently, although it has an able recent defender in Thiselton (2000). Against this, see (i.a.) Wright (2003, esp. 277-374).

nians is incompatible with anything said in Colossians. Could the Colossians not have held those views without difficulty while adhering to everything that was taught in this letter? It seems possible.

Thus, it is apparent that the actual configurations of the data from various Pauline texts used by Ehrman to create a case for the pseudonymity of Colossians on the basis of conceptual incompatibility are dubious (or at least questionable). A more careful reading of the argumentation in parts of Romans, 1 Corinthians, and Colossians, assisted by relevant fragments from Philippians and Galatians, suggests that these texts all plausibly draw from the same basic conceptual configuration, differing from one another only by way of circumstantial emphasis. And Ehrman's case for pseudonymity in these terms consequently deflates. Even granting the validity of an argument in terms of conceptual incompatibility, none is really apparent. Indeed, if anything, the plausibility of including Colossians within the authentic Pauline sample seems enhanced.

Before moving on, one final observation on this type of case might be useful.

(iii) Ehrman's case concerning different ostensible soteriologies and eschatologies in both the undisputed Paul and Colossians rests in part on the application of zero-sum relationships to salvation in terms of being and time. And these assumptions are worth querying.

That is, Ehrman assumes that the relationship within Christians between a present, difficult state, which Paul refers to as "in Adam," and a liberated, joyful state, which Paul refers to as "in Christ," operates in a zero-sum, or essentially quantitative, manner. And in the case of quantities, people can experience more of one only as they experience less of the other. To be in Adam is also, to the equivalent inverse degree, to be lacking Christ, and to be in Christ is to be, to the same inverse proportion, lacking and beyond Adam. Hence, it is almost as if non-Christians are 100 percent Adamic. When Christ comes and converts them, a part of them is now located in him, but because they are still Adamic to some degree, they still lack Christ to some degree. So we could speak of Christians being, say, 50 percent still Adamic and 50 percent in Christ. This is apparently helpful, because the present weakness and difficulties of Christians can be understood in terms of the Adamic material that lingers. And future expectations of Paul can be understood in terms of the elimination of the remaining Adamic elements and the arrival of Christ in fullness, at which point Christians will presumably be 100 percent in Christ. Everything Adamic will have been eliminated. (There is a further assumption operative here in terms of time, but addressing the ontological conceptualization in terms of space and quantity will be more than enough to deal with for now.)[44]

It is in part this conceptuality that allows Ehrman and others arguing as he does to play certain claims in the Pauline texts off against one another.

An initial emphasis on texts proclaiming the future coming of Christ and his resolution at that time of any cosmic struggles and problems suggests in quantitative terms that Christians *must* presently be living in a mixed condition characterized by the ongoing presence of a significant percentage of Adamic material, so to speak. If fullness and perfection lie ahead, then they cannot be present now. And any ongoing emphases on sin or struggles would seem to affirm this view. So texts drawn from any letters emphasizing the perfections inaugurated by the *parousia* will set up "mixed" expectations concerning the present state of Christians.

The citation of fulfillment texts from other letters will then create an apparent problem. Any emphases on the effectiveness of the resurrected and living Christ within the lives of believers in the present will tilt the perceived quantities in a stronger Christian direction. Instead of a strongly mixed condition, then, perhaps 50 percent Adamic and 50 percent Christ, such texts suggest a balance strongly tilted toward Christ and perhaps even completely so. Christians are 90 percent or even 100 percent Christ, and hence presumably only to this degree dwelling in Adam. (Perhaps they are only 10 percent Adam or even 0 percent Adam.) And this condition clearly creates interpretative tensions with future texts, and with data concerning early Christian sinfulness. It is immediately apparent that Adam is alive and well in both Paul and his recipients in these texts. Hence, any such ludicrous perfectionism is best attributed to later church movements known for their overly high estimation of their own sinlessness — various Gnostics and the like.

Ehrman presupposes this quantitative analogy and utilizes the resulting difficulties when he builds his case against Colossians in terms of incompatibility. He emphasizes the future nature of certain undisputed texts — of 1 Corinthians and the like. (First Thessalonians lies in the background of his case here, too.) And he emphasizes the absence of the resurrected Christ from the present lives of Christians even in Romans — as he must. This move is supported, as we have seen, by an

44. See esp. T. F. Torrance (1976; 1986).

appeal to the Corinthian situation. Paul is said there to be resisting the Corinthians' endorsement of the present resurrected Christ in their lives, because this would not be mixed enough; they would be embracing a foolish perfectionism. The present Christian condition, according to these undisputed letters, is characterized by a decidedly mixed ontology. A significant percentage of Adamic material remains, and Christians will receive a decisive dose of Christ only after Christ returns sometime in the future. They are presently 50/50 Christians, and possibly not even that.

Ehrman then turns to Colossians and emphasizes the ascended Christ. This Christ is clearly present to the church in power and glory "now," so he is not, for this reason, future. Ehrman also emphasizes the present resurrected state of Christians in Colossians. And these emphases create a very different picture of the underlying Christian situation if they are interpreted quantitatively. The author of Colossians is not looking forward especially strongly to some future infusion of Christian being; it is here already. The Christians presupposed by Colossians, then, are 10/90 Christians, or perhaps even 0/100, and seem as a result to be very different from the benighted 50/50 Christians presupposed by (Ehrman's account of) the undisputed letters. The two depictions seem, in short, to be incompatible.

What are we to make of this case when it is understood in these terms — with its key ontological assumption identified? A little ironically, it is now apparent that Ehrman's case rests in part on a presupposition that is probably anachronistic.

It is, in the first instance, just an assumption — specifically, that a certain metaphor or analogy that seems self-evident for basic physical quantities and their interactions (although it does not actually hold good even there) applies to divine action on humanity. But we do not need to make this prior decision and go on to support its reductionist interpretative consequences.[45]

Besides being reductionist and unsupported, this assumption also seems characteristically Western and hence quite possibly anachronistic. These spatial and mutually exclusive perceptions of states are familiar to the intellectual traditions of western Europe, but Paul was not an

---

45. That is, unless a prior decision has been made that all historical causality is immanent, and consequently that everything Paul writes about is untrue in the terms in which he understood them. See Kerr's (2009) useful explication and critique of Troeltsch.

inhabitant of these traditions, many of which built up after his epochal period and within the Latin-speaking church, however anomalously. In direct complement to this concern, properly *theological* categories, drawing on the reflections of Nicene orthodoxy, tend to contradict this assumption. Divine-human interactions must in the first instance be understood self-interpretatively, and emphatically not by way of analogy with creation; the latter is one of the mistakes that an emphasis on divine transcendence is supposed to guard against. Moreover, any divine self-interpretation begins by affirming the full mutual indwelling of quite distinct realities — three persons in one God; a God fully present in a person; and so on. This is not necessarily to affirm the truth of those claims but merely to note that completely different ontological assumptions are possible that eliminate the difficulties generated by Ehrman's application of crude spatial analogies to Paul's texts — although those assumptions are more in tune with the central commitments of the church.[46] However, it might be easier to appreciate these objections if we simply switch metaphors.

Rather than thinking of ontologies in terms of mutually exclusive spaces, it might be helpful to think in sonic or musical terms and of ontologies as sounds or musical discourses. So we can conceptualize an Adamic ontology present within humanity as a particular piece of music, perhaps playing loudly and somewhat discordantly. And any ontology present in relation to Christ can be thought of as a completely different piece of music, perhaps playing in a captivating and melodic fashion. It is immediately clear that both discourses can be fully present in Christians, occupying the same human space, at exactly the same time. If we play two pieces of music on the opposite sides of a room, there is no place in that room where the two pieces of music are not both penetrating — although which one is *dominant* depends on which one is being played with the highest volume. But irrespective of whether we can hear both pieces of music, both are fully present.[47]

If Paul's ontological categories are best understood sonically and musically and not visually and spatially, then all of the "incompatibilities" enumerated by Ehrman — even granting both the legitimacy of the coordination at this analytic stage and the characterization of the data — disappear.

46. T. F. Torrance (1986); see also Zizioulas (1985).
47. See esp. Begbie (2013, 141-75).

This analysis should be sufficient to indicate how cases for pseudonymity in substantial terms like Ehrman's are problematic. His claim that a fundamental incompatibility is observable between the eschatological material in the undisputed letters and Colossians is a methodologically invalid argument during preliminary framing; it rests on a series of oversimplifications of the data; and it presupposes an anachronistic and arguably false analogy concerning the ontologies involved (which map, we should recall, interactions between the human and the divine).

It follows that claims of substantive incompatibility in any other terms — concerning the *Haustafeln,* the developments of bodiliness, the role of the assembly — should probably be rejected as well. These claims too are methodologically inadmissible, and they tend to rest on selective interpretations of the data in question.[48]

With these realizations, it can be seen that the last significant element

48. It is unlikely that the brief and generic instance of the *Haustafeln* in Col 3:18–4:1 is incompatible with Paul's advice in 1 Cor regarding various questions of gender and sexuality. Prolonged engagement with these texts has convinced me, rather, that such is the inevitable complication and qualification that takes place when simple binary accounts supposedly structuring social realities encounter those realities on the ground. Actual social reality is rather too complex to be susceptible to straightforward binary ordering. Paul's navigation of these tensions is apparent in Horrell's (2005) important treatment.

Arguments against the authenticity of Col in terms of bodiliness suffer from the basic difficulty that they must comprehend a complex discourse in Paul that is utilized in quite diverse ways rhetorically yet must argue nevertheless that certain elements are nonnegotiable and other developments are inadmissible — an implausible undertaking. One such argument, although richly informative in other respects, is Dawes (1998). A lively postmodern treatment of Paul's engagement with bodiliness at Corinth is D. Martin (1995; and parts of his later collection, 2006, are also informative for this question). On the discourse within early Christianity in general, see the classic account of P. Brown (2008 [1988]). General Jewish and NT background can be found in Wright (2003) within the broader context of a treatment of eschatology. A more recent, controversial analysis is Engberg-Pedersen (2010).

The treatment of the assembly (i.e., ἡ ἐκκλησία) in Col is also arguably in tension with the motif's treatment in the undisputed letters. However, it can simply be granted that the instances in 1:18 and 24 are different, being rather more universal than the signifier's occurrences elsewhere (including in Col 4:15 and 16). The universal sense apparent in Col 1 is probably evocative of the *qahal Israel,* that is, the assembly of Israel, which could also have eschatological connotations. But this signification in Col 1 is not necessarily incompatible with Pauline thinking if Paul in Col is citing an early church hymn or confession in 1:15-20, as many scholars have supposed, and then utilizing the theology of that confession in its immediate context. Moreover, in both 1:18 and 1:24 the notion of "assembly" is overtly qualified by the notion of "body," which is, as we have just seen, an important Pauline discourse. So this data is hardly fatal to Col's authenticity.

within the case for the pseudonymity of Colossians has collapsed. We should turn, then, to our final judgment — bearing in mind that all judgments made during preliminary framing are provisional.

2.5 Judgment and Further Implications

It will be apparent by this stage in our discussion that Colossians fits well into both its own implicit exigence and our developing frame, augmenting the latter in intriguing ways. It reinforces the hints in Philemon that Paul was imprisoned in Asia near the Lycus valley, in 50 CE, most probably a few days' travel to the east of Colossae and hence possibly in Apamea. Moreover, all the usual charges against the authenticity of Colossians have largely wilted under cross-examination — that is, assertions that the text contains small, telltale errors of fact; that its style is unacceptably distinctive; that the teaching it opposes is anachronistic; and that some of its substantive positions, especially in terms of eschatology and soteriology, are incompatible with what we know of Paul from his undisputed letters (even conceding the admissibility of this last type of argument). Indeed, the cumulatively increasing strength of the letter's apparent authenticity — at this preliminary stage in the historical reconstruction of Paul, framing his basic story — has been rather surprising. It remains only to add that later investigation into the original Pauline letter collection, insofar as we can determine its contents with any certainty, will marginally corroborate this judgment, although this determination is most profitably undertaken at the end of the next chapter.

If Colossians is judged authentic, taking our group of authentic letters to nine, then what are the implications for framing? The main consequences have already been introduced, but some broader implications have yet to be noted.

We should recall first that Philemon and Colossians were written during an Asian captivity, probably in Apamea (or, at least, somewhere like this), in the year previous to Paul's (calendar) year of crisis in 51, hence in 50 CE. We can infer, moreover, that Paul was eventually released from this imprisonment, his anticipation of this in Philemon 22 thus proving correct. (He was an experienced detainee.) He then almost certainly visited Colossae, Laodicea, and Hierapolis en route to Ephesus, since those settlements lay on the direct path to the Maeander valley and the road to both Miletus and the great Asian metropolis. And doubtless he spent some time in those small towns on the way, catechizing his new converts, along with any other pagans he could persuade to join them.

We cannot say at this point, however, just how long Paul worked in Ephesus over the winter or what events might have transpired to open a door but also to challenge his mission there. And we do not know what the front end of this entire sequence of events contained beyond Paul's important visits to Antioch and Jerusalem. The letters are silent here (i.e., we have none from this period). Behind this point in the frame, there is simply the long interval back to the Thessalonian correspondence, written in or after 40 CE. Furthermore, while we nurse suspicions that 1 and 2 Thessalonians were written relatively early within this long interval — say in 41 CE itself — we cannot yet confirm this with complete confidence. Beyond this, we know principally of only two specific events that fell into this window, although we know of several more general activities.[49]

Fragmentary epistolary evidence suggests that at some point between 40 and 50 Paul visited Corinth for a second time. His visit anticipated in 1 and 2 Corinthians, and unfolding when Galatians, Philippians, and Romans were written, was his third. And we could be forgiven for surmising a second visit to Thessalonica as well. There is no direct evidence of this, but it does seem likely given Paul's announced wishes in 1 Thessalonians 2:17-18 and 3:11, as well as the fact that of the regions he probably subsequently evangelized, three lay along the Ignatian Way, Illyricum being named specifically.

In fact, Paul's almost inadvertent claim in Romans (15:19) that he evangelized during this period "as far as Illyricum," hence up the eastern coast of the Adriatic Sea, is highly significant. It seems, in the light of this, that Paul evangelized quite distant regions during this interval, although apparently without much success. We have no evidence of any successful church plants in any other areas from this time (with the possible exception of data from Titus, but we are not considering that data yet). But we can still ask how far Paul seems to have reached in this long and apparently fruitless missionary work.

We have already calculated a rough estimate of the time that Paul spent in a given region on the basis of Galatians 1:17-18, that is, one to two years. If we suppose that Paul spent close to two years in Corinth as against one, given the complexity and success of the Achaian mission, this leaves 43-49 CE unaccounted for in specific terms, assuming the maximum possible extent of this

49. We *might* also want to infer the presence of a false teacher at Colossae. The hints in the text suggest to me (as we have already seen) the presence there of a third party. Moreover, it might be that further data about such a figure would allow us to decide more firmly about which of the options concerning the intrusive problematic teaching is actually correct — reversing here the usual flow of analysis. But this sort of result is one of the benefits we expect from sound preliminary framing.

temporal window for the sake of argument. (By the end of 49 or thereabouts he is visiting Antioch and Jerusalem.) And it follows that, moving at his fastest rate, Paul might have evangelized as many as seven regions during this time, one of those being Illyricum.

The regions within the Roman Empire that lie east of Illyricum and west of Jerusalem and Judea (i.e., west of Judea, Arabia/Nabataea, the Decapolis, Cilicia, and Syria; see Rom 15:19), included — enumerating west to east — Moesia, Thrace, Bithynia, Pontus, and Cappadocia. So, astonishing as it appears at first glance, it seems possible that Paul tried at some point to visit and to evangelize all of these regions — six in total, including Illyricum. Moving at his slower speed of two years per region, he could still have evangelized four, so, Illyricum, Moesia, Thrace, and Bithynia. But the slower rate probably held when the missions were successful, so we might think more in terms of the upper limit here of six areas. Moesia and Thrace were quite disturbed areas during the early 40s but might have seemed providentially ordered from around 44 CE onward.[50] However, perhaps we should not exclude the possibility of Paul working outside the borders of the Roman Empire periodically, most probably in Dacia (see esp. Col 3:11 and Rom 1:14). Moreover, Galatia could have been evangelized at this time as well. Whether Paul's Galatians were "ethnic" Galatians from the northern part of the province or provincial Galatians from the southern part (or both) is hard to say; neither option can be obviously excluded at this point from our developing frame. Paul's most relevant terminology seems to be *klimatic* or regional, potentially denoting areas larger than (Rom 15:23), equal to (2 Cor 11:10), or smaller than (Gal 1:21) provinces, hence encompassing any of the foregoing options. Acts might eventually help us here, but that intervention must wait. In the meantime, fortunately, not a great deal changes in specific terms in relation to any of these options. We simply cannot envisage where Paul's Galatian addressees were in absolutely precise terms — whether located on the main northern east-west route from Syria across what is now Turkey, on the southern east-west route, or scattered across both (see Syme 1995).[51] And Paul's remark in 2 Corinthians 11:25 now becomes especially pertinent.

50. See Wilkes in Bowman, Champlin, and Lintott (1996, 545-85).

51. That Paul's designations "Galatia"/"Galatians" (Gal 1:2; 3:1; see also 1 Cor 16:1; also Acts 16:6; 18:23; 2 Tim 4:10; 1 Pet 1:1) could denote all these options has been incontrovertible since Stephen Mitchell (1995; summarized and presaged in his 1992). The advocacy of a "south Galatian," i.e., provincial, provenance for Gal goes back largely to the work of William Ramsay in the late 1800s, which established it as a possibility (see R. Longenecker 1990, lxi-lxxii, esp. lxiii, lxvi-lxvii). As I have suggested earlier, however, in ch. 3, this debate is largely generated

There he writes, τρὶς ἐραβδίσθην, ἅπαξ ἐλιθάσθην, τρὶς ἐναυάγησα, νυχθήμερον ἐν τῷ βυθῷ πεποίηκα.[52] Paul implicitly but obviously affirms here a great deal of travel, and especially of sea travel, much of it apparently at inauspicious times of the year. But this remark nicely confirms the implications of the regional data just noted concerning Paul's activities during this interval. Paul was traveling, as much as he could, by sea, this being by far the easiest and fastest way to travel at the time, although not without risks. And we must envisage him traveling enough to be shipwrecked three times during this period.[53] Furthermore, it is clearly not unreasonable to suppose that from 43 to 49 CE he covered a great deal of ground. Hence, his remarks and implications concerning regional missionary work and his remarks concerning travel confirm one another — and Romans 15:19b now makes rather more sense than is often thought, in what might be a final flourish of confirmation (ὥστε με ἀπὸ Ἰερουσαλὴμ καὶ κύκλῳ μέχρι τοῦ Ἰλλυρικοῦ πεπληρωκέναι τὸ εὐαγγέλιον τοῦ Χριστοῦ). Paul really had evangelized all the areas around the Mediterranean between the two points of Jerusalem and Illyricum.

But Paul also details a series of official punishments near his travel text,

---

by the need to integrate data from Acts with data from the letters. When faced with letter data alone, Ramsay, Mitchell, and those like them have established that a provincial provenance for Gal is possible as against the more traditional northern, ethnic provenance. But I know of no epistolary data allowing a decisive judgment between them. So, for example, any appeals to "biographical markers" like the prominence of Barnabas in Gal (see 2:1, 9, 13) presuppose appeals to data from Acts and so for now must be set to one side (see Longenecker 1990, lxx-lxxii).

That Gal 4:13 implies a second visit by Paul to Galatia in the interim, i.e., prior to the composition of Gal, and as suggested also by 1 Cor 16:1, does seem likely in our reconstruction: "You know that I proclaimed the good news to you formerly / the first time [I was with you] because of a bodily weakness [i.e., an illness]" (οἴδατε δὲ ὅτι δι᾽ ἀσθένειαν τῆς σαρκὸς εὐηγγελισάμην ὑμῖν τὸ πρότερον). Certainly, there is no need to resist this implication; rather, the developing frame suggests it. Paul is in Corinth when he composes Gal. He seems to have founded the Galatian communities some time ago — at least prior to the start of the Asian mission. Since then he has journeyed to Syrian Antioch and Jerusalem and returned to the Aegean by way of Galatia, leaving oral instructions about the collection. The implications of 4:13 dovetail with this reconstruction exactly. Moreover, the use of the expression τὸ πρότερον in 4:13 seems redundant otherwise. This observation will have an influence on our later processing of Acts data, however slight.

52. 2 Cor 11:26 is also suggestive: ὁδοιπορίαις πολλάκις, κινδύνοις ποταμῶν, κινδύνοις λῃστῶν, κινδύνοις ἐκ γένους, κινδύνοις ἐξ ἐθνῶν, κινδύνοις ἐν πόλει, κινδύνοις ἐν ἐρημίᾳ, κινδύνοις ἐν θαλάσσῃ. These denote, in the main, the quite considerable challenges of ancient travel.

53. On this dimension within the Mediterranean Sea's ancient history, see esp. Horden and Purcell (2000).

which are worth considering again (see 2 Cor 11:24: Ὑπὸ Ἰουδαίων πεντάκις τεσσεράκοντα παρὰ μίαν ἔλαβον [25] τρὶς ἐραβδίσθην, ἅπαξ ἐλιθάσθην κ.τ.λ.). Almost all of these would have presupposed an arrest and probable period of detention prior to trial and sentencing. And this seems to confirm the plausibility of the Asian imprisonment presupposed by Philemon and Colossians. Indeed, if Paul visited six more large regions during this period, including Illyricum, and experienced only three of his five synagogual whippings and two of his three beatings with rods, he could still have been punished officially in some way in almost every one of these regions. He was a troublemaker, or at least frequently perceived to be one.

In short, the "years of shadow," as I call them, that fall between the details of the frame discernible in the late 30s and early 40s CE and the details that come into view from 50 CE onward should be filled out with these inferences. It is frustrating that we do not know more about this period, but we do not know *nothing*. Moreover, the hints that we do have nicely confirm the scenario developed from this chapter's analysis of Philemon and Colossians — extensive travel, frequent incarceration, and evangelistic struggle, Paul's preferred term for this activity being "weakness," or perhaps better, "vulnerability" (ἀσθένεια).

We should now augment our developing frame in the following terms.

> . . . mission to Achaia . . .
>
> // 43- //
>
> . . . second visit to Thessalonica . . .
>
> . . . mission to Illyricum . . .[54]
>
> . . . mission to Moesia . . .
>
> . . . mission to Thrace . . .
>
> . . . mission to Bithynia . . .
>
> . . . mission to Galatia? . . .
>
> . . . mission to Pontus . . .
>
> . . . mission to Cappadocia . . .
>
> . . . second visit to Corinth . . .
>
> // -49 //
>
> . . . Antioch incident — second visit to Jerusalem[55] —
>
> // 50 //

54. The following missions would not necessarily have been in this order, although they should pivot around the Macedonian cities plausibly.

55. These events might have taken place early in 50 CE as against late in 49.

mission to Asia begins — imprisonment[56] — Phlm / Col —
visit to Colossae[57] — visit/s to Laodicea/Hierapolis[58] — visit to Ephesus[59] . . .
// 51 //

And with these further framing implications noted, we can turn finally to consider the location and authenticity of Ephesians.

3. Locating "Ephesians"

3.1 The Immediate Implied Exigence

If doubts have not arisen by this stage in our broader analysis concerning Paul's authorship of a letter, they will almost certainly arise now. Paul's letter to the Ephesians, as it is usually known, has numerous features that at first glance trouble any judgment of authenticity. Its instructions are highly generalized and even abstract; few if any specific details or problems are apparent in relation to a particular community. Coupled with this, the style of the letter, whether judged grandiose or ponderous, seems quite distinctive. Various substantive emphases are distinctive as well — most famously, a sustained emphasis on the Christian community usually articulated in terms of "the church." The letter consequently seems to belong to a later, calmer, more ecclesial era than to that of Paul's gritty struggles with small groups of people, many of whom could be named if necessary. Hence, a judgment of pseudonymity is invited quite quickly. However, certain similarities between Ephesians and Romans should probably give us pause.

While the opening and closing of Romans contain a great deal of particular information (not unlike Col 4:7-17), the letter body is similar in style and

---

56. Most likely in Apamea, and more certainly, east of Colossae but west of any town with a successful Galatian congregation. The proxy evangelization of Colossae by Epaphras takes place at this time.

57. First personal visit by Paul to Colossae after his anticipated release (Phlm 22), but not a founding visit in this unusual case.

58. Conflating Paul's contact with Laodicea and Hierapolis, since Col 4:13, 15, and 16 seem to suggest this.

59. We do not know whether this was Paul's first visit to Ephesus, although it is the first one for which we have direct evidence from his letters. More significantly, we do not know whether he then founded the church at Ephesus or whether a successful mission was already underway under the leadership (presumably) of Prisca and Aquila (see 1 Cor 16:19; also Rom 16:3-5a).

generality to Ephesians. We find a series of carefully crafted units that seem
to have little direct contextual relevance or specificity. But I would suggest
that Romans had a highly practical and specific exigence for which its sets
of generalized discussions proved necessary — the pending arrival at Rome
of the Teacher with his sophisticated Judaizing agenda. This necessitated an
extended, somewhat generalized response by letter from Paul, hence Romans.
The question here will be whether a plausible particular exigence can explain
the composition and dispatch of Ephesians in similar terms. That is, we will
here, as usual, assume authenticity at first and see whether any developing
hypothesis in these terms breaks down under close scrutiny.

We should note immediately that the text of Ephesians presents itself
as grounded in some particular Christian community or sequence of congregations, because it expects Tychicus to bear the letter, to explain it, and
to model Paul's *ethos* and ministry (see 6:21:Ἵνα . . . εἰδῆτε καὶ ὑμεῖς τὰ κατ'
ἐμέ, τί πράσσω, πάντα γνωρίσει ὑμῖν Τύχικος ὁ ἀγαπητὸς ἀδελφὸς καὶ πιστὸς
διάκονος ἐν κυρίῳ). He will also bring news of "us" and encourage the letter's
recipients (so 6:22: ὃν ἔπεμψα πρὸς ὑμᾶς εἰς αὐτὸ τοῦτο, ἵνα γνῶτε τὰ περὶ
ἡμῶν καὶ παρακαλέσῃ τὰς καρδίας ὑμῶν). So a specific arrival by the letter's
bearer and interpreter, Tychicus, is articulated, in relation to specific recipients
and from a specific sender. But whom was he actually supposed to visit? Can
a plausible account of the letter's recipients be found in the text?

We would ordinarily expect these sorts of details to be provided first in
an ancient letter's prescript, and that is the case here in Ephesians, although
we now step into murky waters. Identifying the addressees in Ephesians is
complicated by a set of textual variations. Yet there is no way forward without
engaging with this question. Nestlé-Aland[27] provides most of the necessary
data; five variations must initially be considered.

1. τοῖς ἁγίοις τοῖς οὖσιν ἐν Λαοδικείᾳ καὶ πιστοῖς ἐν Χριστῷ Ἰησοῦ . . .[60]
2. τοῖς ἁγίοις οὖσιν καὶ πιστοῖς ἐν Χριστῷ Ἰησοῦ . . .[61]
3. τοῖς ἁγίοις τοῖς οὖσιν καὶ πιστοῖς ἐν Χριστῷ Ἰησοῦ . . .[62]
4. τοῖς ἁγίοις τοῖς οὖσιν ἐν Ἐφέσῳ καὶ πιστοῖς ἐν Χριστῷ Ἰησοῦ . . .[63]
5. τοῖς ἁγίοις πᾶσιν τοῖς οὖσιν ἐν Ἐφέσῳ καὶ πιστοῖς ἐν Χριστῷ Ἰησοῦ . . .[64]

60. Marcion; see also Col 1:2a: τοῖς ἐν Κολοσσαῖς ἁγίοις καὶ πιστοῖς ἀδελφοῖς ἐν Χριστῷ.
61. p[46].
62. a*, B*, 6, 1739 [see p[46]].
63. B[2], D, F, G, Ψ, 0278, 33, 1881, latt, sy, co.
64. a[2], A, P, 81, 326, 629, 2464.

It can be seen immediately from this tabulation that the case for the letter's Ephesian addressees is rather weak. The main uncials, p⁴⁶, and the earliest traceable patristic comments are all against this identification. It cannot be attested in the manuscript tradition before the fifth century, although Tertullian protests in its behalf at the beginning of the third. Corroborating a suspicion of later emendation, many of its witnesses seem to have harmonized the addressees further in the light of Romans 1:7 (πᾶσιν τοῖς οὖσιν ἐν Ῥώμῃ ἀγαπητοῖς θεοῦ, κλητοῖς ἁγίοις . . .). So an Ephesian address should be tabled initially in favor of variations 1, 2, and 3.

But in variant 2 the sole witness, p⁴⁶, has apparently, somewhat typically, made a mistake and elided the article (although not much turns on this). And this reduces the variants essentially to two: one with a Laodicean address — 1 — and one lacking a specific address altogether — 3, supported to a degree by 2. A decision between them is not that difficult, however, at least at this stage in our analysis, with the authenticity of Ephesians being assumed. Paul uses a participle of being on four other occasions in his prescripts, and they are invariably both arthrous (here speaking against p⁴⁶ and variant 2) and possess a local geographical object.

Rom 1:7: πᾶσιν τοῖς **οὖσιν ἐν Ῥώμῃ** ἀγαπητοῖς θεοῦ, κλητοῖς ἁγίοις. . . .

1 Cor 1:2: τῇ ἐκκλησίᾳ τοῦ θεοῦ τῇ **οὔσῃ ἐν Κορίνθῳ**, ἡγιασμένοις ἐν Χριστῷ Ἰησοῦ, κλητοῖς ἁγίοις, σὺν πᾶσιν τοῖς ἐπικαλουμένοις τὸ ὄνομα τοῦ κυρίου ἡμῶν Ἰησοῦ Χριστοῦ ἐν παντὶ τόπῳ, αὐτῶν καὶ ἡμῶν. . . .

2 Cor 1:1b: τῇ ἐκκλησίᾳ τοῦ θεοῦ τῇ **οὔσῃ ἐν Κορίνθῳ** σὺν τοῖς ἁγίοις πᾶσιν τοῖς οὖσιν ἐν ὅλῃ τῇ Ἀχαΐᾳ. . . .

Phil 1:1b: τοῖς ἁγίοις ἐν Χριστῷ Ἰησοῦ τοῖς **οὖσιν ἐν Φιλίπποις** σὺν ἐπισκόποις καὶ διακόνοις. . . .

So, as Lincoln (1990, 3) observes, the construction in Ephesians 1:1b "demands a subsequent geographical location," and we should try to supply one, thereby avoiding the odd situation of a general address created with an unnecessary participle of being. But we are in the happy position of having such a location supplied in what is easily our earliest attested variant by way of Marcion, and so, at the latest, deriving from the mid-second century — namely, Laodicea.⁶⁵

---

65. Marcion's address is triply attested — by Tertullian and Epiphanius, as often noted

Moreover, we can even go on to offer a plausible explanation for the elimination of this address in the next phase of scribal work as Paul's letters were transmitted. It could well have been thought inappropriate that an apostolic letter should address a church that the book of Revelation exposed later to be such an abject failure (see Rev. 3:15-18 in the context of 3:14-22 — Harnack's view, which I find plausible; the much later insertion of Ephesus into the address might then be attributable to the influence of Rev as well [see the glowing account of the Ephesian church in Rev. 2:1-7] or might have been an inference from 2 Tim, as Van Kooten [2003, 199] suggests). Alternatively, this emphatically ecclesial letter could simply have been generalized, as Romans was.

Irrespective of the exact reasons for its later modifications, it is difficult to object cogently to an original address in terms of variant 1.[66] And so we will proceed for the time being on the assumption that the original addressees of our canonical Ephesians were actually the Laodiceans, and will consequently refer from this point onward to canonical Ephesians as Laodiceans (or, alternatively, as "Ephesians," thereby indicating the improbability of this address).[67] And with this initial judgment in place, we need to consider what information Laodiceans gives us about its recipients besides their location in the ancient town of Laodicea, which lay in the mouth of the Lycus valley astride an important crossroads. Does this specific address help us interpret the letter plausibly in contingent terms, or is it a crafty fiction?

According to the letter, its addressees do not seem to have known Paul personally when it was composed. Laodiceans 3:2 suggests that they had only

---

(and in both figures several times), but also by Theodoret of Cyrrhus (ca. 393-466 CE; *Interpretatio XIV epistolarum sancti Pauli apostoli* 82.625C). Full references and quotations of the key claims can be found in Van Kooten (2003, 198 n. 79).

66. Lincoln (1990, 3) resists this final simple solution, but on unconvincing grounds, suggesting that the text is unacceptably awkward because of its syllepsis or zeugma. But he overlooks the decisive relevance of Col 1:2 at this point, which contains almost exactly the same syntax. Hence, Eph 1:1b might not be elegant Greek, but it is certainly acceptable — and rather more so than the introduction of an unattested and more complicated conjectured text. Best (1979; 1982; 1987; 1998) has mounted a vigorous and important campaign in behalf of an original generalized address, but Lincoln (1990, 3) rightly repudiates this on the grounds of its overly complex and unattested early steps in the manuscript tradition. Fortunately, no such steps need to be posited for a Laodicean address.

67. This judgment is rare but not altogether unheralded in previous scholarship; see e.g. BeDuhn 2013, 224, esp. n. 76, 252, 309. Rutherford makes the case tidily (1907/1908). And Coneybeare and Howson — who concur — note the earlier agreement of Paley, although the former combine this view with Usscher's suggestion that a circular letter to Asia based on Laod was sent simultaneously, and this led to the MSS confusion (1878, 812-16).

"heard" of his special benefaction for pagans — although arguably not to the depth and degree that Paul would have liked — and apparently, he had only "heard" of their faith and love in turn (1:15).[68] Paul's address throughout the letter is nevertheless highly consistent in general terms; the letter's addressees are identified as pagan converts in the specific sense of being Christian converts from paganism. In 2:11-12 this is especially clear: [2:11] Διὸ μνημονεύετε ὅτι ποτὲ ὑμεῖς τὰ ἔθνη ἐν σαρκί, οἱ λεγόμενοι ἀκροβυστία ὑπὸ τῆς λεγομένης περιτομῆς ἐν σαρκὶ χειροποιήτου, [12] ὅτι ἦτε τῷ καιρῷ ἐκείνῳ χωρὶς Χριστοῦ, ἀπηλλοτριωμένοι τῆς πολιτείας τοῦ Ἰσραὴλ καὶ ξένοι τῶν διαθηκῶν τῆς ἐπαγγελίας, ἐλπίδα μὴ ἔχοντες καὶ ἄθεοι ἐν τῷ κόσμῳ.

Hence, the addressees are never included by the text within Judaism, nor are they placed outside the Christian community within paganism proper at Paul's time of writing. Their construction in these terms is quite generic but consistent, although their inextricable relationship with Judaism is plainly in view as well, a matter to which we will later need to return.[69] Moreover, the letter supplies a persuasive reason for the lack of personal acquaintance between Paul and the Laodiceans.

Paul is currently incarcerated close by, something he mentions three times overtly (3:1, and see also 13; 4:1; 6:19-20). This is of course a plausible location for Paul when composing a letter. Of the nine letters currently judged authentic, three were written from an imprisonment. If Paul had been incarcerated prior to reaching Laodicea, then clearly the letter's recipients would not have known him personally, although they might have had some distant knowledge of his reputation. This is all fundamentally plausible.

And with these initial observations in place, we should attempt a slightly more detailed description of the letter's immediate implied exigence. Three further, particular, and quite significant dynamics discernible in the text need to be probed.

(1) The Definition of the Addressees' Identity

We do not know how the Laodiceans had converted, but as we just saw, they are defined by the letter consistently as converts from paganism. And that this

---

68. 1:15: Διὰ τοῦτο κἀγὼ ἀκούσας τὴν καθ' ὑμᾶς πίστιν ἐν τῷ κυρίῳ Ἰησοῦ καὶ τὴν ἀγάπην τὴν εἰς πάντας τοὺς ἁγίους κ.τ.λ.; 3:2: εἴ γε ἠκούσατε τὴν οἰκονομίαν τῆς χάριτος τοῦ θεοῦ τῆς δοθείσης μοι εἰς ὑμᾶς κ.τ.λ.

69. See esp. 2:11-19; 3:6; and, more implicitly, 4:4-6.

group of unknown etiology had converted is intriguing but not necessarily problematic. We know of other missionary work among pagans in addition to Paul's from his letters alone. The letter suggests that Paul had been imprisoned not far from these converts, before he had reached their town. So he had had no personal contact with them yet and no influence on their formation. However, technically these converts still fell under his apostolic jurisdiction; Paul was a recognized authority on pagan conversion (Gal 2:1-10, esp. 8-9), and certainly he would have viewed matters in this way. It seems to be this situation that creates the rather fascinating and distinctive exigence for Laodiceans.

Paul had a clear reason to shape the Christian existence of these unknown pagan converts in terms of his own missionary and apostolic agenda, that is, in terms of his coherence. The Laodicean converts knew none of this but clearly ought to have, in his view. This was their basic deficiency. But because of Paul's imprisonment, they would have to be instructed by letter in lieu of a personal visit. Hence, Paul composed Laodiceans — and thereby created a largely unparalleled situation for the modern interpreter. If this reconstruction holds good, then we would observe in Laodiceans as in no other epistolary situation (at least yet) a relatively straightforward account of Paul's missionary agenda in relation to pagan conversion — a presentation, he might say, of his gospel, and that Beker would define in terms of coherence. It was the existence of the mysterious Laodicean converts not far from Paul's incarceration that created this unusual rhetorical "space." We have encountered in this situation, essentially for the first time in our letter sequence thus far, a contingent reason for a largely coherent text. The letter to the Roman Christians would be the closest approximation, but those recipients had some Pauline converts among them and, moreover, were under threat from a third party, complicating any direct presentation of Paul's coherence. No such third party is evident in relation to Laodiceans.

This, then, is the fundamental explanation that the letter provides of its own immediate exigence, and it seems plausible, although certain pitfalls become apparent as we try to articulate it further.

Scholars have often suggested reductionist accounts of this coherence when Laodiceans presents a complex orchestration of themes and symbols. Alternatively, problematic and/or anachronistic organizations of this material have been suggested — for example, into doctrine and ethics. But fortunately, we do not need to press much further at this stage for the purposes of framing. It suffices for now to note that this exigence would have been filled rhetorically by Paul with what we might call an account of pagan Christian identity.

Admittedly, "identity" is a notion fraught with difficulty. It is contested, complex, and unstable.[70] But even admitting its important postmodern quali-fications, the notion that groups and their leaders engaged (and engage) in at-tempts to define themselves is plausible and arguably even ubiquitous. Suitably qualified, then, it seems fair to suggest, following some key hints in Lincoln, that Laodiceans constructs a pagan Christian identity — in Pauline terms! — for its Laodicean recipients.[71] But this account does not exhaust the letter's implications concerning its situation. We need now to note two further, less important but still significant aspects of its genesis.

(2) The Rhetorical Dimension

Paul's letter to the Laodiceans might well be the most straightforward account that we possess of his gospel as it constructs the identity of converts from pa-ganism, but it is not for this reason simply a coherent statement. It still sought to move a group from a location perceived to be deficient to one perceived to be better, that is, it still possessed rhetorical goals and strategies, and these need to be identified, although Laodiceans presents peculiar challenges in this regard. In the first instance, it seems that Paul himself did not know a great deal about the Laodiceans. Moreover, their lack of acquaintance with him, and possibly even lack of much knowledge of him, entailed that he could exert little or no leverage on them in terms of prior personal knowledge, relationship, and friendship. The letter itself had to establish an appropriate account of his au-thority, so this was a rhetorical goal rather than a point of rhetorical leverage. And second, we are one further step removed from this shadowy situation, lacking even Paul's sketchy knowledge of his recipients. We must therefore make certain assumptions about the letter's rhetoric and then qualify them heavily in terms of certitude.

Paul would probably have appealed to views that the Laodicean Chris-

70. Discussions that can usefully introduce some of the sociological and interpretative dynamics in play here are Esler (1987; 1994; 1998; 2003; 2005; with 1994, 1998, and 2003 focusing entirely on Pauline texts). Notions of identity must not be restricted to Henri Tajfel's account, in my view, nor should the interpretation of Rom be restricted to Esler's reading in terms of the creation of social identity (and, in particular, as Tajfel constructs this). It is interesting to contrast, even in this limited purview, the work of Horrell (see his 1996; 2005). (Esler and Horrell exchange views in Esler 2000a and Horrell 2000.) I make some remarks on questions of identity in Paul in 1996; 2005b; 2013.

71. So Lincoln helpfully suggests that, among other things, "the letter was intended to reinforce its readers' identity as participants in the Church" (1990, lxxxvi).

tians already held to build toward his own positions; he would presumably have sought to suggest that, correctly understood, some of their own existing commitments entailed ultimately a Pauline construction of their identity.[72] Moreover, he would probably have effected as much solidarity with those existing commitments as he could, affirming and reiterating them where that was possible. Hence, it would be unwise to understand any affirmations in merely propositional or cognitive terms, although the letter would have included those. The Laodiceans were, like all human groups, located within a set of existing practices (in their case, early Christian), so it is not surprising to find Laodiceans (at least arguably) echoing elements of early Christian worship — eulogy, doxology, songs, and prayers.

In short, then, insofar as Paul knew their views and was able either to build from or simply to affirm them, Laodiceans contains non-Pauline Christian material already assumed to be operative at Laodicea, which he is using as a rhetorical resource. We have little or no way of distinguishing this material from Paul's at present; this exercise must wait (at least) until framing. But we do need to take this dimension of Laodiceans into account when assessing it.

And with this realization about the probable presence of traditional early Christian material in Laodiceans, a second subordinate aspect of the situation now needs to be recognized.

(3) The Compositional Dynamics of Incarceration

If Paul was imprisoned for some time during the composition of Laodiceans — perhaps for a number of months — then several further aspects of the letter might need to be taken into account.

We have already noted that incarceration is often a fertile space for reflection and composition by literate activists (principally by affording time), yielding definitive work, provided that appropriate ways of preserving and disseminating it can be found. So King's "Letter from Birmingham Jail" was written initially on the margins of a newspaper and smuggled out of his cell in a shoe. It is salutary to note further that it was written in stages; other parts were composed on scraps of paper and on a pad used by his attorneys when visiting him, and the final letter was then edited together by someone else,

---

72. Certainly, this strategy is frequently discerned in Rom, often specifically in relation to 1:2-4; see my 2009 (esp. 634-36).

the Rev. Wyatt Walker, at the local campaign headquarters.[73] Consequently, we should note, first, that the letter to the Laodiceans could have been a deeply considered piece, worked over time and time again. We should not regard it as a manifesto or systematic summary per se; we have just seen that a practical exigence elicited its reflections. But Paul's incarceration entailed that these could have been highly considered reflections that were eventually committed to writing in Laodiceans. They also could have been largely oral/aural reflections in their initial stages, something we will need to consider further momentarily.

Second, Paul's incarceration might have restricted his knowledge about the Laodicean situation. We must therefore reckon with the possibility that he possessed very little information about his addressees, which might have generated in turn a certain blandness in his characterizations of them.

Third, Paul might then have filled out his reflections, as all people do, with material from his own emotional and conceptual situation.[74] This would not have been a matter of deliberate, subtle instructions for any *Nebenadressat* so much as the subliminal introduction of aspects of Paul's own context of imprisonment into the constructions of the text. We should be alert to these possibilities, and aware of their implications for any assessment of framing.

This, then, is the account that Laodiceans supplies of its immediate exigence. The letter suggests that the principal situation underlying its composition was created by the presence of a mysterious group of pagan converts at Laodicea and Paul's incarceration not far from them, along with his knowledge of their existence. Paul understandably wanted to shape this group's Christian identity in his own terms, and was forced to do so by letter. But in that letter it seems certain that as part of his broader rhetorical strategy he appealed to and affirmed their own existing Christian location to some degree, although just where and to what extent is difficult to determine; and he also likely subliminally projected aspects of his own incarceration into his highly reflective epistolary account of Christian identity. There is nothing immediately objectionable in this exigence, although it is atypical, but then most of Paul's letters have distinctive aspects to their exigencies. As usual, we will find this account either confirmed or denied as we turn to evaluate where Laodiceans might fit in these terms into our broader developing frame — but this is not a difficult judgment now that we have identified "Ephesians" as Laodiceans.

73. See Oates (1982, 222-30; also 342-43: "Letter from a Selma Jail").

74. Another point where recent advances in neuroscience and psychology prove useful. Gilbert (2005, esp. 83-105) introduces this phenomenon nicely.

318   FRAMING PAUL

3.2 Framing Considerations

Like the disciples at Jesus' last meal in Jerusalem, Paul's letter to the Laodiceans
already has a place prepared for it within our developing biographical framework. His letter to the Colossians notes its existence in 4:16b (. . . καὶ τὴν ἐκ
Λαοδικείας ἵνα καὶ ὑμεῖς ἀναγνῶτε), so it simply slots into our existing biography in this place without further ado. Moreover, this verse and two others
in Colossians confirm the prior existence of the Laodicean congregation (2:1;
4:15, 16a), along with their lack of any direct personal acquaintance with Paul
(see 2:1 in particular: Θέλω γὰρ ὑμᾶς εἰδέναι ἡλίκον ἀγῶνα ἔχω ὑπὲρ ὑμῶν καὶ
τῶν ἐν Λαοδικείᾳ καὶ ὅσοι οὐχ ἑόρακαν τὸ πρόσωπόν μου ἐν σαρκί). These are
important confirmations by Colossians of the key elements in the account that
the letter to the Laodiceans supplies of its immediate exigence: the existence
of the Laodicean converts, their lack of personal acquaintance with Paul, and
Paul's current incarceration close by.[75] The existence of Laodiceans alongside
Colossians and Philemon now deepens our understanding of the entire situation within which all these letters were composed in several interesting ways,
enriching our frame at this point.

First, Colossians in combination with Laodiceans suggests that what
was probably a more reflective situation had become characterized by some
urgency. The time pressure was generated by the arrival at Colossae of a problematic teaching, probably by way of an equally problematic third party, information that was conveyed to Paul by Onesimus. The situation was therefore
urgent at Colossae, necessitating the dispatch of a brief corrective letter. But
Colossae was not far from Laodicea and Hierapolis. So it would have become
apparent at this moment as well that the introduction of Paul's apostolic
agenda at Laodicea would potentially be confused and hindered if it reached
the Laodiceans after the teaching and/or evident third party at Colossae did.
Given the situation at Colossae, catalyzed for Paul by the arrival of Onesimus, it
followed that Paul's intervention at Laodicea by way of Laodiceans now needed
to be made as soon as possible. And certain relationships between the letters
seem discernible in the light of this new urgent exigence.

It seems likely that Laodiceans was *primarily* composed before Colossians (if of course it is authentic). The letter to the Colossians clearly responds
to the urgent exigence in that small town. And it seems unlikely that Paul

75. Data in Acts might arguably confirm this scenario in due course, although this
might not have become noticeable without the initial establishment of the scenario on epistolary grounds.

would have written it and then composed a highly crafted letter in the light of Colossians for the Laodiceans, to be sent with the same messenger, Tychicus — one apparently eliminating many of the specific references in Colossians to the approaching problematic teaching, despite its approach, but expanding elaborately on much else. Such dallying seems less likely than the reverse sequence.

Paul was probably crafting Laodiceans in a more leisurely manner, and then Onesimus interrupted its final dispatch with his urgent news. Paul then composed Colossians rather more quickly, apparently informed significantly by the composition he had just undertaken so carefully for the Laodiceans (and this economy is understandable within both an urgent and an incarcerated situation). But he clearly responded in Colossians as well to the specific information about the Colossian situation brought to him by Onesimus (see esp. the largely unique material in Col 2:8–3:4).[76] He then wrote Philemon, addressing Onesimus's particular difficulties, and sent all these letters off together with Tychicus. But before noting the challenges implicit within this reconstruction, we ought first to note some of its further helpful implications.

Reconstructed in this way, the situation entails that both Laodiceans and Colossians are now to some degree components *in a single extended epistolary event* and *at more than one location*. Paul is explicit in this regard in Colossians 4:16. The letter to the Colossians is to be read to the Colossians but then copied and sent to Laodicea; in this way, the specific teaching in Colossians addressing the problematic Colossian teacher will be heard by the Laodiceans and by Nympha's house gathering. Moreover, the letter to the Laodiceans is to be read to the Colossians (and presumably copied as well) so that they will benefit from its considered account of pagan Christian identity. Thus, the letter to the Colossians no longer addresses just the Colossians, its explicit recipients, but will address the audience of Laodiceans as well; and vice versa, the letter to the Laodiceans will address the audience of Colossians. (Phlm will not apparently be part of this exchange.) Paul is aware of this strategy and its intended results before he authors Colossians 4:16.

This important level of integration between the two main letters before us is confirmed by the phenomenon of the letter bearer. Tychicus is to carry all three letters to Colossae, and two onward to Laodicea and Hierapolis, bearing and reading out at least Colossians and Laodiceans in each location. Paul is clearly envisaging this process as well when he finishes Colossians. So we should not now think in overly discrete terms about the recipients of Colossians and Laodiceans, despite the named addressees. Because of the

---

76. This is usefully tabulated by Van Kooten (2003, 262-63).

peculiarly intertwined and urgent situation that elicited these letters, the Colossians heard Colossians *and Laodiceans* (and some of them, Phlm as well);
and the Laodiceans and Nympha's house gathering heard Laodiceans *and
Colossians*. It seems to me that these two phenomena — Paul's new strategy
of multiple letters and their delivery by way of a single visit from Tychicus
— now greatly complicate any precise assessment of dependence. Indeed,
the situation must now be understood in a rather more complex way than is
arguably often the case. (And it suggests a slightly different approach to any
commentary on these letters; isolating the letters risks producing artificial
historical-critical results.)

Although this reconstruction does envisage Laodiceans as coming first
in principal compositional terms, that does not necessarily entail that it was
completed first — an important distinction to grasp. The three letters being
sent with Tychicus would have received final readings and Paul's signatures
together, along with an explicit notation from Paul of at least two words in
Philemon 19 (ἐγὼ Παῦλος ἔγραψα τῇ ἐμῇ χειρί, ἐγὼ ἀποτίσω), and their dispatch would then have been simultaneous. Hence, that different copies of each
letter might have received final modifications and "tweaks" from Paul just prior
to their finalization cannot be ruled out; indeed, it seems likely. So while we
might assign a principal compositional priority to Laodiceans over Colossians,
we cannot assign an utterly unidirectional sequence in every respect. It seems
more likely that Laodiceans, Colossians, and Philemon were finally written up
by a scribe together, signed together by Paul, and then dispatched together with
Tychicus — to be read largely together on arrival. Fundamentally interactive
relationships therefore seem likely in the final stages of their composition,
despite the unidirectional nature of the initial composition of the main letters,
and that interaction would have begun with the arrival of Onesimus at Paul's
place of imprisonment. This does not entail that matters of dependence cannot be sorted out to some degree; indeed, any account of dependence should
be helped by these realizations. But it qualifies sharply any judgments based
on a rigidly unidirectional account of the causality between Laodiceans and
Colossians (and a further caveat will be introduced here shortly, in the next
subsection).

With this nuanced account in place concerning the probable compositional dependencies between the letters — of initial principal unidirectionality
making a transition into interactivity — we should turn to evaluate whether
this reconstruction can respond adequately to the serious challenges offered by
numerous scholars to the authenticity of "Ephesians." If "Ephesians" was in fact
Laodiceans, how might this affect its frequent designation as pseudonymous?

3.3 Challenges

It seems fair to claim at the outset that although the immediate implied exigence of Laodiceans is distinctive, it is not for this reason implausible in any respect, and one of its advantages is that the relationship of the letter to our developing frame is immediately indicated plausibly as well. It is the letter identified by Colossians 4:16 and consequently fits straightaway into a part of the frame that has already been developed and tested, both clarifying and complicating this locale in several ways. It is now time to place pressure on some of those complications. Any challenges here will tend to fall into the usual categories — concerns in terms of dependence (here especially noticeable), style, and substance, since simple anachronisms or other mistakes by a pseudepigrapher have not been identified decisively.

(1) Dependence

If the dependence of Laodiceans on Colossians could be demonstrated, then it should in my view be designated as pseudepigraphic and we should revert to calling it Ephesians, since it should no longer be identified with the letter described in Colossians as being written simultaneously to Laodicea. We have already noted how unlikely it would have been for Paul, in a situation of some urgency occasioned by the arrival of Onesimus, to have composed this rather generalized letter in complex but indirect dependence on Colossians — after it — as the third part of a set of three letters being composed at the time.[77] It would seem more likely, if the dependence of Laodiceans on Colossians could be decisively proven, that Laodiceans was a later generalization based on Colossians by a cunning pseudepigrapher, who thereby found a brilliant point at which to insert this pseudepigraphon into a Pauline letter collection. It was introduced in place of the lost letter to the Laodiceans, a location further facilitated by its deliberate resonances with the other main letter composed at that time and still extant, Colossians. But the advocacy of the pseudonymity of "Ephesians" on grounds of its demonstrable dependence on Colossians faces

---

77. It has already been intimated that the instructions concerning two principal letters in Col 4:16 are not decisive for the order of their composition (although I used to view them this way); they probably refer simply to the first destination on Tychicus's itinerary, where any copying would have had to take place, and therefore not *necessarily* to the prior existence of a letter addressed to Laodicea. However, reconstruction of the broader situation on other grounds suggests that Laod came first primarily.

some serious challenges. Three particular difficulties within this case need to be appreciated.

(i) As in any attempted resolution of the Synoptic Problem, it is difficult to demonstrate definitively the direction of the relationships of dependence in view. Almost all the arguments used in favor of one relationship can generally (and even invariably) be countered with equally plausible explanations that run in the opposite direction — the recurrence here in another form of the problem of multiple plausible narrativity. That is, that the letters exhibit some sort of dependence is obvious. But we cannot tell in relation to Laodiceans and Colossians — as in many of the relationships between the Gospels — whether Colossians is a compression of the material in Laodiceans that summarizes and reorients it, or whether Laodiceans is an elaborate expansion of selected and more cryptic material found in Colossians. Both accounts of any given textual relationship between Laodiceans and Colossians seem almost invariably to be plausible, rendering the entire contention indecisive.

(ii) The situation is further complicated by the possibility that the relationship between Laodiceans and Colossians was fundamentally oral/aural and not written, a point where we must resist the anachronistic tendency to conceptualize Paul's ancient oral culture in terms of our own written privileges (so of course Ong, esp. 2012 [1982]; also 2002). That is, most scholars seem to conceptualize the dependence in view as textual in the specific senses of texts being written and copied, and at points this seems definite (i.e., Laod 6:21-22 // Col 4:7-8;[78] and quite possibly Laod 1:1-2 // Col 1:1-2 as well[79]). This predilection is evident in the production

---

78. Laod 6:21-22:

[21]Ἵνα δὲ εἰδῆτε καὶ ὑμεῖς **τὰ κατ' ἐμέ**, τί πράσσω, **πάντα γνωρίσει ὑμῖν Τύχικος ὁ ἀγαπητὸς ἀδελφὸς καὶ πιστὸς διάκονος ἐν κυρίῳ**

[22] **ὃν ἔπεμψα πρὸς ὑμᾶς εἰς αὐτὸ τοῦτο**, ἵνα γνῶτε τὰ περὶ ἡμῶν καὶ παρακαλέσῃ τὰς καρδίας ὑμῶν.

Col 4:7-8:

[7] **Τὰ κατ' ἐμὲ πάντα γνωρίσει ὑμῖν Τύχικος ὁ ἀγαπητὸς ἀδελφὸς** καὶ πιστὸς διάκονος καὶ σύνδουλος **ἐν κυρίῳ**,

[8] **ὃν ἔπεμψα πρὸς ὑμᾶς εἰς αὐτὸ τοῦτο**, ἵνα γνῶτε τὰ περὶ ἡμῶν καὶ παρακαλέσῃ τὰς καρδίας ὑμῶν.

79. Laod 1:1-2:

[1] **Παῦλος ἀπόστολος Χριστοῦ Ἰησοῦ διὰ θελήματος θεοῦ τοῖς ἁγίοις** τοῖς οὖσιν ἐν Λαοδικείᾳ **καὶ πιστοῖς ἐν Χριστῷ Ἰησοῦ**

[2] **χάρις ὑμῖν καὶ εἰρήνη ἀπὸ θεοῦ πατρὸς ἡμῶν** καὶ κυρίου Ἰησοῦ Χριστοῦ.

of various synopses of the problem, which assume that it is soluble in these terms.[80] But the texts just noted are small, distinctive segments within a much richer pattern of dependence, and they occur in the letter opening and closing, where we might expect a more standardized approach. Elsewhere the relationship between the two letters is by no means synoptic in the sense that it maps obviously in terms of the use of a prior written source by a later redactor. Some sequences are preserved, but in general, motifs are mixed up and recombined (depending on the assumed flow of dependence) — something that causes the various attempted synopses a lot of difficulty. This situation seems more explicable in terms of a fundamentally oral process of composition as against a written one, in which one deeply reflective and carefully memorized text has filtered through into another compositional "performance," much as improvising actors return to and reuse stock stories, jokes, and verbal sequences in subsequent performances (see here esp. Wells 2004). But when interpreters concede the orality of the process, they lose the right to make strong claims about causality. The direction and causalities of oral reproductions cannot be reconstructed with any confidence simply in their own terms; this would be not unlike trying to eat soup with a knife.[81]

An oral/aural understanding of the process lying behind Laodiceans and Colossians possesses the further virtue of being the most plausible account of Paul's practical compositional situation, in prison. His ability to compose a text orally and aurally would likely not have been obstructed, but any use of written materials might have been much more difficult. Indeed, as was noted earlier, prison literature is often a fundamentally oral process, committed to writing at late stages and in fragile ways.

Col 1:1-2:

[1] Παῦλος ἀπόστολος Χριστοῦ Ἰησοῦ διὰ θελήματος θεοῦ καὶ Τιμόθεος ὁ ἀδελφὸς

[2] τοῖς ἐν Κολοσσαῖς ἁγίοις καὶ πιστοῖς ἀδελφοῖς ἐν Χριστῷ, χάρις ὑμῖν καὶ εἰρήνη ἀπὸ θεοῦ πατρὸς ἡμῶν.

80. So (i.a.) Goodspeed (1933); Mitton (1951); Van Kooten (2003).

81. Attention to oral/aural dynamics has been more prominent in discussions of the Synoptic Gospels recently than it has been within Pauline studies. While a certain amount said in the former relation might be helpful in terms of the latter, I would want to emphasize that quite different temporal, circumstantial, and editorial dynamics are present when we turn from the Synoptics to Paul's letters or vice versa. In the case of Paul, only one person is at present involved, in a relatively constrained situation, for a relatively brief period of time.

In short, if we recognize a primarily oral process of composition lying behind both Laodiceans and Colossians, then the relationship of dependence between them was rather fluid and complex, defying any obvious mapping in terms of causality. The reutilization and redeployment of some material from Laodiceans by Colossians seems just as plausible as the same process running in the other direction; and a significant interaction between the two letters in these terms cannot be ruled out, with Paul perhaps composing and memorizing both penultimate drafts of the letter bodies prior to syllabic dictation to a scribe.

(iii)   The situation is further complicated in the case of any putative dependence by Laodiceans on Colossians by the probable interactivity of the later stages in the composition of these texts. Hence, even if an oral process of composition had a principal causal direction early on, it nevertheless seems likely that as the three letters were committed to print, presumably by a scribe or a scribally adept member of Paul's circle (although none is designated as such), cross-checking and what we might call textual "cross-pollination" might have taken place. This seems to be a plausible explanation for the written dependence in view in the letter openings and closings. In essence, because the final production and dispatch of the letters was simultaneous, any minor moments of dependence and adjustments to the texts during their final stages of composition could have run in multiple directions. We should probably imagine Paul listening to penultimate written versions of all three letters and offering minor comments. These could then have been introduced either in the margins of the letters or in a new copy, after which he would have signed them personally and sent Tychicus on his way.

It is arguably easier to imagine the extra material apparent in Laodiceans 6:21-22 as an adjustment to Colossians 4:7-8 — although this is by no means certain (see Best 1997b). But this sort of addition could well have come from the final stages in the letters' composition and consequently suggests nothing about the principal direction of dependence between them. The text in Colossians could have preceded Laodiceans in this instance, but Laodiceans could still have largely preceded Colossians, after a phase of reflection and oral composition in prison.

In view of these dynamics, it seems to me that any definitive case for the pseudonymity of "Ephesians" because of its evident dependence on Colossians is doomed. The establishment of this conclusion in defiance of all alternatives is effectively impossible. Moreover, it now seems that many advocates of the dependence of "Ephesians" on Colossians have been caught up by broader disciplinary flows of plausibility that have left them vulnerable in the context of our particular method and resulting reconstruction. If it has already been decided that Ephesians is pseudepigraphic but Colossians possibly authentic, then it follows that Ephesians is dependent on Colossians — and with sufficient determination, this construal of the data is possible. But in the context of this framing exercise, with both "Ephesians" as Laodiceans and Colossians currently being treated as authentic, such considerations beg the key question. Indeed, arguably it is now becoming apparent that our whole approach to the assessment of the dependence between Laodiceans and Colossians needs to be reversed, and made to depend *on* framing, not to dictate it. With preliminary framing judgments made, we will be able to return and investigate the dependence in view knowing already, from the frame, what the principal direction was, and what the broader circumstances were that informed its nature. Perhaps only responsible framing will allow us any real hope of reconstructing the main flows within the complex relationship of dependence evident between Laodiceans and Colossians.

So much, then, for arguments in favor of the pseudonymity of "Ephesians" in the light of its evident dependence on Colossians. That relationship is possible, but so are many others. But do other echoes of "Ephesians"/Laodiceans in the undisputed letters call its authenticity into question?

(2) Dependence on Undisputed Pauline Letters

Numerous echoes of Laodiceans can be found in the other undisputed Pauline letters, and this might suggest an influence on the later composition of "Ephesians" from the authentic Pauline letters, and hence pseudepigraphy. But the peculiar circumstances of Laodiceans arguably speak to this concern quite satisfactorily.

Of all the Pauline letters examined thus far, Laodiceans was elicited by particular circumstances that called most directly for an exposition of Paul's most coherent concerns — in effect, for his construction of the Christian identity of a community of pagan converts. Moreover, this letter fits into the frame just prior to Paul's year of crisis, that is, in 50 CE, preceding the troubles of spring 51-spring 52, when 1 Corinthians, 2 Corinthians, Galatians, Philippians, and Romans were composed. It seems possible that the echoes of Laodiceans found in the undisputed letters are not evidence of the later influence on "Ephesians" of the authentic Paulines so much as the filtering through of many of Paul's most significant concerns from Laodiceans to the letters he was forced to write in 51 and the spring of 52 in various rather more difficult and specific circumstances — and its especially concentrated set of echoes with Romans might further encourage confidence in this view. Preliminary framing can proceed, in short, with the hypothesis that Laodiceans articulates many of Paul's central concerns. This would explain the heavy interdependence evident between the undisputed letters and Laodiceans.[82]

It will of course pay a price for doing so. Ultimately, this position will result in a more "Ephesiocentric" account of Paul's thought than might otherwise be the case, and some scholars will be happier paying this price than others. But it is not cogently falsifiable at this stage in our discussion, when framing. That is, any falsification of the authenticity of Laodiceans in terms of evident dependence would have to demonstrate the nature and content of Paul's coherence, and then proceed to show how the positions found in "Ephesians" in echo with the undisputed letters are a demonstrably impossible account of that coherence. This case can be made only after preliminary framing and not during it (because it presupposes a biographical frame within which Paul's coherence can be reconstructed and assessed). So framing can proceed for now, with the caveat that — probably — Laodiceans may ultimately have to figure centrally in any account of Paul's coherence. (I say "probably" because Paul's coherence could ultimately be deemed incoherent or markedly developmental, with Laodiceans representing the concerns of 50, and his other letters the rather different concerns of 51 and 52 CE.)

But we have raised substantive concerns here and so should now consider the many serious objections that arise to the authenticity of "Ephesians" in these terms.

(3) Unacceptable Generality

Perhaps the principal initial difficulty that many scholars have with the authenticity of "Ephesians" is its generality, which can be described in different ways. One can speak of its level of abstraction, and even of its blandness. What is generally being articulated here is the sense that "Ephesians" lacks any of

82. Echoes of 1 and/or 2 Thess would involve different explanatory dynamics. But we have already touched on the possible influence of these letters long after their composition, partly since Paul seems to have retained copies of them and referred to them when he thought it useful. So later echoes of these letters will be informative but are unlikely to be fatal to the developing frame.

the particularity or specificity that we invariably find elsewhere in a genuine Pauline letter. One line of defense offered against this criticism in the past has been the hypothesis that "Ephesians" was actually a circular letter or, in a variation on this view, a treatise or manifesto that was freighted in an epistolary form — and this might explain some of the textual confusion in the prescript as well. But we have already briefly noted why this rejoinder is inadequate.

Most forms of the letter have addressees, and those that lack them are grammatically odd and stylistically atypical. Moreover, the letter presents itself as being carried and delivered by Tychicus, who has been entrusted with quite concrete personal duties; one of them is to remind his recipients of how Paul lives. So the letter is not really a circular (except perhaps in a highly localized sense) or a manifesto, and the letter's blandness consequently cannot be explained in this way. However, the identification of "Ephesians" as Laodiceans does seem to speak to this perceived difficulty adequately.

Once it is grasped that the Laodiceans had not been converted by Paul, and barely knew him, and that Paul was prevented from instructing them by his incarceration, and may in turn have known very little about them, the scene is set in quite specific terms for a highly generalized discussion — an account of Christian identity for pagan converts. The key to Ephesians in this relation is then its hidden identity as Laodiceans, along with the location of the Laodiceans in relation to Paul. The letter's level of abstraction seems well explained in these practical terms. However, having made this general observation about the genesis of the letter's distinctive approach, we can still ask whether certain substantive emphases within it are unacceptable and/or anachronistic in relation to Paul.

(4) Unacceptable Substantive Emphases

Scholars have suggested that the realized eschatology evident in "Ephesians" is as unacceptable in relation to Paul here as it was in Colossians. But we have already noted a series of difficulties with this objection, not least of which is its own anachronistic interpretative projections. The letter to the Laodiceans affords several other themes susceptible to this objection, however, most notable of which is its emphasis on "the church."

The *ekklēsia* (ἐκκλησία) is named specifically nine times in Laodiceans, and always in its general, universal sense (1:22; 3:10, 21; 5:23-25, 27, 29, 32). But this usage is rare elsewhere in the Pauline corpus, occurring only seven times in other letters (see esp. Col 1:18 and 24; but also Gal 1:13; 1 Cor 10:32; 12:28;

15:9; Phil 3:6). Paul usually uses this signifier to refer to a local gathering or congregation, a usage entirely absent from Laodiceans. This seems to be a peculiar configuration, although it could be explained quite easily in terms of a later pseudepigrapher's desire to provide an account of "the church."

But while this challenge identifies an important emphasis within the data, it does not seem fatal to Pauline authorship. The presence of the universal sense for *ekklēsia* in four other authentic letters might reinforce the hypothesis that Laodiceans articulates Paul's most central, coherent concerns. And we may now add a secondary argument to this rejoinder.

We noted earlier that, although it is difficult to detect, Laodiceans doubtless uses traditional Christian material at Laodicea to generate leverage on its auditors. And arguably, the universal sense of "the assembly" is one such traditional point of purchase. This motif is poorly translated as "the church," a rendering that will instantly generate a spectrum of anachronistic connotations. It is actually a reference to an assembly or gathering, and hence, in its singular usage, to *the* assembly, drawing here most probably on the OT notion of the assembly of all Israel *(qahal Israel)*. This was thought by many in Paul's day to be eschatologically consummated and hence could well have been appropriated by the first followers of Jesus to define themselves. Paul's use of this meaning in three references to his pre-call persecutions seems tentatively to corroborate this reconstruction (Gal 1:13; 1 Cor 15:9; Phil 3:6), as does its occurrence in this sense in Colossians 1:18, a section of material widely viewed as traditional, if not quoted directly from tradition. These realizations combine to respond more than adequately to the objection that Laodiceans is overly ecclesial.

Not only is this emphasis on the *ekklēsia* possibly a part of Paul's coherence, but it might, in either complementary or alternative terms, have been a part of the Laodiceans' traditions to which Paul was appealing for rhetorical leverage as he sought to construct his richer account of Christian community — glossing this image in turn with connotations in terms of a temple (which might also have been traditional material), a new humanity (here Adamic, and so traditional in some sense as well), a family, a bride, a body, and a place characterized by fullness or overflow (i.e., πλήρωμα). It seems an entirely plausible candidate for this role; hence, its heavy representation in Laodiceans is, a little ironically, plausibly explicable in contingent terms.

Moreover, we learn from this that any argument for the pseudonymity of Laodiceans in terms of its unacceptable substantive emphases must demonstrate not only that these could not have inhabited any plausible reconstruction of Paul's coherence (something that must, strictly speaking, take place after framing in any case); it must demonstrate in addition that these could not have been traditional resources within the early church to which Paul might have been appealing in Laodiceans for rhetorical leverage. And this type of challenge now seems to be a very tall order. But the defender of the letter's authenticity can make a further appeal in this relation that we should note before moving on.

It might be objected that Laodiceans contains an implausible account of Judaism, a challenge that can be couched in slightly more aggressive and comprehensive terms than the contention in terms of the church. On the one hand, certain recognizably Jewish motifs found frequently elsewhere in Paul are almost entirely absent. "Works of Torah" and "faith" are found only vestigially, in 2:8-10,[83] while the language of justification (i.e., using the verb δικαιόω or its substantive cognates) is absent altogether. However, there is an evident concern to locate the Christian community in a tightly unified way alongside converts from Judaism. These two groups convert from the same desperate location (2:1-5; see also vv. 11-12) and then form one single body and temple (2:15b, 18), having had their mutual hostility put to death (2:14, 16). Moreover, this unity between Jew and pagan is reinforced by the letter's later calls for communal unity (4:3-6). The letter breathes a certain sort of ecumenicity.

The ostensible absences from Laodiceans, which raise slightly different methodological issues, will be addressed in the next subsection. Here we will concentrate on the rather programmatic account of Jewish-pagan relations articulated in Laodiceans, along with its emphasis on unity. Certainly, it can be suggested that a later pseudepigrapher, concerned at "the parting of the ways," might have crafted this impressively interreligious material. But is it implausible to suggest that Paul might have voiced these concerns? Addressing this challenge will in fact highlight the way in which the identification of "Ephesians" as Laodiceans within our developing frame can provide distinctive rejoinders to various challenges to its authenticity.

According to our frame, Laodiceans was written during an incarceration in 50 CE, while Paul was returning to the Aegean from a critical meeting in Jerusalem that took place in turn on the heels of a dramatic confrontation in Syrian Antioch over the status of Paul's pagan converts. Thus, it is possible that the carefully nuanced account of Christian unity found in Laodiceans may reflect in part these meetings that had just preceded it. (Certainly, they

---

83. [2:8] Τῇ γὰρ χάριτί ἐστε σεσῳσμένοι διὰ πίστεως· καὶ τοῦτο οὐκ ἐξ ὑμῶν, θεοῦ τὸ δῶρον. [9] οὐκ ἐξ ἔργων, ἵνα μή τις καυχήσηται. [10] αὐτοῦ γάρ ἐσμεν ποίημα, κτισθέντες ἐν Χριστῷ Ἰησοῦ ἐπὶ ἔργοις ἀγαθοῖς οἷς προητοίμασεν ὁ θεός, ἵνα ἐν αὐτοῖς περιπατήσωμεν.

would have informed it.)[84] And it is important to recall that the immediate outcome of Paul's second visit to Jerusalem was positive. The leaders of the two main missions in the early church — to Jews and to pagans — had shaken hands in a binding mutual acknowledgment of their participation in a society together (Gal 2:1-10, esp. vv. 8-9), and the collection was now tangible evidence of Paul's and his pagan converts' commitment to that society. Hence, argu-ably, the carefully nuanced account of communal unity found in Laodiceans, embracing the execution within the assembly of the enmity often existing in general between Jews and pagans, fits this situation like the proverbial hand in a glove — and may in turn shed light on some of the content of those earlier meetings, which was so critical and yet whose attestation is so limited.[85] That is, the presence of both the Jewish and the "ecumenical" material in Laodiceans seems well explained by its location in our broader letter sequence just after the Jerusalem conference.

This response should also serve to indicate how challenges to the au-thenticity of Laodiceans on grounds of any inappropriate substantive empha-sis are quite difficult to make cogently, and reasonably easy to rebut. Such a defense can appeal, first, to the distinctive contingency of Laodiceans (with countervailing accounts of Paul's coherence lacking viability or validity at this point); second, to the way Paul might be utilizing traditional material from the early church that was shared by the Laodiceans for rhetorical leverage; and third, to the location of Laodiceans in a distinctive window within Paul's life, after important discussions in Syrian Antioch and Jerusalem that had affirmed

84. I do not want to insist on this point but simply to list it as an interpretative possibil-ity. The concern in Laod with Judaism may have arisen from a specific aspect of the exigence in Laodicea — although probably drawing in response to that on the material that had been discussed earlier in Jerusalem. Alternatively, Paul might simply have been projecting material from Jerusalem into his current vision of the identity of pagan converts. At this point, during preliminary framing, we cannot tell.

85. Lincoln (1990, lxiv, xciii) suggests that the account of Judaism found in Laod is ir-reconcilable with the discussion of Rom 9–11. But I find this contention rather odd. Rom 9–11 is concerned at first with pagan inclusion, and it makes no claims that are in serious tension with the fuller account of this dynamic supplied by Laod; indeed, both appeal strongly to the divine initiative, i.e., to election, properly understood. The rest of Rom 9–11 then addresses the general Jewish rejection of the gospel, providing several interlocking explanations of this tragedy. Conversely, Laod does not specifically address the Jewish rejection of Christian claims. It provides an account of Jewish and pagan conversion that creates a new united community (something that might then arguably look like two types of branches being grafted into one single tree). So the two texts basically address different questions. That they consequently often look different may be conceded, but this hardly establishes any irreducible tensions between them. And arguably when they do touch on the same questions, they say much the same things.

the unity of the early church and the validity of Paul's distinctive mission to paganism. These are powerful interpretive resources for any advocate of authenticity against any charges of inappropriate substantive emphases in Laodiceans. But if distinctive substantive emphases can be accounted for, does the same apply to distinctive absences, one of which we have already noted?

(5) Unacceptable Substantive Omissions

In a mirror image to the preceding concern, it might be objected that certain key emphases found elsewhere in the authentic Paul are missing from Laodiceans, thereby calling its authenticity into question. We have already noted briefly the main candidate in this relation, namely, Paul's "justification discourse," as I refer to it elsewhere (2009). This is a distinctive cluster of words and phrases centered on the phrase "works of Torah" (ἔργων νόμου) and words using πιστ- and δικαιο- stems, usually translated in terms of faith and belief or of righteousness and justification, respectively. (Other words and motifs are associated with this central group but need not detain us here.) Protestant interpreters of Paul have frequently argued that this cluster of material is either the heart of his coherence or a significant part of it. So the vestigial acknowledgment by Laodiceans of just two of the three critical motifs in this cluster, in 2:8-10, is troubling to such interpreters, and they tend to query the letter's legitimacy accordingly.

However, this challenge in terms of absence is as inadequate as the preceding challenges in terms of unacceptable presence. In the first instance, it should be recalled that all such substantive assertions are moot during preliminary framing. But even granting them here for the sake of argument, it is questionable simply on its own terms that this cluster is necessarily coherent for Paul.

It occurs only in parts of Romans (principally 1:16–5:2 and from 9:30, fading by 10:17) and Galatians (from 2:15, fading through to 3:26, recurring in 5:5-6), and much more briefly in Philippians (see 3:6 and 9 in the context of 3:1-11, i.e., it seems to have characterized the Previous Letter to Philippi). This is not a promising distribution for material supposedly coming from Paul's properly basic convictions. Hence, when we turn to Laodiceans, its passing acknowledgment in 2:8-10 might well be an appropriate reflection of its relative importance alongside the rest of Paul's concerns, viewed in the broader context of his authentic letters — and this is, in any case, a stronger representation of the material than we find in 1 and 2 Thessalonians, Colossians, and Philemon.

(There are fragmentary occurrences in 1 Cor 1:30; 6:11; and 2 Cor 5:21; although none of these instances is as full as Laod 2:8-10.) But Laodiceans has an even stronger card to play in its own defense at this point, indicating here how it can defend itself against any or all charges of substantive silences concerning material well represented in the major letters.

Because of its location prior to the composition of these letters, Laodiceans can turn the tables on these objections and suggest that when this distinctive material occurs in a letter written later, we have a good prima facie case for *that* material's fundamental contingency. The boot, it seems, is on the other foot. Advocates of the importance of material deemed absent from Laodiceans but present only in parts of 1 Corinthians, 2 Corinthians, Galatians, Philippians, and/or Romans must now make a case for the importance and centrality of that material — a job that will have to take place after preliminary framing. Conversely, Laodiceans itself might suggest that this material was highly circumstantial. So, for example, Paul's justification discourse might have been mobilized in depth only when the Teacher was in view, an overtly circumstantial exigence. Otherwise, Paul barely mentions this distinctive material, indicating thereby that it should perhaps be excluded from any significant role in his coherence, or, at least, positioned toward the edge of it.

In short, this challenge in terms of a supposedly pregnant substantive silence in Laodiceans should be laid to one side — although by considering it, we have identified another strength in the location of Laodiceans in 50 CE within our broader frame. Not only does this allow us to explain certain emphases within Laodiceans (and Col) as possible echoes from the meetings that had just taken place in Syrian Antioch and Jerusalem, but it removes the need for Laodiceans to justify any of its silences concerning material that occurs in the later letters. Because these letters did not exist when Laodiceans was written, any silences in relation to their concerns are hardly a problem automatically. Still, if various substantive silences are no longer threatening to Laodiceans, certain initially more innocuous personal silences might be.

(6) An Absence of Particular Features

One of the most troubling features in the case for the authenticity of "Ephesians" as Laodiceans is not its set of substantive absences so much as its cluster of personal omissions.

The letter ending is abrupt, and it contains a number of distinctive features. It reproduces material from Colossians on the role of Tychicus almost exactly in 6:21-22 (without pronouncing on the underlying causality here). A somewhat elaborate peace wish follows in v. 23 (Εἰρήνη τοῖς ἀδελφοῖς καὶ ἀγάπη μετὰ πίστεως ἀπὸ θεοῦ πατρὸς καὶ κυρίου Ἰησοῦ Χριστοῦ), and then a grace wish in v. 24. But this last is directed in atypical fashion, in the third person, to "those who love our Lord Jesus Christ,"[86] as against in the second person, to those who are receiving the letter, Paul's invariable practice elsewhere. And it is combined with a troublesome phrase — "through immortality" (ἐν ἀφθαρσίᾳ).[87]

Admittedly, we have seen many times already that distinctiveness alone is not enough to call Paul's authorship of a text into question, but here it combines with a puzzling omission. Alone among the letters considered thus far — all of which have been judged authentic — Laodiceans omits any greetings. This is odd in and of itself. But it is especially troubling when we note that the two letters addressing congregations personally unknown to Paul — namely, Romans (16:3-16, 21-23) and Colossians (4:10-15, also 18a) — seem to go out of their way to craft especially elaborate greetings. To make matters worse, both of those sets of greetings emphasize Jewish connections where possible, something that would presumably have been especially useful in Laodiceans, which is evidently concerned to promote unity between pagan and Jewish converts. This is an argument from silence, but the silence in Laodiceans does seem to be a pregnant one. We have strong expectations that Laodiceans would send numerous personal greetings to the Laodiceans, and emphasize any Jewish converts in doing so, but it does not, prompting doubt about the letter's authenticity.

It is also slightly odd that Colossians emphasizes Jewish connections in its elaborate greetings when the letter itself is *not* especially concerned with Jewish-pagan relations or unity in the way that Laodiceans is. But herein may lie the first important clue to a possible solution to this problem. Perhaps tellingly, the Laodiceans figure prominently in these greetings. Epaphras is said to struggle for them as well as the Colossians and those in Hierapolis in v. 13; the Colossians are told to greet them in v. 15; and the letter is to be sent to them in v. 16, and their letter read to the Colossians as well. And this last set of instructions by Paul recalls the claim made earlier in our initial consideration of the immediate implied exigencies of both letters.

By the time Paul writes Colossians 4:16, he is envisaging an integrated

---

86. ἡ χάρις μετὰ πάντων τῶν ἀγαπώντων τὸν κύριον ἡμῶν Ἰησοῦν Χριστὸν ἐν ἀφθαρσίᾳ.

87. This is probably best linked with the benefaction in view, denoting it to be glorious and immortal; for discussion and a list of supporters, see Lincoln (1990, 467-68).

epistolary event at Colossae and Laodicea; both letters are to be read out at both locations. So the poverty of greeting at the end of Laodiceans is potentially explicable in terms of the wealth of contact and information that Paul provides at the end of Colossians. All of this would have been heard by the Laodiceans, and they are explicitly engaged by the material. This explanation has the added virtue of explaining why the Jewish credentials of some of Paul's companions are emphasized so strongly in Colossians when this seems otiose in the context of the Colossian difficulties. These emphases speak directly to the situation at Laodicea. Paul's circle of coworkers, which labors vigorously together and includes converts from both Judaism and paganism, is an instantiation of the community that he advocates in Laodiceans. (It is not inconsistent with the ecclesiology advocated by Col, but such concerns are not especially overt there.)

Once all these pieces of evidence have been grasped, any doubts in this relation tend to evaporate — although in confronting them, we do seem to learn more about the urgency gripping the final stages of these letters' preparation.[88] Time, access, and/or energy seem to have been so lacking that parts of the letter openings and closings were mechanically reproduced, and the extensive greetings and practical instructions occurring at the end of one of the letters were effectively made to do double duty in relation to the recipients in both key locations. An epistolary process that seems to have begun with nothing but time apparently ended under pressure from an acute lack of it.

And with this concern addressed — in my view one of the most serious — we can turn to our final challenge in this relation.

(7) Style

The authenticity of "Ephesians" has often been challenged on grounds of its ostensibly distinctive style. But what we have said before remains relevant. It is true that tabulations can be made of various stylistic features that are particularly distinctive to "Ephesians," most notably, sentence length. But many stylistic features are shared unremarkably with other undisputed letters.[89] So the key question is, again, not so much whether "Ephesians" has distinctive

88. There might also be a suggestion here that Paul composed the letter body first, appending an appropriate address and postscript later, during the letters' final stages of preparation, and probably leading up to his signature — an interesting compositional practice to reflect on.

89. See Kenny (1986).

stylistic features, because it does, as whether those are different enough from the style of the other Pauline letters to suggest a judgment of pseudonymity. The statistical analysis of this question is at best ambiguous, and at worst negative.

Those statistically astute analysts who have addressed the issue differ in their results. Ledger and Mealand view the differences apparent in "Ephesians" at certain points as significant, while Neumann does not. But not all the samples used by Ledger and Mealand are in fact significantly different — only those taken from the first part of the letter (see the plots introduced earlier in relation to Colossians). And Kenny does not detect any statistically significant variations. However, we can add some further dimensions to this rejoinder in the case of Laodiceans, looking in particular at Paul's crafted rhetorical engagement with his audience.[90]

I have already suggested that Paul utilized traditional material to appeal to the Laodiceans. That is, Laodiceans is a sophisticated account of Christian identity that offers far more than merely cognitive suggestions. It was a rhetorical intervention. As such, it probably sought to affirm where it could the Laodiceans' existing Christian identity, as well as to build on that. And it seems to have done so by working its claims into the language of Jewish worship. The letter is strongly infused with eulogy and prayer. There are moments of doxology, and probable hymnic fragments.[91] And this all stands to reason. The Laodiceans, although consistently described as pagan converts, most likely came from the fringes of Judaism. If they were familiar with the synagogue and its worship practices, then these appeals on Paul's part are quite understandable. That they have interacted previously with Judaism seems, moreover, to be probable.

Paul's mission seems to have had a radical reputation, garnered by engaging with pagans directly and then refusing, after any conversions, to teach a Christian ethic based on full Jewish Torah observance. This mission and ethic caused conflict in the early church, and he had to defend it cleverly and vigorously — which he seems to have done successfully (at least for the time being) when Laodiceans and Colossians were composed. But it follows from this that most other evangelizing of pagans was probably less radical than Paul's. We gain a sense of the resulting different ethical locations of various

90. We noted earlier the probability that Laodiceans was composed initially in an oral/aural fashion, a process that makes particular sense in a carceral setting. And some of the distinctive features of Laodiceans noted by scholars are arguably explicable in terms of the standard practices of oral/aural composition; see Ong (2002; 2012 [1982]).

91. I treat this in more detail in my 2009 (624-38).

pagan converts when Paul addresses the practices of the weak and the strong in Rome and Corinth (see esp. Rom 14; 1 Cor 8, 10). Some pagan converts were clearly comfortable with abandoning more of the Torah than others. Hence, the weak apparently continued to observe Jewish dietary and temporal regulations. All of this combines to suggest that any pagan converts not converted by Paul or one of his proxies would have been rather more likely to have come from a more observant Jewish context than not. They would, in short, most probably have been God-fearers. And if this was the case, then it goes some way toward explaining the distinctive style of Laodiceans.[92]

Recalling Paul's probable rhetorical strategy of affirming and building from the Laodiceans' own traditions, as well as the distinctive commitment of the text to different aspects of the language of worship, we might surmise that in Laodiceans Paul deliberately wrote a text that a gathering of former God-fearers would recognize and appreciate by evoking the language of the synagogue or some similar context involving Jewish worship. And this language, with its special rhythms and ritual uses, would have affected his vocabulary and syntax. It is unnecessary to press any deeper at this point to an identification of where the Laodiceans might have fallen on a broad map of Judaism in Paul's day.[93] Such specificity is not necessary for our present purposes. We need only to note here that the distinctive features of the letter's style are plausibly explained by a deliberate evocation on Paul's part of some of these forms. The Laodiceans' location and his rhetoric, moreover, would have made these appeals quite distinctive within his corpus as a whole (as it is extant). With this realization, any concerns about the authenticity of Laodiceans in terms of style should dissipate, at which point we are ready finally to reach a judgment concerning its authenticity.

3.4 Judgment

Our consideration of this question began, as usual, by assuming the letter's authenticity, something that led in this instance to the identification of "Ephesians" as Paul's "lost" letter to the Laodiceans (Col 4:16b). This led quickly in turn to the location of Laodiceans alongside Colossians and Philemon within

---

92. Cohen (1999) is a helpful orientation in the broader context of a nuanced discussion of ancient Jewish identity. The key restoration of the "God-fearers" to validity, on inscriptional grounds, after their characterization as a fictitious literary construction by Kraabel et al. is Reynolds and Tannenbaum (1987). For further discussion, see Trebilco (1991, 145-66).

93. Lincoln (1990, lxxv, xcii-xciii) makes some preliminary observations here.

our developing frame, in 50 CE. Hence, the letter now falls, like Colossians and Philemon, in Paul's mission to Asia that took place just after the important events surrounding his second visit to Jerusalem, but prior to the tempestuous year of crisis that unfolded through 51 and the spring of 52 CE, the year in which he wrote most of his extant letters. And in the light of these initial framing decisions, all the different challenges to the authenticity of "Ephesians" have proved to be indecisive or have simply collapsed.

The contention of pseudonymity can point to no decisive evidence in terms of incontestable anachronisms or the like. Nor are any problems evident in the letter's later transmission (although we have yet to discuss this question fully; but the next chapter will supply further grounds for our confidence in the letter's authenticity in these terms). So the case for pseudonymity had to rely on different challenges, and consequently on the usual suspects — purported problems in the letter's dependence, substance, and style.

These were by no means inconsiderable. But closer scrutiny has suggested that they are all answerable. It is worth emphasizing, moreover, that this defense has drawn frequently on the particular location of Laodiceans in the frame, in 50, after Paul's second visit to Jerusalem but before Paul's year of crisis. This location offered a number of quite specific insights into the composition of Laodiceans, many of which went on to defuse concerns with the letter's authenticity.

Hence, it follows that the letter should be judged authentic. But it also follows that it has been judged so only in these terms and in this particular location — with "Ephesians" identified as Laodiceans and located in 50 CE. That is, I am not convinced that my defensive rejoinders hold good in any other location (i.e., later). Pseudonymity seems to me to be a better explanation for this letter's dynamics than its authentic composition either as a circular or in a later imprisonment in Rome (although, strictly speaking, we are not considering this location yet). But this is possibly not surprising. It seems that when we remove Laodiceans from this particular identification and from a relatively early location in our frame, we *generate* a number of the interpretative difficulties that have elicited a judgment of pseudonymity. That is, many modern scholars seem to have reacted to other improbable provenances for Laodiceans understandably, with a judgment of pseudonymity. But my principal suggestion here is that these difficulties can be resolved by the biographical expedient, achieved by accurate preliminary framing, of an alternative provenance.

Hence, we will proceed here on the assumptions that the designation and identification of "Ephesians" as Laodiceans is correct, along with its location in 50 CE, and that the letter is authentic. We have now affirmed the genuineness of ten Pauline letters in total, although the name of one of the letters so identified will probably strike most interpreters as a little unexpected. Nevertheless, we are now working with a "ten-letter canon" — in chronological sequence, 1 Thessalonians, 2 Thessalonians, Laodiceans/Colossians/Philemon, 1 Corinthians, 2 Corinthians, Galatians, Philippians, and Romans. And if this judgment proves correct, I recommend that Bibles and New Testaments be amended accordingly. (There is of course nothing sacred about a letter's later canonical designation.) Paul did not write a letter to the Ephesians, and it causes a lot of trouble to think that he did so. The letter so designated was sent to the Laodiceans as referenced by Colossians 4:16b.

CHAPTER SIX

Locating Titus and 1 and 2 Timothy

1. Preliminary Methodological Considerations

We turn in this final chapter to consider the two letters in the canon written to Timothy and the letter to Titus. Methodological consistency will continue to dictate a certain approach to the assessment of these texts, which are viewed by so many modern scholars as pseudonymous.

We have consistently excluded question begging and potentially circular argumentation from preliminary framing and so have not appealed previously to putative differences between any letters in terms of substance. We do not know at this stage in our work what Paul's "substance" was, and cannot make judgments in these terms until preliminary framing has been completed. Similarly, overly specific appeals to differences in terms of style have been avoided. Only statistically significant appeals to the overarching stylistic fingerprints of texts have been admitted, and we have yet to encounter any indubitable instances of this, although the text of Titus will reintroduce this contention here in earnest. But past debate of 1 Timothy, 2 Timothy, and Titus has often used additional broad arguments. Scholars have appealed to the communal organization and opposition ostensibly apparent in the texts, to their atypical letter structure and genre for Paul, and to the implications of their grouping. So we need to ask quickly whether these arguments are valid in terms of preliminary framing or whether they are excluded — or at least mitigated — by the strictures that have already curtailed circular appeals to substance and style.

Insofar as these types of arguments also make circular and related question begging claims, they should (of course) be excluded. This might seem to place the following analysis quite close to the spirited defenses of the authenticity of these letters that have been offered relatively recently (see esp. L. Johnson 2001; Towner 2006) — and in certain respects, it is. Commentators like Marshall, Johnson, and Towner — a disparate group — have rightly complained that many arguments against the authenticity of 1 Timothy, 2 Timothy, and Titus beg key questions. And they are correct, as much of the preceding analysis here would suggest.

Johnson and others have argued further that 1 Timothy, 2 Timothy, and Titus should not be grouped together and assessed in the first instance as "the Pastorals." This prejudices any judgment of authenticity, artificially emphasizing their problematic differences with the letters already judged authentic and their (supposedly) problematic similarities with each other. Various points of overlap in the former direction and of distinctiveness in the latter are effectively narcotized by this judgment, to use Eco's (1976) term.[1]

Clearly, our analysis endorses this complaint as well, not least because treating the group as a whole obscures any consideration of possible relationships of dependence between authentic and falsified letters within it. This concurs with Kenny's judgment that 1 and 2 Timothy and Titus should *not* be grouped over against other Pauline letters on grounds simply of style.[2] So we will assess each letter here in its own terms. We will analyze 1 and 2 Timothy and Titus rigorously in terms of our usual approach, something the foregoing commentators do not always do. We will interrogate the letters' accounts of their immediate exigence and their possible fit with our existing frame; and we will consider challenges to their authenticity in terms of mistakes, at which point elements from the preceding, broadly circular arguments may find themselves being reintroduced in a different methodological mode. It will be interesting to discover whether the more methodologically constrained approach being advocated throughout this study will deliver the usual judgment

---

1. Kahneman (2011) might call this an instance of "confirmation" bias (see 80-81, 324, 333).

2. See Kenny (1986, 98). Kenny orders the letters in terms of their demonstrable statistical correlations (as we have already seen), as Rom, Phil, 2 Tim, 2 Cor, Gal, 2 Thess, 1 Thess, Col, Eph, 1 Tim, Phlm, 1 Cor, and Titus. The positions of the so-called Pastorals here directly undermine any suggestion that the letters necessarily group together over against the other Paulines on grounds of style alone. An earlier, indirect protest in these terms was made by B. Metzger (1958), against Harrison's (1921; 1955) attempted determination of the provenance of the Pastorals in the second century on quasi-statistical grounds. Metzger appeals to the methodological cautions urged by a relatively contemporary statistical study of authorship (whether *De Imitatione Christi* was written by Thomas à Kempis or John Gerson) by the statistician G. Udny Yule (1944). Metzger articulates all the key limitations on statistical analyses noted earlier here, in chs. 4 and 5.

of pseudonymity for these texts, thereby confirming the intuitions of many modern scholars (if not their methods), or whether it will suggest instead that scholarly skepticism with respect to 1 and 2 Timothy and Titus is informed fundamentally by distorted assumptions and procedures.

With these methodological iterations in mind, we can turn to consider the three remaining ancient canonical letters bearing Paul's name. It is not obvious whether we should begin with 1 Timothy or Titus. (Second Timothy clearly seems best left for last.) So we will follow Klauck's somewhat optimistic suggestion that the Muratorian Canon attests to an original position for Titus ahead of 1 Timothy and begin with that letter. Not much turns on this decision in any case.

Is Paul's letter to Titus authentic? And if authentic, where would it belong within our developing frame? Alternatively, does our developing frame cause any problems for Titus? Can we detect any mistakes or overt anachronisms?

2. Locating Titus

2.1 The Immediate Implied Exigence

Paul's letter to Titus appears to be something new under the sun in terms of a Pauline letter, at least initially: it is written to an individual. What account does it give of this distinctive exigence?

The most important practical remark concerning the letter's original purpose and implicit surrounding situation is given in 1:5, where Titus is told that he has been left on Crete to "straighten out what was left unfinished," in part "by appointing elders in every town" (τούτου χάριν ἀπέλιπόν σε ἐν Κρήτῃ, ἵνα τὰ λείποντα ἐπιδιορθώσῃ καὶ καταστήσῃς κατὰ πόλιν πρεσβυτέρους, ὡς ἐγώ σοι διεταξάμην). These instructions are then supplemented by further specific orders in 3:12-13. Titus is to wait until Artemas or Tychicus comes, after which he should join Paul in Nicopolis, where Paul plans to winter (Ὅταν πέμψω Ἀρτεμᾶν πρὸς σὲ ἢ Τύχικον, σπούδασον ἐλθεῖν πρός με εἰς Νικόπολιν, ἐκεῖ γὰρ κέκρικα παραχειμάσαι). Meanwhile, when Apollos and Zenas come, he should assist them on their way (Ζηνᾶν τὸν νομικὸν καὶ Ἀπολλῶν σπουδαίως πρόπεμψον, ἵνα μηδὲν αὐτοῖς λείπῃ).

These remarks contain the most important information for framing purposes, so we will scrutinize them carefully in the next subsection. However, more importantly for our current question, it is clear that they do not exhaust much of the letter's remaining content. If this was all that Paul wanted to say, he could have written a letter consisting largely of these three verses; many papyri attest to the existence of such short, practical communications. But more generic instructions are found in 2:1-3, 6, 9, 15; 3:1, 8, 9-10.

Titus is to teach, encourage, and exhort the Cretan communities and their elders in terms of certain things, largely by way of reminder. Titus 1:1-3 indicates that this teaching goes back ultimately to Paul. Titus is to promote a tradition that preserves it by appointing elders who are responsible tradents and virtuous examples (1:5, 9; 2:1, 15; 3:8). He is to teach accurately, in certain terms, about the divine act in Christ that has established the community (see esp. 2:11, 13-14; 3:4-7). And he is clearly supposed to articulate the way in which this act has moved its members from a state characterized by deception and a brutish enslavement to the passions (1:10a, 12-14; [2:3b], [12a], [14a]; 3:3) into a community of order, self-control, and virtue (the nature of the appropriate elders is described in 1:6-9; further community ordering is described in 2:2-10, in a variation on the Household Codes). Hence, something of a boundary is apparent within this entire depiction around the community. Moreover, this boundary is to be policed in relation to false teaching. Titus is to warn, to avoid, and, if necessary, to expel those who oppose this tradition unprofitably (3:9-10; see also 2:10b-11, 14-15). But what are we to make of this material in terms of the letter's immediate implied exigence? Clearly, it raises some distinctive questions.

Is it plausible to suggest that Paul wrote to an individual a letter containing such a weight of generic material — material that the individual in question would already have known? Up to this point, we have encountered only letters written to communities, generally addressing very practical concerns, although it must be conceded that certain practical situations can elicit quite abstract discussions from Paul (i.e., at Laodicea and Rome). This concern overlaps with a quest for the genre of Titus. Are letters constructed in this fashion apparent in Paul's general cultural context? If not, then we would have further grounds for doubt. It seems, however, that Paul's epistolary context can go some way toward answering this set of questions.

Not much of Epicurus's voluminous correspondence has been preserved, but it does seem clear that he wrote letters to both communities and individuals. And letters written to his individual disciples could contain quite generic instructional material. Similarly, Cicero wrote to groups and to individuals, and some of his letters contained extremely specific, practical material, while others were little more than an excuse for extensive general treatments of various topics. (Admittedly, these would have been composed with an eye on later publication, which may not necessarily have been the case for Paul, but a degree of self-consciousness on Paul's part cannot be ruled out.)³ Moreover, it does not matter whether Titus conforms to these letters precisely. Paul's community letters in many respects defy specific categorization in terms of genre. If we can find points at which Titus overlaps with epistolary texts from Paul's day — bearing in mind that this applies to related material as well, such as rhetorical manuals and speeches and exegetical texts and practices — we cannot object strongly to its plausibility in terms of an unattested genre.⁴ And we should recall, further, that Paul seems quite conscious of "audiences along-side" (i.e., *Nebenadressat*) in his letters that have already been judged authentic. So while Titus might be addressed to Titus, so to speak, this need not preclude various public readings of the letter affirming Titus's authority and instructing all of its listeners in general terms. All of which is to say that although the immediate implied exigence of Titus is clearly distinctive for Paul, at least thus far — addressing an individual, and in unusually generic, bland terms — this does not seem to be demonstrably fatal to its fundamental plausibility.

In sum, we can responsibly conceive of Paul writing such a letter in the terms that it sets out for itself. Conversely, we cannot insist that Paul always wrote the same sort of letter, thereby excluding Titus from his extant letters at the outset of its consideration. We will proceed for the moment, then, on the assumption that Titus was genuine and was written specifically to Titus after a highly successful mission on Crete, to affirm his authority there and to remind the Cretan communities of their founding narrative, order, and virtues. But

3. Seneca might also be a useful point of comparison. However, Seneca's instructional letters, the *Epistulae morales,* were most probably only artificially composed and sent (although this *might* apply to Titus as well). Moreover, other instructional letters are overtly pseudepigraphic — the extant "Socratic" and "Cynic" epistles, for example. However, Wolter (1988) suggests that the genuinely circumstantial letter from Ignatius to Polycarp is a further possible parallel with Titus and 1 Tim, along with some of the emperor Julian's epistles (see also Fiore 1986), although the authenticity of Ign. *Pol.* could be disputed. And although Paul was not an upper-class Roman writing self-consciously for posterity, he was the founder (or key tradent) of a new cult and thus self-conscious of the importance of his writings, perhaps envisaging a form of publication and further circulation (see esp. 2 Thess 2:15; and perhaps also 1 Cor 4:6 [so Hanges 2012, although not always persuasively]). In this entire relation, see Klauck (2006 [1998], 122-24, 149-82).

4. M. Mitchell's (2002b) caution that *PTebt* has been overinterpreted in this relation should be heeded (see, i.a., Spicq 1933). This is too small a sample, too distant, and too ambiguous — reading this evidence generously — to ground the claim that Titus and 1 Tim were instructional letters analogous to letters (ostensibly) reproducing organizational instructions from the imperial chancery for delegates. But the collapse of this particular claim does not, it seems to me, invalidate appeals to broadly similar letters composed by ancient philosophers; see Fiore (1986).

this position leads us directly to a consideration of where Titus might fit into our developing frame.

2.2 Framing Considerations

Paul's letter to Titus seems at first to slot effortlessly into our developing schema.

From 43 through 48 CE, we largely lost sight of Paul (assuming the early composition of the Thessalonian letters). He came back into view in late 49 or early 50, from which point we have an increasingly detailed account of his life through the spring of 52, when we lose sight of him again. In that spring, he writes that he is satisfied that he has evangelized from Jerusalem all the way around to the region of Illyricum (Rom 15:19), so that he is now able to depart for Rome, after a visit to Jerusalem, and then journey on to Spain. From there he would presumably begin to evangelize the Roman Empire and the Mediterranean littoral, likely viewed by him as the center of the world, from its westernmost extremity. Much of Paul's work up to this declaration has taken place around the shores of the Aegean Sea, and the large island of Crete falls squarely into this area. So it seems at first glance as if Titus might nicely illuminate our years of shadow, not to mention corroborate our developing epistolary frame, when it speaks of a highly successful mission to Crete. (Communities have been founded in various towns; see Titus 1:5.) Moreover, Paul's location in Nicopolis seems at first glance to corroborate this view.

Two places in the Roman Empire named Nicopolis, or "city of victory," are particularly noteworthy in this relation: the city founded in 28 BCE on the shores of the Adriatic Sea to commemorate Octavian's victory at Actium (31 BCE), which was technically part of the province of Achaia at this time; and the city founded by Pompey in 63 BCE after his victory over Mithridates VI in the third Mithridatic war (Appian, *Mithridatic War* 115; see also Strabo 12.3.28), which lay in Pontus (near the modern Turkish city of Koyulhisar).[5] Both cities are basically plausible locations for Paul according to our reconstruction, although if Paul worked regionally, we might ask why he would want to winter in the former, in a region where he had already established a significant set

---

5. That Paul would have been in the city of this name founded by Augustus in Egypt is excluded by Rom 15:19. And it is unlikely that he was in the cities of this name lying in modern Bulgaria (Nikopol, named Nicopolis in 1059 CE) and Israel (Emmaus, renamed Emmaus Nicopolis in 221 CE). The city bearing this name in Turkey, now known as Afyonkarahisar, was most probably named Nicopolis after Paul's time as well — by Leo III in 740 CE.

of communities. Having said this, Nicopolis in Pontus was a long way away from Paul, at the farthest extremity of his missionary activity, according to our reconstruction. Prior to attempting any decision here, we should note some problems within this entire developing scenario.

The letter warns both Titus and any other auditors parenthetically in 1:10b-11 against deceivers, "especially those of the circumcision, whom it is necessary to silence" (Εἰσὶν γὰρ πολλοὶ . . . φρεναπάται, μάλιστα οἱ ἐκ τῆς περιτομῆς [11] οὓς δεῖ ἐπιστομίζειν). The letter's auditors are "not to pay attention to Jewish myths and human commands" ([14] μὴ προσέχοντες Ἰουδαϊκοῖς μύθοις καὶ ἐντολαῖς ἀνθρώπων). These warnings are repeated in 3:9-11, being expanded to include unnecessary disputes over genealogies and legal quarrels (γενεαλογίας καὶ . . . μάχας νομικάς).

If the letter is genuine, then these warnings evoke a familiar problem — the Teacher and his followers, who swept through Paul's communities in late 51 CE, along with the first phase (at least) of the teaching Paul encountered at Colossae when he was imprisoned near the Lycus valley in 50. (That they are simply straightforward anti-Jewish polemic seems unlikely.)[6] These controversies seem to have lain behind his confrontation at Syrian Antioch and second apostolic visit to Jerusalem, which took place six months to a year earlier, so we can push the window for the presence of this dynamic in Paul's life back into late 49 CE. But we cannot realistically push it any further.

These challenges were so critical that they elicited immediate address from Paul wherever he found them, including intense engagements in both Antioch and Jerusalem (see Gal 2:1-14). Hence, the abbreviated warnings found in Titus are not a plausible candidate for the first arrival of the Teacher within Paul's mission fields, and especially given that his response in Titus supposedly emanates from a city called Nicopolis where he is going to stay for the winter. The warnings in Titus are not extensive, specific, or urgent enough

---

6. This seems unlikely in terms of Paul's cultural location and program, as well as the circumstances that underlay the composition of his letters. Paul did not deal in abstractions. He wrote to Christian communities about real problems — often, more specifically, about groups of people and rival teachers who had some degree of Christian integrity and so could plausibly approach and influence his communities. So if Titus is authentic, the most likely candidate for these warnings would have been the Teacher and his group, who advocated circumcision for pagan converts. In further support of this claim, there is little or no support elsewhere in Paul's writings for a programmatic anti-Jewishness in communal and sociological terms, as we find here. (That Paul could get angry with Judeans has already been conceded, but this would not explain 1:10-11 and 3:9-11.) If Titus proves to be pseudonymous, however, the identity of the group lying behind this polemic will have to be reassessed.

to fill the requisite biographical space. Consequently, they cannot predate the arrival of these challenges within Paul's biography, from late 49 onward. But this moves the letter out of its current location, within Paul's years of shadow, where it seemed initially to fit so comfortably. We must find another plausible location for it later within the frame. First, however, we should note that further details in the letter arguably confirm the inappropriateness of its location somewhere in the years of shadow that ran from 43 through 48 or mid-49 CE.

Paul states in 3:12 that Artemas or Tychicus will be sent to Crete shortly. And he asks in 3:13 for Titus to assist the onward journey of Apollos. Neither of these biographical markers is as decisive as the sense of the Judaizing crisis just noted, but they are both troubling.

Tychicus has appeared in Paul's letters up to this moment only in relation to Asia (Col 4:7; see Laod 6:21 — an association that Acts will later corroborate in 20:4). We do not yet know for certain when this mission began. But it may have begun with Paul's imprisonment in Apamea or somewhere close by, sometime in 50 CE, when he was journeying back from Antioch and Jerusalem, after his second visit to the holy city, to the Aegean by way of Galatia, using roads through the interior of Asia Minor. The Ephesian mission certainly is not yet in full swing (see 1 Cor 16:8-9). Moreover, we suspect by this point that Paul generally likes to evangelize a key city or sequence of cities in a region and then move on, suggesting that the Lycus valley mission could have been his first significant incursion into the province of Asia, one shortly to be extended by work in Ephesus. So the presence of Tychicus in the letter to Titus seems marginally to corroborate the doubts already introduced by the presence of the Teachers or of those like him. If it is genuine, Titus does not seem to belong to Paul's missionary work that took place before 49 CE and hence before all the events in Asia that began to unfold during 50. Similarly, the letter asks that Apollos be assisted and sent on his way (Titus 3:13), but we have encountered Apollos explicitly only in 51 CE, learning then that he probably arrived on Paul's turf sometime in 50 CE (1 Cor 1:12; 3:1-16; 4:6; 16:12). So once again, Titus does not seem to fall into the years of shadow.

It could be replied that the group of deceptive Judaeophiles in 1:10b-11, 14, and 3:9-11 are not the same as the Teacher and his group; that Tychicus, although Asian, was not converted *in* Asia; and that the Apollos in view in Titus was not the same figure as the rival evident in the Corinthian letters. With three instances of special pleading, however, the plausibility of the entire scenario begins to unravel. Might these problems be resolved simply by repositioning Titus later in the frame? We could explain the foregoing pieces of data — the presence of the Teacher and his characteristic program, and of Tychicus and Apollos — just by positioning Titus at the end of the letter sequence, sometime after Romans. Unfortunately, however, this suggestion runs into difficulties as well.

Paul states programmatically in Romans 15:19-24 that his work in the northeast quadrant of the Mediterranean littoral is done. He is heading toward Rome and then on to Spain. So to accommodate a later position in the sequence for Titus, we have to posit a significant change of plans on Paul's part. He must return to the area *and* undertake an extensive and successful mission on Crete. Moreover, he himself must stay for a time in the vicinity of (probably) one of the two principal cities named Nicopolis — either in Epirus, in the province of Achaia, or in Pontus. So we must posit *two* significant evangelistic undertakings in the very quadrant that Paul declared in Romans 15:19 to have been satisfactorily evangelized.

Now admittedly, Paul can change his mind about things like travel plans, and perhaps about what we might call "doctrinal matters" as well, but a scenario presupposing these two later missions in the Mediterranean quadrant he earlier declared definitively evangelized looks again like special pleading. It will prove difficult to glean any corroborations from other sources of a return by Paul to the entire area and of a highly successful Cretan mission at this time, although we must wait until we have assessed 1 and 2 Timothy, not to mention the relevant data from Acts, before we insist on this point. Suffice it to say that a relocation of Titus later in the frame, to a further period of extensive missionary work in the northeastern quarter of the Mediterranean, looks suspicious.

In sum, the letter's missional presuppositions initially fit nicely into the underdeveloped part of our sequence, the years of shadow, after the missions to Macedonia and Achaia in the late 30s and through 40 (and hence after the composition of 1 and 2 Thess) but before the intensive sequence that began (probably) in 49 CE, during which Paul fought off rivals and enemies and evangelized Asia. The missions on Crete and in the region around Nicopolis presupposed by Titus make perfect sense between these two periods. But the letter's partisan and biographical details push it inexorably out of this location and later in Paul's life — where these missions then make little sense and find less confirmation. (Note also that this difficulty with later *missions* in the northeast is peculiar to Titus; they are more difficult to explain than a mere return by Paul to the area on a visit, this being the scenario we might find in 1 and 2 Timothy.) And to this basic problem in the exigence of the letter against its broader frame we must now add suspicions about the travelogue of Zenas and Apollos.

As we have already noted, Titus is told in 3:13 to assist Zenas and Apollos on their way (Ζηνᾶν τὸν νομικὸν καὶ Ἀπολλῶν σπουδαίως πρόπεμψον, ἵνα μηδὲν αὐτοῖς λείπῃ).[7] For Paul to issue these instructions, Zenas and Apollos would presumably be in some proximity to him (i.e., in close contact), and he is, as we have seen, most probably located in one of the two major cities named Nicopolis. But the difficulty now arises that a journey from the vicinity of one of these cities by way of Crete to somewhere else makes little sense.

Crete is not on the way from either city to anywhere significant or plausible. That travelers would journey from a far distant city in Pontus to any destination by way of Crete is baffling. ORBIS (June 24, 2013) plots a journey in these basic terms only to the North African town of Petras Megas (in modern Libya). Not even journeys to Paraetonium (to the east of Petras Megas) or Petrass (to the west) would take a traveler rationally through Crete. And that travelers would journey from the city in Epirus to anywhere via Crete is even more implausible (a broadly southeastern journey). Only the deliberately coast-hugging east-west voyage from Asia Minor on to Sicily or Rome is a plausible itinerary, one that Acts famously associates with Paul. But this is a very distinct journey, and from nowhere near (a) Nicopolis. Crete is simply not located on important travel routes around the Mediterranean. It is a destination, and little more.

We should not press this suspicion too far. Our knowledge of ancient travel is by no means exhaustive — and Paul did himself travel at least somewhere by way of Crete, if Acts is to be trusted (although we will not of course insist on this claim yet). However, it does seem that a further doubt concerning the authenticity of Titus has become apparent as its framing implications are being pressed. Its implicit travelogue for Zenas and Apollos seems more fictitious than practical.

Having noted these two main concerns generated by a close look at the letter's framing implications, we can turn to consider some of the more common challenges to the letter's authenticity.

2.3 The Challenge of Style

Up to this point, we have consistently rejected arguments for pseudonymity on the basis of style, on two principal grounds. First, uncontrolled appeals to

---

7. This command uses a technical term for concrete assistance to travelers — προπέμπειν; see also Rom 15:24; 1 Cor 16:6, 11; 2 Cor 1:16; also Acts 15:3; 20:38; 21:5; 3 Jn 6. This connotation is noted esp. by Malherbe (1977, 222-32).

certain specific stylistic indicators have appeared slanted in their presentations of the data — what Kahneman would say was an instance of confirmation bias, and what others might describe more colorfully as "cherry-picking."[8] Second, when statistically controlled appeals have been made (see Kenny, Neumann, Ledger, and Mealand), these have generally not confirmed one another and, moreover, when making strong claims about pseudepigraphy, have seemed to overinterpret the data, finding meaningful information in patterns that arguably are equally explicable in terms of sampling error or statistical "noise." (Hence, the principal use of the more statistically sophisticated studies here has been negative, namely, to expose the error of confirmation bias in the selection of any stylistic markers within a broader case for pseudepigraphy.) But in the case of Titus, we come to the first — and the last — canonical letter by Paul on which all the more sophisticated studies of style agree. Even the cautious Kenny (1986) suggests that this letter has a demonstrably distinctive style over against the other Pauline letters, a judgment echoed by Neumann (1990), Ledger (1995), and Mealand (esp. 1989; 1995). As Kenny puts it: "Only Titus . . . is . . . deserving of the suspicion cast on the Pastorals"; hence, "on the basis of the [statistical] evidence . . . for my part I see no reason to reject the hypothesis that twelve of the Pauline Epistles are the work of a single, unusually versatile author" (100) — Titus being the unlucky thirteenth epistle that should be under a stylistic cloud. Suffice it to say, then, that Titus — and Titus alone — *is* under immediate suspicion of pseudepigraphy on grounds of a statistically corroborated analysis of its style. And this doubt must now be added to those concerns generated by a consideration of the letter's framing implications. Indeed, with this realization, we are now in a position to make a preliminary judgment concerning the authenticity of Titus.

2.4 Judgment

The three doubts raised — in relation to the frame, where we found two, and style — are independently generated and hence cumulative in force, and they combine to suggest a tentative preliminary judgment of pseudepigraphy for Titus, leading to its exclusion from further involvement in the reconstruction of the Pauline frame. Furthermore, I expect this judgment to be cumulatively corroborated in analyses that follow, both here and elsewhere. Subsequently in this chapter, we will consider the earliest attestation to the transmission of

8. See Kahneman (2011, esp. 80-81, 324, 333); also Rudman (1998).

the Pauline letters by reconstructing, as best we can, the original edition of the letter collection, something that will confirm our judgment here. Paul's letter to Titus was not, as far as I can tell, part of the original collection of Paul's letters. This is not a definitive demonstration of pseudepigraphy, for obvious reasons to be noted shortly, but it is an important corroborative contention.[9] So we will proceed for now on the assumption that our collection of genuine Pauline letters does not need to be expanded to include Titus. And with this decision made, we can turn to consider 1 Timothy.

3. Locating 1 Timothy

3.1 The Immediate Implied Exigence

With its authenticity assumed at the outset of our analysis, 1 Timothy provides a number of details about its immediate exigence.

First Timothy 1:3 suggests that Paul has traveled to Macedonia, leaving Timothy in Ephesus to manage the Christian community there. Paul's entreaty to Timothy to continue to stay is followed immediately by a warning about false teaching (καθὼς παρεκάλεσά σε προσμεῖναι ἐν Ἐφέσῳ πορευόμενος εἰς Μακεδονίαν, ἵνα παραγγείλῃς τισὶν μὴ ἑτεροδιδασκαλεῖν κ.τ.λ.). And 3:14-15 expands on this situation, stating that Paul hopes to return soon but, because he might be delayed, is writing now so that Timothy "might know how life is to be conducted in God's household" and "assembly" ([14] Ταῦτά σοι γράφω ἐλπίζων ἐλθεῖν πρὸς σὲ ἐν τάχει, [15] ἐὰν δὲ βραδύνω, ἵνα εἰδῇς πῶς δεῖ ἐν οἴκῳ θεοῦ ἀναστρέφεσθαι, ἥτις ἐστὶν ἐκκλησία θεοῦ ζῶντος κ.τ.λ.). This narrative is corroborated in 4:13, which speaks again of Paul's return — "Until I come . . ." (ἕως ἔρχομαι κ.τ.λ.). Then in 6:13-14 this space is expanded rather dramatically, with Timothy charged to keep "the commandment," which in context seems in particular to be "true confession" (see vv. 12-13), until the *parousia* of Jesus Christ, whenever that might be ([13] παραγγέλλω σοι ἐνώπιον τοῦ θεοῦ τοῦ ζῳογονοῦντος τὰ πάντα καὶ Χριστοῦ Ἰησοῦ τοῦ μαρτυρήσαντος ἐπὶ Ποντίου Πιλάτου τὴν καλὴν ὁμολογίαν, [14] τηρῆσαί σε τὴν ἐντολὴν ἄσπιλον ἀνεπίλημπτον μέχρι τῆς ἐπιφανείας τοῦ κυρίου ἡμῶν Ἰησοῦ Χριστοῦ κ.τ.λ.). So Timothy's instructions are clear, even if Paul never returns to Ephesus.

---

9. And I suspect that a later consideration of the data found in Acts will reinforce this judgment, in part by further problematizing any shift of the missionary and travel scenarios envisaged by Titus from the intermediate years of shadow into a late phase in Paul's ministry.

The letter's final instruction to Timothy, in 6:20a, is "to guard what has been entrusted to you" (Ὦ Τιμόθεε, τὴν παραθήκην φύλαξον), again, turning away from false teaching.

The content of the letter is thus recognizably similar to Titus, although not identical with it (and this suggests, at least for the moment, that the pseudepigraphic Titus utilized 1 Timothy as its primary textual template).

Emphases resonant with those found in Titus are the basic confessions of the divine act in Christ that called the Christian community into existence (see 1:15-17; 2:3-6; 3:16; 4:3-5 [things created], 9-10; possibly along with a repeated emphasis on one immortal, only God in 1:17; 6:15-16); the appropriate transmission of these claims and related teaching from Paul's witness through trusted delegates like Timothy to appropriately selected groups of leaders (see just below); the ordering of the community under their leadership, in terms of both suitable relationships of authority and virtues (2:8-15; 5:1-16; 6:1-2);[10] and the exclusion of harmful teaching from any influence (see just below). But variations are also apparent.

The letter provides instructions about two groups of leaders. Whereas Titus speaks of a single body of "elders," in 1:5-9 (denoted as πρεσβύτεροι in v. 5 but developed in terms of a generic ἐπίσκοπός from v. 7), 1 Timothy provides advice about two distinguishable groups — about "overseers" (ἐπίσκοπός) in 3:1-7, and about "deacons" (sg. διάκονος) in 3:8-13 — along with more general admonitions to elders in 5:17-20 (πρεσβύτεροι). A "body of elders" (πρεσβυτέριον) is also mentioned in 4:14. Rather significantly, these leaders are to be paid, as "Scripture says . . ." (5:17-19). Timothy personally exemplifies the work of the Holy Spirit in relation to this ordered process of transmission. He is exhorted in 1:18 to fulfill the prophecy first made about him by fighting for sound teaching. Moreover, 4:14 details that his gift was given to him, accompanied by prophecy, when the elders laid hands on him (μὴ ἀμέλει τοῦ ἐν σοὶ χαρίσματος, ὃ ἐδόθη σοι διὰ προφητείας μετὰ ἐπιθέσεως τῶν χειρῶν τοῦ πρεσβυτερίου).

New flourishes vis-à-vis the ordering of the community are also apparent in 1 Timothy. There is instruction to be prayerful and peaceful in relation to political rulers (2:1-2). The letter famously excludes women from teaching or "having authority over a man" (2:11-15; see esp. v. 12: διδάσκειν δὲ γυναικὶ οὐκ ἐπιτρέπω οὐδὲ αὐθεντεῖν ἀνδρός, ἀλλ' εἶναι ἐν ἡσυχίᾳ). And there is extensive instruction concerning widows (5:3-16).

---

10. See similar "Household Codes" material in Titus 2:2-10; 3:1; also Col 3:18–4:1; Eph 5:21–6:9; and, less overtly, 1 Cor 7:17-24; Rom 13:1-7; also 1 Pet 2:11–3:12.

The false teaching in view is somewhat different as well. The anti-Jewish cast in the teaching rejected by Titus has been displaced by a rather positive view of the law, which is contrasted with "foolish" and "meaningless" "teachers of the law" (1:3b-11; see esp. vv. 7-8: [7] θέλοντες εἶναι νομοδιδάσκαλοι, μὴ νοοῦντες μήτε ἃ λέγουσιν μήτε περὶ τίνων διαβεβαιοῦνται. [8] Οἴδαμεν δὲ ὅτι καλὸς ὁ νόμος, ἐάν τις αὐτῷ νομίμως χρῆται). Nevertheless, the law does not order the Christian community explicitly but is intended only for wicked people ([9] ὅτι δικαίῳ νόμος οὐ κεῖται ἀνόμοις δὲ καὶ ἀνυποτάκτοις, ἀσεβέσι καὶ ἁμαρτωλοῖς, ἀνοσίοις καὶ βεβήλοις, πατρολῴαις καὶ μητρολῴαις, ἀνδροφόνοις). Celibacy and dietary scruples are excoriated (4:3 in the context of vv. 1-4). And in the final sections of the letter, false teaching is linked to the love of money (see 6:3-5, 10, 20b-21, as well as vv. 6-10 and 17-19).

Paul's own biography protrudes marginally more obviously into 1 Timothy than it does into Titus (as does Timothy's).[11] Timothy's response to false teachers and their instructions is presumably then to be modeled on Paul's actions in 1:18-20. Timothy is to fight to maintain the appropriate teachings and so, if necessary, like Paul, to hand "shipwrecked" "blasphemers" like Hymenaeus and Alexander "over to Satan" ([1:18] Ταύτην τὴν παραγγελίαν παρατίθεμαί σοι, τέκνον Τιμόθεε, κατὰ τὰς προαγούσας ἐπὶ σὲ προφητείας, ἵνα στρατεύῃ ἐν αὐταῖς τὴν καλὴν στρατείαν [19] ἔχων πίστιν καὶ ἀγαθὴν συνείδησιν, ἥν τινες ἀπωσάμενοι περὶ τὴν πίστιν ἐναυάγησαν [20] ὧν ἐστιν Ὑμέναιος καὶ Ἀλέξανδρος, οὓς παρέδωκα τῷ σατανᾷ, ἵνα παιδευθῶσιν μὴ βλασφημεῖν; see 1 Cor 5:1-5). And references to Paul's apostolic commission in the context of his sinful past in 1:12-13 and 1:15a-16 ground broader claims about the Lord's grace and love and consequent salvation of sinners in 1:14-15a (see also 2:7). Moreover, in view of this material, 1 Timothy lacks the strong demarcation of a boundary between sinners and the Christian community that was apparent in Titus; while a boundary is implicit within this biographical fragment, it is overshadowed here by the divine kindness.

With these brief observations concerning the letter's content in place, it is time to ask whether its account of its immediate exigence encompasses them plausibly.

We have already conceded the possibility in relation to Titus that Paul could have written a letter to a delegate that was intended to affirm the delegate's authority within the broader community and to provide instructions about the ordering of that listening community. Clearly, this account can also

---

11. An important detailed account of this feature — although assuming pseudonymity — is provided by Merz (2004); it is handily summarized by M. Mitchell (2008, esp. 43, 45-47).

explain the potentially problematic redundancy and generality in 1 Timothy. Paul is not instructing Timothy so much as his broader constituency, and these instructions are consequently understandably general. But the exigence constructed so carefully by 1 Timothy in 1:3; 3:14-15; 4:13; and, to a degree, 6:13-14 introduces a significant note of doubt into this explanation.

The letter steps beyond the scenario in which it authorizes and instructs a delegate in public when it says that it was caused by a potential delay in Paul's return from Macedonia in 3:14-15. It thereby states explicitly that the letter was written for Timothy's own benefit ahead of Paul's later arrival, when he would impart these instructions in person. Paul was *not* therefore apparently reinforcing something that Timothy already knew from the past and/or principally writing for the benefit of the wider listening community in the present, as he might have been in Titus. He was providing instructions to Timothy by letter ahead of a future visit, suggesting directly that this information was largely unknown to Timothy at present. And this undermines the justification for the material's redundancy and generality offered by an explanation in terms of public authorization and corroboration. As we will see in more detail shortly, Timothy has been accompanying Paul for many years by this point in their missionary work, so the suggestion that he would need this sort of general instruction now seems implausible. This would hardly be new information that Paul would need to impart in case he did not eventually return from Macedonia; it cannot conceivably have newly arisen during that recent journey. Hence, we should introduce an element of doubt into our appraisal of the account that 1 Timothy supplies concerning its immediate exigence. We should turn now to consider where this letter might fit into the broader biographical frame.

3.2 *Framing Considerations*

There are three initial possibilities for the location of 1 Timothy within our broader frame: relatively early, in the years of shadow (43-49 CE); in an intermediate position, within or immediately adjacent to Paul's calendar year of crisis (spring 51-spring 52 CE); or later, after our current sequence altogether, that is, after Paul's trip to Jerusalem, about which and after which we do not yet have epistolary evidence. This last scenario would place 1 Timothy sometime after mid-52 CE. The first two possibilities collapse fairly quickly on closer examination, leaving us with scenario three and a later placement — and this, in any case, is the most defensible position for the authenticity of 1 Timothy in substantive terms, as we will see shortly.

As we have just noted, the letter suggests that Paul has left Timothy in Ephesus to manage the church there, partly by appointing elders and partly by excluding various false teachers. Among other things, he is not to appoint anyone to the position of overseer who is a recent convert (3:6). There are also extensive instructions concerning an apparently significant number of widows. And this all implies a well-established and burgeoning church in Ephesus and consequently seems to exclude an early location for 1 Timothy.

In the middle of 50 CE Paul was incarcerated somewhere near the Lycus valley. In the spring of 51 Paul wrote 1 Corinthians from Ephesus, our first notice from a letter of his presence in that city, and he tells us there that he wants to remain in the city until Pentecost (i.e., around 50 days, if he is writing near the time of Passover; see 5:6-8), "because a great and powerful door [for ministry] has opened to me" ([16:8] ἐπιμενῶ δὲ ἐν᾽Εφέσῳ ἕως τῆς πεντηκοστῆς· [9] θύρα γάρ μοι ἀνέῳγεν μεγάλη καὶ ἐνεργής, καὶ ἀντικείμενοι πολλοί). It seems most likely, then, that Paul's mission in Ephesus had begun in the interim, and that it had only just begun to flourish after some months of struggle over the winter of 50-51. In the light of this data from 1 Corinthians, it is difficult to posit a successful mission and a large church in Ephesus prior to this period, during which 1 Timothy could have been written — a letter assuming a large leadership group, which, moreover, is not to be drawn from neophytes, and a sizable number of widows. (The developmental challenges noted just below will corroborate this decision.) Prior to recent months, next to no one seems to have converted to Paul's community in Ephesus. The great door for ministry has only just opened, whereas 1 Timothy seems to suggest that it has been open for some time. It is equally difficult to posit an intermediate location for 1 Timothy in our frame, during the year of crisis and shortly after the door for ministry has opened wide in Ephesus.

Paul does at least travel through the right areas during this time as he sets out on his third visit to Corinth. But nothing else really matches the details found in 1 Timothy, which leaves Timothy in Ephesus with Paul speaking from Macedonia of a return in short order. Paul's year of crisis had a very different shape.

Timothy seems to have accompanied Paul on his journey through Macedonia to Corinth on his third visit to that city. He coauthored 2 Corinthians from Macedonia (1:1) and Philippians from Corinth (1:1) and then apparently visited Philippi (Phil 2:19-23), returning in time to greet the Romans when that letter was composed in Corinth (Rom 16:21a).[12]

---

12. Moreover, we can tentatively infer from the various travelogues in 1 Cor, 2 Cor, Phil,

Thus, while the exigence of 1 Timothy bears an initial resemblance to Paul's year of crisis in the Aegean, this is superficial and collapses on closer examination. At no point did Paul travel to Macedonia leaving Timothy in charge of a flourishing church in Ephesus, planning to return shortly thereafter. More could be said at this point, in developmental terms, but it does not really need to be. We turn, then, to consider the final possibility for the provenance of 1 Timothy.

The only possible location remaining for 1 Timothy within our developing frame is later, sometime after the sequence that is already in place. So we have to posit a return to the Aegean by Paul after his third visit to Jerusalem (and so on), during which he visits Ephesus and then leaves Timothy in charge of that church, traveling on to Macedonia. Paul was apparently planning to return to Ephesus but, fearing a delay, penned 1 Timothy in the interim. This location might offer some useful narrative leverage in relation to various challenges to the authenticity of 1 Timothy on grounds of contradiction that will be noted shortly. But we should first register some of the doubts concerning the late scenario that have already been noted with respect to Titus, along with certain variations in the explanation in question.

It is possible in the first instance that the events surrounding 1 Timothy took place after Paul left Jerusalem and was on the way to Rome. A journey to Rome would ordinarily have proceeded more directly, but it is not inconceivable that Paul could have chosen to travel from Jerusalem to Rome by way of his Aegean churches, thereby returning to the area quite quickly, and imparting important new pieces of information that he might have picked up in Jerusalem — perhaps about church organization and the role of women. But that he would have planned a round trip to Macedonia from Ephesus at this time is much harder to imagine. Indeed, it is next to impossible (Paul both pausing and then backtracking in this scenario away from Rome). If this was the case, then Paul's plans as announced in Romans 15:19-24 would have shifted completely. And so we really would have to suppose that Paul is involved in some new venture in 1 Timothy, either abandoning the intentions of Romans 15:19-24 or returning to the area after his trip to Rome, and perhaps also Spain, has been completed.

This last scenario could involve the elapse of a considerable amount of time between his third Jerusalem visit and subsequent visit to Rome and the

---

and Rom that Paul's journey to Jerusalem by way of Macedonia and Asia was a late adjustment made in response to the depredations of the enemies, and hence was conceived only after he had left Ephesus and traveled through Macedonia (Phil 2:24).

composition of 1 Timothy — perhaps many years. But given the significant shifts in organization in view in 1 Timothy, and the absence of any need to abandon Romans 15:19-24, the late scenario probably commends itself the most. It must be conceded that, in and of itself, this scenario is not implausible, although it is largely unattested. Moreover, it seems that we must prescind from further, stronger judgments in relation to framing, because any further analysis must engage with extra-epistolary evidence, especially with data supplied by Acts, and our current project is working solely with epistolary data. Suffice it to say that it does not seem impossible to suppose that Paul changed his mind and returned to the Aegean after his planned trip to Jerusalem, undertaking a longer season of work in and around Asia and Macedonia. Or, alternatively — and rather more plausibly — he may have made this visit after years of further missionary work in Rome and Spain. These possibilities cannot be ruled out yet, on the basis of epistolary evidence alone, because Paul's genuine letters, somewhat understandably, do not tell us how and when he died. Moreover, his extant corpus falls silent at present in the spring of 52 CE. So we cannot definitively exclude a later provenance and date for 1 Timothy at this stage in our analysis, however many doubts it might produce in framing terms. (Many of these presumably arise from clashes between this scenario and the implications of Acts, but they should of course be resisted.)

However, this framing decision does function as a caveat. Any case for the authenticity of 1 Timothy must locate it late in the letter sequence, during some return by Paul to the Aegean, and hence at least after mid-52 CE, a position with some vulnerabilities, although it does at least fill out a part of the frame where we currently lack information. But before placing too much weight on this new addition, we should consider some further challenges to the letter's integrity.

3.3 Challenges

As usual, many of the most popular challenges to the authenticity of 1 Timothy are shown to be unconvincing when they are subjected to this project's methodological strictures.

Many scholars have suggested that the style of 1 Timothy is overtly non-Pauline. But Kenny (1986, 98) demonstrates that the style of 1 Timothy is at least arguably acceptable, being closer to the Pauline mean in his analysis than either 1 Corinthians or Philemon (and Mealand's plots displayed in ch. 5 make a similar point).

Others have suggested that the differences apparent in the role of the law between the letters written to combat the enemies (i.e., the Teacher and his followers, so Rom, Gal, and the Previous Letter to Philippi / Phil 3:2–4:3) and the instructions directed to Timothy in 1 Timothy 1 (esp. vv. 8-11) cannot be accommodated within one author's thinking. That Paul would have developed from the Torah-free ethical position he elaborated with such sophistication in Romans (esp. 5-8) — and apparently defended so doggedly (see Gal 2:1-10, 11-14) — to the endorsement of a "proper use" of the law in relation to evildoers in 1 Timothy defies any obvious explanation in terms of conceptual progress, it might be said.

But as we have already seen many times, in all essentially substantive appeals of this nature, we cannot yet exclude opportunism or some combination of sheer confusion and later degeneration from Paul's coherent thinking. He may have written and defended one set of things about the Torah through the spring of 52 CE and then, for whatever reason, softened or blunted this position by the time that 1 Timothy was written later on — perhaps as late as 58 or 59 CE — even granting that a fundamental contradiction is present in this material. So this type of observation is indecisive in relation to authenticity — although its implications for Paul's acumen might be somewhat depressing.[13]

Others have suggested that the level of communal organization in view in 1 Timothy is anachronistic, a challenge worth spending a little more time on.

Several features of 1 Timothy are arguably troubling in relation to authentic Paulinism. The letter provides instructions for two distinct sets of community leaders — overseers and deacons — who together composed the eldership of a given church. The instructions are not overly detailed, but apparently overseers were to teach (see διδακτικόν in 3:2; and perhaps also implicitly from 4:11, 13, 15-16; see also 5:17b), while deacons, as their name suggests, merely served (see 3:10b, 13; see also Acts 6:1-6). Both groups were involved in

---

13. This challenge is further complicated by the complex debate currently unfolding within Pauline scholarship over the exact nature of Paul's argumentation in his "justification" texts. A conventional account of that material need not see a strong contradiction between Rom, Gal, and Phil 3:1-11 on the one hand and 1 Tim 1:8-11 on the other, since it views sinful non-Christians as being subject to God's law (see esp. Rom 1:18-32; 2:12-16). Indeed, it might see no difficulties here at all. Moreover, 1 Tim 1:8-11 would endorse the "third use of the law." However, alternative views of this argumentation in Paul, whether "apocalyptic" or informed by "the new perspective" or some other revisionist approach, might perceive more tensions between these two groups of texts (or they might not). See my 2009 (esp. 15-24 within ch. 1, a section entitled "The First Phase: The Rigorous Contract"; and ch. 12, "Wide and Narrow Paths," 412-66).

praying and ordination, however (4:14; 5:22). There is no distinction in their wages either (5:17). The leadership is to be entirely male, and its members married, although to "but one wife" (3:2, 12). The Holy Spirit, insofar as 1 Timothy mentions it, works through this arrangement as well; there was prophecy at Timothy's ordination, at which time this gift was also imparted to him (1:18; 4:14; 5:22). Complementing the male hierarchy, women were not permitted to teach and thereby to hold authority over men. They were allowed to learn, albeit quietly (2:11-15). And complementing the married norm, women were to fulfill roles of childbearing (2:15), along with child rearing, hospitality, and acts of charity (implicit in 5:10). They were to avoid ostentatious dress and behavior (2:9-10). The liminal category of widows is then carefully parsed in 5:3-16.

Many aspects of the general account of the church supplied here concern readers of the Pauline letters that have already been judged authentic. Leadership does not seem to be so well defined in those letters. Senior figures and perhaps even an eldership are occasionally discernible — as the defenders of the authenticity of 1 Timothy have noted (see, i.a., L. Johnson 1996, 13-16) — but never overtly in terms of two distinct groups of overseers and deacons. Moreover, teaching is one charismatic office among others (see Rom 12:7; 1 Cor 12:28; Laod 4:11). There is no obvious process of "ordination," nor is the work of the Spirit limited to this channel. Rather, all participants are encouraged to make a contribution to worship and thereby to speak (at least at Corinth; see 1 Cor 14:26). Hence, even if Paul silences the Corinthian women in certain respects (14:33b-36), he does not silence their speech in the Spirit, specifically in prayer, tongues, and prophecy, and presumably such utterances were authoritative for male auditors (11:2-16). Female figures are also detectable in leadership positions elsewhere (Rom 16:1-3). The question of widows is never addressed, and there is no evidence elsewhere of a "widow's list." In short, the organization of the Christian community in the ten letters already treated seems subtly but significantly different in multiple respects from the organization depicted by 1 Timothy — and is at times contrary to it. And some key differences are arguably apparent in relation to Paul himself.

Paul and some of his closest associates seem to have been celibate, and to have endorsed this state as superior to marriage (1 Cor 7:17-40; 9:5). Similarly, they seem to have refused payment, relying on donations from distant churches and on the work of their hands to support themselves, practices at some variance with those named as normative for church leaders in 1 Timothy. But are these differences fatal to the authenticity of 1 Timothy?

I would say not. The late location of 1 Timothy allows it to respond in developmental terms to these challenges. After many years in prison, an advocate of 1 Timothy might say, Paul, faced with reports of various disturbing aberrations and problems in his communities, had formulated a more tightly structured account of local communal organization, which he proceeded to spread and to enforce when traveling again through his mission fields around the Aegean Sea.[14] (Perhaps this was also — or even primarily — an accommodation to Judean practices.) And it is not necessarily surprising that we do not find specific apologies in 1 Timothy for its corrections and alterations of earlier teachings as we do in 2 Corinthians. Paul's first letter to Timothy is a general document conveying generic instructions. And any local apologies could have been undertaken orally and in specific letters if they proved necessary — as they would have at Corinth. (Paul would have had to address his reasons for altering his views on celibacy, female leadership, charismatic utterances by women, the charismatic assignment of offices, and his financial practices there, at the least, and his silences in all these respects in the Corinthian correspondence and related texts is a further indication that earlier and intermediate provenances for 1 Timothy are unlikely.)[15]

But some scholars make a slightly more programmatic claim at this point (see, i.a., MacDonald 1988). Instead of pointing to seriatim differences, they suggest that the two levels of organization depicted in the two sets of texts simply fall at different points on the well-trodden path that runs from the first establishment of local communities by charismatic individuals on through their institutionalization. This claim is rooted ultimately in Weber's (1978 [1956]) famous thesis that without such institutionalization no original charismatic movement can survive, thus resulting inevitably in "the routinization of charisma." And so it is argued that the depictions in the different Pauline texts in view necessarily belong to different eras in the development of the early church, and the texts in question consequently to different authors. Paul was clearly the charismatic founder running his communities on a fairly ad hoc and personal basis in the letters already judged authentic, but 1 Timothy depicts a time after his death during which the leadership of those communities had become more structured and even bureaucratized in order to survive. This would have resulted in the institution of various standard operating procedures, one consequence of which was — somewhat ironically — resistance to further disruptions from charismatic phenomena.

14. That is, the suggestion that "early Catholicism" is evident in certain Pauline texts can be reversed in relation to 1 Tim and used against advocates of its pseudonymity.

15. But a further line of inquiry is arguably opened by this contention: Do we sense an appropriate set of practices at Corinth, given a late provenance for 1 Timothy, in *1 Clement*? This is too delicate a case to warrant pursuit here; however, it is an intriguing one.

It is an attractive thesis and arguably rests on a profound truth. But appeals to Weber's thesis to resolve questions of authenticity are unwise. It seems best to refrain from strong claims concerning both the interrelationship between unstructured charisma and routinized authority and (perhaps more importantly) the development of this relationship over time.[16] The first relationship here is rather more complicated than Weber first suggested, as evidenced by a close reading of Paul's letters that have already been affirmed; various procedures, routines, and inchoate institutions are found coexisting and interacting in and around them with more flexible and unpredictable charismatic phenomena. And we should bear in mind that Paul's context contained numerous organizational examples, whether in terms of Diaspora Jewish or Greco-Roman models.[17] The second claim in this relation is best abandoned as well. Movements simply do not evolve institutionally in fixed and steady patterns, allowing different levels of organization to be plotted neatly on a timeline and authorship assigned accordingly. As more recent studies than Weber's suggest, organizations are highly diverse, complex, and somewhat unpredictable.[18] Hence — as we have had cause to observe frequently in our preceding analysis — the relationship between these substantive claims about Pauline texts and framing is really best reversed.

Rather than making important framing claims on the basis of perceived organizational patterns and their supposed evolution, the letters should be sequenced and framed first on independent grounds, and conclusions then drawn about the organizational patterns that seem in fact to have evolved (if they did). It may be that different strata in relation to different stages in the development of the early church are discernible. But this judgment will be a consequence of framing and not its presupposition. It is not so much that Weber's basic insight is being denied; it is simply that organizational patterns cannot be mapped in temporal terms with sufficient precision to allow strong conclusions about texts written within the developing ancient organization that was the early church. At bottom, we cannot tell initially whether the organizational recommendations in 1 Timothy could have arisen within Paul's

16. The anti-Catholic prejudices of Weber and of many of his recent Protestant followers in the modern period should also be taken into account, not to mention the anti-institutional biases of any modern, fundamentally liberal readers. Some of MacIntyre's (1990) warnings are salutary in this relation.

17. See (i.a.) Kloppenborg and Wilson (1996).

18. See esp. Burke (2011 [2002]); Aldrich (1999); see also, to a degree, Rogers (2003 [1962]), discussing the relationship between organizations and innovation, and the astonishingly unpredictable and diverse patterns of dissemination that result.

lifetime or had to have developed well after it. And only framing will help us answer this question definitively.

It seems that many of the major challenges to the authenticity of 1 Timothy have collapsed — and certainly those made in terms essentially of substantive differences, often played out for 1 Timothy in specifically organizational terms. I do not always find the rebuttals of these challenges by advocates of authenticity particularly satisfying; they amount at this stage to the endorsement of 1 Timothy as the climactic point of Pauline instruction. At the same time, I do not think that any of these attacks on the authenticity of 1 Timothy are definitive.

However, our discussion is not yet over. The veracity of 1 Timothy may not need to be challenged in the rather programmatic, substantive ways just noted, a mode of address that is almost invariably indecisive for this question during framing. In the case of 1 Timothy, we might encounter the first instance in a Pauline letter of a small but overt anachronism — a telltale "smoking gun" — on the basis of which a hypothesis of pseudepigraphy can immediately be asserted.

As we have already seen, 1 Timothy 5:18 instructs its communities to pay its leaders, thus generating a point of tension with the characterization of Paul's financial policy in the communal letters. But 5:18 issues its command by combining an explicit quotation of a scriptural text, Deuteronomy 25:4, with a quotation of Luke 10:7 (// Mt 10:10): "for the Scripture says 'do not muzzle a threshing ox' and 'the worker is worthy of his wages'" (λέγει γὰρ ἡ γραφή· βοῦν ἀλοῶντα οὐ φιμώσεις καί ἄξιος ὁ ἐργάτης τοῦ μισθοῦ αὐτοῦ).[19] The syntax of this command seems to combine Deuteronomy 25:4 and Luke 10:7 as scriptural texts (ἡ γραφή), thereby indicating that Luke was a scriptural resource at the time when 1 Timothy was written. And if this is the case, it seems clear that both the author of 1 Timothy and his auditors knew a Gospel, and this would place the letter well beyond the boundaries of Paul's life, during a later stage in the life of the early church, after the Gospels had been written, circulated widely, and given scriptural status alongside the Jewish Bible (here the LXX). Scholars are divided over exactly when this happened, but most if not all would agree that these stages did not unfold during the lifetime of Paul.

One rejoinder to this problem might be to appeal to the widespread circulation of a written and very early version of Q that contained Luke 10:7

---

19. Cf. Mt 10:10: ἄξιος γὰρ ὁ ἐργάτης τῆς τροφῆς αὐτοῦ; Lk 10:7: ἄξιος γὰρ ὁ ἐργάτης τοῦ μισθοῦ αὐτοῦ. Note also that Deut 19:15 is echoed in the following verse in 1 Tim, an appeal paralleled by Mt 18:16.

and was already denoted as Scripture in Paul's day. Paul was familiar with oral traditions concerning Jesus; he seems to have been familiar with a rudimentary passion narrative, and occasionally quotes Jesus' sayings.[20] But he never refers to these sayings as Scripture; they are the Lord's commands or instructions, or something similar (1 Cor 7:10, 12). Nor does he supply convincing evidence that an authoritative written text containing sayings from Jesus and denoted as Scripture circulated in his lifetime from which he could quote (and in fact I share the doubts of some that such a source even existed, let alone was written down or functioned as Scripture; see, i.a., Goodacre 2002; Goodacre and Perrin 2004). So this rejoinder extends beyond special pleading to overt implausibility.

However, it might be suggested that "Scripture" in 5:18 refers only to the first quotation, from Deuteronomy 25:4. The second quotation would then be a simple appending of a Jesus logion. In a variation on this proposal, the καί might be explicative and the logion added to explain the implication in the quotation of Deuteronomy 25:4, which is possibly a little opaque: "for the Scripture says, 'do not muzzle a threshing ox,' that is to say, 'the worker is worthy of his wages.'"

But the logion does not really explain the Deuteronomic command so much as supplement it. When either animals or people were working, it was cruel to prevent them from sharing in some of the results of that toil, especially when it was inadvertent, the Deuteronomic text suggests. The Lukan word then adds that leaders are, moreover, *worthy* of their wages, as v. 17 in the letter has just affirmed. Indeed, this neat double function of two quotations in support of a single point suggests quite strongly that the bald καί linking them is supposed to draw both statements under the initial heading of affirmation(s) from Scripture: "The Scripture says X *and* Y." To avoid this construal would be to introduce an unstated disjunction between an authoritative quotation from Deuteronomy and an authoritative quotation from Jesus and thereby to risk falling again into special pleading.

It seems, then, that the best construal of 1 Timothy 5:18 includes a saying of Jesus found in the Gospel of Luke within the general rubric of Scripture. And this suggests in turn the composition and reception of 1 Timothy sometime after the life of Paul, when the canonical Gospels had been written, widely circulated, and widely used, and thereby given scriptural status. And our earlier doubts in terms of the letter's immediate implied exigence now

---

20. The extent and implications of this phenomenon are much debated, but its brute fact and basic contours in the data are not in dispute; see (i.a.) Hays (2008).

seem to have found a small but decisive piece of confirmation. Meanwhile, two small further details in the letter, while not decisive, might corroborate our gathering suspicions.

For some time, I thought that 4:12a contained another smoking gun, namely, Paul's admonition to Timothy to let no one despise his "youth" (μηδείς σου τῆς νεότητος καταφρονείτω). If 1 Timothy was composed after mid-52 CE, then Timothy would have been accompanying Paul for some time by this date — at least from the Macedonian mission, which began as early as 39 CE (2 Cor 1:19; 1 Thess 1:1; 2 Thess 1:1), hence some thirteen years earlier. It seems almost certain, then, that Timothy was in his twenties and perhaps even nearing thirty when 1 Timothy arrived, and so hardly would have been a mere youth. At first glance, this just looks like a mistake by a later pseudepigrapher whose mental image of Timothy was understandably youthful, although here incorrectly (see Ehrman 2013, 209-10, although here pressing the point in relation to 2 Tim). But things are not quite so straightforward, because the word in question does not necessarily denote "youth," nor did ancient society necessarily construct this life stage in modern terms.

Timothy could have been a relatively *inexperienced* man by ancient standards and not a youth literally, especially as modern readers might construe this data (so Spicq 1969 [1947], 511-12). That is, the word means by analogy "(relatively) inexperienced." Jerome's comments on the ordination of a friend at the age of thirty are instructive: "Porro aetas ejus et Beatitudini tuae nota est, et cum ad triginta annorum spatia jam pervenerit, puto eam in hoc non esse reprehendendam. . . . Audiat cum Timotheo: *Adolescentiam tuam nemo contemnat* (1 Tim 4:12). Certe ipse quando Episcopus ordinatus est, non multum ab ea, in qua nunc frater meus est, distabat aetate" (PL 22:740-41; cited in Quinn and Wacker 2000, 382, 387-89). And a story recounted by Appian in *Bellum civile* makes the same point. There Sulla mocks the head of Marius the younger, who was probably around twenty-eight years old at the time of his death. "Marius hid himself in an underground tunnel and shortly afterward committed suicide. Lucretius cut off his head and sent it to Sulla, who exposed it in the forum in front of the rostra. It is said that he indulged in a jest at the youth of the consul (ἐπιγελάσαι λέγεται τῇ νεότητι τοῦ ὑπάτου) saying 'First learn to row, before you try to steer'" (1.94).[21]

Having said this, however, it still seems a little odd for Paul to exhort

---

21. Further discussion can be found in W. Metzger (1977); see also Ignatius, *Magn.* 3.1. (My thanks to Brendan Case for his investigations into, and trenchant discussions concerning, this issue.)

Timothy not to let anyone despise his "inexperience." Timothy has, as we just noted, been working with Paul by this time for as many as thirteen years, and possibly — presupposing a return to the Aegean by Paul after a Roman imprisonment — for something approaching twenty. So he is hardly inexperienced. This textual oddity falls short of being a decisive contention. But it does seem suggestive to me of pseudepigraphy rather than authenticity.

Furthermore, the letter's final exhortation in 6:20-21a, preceding the brief grace wish in v. 21b (Ἡ χάρις μεθ᾽ ὑμῶν), is suggestive. The sentence is oddly complex and negative: "Oh Timothy, guard what you have been entrusted with, turning away from the vile empty talking and contradictions of falsely named knowledge — by the proclamation of which concerning the faith, some have lost their way" ([6:20] Ὦ Τιμόθεε, τὴν παραθήκην φύλαξον ἐκτρεπόμενος τὰς βεβήλους κενοφωνίας καὶ ἀντιθέσεις τῆς ψευδωνύμου γνώσεως, [21a] ἥν τινες ἐπαγγελλόμενοι περὶ τὴν πίστιν ἠστόχησαν). This injunction draws together the letter's previous threads of warning about false teaching. The false teachers are designated as Christians in some sense, but illegitimately. They are rejected in no uncertain terms, as speakers of vile and empty things. But the second element that Timothy is to abandon is less polemical and more substantive; he is to turn away from their "contradictions," literally, from their "antitheses" (ἀντιθέσεις), which are then glossed with the further information that any such "knowledge" is "falsely named" (τῆς ψευδωνύμου γνώσεως). And the letter's use of the word "antitheses" here is possibly important.

This word is not uncommon in extant Greek but occurs mainly in earlier, technical philosophical discussions to denote contrary pairs like the beautiful and the ugly.[22] It occurs nowhere else in the NT, and is rare in Christian literature in Greek before the fourth century.[23] Nevertheless, Tertullian uses it — here transliterating a Greek word into Latin — because it was the name of Marcion's much-vilified theological work that sought to contrast the vengeful God of the Old Testament and Judaism with the loving deity of the New.[24] And

---

22. See (i.a.) Plato, *Theat.* 257e; 258b; Aristotle, *Metaphysics* passim (1054a-67b); *Rhetoric* 3.9-11; *Ethics* 1222a-24a; Plutarch, *Mor.* 953b; Lucian, *Dial. mort.* 10.10; *Hermetic Writings* 10.10; Philo, *Ebr.* 187.

23. See the *Clementine Recognitions* 8.15.1; Clement of Alexandria (see more below); Hippolytus (see more below); also Irenaeus, *Adv. haer.* 4.28.1, which uses the participle *antithentas* in relation to Marcion.

24. Tertullian claims that Marcion's *Antitheses* presented "confronting oppositions, which attempt to establish the discord between the Gospel and the Law, in order to demonstrate from the contrast of statements from both documents a contrast of Gods also" (*Adv. Marc.* 1.19.4).

this raises the question whether 1 Timothy 6:20-21a is a subtle repudiation of Marcion, an act that, if true, would locate the letter in the middle of the second century CE or shortly thereafter.[25]

There are two possibilities. Either this word was used coincidentally by an earlier author — possibly Paul himself — or it was a specific and pseudepigraphic reference to the infamous second-century heretic. But the advocate of coincidence needs to explain more than the mere fact of this word choice, which is common enough outside the Christian tradition, although distinctive within it. Certain factors indicate that its use by the letter's author here was entirely deliberate.

To be antithetical is not necessarily bad; this is a technical term concerning the structure of an argument. As we noted earlier, the author seems to have included this term in 6:20-21a to indicate the content of the false teaching he is warning against. But the term is carefully glossed by a phrase stating that this "knowledge" is "falsely named"; it is false knowledge. The knowledge, moreover, is linked with a particular group of people who could lay claim to a semblance of legitimacy. They were proclaiming this false knowledge in relation to the faith and thereby had, in the opinion of the author of 1 Timothy, lost their way. And this warning occurs, as we have also seen, in a nuanced and complex sentence, which, even more importantly, is positioned in an inordinately strategic place — at the end of the letter, just prior to the concluding grace wish, which itself contains only four words. The letter's auditors would consequently be left with this negative warning to turn away from certain antitheses ringing in their ears. To ignore it would be to lose their way and to stray into empty and vile doctrine. They must avoid the false knowledge — characterized by antitheses or contraries — being professed by certain deceptive and deceived Christian teachers. And then "Paul" signs off.

Now, all of this might be coincidence. But it seems that these accumulating markers *might* suggest a final deliberate polemical thrust by the letter's author, one centered in terms of content on certain antitheses, at which point an allusion to Marcion's *Antitheses* seems likely (assuming that any later objections to this reconstruction prove inadequate).

Clearly, this argument falls short of definitive proof. Other plausible

---

25. This hypothesis has been advocated for some time in NT circles, although it has not been favored universally; see more in this relation just below. A. Yarbro Collins (2011) does reach this conclusion in a relatively recent study, although presupposing pseudepigraphy.

explanations of the data are possible. So the author's use of "[the] Antitheses" in 6:20 is not a smoking gun — although perhaps it is a telltale strand of fiber left at the scene of the crime. Put slightly more formally, this statement can function as corroborative evidence of pseudepigraphy, although it falls short of being itself decisive. But it is worth noting that it can ultimately contribute helpfully to an important aspect of a pseudepigraphic reading by supplying a plausible alternative location for the faked text's composition — in this case, in the aftermath of Marcion's controversial appeal to Paul, where the composition of an alternative account of Paul by a horrified and rather less radical Paulinist makes excellent sense. That is, if it is faked, 1 Timothy 6:20-21a suggests that, at least in part,[26] the second-century bête noire Marcion was in view. And something of a Pandora's box of evidence arguably opens up once this location has been established.[27]

---

26. It is important to appreciate that 1 Tim does not need to respond just to Marcion; if it was late, then it probably targeted a range of perceived heresies at the time, including Montanists, Judaizers, and Gnostics. A useful indication of the potential diversity and complexity of different trajectories within early Christianity is given by Lampe (2003 [1989]), speaking specifically of Rome.

27. Hippolytus, *Ref.* 7.30.1, suggests that the Marcionites bring forth theological contrasts — ἐκ τῆς ἀντιπαραθέσεως ἀγαθοῦ καὶ κακοῦ προφέρων λόγους. He then goes on to cite 1 Tim extensively as a directly anti-Marcionite text: "You forbid marriage, the procreation of children, [and] the abstaining from meats which God has created for participation by the faithful, and those that know the truth" (7.30.3; see κωλύεις γαμεῖν, τεκνοῦν, ἀπέχεσθαι βρωμάτων, ὧν ὁ θεὸς ἔκτισεν εἰς μετάλημψιν μετὰ εὐχαριστίας τοῖς πιστοῖς καὶ ἐπεγνωκόσι τὴν ἀλήθειαν; this is largely a direct quotation of 1 Tim 4:3: see κωλυόντων γαμεῖν, ἀπέχεσθαι βρωμάτων, ἃ ὁ θεὸς ἔκτισεν εἰς μετάλημψιν μετὰ εὐχαριστίας τοῖς πιστοῖς καὶ ἐπεγνωκόσι τὴν ἀλήθειαν). See also 8.20.2.

Clement also cites 1 Tim against Gnostics, specifically 6:20-21a (!), but may well have had Marcion in mind, because he goes on immediately to note that "convicted by this utterance the heretics reject the epistles to Timothy" (*Strom.* 2.11.52). In §12 he then notes that certain virtues "dwell together in pairs." One wonders, then, whether the reference in 1 Tim 6:21a to shipwreck is not a subtle joke at Marcion's expense, since he was a shipbuilder. He was also wealthy, and the repeated admonitions in 1 Tim against wealth can therefore also function specifically against him (further details can be found in Moll 2010, 29-30). (My thanks to T. J. Lang for his help with much of this material.)

Note also the possible pun on two second-century papal names, Hyginus and Pius, in 1 Tim 6:3 (a pun arguably echoed in other texts): εἴ τις ἑτεροδιδασκαλεῖ καὶ μὴ προσέρχεται ὑγιαίνουσιν λόγοις τοῖς τοῦ κυρίου ἡμῶν Ἰησοῦ Χριστοῦ καὶ τῇ κατ᾽ εὐσέβειαν διδασκαλία . . . These bishops presided over the church in Rome in the middle of the second century, when Marcionism arrived and temporarily flourished. (This possibility was first brought to my attention by Stephen Carlson.)

3.4 Judgment

It is time for us to try to reach a final judgment concerning the authenticity and location of 1 Timothy.

We began our more detailed analysis by concluding — rather unusually — that the letter's immediate implied exigence is somewhat implausible. The careful narrative it supplies of Paul's journey away from Ephesus to Macedonia and back again actually undermines an appeal to more programmatic letters by way of analogy to some philosophical letter writers — a provenance that could have explained the letter's general and instructional content. The letter suggests that it is being written ahead of eventual instruction from Paul in person; however, such programmatic instruction seems implausibly offered after their decade or more of missionary work together.

If the letter is genuine, it needs to be positioned after our existing frame, which ends with Romans in the spring of 52 CE. But there it runs into some of the same problems that Titus faced, although not as acutely. Paul's first letter to Timothy does not need to presuppose later periods of mission in an area declared by Paul in Romans 15:19b-21 to have already been evangelized, as Titus did, and a mere visit back to the area is more understandable, although the sustained and circular journey in view is rather harder to comprehend if Paul is on his way to Rome after his third visit to Jerusalem. But a later visit to the area cannot yet be excluded. So this judgment of a later provenance for 1 Timothy, despite its vulnerabilities, functions largely as a caveat on the letter's further explanation.

The usual essentially substantive challenges to the letter's integrity have been rejected here — challenges in terms of style, theology, and, most significantly for 1 Timothy, the evident organization and ordering of the Christian community. Some of the differences noted were by no means insignificant, but they risked introducing circularity into the frame as arguments against authenticity and so had to be set to one side. And the late provenance of the letter helped defuse some of the tensions evident here as well. It could be suggested that 1 Timothy was a later phase of ecclesial reflection and instruction by Paul, written after many years of further work and experience.

But after these demurrals, it became evident that the reference by 5:18 to Luke 10:7 as Scripture was intractable for the letter's authenticity. This instruction, it seems, is a proverbial smoking gun, directly suggesting the letter's pseudepigraphy. Indeed, largely in view of this evidence, combined with suspicions surrounding the letter's account of its immediate exigence, we ought to conclude that 1 Timothy, like Titus, is pseudepigraphic, and so exclude it from further involvement in framing.

Moreover, with this decision made, we can see that 6:20 — potentially along with quite a bit of other data — plays a useful corroborative role, suggesting the composition of 1 Timothy in a completely understandable location, namely, after Marcion, in the middle of the second century CE. (It is unnecessary to suppose, however, that the letter responds to Marcion alone.) This has the happy consequence of pushing the organizational tensions noted previously into the second century and in relation to a particular opponent. Hence, the institutionalization evident in 1 Timothy did indeed develop rather later than Paul's lifetime. As in the case of Titus, this judgment concerning 1 Timothy should be corroborated in due course by further investigations. In particular, we will consider evidence shortly that the original edition of Paul's letters excluded 1 Timothy. (Certain objections will have to be met before this evidence can be used with confidence, but arguably they can be refuted.)[28]

Having made this decision concerning 1 Timothy, we now have two pseudepigraphic letters — Titus and 1 Timothy — that in certain distinctive respects are similar to one another. These particular similarities will prove helpful — although not decisive — during the assessment of 2 Timothy, the final Pauline letter in the canon remaining for our consideration.

4. Locating 2 Timothy

4.1 The Immediate Implied Exigence

Paul's second letter to Timothy was written from an immediate exigence already familiar to us: imprisonment (1:8; 2:9a; 4:16-17 implicitly). Unlike the other Pauline prison letters, however, 2 Timothy does not leave Paul's location to be inferred; 1:17 identifies it as Rome. And this basic exigence is of course plausible (see Rom 15:18-29).

We do not know the exact cause of Paul's incarceration. The letter states in 4:14a that "Alexander the metalworker did me a great deal of harm"

---

28. And in due course, the evidence in Acts will call any later provenance for 1 Timothy into question as well. Indeed, once the letter is returned to its probable intended location, in relation to Acts 20:1, its pseudepigraphic character becomes still more apparent. But this investigation lies well ahead of us and so cannot be counted on here; its possible future support should merely be noted.

('Αλέξανδρος ὁ χαλκεὺς πολλά μοι κακὰ ἐνεδείξατο). So we may surmise that his charge was responsible for Paul's current predicament. Unfortunately, we do not know anything reliable beyond this — for example, the circumstances, location, or timing of Paul's arrest.

The letter was composed and dispatched to an individual, a unique address in the present collection, with the other ten genuine letters being written to communities. In terms of content, it is in part an urgent summons to Timothy to travel to a rather isolated Paul before his death, ideally arriving before the winter (1:4; 4:9, 21a). But this practical and understandable request by no means exhausts the letter's content. There is an extensive set of exhortations and charges from Paul, certain aspects of which are already familiar to us from our considerations of Titus and 1 Timothy.

Various fragments of biographical information about Paul scattered through the letter (1:3, 11, 13; 3:10-11) undergird his integrity and the integrity of his teaching, and his final situation, facing death in prison, evokes a powerful *pathos* and *ethos* that generate much of the letter's considerable rhetorical impact (4:6-8, 16-18; see also 1:8, 12, 16; 2:9-10). The particular content of this teaching is summarized in certain key strategic statements (1:9-10; 2:8, 11-13). The letter is especially explicit in its inclusion within this remit of "the holy writings," which are "God-breathed" (3:15-16: πᾶσα γραφὴ θεόπνευστος). Timothy is exhorted to hold on to this "deposit" firmly (1:13-14; see also 1:12) and to discharge his duties (2:1, 3-7, 14-15, 19-26; 3:10-4:2, 5), to defend the faith against false teachers and deviation (2:16-18, 23-26; 3:2-9, 13; 4:3-4), and even to appoint other trustworthy people to transmit it onward (2:2). Moreover, by implication, these followers too are, if necessary, to die for it (4:7). This brief summary should suffice for us to consider the plausibility of the letter's immediate exigence in terms of its own data.

There is widespread attestation in and around Paul's day to pseudonymous literature written effectively on the author's deathbed — the testamentary genre (see R. Collins 2002, 182-85). The importance of the final speech of an august figure is well attested in the ancient Near East and in the OT (see Gen 27; 48:8–49:33; Deut 33; Josh 24). And the example of Socrates arguably further reinforced the importance of and literary possibilities within this context. Hence, much Jewish apocalyptic literature makes use of the testamentary device, as do texts in the NT authored after the time of Paul (see esp. Jn 13–17; Acts 20:17-38). And this might seem to call the authenticity of 2 Timothy immediately into question.

But having said this, it is worth noting that there were good reasons for the existence of these traditions. They resonated with the dramatic scenes

that did take place at the ends of many famous lives, not to mention simply at
the ends of the lives of many. And of course genuine letters have frequently
been written from prison just prior to execution. All manner of letters are attested later in the Christian tradition as being dispatched from prison in this
dire circumstance — to a generic audience, to specific churches, to groups of
friends, to judges, as well as to individual family members, whether spouses
or children (and these last texts often make especially hard reading; see Van
Braght 1951 [1660], 413-1141, for a massive sample from a relatively short
historical window). So it would not seem wise to exclude a combination of
these possibilities for an incarcerated Paul. That is, his second letter to Timothy could simply be a canonical instance of a dramatic final exhortation
written from prison just prior to execution. In these circumstances, it seems
plausible for Paul to include within a letter to a special disciple a range of
exhortations that he considered especially important — namely, to guard
correct teaching courageously, in part by living a life with the appropriate
integrity, and to repudiate false teaching and teachers firmly. There seems
little need to introduce serious doubts about 2 Timothy, then, related to the
account that it supplies of its own immediate exigence. And with this initial
decision made, we can turn to consider the location of 2 Timothy in relation
to our existing frame.

4.2 Framing Considerations

Clearly, 2 Timothy asks to be placed at the end of the frame, just before Paul's
probable death; if genuine, it would supply us with some welcome biographical
closure, however tragically. But we do not yet know exactly where that closure
would fall in relation to our existing biography, that is, whether the circumstances depicted in 2 Timothy should fall shortly after our existing frame,
which terminates explicitly in the spring of 52 CE, although it anticipates some
further key events, or sometime later. When considering this question in more
detail, we tend to strike the same issues that we already encountered in relation
to Titus and 1 Timothy.

What we know as Paul's second letter to Timothy, like Titus and 1 Timothy, looks back on a previous journey through the Aegean. Moreover, it must
have been fairly recent. Paul has left his cloak, scrolls, and parchments with
Carpus in Troas (4:13), which he asks Timothy to fetch. Erastus has remained
in Corinth (4:20a). And an ailing Trophimus has been left in Miletus (4:20b).
Hence, some of the same options exist for the location of this journey in rela-

tion to the existing frame as for the journey implicit in 1 Timothy, as well as, to a lesser extent, the events implied by Titus.

These events in the Aegean could have taken place when Paul was traveling, after his third visit to Jerusalem, to Rome. Or they could have taken place sometime later, after missionary work in Rome and Spain had been completed, with Paul returning to visit his Aegean communities before traveling back to Rome and being arrested — or perhaps even being arrested during this return visit to the Aegean littoral.

Whatever our judgment here — and it is difficult to make one at this moment — 2 Timothy is rather isolated with respect to the rest of the letter sequence. It basically floats off from 52 CE into the future with no indication of exactly when its implied events took place in relative or absolute terms. But there is no need to doubt its authenticity on these grounds. These later possible locations merely function as a caveat on further interpretation (that is, until the relevant data from Acts is introduced). Having said this, however, it is hardly surprising that 2 Timothy does not raise difficulties for the frame, since a letter written from Rome just prior to Paul's death can effectively assign its own framing implications sometime after our existing frame has tailed off. Our existing data by definition has little or nothing to say here (see only Rom 15:19-21). And with this decision made, it is time to consider various challenges to our tentative reconstruction.

4.3 Possible Mistakes

Although the immediate implied exigence and framing location of 2 Timothy are broadly plausible, its data occasionally raise suspicions. Setting aside here, as usual, the customary but circular challenges to authenticity in terms of style and substance, seven specific problems should be noted.[29]

(1) Geographical References

We observed earlier, in chapter 5, that Paul seems to have thought about combinations of places in a way typical for an ancient traveler, in terms of sequences

---

29. I will not be introducing concerns about the reference to "parchment codices" (4:13) or the Romans who send greetings (4:21b), as fascinating as some of these are. H. F. Gamble (1995, 43-54) provides brief background information on parchments as against papyrus documents, and on a probable consequent reference in 4:13 to codices.

or itineraries, and not as a modern person might, as a map-like arrangement of topographically precise spaces. Sequences facilitated efficient and reliable travel in an ancient context that could not presuppose topographically accurate maps, or perhaps any maps at all. And the final geographical designations supplied by the letter in 4:19-21 are therefore disquieting: [4:19] Ἄσπασαι Πρίσκαν καὶ Ἀκύλαν καὶ τὸν Ὀνησιφόρου οἶκον. [20a] Ἔραστος ἔμεινεν ἐν Κορίνθῳ, [20b] Τρόφιμον δὲ ἀπέλιπον ἐν Μιλήτῳ ἀσθενοῦντα. [21a] Σπούδασον πρὸ χειμῶνος ἐλθεῖν. [21b] Ἀσπάζεταί σε Εὔβουλος καὶ Πούδης καὶ Λίνος καὶ Κλαυδία καὶ οἱ ἀδελφοὶ πάντες.

The comments begin by focusing on Ephesus, where Prisca and Aquila and the household of Onesiphorus are currently living (see 1:16-18). After this, the letter's purview moves to Corinth, where Erastus has remained (and so back plausibly toward Rome; 4:20a). But its attention then moves back to Miletus, a city close by Ephesus, where Trophimus has been left ill (4:20b). It next focuses on Timothy, although we do not know where he is located — necessarily somewhere beyond both Troas and Ephesus. And after this the letter's purview returns to Rome, where various brothers and sisters greet Timothy (4:21b).

It is simply worth noting that this is a completely unworkable itinerary (Ephesus — Corinth — Miletus — Inner Asia? — Rome), returning any traveler heading west to Rome by way of Corinth back to Miletus — having just left Ephesus — before turning again and heading westward to Rome. (The most plausible sequence would have been Inner Asia? — Ephesus — Miletus — Corinth — Rome, giving the benefit of the doubt here to Timothy's unknown location somewhere beyond Troas.) This data suggests that the author of 2 Timothy is not thinking about cities and regions in practical terms. But Paul was an experienced traveler and seems to have thought elsewhere about his surrounding context in a concrete, connected, sequential fashion. That Paul's final letter would be so removed from geographical realities is a ground for suspicion that he did not actually write it.

(2) Personalia

In like manner, the figures mentioned by 2 Timothy overlap suspiciously with the greetings found in Colossians 4:7-14, as the following chart indicates. (Note that there are many more individuals named in 2 Tim than this; we are discussing here only those named in 2 Tim 4:10-13.)

	2 Timothy	Colossians
Timothy	**Entire, esp. 1:2**	**1:1b**
Demas	**4:10a**	**4:14b**
Luke	**4:11a**	**4:14a**
Mark	**4:11b**	**4:10b**
Tychicus	**4:12**	**4:7-8**
Titus	4:10c	-
Crescens	4:10b	-
Carpus	4:13	
Aristarchus	-	4:10a
Jesus/Joshua/Justus	-	4:11a
Onesimus	-	4:9 [distinctively Colossian]
Epaphras	-	4:12-13 [distinctively Colossian]

This overlap is not sufficiently precise to create another smoking gun. But the partial degree of overlap apparent between these two groups and situations remains troubling.

Colossians was written in 50 CE from within or near Apamea, whereas 2 Timothy was written possibly many years later from Rome. That Timothy and Tychicus are both still associated with Paul in 2 Timothy is understandable, and the presence of Titus until he deserted seems plausible as well, since they all seem to have been members of Paul's itinerant circle. That a previously unknown figure, Crescens, would have been present in Rome too seems plausible, although if he was a Galatian, then we might have expected him to have appeared in a Pauline letter before this point. And the absences of Aristarchus and Joshua-Justus from Rome are not necessarily troubling (although Acts data will introduce a concern here, namely, that Aristarchus was part of Paul's circle and accompanied him on his journey to Rome after his third visit to Jerusalem; see 20:4). But that Luke and Demas would have been with Paul in Apamea and in Rome, in addition to Tychicus, Titus, and Timothy, perhaps stretches credulity just a little, especially when we realize that the overlap between the figures in 2 Timothy and Colossians takes place almost entirely in relation to 2 Timothy 4:10-12. No Colossian figures are found in 4:19-21 (i.e., except the implicit subject, Timothy). Hence, it seems that Colossians 4:7-14 could have functioned as the principal source for the personalia found in 2 Timothy 4:10-12, if the letter is pseudepigraphic. It is fair for defenders of the authenticity of 2 Timothy to appeal to chance combined with modern interpretative ignorance and thereby excuse the recurrence of Demas, Luke, Mark, Tychicus, and of course Timothy from Colossians in 2 Timothy 4:10-12.

The overlap is not decisive proof of copying and hence of pseudepigraphy. But this data does seem again to arouse suspicions.

(3) Paul's Sufferings

In 3:11 Timothy is reminded of the persecutions that Paul endured in Antioch, Iconium, and Lystra, to illustrate Paul's "teaching, way of life, purpose, faith, patience, love, endurance . . . and sufferings" ([3:10] Σὺ δὲ παρηκολούθησάς μου τῇ διδασκαλίᾳ, τῇ ἀγωγῇ, τῇ προθέσει, τῇ πίστει, τῇ μακροθυμίᾳ, τῇ ἀγάπῃ, τῇ ὑπομονῇ [11a] τοῖς διωγμοῖς, τοῖς παθήμασιν, οἷά μοι ἐγένετο ἐν Ἀντιοχείᾳ, ἐν Ἰκονίῳ, ἐν Λύστροις οἵους διωγμοὺς ὑπήνεγκα), not to mention the way that God rescued him from all of them ([11b] καὶ ἐκ πάντων με ἐρρύσατο ὁ κύριος). Moreover, these illustrate that those who want to "live a godly life in Christ Jesus will be persecuted" ([12] καὶ πάντες δὲ οἱ θέλοντες εὐσεβῶς ζῆν ἐν Χριστῷ Ἰησοῦ διωχθήσονται).

These particular persecutions have not been documented by any other Pauline letters thus far in our analysis, although generic sufferings have been mentioned frequently. (They are, incidentally, the first concrete indication in a letter that Paul evangelized the southern part of the province of Galatia, but we should not affirm this evidence too strongly just yet.) However, the sufferings named here will be familiar to any reader of the book of Acts, since a series of fitting difficulties is described there for Paul and Barnabas as they traverse the Roman province of Galatia in chapters 13 and 14. At the end of this troubled trajectory, they arrive in the small community of Derbe, near Lystra, where they seem to recover before retracing their steps, returning finally to Syrian Antioch. When Paul passes through Derbe again, at the beginning of his next major missionary trajectory in Acts, recounted from 15:36 onward, he recruits Timothy into his missionary team (see 16:1-3). So at this moment the reader of both 2 Timothy and Acts can infer that Timothy must have heard of Paul's troubles during the apostle's previous visit, when he was recovering from them, and the reference in 2 Timothy 3:11 makes sense. Paul would have arrived, effectively still bleeding, in Derbe, and perhaps shortly afterward at Timothy's house (the home of his grandmother and mother), after suffering painful rejections in Pisidian Antioch and Iconium, and being stoned in Lystra. So Timothy would have known "what kinds of things happened to [Paul] in Antioch, Iconium, and Lystra" (3:11). But how plausible is this scenario?

The letter refers here to sufferings that Paul endured before arriving in

Derbe and meeting Timothy, and consequently that Timothy only hears of. The reader of Acts would therefore be as familiar with them as Timothy himself; they existed by way of narration. And it seems strange that the letter makes this slightly distanced and highly specific reference, and even stranger that it nevertheless fails to mention the numerous sufferings that Timothy must have experienced concretely with Paul *himself.* They had evangelized together for as many as fifteen or even twenty years by the time 2 Timothy was written, and the other letters testify to specific sufferings every bit as trying as those documented in Acts 13–14 (see esp. 2 Cor 11:23-27). Yet 2 Timothy passes over these in silence. Why does the letter refer to a narrative of suffering that Timothy only knew of, overlooking the direct participation in sufferings that Timothy experienced with Paul personally and hence — presumably — rather more memorably, dramatically, and significantly?

Clearly, these are not decisive contentions for pseudepigraphy. Paul could choose to reference whatever sufferings he wished when writing in desperate straits to Timothy. And there are no reasons to question that these sufferings took place. However, his selections here seem better explained in terms of a pseudepigrapher's recourse to particular stories about Paul's sufferings that did not need to be critically reconstructed from the genuine letters but could simply be read off the pages of the book of Acts from the specific point in the story where Timothy was implicitly being inserted. A later reader would find these narrative sufferings rather more significant and memorable than those that Paul and Timothy actually experienced together but that were not recorded in detail in a text for posterity. Once again, then, it seems that we have grounds for doubt.

(4) The Prescript

Paul's second letter to Timothy begins in the following way:

[1:1] Παῦλος
ἀπόστολος Χριστοῦ Ἰησοῦ
διὰ θελήματος θεοῦ
κατ᾽ ἐπαγγελίαν ζωῆς τῆς ἐν Χριστῷ Ἰησοῦ
[2a] Τιμοθέῳ
ἀγαπητῷ τέκνῳ,
[2b] χάρις ἔλεος εἰρήνη
ἀπὸ θεοῦ πατρὸς καὶ Χριστοῦ Ἰησοῦ τοῦ κυρίου ἡμῶν.

This opening reproduces the same three principal elements in the opening of a communal Pauline letter — and in fact of most extant letters from
Paul's day (although Paul's contained characteristic Christian flourishes) —
namely, the letter's sender, its recipient(s), and a greeting.

The sender's name is provided — Paul — along with a title and an expansion. Only 1 and 2 Thessalonians lack titular expansions for Paul, so the
form in 2 Timothy is typical. The use of an apostolic title here is also common,
echoing Romans, 1 and 2 Corinthians, Galatians, Laodiceans ("Ephesians"),
and Colossians (also 1 Tim and Titus). This apostolic reference is usually expanded elsewhere by the short phrase διὰ θελήματος θεοῦ, which also occurs
here; see 1 and 2 Corinthians, Laodiceans ("Ephesians"), and Colossians. Only
Romans and Galatians among the genuine letters, however, expand this designation more extensively, as 2 Timothy does, along with Titus and 1 Timothy.

The recipient of 2 Timothy is of course distinctive, being an individual
unaccompanied by other figures or a community, as in Philemon. But the form
in 2 Timothy is close to Titus 1:4 (Τίτῳ γνησίῳ τέκνῳ κατὰ κοινὴν πίστιν) and
1 Timothy 1:2 (Τιμοθέῳ γνησίῳ τέκνῳ ἐν πίστει). It should also be noted that
Timothy's faith is the subject of immediate acknowledgment in 2 Timothy,
something we will consider in more detail momentarily (see 1:5: ὑπόμνησιν
λαβὼν τῆς ἐν σοὶ ἀνυποκρίτου πίστεως, ἥτις ἐνῴκησεν πρῶτον ἐν τῇ μάμμῃ
σου Λωΐδι καὶ τῇ μητρί σου Εὐνίκῃ, πέπεισμαι δὲ ὅτι καὶ ἐν σοί).

The greeting is somewhat distinctive as well. As in Titus and 1 Timothy,
the benediction in 2 Timothy adds "mercy" to the bestowal of "grace" and
"peace," this last couplet being something of a staple in the genuine communal letters. The designation of the source(s) of these blessings is then typical,
although the position of the possessive pronoun is atypical, as it is in Titus and
1 Timothy. In the authentic communal letters, with the exceptions of 1 Thessalonians, which has just used the phrase to detail the addressees and so drops it,
and 2 Thessalonians, which in some manuscripts omits it, this qualifies "God
the Father" and not "the Lord Jesus."

In sum, the form of the letter opening in 2 Timothy is a little odd. It
is close to the form of the openings in the pseudepigraphic letters Titus and
1 Timothy, including the addition of "mercy" to the usual benedictions of
"grace and peace." But its titular expansion of Paul's name in terms of his
apostleship is arguably especially problematic.

While, as we have just noted, many of Paul's letters name him as an
apostle and expand this briefly, his status is invariably under pressure in some
way in those communications. Hence, at the outset of Philippians, written to a
devoted community where his leadership is neither unknown nor in question,

he characterizes himself only as a servant. And in 1 and 2 Thessalonians, he seems to feel sufficiently secure to avoid any self-designation at all (although this might be explicable in terms of the much earlier composition of those letters). In Philemon, the titular role has already been fulfilled by Colossians 1:1. In all the other communal letters, however, there is a clear need for him to assert his status, whether because his recipients do not appreciate it fully, not knowing him very well, if at all (Rom, Col and Laod), or because it is being challenged quite directly (1 Cor, 2 Cor, and Gal). So we find emphases in the prescripts of those letters on Paul's apostleship. But these explanations do not obviously apply to 2 Timothy (or indeed to Titus or 1 Tim).

Second Timothy would have occupied the same devoted and loyal space as the letter to the Philippians. And while Titus and 1 Timothy could arguably assert Paul's apostleship usefully in relation to their broader ecclesial audiences, this explanation does not apply to 2 Timothy, which seems to have been written to Timothy as a last exhortation before Paul's execution, and to various other loyal followers "listening alongside" (e.g., Mark [4:11], Prisca and Aquila, and the faithful household of Onesiphorus [4:19]). It is not inconceivable that Paul would want to say something about his apostleship in this letter at some point, but it seems odd that he would expand his prescript in this way to emphasize his own authority and status when writing to his devoted disciples, who would not have questioned it. A pseudepigraphic explanation therefore beckons at this point.

(5) The Thanksgiving

Unlike Titus and 1 Timothy, 2 Timothy contains a thanksgiving, which is helpful for its claim to authenticity.[30] But closer examination suggests that it contains certain troubling features as well.

[1:3] Χάριν ἔχω τῷ θεῷ,
ᾧ λατρεύω ἀπὸ προγόνων ἐν καθαρᾷ συνειδήσει,
ὡς ἀδιάλειπτον ἔχω τὴν περὶ σοῦ μνείαν ἐν ταῖς δεήσεσίν μου νυκτὸς
καὶ ἡμέρας
[4] ἐπιποθῶν σε ἰδεῖν,
μεμνημένος σου τῶν δακρύων,
ἵνα χαρᾶς πληρωθῶ

---

30. 1 Tim 1:12-14(-17) is not a thanksgiving paragraph, although it begins in the same way as 2 Tim 1:3-5: Χάριν ἔχω τῷ ἐνδυναμώσαντί με Χριστῷ Ἰησοῦ τῷ κυρίῳ ἡμῶν κ.τ.λ.

[5] ὑπόμνησιν λαβὼν τῆς ἐν σοὶ ἀνυποκρίτου πίστεως,
ἥτις ἐνῴκησεν πρῶτον ἐν τῇ μάμμῃ σου Λωΐδι καὶ τῇ μητρί σου Εὐνίκῃ,
πέπεισμαι δὲ ὅτι καὶ ἐν σοί.

Building on seminal work undertaken by Paul Schubert (1939), as extended and nuanced by other scholars, L. Ann Jervis (1991) identifies five typical elements within a Pauline thanksgiving:[31]

A. The principal verb εὐχαριστῶ and its personal object τῷ θεῷ [μου].
B. Adverbial and/or participial constructions indicating the *indirect object* of thanksgiving (Jervis speaks here of manner). A similar pronominal object phrase usually occurs here, περὶ πάντων ὑμῶν or ὑπὲρ πάντων ὑμῶν.
C. Indications of the *reasons* or *causes* for thanksgiving, using the prepositions ἐπί or ὅτι and/or participial clauses, usually constructed with verbs of learning or hearing.
D. An *explanatory* construction using καθώς or some other consecutive explanatory signal (using ὥστε or γάρ) that elaborates on the preceding account of the cause.
E. A *prayer report* indicating Paul's specific concerns. The content of these concerns is not always present (e.g., 1 Cor), and can, alternatively, be articulated by multiple final clauses (e.g., Phil, 2 Thess). Alternatively, *explanatory* statements are present. This subsection tends to be especially indicative of Paul's particular concerns in writing.

How does the thanksgiving in 2 Timothy fare in relation to this arrangement of the data associated with thanksgivings in the Pauline letters that have already been judged authentic?

We can observe first that the verb εὐχαριστῶ — component A in Jervis's structure, elsewhere used invariably in this position in Pauline thanksgivings — is absent altogether from 2 Timothy. The closest parallel to the initial phraseology of the 2 Timothy thanksgiving is found in 1 Timothy 1:12. This is a troubling beginning.

The indirect object of Paul's thanks, component B, which is usually designated quite simply with a περί or a ὑπέρ phrase ("I give thanks to my God for you"), occurs here after a parenthesis (ᾧ λατρεύω ἀπὸ προγόνων ἐν

31. Jervis (1991, 48-52, 86-109, esp. 89-91). See earlier O'Brien (1977); see also esp. in this relation Lambrecht (1990; 2000).

and all three letters were written by the same second-century figure in behalf of perceived orthodoxy in terms of the foregoing scenario.[37]

It is clear after our preceding analysis that 2 Timothy does not belong obviously to either group of existing letters. Depending on the markers se-lected, it belongs to one or the other group equally comfortably and overtly. Moreover, there are no explicit smoking guns — no telltale anachronisms betraying later authorship. And this makes our judgment here rather more difficult than it was for Titus and 1 Timothy. Nevertheless, the doubts that were enumerated are powerful enough in my opinion to generate a significant degree of doubt and thereby elicit the judgment that 2 Timothy should be assigned to the category of pseudonymous letters ostensibly written by Paul to individuals, a group that already includes Titus and 1 Timothy. So these three letters can now appropriately be called "the Pastoral Letters" and grouped together as the work in all probability of a single pseudepigrapher. However, it must be emphasized that this is a preliminary and provisional judgment in terms of framing. Our later investigations, into the shape of the original edition of the Pauline letters, and into any reliable and relevant evidence that might be drawn from Acts, will be especially important corroborations of it (or not).[38] And having reached this decision, we should quickly note the plausibility of a second-century location for 2 Timothy before turning to consider our first significant avenue of independent attestation: the shape of the original Pauline letter collection.

An anti-Marcionite provenance works just as well for 2 Timothy as it did

37. In something of a mediating position, to accommodate the many features 2 Tim shares with the genuine communal letters, it has been suggested by some that 2 Tim is not genuine in its current form but is based on genuine Pauline material that is still present in a fragmentary form — see esp. Harrison (1921, reprised in 1955; also 1956; 1964). For framing purposes, however, this option collapses into option two. We would exclude the letter in its current form and then reintroduce reconstructed parts of it under the control of the rest of the frame and what has subsequently been built on it.

38. It is only fair to acknowledge that while I expect these later investigations to confirm my judgment here, others will find them less than convincing — along with, perhaps, the pre-ceding articulation of doubts — and so might continue to include 2 Tim among Paul's genuine letters. And I do not believe that this position can be confidently and completely repudiated, although I do not myself share it at this point. I do think, however, that in due course it will be difficult if not impossible to maintain the authenticity of 2 Tim *and* to endorse strongly the relevant data from Acts; conversely, if interpreters have good grounds for doubting most of the data in Acts, it will become a little more difficult, somewhat ironically, to confirm the pseudepigraphy of 2 Tim.

for Titus and 1 Timothy, bearing in mind that these letters probably targeted
other perceived heretics as well. "Paul's second letter to Timothy" reinforces
especially overtly the importance of Scripture within the Christian community, clearly endorsing the inspiration of all the holy writings (3:16a: πᾶσα
γραφὴ θεόπνευστος κ.τ.λ.), along with their usefulness for salvation (3:15b:
τὰ δυνάμενά σε σοφίσαι εἰς σωτηρίαν), and commending Timothy for having
known these texts from his infancy (3:15a: ἀπὸ βρέφους τὰ ἱερὰ γράμματα
οἶδας). Indeed, one wonders in passing why scriptural inspiration would have
needed to be affirmed to Timothy by Paul so overtly if he had known and
studied them from infancy; this would have been distinctly otiose — but it
would have been a vital thing to assert against Marcionites, who denied the
legitimacy of the Jewish Scriptures.

The generational perspective that was evident in the other pseudonymous texts is even more apparent in 2 Timothy. Timothy is said, as we have
seen earlier, to have inherited his faith from his grandmother and his mother
(1:5); Paul has worshipped God within his ancestral tradition (1:3); and, as
we have just seen, Timothy has been tutored in the Scriptures from infancy
(3:15). And this emphasis is again readily comprehensible as an attack on the
leadership of Marcion, who deviated from the faith he received from his fore-
bears. The emphases on opposing false teaching and guarding the true that
are apparent in the other Pastorals are apparent in 2 Timothy as well (see,
i.a., 1:13-14; 2:1-2, 8, 14-19; 3:14-15; 4:1-5), and could clearly have been effective
against Marcion and other perceived deviations from orthodoxy in the second
century. And the theme of desertion developed through the letter would also
have been effective in this later context.

The letter suggests that Paul has been abandoned by many of his followers, including trusted companions like Titus (4:10b), and many from Asia (1:15).
Only courageous leaders like Timothy are left, who are to stand firm as Paul
has, if necessary in the face of imprisonment and death. The letter's auditors
are told that great division and desertion took place even in Paul's lifetime,
something that is occurring again in their day. To have followed Paul's gospel
at some point — or even to claim to follow Paul still — is not necessarily to be
trustworthy. Such figures might be nothing more than cowardly deserters like
Demas, Crescens, and Titus. Hence, the letter's auditors are exhorted to identify
with and support the leadership of the trustworthy figures that remain, walking in the footsteps of Paul in terms of teaching, integrity, and courage, and,
among other things, continuing to teach the sufficiency of all the Scriptures.[39]

39. Tertullian deploys just this language against Marcion in *Adv. Marc.* 1.1.6: "His dis-

The suitability of 2 Timothy within a second-century, largely anti-Marcionite provenance does not establish the likelihood of that location but rather is compatible with a hypothesis of pseudonymity there, and this distantly corroborates a judgment of pseudonymity for the letter as long as it has been reached primarily on other grounds. It will be useful to bear this context in mind as we turn to consider the shape of the original Pauline letter collection and its implications for framing.

5. The Implications of the Original Pauline Letter Collection

5.1 Preliminary Methodological Considerations

With this section, we reach finally the more detailed discussion of the phenomenon of external attestation. That is, as the case of the Getty's fake *kouros* showed, it has always been important when assessing the authenticity of ancient artifacts to press two complementary lines of investigation. The items in question must be examined carefully in their own right, and against other authentic items from the period in question, something we have done here for almost five chapters — what we might call an internal investigation. And the external documentation of the item's provenance that accompanies it must be scrutinized as well. In the case of the canonical letters bearing Paul's name, however, this second task will always be both difficult and limited. It is not possible to document externally the first copying and transmission of the letters, which were presumably not famous enough when they were first penned to warrant this attention; the letters themselves were this external documentation, including things like signatures in Paul's hand. However, we do possess evidence concerning the next best thing, namely, the first collection and publication as a group of certain letters within an edition. If the approximate date and shape of this edition can be determined, then we will generate useful complementary information concerning the authenticity of the individual letters that fell within and outside it.

This will not be definitive, because the original editor of this collection

---

ciples will not deny that his first faith he held along with ourselves . . . so that for the future a heretic may from his case be designated as one who, forsaking that which was prior, afterwards chose out for himself that which was not in times past." This is not to suggest, however, that the theme of desertion evident in 2 Tim must be applied to Marcion.

might have included pseudonymous letters within the collection, or, in one celebrated theory, might even have composed a pseudonymous introductory letter to it himself. Moreover, he (more likely) may not have included all the extant authentic letters in the collection, its contours being governed by principles other than sheer inclusion. Hence, he might have excluded genuine texts that may have then circulated independently, showing up later historically in some way. Nevertheless, the editor presumably wanted to include at least some authentic letters — few scholars want to claim that all the Pauline letters in the NT are fake, a position that is, in any case, self-defeating — so our presumption can be that if a letter was found in the original edition of Paul's letters, then this finding can function to further corroborate an existing judgment of authenticity reached on internal grounds. Similarly, letters excluded from this original edition are not automatically pseudonymous, but they lack this confirmatory evidence of inclusion and consequently have a harder row to hoe in terms of authenticity. Their case must come from internal evidence alone. Hence, inclusion within the original edition functions more strongly in positive support of authenticity than exclusion as negative evidence against, because the likelihood of original letters being left out is high. (Indeed, the inference that exclusion *entails* pseudonymity is, strictly speaking, a non sequitur.) It is just that a letter judged pseudonymous on internal grounds will lack any countervailing evidence from inclusion that might alter a judgment of exclusion, so it is likely to remain excluded. In short, any external attestation in relation to individual letters from the original edition — if this can be ascertained — is worth something. And it will be worth even more if the original edition matches the groupings of Pauline letters that have already been determined on internal grounds.

Thus, if the original edition of Paul's letters was a ten-letter edition that included the communal letters already judged authentic but excluded all others, including the Pastorals, then we would have a perfect match between internal and external evidence. And this would greatly increase our confidence in the importance of the external evidence. Inclusion within the original edition would be a significant corroboration of authenticity, and exclusion would be a significant loss of support for the same. A match would suggest, in short, that our original editor was interested to a degree in historicity and basically got things right, taking our external attestation to Paul's letters back to an impressively early date. But we would have to determine this correlation between internal and external judgments independently, on its own terms, the question to which we now turn as we investigate the probable shape of the first edition of Paul's letter collection.

tion of the fragment's date. The evidence suggesting a fourth-century date is equally, if not more, fragile (see Hahneman 1992, reviewed by Ferguson 1993; and Ferguson's attack on Sundberg's earlier case in 1982). However, even a date "in the latter part of the second century and certainly not later than the year 200" (B. Metzger 1987, 194), conceding the early case for the sake of argument, does not offer strong grounds for the existence of the Pastorals prior to Marcion. Marcion, and his possible predecessor, Cerdo, arrived in Rome during the preceding "papacy" of Hyginus (ca. 136-40 CE), or shortly thereafter, so we might even expect an anti-Marcionite pseudepigrapher to be at work in the subsequent decade and papacy, that is, from approximately 150 onward.[57]

Third, Tertullian states that Marcion "rejected" the Pastorals ("recusaverit"; *Adv. Marc.* 5.21), suggesting their prior existence. But it would be unwise to place too much weight on Tertullian's exact wording. We cannot be certain that Tertullian is speaking with complete precision as against polemically exaggerating a useful fact, namely, that Marcion was known simply not to have included 1 and 2 Timothy and Titus within his original collection. Tertullian does not go into any further details concerning this fairly shocking omission. Moreover, he berates Marcion for changing the addressees of "Ephesians" to "Laodiceans." It is, however, highly unlikely that Marcion did so. As we have already seen in chapter 5, it is almost certain that this change took place after Marcion's time and in the opposite direction. So Tertullian's comments here — which are more emphatic than his comment on the exclusion of the Pastorals — are not rooted in accurate evidence; they are polemical calumnies and

---

of Hermas and the other scriptural books just listed, while — more importantly — "temporibus nostris" could refer to the entire post-apostolic age as against the age of the authentic, apostolic Scriptures' authorship (see Irenaeus, *Adv. haer.* 5.30.3). Hence, Sundberg argues that the text could be suggesting simply that the *Shepherd* was written too late — in the post-apostolic age, during the papacy of Pius — to be included in the canon. And speaking in these terms, it would tell us nothing about when it was itself written. Sundberg translates the key sentence: "But Hermas wrote the Shepherd most recently, in our time (i.e., in post-apostolic times), in the city of Rome, while his brother Pius was the bishop occupying the episcopal chair of the church of the city of Rome" (11). Note that Sundberg affirms only the ambiguity of this data. But the higher likelihood of formal as against biographical statements in the text, coupled with the elevated notion of the Roman episcopacy evident in relation to ca. 150 CE, seems to confirm his skepticism concerning Zahn's reading and consequent proposed date. And with the collapse of this datum, only more general and ambiguous considerations remain in relation to dating for the acceptance or rejection of texts as canonical.

57. Moll (2010, 25-46) would date things a little later than this — from ca. 144 CE onward — but not much alters as a result. Moll is also dubious about the role and even the existence of Cerdo. But most famous figures in human history have less-well-known precursors.

hence of no historical value. And it is likely that his comment on the exclusion of the Pastorals is of similar quality.

However, fourth, a more formidable case than the foregoing can be made suggesting that the Pastorals demonstrably predated Marcion, although it is also more complex. This needs to be considered more carefully. It contains three steps.

Polycarp alludes to the Pastorals numerous times in his extant letter to the Philippians. (*Philippians* 4:1 echoes 1 Tim 6:10 and 7; and, less obviously, *Phil* 5:2 echoes 2 Tim 2:12; 8:1 echoes 1 Tim 1:1; 9:2 echoes 2 Tim 2:11 and 4:10; 11:3 echoes 2 Tim 2:25; and 12:3 echoes 1 Tim 2:2.) So this text seems aware of the existence of at least 1 and 2 Timothy, texts we would group with Titus (with grouping working in favor of authenticity here).[58]

But this letter is also explicitly bound to the letters and fate of Ignatius of Syria. Ignatius's extant letters, taken by most modern scholars to be seven, suggest that he was martyred after journeying through Asia Minor and corresponding extensively with the various Christian communities there. He ostensibly wrote four letters from Smyrna, to the churches in Ephesus, Magnesia, Tralles, and Rome; and three more from Troas, to the churches in Philadelphia and Smyrna, and to the famous bishop of the Smyrneans, Polycarp.

Polycarp's single extant letter to Philippi inquires about Ignatius's fate from the Philippians, and responds to a request from them for Ignatius's letters (13:2). And it responds to a further request from both the Philippians and Ignatius to have a Philippian letter sent on to Syria (13:1). So the text of *Philippians*, at least at certain points, seems to follow closely on the heels of Ignatius's journey and local correspondence. It remains only to determine when this was.

Eusebius provides specific information about the date of the martyrdom of Ignatius, suggesting in both *Historia ecclesiastica* and the *Chronicon* that it occurred during the reign of Trajan (98-117 CE).[59] Neither entry supplies details about the martyrdom itself, and each provides a different precise date, the *Historia ecclesiastica* placing Ignatius's martyrdom close by Clement's death in Trajan's third year (100 CE), and the *Chronicon* listing it near Trajan's tenth year (107 CE). However, Lightfoot (1891, 1.30), in one of the first scholarly analyses of Ignatius, opined that it fell a little later on, somewhere between 110 and 118 CE, and this period has subsequently passed into the scholarly literature.

---

58. So (i.a.) Berding (1999); textual relationships with other NT texts and *1 Clement* are charted helpfully on pp. 353-55.

59. The information supplied by the *Apostolic Constitutions* (7.46) is, as Foster (2006a, 490) notes, largely worthless.

second-century date, has crumbled. Doubts surround each of three key steps — concerning the integrity of Polycarp's letter to the *Philippians*, along with the authenticity of its final critical sub-sections, the authenticity of Ignatius's letters, and Eusebius's suggestion that Ignatius's martyrdom took place early in the second century. A mathematical proof is only as strong as the multiplication (not the sum) of its parts. Hence this case, which needs three complex but fragile hypotheses to hold good, is beginning to look extremely unlikely. Although the case for the later date, in response to Marcion, has not been made here definitively, it is intact, and the frequent resonances between *Philippians* 1–9 and the Pastorals, and the frequent use by the former of the latter, encourage still further confidence in the appropriateness of this view. And with this broad judgment, the argument in this chapter is largely complete.

It has been suggested — paying due attention to circularity and other pervasive methodological errors — that Titus, 1 Timothy, and 2 Timothy are best designated pseudepigraphic and excluded from further involvement in preliminary framing. The evidence has generally been indubitable, although the case against 2 Timothy is less decisive than against Titus and 1 Timothy. Moreover, despite the best countervailing arguments, the earliest Pauline letter collection, dimly apparent in advance of Marcion, affirms these judgments. The shape of the collection that immediately preceded Marcion, which is our earliest documentable window onto this process, is best explained by his inheritance of an edition of ten authentic Pauline letters addressed to seven Christian churches (three communities being addressed by two letters and four by one). Moreover, this original edition and our previous internal judgments can now be seen to correlate exactly, considerably increasing our confidence in the value of the external evidence, and in the consequent strength of our internal judgments.

It will now be a little harder than it was before to exclude certain letters from the ten-letter canon as pseudonymous, and to affirm other letters from outside this group as genuine — although the former task will be harder than the latter, and neither task is impossible. And with these judgments in place, it can be seen that we have crossed an important threshold, into the world of pseudonymous Pauline material, something indicating that our preliminary, provisional construction of a frame for Paul's authentic letters on the basis of the canonical Pauline evidence is complete. From this point onward this frame can be augmented, but I actually doubt that it will be significantly altered. Further evidence may corroborate and supplement it but will struggle to displace any of its principal structures.

Conclusion

What has the argument of this book achieved? Although at times the discussion has spiraled into quite technical points — although, by design, only where absolutely necessary — the basic picture of the writing of Paul's letters that has emerged is a relatively simple one, generating a frame that can ground all subsequent interpretive work on Paul rather more accurately and firmly than has hitherto been the case.

We have judged ten of the letters in the canon to be authentic in preliminary and provisional terms — notably, all the communal letters. So "Ephesians," Colossians, and 2 Thessalonians should now join Romans, 1 and 2 Corinthians, Galatians, Philippians, 1 Thessalonians, and Philemon in more frequent use by Pauline scholars. There seem to be no good reasons for doubting their authenticity in initial terms, although later considerations might arise and call a particular letter's authenticity into question. However, the burden of proof lies from this moment forward on those who would exclude one of these; the case for pseudonymity in relation to these letters needs to be made presupposing inclusion. And indeed, it has become apparent that many of the arguments often made in favor of pseudonymity need to be scrutinized if not rejected. Circular appeals to Paul's theology, development, and biography must be abandoned, as must subjective and partial selections of statistical data. ("Cherry-picked" data reads impressively to the statistically uninformed but establishes nothing, as our brief foray into the work of computer-assisted authorship ascription has indicated.) So the shape of these discussions needs to change considerably.

Nevertheless, by investigating in these more rigorous terms, we have still judged that the Pastorals — appropriately so called after their investigation, although not necessarily before it — should continue to be excluded initially from authenticity. This became apparent upon scrutiny of their immediate implied exigencies, that is, the accounts that they themselves supplied of their immediate circumstances, along with their fit, or not, with the developing biographical frame; and it was indicated decisively by the occasional presence of an overt and unambiguous anachronism — the proverbial smoking gun. But the judgments here were at times finely balanced, especially in relation to 2 Timothy, and so I recommend that 1 and 2 Timothy and Titus be fully included in further discussion. This secondary inclusion will protect Pauline interpreters from falling prey to the heuristic bias of availability when evaluating them. That is, the letters can be assessed fairly only if the Pauline scholar is as familiar with their data as with the data of the letters judged to be authentic. So they should probably be in play rather more than they are at present, if only in footnotes and endnotes for comparative purposes. They also provide priceless information concerning how Paul was actually read by earlier interpreters as against how modern scholars think he was read, not to mention concerning later ecclesial organization.

We have judged as well that there are no good reasons at present for partitioning any of Paul's letters. Hence, in particular, 2 Corinthians and Philippians can be left in their canonical shape, as can Romans. Claims for partition can of course continue to be made, but the burden of proof rests on their advocates, who need to give a better account of ancient editorial practice than has been supplied thus far (i.e., at the least, in terms of Klauckian simplicity). They need to supply more decisive arguments as well — in terms of overt contradictions and the like (here again as Klauck intimated). So, for example, appeals to apparent shifts in the rhetorical texture of a letter are too weak to justify partition, these being fundamentally cross-cultural judgments that modern interpreters are perilously underequipped to make but are seldom corrected for positing. Our preliminary investigations have suggested, in short, injecting a large dose of interpretative humility into the discussion of Paul's sources in terms of collation and partition.

It is worth noting now that these judgments reached on internal grounds — principally by a careful assessment, where necessary, of the letters' immediate implied exigencies and fit with our developing frame, along with an assessment of style in the case of Titus, and the detection of overt anachronisms where those were identifiable — were corroborated by our most important piece of external attestation, namely, the probable shape of the first edition of Paul's letters. This original edition, dimly apparent in various patristic engagements with Marcion, probably preceded him and contained precisely these ten letters. This evidence also confirmed our earlier judgment that Ephesians

should from this point on be identified with and treated as Laodiceans — Paul's
letter to the Christian community at Laodicea noted in Colossians 4:16. The
other organizing principle apparent in the original edition was an address by
ten particular letters to seven churches, an overt hint of universality, and a
piece of data that aligned, at the least, with the strange letter collection apparent in chapters 2-3 of the book of Revelation. So we could safely suggest that
the actual collection and publication of Paul's letters preceded the redaction
of this material into the book of Revelation, although doubts about that process entailed that a date could not be advanced confidently for the collection's
publication other than a probable *terminus ad quem* at the end of the first
century. Nevertheless, this still placed the edition's collection and publication
well in advance of Marcion.

Beyond assessing the letters' authenticity and integrity, we have also
spent a great deal of time sequencing and dating them in terms of their original
composition and dispatch by Paul, these questions necessarily being answered
largely simultaneously. And despite the apparent complexities of the resulting
minimal account of Paul's life as it unfolded around these texts (see the appen-
dix), the basic underlying story is a simple one. It has placed the ten authentic letters in both a relative and an absolute sequence, dating that sequence
principally by anchoring it to Paul's escape in late 36 CE from a governor over
Damascus appointed by King Aretas IV of Nabataea, this date being broadly
corroborated by the shadow falling across 2 Thessalonians from the Gaian
crisis that began in late 39 CE.

The sequence has an early cluster of letters, 1 and 2 Thessalonians, which
must be dated after the Gaian crisis although not necessarily well after it.
Written from Athens to stabilize the struggling Thessalonians, these letters
were probably penned just after the Macedonian mission and in the midst of
the Achaian mission, both of which were unfolding through the late 30s and
early 40s, as the Gaian intimations suggest. They are remarkably early sources
for the early Christian movement, which attest, furthermore, to its extraordinarily rapid diversification and spread through the Roman Empire and the
Mediterranean basin. On the basis of information in Galatians, we were also
able to posit an important narrative segment just prior to these missions and
their letters, namely, Paul's call near Damascus and subsequent missionary
activity in Arabia, Syria, and Cilicia. Paul's first visit to Jerusalem took place
at this time as well, along with his escape from Damascus. So a sequence of
events and letters spreading across several years, through roughly 34-41 CE,
composes the first part of the frame.

The frame then largely loses sight of Paul until he comes into view again writing letters to various communities in Asia's Lycus valley in 50 CE. We have designated this intermediate period the "years of shadow," filled only by implication with extensive travels that seem to have been conspicuously far-reaching, difficult, and unsuccessful. But Paul does come back into focus in 50, just after a confrontation at Antioch with Cephas, followed by his second visit to Jerusalem in late 49 or early 50, at which time the collection project so apparent in his later longer letters is initiated (so Gal 2:10). By mid-50 we find Paul incarcerated on his way back from Syrian Antioch and Jerusalem to the Aegean, most likely in Apamea or a city like it and close by the Lycus valley. From prison Paul writes a cluster of letters — Laodiceans ("Ephesians"), Colossians, and Philemon — to fledgling communities in the Lycus valley, whose circumstances were notably distinctive.

The initial exigence was the heretofore unparalleled need for Paul to write to a group of converts from paganism at Laodicea who had not been converted by either him or a member of his circle. (There are Pauline associates at Rome, so Romans is only a partial exception to this observation, and its composition was greatly complicated by other factors.) So of any letter extant, Laodiceans is a unique introduction to the Pauline way for those who knew next to nothing about it. However, as this letter was being crafted — quite possibly as an oral/aural event composed for much of the time in the darkness of a detention cell — an emergency arose at a small congregation of a Pauline nature founded by proxy at Colossae. So Paul, heavily informed by his initial composition, composed another, briefer letter — Colossians — more specifically directed to an unhelpful intrusive teaching. And he wrote an even shorter letter to Philemon, the owner of the troubled slave Onesimus, who had brought him all this disturbing information, although the letter also addresses Philemon's wife (or sister), Apphia, and the leader of their house church, Archippus. Moreover, Paul instructed that the two main letters be read at both destinations, thereby effecting an integrated epistolary event in which the roles of both explicit addressees and *Nebenadressat,* or addressees alongside, become especially obvious. That is, we had already long suspected this multiple reception dynamic — something with important implications for commentary — but these letters overtly confirm it.

Following this activity in the Roman province of Asia, we enter a brief but very busy and contentious period in Paul's life that lasted for about a year and a half. It was characterized by two waves of difficulty; just as he seems to have dealt with one wave, another, even more serious disturbance seems to have washed through his communities and even threatened him directly. The first wave was the contentious period Paul experienced vis-à-vis the

Corinthian congregation. We found a minimal account of Paul's management of this conflict to be the most plausible, but even that is complex enough. Beginning in 50 CE, after his release from an Apamean incarceration, visit to the Lycus valley communities, and arrival in Ephesus, Paul penned a letter to the Corinthians that has not been preserved. This letter, which we designated the Previous Letter to Corinth, seems to have articulated, among other things, instructions about the collection. The Corinthians responded somewhat assertively with a written reply, and several oral reports of varying loyalty seem also to have reached Paul in Ephesus at this time. One of the difficult factors in play at Corinth seems to have been a group of followers of another leader, probably Apollos. As a result, Paul seems to have decided "to triangulate" the fractured and deteriorating situation, traveling to see the Corinthians by way of Macedonia so he could, at the least, arrive with a posse of loyal Macedonians at his back. In the meantime, Timothy (presumably) took a stinging letter to the Corinthians in Paul's stead — our 1 Corinthians. Paul then left Asia a little earlier than planned after some sudden crisis (2 Cor 1:8-9) but arrived to good news when he met up with Titus in Macedonia, who was returning from Corinth in a clockwise direction around the Aegean; he had been sent to monitor the aftereffects of the devastating "Letter of Tears." Indeed, in response to the success of his epistolary strategy at Corinth with 1 Corinthians / the Letter of Tears, Paul penned another letter, our 2 Corinthians, in which it is clear that not everything had been resolved. Arguably a small group of Corinthian converts remained deeply hostile to Paul, not to mention archly abusive, in an opposition exacerbated by third parties, whether they were Apollos and his retainers or certain "super-apostles." Many of Paul's supporters were hurt and diffident. Nevertheless, the letter seems to have had a positive impact, and Paul arrived in Corinth, on what was his third visit to the city, to a congregation that in the main still supported him. But just as things seem to have settled down at Corinth, at least to some degree, another, even worse crisis suddenly appeared.

A group of hostile Jewish Christian missionaries seems to have arrived on Paul's doorstep, seeking to subvert his congregations and attack him (see perhaps Gal 2:4; more certainly, 5:7-12). Paul responded in part by penning a volley of letters to the congregations he suspected had been turned, or who might yet be threatened. The Galatians, who were said to have abandoned Paul's gospel (at least in his mind), received a powerful letter. And the Philippians received a stringent exhortation to vigilance — what we have called the Previous Letter to Philippi — which has been lost but was fortuitously preserved in part when Paul quoted it in another letter written to the Philippians (Phil 3:2–4:3). Indeed, Paul soon wrote a second letter to Philippi — our Philippians — although at the time of writing he was in prison at Corinth in a capital trial (making Phil his fourth extant letter written from prison).

Nevertheless, as he anticipates in the letter, he survived this trial and prepared to resolve the current crisis by returning for another visit to Jerusalem, his third as an apostle, which would enable him to carry out the collection project personally (although he would travel by way of Macedonia, to settle those congregations in view of the threat posed by the enemies). But to preempt an arrival in the meantime of his enemies at Rome, and a resultant disruption of his plan to set out from that city to evangelize Spain and the northwestern quadrant of the empire, Paul wrote a comprehensive account of his gospel over against their inadequate and moralizing ethic — our Romans — and dispatched it to the Roman communities. And with this, Paul's year of crisis came to a close, although it was really closer to a year and a half of trouble; Paul composed Romans in all probability in the spring of 52 CE.

It had indeed been an *annus horribilis* for Paul, but this of course redounded to our good, since he wrote five of the ten letters later preserved in the original edition of his texts at this time — in order: 1 Corinthians, 2 Corinthians, Galatians, Philippians, and Romans. Three more were composed just prior to it — in order: Laodiceans ("Ephesians"), Colossians, and Philemon. And with these realizations, it is apparent that our epistolary frame is complete.

The actual sequence of the composition of the authentic letters, then:

1 Thess — 2 Thess — Laod ("Eph") / Col / Phlm —
1 Cor — 2 Cor — Gal — Phil — Rom

However, as we have seen, considerable gaps lay between some of these clusters of writing. So with the correct dates and intervals added, the sequence looks more like the following, although it should be recalled that we cannot say for certain whether the composition of Philippians fell into the end of 51 or the beginning of 52 (a judgment pertaining to the Corinthian reply and Corinthian visitors during the previous winter as well); Paul was probably imprisoned during the winter. However, fortunately, not much turns on this:

// ca. 40 CE //
. . . 1 Thess — 2 Thess . . .
// years of shadow //

// 50 //
. . . Laod ("Eph") / Col / Phlm —
// 51 //
— 1 Cor — 2 Cor — Gal — Phil —
// 52 //
(— Phil?) — Rom . . .

With lost letters and other events added, the sequence becomes rather more complicated; however, it should not be forgotten that the key decisions generate the essentially simple arrangement just noted. Paul's authentic extant letters fall into two groups. The first consists of just two, 1 and 2 Thessalonians, written in that order, although rapidly, perhaps as early as 40 CE. The remaining eight were written about ten years later, within a two-year period in or around the Aegean, between mid-50 CE and the spring of 52 CE.

It is important to emphasize in closing that this frame for Paul's letters has been generated solely from epistolary data, and without appealing even in terms of that evidence to arguments vulnerable to vicious circularity, hence to claims rooted in prior judgments — or prejudices — about the nature of Paul's theology and thinking in general (i.e., confused, developmental, or coherent) or some of his particular commitments (i.e., to eschatology or the nature and extent of the church or some such). Indeed, interpreters will now be able to reach more accurate judgments about these important substantive questions by presupposing this frame and determining Paul's thinking accordingly.

This frame will be supplemented in due course by a consideration of the evidence in Acts. But although it will be greatly enriched by that evidence, and the value of a great deal of the material in Acts will in turn be strikingly affirmed, it is unlikely that the frame itself will be changed fundamentally by data from Acts. Only countervailing eyewitness testimony in Acts could suggest significant alterations, and this is a plausible option for Acts data (rather intriguingly) only just after the epistolary frame finishes, with Paul in Corinth about to head to Jerusalem, since this is where the sustained presence of the "we source" in Acts begins (see 20:5). So we can expect our epistolary frame to hold firm. But this engagement with Acts is best undertaken in an entirely separate study.

It is vital that Paul's interpreters discipline their thinking and interpret his letters initially only in terms of data found in those texts, that is, data from his own hand. After all, he was there, however biased his participation in certain events, something modern scholars tend to forget when faced with a more obvious story about Paul written by someone else. Only when the epistolary process has run its course, then, and each item of information has been squeezed dry for every last drop of insight, should interpreters turn and introduce evidence from Acts, although now into a situation characterized by both simplicity and control. This study is an instance of just this exclusively epistolary process — one that many scholars have previously believed was not even possible but that seems reasonably straightforward once a few small puzzles have been solved.

The framing of Paul's letters is now complete. We know the basic story that surrounded their composition, and in their own terms. We are now prepared to pose further exciting questions to the apostle — and with perhaps more hope that we will hear his answers, undistorted by our own concerns, in reply.

Appendix: The Pauline Letter Frame

The Basic Sequence of Paul's Letters

// ca. 40 CE //
... 1 Thess — 2 Thess ...
// 43-49: years of shadow //
// 50 //
... Laod ("Eph") / Col / Phlm ... [PLC] —
// 51 //
... 1 Cor — 2 Cor — Gal / [PLP]$^{Phil\ 3:2–4:3}$ — Phil —
// 52 //
(— Phil?) — Rom ...

The Detailed Sequence of Events Surrounding Paul's Letters

Prior to 34 CE:	Previous life as a Pharisee
	Persecution of the early church in Jerusalem
Early/mid-34:	Apostolic commission near Damascus
Early 34–mid-36:	Activity in the region of Damascus
	Activity in "Arabia"
	Return to Damascus
Late 36:	Escape from Damascus, from a governor appointed by King Aretas IV
	Paul's first visit to Jerusalem, 2.x years after commission
	Activity in Syria and Cilicia presumably begins

37-38:	Probable activity in Syria and Cilicia, including in Antioch
(Late 39/early 40):	Announcement of Gaian plan to desecrate the Jerusalem temple
Ca. 40-42:	Mission to Macedonia:
	Founding visit to Philippi
	Founding visit to Thessalonica
	Mission to Achaia:
	Founding visit to **Athens**
	Timothy's visit from Athens to Thessalonica and back
	1 Thessalonians
	Arrival of further news from Thessalonica
	2 Thessalonians
	Founding visit to Corinth
Ca. 43-49:	Years of shadow: extensive travel
	Mission to Illyricum
	Mission to Galatia (the most plausible location currently)
	Possible missions to Moesia, Thrace, Bithynia, Pontus, and Cappadocia
	Sufferings from travel (shipwrecks) and disciplinary measures (whippings and beatings with rods)
	Paul's second visit to Corinth (during or adjacent to this period)
Late 49/early 50:	Antioch incident (Gal 2:11-14)
	Paul's second visit to Jerusalem, 13.x years after first visit; collection inaugurated
Mid-50:	Return to the Aegean by way of Antioch and Galatia
	Mission to Asia:
	Imprisonment en route, possibly in **Apamea**
	Founding of congregation at Colossae by proxy
	Laodiceans ("Ephesians") / *Colossians* / *Philemon*
	Release from prison; visits to Lycus valley communities
	Founding visit to **Ephesus**
Late 50:	[Previous Letter to Corinth]
	Apollos's first visit to Corinth
Winter 50-51:	[Corinthian reply]
	Informal oral reports from Corinth

Spring 51:   **1 Corinthians**, later defined as Letter of Tears (2 Cor
                        2:4), probably dispatched with Timothy
                        Apollos's second visit to Corinth
                        Super-apostles' visit to Corinth (if they are different
                        from the foregoing)
                        Titus's first visit to Corinth, with instructions to rendez-
                        vous with Paul in Macedonia or northern Asia
                        Asian crisis, probably in Ephesus (2 Cor 1:8-10)
                        Paul's departure from Ephesus for Troas and then
                        Macedonia
Ca. summer 51:   Rendezvous with Titus in **Macedonia**
                        2 Corinthians
                        Titus's second visit to Corinth, bearing 2 Corinthians
                        Paul's third visit to **Corinth**
Fall 51-winter 51-52:   Enemies' arrival in Corinth (see Phil 3:18)
                        [Previous Letter to Philippi] (Phil 3:2–4:3)
                        Galatians
                        Paul's *imprisonment* and capital trial
                        Epaphroditus's visit from Philippi and ensuing illness
                        Philippians, dispatched with Epaphroditus
                        Timothy's visit to Philippi
                        Paul's release from prison
Spring 52:   **Romans**
                        Paul's departure with the collection for his third visit to
                        Jerusalem, via Macedonia, and presumably also Asia —
                        ultimately bound for Rome

The authentic epistolary sources lose sight of Paul at this point. (A pseudonymous epistolary source — 2 Timothy — suggests that he was executed in due
course at Rome.)

References

Aageson, James W.
2008   *Paul, the Pastoral Epistles and the Early Church.* LPS. Peabody, Mass.: Hendrickson.

Abakuks, Andris
2006a   "A Statistical Study of the Triple-Link Model in the Synoptic Problem." *Journal of the Royal Statistical Society: Series A (Statistics in Society)* 169:49-60.
2006b   "The Synoptic Problem and Statistics." *Significance* 3:153-57.
2007   "A Modification of Honoré's Triple-Link Model in the Synoptic Problem." *Journal of the Royal Statistical Society: Series A (Statistics in Society)* 170:841-50.
2012   "The Synoptic Problem: On Matthew's and Luke's Use of Mark." *Journal of the Royal Statistical Society: Series A (Statistics in Society)* 175:959-75.

Aldrete, G.
1999   *Gestures and Acclamations in Ancient Rome.* Baltimore: Johns Hopkins University Press.

Aldrich, Howard E.
1999   *Organizations Evolving.* London: Sage. (2nd ed., with Martin Ruef, 2006.)

Anderson, Graham
1994   *Sage, Saint, and Sophist: Holy Men and Their Associates in the Early Roman Empire.* London: Routledge.

Arneson, Hans
2014   "In Defense of Divine Conduct: Theology and Apology in 2 Corinthians." PhD diss., Duke University.

Arnold, C. E.
1989   *Ephesians: Power and Magic.* SNTSMS 63. Cambridge: Cambridge University Press.
1992   *Powers of Darkness: Principalities and Powers in Paul's Letters.* Downers Grove, Ill.: IVP Academic.

415

1996   *The Colossian Syncretism: The Interface between Christianity and Folk Belief at Colossae.* Grand Rapids, Mich.: Baker.

Arzt-Grabner, Peter
2003   *Philemon: Papyrologische Kommentare zum Neuen Testament.* Tübingen: Vandenhoeck & Ruprecht.
2010   "How to Deal with Onesimus? Paul's Solution within the Frame of Ancient Legal and Documentary Sources." In Tolmie 2010, 113-42.

Aune, David E.
1997   *Revelation 1–5.* WBC 52A. Dallas: Word.

Bahr, G. J.
1966   "Paul and Letter Writing in the First Century." *Catholic Biblical Quarterly* 28:465-77.

Barabási, Albert-László
2003   *Linked: How Everything Is Connected to Everything Else and What It Means for Business, Science, and Everyday Life.* New York: Penguin/Plume.

Barclay, John M. G.
1987   "Mirror-Reading a Polemical Letter: Galatians as a Test Case." *Journal for the Study of the New Testament* 31:73-93.
1991   "Paul, Philemon and the Dilemma of Christian Slave-Ownership." *New Testament Studies* 37:161-86.
2004   "The Politics of Contempt: Judeans and Egyptians in Josephus' *Against Apion.*" In *Negotiating Diaspora: Jewish Strategies in the Roman Empire,* edited by J. Barclay, 109-27. London: T&T Clark.
2011a   "Paul, Roman Religion and the Emperor" and "Why the Roman Empire Was Insignificant to Paul." In *Pauline Churches and Diaspora Jews,* 345-88. Tübingen: Mohr Siebeck.
2011b   "Pushing Back: Some Questions for Discussion." *Journal for the Study of the New Testament* 33:321-26.

Barnes, T. D.
1980   "The Editions of Eusebius' *Ecclesiastical History.*" *Greek, Roman and Byzantine Studies* 21:191-201.
2008   "The Date of Ignatius." *Expository Times* 120:119-30.
2009   "Eusebius of Caesarea." *Expository Times* 121:1-14.

Barr, George K.
2004   *Scalometry and the Pauline Epistles.* JSNTSup 261. London: T&T Clark.

Barrett, C. K.
1973   *Second Epistle to the Corinthians.* London: A&C Black.
1982 [1969]   "Titus." In *Essays on Paul,* 118-31. London: SPCK.

Barth, Markus, and Helmut Blanke
2000   *The Letter to Philemon: A New Translation with Notes and Commentary.* Grand Rapids, Mich.: Eerdmans.

Bauer, Walter
1971 [1934]   *Orthodoxy and Heresy in Earliest Christianity.* Edited by Robert A. Kraft and Gerhard Krodel. Translated from 2nd German ed. (1964)

by the Philadelphia Seminar on Christian Origins. Philadelphia: Fortress.

Baur, F. C.
2003 [1845]   *Paul the Apostle of Jesus Christ: His Life and Works, His Epistles and Teachings.* 2 vols. Peabody, Mass.: Hendrickson.

Becker, Eve-Marie
2009   "Ὡς δι' ἡμῶν in 2 Thess als Hinweis auf einen verlorenen Brief." *New Testament Studies* 55:55-72.

Becker, J.
1993 [1989]   *Paul: Apostle to the Gentiles.* Translated by O. C. Dean Jr. Louisville, Ky.: Westminster John Knox.

BeDuhn, Jason D.
2013   *The First New Testament: Marcion's Scriptural Canon.* Salem, Ore.: Polebridge.

Begbie, Jeremy
2013   *Music, Modernity and God: Essays in Listening.* Oxford: Oxford University Press.

Beker, J. C.
1984 [1980]   *Paul the Apostle: The Triumph of God in Life and Thought.* Philadelphia: Fortress. Paperback ed. with new introduction.

Bellen, H.
1971   *Studien zur Sklavenflucht im römischen Kaiserreich.* FASk 4. Wiesbaden: F. Steiner.

Bercovitz, J. Peter
2013   *As Paul Tells It.* http://www.paulonpaul.org.

Berding, K.
1999   "Polycarp of Smyrna's View of the Authorship of 1 and 2 Timothy." *Vigiliae Christianae* 53:349-60.

Best, E.
1972   *A Commentary on the First and Second Epistles to the Thessalonians.* BNTC. London: Black.
1979   "Ephesians i.1." In *Text and Interpretation,* edited by E. Best and R. McL. Wilson, 29-41. Cambridge: Cambridge University Press.
1982   "Ephesians 1.1 Again." In *Paul and Paulinism,* edited by M. D. Hooker and S. G. Wilson, 273-79. London: SPCK.
1987   "Recipients and Title of the Letter to the Ephesians: Why and When the Designation 'Ephesians'?" *ANRW* 2.25.4:3247-79.
1997a   *Essays on Ephesians.* Edinburgh: T&T Clark.
1997b   "Who Used Whom? The Relationship of Ephesians and Colossians." *New Testament Studies* 43:72-96.
1998   *A Critical and Exegetical Commentary on Ephesians.* London: T&T Clark / Continuum.

Betz, H. D.
1973   "2 Cor 6:14–7:1: An Anti-Pauline Fragment?" *Journal of Biblical Literature* 92:88-108.
1985   *2 Corinthians 8 & 9.* Philadelphia: Fortress.

1992   "Paul." *ABD* 5:186-201.

Beyschlag, W.

1871   "Zur Streitfrage über die Paulusgegner des zweiten Korintherbriefs." *TSK* 44:635-76.

Bickerman, E. J.

1980 [1968]   *Chronology of the Ancient World.* Rev. ed. London: Thames & Hudson.

Bitzer, Lloyd

1968   "The Rhetorical Situation." *Philosophy and Rhetoric* 1:1-14.

Bleek, F.

1830   "Erörterungen in Beziehung auf die Briefe Pauli an die Korinther." *TSK* 3:614-32.

1869 [1866]   *An Introduction to the New Testament.* Vol. 1. Translated by W. Urwick. Edinburgh: T&T Clark.

Bockmuehl, M.

1997   *The Epistle to the Philippians.* Peabody, Mass.: Hendrickson.

2001   "1 Thessalonians 2:14-16 and the Church in Jerusalem." *Tyndale Bulletin* 52:1-31.

Boegehold, A. L.

1961   *When a Gesture Was Expected: Selected Examples from Archaic and Classical Greek Literature.* Princeton, N.J.: Princeton University Press.

Boers, Hendrickus

1976   "The Form Critical Study of Paul's Letters: 1 Thessalonians as a Case Study." *New Testament Studies* 22:140-58.

Bonhoeffer, Dietrich

2010 [1953]   *Letters and Papers from Prison.* Edited by John de Gruchy. Translated by I. Best. Minneapolis: Augsburg Fortress. (1st German ed. edited by Eberhard Bethge; 1st English ed. 1953.)

Bowersock, G.

1983   *Roman Arabia.* Cambridge, Mass.: Harvard University Press.

Bowman, A. K., Edward Champlin, and Andrew Lintott

(eds.) 1996   *The Cambridge Ancient History.* Vol. 10, *The Augustan Empire, 43 BC–AD 69.* 2nd ed. Cambridge: Cambridge University Press.

Bradley, Keith R.

1987 [1984]   *Slaves and Masters in the Roman Empire: A Study in Social Control.* Oxford: Oxford University Press.

1994   *Slavery and Society at Rome.* Cambridge: Cambridge University Press.

Braun, Herbert

1952-53   "Zur nachpaulinischen Herkunft des zweiten Thessalonicherbriefes." *ZNW* 44:152-56.

Bray, G. L.

(ed.) 2006   *1-2 Corinthians.* ACCS. Downers Grove, Ill.: IVP Academic.

(ed.) 2009   *Commentaries on Romans and 1-2 Corinthians: Ambrosiaster.* ACT. Downers Grove, Ill.: IVP Academic.

Brent, Allen

2006   *Ignatius of Antioch and the Second Sophistic.* STAC 36. Tübingen: Mohr Siebeck.

2007   *Ignatius of Antioch: A Martyr Bishop and the Origins of Episcopacy.*
                London: T&T Clark/Continuum.

Briones, David
2011   "Paul's Intentional 'Thankless Thanks' in Philippians 4.10-20." *Journal
                for the Study of the New Testament* 34:47-69.

Broer, Ingo
1990   " 'Der ganze Zorn ist schon über sie gekommen': Bemerkungen zur
                Interpolationshypothese und zur Interpretation von 1 Thes 2, 14-16."
                In R. Collins 1990, 137-59.

Brown, Peter
2008 [1988]   *The Body and Society: Men, Women, and Sexual Renunciation in Early
                Christianity.* 2nd ed. New York: Columbia University Press.

Brown, Raymond E.
1997   *An Introduction to the New Testament.* ABRL. New York: Doubleday.

Bruce, F. F.
2006 [1985]   *The Pauline Circle.* Eugene, Ore.: Wipf & Stock.

Buck, C. H., and G. Taylor
1969   *Saint Paul: A Study of the Development of His Thought.* New York:
                Scribner.

Bujard, Walter
1973   *Stilanalytische Untersuchungen zum Kolosserbrief als Beitrag zur
                Methodik von Sprachvergleichen.* SUNT 11. Göttingen: Vandenhoeck
                & Ruprecht.

Bultmann, Rudolf
1951-55   *Theology of the New Testament.* 2 vols. Translated by K. Grobel. New
                York: Scribner.

Burgess, R. W.
1997   "The Dates and Editions of Eusebius' *Chronici Canones* and *Historia
                Ecclesiastica.*" *Journal of Theological Studies* 48:471-504.

Burgoon, J. K.
1994   "Nonverbal Signals." In *Handbook of Interpersonal Communication,* ed-
                ited by M. L. Knapp and G. R. Miller, 229-85. Thousand Oaks, Calif.: Sage.

Burke, W. Warner
2011 [2002]   *Organization Change: Theory and Practice.* 3rd ed. London: Sage.

Burrows, John F.
1987   "Word Patterns and Story Shapes: The Statistical Analysis of Narrative
                Style." *Literary and Linguistic Computing* 2:61-70.

1989   " 'An Ocean Where Each Kind . . .': Statistical Analysis and Some Ma-
                jor Determinants of Literary Style." *Computers and the Humanities*
                23:309-21.

1992a   "Computers and the Study of Literature." In *Computers and Written
                Texts,* edited by C. S. Butler, 167-204. Oxford: Blackwell.

1992b   "Not Unless You Ask Nicely: The Interpretative Nexus between Anal-
                ysis and Information." *Literary and Linguistic Computing* 7:91-109.

2002   "Delta: A Measure of Stylistic Difference and a Guide to Like Author-
                ship." *Literary and Linguistic Computing* 17:267-87.

2003   "Questions of Authorship: Attribution and Beyond." *Computers and the Humanities* 37:5-32.

Burton, Ernest De Witt
1920   *A Critical and Exegetical Commentary on the Epistle to the Galatians.* New York: Scribner.

Caird, George B.
1994   *New Testament Theology.* Completed and edited by L. D. Hurst. Oxford: Clarendon.

Campbell, Charles L., and Stanley P. Saunders
2000   *The Word on the Street: Performing the Scriptures in the Urban Context.* Grand Rapids, Mich.: Eerdmans.

Campbell, Douglas A.
1994   "Determining the Gospel through Rhetorical Analysis in Paul's Letter to the Roman Christians." In Jervis and Richardson 1994, 327-49.
1996   "Unravelling Colossians 3.11b." *New Testament Studies* 42:120-32.
2002   "An Anchor for Pauline Chronology: Paul's Flight from 'The Ethnarch of King Aretas' 2 Cor 11:32-33." *Journal of Biblical Literature* 121:279-302.
2005a   "Inscriptional Attestation to Sergius Paul[l]us (Acts 13.6-12) and the Implications for Pauline Chronology." *Journal of Theological Studies* 56:1-29.
2005b   *The Quest for Paul's Gospel: A Suggested Strategy.* London: T&T Clark / Continuum.
2009   *The Deliverance of God: An Apocalyptic Rereading of Justification in Paul.* Grand Rapids, Mich.: Eerdmans.
2011   "Galatians 5.11: Evidence of an Early Law-Observant Mission by Paul?" *New Testament Studies* 57:325-47.
2013   "Paul's Apocalyptic Politics." *Pro Ecclesia* 22:129-52.

Campenhausen, Hans von
1963   "Polykarp von Smyrna und die Pastoralbriefe." In *Aus der Frühzeit des Christentums*, 197-252. Tübingen: Mohr Siebeck.

Childs, Brevard S.
1992   *Biblical Theology of the Old and New Testaments.* Minneapolis: Fortress.

Cohen, S. J. D.
1999   *The Beginnings of Jewishness: Boundaries, Varieties, Uncertainties.* Berkeley: University of California Press.

Collins, Raymond
1979   "Apropos the Integrity of 1 Thes." *ETL* 55:67-106. (Reprinted in R. Collins 1984, 96-135.)
1984   *Studies on the First Letter to the Thessalonians.* BETL 66. Leuven: Peeters.
(ed.) 1990 *The Thessalonian Correspondence.* BETL 87. Leuven: Peeters.
2002   *I & II Timothy and Titus: A Commentary.* NTL. Louisville, Ky.: Westminster John Knox.

Coneybeare, W. J., and J. S. Howson
1878   *The Life and Epistles of St. Paul.* Hartford, Conn.: Columbian Book Company.

Corssen, Peter M.
1909   "Zur Überlieferungsgeschichte des Römerbriefes." *ZNW* 10:1-45, 97-102.

Crook, J. A., Andrew Lintott, and Elizabeth Rawson
(eds.) 1994   *The Cambridge Ancient History*. Vol. 9, *The Last Age of the Roman Republic, 146-43 BC*. 2nd ed. Cambridge: Cambridge University Press.

Dahl, Nils A.
1978   "The Origin of the Earliest Prologues to the Pauline Letters." *Semeia* 12:233-77. (Reprinted in *Studies in Ephesians: Introductory Questions, Text- and Edition-Critical Issues, Interpretation of Texts and Themes*, edited by D. Hellholm, V. Blomkvist, and T. Fornberg, 179-209. Tübingen: Mohr Siebeck, 2000.)

Dawes, Gregory
1998   *The Body in Question: Metaphor and Meaning in the Interpretation of Ephesians 5:21-33*. BIS 30. Leiden: Brill.

de Boer, Martinus C.
1994   "The Composition of 1 Corinthians." *New Testament Studies* 40:229-45.
2011   *Galatians: A Commentary*. Louisville, Ky.: Westminster John Knox.

De Bruyn, Donatien
1907   "Prologues Bibliques D'Origine Marcionite." *RBén* 24:1-16.

Deissmann, G. A.
1923   "Zur ephesinischen Gefangenschaft des Apostels Paulus." In *Anatolian Studies Presented to Sir William Ramsay*, edited by W. H. Buckler and W. M. Calder, 121-27. Manchester: Manchester University Press.

DeMaris, Richard E.
1994   *The Colossian Controversy: Wisdom in Dispute at Colossae*. JSNTSup 96. Sheffield: Academic.

De Morgan, Sophie Elizabeth
(ed.) 1882   *Memoir of Augustus de Morgan (With Selections from His Letters)*. London: Longmans, Green.

De Wette, W.
1841   *Kurze Erklärung der Briefe an die Corinther*. Leipzig: Weidmann.

Diamond, Jared
2012   *The World until Yesterday: What Can We Learn from Traditional Societies?* New York: Viking.

Dillon, J. M.
1977   *The Middle Platonists*. Ithaca, N.Y.: Cornell University Press.

Donfried, Karl P.
1991 [1974]   "False Presuppositions in the Study of Romans." In Donfried 1991, 102-24.
(ed.) 1991   *The Romans Debate*. Rev. and exp. ed. Peabody, Mass.: Hendrickson. (1st ed. 1977.)
1992   "Chronology, New Testament." *ABD* 1:1011-22.
(ed.) 2008   *1 Timothy Reconsidered*. COP 18. Leuven: Peeters.
forthcoming   *1 & 2 Thessalonians: A Critical and Exegetical Commentary*. ICC. London: T&T Clark / Continuum.

Donfried, Karl P., and Johannes Beutler
(eds.) 2000   *The Thessalonians Debate: Methodological Discord or Methodological Synthesis?* Grand Rapids, Mich.: Eerdmans.
Downs, D. J.
2006   "Paul's Collection and the Book of Acts Revisited." *New Testament Studies* 52:50-70.
2008   *The Offering of the Gentiles: Paul's Collection for Jerusalem in Its Chronological, Cultural, and Cultic Contexts.* Tübingen: Mohr Siebeck.
Duff, J.
1998   "P46 and the Pastorals: A Misleading Consensus?" *New Testament Studies* 44:578-90.
Duncan, G. S.
1929   *St. Paul's Ephesian Ministry: A Reconstruction with Special Reference to the Ephesian Origin of the Imprisonment Epistles.* London: Hodder & Stoughton.
1931-32   "A New Setting for Paul's Epistle to the Philippians." *Expository Times* 43:7-11.
Dunn, James D. G.
1998   *The Theology of Paul the Apostle.* Edinburgh: T&T Clark; Grand Rapids, Mich.: Eerdmans.
2003a   "Altering the Default Setting: Re-envisaging the Early Transmission of the Jesus Tradition." *New Testament Studies* 49:139-75.
(ed.) 2003b   *The Cambridge Companion to St Paul.* Cambridge: Cambridge University Press.
Dupont-Sommer, A.
1939   *Le quatrième livre des Macchabées.* BEHE 274. Parish: H. Champion.
Eastman, S. G.
2010   "Israel and the Mercy of God: A Re-reading of Galatians 6.16 and Romans 9–11." *New Testament Studies* 56:367-95.
Eco, Umberto
1976   *A Theory of Semiotics.* Bloomington, Ind.: Indiana University Press.
Ehrman, Bart D.
1993   *The Orthodox Corruption of Scripture. The Effect of Early Christological Controversies on the Text of the New Testament.* Oxford: Oxford University Press.
(ed.) 2003   *The Apostolic Fathers.* 2 vols. LCL. Cambridge, Mass.: Harvard University Press.
2013   *Forgery and Counterforgery: The Use of Literary Deceit in Early Christian Polemics.* Oxford: Oxford University Press.
Ellis, E. Earle
1971   "Paul and His Co-workers: For the Very Rev. Professor James S. Stewart on His Seventy-Fifth Birthday." *New Testament Studies* 17:437-52.
1993   "Coworkers, Paul and His." *DP&L*, 183-89.
Engberg-Pedersen, Troels
2010   *Cosmology and Self in the Apostle Paul: The Material Spirit.* Oxford: Oxford University Press.

Esler, P.

1987   *Community and Gospel in Luke-Acts: The Social and Political Motiva-
            tions of Lucan Theology.* SNTSMS. Cambridge: Cambridge University
            Press.

1994   *The First Christians in Their Social World: Social Scientific Approaches
            to New Testament Interpretation.* New York: Routledge.

1998   *Galatians.* New York: Routledge.

2000a   "Models in New Testament Interpretation: A Reply to David Horrell."
            Journal for the Study of the New Testament 78:107-13.

2000b   "2 Thessalonians." In *The Oxford Bible Commentary,* edited by J. Barton
            and J. Muddiman, 1213-20. Oxford: Oxford University Press.

2003   *Conflict and Identity in Romans: The Social Setting of Paul's Letter.* Min-
            neapolis: Fortress.

2005   *New Testament Theology: Communion and Community.* Minneapolis:
            Fortress.

Fee, Gordon

1977   "II Corinthians vi.14-vii.1 and Food Offered to Idols." *New Testament
            Studies* 23:140-61.

Ferguson, Everett

1982   "Canon Muratori: Date and Provenance." *Studia Patristica* 18:677-83.

1993   Review of *The Muratorian Fragment and the Development of the Canon,*
            by Geoffrey M. Hahneman. *Journal of Theological Studies* 44:691-97.

Finegan, Jack

1956   "The Original Form of the Pauline Collection." *Harvard Theological
            Review* 49:85-103.

Fiore, Benjamin, SJ

1986   *The Function of Personal Example in the Socratic and Pastoral Epistles.*
            AnBib 105. Rome: Biblical Institute.

Foster, Paul

2006a   "The Epistles of Ignatius of Antioch (Part I)." *Expository Times*
            117:487-95.

2006b   "The Epistles of Ignatius of Antioch (Part II)." *Expository Times* 118:2-11.

(ed.) 2007 *The Writings of the Apostolic Fathers.* London: T&T Clark.

2012   "Who Wrote 2 Thessalonians? A Fresh Look at an Old Problem." *Jour-
            nal for the Study of the New Testament* 35:150-75.

Francis, F. O.

1962   "Humility and Angelic Worship in Col 2:18." *Studia Theologica*
            16:109-34.

1967   "Visionary Discipline and Scriptural Tradition at Colossae." *Lexington
            Theological Quarterly* 2:71-78.

1975a   "The Background of *Embateuein* (Col 2:18) in Legal Papyri and Oracle
            Inscriptions." In Francis and Meeks 1975, 197-207.

1975b   "Humility and Angelic Worship in Col. 2:18." In Francis and Meeks
            1975, 163-96.

Francis, F. O., and Wayne A. Meeks

(eds.) 1975 *Conflict at Colossae: A Problem in the Interpretation of Early Christian-*

ity Illustrated by Selected Modern Studies. Rev. ed. SBLSBS 4. Missoula: Scholars Press.

Fredrickson, D. E.

2001   "'Through Many Tears' (2 Cor 2:4): Paul's Grieving Letter and the Occasion of 2 Corinthians 1–7." In *Paul and Pathos,* edited by Thomas H. Olbricht and Jerry L. Sumney, 161-79. Atlanta: SBL.

Friedrich, Gerhard

1981   "1-2 Thessalonians." In *Die Briefe an die Galataer, Epheser, Philipper, Kolosser, Thessalonicher und Philemon: Übersetzt und Erklärt,* edited by J. Becker, H. Conzelmann, and G. Friedrich, 252-57. NTD. Göttingen: Vandenhoeck & Ruprecht.

Fuhrmann, Christopher J.

2012   *Policing the Roman Empire: Soldiers, Administration, and Public Order.* Oxford: Oxford University Press.

Furnish, V. P.

1984   *II Corinthians: A New Translation with Introduction and Commentary.* AB 32A. New York: Doubleday.

1989   "Pauline Studies." In *The New Testament and Its Modern Interpreters,* edited by E. J. Epp and G. W. McRae, 321-50. Atlanta: Scholars Press.

Gamble, Harry F.

1995   *Books and Readers in the Early Church: A History of Early Christian Texts.* New Haven: Yale University Press.

Gamble, H. Y.

1977   *The Textual History of the Letter to the Romans.* Grand Rapids, Mich.: Eerdmans.

Garland, D.

1985   "The Composition and Unity of Philippians: Some Neglected Literary Factors." *Novum Testamentum* 27:141-73.

Gaventa, Beverly Roberts, and Richard B. Hays

(eds.) 2008   *Seeking the Identity of Jesus: A Pilgrimage.* Grand Rapids, Mich.: Eerdmans.

Gawande, Atul

2009   "Annals of Human Rights: Hellhole." *New Yorker,* March 30, 2009. http://www.newyorker.com/reporting/2009/03/30/090330fa_fact _gawande.

Gellner, Ernst

1988   *Plough, Sword, and Book: The Structure of Human History.* Chicago: University of Chicago Press.

Georgi, D.

1991 [1965]   *Remembering the Poor: The History of Paul's Collection for Jerusalem.* Nashville: Abingdon.

Gibson, Roy

2012   "On the Nature of Ancient Letter Collections." *Journal of Roman Studies* 102: 56-78.

Gilbert, Daniel
2005   *Stumbling on Happiness.* New York: Vintage.
Gladwell, Malcolm
2005   *Blink: The Power of Thinking without Thinking.* New York: Little, Brown.
Glancy, Jennifer A.
2006   *Slavery in Early Christianity.* Minneapolis: Fortress.
Gnilka, Joachim
1994   *Theologie des Neuen Testaments.* HTKNT Supp. 5. Freiburg: Herder.
Goguel, Maurice
1925   *Introduction au Nouveau Testament.* 4 vols. Paris: Leroux.
Goodacre, Mark
2002   *The Case against Q: Studies in Markan Priority and the Synoptic Problem.* Harrisburg, Pa.: Trinity Press International.
Goodacre, Mark, and Nicholas Perrin
(eds.) 2004 *Questioning Q: A Multidimensional Critique.* With a foreword by N. T. Wright. Downers Grove, Ill.: IVP Academic.
Goodspeed, Edgar J.
1933   *The Meaning of Ephesians.* Chicago: University of Chicago Press.
1937   *An Introduction to the New Testament.* Chicago: University of Chicago Press.
1956   *The Key to Ephesians.* Chicago: University of Chicago Press.
Goulder, M.
1994   "2 Cor 6:14–7:1 as an Integral Part of 2 Corinthians." *Novum Testamentum* 36:47-57.
Graf, F.
1992   "Gestures and Conventions: The Gestures of Roman Actors and Orators." In *A Cultural History of Gesture,* edited by Jan Bremmer and Herman Roodenburg, 3-58. Ithaca, N.Y.: Cornell University Press.
Grotius, Hugo
1679 [1640] *Commentatio ad loca Novi Testamenti, quae de Antichristo agunt aut agere putantus, expedenda eruditis.* In *Opera omnia theologica.* London: Moses Pitt.
1829 [1641] *Annotationes in novum Testamentum. VII. Continens Annotationes in Pauli Epistolas ad Ephesios-Philemonem et in Epist. Ad Hebraeos.* Groningae: W. Zuidema.
Guerrero, L. K., Joseph A. Devito, and Michael L. Hecht (eds.)
1999   *The Nonverbal Communication Reader.* Prospect Heights, Ill.: Waveland.
Gumerlock, F.
2006   "NERO ANTICHRIST: Patristic Evidence of the Use of Nero's Name in Calculating the Number of the Beast (Rev. 13:18)." *Westminster Theological Journal* 68:347-60.
Haacker, K.
2003   "Paul's Life." In Dunn 2003b, 19-33.
Hahn, Ferdinand
2001-5 [2002] *Theologie des Neuen Testaments.* 2nd ed. 2 vols. Tübingen: Mohr Siebeck.

Hahneman, Geoffrey M.
1992   *The Muratorian Fragment and the Development of the Canon.* Oxford:
               Clarendon.
Hanges, James C.
2012   *Paul, Founder of Churches: A Study in Light of the Evidence for the
               Role of "Founder-Figures" in the Hellenistic-Roman Period.* WUNT 292.
               Tübingen: Mohr Siebeck.
Hare, Douglas R. A.
1987 [1950]   "Introduction." In Knox 1987 [1950], ix-xxii.
Harnack, Adolf von
2007 [1921]   *Marcion: The Gospel of the Alien God.* Translated by John E. Steely
               and Lyle D. Bierma. Eugene, Ore.: Wipf & Stock. Reprint of 1990 ET,
               Labyrinth Press. (3rd German ed. 1996; 1st 1921.)
Harrill, J. Albert
1999   "Using the Roman Jurists to Interpret Philemon: A Response to Peter
               Lampe." *ZNW* 90:135-38.
Harris, J. Rendell
1898   "A Study in Letter-Writing." *The Expositor,* 5th ser., 8:161-80.
Harris, William V.
1989   *Ancient Literacy.* Cambridge, Mass.: Harvard University Press.
Harrison, P. N.
1921   *The Problem of the Pastoral Epistles.* London: Oxford University Press.
1936   *Polycarp's Two Epistles to the Philippians.* Cambridge: Cambridge Uni-
               versity Press.
1955   "Important Hypotheses Reconsidered, III: The Authorship of the Pas-
               toral Epistles." *Expository Times* 67:77-81.
1956   "The Pastoral Epistles and Duncan's Ephesian Theory." *New Testament
               Studies* 2:250-61.
1964   *Paulines and Pastorals.* London: Villiers.
Hartwig, Charlotte, and Gerd Theissen
2004   "Die Korinthische Gemeinde als Nebenadressat des Römerbriefs.
               Eigentextreferenzen des Paulus und Kommunikativer Kontext des
               Längsten Paulusbriefes." *Novum Testamentum* 46:229-52.
Hauerwas, Stanley
2002   *With the Grain of the Universe: The Church's Witness and Natural The-
               ology.* London: SCM.
Hays, Richard B.
2002 [1983]   *The Faith of Jesus Christ: The Narrative Substructure of Galatians 3:1–
               4:11.* 2nd ed. Grand Rapids, Mich.: Eerdmans. (1st ed. 1983.)
2008   "The Story of God's Son: The Identity of Jesus in the Letters of Paul."
               In Gaventa and Hays 2008, 180-99.
Head, P. M.
2009a   "Letter Carriers in the Ancient Jewish Epistolary Material." In *Jew-
               ish and Christian Scripture as Artifact and Canon,* edited by Craig A.
               Evans and H. Daniel Zacharias, 203-19. London: T&T Clark /
               Continuum.

2009b   "Named Letter-Carriers among the Oxyrhynchus Papyri." *Journal for the Study of the New Testament* 31:279-99.

Hodge, Charles
1974 [1859]   *A Commentary on 1 & 2 Corinthians.* Edinburgh: Banner of Truth Trust.

Holland, Glenn S.
1986   *The Tradition That You Received from Us: 2 Thessalonians in the Pauline Tradition.* HUT 24. Tübingen: Mohr Siebeck.
1990   " 'A Letter Supposedly from Us': A Contribution to the Discussion about the Authorship of 2 Thessalonians." In R. Collins 1990, 394-402.

Holmes, David
1994   "Authorship Attribution." *Computers and the Humanities* 28:87-106.
1998   "The Evolution of Stylometry." *Literary and Linguistic Computing* 13:111-17.

Holmes, Michael W.
2005   "Polycarp's *Letter to the Philippians* and the Writings That Later Formed the New Testament." In *The Reception of the New Testament in the Apostolic Fathers,* edited by A. Gregory and C. Tuckett, 187-227. Oxford: Oxford University Press.
2006   "The Apostolic Fathers: Polycarp of Smyrna, *Letter to the Philippians.*" *Expository Times* 118:53-63. (Reprinted as "Polycarp of Smyrna, *Letter to the Philippians*" in Foster 2007, 108-25.)
2007   *The Apostolic Fathers: Greek Texts and English Translations.* After the earlier work of J. B. Lightfoot and J. R. Harmer. 3rd ed. Grand Rapids, Mich.: Baker Academic.
2011   "Paul and Polycarp." In *Paul and the Second Century,* edited by Michael F. Bird and Joseph R. Dodson, 57-69. LNTS 412. New York: T&T Clark.

Holtzmann, H.
1879   "Das gegenseitige Verhältniss der beiden Korintherbriefe." *ZWT* 22:455-92.
1901   "Zum zweiten Thessalonicherbrief." *ZNW* 2:97-108.

Holz, Traugott
1990   "The Judgment on the Jews and the Salvation of All Israel: 1 Thes 2, 15-16 and Rom 11, 25-26." In R. Collins 1990, 284-94.

Hooker, M. D.
1973   "Were There False Teachers in Colossae?" In *Christ and Spirit in the New Testament,* edited by B. Lindars and S. S. Smalley, 315-31. Cambridge: Cambridge University Press.

Hoover, David L.
2003   "Another Perspective on Vocabulary Richness." *Computers and the Humanities* 37:151-78.
2004a   "Delta Prime?" *Literary and Linguistic Computing* 19:477-95.
2004b   "Testing Burrows's Delta." *Literary and Linguistic Computing* 19:453-75.
2013   "Textual Analysis." Literary Studies in the Digital Age: An Evolving Anthology. MLA Commons. Accessed May 16. http://dlsanthology .commons.mla.org/textual-analysis/.

Horden, Peregrine, and Nicholas Purcell
2000   *The Corrupting Sea: A Study of Mediterranean History.* Oxford: Wiley-Blackwell.

Horrell, David G.
1996   *The Social Ethos of the Corinthian Correspondence: Interests and Ideology from 1 Corinthians to 1 Clement.* Edinburgh: T&T Clark.
2000   "Models and Methods in Social-Scientific Interpretation: A Response to Philip Esler." *Journal for the Study of the New Testament* 78:83-105.
2005   *Solidarity and Difference: A Contemporary Reading of Paul's Ethics.* London: T&T Clark International / Continuum.
2007   "The Label Χριστιανός: 1 Peter 4:16 and the Formation of Christian Identity." *Journal of Biblical Literature* 126:361-81.

Horsley, Richard
(ed.) 1997   *Paul and Empire: Religion and Power in Roman Imperial Society.* Harrisburg, Pa.: Trinity Press International.
(ed.) 2000   *Paul and Politics: Ekklēsia, Israel, Imperium, Interpretation: Essays in Honor of Krister Stendahl.* Harrisburg, Pa.: Trinity Press International.
(ed.) 2004   *Paul and the Roman Imperial Order.* Harrisburg, Pa.: Trinity Press International.

Hübner, Reinhard M.
1997   "Thesen zur Echtheit und Datierung der sieben Briefe des Ignatius von Antiochien." *ZAC* 1:44-72.

Hughes, Frank W.
1989   *Early Christian Rhetoric and 2 Thessalonians.* JSNTSup 30. Sheffield: JSOT.

Hughes, P. E.
1962   *Paul's Second Epistle to the Corinthians.* NICNT. Grand Rapids, Mich.: Eerdmans.

Hurd, J. C.
1983 [1965]   *The Origin of I Corinthians.* Macon, Ga.: Mercer University Press.

Hurtado, L.
2009   "Monotheism, Principal Angels, and the Background of Christology." In *The Oxford Handbook of the Dead Sea Scrolls,* edited by Timothy H. Lim and John J. Collins, 546-64. Oxford: Oxford University Press.

Hyldahl, N.
1973   "Die Frage nach der literarischen Einheit des Zweiten Korintherbriefes." *ZNW* 64:289-306.
1986   *Die Paulinische Chronologie.* Leiden: Brill.

Jaffee, Martin S.
2001   *Torah in the Mouth: Writing and Oral Tradition in Palestinian Judaism 200 B.C.E.-200 C.E.* Oxford: Oxford University Press.

Jasinski, James
2001   "Rhetorical Situation." In *Encyclopedia of Rhetoric,* edited by Thomas O. Sloane. Oxford: Oxford University Press. (Online version, http://www .oxfordreference.com.)

Jervis, L. Ann

1991   *The Purpose of Romans: A Comparative Letter Structure Investigation.*
            JSNTSup 55. Sheffield: Academic.

Jervis, L. Ann, and Peter Richardson

(eds.) 1994 *Gospel in Paul: Studies on Corinthians, Galatians and Romans for Richard N. Longenecker.* JSNTSup 108. Sheffield: JSOT.

Jewett, Robert

1979   *A Chronology of Paul's Life.* Philadelphia: Fortress.

1986   *The Thessalonian Correspondence: Pauline Rhetoric and Millenarian Piety.* FFNT. Philadelphia: Fortress.

2007   *Romans.* Herm. Minneapolis: Fortress.

Johnson, Barbara

1980 [1978] "The Frame of Reference: Poe, Lacan, Derrida." In *The Critical Difference: Essays in the Contemporary Rhetoric of Reading,* 110-46, 152-54. Baltimore: Johns Hopkins University Press.

Johnson, L. T.

1996   *Letters to Paul's Delegates: 1 Timothy, 2 Timothy, Titus.* NTC. Valley Forge: Trinity Press International.

2001   *The First and Second Letters to Timothy: A New Translation with Introduction and Commentary.* AB 35A. New York: Doubleday.

Johnson, W. A.

2000   "Toward a Sociology of Reading in Classical Antiquity." *American Journal of Philology* 121:593-627.

2010   *Readers and Reading Culture in the High Roman Empire: A Study of Elite Communities.* Oxford: Oxford University Press.

Juola, Patrick

2004   "Ad-hoc Authorship Attribution Competition." Proceedings of the Joint International Conference of the Association for Literary and Linguistic Computing and the Association for Computers and the Humanities, Göteborg, Sweden, June 2004.

2006   "Authorship Attribution." *Foundations and Trends in Information Retrieval* 1:233-334.

Kahneman, Daniel

2011   *Thinking, Fast and Slow.* New York: Farrar, Straus and Giroux.

Karris, R. J.

1991 [1973] "Romans 14:1–15:13 and the Occasion of Romans." In Donfried 1991, 65-84.

Käsemann, E.

1971   *Perspectives on Paul.* Translated by M. Kohl. London: SCM.

Kenny, Anthony

1986   *A Stylometric Study of the New Testament.* Oxford: Clarendon.

Kern, Friedrich H.

1839   "Über 2. Thess 2,1-12. Nebst Andeutungen über den Ursprung des zweiten Briefs an die Thessalonicher." *TZT* 2:145-214.

Kerr, Nathan

2009   "Ernst Troeltsch: The Triumph of Ideology and the Eclipse of Apocalyptic." Ch. 2 in *Christ, History, and Apocalyptic: The Politics of Christian Mission*, 23-62. London: SCM.

Kiley, M.
1986   *Colossians as Pseudepigraphy.* Sheffield: JSOT.

Kilpatrick, G. D.
1968   "ΒΛΕΠΕΤΕ, Philippians 3:2." In *In Memoriam Paul Kahle*, edited by M. Black and G. Fohrer, 146-48. BZAW 103. Berlin: Töpelmann.

King, Martin Luther Jr.
2004 [1963]   "Letter from Birmingham Jail." In *The Norton Anthology of African American Literature*, edited by H. L. Gates and N. Y. McKay, 1896-1908. 2nd ed. New York: Norton.

Klauck, H.-J.
2003   "Compilation of Letters in Cicero's Correspondence." In Olbricht, Fitzgerald, and White 2003, 131-55.

2006 [1998]   *Ancient Letters and the New Testament: A Guide to Context and Exegesis.* Translated, revised, expanded, and edited by Daniel P. Bailey. Waco: Baylor University Press.

Kloppenborg, John S., and Stephen G. Wilson
(eds.) 1996   *Voluntary Associations in the Graeco-Roman World.* New York: Routledge.

Knopf, Rudolf
1905   *Das nachapostolische Zeitalter. Geschichte der Christlichen Gemeinden vom Beginn der Flavierdynastie bis zum ende Hadrians.* Tübingen: Mohr.

Knox, John
1936   "Fourteen Years Later: A Note on the Pauline Chronology." *Journal of Religion* 16:341-49.

1939   "The Pauline Chronology." *Journal of Biblical Literature* 58:15-29.

1959   *Philemon among the Letters of Paul.* Rev. ed. Nashville: Abingdon.

1983   "Chapters in a Life of Paul — A Response to Robert Jewett and Gerd Luedemann." In *Colloquy on New Testament Studies: A Time for Reappraisal and Fresh Approaches*, edited by Bruce C. Corley, 339-64. Macon, Ga.: Mercer University Press.

1987 [1950]   *Chapters in a Life of Paul.* Rev. ed. London: SCM.

1990   "On the Pauline Chronology: Buck-Taylor-Hurd Revisited." In *The Conversation Continues: Studies in Paul and John in Honor of J. Louis Martyn*, edited by B. R. Gaventa and R. T. Fortna, 258-74. Nashville: Abingdon.

Koester, H.
1979   "1 Thessalonians — Experiment in Christian Writing." In *Continuity and Discontinuity in Church History: Essays Presented to G. H. Williams*, edited by F. F. Church and T. George, 33-44. Leiden: Brill.

1982   *Introduction to the New Testament.* Vol. 2, *History and Literature of Early Christianity.* Philadelphia: Fortress.

1990   "From Paul's Eschatology to the Apocalyptic Schemata of 2 Thessalonians." In R. Collins 1990, 441-58.

1995	"Ephesos in Early Christian Literature." In *Ephesos, Metropolis of Asia: An Interdisciplinary Approach to Its Archaeology, Religion, and Culture,* edited by H. Koester, 119-40. Harrisburg, Pa.: Trinity Press International.
1997	"Imperial Ideology and Paul's Eschatology in 1 Thessalonians." In Horsley 1997, 158-66.

Koperski, V.

1993	"The Early History of the Dissection of Philippians." *Journal of Theological Studies* 44:599-603.

Krenkel, M.

1890	*Beiträge zur Aufhellung der Geschichte und der Briefe des Apostels Paulus.* Braunschweig: Schwetschke.

Lakoff, George

2002	*Moral Politics. How Liberals and Conservatives Think.* Chicago: University of Chicago Press.

Lambrecht, J.

1990	"Thanksgivings in 1 Thessalonians 1-3." In R. Collins 1990, 183-205. (Reprinted in Donfried and Beutler 2000, 135-62.)
2000	"A Structural Analysis of 1 Thessalonian 4-5." In Donfried and Beutler 2000, 163-78.

Lampe, P.

1985a	"Keine 'Sklavenflucht' des Onesimus." *ZNW* 76:135-37.
1985b	"Zur Textgeschichte des Römerbriefes." *Novum Testamentum* 27:273-77.
1991	"The Roman Christians of Romans 16." In Donfried 1991, 216-30.
2003 [1989]	*From Paul to Valentinus: Christians at Rome in the First Two Centuries.* Translated by M. Steinhauser. Minneapolis: Fortress.

Lechner, T.

1999	*Ignatius adversus Valentinianos? Chronologische und theologiegeschichtliche Studien zu den Briefen des Ignatius von Antiochen.* VCSup 47. Leiden: Brill.

Ledger, Gerard

1995	"An Exploration of Differences in the Pauline Epistles Using Multivariate Statistical Analysis." *Literary and Linguistic Computing* 10:85-97.

Leppä, Outi

2003	*The Making of Colossians: A Study on the Formation and Purpose of a Deutero-Pauline Letter.* PFES 86. Göttingen: Vandenhoeck & Ruprecht.
2006	"2 Thessalonians among the Pauline Letters: Tracing Literary Links between 2 Thessalonians and the Other Pauline Epistles." In *The Intertextuality of the Epistles: Explorations of Theory and Practice,* edited by T. L. Brodie, D. R. MacDonald, and S. E. Porter, 175-95. Sheffield: Phoenix.

Lietzmann, H.

1969	*An Die Korinther I/II.* Tübingen: Mohr Siebeck.

Lightfoot, J. B.

1891	*The Apostolic Fathers: Revised Texts with Short Introductions and En-*

glish Translations. Edited and completed by J. R. Harmer. London: Macmillan.

1896   *Saint Paul's Epistle to the Philippians: A Revised Text with Introduction, Notes, and Dissertations.* London: Macmillan.

Lincoln, Andrew T.

1990   *Ephesians.* WBC 42. Dallas: Word.

Lindbeck, George A.

1984   *The Nature of Doctrine: Religion and Theology in a Post-Liberal Age.* Louisville, Ky.: Westminster John Knox.

Lindemann, Andreas

1977   "Zum Abfassungszweck des Zweiten Thessalonicherbriefes." *ZNW* 68:35-47.

Loh, I.-J., and E. A. Nida

1977   *A Translator's Handbook on Paul's Letter to the Philippians.* London, New York, Stuttgart: United Bible Societies.

Longenecker, Bruce W.

(ed.) 2002   *Narrative Dynamics in Paul: A Critical Assessment.* Louisville, Ky.: Westminster John Knox.

2007   "Good News to the Poor: Jesus, Paul and Jerusalem." In *Jesus and Paul Reconnected,* edited by T. Still, 37-66. Grand Rapids, Mich.: Eerdmans.

2010   *Remember the Poor: Paul, Poverty, and the Greco-Roman World.* Grand Rapids, Mich.: Eerdmans.

Longenecker, Richard N.

1990   *Galatians.* WBC 41. Dallas: Word.

1998   "Is There Development in Paul's Resurrection Thought?" In *Life in the Face of Death: The Resurrection Message of the New Testament,* edited by R. Longenecker, 171-202. Grand Rapids, Mich.: Eerdmans.

Looks, Carsten

1999   *Das Anvertraute bewahren: Die Rezeption der Pastoralbriefe im 2. Jahrhundert.* MTB 3. München: Herbert Utz Verlag.

Luedemann, Gerd

1984 [1980]   *Paul, Apostle to the Gentiles: Studies in Chronology.* Translated by F. Stanley Jones. Philadelphia: Fortress.

1989a   *Early Christianity according to the Traditions in Acts.* Minneapolis: Fortress.

1989b [1983]   *Opposition to Paul in Jewish Christianity.* Translated by M. E. Boring. Minneapolis: Fortress.

Lütgert, W.

1919   *Gesetz und Geist: Eine Untersuchung zur Vorgeschichte des Galaterbriefes.* Gütersloh: Bertelsmann.

Lyons, G.

1985   *Pauline Autobiography: Toward a New Understanding.* Atlanta: SBL.

2012   *Galatians: A Commentary in the Wesleyan Tradition.* NBBC. Kansas City, Mo.: Beacon Hill.

MacDonald, M. Y.

1988   *The Pauline Churches: A Socio-historical Study of Institutionalization in the Pauline and Deutero-Pauline Writings.* SNTSMS 57. Cambridge: Cambridge University Press.

MacIntyre, Alasdair C.

1988   *Whose Justice? Which Rationality?* Notre Dame, Ind.: University of Notre Dame Press.

1990   *Three Rival Versions of Moral Enquiry: Encyclopaedia, Genealogy, and Tradition.* Notre Dame, Ind.: University of Notre Dame Press.

2007 [1981]   *After Virtue.* 3rd ed. Notre Dame, Ind.: University of Notre Dame Press.

Malherbe, Abraham J.

1977   "The Inhospitality of Diotrephes." In *God's Christ and His People: Studies in Honor of Nils A. Dahl,* edited by Jacob Jervell and Wayne Meeks, 222-32. Oslo: Universitetsforlaget. (Reprinted as "Hospitality and Inhospitality in the Church" in Malherbe 1983b, 92-112.)

1983a   "Antisthenes and Odysseus, and Paul at War." *Harvard Theological Review* 76:143-73.

1983b   *Social Aspects of Early Christianity.* 2nd ed. Philadelphia: Fortress.

2000   *The Letters to the Thessalonians.* AB 32B. New York: Doubleday.

Manson, T. W.

1953   "St Paul in Greece: The Letters to the Thessalonians." *BJRL* 35:428-47.

1991 [1962]   "St. Paul's Letter to the Romans — and Others." In Donfried 1991, 3-15.

Marcus, Joel

1989   "The Circumcision and the Uncircumcision in Rome." *New Testament Studies* 35:67-81.

2006   "Idolatry in the New Testament." *Interpretation* 60:152-64.

Marshall, Christopher D.

2012   *Compassionate Justice: An Interdisciplinary Dialogue with Two Gospel Parables on Law, Crime, and Restorative Justice.* TV 15. Eugene, Ore.: Cascade.

Marshall, I. Howard

1999   *A Critical and Exegetical Commentary on the Pastoral Epistles.* In collaboration with Philip H. Towner. ICC. Edinburgh: T&T Clark.

2004   *New Testament Theology: Many Witnesses, One Gospel.* Downers Grove, Ill.: IVP Academic.

Marshall, P.

1987   *Enmity at Corinth: Social Conventions in Paul's Relations with the Corinthians.* WUNT 2/23. Tübingen: Mohr Siebeck.

Martin, Dale

1995   *The Corinthian Body.* New Haven: Yale University Press.

2006   *Sex and the Single Savior: Gender and Sexuality in Biblical Interpretation.* Louisville, Ky.: Westminster John Knox.

Martin, Troy
1996   *By Philosophy and Empty Deceit: Colossians as Response to a Cynic
             Critique.* JSNTSup 118. Sheffield: Academic.
Martyn, J. L.
1985   "Apocalyptic Antinomies in Paul's Letter to the Galatians." *New Testa-
             ment Studies* 31:410-24. (Reprinted in Martyn 1997b, 111-24.)
1997a   *Galatians: A New Translation with Introduction and Commentary.* AB
             33A. New York: Doubleday.
1997b   *Theological Issues in the Letters of Paul.* Edinburgh: T&T Clark.
Marxsen, Willi
1968   *Introduction to the New Testament: An Approach to Its Problems.* Ox-
             ford: Blackwell.
1969   "Auslegung von 1 Thess 4,13-18." *ZTK* 66:23-37.
Mascoll, Conrad
1888a   "Curves of Pauline and Pseudo-Pauline Style I." *Unitarian Review*
             30:452-60.
1888b   "Curves of Pauline and Pseudo-Pauline Style II." *Unitarian Review*
             30:539-46.
Matera, Frank
2005   "New Testament Theology: History, Method, and Identity." *Catholic
             Biblical Quarterly* 67:1-21.
2007   *New Testament Theology: Exploring Diversity and Unity.* Louisville, Ky.:
             Westminster John Knox.
Mealand, David L.
1988   "Computers in New Testament Research: An Interim Report." *Journal
             for the Study of the New Testament* 33:97-115.
1989   "Positional Stylometry Reassessed: Testing a Seven Epistle Theory of
             Pauline Authorship." *New Testament Studies* 35:266-86.
1995   "The Extent of the Pauline Corpus: A Multivariate Approach." *Journal
             for the Study of the New Testament* 59:61-92.
1997   "Measuring Genre Differences in Mark with Correspondence Analy-
             sis." *Literary and Linguistic Computing* 12:227-45.
1999   "Style, Genre, and Authorship in Acts, the Septuagint, and Hellenistic
             Historians." *Literary and Linguistic Computing* 14:479-506.
Mendenhall, T. C.
1887   "The Characteristic Curves of Composition." *Science,* n.s., 9.214:237-49.
Merz, Annette
2004   *Die fiktive Selbstauslegung des Paulus: Intertextuelle Studien zur Inten-
             tion und Rezeption der Pastoralbriefe.* NTOA 52. Göttingen: Vanden-
             hoeck & Ruprecht.
Metzger, Bruce
1958   "A Reconsideration of Certain Arguments against the Pauline Author-
             ship of the Pastoral Epistles." *Expository Times* 70:91-94.
1987   *The Canon of the New Testament: Its Origin, Development, and Signif-
             icance.* Oxford: Clarendon.

Metzger, Wolfgang
1977   "Die neōterikaì epithymiai in 2. Tim. 2, 22." *TZ* 33:129-36.
Michael, J. Hugh
1922   "The First and Second Epistles to the Philippians." *Expository Times*
                34:106-9.
Millar, F.
1977   *The Emperor in the Roman World, 31 BC-AD 337.* Ithaca, N.Y.: Cornell
                University Press.
1984   "Condemnation to Hard Labour in the Roman Empire, from the Julio-
                Claudians to Constantine." *Papers of the British School at Rome* 52:124-47.
Miller, Colin Douglas
forthcoming   *The Practice of the Body of Christ.* Eugene, Ore.: Pickwick.
Mitchell, Margaret M.
1989   "Concerning Περὶ δέ in 1 Corinthians." *Novum Testamentum* 31:229-56.
1992   "New Testament Envoys in the Context of Greco-Roman Diplomatic
                and Epistolary Conventions: The Example of Timothy and Titus." *Jour-*
                nal of Biblical Literature 111:641-62.
2001   "Reading Rhetoric with Patristic Exegetes: John Chrysostom on Ga-
                latians." In *Antiquity and Humanity: Essays on Ancient Religion and*
                Philosophy Presented to Hans Dieter Betz on His 70th Birthday, ed-
                ited by A. Yarbro Collins and M. M. Mitchell, 333-55. Tübingen: Mohr
                Siebeck.
2002a   *The Heavenly Trumpet: John Chrysostom and the Art of Pauline Inter-*
                pretation. Louisville, Ky.: John Knox.
2002b   "PTebt 703 and the Genre of 1 Timothy: The Curious Career of a Ptole-
                maic Papyrus in Pauline Scholarship." *Novum Testamentum* 44:344-70.
2003   "The Corinthian Correspondence and the Birth of Pauline Herme-
                neutics." In *Paul and the Corinthians: Studies on a Community in Con-*
                flict. Essays in Honour of Margaret Thrall, edited by J. Keith Elliott and
                Trevor J. Burke, 17-53. Leiden: Brill.
2005   "Paul's Letters to Corinth: The Interpretive Intertwining of Literary
                and Historical Reconstruction." In *Urban Religion in Roman Corinth:*
                Interdisciplinary Approaches, edited by D. N. Schowalter and Steven J.
                Friesen, 307-38. Cambridge, Mass.: Harvard University Press.
2008   "Corrective Composition, Corrective Exegesis: The Teaching on Prayer
                in 1 Tim 2:1-15." In Donfried 2008, 41-62.
2010   *Paul, the Corinthians, and the Birth of Christian Hermeneutics.* Cam-
                bridge: Cambridge University Press.
Mitchell, Stephen
1992   "Galatia (Place)." *ABD* 2:870-71.
1995   *Anatolia: Land, Men, and Gods in Asia Minor.* Vol. 1, *The Celts in Ana-*
                tolia and the Impact of Roman Rule. Oxford: Oxford University Press.
Mitton, C. Leslie
1951   *The Epistle to the Ephesians: Its Authorship, Origin, and Purpose.* Ox-
                ford: Clarendon.
1955   *The Formation of the Pauline Corpus of Letters.* London: Epworth.

Moll, Sebastian
2010   *The Arch-Heretic Marcion.* WUNT 250. Tübingen: Mohr Siebeck.
Moore, David, and John McDonald
2000   *Transforming Conflict in Workplaces and Communities.* Maryborough,
              Victoria: Australian Print Group.
Morton, A. Q.
1978   *Literary Detection: How to Prove Authorship and Fraud in Literature
              and Documents.* New York: Scribner.
Morton, A. Q., and J. J. McLeman
1966   *Paul, the Man and the Myth: A Study in the Authorship of Greek Prose.*
              London: Hodder & Stoughton.
Moses, Robert Ewusie
2014   *Practices of Power: Revisiting the Principalities and Powers in the Pau-
              line Letters.* ES. Minneapolis: Fortress.
Mosteller, F., and D. L. Wallace
1964   *Inference and Disputed Authorship: The Federalist.* Reading, Mass.:
              Addison-Wesley.
1984   *Applied Bayesian and Classical Inference: The Case of the "Federalist
              Papers."* 2nd ed. New York: Springer.
Muddiman, John
2001   *The Epistle to the Ephesians.* BNTC. London: Continuum.
Mullins, T. Y.
1964   "Disclosure, A Literary Form in the New Testament." *Novum Testa-
              mentum* 7:44-50.
Murphy-O'Connor, Jerome
1991   "2 Timothy Contrasted with 1 Timothy and Titus." *RB* 98:403-18.
1995   *St Paul the Letter Writer: His World, His Options, His Skills.* GNS 41.
              Collegeville, Minn.: Liturgical Press.
1996   *Paul: A Critical Life.* Oxford: Oxford University Press.
Neumann, Kenneth J.
1990   *The Authenticity of the Pauline Epistles in the Light of Stylostatistical
              Analysis.* SBLDS 120. Atlanta: Scholars Press.
Nicholl, Colin R.
2004   *From Hope to Despair in Thessalonica: Situating 1 and 2 Thessalonians.*
              SNTSMS 126. Cambridge: Cambridge University Press.
Noormann, Rolf
1994   *Irenäus als Paulusinterpret: Zur Rezeption und Wirkung der paulin-
              ischen und deuteropaulinischen Briefe im Werk des Irenäus von Lyon.*
              WUNT 2/66. Tübingen: Mohr Siebeck.
Oates, Stephen B.
1982   *Let the Trumpet Sound: A Life of Martin Luther King, Jr.* New York:
              HarperCollins.
O'Brien, P. T.
1977   *Introductory Thanksgivings in the Letters of Paul.* NovTSup 49. Leiden:
              Brill.

1991	*The Epistle to the Philippians: A Commentary on the Greek Text.* Grand Rapids, Mich.: Eerdmans.

Ogereau, J. M.

2012	"The Jerusalem Collection as Κοινωνία: Paul's Global Politics of Socio-Economic Equality and Solidarity." *New Testament Studies* 58:360-78.

Olbricht, Thomas H., John T. Fitzgerald, and L. Michael White

(eds.) 2003	*Early Christianity and Classical Culture: Comparative Studies in Honor of Abraham J. Malherbe.* Leiden: Brill.

Ollrog, W. H.

1979	*Paulus und seine Mitarbeiter: Untersuchungen zu Theorie und Praxis der paulinischen Mission.* WMANT 50. Neukirchen-Vluyn: Neukirchener.

Ong, Walter J.

2000 [1967]	*The Presence of the Word: Some Prolegomena for Cultural and Religious History.* 2nd ed. Binghamton, N.Y.: Global Publications.
2002	*An Ong Reader: Challenges for Further Inquiry.* Edited by T. J. Farrell and P. A. Soukup. Cresskill, N.J.: Hampton Press.
2012 [1982]	*Orality and Literacy: The Technologizing of the Word.* 2nd 30th anniversary ed. New York: Routledge.

ORBIS

2013	http://orbis.stanford.edu. Accessed May-July.

Pagels, Elaine

1992 [1975]	*The Gnostic Paul.* 2nd ed. London: Continuum International.

Paley, William

1790	*The Horae Paulinae.* London: Ward, Lock. http://www.tracts.ukgo.com/paley_horae_paulinae.pdf.

Patterson, Orlando

1982	*Slavery and Social Death: A Comparative Study.* Cambridge, Mass.: Harvard University Press.

Pearson, Birger

1971	"I Thessalonians 2:13-16: A Deutero-Pauline Interpolation." *Harvard Theological Review* 64:79-94.

Perelman, C., and L. Olbrechts-Tyteca

1969 [1958]	*The New Rhetoric: A Treatise on Argumentation.* Notre Dame, Ind.: University of Notre Dame Press.

Pervo, Richard I.

2010	*The Making of Paul: Constructions of Paul in Early Christianity.* Minneapolis: Fortress.

Peterman, G. W.

1991	"'Thankless Thanks': The Epistolary Social Conventions in Philippians 4:10-20." *Tyndale Bulletin* 42:261-70.
1997	*Paul's Gift from Philippi: Conventions of Gift Exchange and Christian Giving.* Cambridge: Cambridge University Press.

Pfitzner, V.

1967	*Paul and the Agon Motif: Athletic Imagery in the Pauline Literature.* Leiden: Brill.

Polanyi, Michael
1964 [1958]   *Personal Knowledge: Towards a Post-Critical Philosophy.* New York: Harper Torchbooks.
1966   *The Tacit Dimension.* New York: Doubleday.
Poole, Ross
1991   *Morality and Modernity.* New York: Routledge.
Porter, Stanley E.
1989   *Verbal Aspect in the Greek of the New Testament with Reference to Tense and Mood.* Frankfurt: Peter Lang.
Porter, Stanley E., and Andrew W. Pitts
2008   "τοῦτο πρῶτον γινώσκοντες ὅτι in 2 Peter 1:20 and Hellenistic Epistolary Convention." *Journal of Biblical Literature* 127:165-71.
2013   "The Disclosure Formula in the Epistolary Papyri and in the New Testament: Development, Form, Function, and Syntax." In *The Language of the New Testament,* edited by Porter and Pitts, 421-38. Vol. 3 of *Early Christianity in Its Hellenistic Context.* LBS 6. Leiden: Brill.
Pranis, Kay
2005   *The Little Book of Circle Processes: A New/Old Approach to Peacemaking.* Intercourse, Pa.: Good Books.
Price, Simon R. F.
1984   *Rituals and Power: The Roman Imperial Cult in Asia Minor.* Cambridge: Cambridge University Press.
Quinn, Jerome D.
1974   "P⁴⁶ — the Pauline Canon?" *Catholic Biblical Quarterly* 36:379-85.
Quinn, Jerome D., and William C. Wacker
2000   *The First and Second Letters to Timothy: A New Translation with Notes and Commentary.* Grand Rapids, Mich.: Eerdmans.
Räisänen, H.
1987 [1983]   *Paul and the Law.* 2nd ed. WUNT 29. Tübingen: Mohr Siebeck.
1988   Paul, God, and Israel: Romans 9–11 in Recent Research." In *The Social World of Formative Christianity and Judaism,* edited by J. Neusner, P. Borgen, E. S. Frerichs, and R. Horsley, 178-206. Philadelphia: Fortress.
2000 [1990]   *Beyond New Testament Theology: A Story and a Program.* 2nd ed. London: SCM.
Rapske, Brian
1996 [1994]   *The Book of Acts and Paul in Roman Custody.* Vol. 3 of *The Book of Acts in Its First Century Setting.* Grand Rapids, Mich.: Eerdmans.
Readings, Bill
1996   *The University in Ruins.* Cambridge, Mass.: Harvard University Press.
Reed, J. T.
1996   "Philippians 3:1 and the Epistolary Hesitation Formulas: The Literary Integrity of Philippians, Again." *Journal of Biblical Literature* 115:63-90.
Rensberger, David
1981   "As the Apostle Teaches: The Development of the Use of Paul's Letters in Second-Century Christianity." PhD diss., Yale University.

Reynolds, Joyce, and Robert F. Tannenbaum
1987   *Jews and God-Fearers at Aphrodisias: Greek Inscriptions with Commentary: Texts from the Excavations at Aphrodisias Conducted by Kenan T. Erim.* Proceedings of the Cambridge Philological Society, Supp. 12. Cambridge: Cambridge Philological Society.

Richard, E. J.
1995   *First and Second Thessalonians.* SP 11. Collegeville, Minn.: Liturgical Press / Michael Glazier.

Richards, E. Randolph
1991   *The Secretary in the Letters of Paul.* WUNT 2/42. Tübingen: Mohr Siebeck.

2004   *Paul and First-Century Letter Writing: Secretaries, Composition and Collection.* Downers Grove, Ill.: IVP Academic.

Ridderbos, H.
1975 [1966] *Paul: An Outline of His Theology.* Translated by J. R. de Witt. Grand Rapids, Mich.: Eerdmans.

Riddle, Donald
1940   *Paul, Man of Conflict: A Modern Biographical Sketch.* Nashville: Cokesbury.

Riesner, R.
2011   "Pauline Chronology." In Westerholm 2011, 9-29.

Rigaux, B.
1956   *Saint Paul: Les épitres aux Thessaloniciens.* Paris: J. Gabalda.

Robinson, B. W.
1910   "An Ephesian Imprisonment of Paul." *Journal of Biblical Literature* 29:181-89.

Rogers, Everett M.
2003 [1962] *Diffusion of Innovations.* 5th ed. New York: Simon & Schuster / Free Press.

Roose, Hanna
2006   "'A Letter As by Us': Intentional Ambiguity in 2 Thessalonians 2.2." *Journal for the Study of the New Testament* 29:107-24.

Ropes, J. H.
1929   *The Singular Problem of the Epistle to the Galatians.* Cambridge, Mass.: Harvard University Press.

Rowe, C. Kavin
2005   "Luke-Acts and the Imperial Cult: A Way through the Conundrum?" *Journal for the Study of the New Testament* 27:279-300.

2006   "New Testament Theology: The Revival of a Discipline; A Review of Recent Contributions to the Field." *Journal of Biblical Literature* 125:393-419.

2009   *World Upside Down: Reading Acts in the Graeco-Roman Age.* Oxford: Oxford University Press.

2011   "Reading *World Upside Down*: A Response to Matthew Sleeman and John Barclay." *Journal for the Study of the New Testament* 33:335-46.

Rückert, L.
1837   *Der zweite Brief Pauli an die Korinther.* Leipzig: Kohler.

Rudman, Joseph
1998   "The State of Authorship Attribution Studies: Some Problems and
             Solutions." *Computers and the Humanities* 31:351-65.
Rutherford, J.
1907-1908   "St. Paul's Epistle to the Laodiceans." *Expository Times* 19:311-14.
Sanders, E. P.
1966   "Literary Dependence in Colossians." *Journal of Biblical Literature*
             85:28-45.
1977   *Paul and Palestinian Judaism.* Philadelphia: Fortress.
1983   *Paul, the Law, and the Jewish People.* Philadelphia: Fortress.
2008   "Did Paul's Theology Develop?" In *The Word Leaps the Gap: Essays on
             Scripture and Theology in Honor of Richard B. Hays,* edited by J. Ross
             Wagner, C. Kavin Rowe, and A. Katherine Grieb, 325-50. Grand Rap-
             ids, Mich.: Eerdmans.
Sandnes, K. O.
2002   *Belly and Body in the Pauline Epistles.* Cambridge: Cambridge Univer-
             sity Press.
Sappington, Thomas J.
1991   *Revelation and Redemption at Colossae.* JSNTSup 53. Sheffield: JSOT.
Scheidel, Walter
2013   "The Shape of the Roman World." Princeton/Stanford Working Papers
             in Classics. http://orbis.stanford.edu/assets/Scheidel_59.pdf.
Scheidel, Walter, Elijah Meeks, and Jonathan Weiland
2012   "ORBIS: The Stanford Geospatial Network Model of the Roman
             World." http://orbis.stanford.edu/ORBIS_v1paper_20120501.pdf.
Schenk, Wolfgang
1983   "Christus, das Geheimnis der Welt, als dogmatisches und ethisches
             Grundprinzip des Kolosserbriefes." *EvT* 43:138-55.
1987   "Der Kolosserbrief in der neueren Forschung (1945-1985)." *ANRW*
             2.25.4:3327-64.
Schlosser, Eric
1998   "The Prison-Industrial Complex." *The Atlantic,* December 1998. http://
             www.theatlantic.com/magazine/print/1998/12/the-prison-industrial
             -complex/4669/.
Schmidt, Darryl
1990   "The Syntactical Style of 2 Thessalonians: How Pauline Is It?" In
             R. Collins 1990, 383-93.
Schmidt, J. E. Christian
1801   "Vermuthungen über die beiden Briefe an die Thessalonicher." In *Bib-
             liothek für Kritik und Exegese des N. T. und älteste Christengeschichte,*
             vol. 2, fasc. 3, 380-86. Hadamar: Neue Gelehrtenbuchhandlung. (Re-
             printed in Trilling 1972, 159-61.)
Schmithals, W.
1972 [1965] "The Historical Situation of the Thessalonian Letters." In *Gnosticism
             in Corinth,* 128-318. Nashville: Abingdon.

| 1984 | *Die Briefe des Paulus in ihrer ursprünglichen Form.* ZWKB. Zürich: Theologischer Verlag. |

Schnabel, Eckhard J.

2004   *Early Christian Mission.* Vol. 2, *Paul and the Early Church.* Downers Grove, Ill.: IVP Academic.

Schnelle, Udo

2005 [2003]   *Apostle Paul: His Life and Theology.* Translated by M. Eugene Boring. Grand Rapids, Mich.: Baker Academic.

Schreiner, Thomas R.

2001   *Paul, Apostle of God's Glory in Christ: A Pauline Theology.* Downers Grove, Ill.: InterVarsity.

Schubert, Paul

1939   *Form and Function of the Pauline Thanksgiving.* BZNW 20. Berlin: Töpelmann.

Schulz, David

1829   Review of Eichhorn's *Einleitung in das Neue Testament* and de Wette's *Lehrbuch der historisch-kritischen Einleitung in die kanonischen Bücher des Neuen Testaments. TSK* 2:563-636, esp. 609-12.

Schweizer, Eduard

1982 [1976]   *The Letter to the Colossians.* Translated by Andrew Chester. Minneapolis: Augsburg Fortress.

1988   "Slaves of the Elements and Worshipers of Angels: Gal 4:3, 9 and Col 2:8, 18, 20." *Journal of Biblical Literature* 107:455-68.

Scott, James C.

1990   *Domination and the Arts of Resistance: Hidden Transcripts.* New Haven: Yale University Press.

Shiell, W. S.

2004   "Conventions of Greco-Roman Delivery." In *Reading Acts: The Lector and the Early Christian Audience,* 34-101. Leiden: Brill.

Smith, Ian K.

2006   *Heavenly Perspective: A Study of the Apostle Paul's Response to a Jewish Mystical Movement at Colossae.* London: T & T Clark / Continuum.

Smith, Peter W. H., and W. Aldridge

2011   "Improving Authorship Attribution: Optimizing Burrows' Delta Method." *Journal of Quantitative Linguistics* 18:63-88.

Smith, R. R. R.

1993   *The Monument of C. Julius Zoilos.* Mainz: Zabern. [*Aphrodisias I. Results of the Excavations at Aphrodisias in Caria conducted by New York University.* Figure drawings by C. H. Hallett.]

Spicq, Ceslas

1933   *The Tebtunis Papyri.* Vol. 3, pt. 1. Edited by A. S. Hunt and J. G. Smyly. London: Cambridge University Press. [*PTebt* 703 on pp. 66-102.]

1969 [1947]   *Saint Paul, Les Épîtres Pastorales.* 4th ed. 2 vols. Paris: Gabalda.

Stamatatos, Efstathios

2009   "A Survey of Modern Authorship Attribution Methods." *Journal of the American Society for Information Science and Technology* 60:538-56.

Stanley, Christopher, and Stanley E. Porter
(eds.) 2008   *As It Is Written: Studying Paul's Use of Scripture.* SBLSymS 50. Atlanta:
                 SBL.
Staples, Jason A.
2011   "What Do the Gentiles Have to Do with 'All Israel'? A Fresh Look at
                 Romans 11:25-27." *Journal of Biblical Literature* 130:371-90.
Stark, Rodney
1996   *The Rise of Christianity: A Sociologist Reconsiders History.* Princeton,
                 N.J.: Princeton University Press.
Stephenson, A. M. G.
1968   "On the Meaning of ὡς ὅτι ἐνέστηκεν ἡ ἡμέρα τοῦ κυρίου in 2 Thes-
                 salonians 2,2." In *Studia Evangelica IV,* edited by F. L. Cross, 442-51.
                 Berlin: Akademie-Verlag.
Stettler, C.
2005   "The Opponents at Colossae." In *Paul and His Opponents,* edited by
                 S. E. Porter, 169-200. PS 2. Leiden: Brill.
Stirewalt, M. Luther
2003   *Paul, the Letter Writer.* Grand Rapids, Mich.: Eerdmans.
Stowers, S. K.
1990   "PERI MEN GAR and the Integrity of 2 Cor. 8 and 9." *Novum Testa-
                 mentum* 32:340-48.
Strecker, Georg
2000 [1996]   *Theology of the New Testament.* Edited by F. W. Horn. Translated by
                 E. Boring. Berlin: de Gruyter; Lousiville: Westminster John Knox.
Stuckenbruck, Loren T.
1995   *Angel Veneration and Christology.* WUNT 2/70. Tübingen: Mohr
                 Siebeck.
Stuhlmacher, Peter
1991-99   *Biblische Theologie des Neuen Testaments.* 2 vols. Göttingen: Vanden-
                 hoeck & Ruprecht.
Sumney, J. L.
1990   *Identifying Paul's Opponents: The Question of Method in 2 Corinthians.*
                 Sheffield: JSOT.
Sundberg, Albert C.
1973   "Canon Muratori: A Fourth-Century List." *Harvard Theological Review*
                 66:1-41.
Swartley, Willard M.
2006   *Covenant of Peace: The Missing Peace in New Testament Theology and
                 Ethics.* Grand Rapids, Mich.: Eerdmans.
Syme, Ronald
1995   *Anatolica: Studies in Strabo.* Edited by Anthony Birley. Oxford:
                 Clarendon.
Talbert, Richard J. A.
2010   *Rome's World: The Peutinger Map Reconsidered.* Cambridge: Cam-
                 bridge University Press.

Tatum, Gregory
2006   *New Chapters in the Life of Paul: The Relative Chronology of His Career.* CBQMS 41. Washington, D.C.: Catholic Biblical Association.

Taylor, Charles
1989   *Sources of the Self: The Making of the Modern Identity.* Cambridge: Cambridge University Press.

Taylor, J.
1994   "Why Were the Disciples First Called 'Christians' at Antioch?" *RB* 101:75-94.

Taylor, Nicholas
1996   "Palestinian Christianity and the Caligula Crisis. Part I. Social and Historical Reconstruction." *Journal for the Study of the New Testament* 61:101-24.

Thielicke, Helmut
1974 [1968]   *The Evangelical Faith.* Vol. 1, *Prolegomena.* Translated by G. W. Bromiley. Edinburgh: T&T Clark.

Thielman, Frank
2005   *Theology of the New Testament: A Canonical and Synthetic Approach.* Grand Rapids, Mich.: Zondervan.

Thiessen, Matthew
2011   *Contesting Conversion: Genealogy, Circumcision, and Identity in Ancient Judaism and Christianity.* Oxford: Oxford University Press.

Thiselton, Anthony J.
2000   *The First Epistle to the Corinthians: A Commentary on the Greek Text.* NIGTC. Grand Rapids, Mich.: Eerdmans.
2011   *1 & 2 Thessalonians: Through the Centuries.* Chichester: Wiley-Blackwell.

Thisted, R., and B. Efron
1987   "Did Shakespeare Write a Newly-Discovered Poem?" *Biometrika* 74:445-55.

Thomson, I. H.
1995   *Chiasmus in the Pauline Letters.* JSNTSup 111. Sheffield: JSOT.

Thrall, M. E.
1987   "The Offender and the Offence: A Problem of Detection in 2 Corinthians." In *Scripture: Meaning and Method,* edited by B. P. Thompson, 65-78. Hull: University of Hull Press.
1994   *A Critical and Exegetical Commentary on the Second Epistle to the Corinthians.* 2 vols. ICC. London: T&T Clark / Continuum.

Tolmie, D. François
(ed.) 2010   *Philemon in Perspective: Interpreting a Pauline Letter.* BZNW 169. Berlin: de Gruyter.

Tomkins, S. S.
2008   *Affect, Imagery, and Consciousness: The Complete Edition.* New York: Springer.

Torrance, T. F.
1969a   *Space, Time, and Incarnation.* London: Oxford University Press.
1969b   *Theological Science.* London: Oxford University Press.

1971   *God and Rationality.* London: Oxford University Press.
1976   *Space, Time, and Resurrection.* Edinburgh: Handsel.
1986   "Karl Barth and the Latin Heresy." *Scottish Journal of Theology* 39:
                461-82.

Towner, Philip H.
2006   *The Letters to Timothy and Titus.* Grand Rapids, Mich.: Eerdmans.

Trebilco, Paul
1991   *Jewish Communities in Asia Minor.* Cambridge: Cambridge University
                Press.
2007 [2004]   *The Early Christians in Ephesus from Paul to Ignatius.* Grand Rapids,
                Mich.: Eerdmans.

Trilling, W.
1972   *Untersuchungen zum 2. Thessalonicherbrief.* ETS 27. Leipzig: Benno.

Trobisch, David
1994   *Paul's Letter Collection: Tracing the Origins.* Minneapolis: Fortress.

Van Braght, Thieleman J.
(ed.) 1951 [1660] *The Bloody Theater; Or, Martyr's Mirror of the Defenseless Christians
                Who Baptized Only upon Confession of Faith, and Suffered and Died for
                the Testimony of Jesus, Their Saviour, from the Time of Christ to the Year
                A.D. 1660.* Translated by Joseph F. Sohm. Scottdale, Pa.: Mennonite
                Publishing House.

Van Kooten, George H.
2003   *Cosmic Christology in Paul and the Pauline School.* WUNT 2/171.
                Tübingen: Mohr Siebeck.

Vegge, I.
2008   *2 Corinthians: A Letter about Reconciliation.* Tübingen: Mohr Siebeck.

Vielhauer, Philipp
1978   *Geschichte der urchristlichen Literatur: Einleitung in das Neue Testa-
                ment, die Apokryphen und die Apostolischen Väter.* 2nd ed. Berlin: de
                Gruyter.

Vincent, M. R.
1897   *A Critical and Exegetical Commentary on the Epistles to the Philippians
                and to Philemon.* ICC. Edinburgh: T&T Clark.

Vouga, F.
2001   *Une théologie du Nouveau Testament.* MdB 43. Geneva: Labor et Fides.

Walters, Patricia
2009   *The Assumed Authorial Unity of Luke and Acts: A Reassessment of the
                Evidence.* SNTSMS 145. Cambridge: Cambridge University Press.

Wanamaker, Charles
1990   *The Epistles to the Thessalonians: A Commentary on the Greek Text.*
                Grand Rapids, Mich.: Eerdmans.

Wansink, Craig S.
1993   "'Imprisonment for the Gospel': The Apostle Paul and Roman Prisons."
                PhD diss., Yale University.
1996   *Imprisonment for the Gospel: The Apostle Paul and Roman Prisons.*
                JSNTSup 130. Sheffield: JSOT.

Watson, D. F.

1988   "A Rhetorical Analysis of Philippians and Its Implications for the Unity Question." *Novum Testamentum* 30:57-88.

2003   "A Reexamination of the Epistolary Analysis Underpinning the Arguments for the Composite Nature of Philippians." In Olbricht, Fitzgerald, and White 2003, 157-77.

Weaver, P. R. C.

1972   *Familia Caesaris: A Social Study of the Emperor's Freedmen and Slaves.* Cambridge: Cambridge University Press.

Weber, Max

1978 [1956] *Economy and Society.* 2 vols. Edited by G. Roth and C. Wittich. Based on the 4th German ed., edited by J. Winckelmann. Berkeley: University of California Press.

Wedderburn, A. J. M.

2002   "Paul's Collection: Chronology and History." *New Testament Studies* 48:95-110.

Weima, J. A. D.

1994a   *Neglected Endings: The Significance of the Pauline Letter Closings.* Sheffield: JSOT.

1994b   "Preaching the Gospel at Rome: A Study of the Epistolary Framework of Romans." In Jervis and Richardson 1994, 337-66.

2012   "'Peace and Security' (1 Thess 5.3): Prophetic Warning or Political Propaganda?" *New Testament Studies* 58:331-59.

forthcoming *1 and 2 Thessalonians.* BECNT. Grand Rapids, Mich.: Baker Academic.

Weima, J. A. D., and Stanley E. Porter

1998   *An Annotated Bibliography of 1 and 2 Thessalonians.* Leiden: Brill.

Weiss, Johannes

1959 [1917] *Earliest Christianity: A History of the Period AD 30-150, Books I-V in Two Volumes.* Translated by F. C. Grant. New York: Harper.

Welborn, L. L.

1999   "Primum tirocinium Pauli 2 Cor 11,32-33." *BZ* 43:49-71.

2005   *Paul, the Fool of Christ: A Study of 1 Corinthians 1–4 in the Comic-Philosophic Tradition.* London: T&T Clark / Continuum.

2011   "Paul and Pain: Paul's Emotional Therapy in 2 Corinthians 1.1–2.13; 7.5-16 in the Context of Ancient Psychagogic Literature." *New Testament Studies* 57:547-70.

Wells, Sam

2004   *Improvisation: The Drama of Christian Ethics.* Grand Rapids, Mich.: Brazos.

Wengst, K.

2006   *Der Brief an Philemon.* ThKNT 16. Stuttgart: Kohlhammer.

Westerholm, S.

(ed.) 2011   *The Blackwell Companion to Paul.* Chichester: Wiley-Blackwell.

White, Benjamin L.

2011   "How to Read a Book: Irenaeus and the Pastoral Epistles Reconsidered." *Vigiliae Christianae* 65:125-49.

White, John L.
1984   *Light from Ancient Letters*. Philadelphia: Fortress.
Whiteley, D. E. H.
1964   *The Theology of St. Paul*. Oxford: Oxford University Press.
Wilckens, Ulrich
2002-5   *Theologie des Neuen Testaments*. 4 vols. Neukirchen-Vluyn: Neukirchener.
Wilson, Robert McLachlan
2005   *Colossians and Philemon*. ICC. London: T&T Clark / Continuum.
Windisch, H.
1970 [1924]   *Der Zweite Korintherbrief*. KEK 6. Göttingen: Vandenhoeck & Ruprecht.
Wire, A. C.
1990   *The Corinthian Women Prophets: A Reconstruction through Paul's Rhetoric*. Minneapolis: Fortress.
Wolter, Michael
1988   *Die Pastoralbrief als Paulustradition*. FRLANT 146. Göttingen: Vandenhoeck & Ruprecht.
Wrede, W.
1903   *Die Echtheit des zweiten Thessalonikerbriefs untersucht*. TU. Leipzig: Hinrichs.
Wright, N. T.
2003   *The Resurrection of the Son of God*. Vol. 3 of *Christian Origins and the Question of God*. Minneapolis: Fortress.
Wuellner, W.
1979   "Greek Rhetoric and Pauline Argumentation." In *Early Christian Literature and the Classical Intellectual Tradition: In Honorem Robert M. Grant*, edited by W. R. Schoedel and R. L. Wilken, 177-88. Paris: Beauchesne.
Yarbro Collins, Adela
2011   "The Female Body as Social Space in 1 Timothy." *New Testament Studies* 57:155-75.
Yule, G. Udny
1944   *The Statistical Study of Literary Vocabulary*. Cambridge: Cambridge University Press.
Zahn, T.
1909 [1897]   *Introduction to the New Testament*. Vol. 1. Translated by J. M. Trout from 3rd German ed. Edinburgh: T&T Clark. (1st German ed. 1897.)
Zehr, Howard
1990   *Changing Lenses: A New Focus for Crime and Justice*. Scottdale, Pa.: Herald.
2002   *The Little Book of Restorative Justice*. Intercourse, Pa.: Good Books.
Zizioulas, John
1985   *Being as Communion*. Crestwood, N.Y.: SVS Press.

Index of Authors

447

Index of Subjects

Acts: and Galatians, 154-55, 177-81, 306n.51; and 2 Timothy, 374-75, 383n.38; as source, 20-26; and Thessalonian correspondence, 191
Antioch incident, 177-81
Antitheses, 364-66
Apamea, 274, 276
Apollos: in Corinthian correspondence, 59-60, 70-71, 95-97; in Titus, 341, 346-48
Apphia, 254, 256, 274
Archippus, 254, 270-71
Aretas datum, 30, 182-89
Aristarchus, 278-80
Asian crisis, 96-97, 121
Athens, Paul's founding visit to, 188-92, 202
Authenticity. *See individual letters*

Caesar's household, 123-24
Chronology, Pauline: dating, 30-31, 182-89, 220-29; difference from framing account, 24-25
Church organization, 357-61
Co-authors, 247n.98
Coherence in Paul's thought: as problem, 1-10; solution to, 11-13
Collection for Jerusalem: absence from Philemon and Colossians, 282; in Ga-

latians, 122, 157-66; in Romans, 1 and 2 Corinthians, 28-29, 37-41
Collection, original, of Paul's letters: content of, 387-91; methodological utility of, 385-86
Colossae, founding visit to, 255, 261-64, 278-80
Colossians: authenticity vs. pseudepigraphy, 276-304; date and provenance, 274-76; implications for frame, 304-9; occasion, 260-68; position in frame, 282; relationship to Ephesians, 32-33, 318-25; relationship to Philemon, 32, 259-60, 270-74
Computer-assisted authorship ascription, 32, 210-16, 250-51, 286-92
Computer-assisted mapping of ancient travel. *See* ORBIS
Contingency in Paul's thought: as problem, 1-10; solution to, 11-13
Copies of Paul's letters, 201-3, 284
Corinth, Paul's previous letter to, 56-59
Corinth, Paul's visits to: founding, 188-92, 196, 202; second, 62-63, 80-90, 94-97; third, 39, 62, 305
Corinthian correspondence: events before 1 Corinthians, 56-60; events between 1 and 2 Corinthians, 61-63, 94-97. *See also* Corinth, Paul's visits

453

Index of Scripture and Other Ancient Literature